Teacher's Annotated Edition

Parents and Their Children

Verdene Ryder
Family Life Education Consultant
Houston, Texas

Celia A. Decker, Ph.D.
Professor of Family and Consumer Sciences, Retired
Northwestern State University of Louisiana
Natchitoches, Louisiana

Publisher
The Goodheart-Willcox Company, Inc.
Tinley Park, Illinois

Contents

Features of the Student Edition T4
Features of *Student Activity Guide* T5
Features of *Teacher's Annotated Edition* T6
Features of *Teacher's Resource Portfolio* T8
Other *Parents and Their Children* Teaching Resources T9
Strategies for Successful Teaching T10
    Helping Your Students Develop Critical Thinking Skills T10
    Decision-Making Skills T11
    Using Cooperative Learning T11
    Helping Students Recognize and Value Diversity T11
    Teaching the Learner with Special Needs T13
Assessment Techniques T15
    Performance Assessment T15
    Portfolios T15
Using Other Resources T16
National Standards for Parenting with
Parents and Their Children T20
Scope and Sequence T20
Correlation of National Standards for Parenting with
Parents and Their Children T21
Scope and Sequence Chart T28
Lesson Planning Guides T36
Chapter 1 ....T36
Chapter 2 ....T38
Chapter 3 ....T41
Chapter 4 ....T44
Chapter 5 ....T46
Chapter 6 ....T49
Chapter 7 ....T52
Chapter 8 ....T55
Chapter 9 ....T58
Chapter 10 ....T61
Chapter 11 ....T64
Chapter 12 ....T67
Chapter 13 ....T70
Chapter 14 ....T73
Chapter 15 ....T76
Chapter 16 ....T78
Chapter 17 ....T81
Chapter 18 ....T84
Chapter 19 ....T86
Chapter 20 ....T88
Chapter 21 ....T91
Chapter 22 ....T94

Parents and Their Children

Student Text

This text will help your students develop insight into parenting. The text is designed to educate students about the decisions and preparations related to parenting, as well as an understanding of the development of children.

- **Objectives** give students a glimpse of the topics they will be studying as they read the chapter.

- **Full-color photos** are complete with in-text references, designed to illustrate the importance of material to students.

- **New terms** are distinguished in boldface as they are defined.

- **Logical organization, colorful headings,** and **readable typeface** facilitate reading comprehension.

- **Summary** provides a review of major chapter concepts.

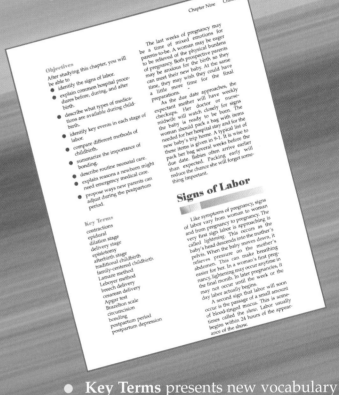

- **Child Development Charts** give general descriptions of physical, intellectual, emotional, and social development for children from 1 month to 18 years old.

- **Key Terms** presents new vocabulary terms, in order of appearance, that emphasize important concepts of the chapter.

More features of the Student Text

- **Reviewing Key Points** questions have students recall chapter information.

- **Learning by Doing** activities provide students with opportunities to gain knowledge through experience.

- **Thinking Critically** challenges students to understand and reflect on chapter concepts in relation to themselves.

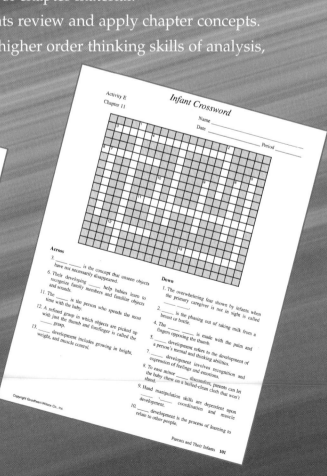

Summary

- Many work opportunities exist in child and family services. There are exciting careers working directly and working on behalf of children and families.
- Some careers involve creating or selling child-related products. Others exist in the children's entertainment field. Still other people work as entrepreneurs.
- Knowing your interests, aptitudes, and abilities is essential before making career plans.
- People who enter a child and family services career must have certain personal characteristics and professional qualifications.
- Developing a career plan can help you determine goals and begin to work toward them.
- Many of the trends in the child and family services careers are related to the growing number of children in child care and the need for more family services.
- You can prepare for future roles now by joining student organizations, developing leadership, teamwork, and communications skills, finding part-time jobs in child and family services, and developing employability skills.

Reviewing Key Points

1. What is the difference between a job and a career?
2. Briefly describe the differences among entry-level, paraprofessional, and professional positions.
3. Briefly describe the procedure for receiving the Child Development Associate (CDA) Credential.
4. List at least three positions social workers might fill if they are involved in child welfare and family services.

5. Briefly describe three careers in which people work on behalf of children and families.
6. Describe two pros and two cons of operating your own business.
7. Explain why your own interests, aptitudes, and abilities should be considered in career planning.
8. Briefly explain what is involved in writing a career plan.
9. Why are child care workers in such demand today?
10. What is an accredited child care program?
11. Name three expanding job opportunities in child and family services.
12. Why is it beneficial for teens to learn parliamentary procedure?
13. List five qualities of a good leader.
14. List three part-time jobs working with children you might be able to obtain now.
15. How can you find out about job openings?
16. What types of information are included on a resume?
17. What items should you take with you on a job interview?

Learning by Doing

1. Scan a newspaper's classified ads section and list job opportunities in child-related areas.
2. Contact community colleges and universities in your area. Research child-related course offerings.
3. Create a brochure for parents on selecting an accredited child care program.
4. Conduct a mock meeting in your classroom using parliamentary procedure.
5. Role-play a job interview. Videotape and evaluate the interview.

Features of the Student Activity Guide

The *Student Activity Guide* reinforces knowledge students gain from the text. It is full of activities touching on every major topic in the text.

Activities range from opinion polls for personal reflection to crossword puzzles encompassing the key terms for reinforcement of chapter material.

Includes numerous activities to help students review and apply chapter concepts.

Many activities require students to use the higher order thinking skills of analysis, synthesis, and evaluation.

Helping Toddlers Learn Their Limits

Activity E
Chapter 12

Name _____
Date _____ Period _____

Indicate whether you agree or disagree with the following statements. Then discuss them in class.

Agree Disagree

1. Children need to be taught behavioral boundaries and limits.
2. Children should be told what is expected of them.
3. Parents should be flexible to change.
4. Limits should let their children know what they can do as well as what they cannot do.
5. Toddlers need to learn they cannot always have their own way.
6. Children should be allowed to feel their ideas and desires are worthwhile.
7. Parents expect firmness and caring guidance.
8. Toddlers should not offer a choice when there is no choice available.
9. Parents should use slight spankings to reinforce their stands on rare occasions.
10. The role of guidance is to achieve results without being abusive.
11. Discipline that is right for one child may be too strong for a more sensitive child.
12. Parents should establish limits but give their toddlers guidelines and freedom within those limits.
13. Firm limits allow toddlers to sense their parents care about them.
14. Parents should use psychological approaches to reinforce their standards.
15. Parents can help their children avoid temper tantrums by meeting their children's reasonable needs.

Choose a statement from the checklist above. Explain why you strongly agree or strongly disagree with that statement.

I strongly (agree/disagree) with statement number _____ because _____

Copyright Goodheart-Willcox Co., Inc.

Parents and Their Toddlers **113**

Infant Crossword

Activity E
Chapter 11

Name _____
Date _____ Period _____

Across

3. _____ have not necessarily disappeared. is the concept that unseen objects
6. Their developing _____ help babies learn to recognize family members and familiar objects and sounds.
11. The _____ is the person who spends the most time with the baby.
12. A refined grasp in which objects are picked up with just the thumb and forefinger is called the _____ grasp.
13. _____ development includes growing in height, weight, and muscle control.

Down

1. The overwhelming fear shown by infants when the primary caregiver is not in sight is called _____
2. _____ is the phasing out of taking milk from a breast or bottle.
4. The _____ is made with the palm and fingers opposing the thumb.
5. _____ development refers to the development of a person's mental and thinking abilities.
7. _____ development involves recognition and expression of feelings and emotions.
8. To ease minor _____ discomfort, parents can let the baby chew on a boiled-clean cloth that won't shred.
9. Hand manipulation skills are dependent upon _____ coordination and muscle development.
10. _____ development is the process of learning to relate to other people.

Copyright Goodheart-Willcox Co., Inc.

Parents and Their Infants **101**

Features of the Teacher's Annotated Edition

A variety of types of annotations appear on each page to guide you in reviewing and reinforcing the chapter content.

- **Note**—Additional information to expand content or spark student interest. Includes statistics, facts, and historical notes.

- **Enrich**—More involved and challenging activities for students. Includes role-playing, research topics, and field trips.

- **Resource**—Related material from the *Student Activity Guide* and the *Teacher's Resources*.

- **Vocabulary**—Reinforcement activities, such as defining, using in sentences, using glossary, or comparing.

- **Discuss**—Questions to reteach or reinforce learning.

- **Reflect**—More personal than discussion questions; often ask the student to apply content to their own lives.

- **Activity**—Activities that reteach and reinforce chapter concepts.

- **Example**—Use to illustrate an important point in chapter material.

- **Answers**—Indicate where answers to *Reviewing Key Points* questions may be found.

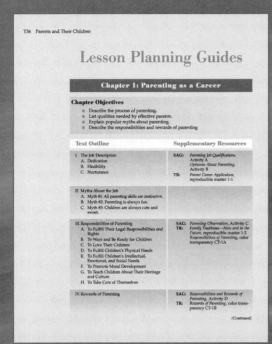

A complete *Lesson Planning Guide* is provided for each chapter of the text to help you plan your teaching strategies.

Chapter Outlines give you an overview of the content and organization of chapter material.

Supplementary Resources include related activities from the *Student Activity Guide* and *Teacher's Resources*.

Assessment includes answers to *Reviewing Key Points* questions assist you in clarifying student understanding of chapter concepts.

Technology Applications include suggestions for activities and projects that focus on the use of technology, particularly the Internet and computer software programs.

Academic Connections give ideas for relating the chapter content to other curriculum areas, such as math, history, social studies, and science.

National Standards Correlation Chart indicates where topics related to the National Standards for Family and Consumer Sciences Education are covered in the text.

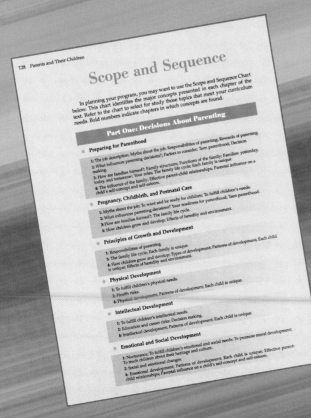

Scope and Sequence lists the major concepts presented in each chapter to help you tailor lessons to student learning needs.

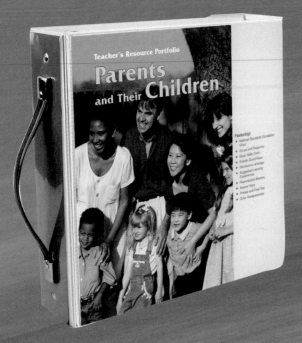

Teacher's Resource Portfolio
Parents
and Their **Children**

Features of the Teacher's Resource Portfolio

Everything you need for teaching a chapter in *Parents and Their Children* is conveniently grouped together in an easy-to-use portfolio!

Basic Skills Chart identifies activities in the text and supplements that encourage the development of verbal, reading, writing, math, science, and analytical skills.

National Standards Correlation Chart indicates where topics related to the National Standards for Parenting are covered in the text.

Teaching Materials are listed to assist planning of daily lessons.

Bulletin Board ideas are described and illustrated.

Student Learning Experiences described for each major concept make it easy for you to plan stimulating lessons.

Activities to **Reteach, Reinforce, Enrich,** and **Extend Concepts** are described. These include diverse experiences—debates, field trips, and speakers. Many activities promote critical thinking, problem solving, and decision-making skills.

Answer Key for text review questions, chapter tests, and activities in the *Student Activity Guide.*

A comprehensive **Pretest** and **Final Test** are included to cover all text material.

Introductory Activities motivate students, stimulating their interest in the chapter.

A reproducible **Chapter Test** is provided for each chapter.

Reproducible Masters and ready-to-use **Color Transparencies** are provided for all chapters in the text.

Other *Parents and Their Children* Teaching Resources

Use these additional resources to reteach, reinforce, enrich, and assess student learning!

The *Teacher's Resource Guide*

Contains all of the items included in the *Teacher's Resource Portfolio* except for the color transparencies.

Some teachers like to keep a copy of the *Teacher's Resource Guide* at home and the *Teacher's Resource Portfolio* at school!

Teacher's Resource CD with GW Test Creation Software

This exciting NEW ancillary puts all the contents of the *Teacher's Resource Portfolio* <u>plus</u> <u>GW Test Creation Software</u> on one CD-ROM!

Everything you'll need for planning lessons and creating tests is only a few keystrokes away. Print off just what you need. Quick and convenient access to all the resources in the portfolio.

Available in Windows.

Features of *GW Test Creation Software:*

- 25 percent more questions in addition to those found on the printed tests.
- Create customized tests using any chapters or chapter questions; alter questions; add your own questions to the database.
- Questions in a variety of formats: true/false, multiple choice, matching, and essay.

Introduction

Parents and Their Children is designed to promote family interactions that are enjoyable, supportive, encouraging, and rewarding. Information is presented to help today's families successfully meet the unique challenges they may face.

Strategies for Successful Teaching

You can make the *Parents and Their Children* subject matter exciting and relevant for your students by using a variety of teaching strategies. Many suggestions for planning classroom activities are given in the various teaching supplements that accompany this text. As you plan your lessons, you might also want to keep the following points in mind.

Helping Your Students Develop Critical Thinking Skills

As today's students leave their classrooms behind, they will face a world of complexity and change. They are likely to work in several career areas and hold many different jobs. Providing young people with a base of knowledge consisting only of facts, principles, and procedures will be doing them a disservice. They must, in addition, be prepared to solve complex problems, make difficult decisions, and assess ethical implications. In other words, students must be able to use critical thinking skills. These skills are often referred to as the higher order thinking skills. Benjamin Bloom listed these as

- analysis—breaking down material into its component parts so that its organizational structure may be understood;

- synthesis—putting parts together to form a new whole; and

- evaluation—judging the value of material for a given purpose.

In a broader perspective, students must be able to use reflective thinking in order to decide what to believe and do. According to Robert Ennis, students should be able to

- define and clarify problems, issues, conclusions, reasons, and assumptions;

- judge the credibility, relevance, and consistency of information; and

- infer or solve problems and draw reasonable conclusions.

Students have the right to be taught how to think critically—it cannot be an option. To think critically, one must have knowledge. However, critical thinking goes beyond memorizing or recalling information. Critical thinking cannot occur in a vacuum; it requires individuals to apply what they know about the subject matter. It requires students to use their common sense and experience. It may also involve controversy.

Critical thinking also requires *creative thinking* to construct all the reasonable alternatives, consequences, influencing factors, and supporting arguments. Unusual ideas are valued and perspectives outside the obvious are sought.

Finally, the teaching of critical thinking does not require exotic and highly unusual classroom approaches. Complex thought processes can be incorporated in the most ordinary and basic activities, even reading, writing, and listening, if these activities are carefully planned and skillfully executed.

Help your students develop their analytical and judgmental skills and to go beyond what they see on the surface. Rather than allowing students to blindly accept what they read or hear, encourage them to examine ideas in ways that show respect for others' opinions and different perspectives.

Encourage students to think about points raised by others. Ask them to evaluate how new ideas relate to their attitudes about various subjects.

Debate is an excellent way to explore opposite sides of an issue. You may want to divide the class into two groups, each to take an opposing side of the issue. You can also ask students to work in smaller groups and explore opposing sides of different issues. Each group can select students from the group to present the points for their side.

Decision-Making Skills

An important aspect in the development of critical thinking skills is learning how to solve problems and make decisions. This is such an important skill for students to have in today's world that it is explained fully in Chapters 2 and 15 of *Parents and Their Children*. Some very important decisions lie ahead for your students, particularly those related to their future education and career choices. The steps in the decision-making process are outlined in Chapter 2. An example is provided that will allow your students to see how other young people used the decision-making process to help them reach their goals.

Simulation games and role-plays allow students to practice solving problems and making decisions under nonthreatening circumstances. Role-playing allows students to examine others' feelings as well as their own. It can help them learn effective ways to react or cope when confronted with similar situations in real life.

Using Cooperative Learning

Because of the new emphasis on teamwork in the workplace, the use of cooperative learning groups in your classroom will give students an opportunity to practice teamwork skills. During cooperative learning, students learn interpersonal and small-group skills that will allow them to function as part of a team. These skills include leadership, decision making, trust building, communication, and conflict management.

When planning for cooperative learning, you will have a particular goal or task in mind. You will first specify the objectives for the lesson. Small groups of learners are matched for the purpose of completing the task or goal, and each person in the group is assigned a role. The success of the group is measured not only in terms of outcome but in terms of the successful performance of each member in his or her role.

In cooperative learning groups, students learn to work together toward a group goal. Each member is dependent upon others for the outcome. This interdependence is a basic component of any cooperative learning group. Students understand one person cannot succeed unless everyone succeeds. The value of each group member is affirmed as learners work toward their goal.

The success of the group depends on individual performance. Groups should be mixed in terms of abilities and talents so that there are opportunities for the students to learn from one another. Also, as groups work together over time, the roles should be rotated so that everyone has an opportunity to practice and develop different skills.

You will also need to monitor the effectiveness of the groups, intervening as necessary to provide task assistance or to help with interpersonal and group skills. Finally, evaluate students' achievement, and help them discuss how well they collaborated with each other.

Helping Students Recognize and Value Diversity

Your students will be entering a rapidly changing workplace—not only in the area of technology, but also in the diverse nature of its workforce. Years ago, the workforce was dominated by white males, but 85 percent of the new entrants into the workforce at the start of this century will be women, minorities, and immigrants. The workforce is also aging. Over half of the workforce will be people between the ages of 35 and 54. Because of these changes, young workers will need to be able to interact effectively with those who are different from themselves.

The appreciation and understanding of diversity is an ongoing process. The earlier and more frequently young people are exposed to diversity, the better able they will be to bridge cultural differences. If your students are exposed to different cultures within your classroom, they can begin the process of understanding cultural differences. This is the best preparation for success in a diverse society. In addition, teachers have found the following strategies to be helpful:

- Actively promote a spirit of openness, consideration, respect, and tolerance in your classroom.

- Use a variety of teaching styles and assessment strategies.

- Use cooperative learning activities whenever possible. Make sure group roles are rotated so that everyone has leadership opportunities.

- When grouping students, make sure the composition of each group is as diverse as possible with regard to gender, race, and nationality. If the groups present information to the class, make sure all members have a speaking part. (Sometimes females and minorities do not do the speaking.)

- Make sure one group's opinions are not over-represented during class discussions. Seek opinions of under-represented persons/groups if necessary.

- If a student makes a sexist, racist, or other comment that is likely to be offensive, ask the student to rephrase the comment in a manner that it will not offend other members of the class. Remind students that offensive statements and behavior are inappropriate in the workplace as well as the classroom.

- If a difficult classroom situation arises based on a diversity issue, ask for a time out and have everyone write down their thoughts and opinions about the incident. This allows everyone to cool down and allows you to plan a response.

- Arrange for guest speakers who represent diversity in gender, race, and ethnicity even though the topic does not relate to diversity.

- Have students change seats from time to time throughout the course, having them sit next to people they do not know, and introducing themselves.

Teaching the Learner with Special Needs

The students in your classroom will represent a wide range of ability levels and needs. Special needs students in your classes will require unique teaching strategies. The chart below provides descriptions of several of the types of special needs students you may find in your classes, followed by some strategies and techniques to keep in mind as you work with these students. You will be asked to meet the needs of all of your students in the same classroom setting. It is a challenge to adapt daily lessons to meet the demands of all your students.

Learning Disabled*	Mentally Disabled*	Behaviorally Emotionally Disabled*
Teaching Strategies — Students with learning disabilities (LD) have neurological disorders that interfere with their ability to store, process, or produce information, creating a "gap" between ability and performance. These students are generally of average or above average intelligence. Examples of learning disabilities are distractibility, spatial problems, and reading comprehension problems.	The mentally disabled student has subaverage general intellectual functioning that exists with deficits in adaptive behavior. These students are slower than others their age in using memory effectively, associating and classifying information, reasoning, and making judgments.	These students exhibit undesirable behaviors or emotions that may, over time, adversely affect educational performance. Their inability to learn cannot be explained by intellectual, social, or health factors. They may be inattentive, withdrawn, timid, restless, defiant, impatient, unhappy, fearful, unreflective, lack initiative, have negative feelings and actions, and blame others.

Description

Learning Disabled*

- Assist students in getting organized.
- Give short oral directions.
- Use drill exercises.
- Give prompt cues during student performance.
- Let students with poor writing skills use a computer.
- Break assignments into small segments and assign only one segment at a time.
- Demonstrate skills and have students model them.
- Give prompt feedback.
- Use continuous assessment to mark students' daily progress.
- Prepare materials at varying levels of ability.
- Shorten the number of items on exercises, tests, and quizzes.
- Provide more hands-on activities.

Mentally Disabled*

- Use concrete examples to introduce concepts.
- Make learning activities consistent.
- Use repetition and drills spread over time.
- Provide work folders for daily assignments.
- Use behavior management techniques, such as behavior modification, in the area of adaptive behavior.
- Encourage students to function independently.
- Give students extra time to both ask and answer questions while giving hints to answers.
- Avoid doing much walking around while talking to MD students as this is distracting for them.
- Give simple directions and read them over with students.
- Use objective test items and hands-on activities because students generally have poor writing skills and difficulty with sentence structure and spelling.

Behaviorally Emotionally Disabled*

- Call students' names or ask them questions when you see their attention wandering.
- Call upon students randomly rather than in a predictable sequence.
- Move around the room frequently.
- Improve students' self-esteem by giving them tasks they can perform well, increasing the number of successful achievement experiences.
- Decrease the length of time for each activity.
- Use hands-on activities instead of using words and abstract symbols.
- Decrease the size of the group so each student can actively participate.
- Make verbal instructions clear, short, and to the point.

We appreciate the assistance of Dr. Debra O. Parker, North Carolina Central University, with this section.

(Continued)

Academically Gifted	Limited English Proficiency	Physical Disabilities
Description Academically gifted students are capable of high performance as a result of general intellectual ability, specific academic aptitude, and/or creative or productive thinking. Such students have a vast fund of general knowledge and high levels of vocabulary, memory, abstract word knowledge, and abstract reasoning.	For many of these students, English is generally a second language. Such students may be academically quite capable, but they lack the language skills needed to reason and comprehend abstract concepts in English.	Includes individuals who are orthopedically impaired, visually impaired, speech-impaired, deaf, hard-of-hearing, hearing-impaired, and health-impaired (cystic fibrosis, epilepsy). Strategies will depend on the specific disability.

Teaching Strategies

Academically Gifted	Limited English Proficiency	Physical Disabilities
■ Provide ample opportunities for creative behavior. ■ Make assignments that call for original work, independent learning, critical thinking, problem solving, and experimentation. ■ Show appreciation for creative efforts. ■ Respect unusual questions, ideas, and solutions these students provide. ■ Encourage students to test their ideas. ■ Provide opportunities and give credit for self-initiated learning. ■ Avoid overly detailed supervision and too much reliance on prescribed curricula. ■ Allow time for reflection. ■ Resist immediate and constant evaluation. This causes students to be afraid to use their creativity. ■ Avoid comparisons with other students, which applies subtle pressure to conform.	■ Use a slow but natural rate of speech; speak clearly; use shorter sentences; repeat concepts in several ways. ■ Act out questions using gestures with hands, arms, and the whole body. Use demonstrations and pantomime. Ask questions that can be answered by a physical movement such as pointing, nodding, or manipulation of materials. ■ When possible, use pictures, photos, and charts. ■ Write key terms on the chalkboard. As they are used, point to the terms. ■ Corrections should be limited and appropriate. Do not correct grammar or usage errors in front of the class, causing embarrassment. ■ Give honest praise and positive feedback through your voice tones and visual articulation whenever possible. ■ Encourage students to use language to communicate, allowing them to use their native language to ask/answer questions when they are unable to do so in English. ■ Integrate students' cultural background into class discussions. ■ Use cooperative learning where students have opportunities to practice expressing ideas without risking language errors in front of the entire class.	■ For visually and hearing-impaired students, seat them near the front of the classroom. Speak clearly and say out loud what you are writing on the chalkboard. ■ In lab settings, in order to reduce the risk of injury, ask students about any conditions that could affect their ability to learn or perform. ■ Rearrange lab equipment or the classroom and make modifications as needed to accommodate any special need. ■ Investigate assistive technology devices that can improve students' functional capabilities. ■ Discuss solutions or modifications with the student who has experience with overcoming his or her disability and may have suggestions you may not have considered. ■ Let the student know when classroom modifications are being made and allow him or her to test them out before class. ■ Ask advice from special education teachers, the school nurse, or physical therapist. ■ Plan field trips that can include all students.

Assessment Techniques

Various forms of assessment need to be used with students in order to evaluate their achievement. Written tests have traditionally been used to evaluate performance. This method of evaluation is good to use when assessing knowledge and comprehension. Other methods of assessment are preferable for measuring the achievement of the higher-level skills of application, analysis, synthesis, and evaluation.

Included in the *Parents and Their Children Teacher's Resource Guide* and the *Teacher's Resource Portfolio* are objective tests for each chapter in the text. The *Reviewing Key Points* sections in the text can be used to evaluate students' recall of key concepts. The activities suggested in *Learning by Doing* and the questions given in *Thinking Critically* will provide opportunities for you to assess your students' abilities to use critical thinking, problem solving, and application.

Performance Assessment

When you assign students some of the projects described in the text, a different form of assessing mastery or achievement is required. One method that teachers have successfully used is a rubric. A **rubric** consists of a set of criteria that includes specific descriptors or standards that can be used to arrive at performance scores for students. A point value is given for each set of descriptors, leading to a range of possible points to be assigned, usually from 1 to 5. The criteria can also be weighted. This method of assessment reduces the guesswork involved in grading, leading to fair and consistent scoring. The standards clearly indicate to students the various levels of mastery of a task. Students are even able to assess their own achievement based on the criteria.

When using rubrics, students should see the criteria at the beginning of the assignment. Then they can focus their effort on what needs to be done to reach a certain level of performance or quality of project. They have a clear understanding of your expectations of achievement.

Portfolios

Another type of performance assessment that is frequently used by teachers today is the portfolio. A **portfolio** consists of a selection of materials that students choose to document their performance over a period of time. Students select their best work samples to showcase their achievement. These items might provide evidence of employability skills as well as academic skills. Some of the items students might include in portfolios are

- work samples (including photographs, videotapes, assessments, etc.) that show mastery of specific skills
- writing samples that show communication skills
- a resume
- letters of recommendation that document specific career-related skills
- certificates of completion
- awards and recognition

The portfolio is assembled at the culmination of a course to provide evidence of learning. A self-assessment summary report should be included that explains what has been accomplished, what has been learned, what strengths the student has gained, and any areas that need improvement. Portfolios may be presented to the class by the students. The items in the portfolio can also be discussed with the teacher in light of educational goals and outcomes. Portfolios should remain the property of students when they leave the course. They may be used for interviews with potential employers.

Portfolio assessment is only one of several evaluation methods teachers can use, but it is a powerful tool for both students and teachers. It encourages self-reflection and self-assessment of a more global nature. Traditional evaluation methods of tests, quizzes, and papers have their place in measuring the achievement of some course objectives, but other assessment tools should also be used to fairly assess the achievement of all desired outcomes.

Using Other Resources

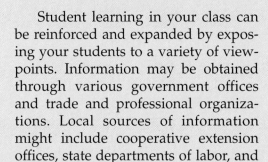

Student learning in your class can be reinforced and expanded by exposing your students to a variety of viewpoints. Information may be obtained through various government offices and trade and professional organizations. Local sources of information might include cooperative extension offices, state departments of labor, and employment agencies.

The following is a list of various trade and professional organizations, government resources, and companies that may be able to provide you with resources for use in your classroom. Names, phone numbers, and Web site addresses are included. Please note that these addresses may have changed since publication of this resource book.

Trade and Professional Organizations*

American Association of Family and Consumer Sciences (AAFCS)
(703) 706-4600
aafcs.org

American Educational Research Association (AERA)
(202) 223-9485
aera.net

American Montessori Association (AMS)
(212) 358-1250
amshq.org

Association for Supervision and Curriculum Development (ASCD)
(703) 578-9600;
(800) 933-ASCD
ascd.org

Children's Defense Fund
(202) 628-8787
childrensdefense.org

Child Welfare League of America (CWLA)
(202) 638-2952
cwla.org

Council for Exceptional Children
(703) 620-3660;
(888) CEC-SPED
cec.sped.org

International Reading Association
(302) 731-1600
reading.org

National Association for the Education of Young Children (NAEYC)
(800) 424-2460
naeyc.org

National Association for Gifted Children
(202) 785-4268
nagc.org

National Black Child Development Institute (NBCDI)
(202) 833-2200
nbcdi.org

National Committee to Prevent Child Abuse
(312) 663-3520
childabuse.org

National Education Association (NEA)
(202) 833-4000
nea.org

Society for Research in Child Development
(734) 998-6578
srcd.org

Government and Allied Organizations

Centers for Disease Control and Prevention (CDC)
(404) 639-3534
cdc.gov

National Center for Health Statistics
(301) 458-4636
cdc.gov/nchs/

National Center for Injury Prevention and Control
(770) 488-1506
cdc.gov/ncipc

National Prevention Information Network
(800) 458-5231
cdcnpin.org

National STD and AIDS Hot Line
(800) 342-AIDS
(800) 344-7432 (Spanish)
(800) 243-7889 (TTY/Deaf Access)
ashastd.org/NSTD/

Consumer Product Safety Commission
(800) 638-2772
cpsc.gov

Department of Education
(800) USA-LEARN
ed.gov

National Center for Educational Statistics
(202) 502-7300
nces.ed.gov

Department of Health and Human Services
(877) 696-6775
hhs.gov

Assistant Secretary for Planning and Evaluation
(202) 690-6461
aspe.hhs/gov

National Clearinghouse for Alcohol and Drug Information, Center for Substance Abuse Prevention
(800) 729-6686
health.org

National Institutes of Health
(800) 370-2943 (Child Health and Human Development)
nih.gov

Government Printing Office
(202) 512-1800
gpo.gov

U.S. House of Representatives
house.gov

U.S. Senate
senate.gov

Allied Organizations

Peace Corps
(800) 424-8580
peacecorps.gov

Educational Resources

AGC Educational Media
(800) 323-9084
agcmedia.com

Cambridge Educational
(800) 468-4227
cambridgeeducational.com

Creative Educational Video
(800) 922-9965

*Distinctive Home Video
Productions*
> (415) 344-7756
> distinctivehomevideo.com

*Films for the Humanities and
Sciences*
> (800) 257-5126
> films.com

The Health Connection
> (800) 548-8700
> healthconnection.org

*Human Relations Media Video
(HRM)*
> (800) 431-2050
> hrmvideo.com

Injoy Videos
> (800) 326-2083
> injoyvideos.com

The Learning Seed
> (800) 634-4941
> learningseed.com

Nasco
> (800) 558-9595
> enasco.com

Sunburst Communications Inc.
> (800) 431-1934
> sunburst.com

Teaching Aids Inc.
> (714) 786-8794

Publications for Students

*The American Montessori Society
Bulletin*
> (212) 358-1250
> amshq.org

The Black Child Advocate
> (202) 833-2200
> nbcdi.org

Child and Youth Care Forum
> (212) 620-8495
> kluweronline.com

*Child Development and Child
Development Abstracts and
Bibliography*
> (734) 998-6578
> srcd.org

Childhood Education
> (800) 423-3563
> udel.edu

Child Health Alert
> (781) 239-1762
> childhealthalert.com

Children Today
> access.gpo.gov/catalog

Child Welfare
> (202) 638-2952
> cwla.org

Developmental Psychology
> (800) 374-2721
> apa.org/journals

Dimensions of Early Childhood
> (800) 305-7322
> seca50.org/dimensions.html

Early Child Development and Care
> (800) 354-1420
> taylorandfrancis.metapress.com

*Early Childhood Education
Journal*
> (212) 620-8495
> kluweronline.com

Early Childhood News
> earlychildhood.com

*Early Childhood Research
Quarterly*
> (800) 424-2460
> naeyc.org

Early Childhood Today
> (800) SCHOLASTIC
> teacher.scholastic.com

Educational Researcher
> (202) 223-9485
> aera.net

Education International
   (800) 423-3563
   udel.edu/bateman/acei/

Education Leadership
   (703) 578-9600; (800) 933-ASCD
   ascd.org

ERIC/EECE Newsletter
   (800) 583-4135
   ericeece.org/pubs/eece-nl.html

Exceptional Children
   (703) 620-3600; (888) CEC-SPED
   cec.sped.org

Gifted Child Quarterly
   (202) 785-7628
   nagc.org

Instructor
   (212) 343-6100
   scholastic.com/instructor

Journal of Family and Consumer Sciences
   (703) 706-4600
   aafcs.org

Journal of Research in Childhood Education
   udel.edu

Report on Preschool Education
   (800) 274-6737
   bpinews.com/edu/pages/rpp.htm

Young Children
   naeyc.org

Publications for Children

Babybug, Cricket, Ladybug, **and** *Spider* **magazines**
   (800) 827-0227
   cricketmag.com

Highlights for Children Inc.
   (800) 603-0349
   highlights.com

Ranger Rick **and** *Your Big Back Yard* **magazines**
   (800) 822-9919
   nwf.org

Sesame Street
   (212) 595-3456
   sesameworkshop.org

Stone Soup
   (800) 447-4569
   stonesoup.com

Turtle
   (317) 634-1100
   cbhi.org

U.S. Kids
   (317) 636-8881
   cbhi.org

*Note: The addresses, phone numbers, FAX numbers, and Web site addresses listed may have changed since the publication of this *Teacher's Annotated Edition.*

National Standards for Family and Consumer Sciences Education

In 1998, the National Standards for Family and Consumer Sciences Education were finalized. This comprehensive guide provides family and consumer sciences educators with a structure for identifying what learners should be able to do. This structure is based on knowledge and skills needed for work life and family life, as well as family and consumer sciences careers. The National Standards Components include 16 areas of study, each with a comprehensive standard that describes the overall content of the area. Each comprehensive standard is then broken down into content standards that describe what is expected of the learner. Competencies further define the knowledge, skills, and practices of the content standards and provide the basis for measurement criteria.

By studying the text *Parents and Their Children*, students will be prepared to master the competencies listed for the area of study called Parenting. To help you see how this can be accomplished, a *Correlation of National Standards for Parenting with Parents and Their Children* has been included in the *Teacher's Annotated Edition* and *Teacher's Resources*. If you want to make sure you prepare students to meet the National Standards for Family and Consumer Sciences Education, this chart should be of interest to you.

Scope and Sequence

A *Scope and Sequence Chart*, beggining on page T28 of this introduction, identifies the major concepts presented in each chapter of the text. This special resource is provided to help you select for study those topics that meet your curriculum needs.

Goodheart-Willcox Welcomes Your Comments

We welcome your comments or suggestions regarding *Parents and Their Children* and its ancillaries as we are continually striving to publish better educational materials. Please send any comments you may have to:

Editorial Department
Goodheart-Willcox Publisher
18604 West Creek Drive
Tinley Park, IL 60477-6243

or to send a memo to the editor, visit our Web site at
www.goodheartwillcox.com

Correlation of National Standards for Parenting with *Parents and Their Children*

In planning your program, you may want to use the correlation chart below. This chart correlates the Family and Consumer Sciences Education National Standards with the content of *Parents and Their Children.* It lists the competencies for each of the content standards for Parenting. It also identifies the major text concepts that relate to each competency. Bold numbers indicate chapters in which concepts are found.

After studying the content of this text, students will be able to achieve the following comprehensive standard:

15.0 Evaluate the impact of parenting roles and responsibilities on strengthening the well being of individuals and families.

Content Standard 15.1 Analyze roles and responsibilities of parenting.	
Competencies	**Text Concepts**
15.1.1 Examine parenting roles across the life span.	**1:** Responsibilities and rewards of parenting **2:** What influences parenting decisions; Factors to consider; Teen parenthood; Decision making **3:** How are families formed?; Family structures; Functions of the family; Your roles; The family life cycle **4:** The influence of the family; The family is the primary nurturing unit; Characteristics of strong families; Effective parent-child relationships **5:** Human reproduction; The man's role; The woman's role **6:** Conception **7:** Medical care, nutrition, and weight gain during pregnancy; Factors that increase health risks to mother and baby **8:** Childbirth preparation decisions; What baby supplies will be needed?; Choosing breast-feeding or formula-feeding; Who will share in the baby's care? **9:** Bonding **10:** The first days of parenthood; How parents care for their newborns; Holding, feeding, bathing, and dressing the newborn; When the newborn cries; The husband and wife as parents **11-15:** Physical, intellectual, emotional, and social development **16:** Piaget's theory of intellectual development; Erikson's theory of personality development; Maslow's hierarchy of human needs; Kohlberg's theory of moral development; Parenting strategies **17:** Guiding children's behavior; How parents guide behavior; Effective discipline; Parents as positive role models; Media influences; Developing responsibility; honesty, and a healthy sexuality **18:** Balancing family and work roles **20:** Deciding whether to use child care; Selecting and evaluating child care **21:** Parents' roles in their children's education; Parents' involvement at home and with schools; Children with special needs; Parents' roles in their children's health care; Caring for a sick child at home

(Continued)

Competencies	Text Concepts
15.1.2 Examine expectations and responsibilities of parenting.	**1:** The job description; Myths about the job; Responsibilities and rewards of parenting **2:** What influences parenting decisions; Factors to consider; Teen parenthood; Decision making **3:** How are families formed?; Functions of the family; Families: yesterday, today, and tomorrow; Your roles; The family life cycle **4:** The influence of the family; Characteristics of strong families **5:** Factors that influence family planning decisions; Human reproduction; The role of heredity; Infertility; Options for infertile couples **6:** Physical and emotional changes during pregnancy; Complications during pregnancy **7:** Medical care, nutrition, and weight gain during pregnancy; Factors that increase health risks to mother and baby; Rest **8:** Childbirth preparation decisions; What baby supplies will be needed?; Choosing breast-feeding or formula-feeding; Who will share in the baby's care? **9:** Signs of labor; Childbirth medications; Methods of childbirth; Bonding; Postpartum period **10:** The first days of parenthood; How parents care for their newborns; Holding, feeding, bathing, and dressing the newborn; When the newborn cries; The husband and wife as parents **11:** Physical, intellectual, emotional, and social development; Medical checkups for infants **12:** Physical, intellectual, emotional, and social development; Medical checkups for toddlers; The importance of play to a child's overall development **13:** Physical, intellectual, emotional, and social development; Medical checkups for preschoolers **14:** Readiness for school; Physical, intellectual, emotional, and social development; Children and stress; Medical checkups for school-age children **15:** Physical, intellectual, emotional, and social development; Medical checkups for teens **17:** Guiding children's behavior; How parents guide behavior; Effective discipline; Parents as positive role models; Media influences; Developing responsibility, honesty, and a healthy sexuality **18:** Balancing family and work roles **20:** Deciding whether to use child care; Selecting and evaluating child care; Concerns of parents **21:** Parents' involvement at home and with schools; Children with special needs; Parents' roles in their children's health care; Caring for a sick child at home
15.1.3 Determine consequences of parenting practices to the individual, family, and society.	**1:** The job description; Responsibilities and rewards of parenting **2:** Teen parenthood **3:** Each family is unique **4:** Effects of heredity and environment; Influence of the family; Characteristics of strong families; Effective parent-child relationships; Parental influence on a child's self-concept and self-esteem **5:** Advantages of family planning; Options for infertile couples **6:** Complications during pregnancy **7:** Medical care, nutrition, and weight gain during pregnancy; Factors that increase health risks to mother and baby

Competencies	Text Concepts
	8: Choosing breast-feeding or formula-feeding; Employment decisions; Choosing a caregiver; Choosing the baby's doctor **9:** Bonding **10:** The first days of parenthood; How parents care for their newborns; Holding, feeding, bathing, and dressing the newborn; When the newborn cries; Personal adjustments in family life **11:** Keeping babies safe; Introducing solid foods; Weaning; Teething; Sleeping patterns and problems; The brain grows and develops; Learning by imitation; Play time means learning; Can parents spoil their babies?; Medical checkups for infants **12:** Life skills; Toilet learning; The importance of books; Guiding the toddler's behavior; Temper tantrums; The importance of play to a child's development; Medical checkups for toddlers **13:** Providing for active play; Life skills; Enuresis; Intellectual development; Developing gender roles; The importance of play; Nightmares; Self-care children; Children and stress; Medical checkups for preschoolers **14:** Readiness for school; Physical, intellectual, emotional, and social development; Children and stress; Medical checkups for school-age children **15:** Eating disorders; Health risks of tobacco, drinking, and drug abuse; Sexual health and teens; Decision-making skills; Emotional and social development; Medical checkups for teens **16:** Piaget's theory of intellectual development; Erikson's theory of personality development; Maslow's hierarchy of human needs; Kohlberg's theory of moral development; Parenting strategies **17:** Guiding children's behavior; Parenting styles; Effective discipline; Parents as positive role models; Media influences; Developing responsibility, honesty, and a healthy sexuality **18:** Balancing family and work roles; Divorce; Remarriage and stepfamilies; Serious illness; Explaining death to children; Family moves **19:** What is a crisis?; Unemployment and financial crises; Alcoholism and other drug abuse; Child abuse and neglect; Gangs, bullies, and peer violence; Missing children; Suicide **20:** Deciding whether to use child care; Selecting and evaluating child care **21:** Parents' involvement at home and with schools; Children with special needs; Parents' roles in their children's health care; Caring for a sick child at home
15.1.4 Determine societal conditions that impact parenting across the life span.	**1:** Myths about the job **2:** Teen parenthood **3:** How are families formed?; Family structures; Functions of the family; Families: yesterday, today, and tomorrow; Cultural, lifestyle, media, and technological influences **4:** Effects of heredity and environment; Parent support systems; Support groups **5:** Factors that influence family planning decisions; Options for infertile couples **6:** Sexually transmitted diseases **7:** Medical care, nutrition, weight gain, and exercise during pregnancy; Factors that increase health risk to mother and baby; Rest **8:** Childbirth preparation decisions; Where will the birth take place?; What baby supplies will be needed?; Choosing breast- or formula-feeding; Employment decisions; Choosing a caregiver

(Continued)

Competencies	Text Concepts
	9: Childbirth medications; Methods of childbirth; Neonatal care **15:** Eating disorders; Health risks of tobacco, drinking, and drug abuse; Sexual behavior **17:** How parents guide behavior; Punishment; Television; Music; Computer software and the Internet; Gender roles; Teens and sexuality **18:** Balancing family and work roles; Divorce; Remarriage and stepfamilies **19:** Unemployment and financial crises; Alcoholism and other drug abuse; Gangs, bullies, and peer violence; Missing children; Suicide **20:** Deciding whether to use child care; Types of child care **21:** Children with special needs; Inclusion
15.1.5 Explain cultural differences in roles and responsibilities of parenting.	**1:** To teach children about their heritage and culture **3:** Each family is unique; Cultural influences

Content Standard 15.2 Evaluate parenting practices that maximize human growth and development.

Competencies	Text Concepts
15.2.1 Choose nurturing practices that support human growth and development.	**1:** The job description; To love their children; To fulfill children's needs; To take care of themselves **2:** Desire to be parents; Decision making **3:** Functions of the family **4:** The family is the primary nurturing unit; The influence of the marital relationship on children; Characteristics of strong families; Effective communication techniques; Parental influence on a child's self-concept and self-esteem **6:** The expectant couple as a team **7:** Medical care, nutrition, weight gain, and exercise during pregnancy; Factors that increase risk to mother and baby; Rest **8:** Choosing breast- or formula-feeding; Who will share in the baby's care? **9:** Bonding **10:** The first days of parenthood; How parents care for their newborns; The husband and wife as parents **11:** Keeping babies safe; The brain grows and develops; Can parents spoil their babies? **12:** Guiding the toddler's behavior **14:** School adjustments; Self-care children; Children and stress **16:** Piaget's theory of intellectual development; Erikson's theory of personality development; Maslow's hierarchy of human needs; Kohlberg's theory of moral development; Parenting strategies **17:** Guiding children's behavior; Sibling relationships **20:** Characteristics of the caregivers **21:** Teachable moments; Encouragement; Children with special needs; Caring for a sick child at home **22:** Personal characteristics needed to work with children

(Continued)

Competencies	Text Concepts
15.2.2 Select communication strategies that promote positive self-esteem in family members.	**2:** Decision making **4:** Communicate with one another; The role of communication; The importance of open communication; Inhibitors to open communication; Effective communication techniques; Active listening; Defining problem ownership; Using "I", "you", or "we" messages; Parental influences on a child's self-esteem **6:** Emotional changes during pregnancy; The expectant couple as a team **11:** The brain grows and develops **12-13:** Language development **14:** School adjustments; Parents and friends; Self-care children; Children and stress **16:** Erikson's theory of personality development **17:** Direct teaching; How parents guide behavior; Questions children ask **21:** Teachable moments; Encouragement
15.2.3 Assess common practices and emerging research about discipline on human growth and development.	**1:** To promote moral development **4:** Effects of environment and heredity **12:** Guiding the toddler's behavior; Temper tantrums **14:** Self-care children **17:** How parents guide behavior; Effective discipline; When a child misbehaves; Punishment **19:** Child abuse and neglect; Domestic violence
15.2.4 Assess the impact of abuse and neglect on children and families and determine methods for prevention.	**1:** To want and be ready for children **2:** Desire to be parents; Expectations about parenthood and children; Your readiness for parenthood; Teen parenthood **11:** The brain grows and develops **17:** How parents guide behavior; Effective discipline; Punishment; Parents as positive role models **18:** Managing dual work roles **19:** Alcoholism and other drug abuse; Child abuse and neglect; Types of child abuse and neglect; Shaken Baby Syndrome; Child abusers; Caregivers as abusers; Stopping child abuse; What you can do; Domestic violence; Runaways **20:** Selecting and evaluating substitute child care; Characteristics of the caregivers; Concerns of parents **22:** Child care personnel; Teachers; Social workers; Health services; Personal characteristics needed to work with children; Trends affecting child and family services careers
15.2.5 Determine criteria for selecting care and services for children.	**8:** Who will share in baby's care?; Employment decisions; Parental leave; Choosing a caregiver; Choosing the baby's doctor **18:** Balancing work and family roles; Options to consider **20:** Deciding whether to use child care; Types of child care; Selecting and evaluating child care; The physical setting, program and adult-child ratio; Characteristics of the caregivers; Consistency; Concerns of parents **21:** Children with special needs; Parents' roles in their children's health care **22:** Personal characteristics needed to work with children

(Continued)

Content Standard 15.3 Evaluate external support systems that provide services for parents.

Competencies	Text Concepts
15.3.1 Assess community resources that provide services for parents.	**2:** Teen parenthood **4:** Resources for parents; Parent support systems; Finding help; Support groups **14:** Self-care children; Children and stress **15:** Eating disorders; Health risks of tobacco, drinking, and drug abuse; Sexual health and teens **16:** Parenting strategies **18:** Managing dual work roles; Divorce; Remarriage and stepfamilies; Serious illness; Explaining death to children; Family moves **19:** Unemployment and financial crises; Alcoholism and other drug abuse; Child abuse and neglect; Domestic violence; Gangs, bullies, and peer violence; Missing children; Runaways; Suicide **21:** Parents' involvement with schools; Children with special needs; Parents' roles in their children's health care
15.3.2 Appraise community resources that provide opportunities related to parenting.	**1:** To want and be ready for children; To fulfill children's needs **2:** Expectations about parenthood; Expectations about children; Your readiness for parenthood; Decision making **5:** Genetic counseling; Options for infertile couples; Choosing an option **6:** Pregnancy tests, Emotional changes during pregnancy; Complications during pregnancy **7:** Medical care during pregnancy; Factors that increase health risks to mother and baby **17:** Volunteer work **18:** Balancing family and work roles **19:** What you can do **22:** Preparing for tomorrow's challenges today
15.3.3 Review current laws and policies related to parenting.	**3:** How are families formed? **5:** Options for infertile couples **8:** What baby supplies will be needed?; Parental leave **9:** Neonatal care **14:** Readiness for school; Self-care children **15:** Health risks of tobacco, drinking, and drug abuse **18:** Divorce; Legal proceedings **19:** Child abuse and neglect; Domestic violence **20:** Types of child care **21:** Children with special needs; Inclusion **22:** Child care personnel; Trends affecting child and family services careers

Content Standard 15.4 Analyze physical and emotional factors related to beginning the parenting process.

Competencies	Text Concepts
15.4.1 Examine biological processes related to prenatal development, birth, and health of mother and child.	**3:** How are families formed?; Family structures **5:** Human reproduction; The man's role; The woman's role; The role of heredity; Genetic counseling **6:** Conception; Prenatal development; Month-by-month development; Gender determination; Physical changes during pregnancy; Complications during pregnancy

(Continued)

Competencies	Text Concepts
	7: Medical care, nutrition, weight gain, and exercise during pregnancy; Factors that increase health risk to mother and baby **8:** Childbirth preparation decisions; Where will birth take place? **9:** Signs of labor; Going to the hospital; Childbirth medications; Three stages of labor; Methods of childbirth; Neonatal care; Emergency care; Postpartum period
15.4.2 Consider the emotional factors of prenatal development and birth in relation to the health of the parents and child.	**5:** Advantages of family planning; Factors that influence family planning decisions **6:** Signs of pregnancy; Pregnancy tests; Emotional changes during pregnancy; The husband's emotions; The couple's relationship; The expectant couple as a team **7:** Medical care, weight gain, and exercise during pregnancy; Factors that increase health risk to mother and baby; Rest; Maternity clothes **8:** Childbirth preparation decisions; Where will birth take place?; What baby supplies will be needed?; Choosing breast-feeding or formula-feeding; Employment decisions; Parental leave; Choosing a caregiver; Choosing the baby's doctor **9:** Signs of labor; Going to the hospital; Childbirth medications; Three stages of labor; Methods of childbirth; Neonatal care; Emergency care; Postpartum period **10:** The first days of parenthood
15.4.3 Examine implications of alternatives to biological parenthood.	**3:** How are families formed? **5:** Infertility; Options for infertile couples; Choosing an option
15.4.4 Determine legal and ethical impacts of technology.	**3:** How are families formed? **5:** Infertility; Options for infertile couples; Choosing an option

Scope and Sequence

In planning your program, you may want to use the Scope and Sequence Chart below. This chart identifies the major concepts presented in each chapter of the text. Refer to the chart to select for study those topics that meet your curriculum needs. Bold numbers indicate chapters in which concepts are found.

Part One: Decisions About Parenting

• Preparing for Parenthood

1: The job description; Myths about the job; Responsibilities of parenting; Rewards of parenting.
2: What influences parenting decisions?; Factors to consider; Teen parenthood; Decision making.
3: How are families formed?; Family structures; Functions of the family; Families: yesterday, today, and tomorrow; Your roles; The family life cycle; Each family is unique.
4: The influence of the family; Effective parent-child relationships; Parental influence on a child's self-concept and self-esteem.

• Pregnancy, Childbirth, and Postnatal Care

1: Myths about the job; To want and be ready for children; To fulfill children's needs.
2: What influences parenting decisions? Your readiness for parenthood; Teen parenthood.
3: How are families formed?; The family life cycle.
4: How children grow and develop; Effects of heredity and environment.

• Principles of Growth and Development

1: Responsibilities of parenting.
3: The family life cycle; Each family is unique.
4: How children grow and develop; Types of development; Patterns of development; Each child is unique; Effects of heredity and environment.

• Physical Development

1: To fulfill children's physical needs.
2: Health risks.
4: Physical development; Patterns of development; Each child is unique.

• Intellectual Development

1: To fulfill children's intellectual needs.
2: Education and career risks; Decision making.
4: Intellectual development; Patterns of development; Each child is unique.

• Emotional and Social Development

1: Nurturance; To fulfill children's emotional and social needs; To promote moral development; To teach children about their heritage and culture.
2: Social and emotional changes.
4: Emotional development; Patterns of development; Each child is unique; Effective parent-child relationships; Parental influence on a child's self-concept and self-esteem.

Personal and Family Relationships

1: To take care of themselves; Rewards of parenting.

2: What influences parenting decisions? Your marital relationship; Decision making.

3: How are families formed? Family structures; Nuclear families; Single-parent families; Stepfamilies; Extended families; Couples without children; Functions of the family; Your roles; Families: yesterday, today, and tomorrow; The family life cycle; Cultural influences.

4: Effects of heredity and environment; The influence of the family; The family is the primary nurturing unit; The influence of the marital relationship on children; Characteristics of strong families; Effective parent-child relationships.

Care and Guidance of Children

1: The job description; Myths about the job; Fulfilling children's needs; To promote moral development; To teach their children about their heritage and culture.

3: Functions of the family; Families: yesterday, today, and tomorrow; Each family is unique.

4: The influence of the family; Effective parent-child relationships.

Education, Health, and Safety

1: To fulfill children's needs; To take care of themselves.

2: Your age and health; Health risks; Education and career risks.

3: Functions of the family.

Special Concerns

1: To want and be ready for children; To take care of themselves.

2: Factors to consider; Teen parenthood.

3: By adoption; By other circumstances; Cultural influences; Lifestyle influences; Community influences; Media influences; Technological influences.

4: Resources for parents; Parent support systems; Finding help; Support groups.

Leadership Development and Careers

2: Your career; Decision making.

3: Lifestyle influences.

Part Two: The Beginning of Parenthood

Preparing for Parenthood

5: Advantages of family planning; Factors that influence family planning decisions; Human reproduction; Genetic counseling; Infertility; Options for infertile couples.

6: Emotional changes during pregnancy; The expectant couple as a team.

7: Medical care, nutrition, and weight gain during pregnancy; Factors that increase risk to mother and baby.

8: Childbirth preparation decisions; Where will the birth take place?; What baby supplies are needed?; Choosing breast-feeding or formula-feeding; Employment decisions; Choosing a caregiver; Choosing the baby's doctor.

Pregnancy, Childbirth, and Postnatal Care

5: Advantages of family planning; Factors that influence family planning decisions; Human reproduction; Genetic counseling; Options for infertile couples.

6: Conception; Gender determination; Prenatal development; Month-by-month development; Signs of pregnancy; Physical changes during pregnancy; Emotional changes during pregnancy; Complications during pregnancy.

7: Medical care during pregnancy; Prenatal tests; Nutrition, weight gain, and exercise during pregnancy; Factors that increase health risks to mother and baby; Medications and over-the-counter drugs; Illegal drugs; Alcohol; Smoking; Caffeine; X rays; Rest; Maternity clothes.

8: Childbirth preparation decisions; Where will the birth take place?; What baby supplies are needed?; Choosing breast-feeding or formula-feeding; Employment decisions; Choosing a caregiver; Choosing the baby's doctor.

9: Signs of labor, Going to the hospital; Childbirth medications; Three stages of labor; Methods of childbirth; Neonatal care; Bonding; Postpartum period.

10: The first days of parenthood; How the newborn looks; What the newborn can do; How parents care for their newborn.

Principles of Growth and Development

5: The role of heredity.

6: Conception; Gender determination; Prenatal development.

9: Three stages of labor; Neonatal care.

10: The newborn reflexes.

Physical Development

5: Human reproduction; The man's role; The woman's role; The role of heredity.

6: Conception; Prenatal development; Month-by-month development.

7: Factors that increase health risks to mother and baby.

9: Three stages of labor; Neonatal care.

10: What the newborn can do, see, hear, smell, taste, and feel; The newborn's reflexes.

Intellectual Development

6: Prenatal development; Month-by-month development.

10: When the newborn cries.

Emotional and Social Development

9: Bonding.

10: What the newborn can feel; Holding the newborn.

Personal and Family Relationships

5: Advantages of family planning; Factors that influence family planning decisions; Human reproduction; The man's role; The woman's role.

6: Emotional changes during pregnancy; The couple's relationship; The expectant couple as a team.

8: Who will share in the baby's care?

9: Bonding; Handling emotional changes.

10: The husband and wife as parents; Personal adjustments in family life.

Care and Guidance of Children

6: Complications during pregnancy.

7: Medical care, nutrition, and weight gain during pregnancy; Factors that increase health risks to mother and baby.

8: What baby supplies will be needed?; Choosing breast-feeding or formula-feeding; Choosing baby's doctor.

9: Neonatal care; Emergency care; Circumcision; Bonding.

10: How parents care for their newborns; Holding, dressing, bathing, and feeding the newborn; The newborn's sleeping habits.

Education, Health, and Safety

5: Advantages of family planning; Factors that influence family planning decisions; Human reproduction; Genetic counseling; Infertility; Options for infertile couples.

6: Conception; Prenatal development; Signs of pregnancy; Pregnancy tests; Physical changes during pregnancy; Complications during pregnancy; Miscarriage and stillbirth; Toxemia; Rubella; Rh factor disorder; Sexually transmitted diseases.

7: Medical care during pregnancy; Prenatal tests; Nutrition, weight gain, and exercise during pregnancy; Factors that increase health risks to mother and baby; Medications and over-the-counter drugs; Illegal drugs; Alcohol; Smoking; Caffeine; X rays; Rest.

8: Childbirth preparation decisions; Baby furniture; Baby clothes; Other equipment and supplies; Choosing breast-feeding or formula-feeding; Choosing the baby's doctor.

9: Going to the hospital; Childbirth medications; Three stages of labor; Methods of childbirth; Neonatal care; Postpartum checkup.

10: Holding, feeding, bathing, and dressing the newborn; Sudden infant death syndrome.

Special Concerns

5: The role of heredity; Infertility; Options for infertile couples.

6: Signs of pregnancy; Pregnancy tests; Complications during pregnancy; Miscarriage and stillbirth; Toxemia; Rubella; Rh factor disorder; Sexually transmitted diseases.

7: Medical care during pregnancy; Prenatal tests; Nutrition during pregnancy; Medications and over-the-counter drugs; Illegal drugs; Alcohol; Smoking; Caffeine; X rays.

8: Childbirth preparation decisions; Where will the birth take place?; Choosing breast-feeding or formula-feeding; Employment decisions; Choosing a caregiver.

9: Breech delivery; Cesarean delivery; Emergency care.

10: Sudden infant death syndrome.

Part Three: Understanding Children's Growth and Development

Preparing for Parenthood

12: Factors to consider when selecting toys.

Principles of Growth and Development

11: Large motor skills; Small motor skills.

12: Types of play; The importance of play to a child's overall development.

13: Handedness.

14: Advances in thinking patterns.

Physical Development

11: Physical development; Large motor skills; Small motor skills; Introducing solid foods; Weaning; Teething; Sleeping patterns and problems; Physical and intellectual development are related.

12: Physical development; Large motor skills; Small motor skills; Toys and play in physical development; Life skills; Teething; Toilet learning; The importance of play to a child's overall development.

13: Physical development; Large motor skills; Small motor skills; Handedness; Life skills; Enuresis.

14: Physical development; Physical fitness and competitive sports; Physical safety.

15: Physical development; Physical changes in boys and girls.

Intellectual Development

11: Intellectual development; The brain grows and develops; Memory develops; Awareness improves; Associations are formed; Simple problems are solved; Babies see similarities and differences; Object permanence appears; Learning by imitation; Play time means learning; Language development; Babies learn the meaning of no.

12: Intellectual development; Toys and play in intellectual development; The importance of books; Language development; The importance of play to a child's overall development.

13: Intellectual development; Language development; Reading and math skills.

14: Readiness for school; Intellectual development; Advances in thinking patterns; Multiple classification; Seriation; Conservation; Reversibility; School adjustments; Schoolwork and homework.

15: Intellectual development; Decision-making skills.

Emotional and Social Development

11: Emotional and social development; Attachment to special objects; New fears; Stranger anxiety; Separation anxiety; Other emotional responses; Babies learn the meaning of no; Can parents spoil their babies?

12: Emotional and social development; Toys and play in emotional and social development; Types of play; Separation anxiety; Guiding the toddler's behavior; Temper tantrums; The importance of play to a child's overall development.

13: Emotional and social development; Developing gender roles; The importance of play; Nightmares.

14: Readiness for school; Emotional and social development; Parents and friends; Conformity; Children and stress.

15: Emotional and social development; Friendships; Dating; Self-concept and self-esteem.

Personal and Family Relationships

11: Emotional and social development; Stranger anxiety; Separation anxiety; Can parents spoil their babies?

12: Emotional and social development; Separation anxiety.

13: Emotional and social development; Developing gender roles.

14: Emotional and social development; Parents and friends.

15: Emotional and social development; Friendships; Dating.

● Care and Guidance of Children

11: Keeping babies safe; Introducing solid foods; Weaning; Teething; Sleeping patterns and problems; The brain grows and develops; Can parents spoil their babies?

12: Life skills; Toilet learning; Guiding the toddler's behavior; The importance of play to a child's overall development.

13: Providing for active play; Life skills; Eating; Dressing; Grooming; Developing gender roles; Nightmares.

14: Readiness for school; Physical fitness and competitive sports; School adjustments; Schoolwork and homework; Self-care children; Children and stress.

● Education, Health, and Safety

11: Keeping babies safe; Teething; Sleeping patterns and problems; The brain grows and develops; Medical checkups for infants.

12: Life skills; Teething; Toilet learning; The importance of books; Factors to consider when selecting toys; Medical checkups for toddlers.

13: Life skills; Enuresis; Language development; Reading and math skills; Medical checkups for preschoolers.

14: Readiness for school; Physical safety; Self-care children; Children and stress; Medical checkups for school-age children.

15: Eating disorders; Health risks of tobacco, drinking, and drug abuse; Sexual health and teens; Medical checkups for teens.

● Special Concerns

11: Sleeping patterns and problems; The brain grows and develops; Stranger anxiety; Separation anxiety.

12: Toilet learning; Separation anxiety; Temper tantrums.

13: Handedness; Enuresis; Nightmares.

14: Self-care children; Children and stress.

15: Eating disorders; Health risks of tobacco, drinking, and drug abuse; Sexual health and teens.

Part Four: The Challenges of Parenting

● Preparing for Parenthood

18: Balancing work and family roles.
20: Deciding whether to use child care.

● Pregnancy, Childbirth, and Postnatal Care

17: Developing a healthy sexuality.

● Principles of Growth and Development

16: Piaget's theory of intellectual development; Erikson's theory of personality development; Freud's theory of personality development; Maslow's hierarchy of human needs; Kohlberg's theory of moral development; An overall view of development.

17: How children learn behavior; Styles of parenting.

19: What is a crisis?

● Physical Development

16: Maslow's hierarchy of human needs.
21: Children with physical disabilities; Inclusion.

● Intellectual Development

16: Piaget's theory of intellectual development; Maslow's hierarchy of human needs.
17: How children learn behavior.
21: Parents' involvement at home; Parents' involvement with schools; Children with mental disabilities; Children with learning disabilities; Attention deficit/hyperactivity disorder; Gifted children; Inclusion.

● Emotional and Social Development

16: Erikson's theory of personality development; Freud's theory of personality development; Maslow's hierarchy of human needs; Kohlberg's theory of moral development.
17: Imitation; Identification; Reinforcement; Parents as positive role models; Sibling relationships; Developing responsibility, honesty, and a healthy sexuality; Gender roles.
18: Children's reactions to divorce.
21: Encouragement; Children with emotional disorders; Inclusion.

● Personal and Family Relationships

16: Erikson's theory of personality development; Freud's theory of personality development; Kohlberg's theory of moral development.
17: Sibling relationships.
18: Balancing family and work roles; Divorce; Remarriage and stepfamilies; A death in the family.
19: What is a crisis?; Unemployment and financial crises; Child abuse and neglect; Domestic violence; Gangs, bullies, and peer violence; Missing children; Runaways; Suicide.
20: Deciding whether to use child care; Concerns of parents.
21: Parents' roles in their children's education; Children with special needs; Parents' roles in their children's health care.

● Care and Guidance of Children

16: Parenting strategies; An overall view of development.
17: Guiding children's behavior; How children learn behavior; How parents guide behavior; Effective discipline; When a child misbehaves; Punishment; Parents as positive role models; Developing responsibility, honesty, and a healthy sexuality; Gender roles; Media influences.
20: Deciding whether to use child care; Types of child care; Selecting child care; Evaluating child care; Concerns of parents.
21: Parents' roles in their children's education; Children with special needs; Parents' roles in their children's health care; Caring for a sick child at home.
22: Child care personnel; Personal characteristics needed to work with children; Trends affecting child and family services careers.

Education, Health, and Safety

17: How children learn behavior.

19: Alcoholism and other drug abuse; Child abuse and neglect; Domestic violence; Missing children; Runaways; Suicide.

20: Deciding whether to use child care; Types of child care; Selecting child care; Evaluating child care; Concerns of parents.

21: Parents' roles in their children's education; Children with mental, physical, and learning disabilities; Children with emotional disorders; Gifted children; Inclusion; Parents' roles in their children's health care; Caring for a sick child at home.

22: Child care personnel; Teachers; Children's librarians; Health services.

Special Concerns

17: Effective discipline; Punishment; Sibling rivalry; Stealing; Television; Music; Computer software and the Internet.

18: Balancing family and work roles; Divorce; Remarriage and stepfamilies; Serious illness; Explaining death to children; Family moves.

19: Unemployment and financial crises; Alcoholism and other drug abuse; Child abuse and neglect; Shaken Baby Syndrome; Domestic violence; Gangs, bullies, and peer violence; Missing children; Runaways; Suicide.

20: Deciding whether to use child care; Concerns of parents.

21: Children with mental, physical, and learning disabilities; Children with emotional disorders; Gifted children; Inclusion; Caring for a sick child at home.

Leadership Development and Careers

17: Volunteer work; Part-time jobs.

18: Balancing family and work roles; Reasons parents work; Options to consider; Managing dual work roles.

19: Unemployment and financial crises.

20: Types of child care; Selecting child care.

21: Children with special needs; Inclusion.

22: Working directly with children; Child care personnel; Nannies; Teachers; Children's librarians; Youth and recreation leaders; Social workers; Health services; Working on behalf of children and their families; Creating and selling products and services for children; Designing and selling children's products; Writers, artists, and entertainers; Entrepreneurship; Considering a Career in child and Family Services; Developing a Career Plan; Personal qualifications for a child and family services career; Trends affecting child and family services careers; Preparing for tomorrow's challenges today; Joining student organizations; Developing your leadership skills; Part-time employment; Interviewing for a job.

Lesson Planning Guides

Chapter 1: Parenting as a Career

Chapter Objectives

- Describe the process of parenting.
- List qualities needed by effective parents.
- Explain popular myths about parenting.
- Describe the responsibilities and rewards of parenting

Text Outline	Supplementary Resources

I. The Job Description
   A. Dedication
   B. Flexibility
   C. Nurturance
	SAG: *Parenting Job Qualifications,* Activity A
	Opinions About Parenting, Activity B
	TR: *Parent Career Application,* reproducible master 1-1

II. Myths About the Job
   A. Myth #1: All parenting skills are instinctive.
   B. Myth #2: Parenting is always fun.
   C. Myth #3: Children are always cute and sweet.	

III. Responsibilities of Parenting
   A. To Fulfill Their Legal Responsibilities and Rights
   B. To Want and Be Ready for Children
   C. To Love Their Children
   D. To Fulfill Children's Physical Needs
   E. To Fulfill Children's Intellectual, Emotional, and Social Needs
   F. To Promote Moral Development
   G. To Teach Children About Their Heritage and Culture
   H. To Take Care of Themselves
	SAG: *Parenting Observation,* Activity C
	TR: *Family Traditions—Now and in the Future,* reproducible master 1-2
	Responsibilities of Parenting, color transparency CT-1A

IV. Rewards of Parenting	**SAG:** *Responsibilities and Rewards of Parenting,* Activity D **TR:** *Rewards of Parenting,* color transparency CT-1B

(Continued)

Assessment

Answers to Reviewing Key Points questions in the text, page 25

1. Parenting is the process of raising a child. (Description is student response.)

2. (Student answers should reflect the following:) Parents need to be dedicated because parenting is a 24-hour-a-day, everyday job. They need to be flexible so they can adjust quickly and easily to new situations. Parents need to be nurturing because children require loving care and attention to grow.

3. (Describe one. Student response.)

4. The seven responsibilities of parenting discussed in the text are: to want and be ready for children; to love their children; to fulfill children's physical needs; to fulfill children's emotional, intellectual, and social needs; to promote moral development; to teach children about their heritage and culture; and to take care of themselves.

5. ethnic identity

6. (Describe two:) parents can set a good example for their children, parents can talk to their children about morals, parents can establish a positive home environment, parents can set rules to guide their children's behavior.

7. (Student response.)

TR: *Chapter 1 Test*, reproducible master
GWTCS: Questions for Chapter 1

Technology Applications

- Have students visit the Web site filmvalues.com. Ask them to research three children's movies. After reading the review, have students write their own review of the movie saying whether they would let a child watch the movie. The review should be from the angle of whether the movie would promote a child's moral development.
- Have students research a cultural tradition different from their own for each month of the year. Using a computer calendar program, have students design a calendar that highlights each tradition. Ask students to share their calendars with the class.
- Using a desktop publishing program, have students design an appreciation certificate for their parents. Explain to students that by recognizing their parents they are rewarding them.

Academic Connections

- Writing. Have students write a cover letter and resume for a person they believe would be a qualified parent. The cover letter and resume should include qualities of a good parent, why this person would be a good parent, and past experiences with children. Resumes could be tailored in the typical format to include information such as previous experience.
- Drama. Have students write short skits about the myths of parenting. Ask the students to perform the skits in class. The skits could also be performed at a community parenting class.

Web Sites

National Parent Information Network
http://npin.org

Chapter 2: Parenting: A Choice

Chapter Objectives

- Describe factors that influence parenting decisions.
- Evaluate reasons some people choose parenting and others do not.
- Identify factors couples should consider when deciding about parenting.
- Describe challenges and risks faced by teen parents.
- Demonstrate how people can use the decision-making process to decide about parenting.

Text Outline	Supplementary Resources

I. What Influences Parenting Decisions?
  A. Desire to Express Marital Love
  B. Desire to Be Parents
  C. Expectations About Parenthood
  D. Expectations About Children
  E. Pressure from Family and Friends
  F. Desire to Influence a Partner
	SAG: *The Personal Choice,* Activity A
	Parenting Views, Activity B
	Your Feelings About Parenting, Activity C

II. Factors to Consider
  A. Your Goals
  B. Your Marital Relationship
  C. Your Finances
  D. Your Career
  E. Your Readiness for Parenthood
  F. Your Age and Health
	SAG: *Time/Life Lines,* Activity D
	Characteristics of Parents, Activity E
	Couples and Children, Activity F
	Costs of Having a Baby, Activity G
	Children, Marriage, and Careers, Activity H
	Couple Profile, Activity I
	TR: *What Are Your Role Expectations as a Parent?* reproducible master 2-1
	Parents Spend $ for…, color transparency CT-2A
	Parents Save $ for…, color transparency CT-2B
	Two Couples—Two Solutions, reproducible master 2-2

III. Teen Parenthood
  A. Health Risks
  B. Social and Emotional Changes
  C. Education and Career Risks
  D. Financial Risks
	SAG: *Teen Parents: The Risks and Challenges,* Activity J

IV. Decision Making	**SAG:** *The Parenting Decision,* Activity K **TR:** *Decision-Making Chain for Marriage and Parenting,* transparency master 2-3 *Decision-Making Chain for Parenting,* transparency master 2-4 *Role-Playing the Parenting Decision,* reproducible master 2-5

(Continued)

Assessment

Answers to *Reviewing Key Points* questions in the text, page 48

1. A desire to express marital love may be the best reason for having a child.

2. (Describe two:) giving in to family and peer pressure, trying to influence a partner, wanting children for friends, wanting children for companionship during old age, having children only to satisfy curiosity

3. (List four:) may not want to be parents, may have negative expectations about parenthood, may have negative expectations about children, may have goals that conflict with parenting, may not have a strong marriage, may want to focus on marriage, may not be financially able or willing to have children, may want to focus on career, career and parenting may not fit together, may not be ready for parenthood, may not want to give up lifestyle, may not be a good age to have children, may have health concerns

4. (Explain two:) their goals, marital relationship, finances, careers, readiness for parenthood, age, and health (Explanation is student response.)

5. The purpose of designing a time/life line is to help you to set future goals and see how different goals fit together.

6. (Possible answers may include the following:) A couple should have a strong marital relationship before having children. If they do not have a strong marriage, they should focus on their marriage before having children. A couple should make parenting decisions before marriage.

7. The cost of raising a child increases as a child grows older because older children eat more, wear more clothes, go more places, and participate in more activities. They also need more space and indirectly may force the family to move to a larger, more expensive home.

8. (Describe one:) pregnant teens—bodies are not fully grown, may compete with baby for nutrients, faces even greater risk if pregnancy occurs again too soon, higher risk for complications during pregnancy; (Describe one:) their infants—may be born too early; may be born too small; may have complications such as brain, lung, liver, and heart problems; more likely to die during infancy (Description is student response.)

9. (Explain one:) one or both partners may feel trapped by the sudden awareness of how their lives have changed, they may feel isolated from friends, they find they have less freedom and little time to go out with friends, they may no longer have as much in common with their friends, they are more likely to drop out of school, they may be forced into low-paying jobs, they are less likely to go to college, they may not be able to have the careers they wanted, etc. (Explanation is student response.)

TR: *Chapter 2 Test*, reproducible master
GWTCS: Questions for Chapter 2

(Continued)

Assessment *(Continued)*

10. identify the decision to be made, list all possible alternatives, evaluate the consequences of each alternative, choose one alternative, act on the decision, evaluate the results

Technology Applications

- Have students research the challenges of pregnancy for women at different ages. One site to visit is the National Center for Health Statistics at cdc.gov/nchs. Ask students to write a short paper discussing how age affects parenting decisions.
- Have students research teenage pregnancy. One site to visit is the National Campaign to Prevent Teen Pregnancy at teenpregnancy.org. Ask students to design their own campaign that would help reduce teenage pregnancies. Have students make posters with a campaign slogan. With permission, display the posters around school.
- Visit the Web site babycenter.com. In the left hand column, there is an icon called "Cost of Child Calculator." Ask the students to use the calculator. Discuss the students' findings.

Academic Connections

- Math. Have students pair off and congratulate them on the fact that each "couple" is one month from having a baby. For each pair, assign a different yearly income. Have the pair make a budget that would allow them to cover all the costs of raising a child. The budgets should include the types of items they will purchase and at what price. After budgets are determined, lead a class discussion on how the groups made financial decisions.
- Psychology. Invite a marriage counselor to the class. Have him or her discuss factors that influence parenting decisions, reasons couples decide to become parents, the challenges couples face, and how couples use the decision-making process to decide whether to become parents.

Web Sites

Alan Guttmacher Institute
agi-usa.org/pubs/teen_preg_sr_0699.html

National Center for Chronic Disease Prevention and Health Promotion
cdc.gov/nccdphp/teen.htm

Chapter 3: Families

Chapter Objectives

- Explain ways families may be formed.
- Identify the five family structures.
- Evaluate the unique characteristics of each structure.
- List the functions of the family.
- Summarize ways families have changed over time.
- Identify all the roles you may assume in life.
- Describe the stages of the family life cycle.
- Explain how cultural, lifestyle, community, media, and technological influences can make families unique.

Text Outline	Supplementary Resources
I. How Are Families Formed? A. By Birth B. By Marriage C. By Adoption D. Other Ways Families Are Formed	**SAG:** *How Families Are Formed,* Activity A
II. Family Structures A. Nuclear Families B. Single-Parent Families C. Stepfamilies D. Extended Families E Couples Without Children	**SAG:** *Parent Panel,* Activity B *Family Structure Opinions,* Activity C *Family Structures,* Activity D **TR:** *Family Structures,* color transparencies, CT-3A and CT-3B *Challenges of Changing Family Structures,* reproducible master 3-1 *The Shape of Family Structures,* reproducible master 3-2
III. Functions of the Family	
IV. Families: Yesterday, Today, and Tomorrow	**SAG:** *Families: Yesterday, Today, and Tomorrow,* Activity E
V. Your Roles	**SAG:** *Your Family Roles,* Activity F
VI. The Family Life Cycle A. The Beginning Stage B. The Expanding Stage C. The Developing Stage D. The Launching Stage E. The Aging Stage	**SAG:** *Your Family Life Cycle,* Activity G *Grandparents,* Activity H **TR:** *The Family Life Cycle,* transparency master 3-3
VII. Each Family Is Unique A. Cultural Influences B. Lifestyle Influences C. Community Influences D. Media Influences E. Technological Influences	**SAG:** *A Unique Family,* Activity I **TR:** *Each Family Is Unique,* transparency master 3-4

(Continued)

Assessment

Answers to *Reviewing Key Points* questions in the text, page 74

1. A family of origin is the family in which a child grows up.

2. (Explain three:) by birth, by marriage, by adoption, by other circumstances (Explanation is student response.)

3. (List two:) Couples might choose to adopt if they are unable to conceive, if they have hereditary conditions they might pass to biological children, or if they want to give a home to children who need one. (Other answers may be given.)

4. Adoptive parents are permanent parents, while foster parents provide temporary care.

5. A.   nuclear family
   B.   extended family
   C.   stepfamily
   D.   couple without children
   E.   single-parent family

6. (Give two:) offers opportunities for several close relationships, has legal and social approval, offers two parents, offers less complicated family relationships (Other answers may be given.)

7. the single-parent family

8. (List three:) must develop relationships, must blend the lifestyles of two different families, and must adjust budget and financial goals, may have to share space (Other answers may be given.)

9. Providing for the physical needs of all family members involves sharing economic resources, offering safety, and caring for health. Nurturing the growth of all family members involves guiding all aspects of a child's development, including social and intellectual development. It also involves supporting adults' growth. Meeting the emotional needs of all family members involves accepting all family members for who they are.

10. (Student response.)

11. (Student response. See pages 63-66 in the text.)

12. (Describe one:) many of today's grandparents are busy expanding their lives with their own activities, some grandparents are becoming more involved with the lives of their grandchildren, when parents need help with child care, grandparents may fill this need

13. It is important to teach children about ethnic diversity so they can understand and appreciate people from other cultural and ethnic groups. This will help them get along better with others and succeed in a multicultural world.

TR: *Chapter 3 Test*, reproducible master

GWTCS: Questions for Chapter 3

(Continued)

Assessment *(Continued)*

14. (Give two:) the jobs parents have, where the family lives, community involved, how family spends leisure time (Other answer may be given.)
15. (Student response.)

Technology Applications

- Split students into groups. Give each group a video camera. Have the groups act as if they are television reporters. Have the "reporters" ask students around the school to define *family*. With the information obtained, ask the "reporters" to write a news clip on the definition of a family. Ask the reporters to edit their video tapes to correspond with the news clip that was written. Show each group's tape and lead a discussion on why people define families differently.
- Analyze television programs (new shows and old reruns) to determine different family structures. Some examples to watch would include the following: *Leave it to Beaver, The Brady Bunch, The Jeffersons,* and *The Gillmore Girls.* Ask students to discuss the benefits of each family and how family structures and roles have changed over the years.
- Ask students to research adoption or foster parenting using Internet resources. Some sources to suggest are adoption.com, adoption.org, adoptiveparents.com, fostercare.com, and nfpainc.org. Have students pick one aspect of adoption or being a part of foster families. Ask the students to prepare oral reports about the aspects they researched.
- The television industry developed a rating system. The Web site tvguidelines.org explains what the ratings mean. Have students visit the Web site and read the guidelines. Then ask the students to research the Internet to discover why these ratings were established and whether families feel they are effective.

Academic Connections

- Social studies. Expanding on the section *Families: Yesterday, Today, and Tomorrow,* have students research how families have changed in the past decade and what events have caused the change. Ask students to write a short report on the changes and have them include a paragraph on how they think family structures will change in the next 100 years.
- Art. Ask students to draw pictures or make a collage of the different stages of the family life cycle. Students could also make cartoons depicting a stage of the family life cycle. Display the artwork around the class or school. If a student makes a cartoon, consider asking the local newspaper to publish it.
- Family and consumer sciences: Food and Nutrition. Hold a cultural food fair. Invite students to bring in a family dish along with other items representing their culture. Invite guests from different cultures to come to the food fair and present information about their culture. Use the food fair to discuss how bias, prejudices, and stereotypes can be formed about different cultures.
- English. Ask students to use their critical thinking skills to analyze the technological influences on the family. Have them write a paper on the positive and negative technological influences.

Web Sites

National Adoption Information Clearinghouse
calib.com/naic

National Foster Parent Association Inc.
nfpainc.org

National Institute on Media and the Family
mediaandthefamily.org

Center for Media Education
cme.org

Chapter 4: Effective Parenting

Chapter Objectives

- Identify physical, intellectual, emotional, and social forms of development.
- Describe the principles of growth and development.
- Distinguish between the influences of heredity and environment on a child's development.
- Summarize the influence of the family on a child's development.
- Identify characteristics of strong families.
- Analyze the influence of effective communication on parent-child relationships.
- Describe effective communication techniques that can strengthen family relationships.
- Explain how parents can influence their child's self-concept and self-esteem.
- Identify sources of parenting support and assistance.

Text Outline	Supplementary Resources
I. How Children Grow and Develop A. Types of Development B. Patterns of Development C. Each Child Is Unique	**SAG:** *Types of Development*, Activity A *Patterns of Development*, Activity B
II. Effects of Heredity and Environment	**SAG:** *Heredity or Environment?* Activity C
III. The Influence of the Family A. The Family Is the Primary Nurturing Unit B. The Influence of the Marital Relationship on Children C. Characteristics of Strong Families	**SAG:** *Needs of Children and Parents*, Activity D *Balancing Needs of Parents and Their Children*, Activity E *Characteristics of Strong Families*, Activity F
IV. Effective Parent-Child Relationships A. The Role of Communication B. Effective Communication Techniques C. Parental Influence on the Child's Self-Concept D. Parental Influences on the Child's Self-Esteem	**SAG:** *Communication Enhancers and Inhibitors*, Activity G *Building a Child's Self-Concept and Self-Esteem*, Activity H **TR:** *Communication in Families: Communication Enhancers* and *Communication in Families: Communication Inhibitors*, color transparencies CT-4A and CT-4B *A Healthy Self-Concept*, reproducible master 4-1 *Active Listening…*, transparency master 4-2
V. Resources for Parents A. Parent Support Systems B. Finding Help C. Support Groups	**SAG:** *Parent Helpers*, Activity I *Building a Parent Support System*, Activity J

(Continued)

Assessment

Answers to *Reviewing Key Points* questions in the text, page 98

1. Growth is an increase in body size, strength, and ability. Development means a change of function as a result of growth.

2. (Student response.)

3. A. trunk outward
   B. sequence
   C. head to foot

4. (Student response.)

5. By communicating, family members can get to know one another better and become closer.

6. sending messages(speaking) and receiving messages (listening)

7. verbal—speaking, writing; nonverbal—gestures, facial expressions, body movements

8. pay attention to the speaker, acknowledge what is being said, allow the speaker to do most of the talking, acknowledge feelings.

9. (Student response.)

10. (Student response.)

11. (Student response.)

12. A support system includes all the people, institutions, and organizations parents can turn to when in need. A support group may be a part of a person's support system. It is a group of people who share a similar problem or concern.

TR: *Chapter 4 Test*, reproducible master
GWTCS: Questions for Chapter 4

Technology Applications

- Have students visit the Web site babycenter.com/calculator/6546.html. Ask the students to take the quiz to test their child development knowledge. After completing the quiz, ask them to read the articles that correspond with the quiz questions.
- Have each student help a young child learn how to use an unfamiliar technology item. Encourage the students to help the child use the technology in a way that would help the child develop a positive self-concept. Ask the students to use effective praise techniques. (This activity could be done in the elementary schools in collaboration with a teacher who is introducing a new concept to students.)
- Split the class into three groups including the following: parent support systems, finding help, and support groups. Assign each group to do research on their topic. Using a computer drawing program, have the group design a brochure. Make the brochures available to the community.

Academic Connections

- English. Have students write a short children's book showing the characteristics of a strong family. Ask the students to visit a child care center and read their book to the children at the center.
- Speech. Ask students to tape a conversation they have with one of their family members using a tape recorder. Have students analyze the conversation to see whether effective communication techniques are being used. Ask students to suggest ways they could improve communication among family members.

Web Sites

KidsHealth, Nemours Foundation
kidshealth.org

Parenting Toolbox (Support groups)
parentingtoolbox.com

Chapter 5: Planning a Family

Chapter Objectives

- Summarize the advantages of family planning.
- Identify factors that influence family planning decisions.
- Explain the process of reproduction.
- Identify causes of infertility.
- Describe options for infertile couples and the implications of these options.

Text Outline	Supplementary Resources
I. Advantages of Family Planning	**TR:** *Myths and Truths About Conception*, reproducible master 5-1
II. Factors that Influence Family Planning Decisions	**SAG:** *Planning Considerations*, Activity A *Factors to Consider*, Activity B

III. Human Reproduction
  A. The Man's Role
  B. The Woman's Role
  C. The Role of Heredity
  D. Genetic Counseling
	SAG: *Human Reproduction*, Activity C
	TR: *Reproductive Organs*, transparency master 5-2 *The Role of Dominant and Recessive Genes in Heredity*, transparency master 5-3

IV. Issues of Family Planning
  A. Infertility
  B. Options for Infertile Couples
  C. Sterilization
	SAG: *Family Planning Opinions*, Activity D *Options for Infertile Couples*, Activity E
	TR: *Family Planning Issues*, color-transparency CT-5-2

Assessment

Answers to *Reviewing Key Points* questions in the text, page 115

1. (Name two:) helps ensure every child born is wanted; helps a couple achieve their goals; can allow a couple to become emotionally and financially prepared for parenthood; can determine size of family they desire, spacing and timing of children born; can stop having children when family is the right size

2. Most authorities suggest parents space their children three to four years apart because this allows each child to achieve a separate status in the family. The mother has a better chance of maintaining her health and strength. Future education costs are another factor.

TR: *Chapter 5 Test*, reproducible master
GWTCS: Questions for Chapter 5

(Continued)

Assessment *(Continued)*

3. A. endometrium
    B. ovary
    C. sperm
    D. vas deferens
    E. semen
    F. uterus
    G. testes
    H. cervix
    I. egg
    J. fallopian tube
    K. epididymis

4. The man's role in reproduction is to produce and deliver sperm to the woman. One sperm will fertilize the egg and produce a baby. The woman's role in reproduction is to produce and release eggs that can be fertilized. When the egg has been fertilized, it implants in the uterus, where it grows and develops.

5. A baby's traits are determined by the kinds of genes inherited from each parent. A recessive gene is overcome by a dominant gene. A recessive trait will only appear if recessive genes from each parent combine for that particular trait.

6. Genetic counseling is counseling that offers scientific information and advice about heredity, especially about the risks of congenital disorders.

7. Congenital disorders are disorders a person is born with that result from heredity. Genetic counseling can help with the detection of congenital disorders.

8. Infertility means the inability to achieve pregnancy despite having intercourse regularly for at least a year.

9. (Name two:) fertility drugs, surgery, artificial insemination, in vitro fertilization, adoption

10. A couple might adopt a child through independent adoption or agency adoption.

11. Public adoption agencies are run by the government, while private agencies are not. Public adoption agencies place children in the state's custody, they have a shorter wait, and they involve lower fees. Private adoption agencies place more infants, they have a longer wait, and they involve higher fees.

12. The surgical procedure for sterilization of a man is vasectomy. The surgical procedure for sterilization of a woman is tubal ligation.

(Continued)

Technology Applications

- Ask students to visit the Web site noah-health.org. Once they've reached the Web site, have them click on *Health Topics* and then click on *Genetic Diseases*. Ask them to research a congenital disorder. Have them use presentation software to give a speech on the disorder. Have a genetic counselor review the presentations.

Academic Connections

- Biology. Invite the biology teacher to discuss human reproduction. Also ask the teacher to explain Punnett Squares to your class. Have the class fill out Punnett Squares to determine hereditary traits. One Web site having a fun lesson plan dealing with Punnett Squares is teach-nology.com/teachers/lesson_plans/ science/biology/genetics. At the site click on *Easter Egg Genetics*.

Web Sites

Genetic Alliance, Inc
geneticalliance.org

Infertility Resources
ihr.com/infertility

Chapter 6: Pregnancy

Chapter Objectives

- Explain the process of conception.
- Describe the highlights of month-by-month prenatal development.
- Identify signs that may indicate pregnancy.
- Describe physical and emotional changes that occur during pregnancy.
- Propose ways a husband can be involved during his wife's pregnancy.
- Describe possible complications of pregnancy.

Text Outline

I. Conception
   A. Gender Determination

II. Prenatal Development
   A. Month-by-Month Development

III. Signs of Pregnancy
   A. Pregnancy Tests

IV. Physical Changes During Pregnancy

V. Emotional Changes During Pregnancy
   A. The Husband's Emotions
   B. The Couple's Relationship

VI. Complications During Pregnancy
   A. Miscarriage and Stillbirth
   B. Pregnancy-Induced Hypertension (PIH)
   C. Rubella
   D. RH Factor Disorder
   E. Sexually Transmitted Diseases

Supplementary Resources

TR: *Gender Determination,* color transparency CT-6

SAG: *Month-by-Month Development,* Activity A
Pregnancy Changes, Activity B
Pregnancy Terms, Activity C
TR: *Prenatal Development Calendar,* reproducible master 6-1

SAG: *Complications During Pregnancy,* Activity D
TR: *Understanding STDs—Symptoms and Health Risks,* reproducible master 1-2

Assessment

Answers to *Reviewing Key Points* questions in the text, page 135

1. A trimester is a three-month period. Pregnancy has three trimesters.

2. A. The developing baby is a zygote at conception.
   B. The baby is a blastocyst at implantation.
   C. The baby is an embryo from two weeks after conception until the eighth week of pregnancy.
   D. The baby is a fetus from the ninth week of pregnancy until birth.

TR: *Chapter 6 Test,* reproducible master
GWTCS: Questions for Chapter 6

(Continued)

Assessment   *(Continued)*

3. The placenta serves as an interchange between mother and baby. The umbilical cord connects the placenta to the baby. It also helps exchange materials between mother and baby.

4. Amniotic fluid regulates the baby's body temperature, cushions the baby against possible injuries, and allows the baby to move more easily.

5. A.   sixth month
   B.   first month
   C.   ninth month

6. A baby's gender is determined by which sex chromosome the baby receives from its father. If the father gives an X chromosome, the baby will be a girl. If he gives a Y chromosome, the baby will be a boy.

7. missed menstrual periods, changes in woman's breasts, nausea

8. HCG or Human Chorionic Gonadotropin

9. (Student response.)

10. Miscarriage occurs before the fifth month of pregnancy, while stillborn occurs during the fifth month of pregnancy or later.

11. Sixty percent of miscarriages are caused by chromosome problems in the embryo or fetus.

12. an abnormal rise in blood pressure, rapid weight gain, swollen face and fingers, headaches, blurred vision

13. false

14. Carmen, because she is Rh-negative

15. (Name and describe three.) gonorrhea—the baby may be blinded by a gonorrhea infection; syphilis—the baby will be born with congenital syphilis. The baby may be stillborn or develop congenital disabilities; herpes—if the infection is severe, miscarriage or stillbirth may occur. If the baby survives, this STD usually causes physical and mental disabilities. HIV/AIDS—HIV/AIDS can be passed to the unborn child; chlamydia—the baby may develop a serious eye infection and pneumonia, and may die soon after birth.

Technology Applications

- Have students visit the Web site pennhealth.com/health/health_info/pregnancy/index.html. Have students select 9-Month Miracle where they can watch the full-color animations in *Pregnancy TV* to see how a baby develops from a single cell.
- Ask students to research common complications during pregnancy on the Internet. Have students choose one complication and make a poster explaining how to prevent, treat, and cope with the complication.

(Continued)

Academic Connections

- Science. Have students research how the female cardiovascular system, kidneys, respiratory system, gastrointestinal system, skin, hormones, liver, and metabolism are affected by pregnancy. Have students discuss their findings in class.
- Journalism. Have students interview a couple who has recently gone through a pregnancy. Ask the students to investigate how the pregnancy affected each of the person's emotions and the couple's relationship. Have students write a short newspaper article about the couple's pregnancy.

Web Sites

BabyCenter
babycenter.com

Health on the Net Foundation
hon.ch/Dossier/MotherChild/index.html

University of Pennsylvania Health System
pennhealth.com/health/health_info/pregnancy/index.html

StorkNet
pregnancyguideonline.com

Chapter 7: Prenatal Care

Chapter Objectives

- Summarize the importance of quality prenatal care that begins early in pregnancy.
- Describe medical care needed during pregnancy.
- Compare and contrast the three types of prenatal tests.
- Identify basic nutritional needs during pregnancy.
- Plan a daily menu that meets a woman's needs during pregnancy.
- Explain why proper weight gain during pregnancy is important.
- Summarize the importance of exercise.
- Describe various factors that increase health risks to mother and baby.

Text Outline	Supplementary Resources
I. Medical Care During Pregnancy 　A. The First Medical Visit 　B. Medical Checkups During Pregnancy 　C. Prenatal Tests	**TR:** *Prenatal Health Care*, reproducible master 7-1
II. Nutrition During Pregnancy 　A. The Bread, Cereal, Rice, and Pasta Group 　B. The Vegetable Group 　C. The Fruit Group 　D. The Milk, Yogurt, and Cheese Group 　E. The Meat, Poultry, Fish, Dry Beans, Eggs, and Nuts Group 　F. Fats, Oils, and Sweets 　G. Other Nutritional Concerns	**SAG:** *Diet During Pregnancy*, Activity B **TR:** *Prenatal Health Care*, color transparency CT-7A *Food Guide Pyramid*, color transparency CT-7B
III. Weight Gain During Pregnancy	
IV. Exercise During Pregnancy	
V. Factors That Increase Health Risks to Mother and Baby 　A. Medications and Over-the-Counter Drugs 　B. Illegal Drugs 　C. Alcohol 　D. Smoking 　E. Caffeine 　F. X rays	**SAG:** *Pregnancy Considerations*, Activity C *Deadly Consequences*, Activity D **TR:** *Lowering Health Risks*, reproducible master 7-2
VI. Rest	
VII. Maternity Clothes	

(Continued)

Assessment

Answers to *Reviewing Key Points* questions in the text, page 156

1. Prenatal care describes all the special care a woman and her baby need during pregnancy. Prenatal care includes medical care, nutrition, weight gain, exercise, and rest. It also includes avoiding factors that increase health risks to both mother and baby.

2. an obstetrician

3. A. Karen—April 12
   B. Natasha—August 24
   C. Sonia—November 19

4. The ultrasound test can be used to check the physical growth of the fetus to make sure growth and development are proceeding normally. It can also check the baby's position, gender, and due date. CVS and amniocentesis check the baby's genes and chromosomes for possible problems.

5. A. carbohydrates, fiber, B vitamins
   B. vitamins (B, C, E, K, folate) and minerals (iron, magnesium, iodine, zinc, selenium), fiber, carbohydrates
   C. vitamins (A, C), minerals (iron), fiber
   D. vitamins (D), minerals (calcium, phosphorus), protein, fat
   E. protein, iron, B vitamins, fat

6. A woman should drink eight glasses of water, juices, and other nonalcoholic, caffeine-free beverages a day. A woman should talk to her doctor about whether she should limit her salt intake during pregnancy. A woman should talk to her doctor before taking any dietary supplements.

7. 25 to 35 pounds

8. A woman should be able to continue the same exercise she did before she was pregnant. If she did not exercise before pregnancy, she may be advised to walk for exercise. A pregnant woman should check with her doctor about how much and what kinds of exercise she can do.

9. Babies born with FAS may have deficient growth, heart problems, small heads and brains, narrow eyes, a low nasal bridge, and a short, upturned nose. They may also have mental disabilities, poor coordination, short attention spans, and behavioral problems.

10. true

11. Researchers are not sure what caffeine's effects are during pregnancy. Some studies indicate caffeine may be dangerous, so many doctors advise their patients not to use caffeine during pregnancy.

12. X rays are a form of radiation. Exposure to radiation can cause congenital disabilities in the developing baby.

TR: *Chapter 7 Test*, reproducible master
GWTCS: Questions for Chapter 7

(Continued)

Technology Applications

- GE Medical Systems has developed a new ultrasound. Visit its Web site at gemedicalsystems.com/rad/us/4d/index.html. Have students read about the new technology and write a short paper on why the technology could be helpful.
- Visit a neonatal unit at a hospital. Have a representative or nurse talk about the equipment used for premature babies and how it has changed over the years. Have he or she talk about the factors that increase health risks and how to prevent them.

Academic Connections

- Family and consumer sciences. Have students research different foods and their nutritional benefits. Ask students to select two foods from each food group. For each food, have the students explain the nutritional benefit and why it is important for a pregnant woman.
- Social studies. Have students research how the recommended weight gain by doctors for a pregnant woman has changed over time. Ask students to research whether weight gain recommendations are different for other cultures.
- Physical education. Collaborate with the physical education department to explain what exercises are good for a pregnant woman. Choose a variety of exercises and ask students to try them. Discuss with the students the proper way for a pregnant woman to exercise and when she should quit.

Web Sites

Medline Plus Health Information
nlm.nih.gov/medlineplus/prenatalcare.html

National Institute of Child Health and Human Development
nichd.nih.gov

Health Resources and Service Administration
ask.hrsa.gov

The Coalition for Positive Outcomes in Pregnancy
storknet.org/CPOP/pbbc.htm

Chapter 8: Decisions Facing Parent's-to-Be

Chapter Objectives

- Summarize the benefits of taking prepared childbirth classes.
- Describe options a couple has when choosing a location for their baby's birth.
- Determine which baby supplies are essential for a newborn and which are optional.
- Compare breast-feeding and formula-feeding.
- Explain the benefits of parental leave.
- List child care options for working parents.
- Explain factors to consider when selecting a doctor for the baby.

Text Outline	Supplementary Resources
I. Childbirth Preparation Decisions	**SAG:** *Childbirth Preparation Class Observation*, Activity A
II. Where Will the Birth Take Place? A. Hospital Delivery Room B. Hospital Birthing Room C. Birth Center D. At Home	**SAG:** *Birthplace Options*, Activity B
III. What Baby Supplies Will Be Needed? A. Baby Furniture B. Diapers C. Baby Clothes D. Other Equipment and Supplies	**SAG:** *Types of Diapers*, Activity C *The Newborn's Wardrobe*, Activity D **TR:** *Nursery Furniture and Equipment*, reproducible master 8-1 *Choosing a Safe Crib*, color transparency CT-8
IV. Choosing Breast-Feeding or Formula-Feeding A. Breast-Feeding B. Formula-Feeding	**SAG:** *Breast- or Formula-Feeding?* Activity E
V. Who Will Share in the Baby's Care? A. Employment Decisions B. Choosing a Caregiver C. Choosing the Baby's Doctor	**SAG:** *Parental Employment*, Activity F **TR:** *Choosing Baby's Doctor*, transparency master 8-2

Assessment

Answers to *Reviewing Key Points* questions in the text, page 179

1. Prepared childbirth means both expectant parents have been taught about pregnancy, labor, and delivery, usually in childbirth classes.
2. (List three:) foster a closer relationship between spouses; promote the father's involvement; allow couples to meet other expectant parents; answer questions; teach breathing, relaxation, and coaching techniques; build expectant parents' confidence; teach techniques for controlling the woman's pain; provide a successful, pleasant, and less stressful labor

TR: *Chapter 8 Test*, reproducible master
GWTCS: Questions for Chapter 8

(Continued)

Assessment *(Continued)*

3. (Student response. See pages 161-163 in the text.)

4. (List four: Student response or suggested answers:) borrow items, garage sales, second-hand stores, make items, comparison shopping, prepare a budget, get essential items first

5. Cribs made before 1988 may not meet current safety standards. They are also often painted with lead-based paint, which is dangerous for children.

6. Cloth diapers—advantages (list two:) reusable; cost much less; doesn't pollute environment; last for several months; can come prefolded; can have hook-and-tape fasteners. Disadvantages (list two:) parents must launder; must fold each diaper; must use vinyl pants, diaper covers, or over-wraps; less convenient. Disposable diapers—advantages (list two:) convenient, parents don't have to launder; parents don't have to fold; good for traveling; don't need vinyl pants, diaper covers, or overwraps. Disadvantages (list two:) much more expensive; contributes to environmental problems; cannot reuse

7. (List three:) the baby's comfort, ease of care, how easy the garment is to put on the baby and remove, climate, season, price, style, fabric, no drawstrings, flame resistant sleepwear

8. (Student response. See pages 168-169 in the text.)

9. breast-feeding—(list two:) most highly recommended choice, nature's food for babies, contains essential nutrients and anti-bodies, requires no preparation, milk is always available and at the right temperature, doesn't cost anything, easy for baby to digest, promotes feeling of closeness, helps mother's body return to normal; formula-feeding—(list two:) father and others can feed the baby, is convenient, allows more modesty, easier if mother returns to work soon after delivery, can measure how much the baby eats, provides closeness

10. advantages—(list two:) more income, inter-acting with adults, feeling satisfied professionally, continuing career; disadvantages—(list two:) child care costs, time away from the child, having less time, feeling more stress, experiencing role strain in meeting multiple demands

11. to allow workers in certain situations to spend time with their families without fear of losing their jobs

12. so parents can concentrate on learning their parenting role before having to balance work and family roles

(Continued)

Assessment *(Continued)*

13. (List four:) one parent stays home with the baby instead of working, one or both parents work from home, parents work opposite shifts to allow them to care for the child, job-sharing to allow parents more time to be home, grandparents, relatives, friends, neighbors, private caregiver, child care center

14. A pediatrician specializes in providing medical care for infants and children. He or she is specially-trained and experienced in working with child patients. A family doctor has general knowledge about all age groups. He or she is qualified to work with children, but does not specialize in their care.

15. (List three:) type of doctor desired, doctor's training, parents' comfort, impression of the doctor, office location, office hours, emergency and after-hours care, average wait for an appointment, cost of services, payment arrangements

Technology Applications

- Have students research baby supplies at **consumerreports.org**. Have them select the supplies with the best ratings. Ask them to make a poster of the best rated products. With permission, display the posters around the community at appropriate locations.
- Have students research breast-feeding and formula-feeding on the Internet. Then assign a couple's lifestyle to each student such as a working mother, a stay-at-home father, and a couple who smokes. Ask students to make a recommendation as to whether the mother should breast-feed or formula-feed. Have students present an oral report to the class, and then discuss the findings.
- Research the Family and Medical Leave Act on the Web. Visit the Department of Labor at **dol.gov** for information. Have students investigate the Act to determine when and why it was established and who it benefits. Also ask students to research how people who do not fall under the Family and Medical Leave Act can take a leave of absence and still keep their jobs.
- Using a computer, have students research and design a pamphlet of all the caregivers in the area. Make copies of the pamphlets. With permission, distribute them around the community in common places such as the library, hospitals, or community centers.

Academic Connections

- Journalism. Have each student interview one of their parents about the decisions the parents made for the student's birth. Have them ask whether they took childbirth classes, why they did or didn't take the classes, and if there was a benefit to them. Also encourage the students to ask about where the birth took place. Have students write their own baby announcement describing the preparation, where the birth took place, and other information such as birth date, weight, height, and length.
- Math. Have students make a list of baby supplies. Assign students a budget. Have them calculate the costs of each item needed. Ask students to reflect on how much money they will need, what resources they will use, what brands they would purchase, and how to save costs.

Web Sites

U.S. Food and Drug Administration
fda.com

Parenting.com
parenting.com

Parenting: Babies & Toddlers
babyparenting.about.com

Chapter 9: Childbirth

Chapter Objectives

- Identify the signs of labor.
- Explain common hospital procedures before, during, and after birth.
- Describe what types of medications are available during childbirth.
- Identify key events in each stage of labor.
- Compare different methods of childbirth.
- Summarize the importance of bonding.
- Describe routine neonatal care.
- Explain reasons a newborn might need emergency medical care.
- Propose ways new parents can adjust during the postpartum period.

Text Outline	Supplementary Resources
I. Signs of Labor	**SAG:** *Signs and Stages of Labor*, Activity A
II. Going to the Hospital A. Hospital Procedures	**SAG:** *Hospital Procedures*, Activity B
III. Childbirth Medications	

IV. Three Stages of Labor
    A. Dilation Stage
    B. Delivery Stage
    C. Afterbirth Stage
	TR: *The Three Stages of Labor*, transparency master 9-1

V. Methods of Childbirth
    A. Traditional Childbirth
    B. Family-Centered Childbirth
    C. Lamaze Method
    D. Leboyer Method
    E. Breech Delivery
    F. Cesarean Delivery
	SAG: *Methods of Childbirth*, Activity C
	    Childbirth Choices, Activity E
	TR: *Special Deliveries*, color transparency CT-9A

VI. Neonatal Care
    A. Emergency Care
    B. Circumcision
	TR: *Emergency Care*, color transparency CT-9B

VII. Bonding	**TR:** *Understanding Bonding*, reproducible master 9-2

VIII. Postpartum Period
    A. The Mother's Hospital Stay
    B. Going Home from the Hospital
    C. Postpartum Checkup	

(Continued)

Assessment

Answers to *Reviewing Key Points* questions in the text, page 201

1. (Name three:) lightening, the show, Braxton-Hicks or prelabor contractions, regular labor contractions, rupturing of the amnio-chorionic membrane.

2. A contraction is a pain that is felt during labor when the muscles of the uterus tense.

3. As labor progresses, the contractions come closer together. They continue rhythmically, and become stronger. That's how a woman can distinguish between labor contractions and prelabor contractions. Prelabor contractions remain equal in intensity from the start. They occur irregularly, are not rhythmical, and stop if a woman changes position.

4. A couple might fill out the admittance forms early so they can get it out of the way. This makes admittance easier when the woman is in labor.

5. Electronic fetal monitoring is the use of various electronic devices to measure the woman's contractions and the baby's response to them. It is used to check how the baby is doing during labor and delivery.

6. (Describe two:) general anesthesia, regional anesthesia, local anesthesia, and analgesics (Description is student response. See pages 186-187 in the text.)

7. Dilation stage—cervix shortens and opens; delivery stage—baby is pushed out of the uterus and delivered; afterbirth stage—the placenta, or afterbirth, is expelled from the uterus.

8. (Name two:) traditional childbirth, family-centered childbirth, Lamaze method, Leboyer method, cesarean delivery. (Descriptions are student response. See pages 189-193 in the text.)

9. (Give three:) labor has been too long or too difficult, the baby's health is in danger, the mother's health is in danger, the baby is in a breech position, there is a problem with the umbilical cord or placenta, the woman's pelvis is too small for the baby to fit, the mother has an active STD the baby might catch by passing through the birth canal.

10. Bonding is the formation of close emotional ties between parents and their children. (Description is student response.)

11. (Name four:) baby is washed; baby is weighed and measured; footprints are taken; Apgar test is given; Brazelton scale is given; identification bands are put on the baby; baby is given eyedrops; baby is given tests for PKU and anemia; circumcision

12. (Student response. See page 193 in the text.)

13. (Give two:) the baby is born prematurely, the baby had a low birthweight, the baby was addicted to illegal drugs, the baby scored very low on an Apgar test

SAG: *Childbirth Crossword*, Activity D
Childbirth Case Studies, Activity F
TR: *Chapter 9 Test*, reproducible master
GWTCS: Questions for Chapter 9

(Continued)

Assessment *(Continued)*

14. The postpartum period is the time in which the mother's body recovers and heals from pregnancy and childbirth. It lasts about six weeks.

15. The postpartum checkup is important because it helps the mother know how well she is recovering. It is also an opportunity to ask any questions she may have.

Technology Applications

- Have students research the pros and cons of various childbirth medications. Using a spreadsheet program, have students make a chart of childbirth medications that are available along with the pros and cons of each.
- Currently, umbilical cord blood is used in the treatment of nearly 50 life-threatening diseases including a wide range of cancers, genetic diseases, immune deficiencies, and blood disorders. Have students research the Internet for ways umbilical cord blood is being used.
- Have students create a Venn diagram using a drawing program. Use the diagram to show how parents can bond with their child and also maintain a strong marital relationship.

Academic Connections

- English. Have students research the Lamaze method and Leboyer method of childbirth. Ask them to write a paper comparing and contrasting the methods.
- Social studies and science. Ask students to research the doctor who designed the Apgar test, Virginia Apgar. Have them discover why the test was needed and how it has changed neonatal care. Have students write a short report about the test and whether it was common for a woman to be influential on neonatal care during the 1950s.

Web Sites

Pregnancy & Childbirth Information
childbrith.org

NCT Pregnancy and Baby Care
nctpregnancyandbabycare.com

Chapter 10: New Parents, New Baby

Chapter Objectives

- Explain changes that occur during the first days of parenthood.
- Describe the appearance and abilities of a newborn.
- Demonstrate proper techniques for holding, feeding, bathing, and dressing a newborn.
- Describe a newborn's sleeping habits.
- Identify adjustments families with newborns may need to make.

Text Outline / Supplementary Resources

I. The First Days of Parenthood

SAG: *New Parents*, Activity A

II. How the Newborn Looks

SAG: *How Newborns Look*, Activity B

III. What the Newborn Can Do
   A. What the Newborn Can See
   B. What the Newborn Can Hear
   C. What the Newborn Can Smell and Taste
   D. What the Newborn Can Feel
   E. The Newborn's Reflexes

SAG: *Senses of the Newborn*, Activity C
The Newborn's Reflexes, Activity D

IV. How Parents Care for Their Newborns
   A. Holding the Newborn
   B. The Newborn's Sleeping Habits
   C. Feeding the Newborn
   D. Bathing the Newborn
   E. Dressing the Newborn
   F. When the Newborn Cries

SAG: *Care of the Newborn*, Activity E
Facts About Newborns, Activity F
TR: *Self-Demand Versus Scheduled Feeding*, reproducible master 10-1
Bathing a Newborn, reproducible master 10-2
Diapering Detail, color transparency CT-10

V. The Husband and the Wife as Parents
   A. Personal Adjustments in Family Life

SAG: *Personal Adjustments*, Activity G

Assessment

Answers to *Reviewing Key Points* questions in the text, page 222

1. (Student response.)
2. The fontanel is the soft spot on top the baby's head. It should be handled gently, but it is okay to touch it.
3. (Describe three:) skin—usually blotchy and wrinkled; ears—pressed to the head; eyebrows and eyelashes—can barely be seen; cheeks—fat; nose—flattened; chin—receding; head—oversize for the rest of the body; shoulders—sloping; chest—narrow; abdomen—protruding; legs—usually are bowed; heartbeat—twice as fast as an adult's heartbeat; breathing rate—twice as fast as an adult's breathing rate; length—averages 20 to 21 inches; weight—averages 7 to 7 1/2 pounds

TR: *Chapter 10 Test*, reproducible master
GWTCS: Questions for Chapter 10

(Continued)

Assessment   *(Continued)*

4. (Student response. See pages 207-209 in the text.)

5. (Describe two:) rooting reflex-when the cheek or mouth is touched, the newborn will open his or her mouth and turn the head, looking for food; grasping reflex—a reflex that causes a newborn to close his or her hand tightly around an object when it is placed in the palm; Babinski reflex—a reflex that causes a newborn to extend the toes upward and outward when the sole of the foot is touched; Moro or startle reflex—a reflex in which a newborn throws the arms apart, spreads the fingers, extends the legs, arches the back and throws the head back in response to a loud noise or a sudden change in position; stepping reflex—when a newborn is held in an upright position and the sole of a foot touches a surface, the newborn will raise the foot as if walking

6. The baby's neck muscles are weak at birth, so a newborn's head tends to roll about if it is not supported.

7. 18 to 20 hours, back

8. A parent should burp a baby to bring up any air that may have been swallowed. To do this, hold the baby upright, either sitting on your lap or lying up against your shoulder. (You may prefer to lay the baby, stomach-down, across your lap.) Then pat the baby gently on the back until the air bubble is released and you hear the burp. Burp the baby once or twice during feeding and again after feeding.

9. Self-demand feeding means feeding the baby when he or she is hungry rather than on a set schedule.

10. Never leave a baby alone on a table or in a tub, not even for a few seconds.

11. The key to preventing diaper rash is cleanliness. Parents can also protect their baby from diaper rash by changing wet or soiled diapers promptly, and cleansing and drying the skin in the diaper area thoroughly. If washing diapers at home, use special laundry care to keep diapers clean and soft.

12. No, answering cries promptly does not spoil a baby. Instead, it is a good way for parents to express their love and concern. This, in turn, helps babies learn their parents can be trusted to fulfill their needs.

13. Colic is severe and intermittent abdominal pain.

14. (Student response.)

(Continued)

Technology Applications

- Have students research Sudden Infant Death Syndrome (SIDS) on the Web. One site is sids.org, the American SIDS Institute. Ask students to research what SIDS is and how to reduce the risk of SIDS.
- Split the class into five groups. For each group, ask students to pretend they are the producers of a movie. Provide each group with a video camera and a movie topic including one of the following: what a newborn can do, feeding the newborn, bathing the newborn, dressing the newborn, and when the newborn cries. Ask students to make a creative movie about the topic they were given. Show the videos in class.
- Using a card-creation software program, have students design an encouraging card that a new parent could give his or her spouse. Students may keep their cards for future use or give to the hospitals to distribute to new parents.

Academic Connections

- Biology. Split the class into groups. Assign each group a newborn's reflexes. Have the group pretend they are a team of doctors who will explain how the reflexes work. Provide a picture of the nervous system for the "team of doctors" to use during their explanation. Ask the groups to present their reflex to the class.

Web Sites

Sudden Infant Death Syndrome Alliance
sidsalliance.org

National SIDS Research Center
sidscenter.org

Chapter 11: Parents and Their Infants

Chapter Objectives

- Describe the physical, intellectual, emotional, and social development of infants.
- Differentiate between large motor skills and small motor skills.
- Explain how parents can influence their infants' brain development.
- Describe how different types of development relate to one another.
- Explain how stranger anxiety and separation anxiety affect social and emotional development.
- Summarize the importance of parental guidance during a child's first year of life.
- Explain why medical checkups are needed during infancy.

Text Outline	Supplementary Resources

I. Physical Development
  A. Large Motor Skills
  B. Small Motor Skills
  C. Keeping Babies Safe
  D. Introducing Solid Foods
  E. Weaning
  F. Teething
  G. Sleeping Patterns and Problems
	SAG: *Large and Small Motor Skills,* Activity A
	Dangers and Safeguards for Infants, Activity B
	TR: *Hand Manipulation,* color transparency CT-11
	Car Safety Seats, reproducible master 11-1
	Infant Safety, reproducible master 11-2

II. Intellectual Development
  A. The Brain Grows and Develops
  B. Physical and Intellectual Development Are Related
  C. Memory Develops
  D. Awareness Improves
  E. Associations Are Formed
  F. Simple Problems Can Be Solved
  G. Babies Begin to See Similarities and Differences
  H. Object Permanence Appears
  I. Learning by Imitation
  J. Play Time Means Learning
  K. Language Development
	SAG: *Intellectual Development,* Activity C

III. Emotional and Social Development
  A. Attachment to Special Objects
  B. New Fears
  C. Other Emotional Responses
  D. Babies Learn the Meaning of No
  E. Can Parents Spoil Their Babies?
	SAG: *Emotional and Social Development,* Activity D

IV. Medical Checkups for Infants	

Assessment

Answers to *Reviewing Key Points* questions in the text, page 264
  1. triple; 1½
  2. false
	SAG: *Infant Crossword,* Activity E
	Caring for Infants, Activity F
	Observing an Infant, Activity G

(Continued)

Assessment   *(Continued)*

3. A mitten grasp is a grasp made with the palm and fingers opposing the thumb. A pincer grasp is a refined grasp in which objects are picked up with just the thumb and forefinger.

4. Solid food should be introduced into a baby's diet at four to six months, or when recommended by the baby's doctor. Baby cereal mixed with milk or formula is generally introduced first.

5. Weaning is the phasing out of taking milk from a breast or bottle.

6. To ease minor teething discomfort, parents can massage the baby's gums. They can also let the baby chew on a boiled clean cloth that won't shred, a bagel, or a teething biscuit. Some dentists recommend the use of teething rings and ointments.

7. (Student response. See pages 241-248 in the text.)

8. memory

9. Through this game, babies learn more about distance and spatial relationships. They also learn that objects don't disappear when they are dropped; they simply fall to the floor.

10. They are taking their first steps away from dependence on their parents and their first steps toward independence.

11. Object permanence is the concept that unseen objects have not necessarily disappeared.

12. Stranger anxiety is the fear infants have when they are around unfamiliar people. Separation anxiety is an overwhelming fear shown by infants when the primary care-giver is not in sight.

13. (Student response. See page 246 of the text.)

14. five times per year; at ages 2-4 weeks, 2 months, 4 months, 6 months, and 12 months

15. Immunizations are treatments that prevent people from developing certain diseases. They are important because they keep people free of certain deadly diseases.

TR: *Developmental Highlights for Infants*, transparency master 11-3 *Chapter 11 Test*, reproducible master
GWTCS: Questions for Chapter 11

Technology Applications

- Split the class into groups. Assign each group a part of physical development including the following: large motor skills, small motor skills, keeping babies safe, introducing solid foods, weaning, teething, and sleeping patterns and problems. (You might want to split the large motor skill group into two groups.) Have students use presentation software to design a presentation for their area. Present to the class. The program could also be given to the community library to serve as a resource for parents with infants.
- Docosahexaenoic acid (DHA) and arachidonic acid (ARA) are long-chain polyunsaturated fatty acids that, according to research, appear to support brain development. Have students research the Internet for how these fatty acids promote intellectual development in infants and in what foods they are found.
- Many students will have baby videos of themselves. Ask for a few volunteers to bring in videos of themselves as infants. Watch the videos in class to analyze aspects of physical, intellectual, emotional, and social development.

(Continued)

Academic Connections

- Science. Have students analyze the ingredients that are in baby food that comes in jars. Ask students to determine what nutritional benefits babies receive from eating these foods. Students could also make their own baby food. Determine the nutritional benefits of these foods as well.
- Speech. Hold a debate to discuss the following question: Can parents spoil their babies?
- Biology. Have students assume the role of a pediatrician. Ask them to give a general presentation on medical checkups for infants. Have students recommend when the infants should visit the doctor and what the checkup will entail, including immunizations.

Web Sites

Enfamil
enfagrow.com/index.html

National Network for Child Care
nncc.org/Child.Dev/grow.infant.html

Oh Baby!
envisagedesign.com/ohbaby/develop.html

Zero to Three: National Center for Infants, Toddlers, and Families
zerotothree.org

Chapter 12: Parents and Their Toddlers

Chapter Objectives

- Identify major steps in a toddler's physical, intellectual, emotional, and social development.
- Summarize the importance of beginning to learn life skills in the toddler years.
- Describe a toddler's competing needs for independence and dependence.
- Select appropriate toys and books for toddlers.
- Explain how parental guidance can encourage toddlers to develop self-control.
- Explain why play is important to a toddler's development.
- Explain why routine medical checkups are recommended for toddlers.

Text Outline

I. Physical Development
   A. Large Motor Skills
   B. Small Motor Skills
   C. Toys and Play in Physical Development
   D. Life Skills
   E. Teething
   F. Toilet Learning

II. Intellectual Development
   A. Toys and Play in Intellectual Development
   B. The Importance of Books
   C. Language Development

III. Emotional and Social Development
   A. Toys and Play in Emotional and Social Development
   B. Separation Anxiety
   C. Guiding the Toddler's Behavior
   D. Temper Tantrums

IV. The Importance of Play to a Child's Overall Development
   A. Factors to Consider When Selecting Toys

V. Medical Checkups for Toddlers

Supplementary Resources

SAG: *Observing a Toddler*, Activity A
Keeping Toddlers Safe, Activity B
Life Skills of Toddlers, Activity C
TR: *Toddlers' Eating Habits*, color transparency 12-1
Sequence of Teething, color transparency CT-12A

SAG: *Books for Children*, Activity H
Teachable Moments, Activity D

SAG: *Helping Toddlers Learn Their Limits*, Activity E
Handling Toddlers' Behavior, Activity F

SAG: *Selecting Toys for Toddlers*, Activity G
TR: *Choosing Toys*, color transparency CT-12B

Assessment

Answers to *Reviewing Key Points* questions in the text, page 296

1. The head may still seem large, but the trunk, arms, and legs are catching up. The legs grow longer and stronger to meet increasing walking needs. The backbone often seems to come forward, and the abdomen protrudes. The "baby fat" of the plump infant begins to disappear; then gradually a leaner, more muscular shape evolves.

TR: *Developmental Highlights for Toddlers*, transparency master 12-2
Chapter 12 Test, reproducible master
GWTCS: Questions for Chapter 12

(Continued)

Assessment   *(Continued)*

2. To achieve this accomplishment, toddlers must judge distances, back up to chairs, and without looking, sit using controlled muscle movements.

3. Toddlers cannot match the pace and direction of adults' walk. They are also distracted by interesting things they see along the way. Toddlers tire faster than adults.

4. (Name five. Student response.)

5. (Give one:) eating, dressing, grooming, brushing teeth, and toilet learning

6. A parent's job during mealtime are to provide nutritious food and to make mealtimes as enjoyable as possible.

7. No, because linking certain foods, especially sweets, to emotions may set the stage for a lifetime of poor eating habits.

8. Children should make their first dental visit as toddlers, between ages one and three. Teeth should be brushed at least twice a day—after breakfast and before bedtime.

9. (Name two. See pages 276-277 in the text.)

10. false

11. (Student response.)

12. false

13. true

14. Parallel play is play in which two children play separately, but beside one another, in the same play activity. Cooperative play is playing with others in a play activity. Parallel play is more common among toddlers.

15. the concept of object permanence, improved memory, and advances in language skills

16. The best way to deal with temper tantrums is to try to avoid the situations that cause them.

17. Routine medical checkups during toddlerhood at 12 months, 15 months, 18 months, 2 years, and 3 years.

Technology Applications

- Have students research toys promoting physical, intellectual, emotional, and social development. One Web site to use is **consumerreports.org**. After the research is over, ask them to make a pamphlet with their recommendations. Provide the pamphlet to various community organizations.
- Have students produce a before and after video of making a home safe for toddlers. Have them start the project by identifying all the unsafe areas in the home. Ask the students to make the home safe for toddlers and then shoot another video that explains why the home is now safe. Students could also shoot a video of a student properly installing a car safety seat.
- Have students research the physical, intellectual, or emotional and social development of a toddler with special needs. Assign a special need to each student. Ask the student to write a paper on how a parent can help promote development of a special-needs toddler. Have students present their papers to the class.
- Using a computer drawing program, have students make a poster entitled *25 Ways to Avoid a Temper Tantrum*.

(Continued)

Academic Connections

- Reading. Have students visit the library to find appropriate books for toddlers. Ask students to read the book to a toddler. Then write a paragraph on the experience of reading the book to the toddler and how he or she responded to it.
- Foreign language. Have the foreign language teacher visit the class to discuss the benefits of teaching a child another language early in his or her life.

Web Sites

National Information Center for Children and Youth with Disabilities
nichcy.org/

KidSource Online
kidsource.com

Parents Magazine
parents.com

ParentingMe—Toilet Training
parentingme.com/toiltrng.htm

Chapter 13: Parents and Their Preschoolers

Chapter Objectives

- Identify steps in the physical, intellectual, emotional, and social development of preschoolers.
- Propose ways parents can help their children develop life skills.
- Explain why enuresis occurs and how parents can help children overcome it.
- Identify special language problems common among preschoolers.
- List ways parents can encourage the development of reading skills, math skills, and gender roles.
- Explain the importance of play in the preschool years.
- Explain ways parents can encourage their preschoolers' development.

Text Outline

I. Physical Development	
A. Large Motor Skills	
B. Small Motor Skills	
C. Life Skills	
D. Enuresis	

II. Intellectual Development	
A. Language Development	
B. Reading and Math Skills	

III. Emotional and Social Development	
A. Developing Gender Roles	
B. The Importance of Play	
C. Nightmares	

IV. Medical Checkups for Preschoolers

Supplementary Resources

SAG: *Observing a Preschooler*, Activity A
Life Skills of Preschoolers, Activity C
TR: *Introducing Safety to Preschoolers*, color transparency CT-13

SAG: *Intellectual Development Concepts*, Activity D
TR: *Read Me a Story*, reproducible master 13-1

SAG: *Reasoning with Preschoolers*, Activity B
Children's Play, Activity E

Assessment

Answers to *Reviewing Key Points* questions in the text, page 323

1. The baby fat disappears, and the body assumes a more adult shape. The legs become longer and straighter. The abdomen remains large, and the chest becomes broader.

2. (List three:) They can make sure their children have plenty of running room in safe and supervised areas. They can take their children to parks to play on swings, jungle gyms, and other play equipment. They can watch for signs that their children are ready to try new skills and then help them. They can encourage their preschoolers' development by being generous with praise.

TR: *Developmental Highlights for Preschoolers*, transparency master 13-2
Chapter 13 Test, reproducible master
GWTCS: Questions for Chapter 13

(Continued)

Assessment *(Continued)*

3. A three-year-old builds a tower of blocks by placing each block with much concentration, but, most often, the tower is crooked. When four-year-olds build block towers, they try to place the blocks neatly. In fact, they may become so interested in a straight-sided tower that they upset the blocks they had already stacked. Five-year-olds expand their manipulative skills a great deal. With improved eye-hand coordination, they have much better control of their hands and fingers. They are no longer content with towers. Now their construction projects include bridges, houses, and churches with steeples.

4. false

5. Children may have fewer problems at mealtimes if they are involved with the shopping and preparing of food. Children who learn about how food looks, smells, and is prepared are likely to have fewer food dislikes.

6. A common psychological cause of enuresis is a new stress in the life of the child. Parents should react by giving the child more comfort and reassurance.

7. Children at this age have the language skills to listen and the intellectual skills to understand.

8. The line between fact and fantasy is still hazy, and they have great imaginations.

9. true

10. (Student response.)

11. (Student response.)

12. Parents should be ready to offer love and reassurance to calm their children's fears.

13. (Student response.)

14. Alternate play behavior is behavior during which a child does something and waits for a response from playmates, thus encouraging the repetition of the activity.

15. The Denver Developmental Screening Test is a test that measures a preschooler's skills in social, language, small motor, and large motor development. It measures how the child is doing in these areas compared to other children the same age. It can detect developmental delays.

Technology Applications

- Have students go to the Web site for Nick Jr., at nickjr.com. Ask students to select a game or a craft item. Have them play the game or make the craft. Ask the students to write a paper on how the game or craft item will help promote a preschooler's development. Other Web sites for students to consider include the following: pbskids.org/barney/html/games.html, learningplanet.com/stu/kids1.asp, and pbskids.org/caillou/dresscaillou.

- One way to promote small motor skill development in preschoolers is through the use of puzzles. Have students use a computer drawing program to make a picture that would be good for a puzzle. Ask students to affix the picture to a piece of cardboard and cut it into a puzzle. Have students visit a preschool center with their puzzles. Ask students to observe the preschoolers putting together the puzzles and the different stages of small motor development.

(Continued)

Academic Connections

- **Music.** Play a selection of familiar children's songs such as *Old MacDonald*. Have students analyze how songs help promote intellectual and motor skill development.
- **English.** Have students write a compare and contrast paper of the emotional and social development of a three-year-old and a preschooler.
- **Drama.** Have students perform role-plays, pretending they are preschoolers. Ask students to act out an imaginative play situation such as going to the zoo. Have the situations acted out in an impromptu way. Also encourage the students to be in different stages of language development. Discuss the play situations and language development.

Web Sites

Preschoolers Today
preschoolerstoday.com

Parent Soup
parentsoup.com/preschool

Chapter 14: Parents and Their School-Age Children

Chapter Objectives

- Identify steps in the physical, intellectual, emotional, and social development of school-age children.
- Explain the importance of parental guidance and encouragement in the school-age years.
- Describe guidelines parents can use for their school-age children's involvement in sports.
- Propose ways parents can help their children adjust to new roles as students.
- Explain how friendships change over the school-age years.
- Identify some of the causes and symptoms of stress among school-age children.
- Propose ways parents can help their children deal with stress.
- Summarize the importance of regular medical checkups and physical exams for school-age children.

Text Outline / Supplementary Resources

Text Outline	Supplementary Resources
I. Readiness for School	**SAG:** *School-Age Children*, Activity A

II. Physical Development
  A. Physical Fitness and Competitive Sports
  B. Physical Safety
	SAG: *Children and Sports*, Activity B

III. Intellectual Development
  A. Advances in Thinking Patterns
  B. School Adjustments
  C. Schoolwork and Homework
	SAG: *Intellectual Achievements and Teachable Moments*, Activity C
	School Adjustments, Activity F

IV. Emotional and Social Development
  A. Parents and Friends
  B. Conformity	

V. Self-Care Children	**SAG:** *Self-Care Children*, Activity G **TR:** *The Keys to Self-Care*, color transparency CT-14
VI. Children and Stress	**SAG:** *Children and Stress*, Activity H
VII. Medical Checkups for School-Age Children	**SAG:** *Medical Checkups for School-Age Children*, Activity I

Assessment

Answers to *Reviewing Key Points* questions in the text, page 356

1. (List five. See pages 328-329 in the text.)
2. (Name one:) advantages—children can learn to appreciate physical fitness, respect law and authority, and cooperate with others; (Name one:) physical risks—children may risk injury to their still-developing bones and muscles. In a few cases, prolonged exertion may cause heart damage. Some children, if pressured to win, may develop hypertension; (Name one:)

SAG: *Facts About School-Age Children*, Activity D
Observing a School-Age Child, Activity E
TR: *The School-Age Child Crossword*, reproducible master 14-1
Developmental Highlights for School-Age Children, transparency master 14-2
Chapter 14 Test, reproducible master
GWTCS: Questions for Chapter 14

(Continued)

Assessment *(Continued)*

psychological risks—children who are pushed into sports against their wishes may develop negative attitudes toward exercise and physical fitness, children who see their parents and coaches argue with umpires and referees may fail to learn respect for authority, children who try to impress others with their individual achievements may develop conceit rather than a spirit of cooperation, children may feel like losers if they cannot match the athletic success of a parent or older sibling, still other children who seldom, if ever, win may suffer a loss of self-esteem, after awhile, they may not even want to try to participate.

3. The most basic rule is to let children decide for themselves.

4. A. multiple classification—the understanding that objects may fit into more than one category
   B. conservation—the understanding that certain properties remain the same even if they change in shape or appearance
   C. seriation—the ability to order groups of things by size, weight, age, or any other common property
   D. reversibility—the concept that objects can return to their original condition after they have been changed

5. (Student response. See pages 338-339 in the text.)

6. (Student response. See page 341 in the text.)

7. peer

8. (Propose four. Student response.)

9. Tattling is common since they have to check with caregivers to find out if their playmates' actions are really wrong.

10. This same-gender group interest reaches a peak at eight years of age and lasts throughout puberty. It is stronger among boys.

11. Once school-age children understand the reason for rules and the concept of fairness, they are eager to make their own rules.

12. Ten-year-olds are happy with life in general. They like school and their teachers. They like their parents and even their brothers and sisters. They obey adults willingly. They accept responsibility and are fairly dependable if they are given encouragement and praise. If differences arise among friends, they are willing to work them out so everyone is happy.

13. If parents are too critical, their children may feel defensive. They may adopt more of the "in" styles or behaviors just to rebel against their parents and prove loyalty to their peers.

14. (List two:) child is of the appropriate age as determined by state law, child feels comfortable staying home alone, child is self-sufficient, child can provide self-care for short periods of time, child can use telephone, small appliances, and other equipment

(Continued)

Assessment *(Continued)*

15. (List three:) causes—conflict, poor health, unhealthy habits, an overly full schedule, an empty schedule, poor performance, major life changes, divorce, death or illness of a family member, remarriage of a parent, birth of a sibling, and so on. (List three:) symptoms—loss of interest in activities previously enjoyed; explosive crying or screaming; verbal or physical aggressiveness; cruelty to pets and playmates; physical symptoms, such as rapid heartbeat, headaches, fatigue, restlessness, upset stomach, neck pain; loss of sense of humor and joy; nightmares, sleepwalking, or teeth-grinding in sleep; hair twisting; nail-biting; excessive fidgeting; threats of harming someone or destroying property; behaviors of escape; prolonged display of temper; increased behaviors of acting out; jumpiness; fear of sudden sounds

16. ages 6, 8, 10, and 12

Technology Applications

- Have the students research the Internet for your state's requirements for school readiness. Also ask students to find out what programs are available to help school-age children to become ready to begin school. Have students make a brochure. With permission, display the brochures in preschools, child care centers, and elementary schools.
- Ask students to research on the Internet typical dangers to children's physical safety that parents need to discuss with their school-age children. Have students pick one safety area and make a pamphlet about how parents can discuss it with their children. Ask the elementary teachers to pass the pamphlets to the parents of school-age children.
- Have students develop a game of jeopardy using presentation software to prepare slides. On one of the slides the students should ask a question about the intellectual development of school-age children. On the next slide, the answer should appear. Compile the slides and assign point values to each question. Play jeopardy with the slides to review the section on intellectual development.

Academic Connections

- Math. Get a list of heights and weights of children in a class at a grade school. Do not include names but do include gender. Using the children's growth chart at the Web site keepkidshealthy.com/growthcharts, have students determine whether the students in the grade school are below average, average, or above average when it comes to physical development.
- Physical education. Have students observe school-age children in a physical education class. Have them watch for the different physical development levels. Also ask students to observe whether the children are competitive and how it affects the overall environment. (This activity could also be done at an extra-curricular sports activity for school-age children.)
- English. Have students write a poem from the viewpoint of a school-age child who is trying to explain one aspect of his or her life. Ask the students to write the poem about emotional and social development, being a self-care child, or being under stress. Ask students to read their poems to the class.

Web Sites

Family Education Network
familyeducation.com

School Age Health Center and Parenting Advice
keepkidshealthy.com/schoolage/schoolage.html

Chapter 15: Parents and Their Teens

Chapter Objectives

- Identify steps in the physical, intellectual, emotional, and social development of teens.
- Differentiate between primary and secondary sex characteristics.
- Describe the dangers teens face related to eating disorders; tobacco, alcohol, and drug use; and sexual behavior.
- Describe the importance of decision making during the teen years.
- Explain the role parents can play in helping their teens establish healthy friendships and dating relationships.
- Propose ways parents can help their teens develop healthy self-concepts and self-esteems.
- Summarize the importance of medical checkups during the teen years.

Text Outline	Supplementary Resources

I. Physical Development
  A. Physical Changes in Boys
  B. Physical Changes in Girls
  C. Eating Disorders
  D. Health Risks of Tobacco
  E. Health Risk of Drinking
  F. Health Risks of Drug Abuse
  G. Sexual Health and Teens
	SAG: *Smoking*, Activity A
	    Drinking, Activity B
	    Drug Abuse, Activity C
	    Communication About Sexuality, Activity D
	TR: *Is Smoking Really All That Cool?* color transparency CT-15

II. Intellectual Development A. Decision-Making Skills	**SAG:** *Decision-Making Skills*, Activity F

III. Emotional and Social Development
  A. Friendships
  B. Dating
  C. Self-Concept and Self-Esteem
	SAG: *Friendships and Dating*, Activity E
	    Building a Positive Self-Concept and Self-Esteem, Activity G
	    Parents and Teens, Activity H
	TR: *You, the Parent of a Teen*, reproducible master 15-1

IV. Medical Checkups For Teens	

Assessment

Answers to *Reviewing Key Points* questions in the text, page 374
 	
1. puberty
2. true
3. The skull grows larger. The jaw lengthens, the chin becomes more pointed, and the nose increases in size.
4. A. primary
   B. secondary
   C. secondary
   D. secondary
   E. primary
   F. secondary
   G. primary
	TR: *Developmental Highlights for Teens*, transparency master 15-2
	    Chapter 15 Test, reproducible master
	GWTCS: Questions for Chapter 15

(Continued)

Assessment   *(Continued)*

5. A. Anorexics starve themselves for fear they will gain weight. They may also exercise excessively.
    B. Bulimics binge and purge uncontrollably.
    C. Binge eaters binge uncontrollably. They do not purge themselves.

6. (Student response. See pages 362-363 in the text.)

7. (Student response.)

8. true

9. Teens who have accurate knowledge of the effects of drugs are more likely to avoid drug abuse.

10. (List three:) could be involved in a teen pregnancy if they don't, could become teen parents if they don't, could acquire an STD if they don't, are unprepared for emotional consequences, are not ready for responsibilities, want them to prepare for healthy future relationships

11. If parents are enthusiastic about education, they can help their children develop a positive attitude about school.

12. abstract thinking

13. Guidelines keep children safe and teach them right from wrong. When pressured by peers to do something wrong, teens can avoid the situation by following their parents' rules.

14. They can do this by expressing genuine interest in their teens' lives. They can accept their teens' faults without excessive criticism and praise the teens' successes.

TR: *Developmental Highlights for Teens*, transparency master 15-2 *Chapter 15 Test*, reproducible master
GWTCS: Questions for Chapter 15

Technology Applications

- Using a computer design program, have students make a poster that says *10 Things You Should Know About Your Daughter/Son*. Ask students to give the poster to their parents.
- Request that students take a self-esteem test on the Internet. Some can be found at the Queendom Tests Web site at queendom.com/tests/index.html. (There are also other tests on the Web site to consider taking.) Ask students to reflect on their findings in a one-page paper.

Academic Connections

- Journalism/Marketing. Have students design an anti-tobacco, anti-drinking, anti-drug, or anti-eating disorder campaign. Ask students to make a slogan and posters. They could also write a newspaper article about the campaign and design ads or radio commercials. Students should include ways parents can talk to their teens about these behaviors.

Web Sites

Parenting Today's Teen
parentingteens.com

Parenting Adolescents
parentingadolescents.com

Focus Adolescent Services
focusas.com

Partnership for a Drug-Free America
freeamerica.org

Chapter 16: Theories and Guidelines

Chapter Objectives

- Describe each stage of Piaget's theory of intellectual development.
- Identify both positive and negative outcomes for each stage of Erikson's theory of personality development.
- Describe each aspect of human functioning identified by Freud.
- Differentiate among levels of human need as identified by Maslow.
- Explain each level of development in Kohlberg's theory of moral development.
- Identify ways parents can access information about child development, parenting, and parenting strategies.
- Assess how child development theories and guidelines help parents establish good parent-child relationships.
- Summarize the importance of an overall view of child development.

Text Outline	Supplementary Resources

I. Piaget's Theory of Intellectual Development
  A. Sensorimotor Stage
  B. Preoperational Stage
  C. Concrete Operational Stage
  D. Formal Operational Stage
	SAG: *Piaget*, Activity A

II. Erikson's Theory of Personality Development
  A. Stage I: Trust Versus Mistrust
  B. Stage II: Autonomy Versus Shame
  C. Stage III: Initiative Versus Guilt
  D. Stage IV: Industry Versus Inferiority
  E. Stage V: Identity Versus Role Confusion
  F. Stage VI: Intimacy Versus Isolation
  G. Stage VII: Generativity Versus Stagnation
  H. Stage VIII: Integrity Versus Despair
	SAG: *Erikson*, Activity B
	TR: *Toddler's Developing Autonomy*, reproducible master 16-1

III. Freud's Theory of Personality Development
  A. The Id
  B. The Ego
  C. The Superego
	SAG: *Freud*, Activity C

IV. Maslow's Hierarchy of Human Needs
  A. Physical Needs
  B. Safety and Security Needs
  C. Love and Acceptance Needs
  D. Esteem Needs
  E. Self-Actualization Needs
	SAG: *Maslow's Theory of Human Needs*, Activity D
	TR: *Maslow's Hierarchy of Human Needs*, color transparency CT-16

V. Kohlberg's Theory of Moral Development
  A. Preconventional Level
  B. Conventional Level
  C. Postconventional Level
	SAG: *Kohlberg*, Activity E
	Theories and Guidelines, Activity F

(Continued)

VI. Other Child Development Theories	**SAG:** *Book Review*, Activity H **TR:** *Child Specialists*, reproducible master 16-2
VII. Parenting Strategies	**SAG:** *Parenting Strategies*, Activity G **TR:** *Local Resources for Parents*, reproducible master 16-3
VIII. An Overall View of Development	

Assessment

Answers to *Reviewing Key Points* questions in the text, page 397	**TR:** *Chapter 16 Test*, reproducible master **GWTCS:** Questions for Chapter 16

1. A theory is an idea that has been well-proven and accepted by others in the same field of study.

2. Sensorimotor stage: This stage lasts from birth to one and one half or two years of age. In this stage, children learn about the world through their senses and their body movements. Preoperational stage: This stage extends from about age two to seven. In this stage, children learn mostly by using language and mental images. Concrete operational stage: This stage begins at age six or seven and continues until about age 11. In this stage, children learn to solve more complex problems and use basic logic. Formal operational stage: This stage begins at age 11 or 12 and extends into adulthood. People in this stage can think through very complex problems and have abstract ideas.

3. A. trust versus mistrust
   B. initiative versus guilt
   C. intimacy versus isolation
   D. integrity versus despair
   E. identify versus role confusion
   F. generativity versus stagnation
   G. autonomy versus shame
   H. industry versus inferiority

4. yes

5. The ID is the source of psychological and physical tension. It demands immediate satisfaction of wants and needs. The ego deals with logic and controlled behaviors, most importantly, it deals with anxiety. The superego is a person's moral code. It has two parts, the conscience and ego ideal.

6. true

7. self-actualization

8. preconventional level, conventional level, postconventional level

9. (Student response.)

10. (Student response. See pages 394-396 in the text.)

(Continued)

Technology Applications

- Visit Discovery's Web site school.discovery.com/lessonplans/programs/humandev. Following the lesson plan given at the site, ask students to get into groups and search the Web for information. Have students present their research to the class.
- Have students pick a community service project such as working with the homeless, repairing a neighborhood park, or a recycling program. Ask students to research the Internet to find resources and other services to help with their project. Have students design the project according to the priorities given in Maslow's hierarchy of human needs. Ask students to write a reflection paper on the project including the effect on their own needs.
- Split the class into seven groups. Ask each group to research one of the parenting strategies given in the text. Have each group use presentation software to illustrate the strategy. Show the presentations to the class.

Academic Connections

- English. Ask students to write a paper about when they displayed or continue to display the three aspects of Freud's theory of personality development.
- Drama. Have students role-play each stage in Kohlberg's theory of moral development. After the skit is performed, discuss how each stage develops. Discuss what would happen if there wasn't a parent who helped the child develop morals.

Web Sites

Child Development Basics
childdevelopmentinfo.com/development/index.html

Chapter 17: Guiding Healthy Development

Chapter Objectives

- Describe the vital role parents play in their children's development.
- Explain how children learn behavior patterns.
- Describe three styles of parenting.
- Explain effective methods of discipline and punishment.
- Analyze the experiences provided by sibling relationships.
- Evaluate methods of helping children develop responsibility, honesty, and healthy sexuality.
- Summarize the influence of the media upon children.

Text Outline	Supplementary Resources
I. Guiding Children's Behavior A. How Children Learn Behavior B. How Parents Guide Behavior C. Effective Discipline D. When a Child Misbehaves E. Parents as Positive Role Models	**SAG:** *Guiding Children's Behavior,* Activity A **TR:** *Memo,* reproducible master 17-1 *Little Eyes Are Watching,* reproducible master 17-2 *How Children Learn Behavior,* reproducible master 17-3
II. Sibling Relationships A. Sibling Rivalry	**SAG:** *Sibling Relationships,* Activity B *Sibling Rivalry,* Activity C
III. Developing Responsibility A. Volunteer Work B. Allowances C. Part-Time Jobs	**SAG:** *Volunteer Work,* Activity D *An Allowance,* Activity E *Money Values,* Activity F *A Part-Time Job,* Activity G **TR:** *Children and Money,* color transparency CT-17A *Volunteering Pays Off,* color transparency CT-17B
IV. Developing Honesty A. Stealing	**SAG:** *Encouraging Honesty,* Activity I
V. Media Influences A. Television B. Music C. Computer Software and the Internet	**SAG:** *Television Influences,* Activity J **TR:** *TV Guidelines,* color transparency CT-17C
VI. Developing a Healthy Sexuality A. Questions Children Ask B. Gender Roles C. Teens and Sexuality	**SAG:** *Children's Questions About Sex,* Activity H **TR:** *Talking to Children About AIDS,* reproducible master 17-4

Assessment

Answers to *Reviewing Key Points* questions in the text, page 428 1. Positive behavior is behavior that is acceptable, healthy, and satisfying for a child and those around him or her.	**TR:** *Chapter 17 Test,* reproducible master **GWTCS:** Questions for Chapter 17

(Continued)

Assessment *(Continued)*

2. Guidance is directing, supervising, and influencing a child's behavior. It can be direct or indirect. Discipline is intentionally teaching and training a child to behave in appropriate ways.

3. (List three:) direct teaching, imitation, identification, trial and error, reinforcement

4. (Student response. See pages 404-405 in the text.)

5. Some rules must be set to keep children safe. Other rules may be made to help children learn appropriate kinds of social behavior.

6. (List two:) time-out, natural consequences, logical consequences

7. true

8. (Name two. Student response. See pages 410-416 in the text.)

9. Four factors parents should consider when deciding how large an allowance to give their children are the child's needs, the needs of other family members, the income level of the family, and the amount other children of the same age receive as an allowance.

10. (List three positive effects and three negative effects. See pages 414-416 in the text.)

11. Parents can help their children to learn to value honesty by rewarding them when they tell the truth.

12. The child learns that wrongs must be righted. The child also learns that parents will offer support even when the child has done something wrong.

13. (List four. Student response. See page 418 in the text.)

14. Children may become less sensitive to the pain and suffering of others. Children may become more fearful of the world around them. They may show more aggressive or harmful behavior toward others. They are more likely to hit their playmates, argue, disobey class rules, and leave tasks unfinished.

15. (Student response. See pages 421-423 in the text.)

16. Authorities feel teens with accurate knowledge about sex are likely to demonstrate responsible sexual behavior and to postpone sexual activity.

(Continued)

Technology Applications

- Have students watch a nightly news program or read a newspaper. Ask students to analyze the stories that deal with children's behavior or child discipline. Have them identify how the child learned the behavior, how the parents guided the behavior, and whether it was effective. Lead a discussion during the next class period on positive and negative reinforcements and the consequences of each.
- Ask students to contact service organizations in the community to find out how people can volunteer for the organization. Using a computer drawing program, have students make a pamphlet of the volunteering opportunities along with the benefits of volunteering. Provide the pamphlets to members of the community.
- Using a computer drawing program, have students design a shopping bag that discourages shoplifting. With permission, have students display their shopping bag designs around the school.
- Have students watch television for an hour. Ask students to write down all the messages they are receiving that would influence their decisions. After the hour is over, have students analyze whether they received more positive or negative influences.

Academic Connections

- Math. Have students poll local parents to find out how much money they give to their children for an allowance. Students should ask for age of the child. Have students determine the average allowance a school-age child or teenager receives. Ask students to chart the results.
- Social studies. Have students research how the government has tried to manage what children view on television and the Internet. Ask students to write a paper about whether they like government intervention and why.
- English. Have students debate the statements such as the following: "Men should not be nurses;" "Women are only good in the kitchen;" "Boys will be boys;" and "Girls are weaker than boys." Lead a discussion on how gender roles and stereotyping develop.

Web Sites

Parenting: Babies and Toddlers
babyparenting.about.com/cs/disciplinetactics

Chapter 18: Family Concerns

Chapter Objectives

- Describe common parenting concerns including balancing work and family roles, divorce, remarriage, serious illness, death, and family moves.
- Identify skills and knowledge parents need to handle these concerns.
- Propose ways parents can help their children adjust to these concerns.
- Summarize community resources available for parents facing these concerns.

Text Outline	Supplementary Resources
I. Balancing Family and Work Roles 　A. Reasons Parents Work 　B. Options to Consider 　C. Managing Dual Work Roles	**SAG:** *Dual-Career Households*, Activity A **TR:** *Balancing Family and Work*, color transparency CT-18
II. Divorce 　A. Children's Reactions to Divorce 　B. Legal Proceedings 　C. After the Divorce	**SAG:** *Explaining Divorce to Children*, Activity B
III. Remarriage and Stepfamilies	**SAG:** *Stepfamilies*, Activity C
IV. Serious Illness	**SAG:** *An Illness in the Family*, Activity D
V. Explaining Death to Children 　A. A Death in the Family	**SAG:** *Explaining Death to Children*, Activity E **TR:** *Helping Children Grieve*, reproducible master 18-1
VI. Family Moves	**SAG:** *New in Town*, Activity F **TR:** *Managing Parenting Concerns*, reproducible master 18-2

Assessment

Answers to *Reviewing Key Points* questions in the text, page 446	**TR:** *Chapter 18 Test*, reproducible master **GWTCS:** Questions for Chapter 18

1. (List two:) to financially support themselves and their families, to meet financial goals, personal satisfaction, identify benefits, self-expression, satisfying relationships, personal growth, developing new skills, meeting new people

2. These programs can benefit employers by creating a more productive and satisfying work environment. They can benefit parents by helping them settle their child care concerns. They can benefit children by offering quality child care.

3. as soon as they have made a final decision to divorce

4. Both parents. A joint explanation allows the children to see that both parents still care about them. It shows the children their parents can work together to resolve family matters. It reduces the chance of children having to choose sides.

(Continued)

Assessment *(Continued)*

5. After divorce, parents need to maintain as much continuity as possible in their children's lives. They should try to get along with one another and work together to raise their children.

6. true

7. Children's questions should be answered simply and truthfully. (See page 442 in the text.)

8. No, because doing so could interfere with the necessary grieving and adjusting process.

9. false

10. (Student response.)

Technology Applications

- Have students design a "Supermom" and "Superdad" campaign. Ask students to research the Internet for ways parents can balance dual work roles.
- There are many organizations such as the Ronald McDonald House Charities or Make a Wish Foundation that help families cope with serious illnesses. Invite a person who works for one of these organizations to speak to the class. Also have students research these organizations on the Internet. Ask students to develop a service learning project to help and support these organizations. One idea would be to start a soda can tab collection program in the school and community.

Academic Connections

- Music. Listen to the song *Going Through the Big D* by Mark Chesnutt (1994). Use the song as a tool to discuss aspects of divorce. Because the song doesn't refer to children, have students write another verse on the effects on a child.
- Social studies. Invite students to diagram their family trees. Have students share their family trees with the classroom. Ask students to point out the positive aspects of their families, especially those students who have dealt with remarriage and stepfamilies. This could also be used to discuss some of the challenges of remarriage and stepfamilies.

Web Sites

Families and Work Institute
familiesandwork.org

BlueSuitMom
bluesuitmom.com

Divorce Net
divorcenet.com

Family Education Network
familyeducation.com

The Hospital for Sick Children
sickkids.on.ca/KidsHealth/default.asp

Chapter 19: Family Crises

Chapter Objectives

- Describe common family crises, such as substance abuse, unemployment and financial crises, child abuse and neglect, missing children, domestic violence, and suicide.
- Identify possible causes for these crises.
- Assess the knowledge and skills parents need to handle these crises.
- Summarize community resources available for parents facing these crises.

Text Outline	Supplementary Resources
I. What Is a Crisis?	
II. Unemployment and Financial Crises	**SAG:** *Help for Families Facing Financial Crises,* Activity A
III. Alcoholism and Other Drug Abuse A. Dealing with Substance Abuse	**SAG:** *Dealing with Substance Abuse Problems,* Activity B

IV. Child Abuse and Neglect
  A. Types of Child Abuse and Neglect
  B. Child Abusers
  C. Stopping Child Abuse
	SAG: *Child Abuse Laws and Programs,* Activity C

V. Domestic Violence	**SAG:** *The Domestic Violence Cycle,* Activity D **TR:** *The Three-Phase Cycle of Domestic Violence,* color transparency CT-19

VI. Gangs, Bullies, and Peer Violence
  A. What Can Parents and Children Do?
  B. School Violence
	SAG: *Gangs, Bullies, and Peer Violence,* Activity E

VII. Missing Children A. Runaways	**SAG:** *Missing Children and Runaways,* Activity F

VIII. Suicide
  A. Factors Leading to Suicide
  B. Signals That Warn of Possible Suicide
  C. Preventing Suicide
	SAG: *Preventing Teen Suicide,* Activity G
	TR: *Myths and Truths About Teen Suicide,* reproducible master 19-1
	Responding to Family Crises, reproducible master 19-2

Assessment

Answers to *Reviewing Key Points* questions in the text, page 467

1. A crisis is an unforeseen situation that demands adjustment by all members of a family.
2. (Describe three. Student response.)
3. (List four. See pages 450-451 in the text.)
4. Alcohol or drug abuse problems within the family will often worsen when they are covered up or ignored.

TR: *Chapter 19 Test,* reproducible master
GWTCS: Questions for Chapter 19

(Continued)

Assessment *(Continued)*

5. (Describe three. See pages 453-454 in the text.)

6. (List four. See page 455 in the text.)

7. The first phase is the tension-building phase. During this phase, the abused person knows a violent incident is coming. The second phase is the violent incident. In this stage, abuse occurs. The third phase is the honeymoon phase. In this phase, the abuser tries to win the forgiveness and trust of the abused person with gifts, romantic dates, and promises.

8. (Student response.)

9. (List five. See pages 460-462 in the text.)

10. (List five. See pages 462-463 in the text.)

11. They have to rely on their families for housing and other kinds of support. Their years of dependency become lengthened.

12. (List five. See pages 465-466 in the text.)

13. true

Technology Applications

- Have students visit the Prevent Child Abuse America Web site preventchildabuse.org. Then have students develop an action plan of how they, along with other community members, can help prevent child abuse.
- Have students visit the Web site dvsheltertour.org. Ask them to take the quiz on domestic violence. Use the quiz as a discussion board for talking about domestic violence.
- Have students make a video about the factors leading to suicide, signals that warn of possible suicide, and preventing suicide. Show the videos to the class. Provide a copy to the school counselor.

Academic Connections

- Math. Give students the figures for yearly incomes of a dual-career household. Have students role-play to decide how they would spend the incomes. Then tell the students one of the parents has lost his or her job and will be on unemployment. Have students again role-play how they would adjust their spending. Ask students to research ways on the Internet and throughout the community for resources to help deal with financial crises.
- English. Have students write a poem about peer violence. Submit the poems to the school newspaper.

Web Sites

Substance Abuse and Mental Health Service Administration
samhsa.gov

Center On Addiction and Substance Abuse
casacolumbia.org

National Clearinghouse on Child Abuse and Neglect Information
calib.com/nccanch

Child Abuse Prevention Network
child-abuse.com

National Coalition Against Domestic Violence
ncadv.org

Family Violence Prevention Fund
endabuse.org

National Center for Missing and Exploited Children
missingkids.com

American Foundation for Suicide Prevention
afsp.org

Chapter 20: A Look at Child Care Options

Chapter Objectives

- Identify the different types of child care available.
- List factors to consider when selecting child care.
- Evaluate options related to child care.
- Describe common concerns of parents who use child care.

Text Outline	Supplementary Resources
I. Deciding Whether to Use Child Care	**TR:** *Positive and Negative Aspects of Group Child Care*, transparency master 20-1
II. Types of Child Care A. Child Care in the Child's Home B. Child Care in the Caregiver's Home C. Government-Sponsored Child Care D. Church-Linked Child Care E. Employer-Sponsored Child Care F. University-Linked Child Care G. Cooperative Child Care H. Play Groups I. Privately-Owned Child Care Centers J. Nationally-Franchised Child Care Centers K. Drop-In Child Care Centers L. School-Age Child Care	**SAG:** *Home-Based Child Care*, Activity A *Child Care Centers*, Activity B **TR:** *Child Care—Checking out the Options*, color transparency CT-20
III.Selecting Child Care A. The Physical Setting B. The Program C. The Adult-Child Ratio D. Characteristics of Caregivers E. Consistency	**SAG:** *Factors to Consider*, Activity D *Selecting Child Care*, Activity E **TR:** *Home-Based Care Versus Group Care*, reproducible master 20-2
IV. Evaluating Child Care	**SAG:** *Evaluating a Child Care Program*, Activity C
V. Concerns of Parents	

Assessment

Answers to *Reviewing Key Points* questions in the text, page 487

1. Many experts believe the ideal child care situation for a young child is in the home with loving and caring parents.
2. (List three:) local child-related organizations, city and state licensing agencies, elementary school teachers, friends, neighbors, coworkers

TR: *Chapter 20 Test*, reproducible master

GWTCS: Questions for Chapter 20

(Continued)

Assessment   *(Continued)*

3. A nanny is specially-trained child care provider, while an au pair is a young person who comes from another country to live with a family and care for their children. An au pair may have less training and education and may not be fluent in the family's language.

4. (List two:) more convenient, don't have to transport children to and from child care, can hire a caregiver whose availability matches their needs, child has familiar surroundings, child can have one-to-one interaction with caregiver

5. false

6. Some companies provide on-site child care for employee's children. Some offer a "voucher system" where a parent is given coupons or vouchers that can be redeemed at whatever child care facility the parent chooses. Some offer a "cafeteria style" package of benefits in which parents may choose company-paid child care.

7. (List two:) parents can be part of the child's child care experiences, parents can meet each other, lower cost, higher quality

8. In general, these centers have lots of good, safe equipment and well-developed programs designed and supervised by trained personnel. Meals and snacks are usually available. Extended hours allow flexibility in parents' schedules. The fees are in the medium price range for dependable child care.

9. (Student response. See page 479.)

10. physical setting, program, adult-child ratio, characteristics of the caregivers, and consistency

11. Suggested adult ratios in child care settings are one caregiver for every two or three infants, one caregiver for every four toddlers, and one caregiver for every eight preschoolers.

12. (Student response. See page 482 in the text.)

13. They must continually evaluate the care their children receive.

14. Parents may have pangs of jealously because the caregiver can spend more time with the child. The child may develop a special attachment to the caregiver. At times, the child may even show preference for the caregiver.

15. Each person who provides care for a child should have a medical consent form so that medical treatment can be given to a child if it is needed.

(Continued)

Technology Applications

- Using a computer drawing program, have students make a pamphlet listing all the child care options in the community and a description of the care provided. Distribute the pamphlets at various locations within the community.
- Visit Child Care Aware's Web site at childcareaware.org. Have students research various aspects of child care. Then ask students to click on *Evaluating a Provider*. Using the evaluation sheet, analyze child care providers in your area (with permission). Have students compile their results. Chart the findings.

Academic Connections

- Math. Have students use the *Checklist for Choosing Child Care* on page XXX. Ask a sample of parents to rate these questions on a scale of 1 to 10 for their importance, with 10 being the highest score. Have students analyze the results to determine what factors are the most important to parents when choosing child care.
- Journalism. Interview parents to investigate parental concerns. Ask students to interview child care professionals to see how they deal with concerned parents. Have students write an article about the concerns of parents. Submit the articles to a local newspaper.

Web Sites

National Child Care Information Center
nccic.org

National Network for Child Care
nncc.org

Child Care Online
childcare.net

USA Child Care
usachildcare.org

Chapter 21: Children's Education and Health

Chapter Objectives

- Describe parents' roles in their children's education, both at home and at school.
- Propose ways parents can increase their children's desire to learn.
- Identify the special needs of children with learning disabilities, mental disabilities, physical disabilities, emotional disorders, and giftedness.
- Summarize the benefits of inclusion for children with special needs and average learners.
- Describe parents' roles in children's health care.
- List common symptoms of childhood illness.
- Explain how to care for a sick child.

Text Outline

I. Parents' Roles in Their Children's Education
   A. Parents' Involvement at Home
   B. Parents' Involvement with Schools

II. Children with Special Needs
   A. Children with Mental Disabilities
   B. Children with Physical Disabilities
   C. Children with Learning Disabilities
   D. Children with Emotional Disorders
   E. Gifted Children

III. Inclusion

IV. Parents' Roles in Their Children's Health Care
   A. Caring for a Sick Child at Home

Supplementary Resources

SAG: *Using Teachable Moments,* Activity A
Homework, Activity B
TR: *Education Survey,* reproducible master 21-1
When Your Child Starts School, reproducible master 21-2

SAG: *Children with Special Needs,* Activity E
Current Developments in Education, Activity C

SAG: *Education Crossword,* Activity D

SAG: *The Child Who Is Ill,* Activity F
TR: *Childhood Diseases,* color transparency, CT-21

Assessment

Answers to *Reviewing Key Points* questions in the text, page 511

1. (Student response.)
2. false
3. (Student response.)
4. Parents may use positive reinforcement when children practice good study habits and do well in school. Parents can make sure children have a suitable place to study. Parents can guide their children while helping them develop their own resources for problem solving.
5. A mental disability is a limitation in the way a person's mind functions. A person with a mental disability may or may not be mentally retarded. Mental retardation is a condition occurring before a person is 18 years old. A person with mental retardation functions intellectually on a level that is far below average. He or she also has deficits in adaptive skills behavior.

TR: *Chapter 21 Test,* reproducible master
GWTCS: Questions for Chapter 21

(Continued)

Assessment (Continued)

6. An IEP is a written plan that states the educational goals for a child with disabilities. It is used as an agreement among the child, his or her family, and the school about how they will work together to meet the child's special learning needs.

7. (Student response.)

8. A learning disorder is a limitation in the way a person's brain sorts and uses information. (Examples are student response. See pages 500-503 in the text.)

9. ADHD can interfere with a person's ability to learn because it causes a shorter-than-average attention span. A person with ADHD cannot concentrate or focus on one task for very long.

10. emotionally; socially

11. An enrichment program is a program within the school that is designed to meet the needs to gifted students. (Examples are student response. See page 506 in the text.)

12. (List three:) students of varying abilities get the opportunity to interact with one another; nondisabled students can act as role models for disabled students; nondisabled students can learn appreciation for diversity, acceptance, and teamwork; offers least restrictive environment for disabled students.

13. A.   every two years
    B.   five times
    C.   every year
    D.   every two years
    E.   every year

14. (Student response. See page 508 in the text.)

15. No, extra nurturance when a child is sick can help him or her feel better faster.

Technology Applications

- Have students research the Internet for Web sites that provide educational activities that parents and children can do together. After the research is complete, design flyers that tell about the sites. With permission, post the flyers around the community.
- Have students use the Internet to research attention deficit hyperactivity disorder (ADHD) or another learning disability. Find out what causes ADHD or a learning disability and how to manage it in the classroom and at home.

Academic Connections

- Journalism. Have students research the history of the National PTA organizations. Ask students to interview parents in the community who are involved in the PTA. Have students write an opinion article about PTA and why parental involvement is important. If your school doesn't have a PTA or a similar organization, ask students to brainstorm ways to begin an organization in your school and community.
- English. Make a list of physical disabilities. Assign a "physical disability" to each student. Have them role-play using props, such as a blindfold or crutches. Have students spend the class period with the disability. Ask students to write a reflection paper on how they felt about having the disability. Read parts of the papers to the class and use the papers as a springboard to talk about other disabilities.
- Science. Have students assume the role of a doctor. Give students a childhood disease to research. Have students explain what causes the disease, what the symptoms are, and how to care for a child with the disease.

(Continued)

Web Sites

National PTA
pta.org

National Coalition for Parent Involvement in Education
ncpie.org

Education World
education-world.com

National Council on Disability
ncd.gov

National Institute on Disability and Rehabilitation Research
ed.gov/offices/OSERS/NIDRR

ADHD.com—the online community
adhd.com

American Academy of Pediatrics
aap.org

Chapter 22: The Challenge of a Child and Family Services Career

Chapter Objectives

- Identify career opportunities in child and family services.
- Do a self-assessment of your interests, aptitudes, and abilities.
- Explain the personal qualifications needed for a child and family services career.
- Describe the general professional qualifications for a child and family services career.
- Develop a career plan.
- Describe trends that affect careers in child and family services.
- Describe how to find and secure employment.

Text Outline	Supplementary Resources

I. Working Directly with Children
  A. Child Care Personnel
  B. Teachers
  C. Children's Librarians
  D. Youth and Recreation Leaders
  E. Social Workers
  F. Health Services
	SAG: *Child and Family Services Career Opportunities,* Activity A

II. Working on Behalf of Children and Families	

III. Creating and Selling Products and Services for Children
  A. Designing and Selling Children's Products
  B. Writers, Artists, and Entertainers	

IV. Entrepreneurship	**SAG:** *You Can Be an Entrepreneur!* Activity B **TR:** *Success as an Entrepreneur,* reproducible master 22-1

V. Know Your Interests, Aptitudes, and Abilities
  A. Interests
  B. Aptitudes
  C. Abilities
	SAG: *Interests, Aptitudes, and Abilities,* Activity C

VI. Considering a Career in Child and Family Services
  A. Personal Qualifications for a Child and Family Services Career
  B. Professional Qualifications for a Child and Family Services Career
	SAG: *Personal Characteristics,* Activity D
	TR: *Do You See Yourself Working with Children?* color transparency CT-22A

VII. Developing a Career Plan	

(Continued)

Text Outline   *(Continued)*

VIII.   Trends Affecting Child and Family
Services Careers
- A.   More Entry-Level Child Care Career
Openings
- B.   Need for More Accredited Child Care
Programs
- C.   Expanding Education Programs for
Young Children
- D.   New Settings for Child Care
- E.   Growing Child and Family Services
Career Demands
- F.   Employees Must Prepare

IX. Preparing for Tomorrow's Challenges Today
- A.   Joining Student Organizations
- B.   Developing Your Leadership Skills
- C.   Becoming an Effective Team Member
- D.   Developing Your Communication Skills
- E.   Finding Part-Time Employment
- F.   Developing Your Employability Skills

Supplementary Resources

SAG: *Trends in Child Care Careers,*
Activity E

SAG: *Developing Leadership Skills,*
Activity F
Your Resume Worksheet, Activity G
TR: *Aim for Job Success,* color trans-
parency CT-22B
Employment Application, repro-
ducible master 22-2

Assessment

Answers to *Reviewing Key Points* questions in the
text, page 536

1. A job is a single work experience, while a
career is a series of related jobs or work
experiences.
2. An entry-level job is one that requires little
or not training after high school. A paraprofessional position requires some education
and training after high school. A person in
this position might have an associate degree
from a two-year college or technical school.
A professional position requires advanced
education and training after high school. A
person in this position has at least a bachelor's degree in his or her field.
3. Applicants must have experience in child
care and receive some related classroom
training. A team of child care professionals
assesses the applicant's skills in working
with young children. They then decide
whether the candidate qualifies for the
CDA Credential.
4. (Student response. See page 518-519 in the text.)
5. Family life educators provide training for
effective parenting for interested parents.
Child development teachers teach junior
high through college level students the
principles of child development and the
care and guidance of children. Teacher
educators work at the college level to
prepare family life educators and child
development teachers for their positions.
6. (Student response. See page 522 in the text.)
7. to help find a career that brings happiness
and fulfillment

TR: *Chapter 22 Test,* reproducible
master
GWTCS: Questions for Chapter 22

(Continued)

Assessment   *(Continued)*

8. (Student response. See page 526.)

9. More and more parents are working. This increases the demand for child care, which means more child care centers are needed. In these new centers, more employees are needed.

10. An accredited child care program is one that is officially recognized and approved by a leading agency in its field. Parents should look for accredited centers or child care homes because these centers meet criteria set by experts in the child care field. It is an indicator of quality of care.

11. (Student response. See pages 527-529 in the text.)

12. Parliamentary procedure is a way of conducting meetings in an orderly manner. It will be used in most groups you will belong to as an adult. Learning these procedures now will help you feel more comfortable in meetings you will attend as an adult.

13. (Student response. See page 530 in the text.)

14. (Student response. See pages 532-533 in the text.)

15. contact a business or agency directly to see if they have any open positions; talk to family members, friends, and neighbors; look in want ads in a newspaper; look for "help wanted" signs in businesses; read notices on community bulletin boards

16. your name, address, phone number, education, work experience, special skills, activities, references

17. the name of the person you are to see, your resume, a pen

Technology Applications

- Have students research the Internet for student organizations that would be helpful when preparing for a future career. Ask students to make a flyer about the organizations and why they would be beneficial when developing interpersonal and leadership skills.
- Prepare a list of typical job interview questions. Have the students choose partners. Have students role-play being the interviewer and interviewee. Tape the interview using a video camera. Ask students to critique their interviews.

Academic Connections

- Speech. Have students research a career related to children and families. Ask students to prepare a speech about the career. Have students give their speech to the class.
- English. Have students prepare a resume and cover letter for part-time employment in a child and family services career. Ask students to exchange papers with one of their classmates and edit one another's work.

Web Sites

Family, Career, and Career Leaders of America
fcclainc.org
4-H
4-H.org
National Association for Family Child Care
nafcc.org
Occupational Outlook Handbook
bls.gov/oco

Parents
and Their Children

Verdene Ryder
Family Life Education Consultant
Houston, Texas

Dr. Celia A. Decker
Professor of Family and Consumer Sciences, Retired
Northwestern State University of Louisiana
Natchitoches, Louisiana

Publisher
The Goodheart-Willcox Company, Inc.
Tinley Park, Illinois

Copyright 2004

by

The Goodheart-Willcox Company, Inc.

Previous Edition Copyright 2000, 1995, 1990, 1985

Library of Congress Catalog Card Number 2002029960

International Standard Book Number 1-59070-116-X

2 3 4 5 6 7 8 9 10   04   09 08 07 06 05 04 03

Library of Congress Cataloging-in-Publication Data

Ryder, Verdene.
Parents and their children / by Verdene Ryder, Celia A. Decker.
     p. cm.
Includes index.
ISBN 1-59070-116-X
1. Parenting. 2. Parent and child. 3. Child psychology. 4. Parenthood.
I. Decker, Celia Anita. II. Title.

HQ755.8.R93 2004
649'.1--dc21

Cover Photo © Francisco Cruz/SuperStock, Inc.

Introduction

If you are interested in children, *Parents and Their Children* is written for you. You may want to be a parent someday, or have a career working with children. Since most people in our society become parents, this book focuses on the decisions related to parenthood. It covers such decisions as when to have children, what health practices to follow during pregnancy, and how to prepare for childbirth. From the moment of birth, both parents and their children constantly learn, grow, and change. This book will help you recognize children's stages of development. It will also show you how parents' roles change as their children grow. The interactions between parents and their children are powerful influences on children's development and parents'

attitudes and behaviors. This text shows you how to promote enjoyable, supportive, encouraging, and rewarding parent-child interactions. It explores the many decisions related to parenthood and describes the roles of parents in various family structures. This revised edition includes more information about pregnancy, prenatal care, and childbirth, as well as a new chapter on decisions facing parents-to-be. Several other topics have been added throughout the book. *Parents and Their Children* presents current information about helping today's families successfully meet the unique challenges they may face. It can also help you in the future as you make decisions about parenting or a child-related career.

About the Authors

Verdene Ryder is a nationally recognized author and family life specialist. In addition to being the author of *Parents and Their Children*, she is also the author of the popular family living texts *Contemporary Living*; *Human Sexuality: Responsible Life Choices*; and several booklets. She is often consulted in interviews on radio and TV relating to family life issues. Verdene has extensive teaching experience at both the high school and university levels. She is a member of several professional organizations and has received numerous academic and leadership awards. A scholarship has been named in her honor to enable women in financial need to attend college.

After a 38-year career in education, Celia A. Decker retired as a professor in the Department of Family and Consumer Sciences at Northwestern State University of Louisiana. She taught courses in early childhood education, child development, and family relations. Before her position at Northwestern State University, she taught college courses at East Texas State University (now Texas A&M at Commerce) and at the University of Arkansas at Fayetteville. In addition to writing this text and *Children: The Early Years*, she and her husband, Dr. John R. Decker, wrote *Planning and Administering Early Childhood Programs*. Dr. Decker has also published numerous chapters in books and articles. She does extensive consultant work for Head Start, Even Start, and local school systems. During her years of teaching, Dr. Decker was named to Who's Who in Child Development Professionals, Who's Who in Personalities of the South, Who's Who in American Women, and the World's Who's Who in Education. In 1994, she was selected as the Outstanding Professor at Northwestern State University.

Contents

Part One
Decisions About Parenting

Chapter 1
Parenting as a Career   12
The Job Description   14
Myths About the Job   16
Responsibilities of Parenting   18
Rewards of Parenting   23

Chapter 2
Parenting: A Choice   28
What Influences Parenting
   Decisions?   30
Factors to Consider   34
Teen Parenthood   42
Decision Making   46

Chapter 3
Families   50
How Are Families Formed?   51
Family Structures   55
Functions of the Family   60
Families: Yesterday, Today, and
   Tomorrow   61
Your Roles   62
The Family Life Cycle   63
Each Family Is Unique   66

Chapter 4
Effective Parenting   76
How Children Grow and Develop   77
Effects of Heredity and
   Environment   80
The Influence of the Family   81
Effective Parent-Child
   Relationships   85
Resources for Parents   94

Part Two
The Beginning of
Parenthood

Chapter 5
Planning a Family   102
Advantages of Family Planning   103
Factors That Influence Family
   Planning Decisions   104
Human Reproduction   106
Issues of Family Planning   108

Chapter 6
Pregnancy   118
Conception   119
Prenatal Development   121
Signs of Pregnancy   125
Physical Changes During
   Pregnancy   126
Emotional Changes During
   Pregnancy   127
Complications During
   Pregnancy   130

Chapter 7
Prenatal Care   138
Medical Care During Pregnancy   139
Nutrition During Pregnancy   143
Weight Gain During Pregnancy   149
Exercise During Pregnancy   150

Factors That Increase Health Risks to Mother and Baby   151
Rest   154
Maternity Clothes   154

Chapter 8
Decisions Facing Parents-to-Be   158
Childbirth Preparation Decisions   159
Where Will the Birth Take Place?   161
What Baby Supplies Will Be Needed?   163
Choosing Breast-Feeding or Bottle-Feeding   169
Who Will Share in the Baby's Care?   172

Chapter 9
Childbirth   182
Signs of Labor   183
Going to the Hospital   184
Childbirth Medications   186
Three Stages of Labor   187
Methods of Childbirth   189
Neonatal Care   193
Bonding   195
Postpartum Period   197

Chapter 10
New Parents, New Baby   204
The First Days of Parenthood   205
How the Newborn Looks   206
What the Newborn Can Do   207
How Parents Care for Their Newborns   211
The Husband and Wife as Parents   219

Part Three
Understanding Children's Growth and Development

Chapter 11
Parents and Their Infants   226
Physical Development   228
Intellectual Development   240
Emotional and Social Development   249
Medical Checkups for Infants   253
Developmental Charts   255

Chapter 12
Parents and Their Toddlers   266
Physical Development   268
Intellectual Development   277
Emotional and Social Development   282
The Importance of Play to a Child's Overall Development   288
Medical Checkups for Toddlers   289
Developmental Charts   290

Chapter 13
Parents and Their Preschoolers 298
Physical Development 299
Intellectual Development 306
Emotional and Social
    Development 312
Medical Checkups for
    Preschoolers 317
Developmental Charts 319

Chapter 14
Parents and Their School-Age Children 326
Readiness for School 328
Physical Development 329
Intellectual Development 336
Emotional and Social
    Development 342
Self-Care Children 347
Children and Stress 348
Medical Checkups for School-Age
    Children 351
Developmental Charts 352

Chapter 15
Parents and Their Teens 358
Physical Development 360
Intellectual Development 365
Emotional and Social
    Development 366
Medical Checkups for Teens
Developmental Charts 372

Part Four
The Challenges of Parenting

Chapter 16
Theories and Guidelines 378
Piaget's Theory of Intellectual
    Development 379
Erikson's Theory of Personality
    Development 382
Freud's Theory of Personality
    Development 389
Maslow's Hierarchy of Human
    Needs 390
Kohlberg's Theory of Moral
    Development 392
Other Child Development
    Theories 393
Parenting Strategies 394
An Overall View of Development 394

Chapter 17
Guiding Healthy Development 400
Guiding Children's Behavior 401
Sibling Relationships 408
Developing Responsibility 410
Developing Honesty 416
Media Influences 419
Developing a Healthy Sexuality 423

Chapter 18

Family Concerns   430

Balancing Family and Work
    Roles   431
Divorce   435
Remarriage and Stepfamilies   441
Serious Illness   442
Explaining Death to Children   443
Family Moves   444

Chapter 19

Family Crises   448

What Is a Crisis?   449
Unemployment and Financial
    Crises   450
Alcoholism and Other Drug
    Abuse   451
Child Abuse and Neglect   453
Domestic Violence   459
Gangs, Bullies, and Peer Violence   460
Missing Children   462
Suicide   463

Chapter 20

**A Look at Child Care
Options   470**

Deciding Whether to Use
    Child Care   472
Types of Child Care   473
Selecting Child Care   480
Evaluating Child Care   482
Concerns of Parents   483
Managing the Child Care
    Experience   485

Chapter 21

**Children's Education and
Health   490**

Parents' Roles in Their Children's
    Education   492
Children with Special Needs   496
Inclusion   506
Parents' Roles in Their Children's
    Health Care   507

Chapter 22

**The Challenge of a Child and
Family Services Career   514**

Working Directly with Children
    and Families   516
Working on Behalf of Children
    and Families   519
Creating and Selling Products and
    Services for Children   521
Entrepreneurship   522
Know Your Interests, Aptitudes,
    and Abilities   523
Considering a Career in Child and
    Family Services   524
Personal Qualifications for a Child
    and Family Services Career   524
Developing a Career Plan   526
Trends Affecting Child and Family
    Services Careers   526
Preparing for Tomorrow's Challenges
    Today   529

Glossary   538
Photo Credits   547
Index   549

Part One
Decisions About Parenting

Chapter 1
Parenting as a Career

Chapter 2
Parenting: A Choice

Chapter 3
Families

Chapter 4
Effective Parenting

Chapter 1
Parenting as a
Career

Objectives

After studying this chapter, you will be able to

- describe the process of parenting.
- list qualities needed by effective parents.
- explain popular myths about parenting.
- describe the responsibilities and rewards of parenting.

Key Terms

parenting
dedication
flexibility
nurturance
moral development
personal priorities
morals
heritage
ethnic group
cultural traditions
ethnic identity
stress

Parenting is the name given to the process of raising a child. Parents provide the daily care, love, support, and guidance their children need to grow and develop into adults. Parenting is a lifelong process that begins when people bring children into their families by birth, adoption, or other circumstances. At some time in their lives, most people become parents.

This book will help you understand what parenting involves. Parenting does not just mean giving birth—that's only the beginning. From the day a new child enters their family, parents are responsible for meeting this child's needs. Parenting is a lot of work; many say it's a full-time job. In fact, parenting is quite similar in some ways to having a career. Comparing the two can help you understand the level of responsibility parenting requires.

People often prepare for their careers by studying. In the same way, you can prepare for parenting by reading books such as this one. People spend a large portion of their lives working at their careers. Likewise, if you decide to choose parenting, it will consume a large portion of your life. Careers demand commitment, involve responsibilities, present challenges, and offer rewards. Parenting also demands commitment—an irreversible one. It involves many responsibilities, the biggest of which is helping a child become a mature, responsible adult. Parenting presents new challenges daily and offers rewards such as joy, pride, and contentment.

1—**Vocabulary:** Look up terms in the glossary and discuss their meanings.

2—**Resource:** *Opinions About Parenting,* Activity B, SAG.

3—**Discuss:** How is studying a book like this to help you prepare for parenting similar to studying for a career?

4—**Reflect:** Parenting demands an irreversible commitment. What does this mean to you?

The Job Description

If you think you might want to be a parent someday, you should know just what it is parents do. Actually, it's good to understand what parents do even if you don't think you will ever become one. You may pursue a career working with children and their parents. Most of your friends and family members will one day be parents. Recognizing the challenges they face and the rewards they receive may strengthen your relationships with them.

Suppose you were reading the want ads in your local newspaper and discovered the ad in 1-1. Would a job like this interest you? Why or why not? When you read the job description in 1-1, did you notice these key words: dedication, flexibility, and nurturance?

Wanted: Parent

Full-time position available for mature individual. Job requires dedication, flexibility, and nurturance. Must be willing to work seven 24-hour shifts per week. No experience needed, but child development knowledge is a definite plus. Responsibilities include: changing diapers, fixing meals, cleaning up messes, and answering questions, as well as teaching, loving, and guiding a child from infancy to adulthood. A minimum 18-year commitment is required.

Salary: You pay thousands.

Fringe benefits: Excellent, including the opportunity to hear a child's first words, help a child learn to ride a bicycle, and watch with pride as your grown-up son or daughter receives a college diploma.

For an application, contact:

The Stork Company

1-1 _____
Does this sound like the job for you? Parenting is hard work, but it has many rewards.

Each of these qualities is important in parenting and will be described further in the sections that follow.

Dedication

Parenting demands **dedication**, or a deep level of continued commitment. It is a 24-hour-a-day, everyday job. When you become a parent, you must devote yourself to your new role. You can't punch a time card and go off duty. If your baby needs to be fed or changed, it is your job to see those needs are met. You can't say, "Sorry, I'm on my coffee break," when your child comes to you with a bloody knee. You can't resign—or even take a vacation—from parenting when the job is difficult. You have to hang in there, giving whatever help and support is needed, 1-2.

Flexibility

Parents need flexibility to survive the many challenges they face. **Flexibility** means being ready and able to adapt to new and different circumstances. When you become a parent, you must be able to adjust easily and fairly quickly to many different situations.

As children grow and develop, they may pass through phases in which they exhibit certain types of behavior. Some of these behaviors include getting into everything, kicking, tattling, and playing practical jokes. As a parent, you will need to adjust to these passing phases and the behaviors your child displays. Often, your child will grow out of a phase just as you learn how to handle behavior in that phase. You have to stay on your toes mentally and physically to keep up with growing children.

In addition to this type of flexibility, parents must also be flexible in their daily plans. When you become a parent, much of your daily schedule

1-2

Being a parent requires dedication—there are no days off.

Nurturance

Nurturance means loving care and attention. To nurture children is to love, teach, and guide them, and further their development.

From the very beginning of their lives, infants need to be assured they are surrounded by love. Although newborns do not understand words, you can communicate with them. Your tone of voice, facial expressions, and touch send a message. Smiling and talking cheerfully to infants can clearly convey your love. Babies gain a feeling of security when their parents hold them close and soothe them.

As babies grow, they still need their parent's love and nurturance. Parents continue to love and nurture their children even into adulthood. Your children will need to know they can

is determined by the needs and activities of your child. For instance, you may have to miss adult social events to watch your child play in a soccer match. You may have to postpone a business meeting to stay home with a sick child. You may have to push back mealtime when, with your child's "help," preparing dinner takes longer than you had planned, 1-3. (In a case like this, a good sense of humor is just as important as flexibility.)

Being flexible in your daily routine will allow you to enjoy children's spontaneous nature. You can share their delight when they first play in the snow or see themselves in the mirror. You can marvel at their first words and first steps. You can smile proudly as they demonstrate new hopping, running, jumping, or dancing skills. Sharing such unplanned moments with your children is one of the most precious fringe benefits of the job of parenting.

1-3

Flexibility in daily plans allows parents to share special moments with their children. This mother enjoys cooking with her "helper" even though it takes longer.

1—Discuss: Discuss how parents can enjoy the spontaneous nature of children. Cite examples such as watching a bird fly or smelling a flower.

2—Discuss: Even infants respond to the love expressed by nurturing care. Explain how nurturance is a part of loving, teaching, and guiding children.

1—Discuss: Why should parents never use love as a reward or a threat?

2—Activity: Give examples of rules parents make that teach their children what they should and should not do.

3—Enrich: Ask parents to share stories that illustrate various myths about parenting.

4—Activity: Compare instinctive parenting skills to learned parenting skills. Give examples of each.

always count on your love. When your children misbehave, explain that although you dislike their behavior, you still love them. Never, under any circumstances, use love as a reward or threat. Do not tell children you will love them more for eating their vegetables or less for getting bad grades. Parents should give their children love constantly and in large doses, 1-4.

Nurturing children involves guiding and teaching them. A parent is a child's first teacher. It is from your parents you probably learned to eat, talk, walk, dress yourself, and ride a bike. These are only a few of the many skills parents teach their children. Parents warn their children to avoid dangers, such as moving cars and hot ovens. They also teach their children what they should and should not do. Children need this guidance in order to develop into mature, responsible adults.

Parents can also nurture their children by encouraging them to do their best. Children like challenges, and they like being praised when they succeed. Having realistic expectations helps parents guide children to develop appropriate skills. Realistic

1-4

Giving lots of love to a child is an important part of nurturance.

expectations are not too high or low for most children of a certain age. Studying child development helps people understand what to expect from children. For instance, typical three-year-olds are ready to ride tricycles and string large beads. Encouraging a three-year-old to develop these skills will likely lead to success. Parents can nurture their children by helping them master age-appropriate skills.

Myths About the Job

People often think of certain careers as "perfect careers." They might believe and spread myths about what a particular career involves. Actually, no career is perfect. Each career has problems and less favorable aspects. Don't believe the myths about a career option; you may be missing part of the story. Instead, learn all you can about what that career is *really* like.

Similarly, many people believe and spread myths about parenting. You have probably heard some of these myths; you may even have believed them. As you read the following sections, however, consider learning more about what parenting involves before making up your mind.

Myth #1: All parenting skills are instinctive.

Some people say all parenting skills are *instinctive*, or based on a natural skill or capacity. They say people are born knowing how to be parents; it just comes naturally. Many mothers and fathers do seem naturally well suited to being parents. This doesn't mean they instinctively know it all or have nothing to learn. No one is born with all the preparation needed to be an effective parent. Parenting takes work, and it takes practice.

Many people do have a parenting instinct. Some skills required in parenting come naturally to them. Some people have stronger parenting instincts than others. *All* parenting skills are not instinctive, however. This is a myth because many parenting skills must be learned, 1-5.

Learning parenting skills can be a little like learning arithmetic. You were not born knowing 2+2=4, nor were you born knowing how to bathe an infant. Since you were willing to work to learn arithmetic, you can now add, subtract, multiply, and divide. If you are willing to work to learn parenting skills, you will become a more effective parent.

Myth #2: Parenting is always fun.

The second common myth is that parenting is always fun. From the outside looking in, it's easier to see the rewards of parenting than the challenges and responsibilities. People who have not yet been parents cannot foresee all these less-positive aspects. People who have already raised children sometimes look back and remember the good times more easily than the bad.

Like any other job, parenting can be fun, sad, exciting, boring, satisfying,

1-5 _____
This new parent has to learn many skills, including how to burp his baby.

and frustrating. The point is you need to have realistic expectations. You will soon be disappointed if you believe parenting is just one fun day after another. You may even grow to resent your child for not fulfilling your dreams of parenting bliss. On the other hand, if you can accept that there will be bad times, too, you will probably enjoy parenting.

Parenting is not fun all the time, but many parents have lots of fun as they raise their children. An important influence is a person's attitude toward parenting. Keeping a sense of humor can help parents through difficult times. Overall, many people genuinely enjoy being parents.

Myth #3: Children are always cute and sweet.

The third common myth is that children are always cute and sweet. While children can be adorable, parents should be prepared to accept reality, 1-6. Children can also be messy, uncooperative, and downright stubborn.

Many people daydream about having a baby. They look forward to holding a sweet, cuddly bundle of joy. It's not as easy to anticipate times when babies are not so cute and sweet. Babies also cry, scream, and squirm. They are sick and unhappy sometimes. Parents must be able to handle all the noise and messes babies create. It can be a big adjustment if parents have unrealistic expectations about what babies are really like.

Even the cutest and sweetest babies grow quickly into school-age children and teens. Older children can be just as enjoyable, if not more so, than babies. However, some people are not ready to handle older children's needs and demands. They may not find older children as cute and sweet as babies. Babies can't start an argument or run all over the house. People will be

1—Reflect: Do you view parenting as fun or hard work? What conditions might make the difference?

2—Discuss: Babies grow up. How many parents become disenchanted with parenting when they compare a cuddly baby to a stubborn two-year-old? Can studying parenting help?

1-6
Parents must be prepared to accept the reality that cute, cuddly children can be messy eaters.

Responsibilities of Parenting

disappointed if they become parents simply to care for cuddly babies. Parents who look forward to all the stages of growth are more prepared. They will find satisfaction throughout their lives as parents, not just during the first few years.

Television and movies help reinforce the myth that children are cute and sweet. Popular TV shows and commercials rarely show children crying, screaming, hitting, kicking, or whining. Instead, they show children playing quietly, eating peacefully with the family, and talking reasonably with their brothers and sisters. Advertisements are even more biased. Diaper ads show only freshly diapered, smiling, cuddly toddlers. You rarely see the uncomfortable, fussy baby with dirty diapers. You never see a parent struggling to change the diapers of an uncooperative, squirming baby.

The media also often misrepresents older children. Television programs and commercials often feature neatly dressed older children going to school or playing nicely. In reality, children also sometimes have torn shirts, black eyes, beestings, skinned knees, and muddy shoes.

You would not accept a job unless you knew what responsibilities you would have and what wages you would earn. Likewise, you should not become a parent before learning about the responsibilities and rewards parents can expect.

To Fulfill Their Legal Responsibilities and Rights

Regardless of parents' marital status, parents have a major legal responsibility to support and supervise their children. This responsibility continues until the child reaches the age of majority (often age 18), marries, or financially supports himself or herself.

Support involves providing the basic necessities (food, clothing, and shelter), medical care, and an education. Based on support obligations parents have rights to make many decisions about their children's lives. For example, parents determine where children will live, what they will do on a day-to-day basis, which school they will attend, and what medical care they will be given. If the parents' support is not adequate, the courts may intervene on behalf of the child. For example, the courts may place a child in another adult's care or insist on certain medical procedures if a child's life is endangered.

Parents also have the responsibility to supervise and control their child's behavior. Parents are liable for a child's accidental or intentional injury of others, destruction of property, stealing, truancy, and curfew violations. Parents can control their child as they see fit as long as they do not abuse or neglect the child or ask the child to do something illegal.

To Want and Be Ready for Children

A parent's first responsibility is deciding he or she wants children and is ready to have them. People should think carefully about whether they really want children and are ready to be parents. Every child deserves the proper care and guidance. Making rational decisions about parenting is best for both the adult and child.

Being a good parent also means recognizing when it is *not* the right time to start (or add to) a family. Family planning decisions will be described more fully in later chapters.

To Love Their Children

Children need lots and lots of love. Parents should give their love freely and constantly to their children. Children need to know they are loved for who they are—for their own special qualities. Feeling loved gives children a sense of security. This helps children feel good about themselves and develop self-confidence. Parents can begin to meet their children's emotional needs by loving them completely and unconditionally, 1-7.

To Fulfill Children's Physical Needs

Parents have a legal responsibility to provide for children's physical needs. Physical needs are easy to identify.

Children need living space. For a newborn, the amount of space is small. As children grow, they need more

1—Discuss: Why is it important for parents to want and be ready for children? In an unplanned pregnancy, are the parents exhibiting this responsibility?

2—Discuss: How can parents fulfill their children's physical needs? If parents do not fill these needs, how can they be held accountable?

1-7
Parent-child relationships are not equal give-and-take relationships. Parents must give love freely and constantly to their children.

1—Discuss: Parents must stay informed about children's changing nutritional needs as they grow. Where can parents get this information?

2—Enrich: Investigate how parents arrange alternate child care when their children are ill. What resources are available in your community for parents with sick children?

3—Discuss: Why is it easier for parents to identify a child's physical needs than his or her other needs?

4—Discuss: Why is it important for people to behave in ways that are acceptable to society? What happens if they behave in unacceptable ways?

space for their equipment, clothes, and toys. They also need space to take care of their physical needs, play, study, or just be alone.

Parents must provide food for children. Dietary needs change throughout the life cycle. Parents must ensure their child eats enough nutritious foods to be healthy and grow.

Clothing is another physical need. Parents are responsible for dressing their child comfortably in clothes that fit and are appropriate in all types of weather. Parents must continually purchase clothing because children grow rapidly.

Parents are also responsible for ensuring their children's health and safety. They should watch for signs of illness and seek medical advice when needed. Regardless of cost and inconvenience, parents must secure quality medical care.

Costs for meeting the physical needs of children are big expenses. Parents should be prepared for meeting these costs before having a child.

To Fulfill Children's Intellectual, Emotional, and Social Needs

Besides physical needs, children also have other types of needs that parents must meet. Meeting a child's intellectual, emotional, and social needs is also critical to a child's development.

Children need intellectual stimulation to grow and learn. Parents can begin meeting a child's intellectual needs soon after birth. By speaking to children and providing opportunities for play, parents can help them develop language and thinking skills. Also, children learn about the world around them from their parents. Parents greatly influence a child's desire to learn. Children often adopt their parents' attitudes toward education. For instance, children whose parents read to them are more likely to enjoy reading.

Parents take a big step toward fulfilling their children's emotional needs when they offer loving care and attention. Children need to feel loved. Parents can also help their children learn to feel and express their emotions. Children need help to develop these important skills.

To help meet children's social needs, parent should give children chances to interact with other people. Children should be encouraged to play with other children. They also learn important social skills by spending time with other adults. Through these interactions, children learn valuable lessons in sharing, communicating, and compromising.

To Promote Moral Development

Parents want their children to become mature, responsible, and happy adults. For this to happen, children need to learn to behave in ways that are acceptable to society and the family. However, children are not born knowing the difference between right and wrong.

Parents have a responsibility to guide and direct their children in ways that will promote the children's moral development. **Moral development** is the gradual process of learning to behave in ways that reflect an understanding of the difference between right and wrong.

Parents can influence a child's moral development by passing along their personal priorities. **Personal priorities** are the principles, concepts, and beliefs a person holds as important. For instance, a person may believe money and possessions are the best things in life. Another person may believe justice is the most important.

Personal priorities give people direction in their lives. People who consider money to be their top priority will focus their energy on getting more money however they can. People who consider justice their top priority will live their lives seeking justice for themselves and others.

Each family has its own set of personal priorities that defines what is important to that particular family. If family members believe hard work, honesty, and close relationships are important, their actions and decisions will reflect these personal priorities.

Parents hope their children will develop personal priorities similar to theirs. Some of the personal priorities parents may instill in their children are moral standards, which are also called morals. **Morals** are the beliefs people have that help them distinguish between right and wrong behavior. A person uses morals to develop personal standards that will guide his or her behavior. Morals may include such standards as honesty, fairness, responsibility, caring, respect, and loyalty.

Parents may worry about how to talk to their children about morals. Explaining morals to children may be difficult because morals are intangible. People cannot see, hear, or touch morals. Morals are also somewhat abstract—no two people will describe them the same way. Parents may feel frustrated because there is no one right way to teach children morals. Each parent does it differently.

A good first step parents can take is establishing a positive home environment. A positive home environment might include warmth, affection, respect, and mutual trust, 1-8. In this atmosphere, children are more likely to learn from their parents and adopt their parents' personal priorities.

Setting rules is a good second step. Parents establish certain rules to keep their children safe. Parents set other rules to teach children which behaviors are and are not acceptable to the family and society. These rules help guide a child's moral development. Learning that the family will not accept disrespectful

1

1-8
Children are more likely to adopt their parents' morals when they know their parents value and love them.

1—Reflect: How has your home environment influenced your moral development?

behavior can teach a child that disrespect is wrong and respect is right. This sense of right and wrong reflects a moral standard the parents have taught their children through rules.

Talking about morals is another way parents can guide their children's moral development. Parents may initiate these talks in response to the child's behavior. For example, when a child lies, the parent may then talk with the child about the family's moral standard of honesty. Parents may also discuss certain morals to prevent behaviors before they occur. They may talk with their child about stealing and explain why stealing is wrong. When children face situations that test their morals, they will remember what their parents have taught them. Remembering their parents' moral standards gives children a starting point for making sound moral decisions.

Finally, and maybe most important, parents guide their children's moral

1—Discuss: If parents set an example of "getting by the law" (such as minor traffic violations), how will it affect children? Should parents explain their actions to their children?

2—Resource: *Family Traditions—Now and in the Future*, reproducible master 1-2, TR.

3—Activity: Have each student share with the class information about his or her cultural heritage. How many ethnic groups are represented in your classroom?

4—Activity: Make a list of cultural traditions that are often observed by families, such as birthday parties, stories, and certain foods.

5—Discuss: Today's parents may experience more stress than parents in the past. Why is it important for parents to learn how to manage stress? How does choosing a healthy lifestyle contribute to stress?

development by example. Children learn much more about personal priorities from what their parents do than from what their parents say. Children watch their parents on a daily basis and learn to behave as their parents do. A parent's example can guide a child's behavior in both positive and negative ways. Parents who exhibit moral behavior are more likely to raise children who will behave morally. If parents are honest in their interactions, their children will learn honesty. If, on the other hand, children see their parents lie, they are more likely to learn to be dishonest.

When a parent's actions and words do not match, the child gets a mixed message. Parents should try to be consistent with what they say and how they behave. If parents tell a child one thing and set an entirely different example, this can confuse the child. When children receive such missed messages often, they may stop looking to their parents for guidance.

To Teach Children About Their Heritage and Culture

Parents also teach their children about their family's heritage and culture. Your **heritage** is all that has been passed down through generations in your family. Your heritage includes stories, traditions, and the common history and background your family has shared. It may also include items your family has owned for many generations.

Part of your heritage is your ethnic background. You gained this ethnic background from your parents. You were born into your parents' ethnic group(s). An **ethnic group** is a group of people with a common racial, national, tribal, religious, or cultural origin or background. Members of an ethnic group share cultural traditions. **Cultural traditions** are beliefs, customs, and behaviors shared by members of a cultural or ethnic group.

Children can learn about their culture in many ways. Many children love to participate in family and cultural traditions. These traditions may involve food preparation, clothing, or spiritual expressions of a family's ethnic background, 1-9.

Learning about family history and cultural traditions helps children form their ethnic identity. **Ethnic identity** is how a person sees himself or herself as a member of a particular ethnic group. Parents help their children develop an ethnic identity by teaching them about their heritage, cultural traditions, and ethnic group. They can teach their children to have pride in who they are.

As children become aware of their cultural heritage, they learn others have a different cultural heritage. Parents can help children learn about people from other cultures. Learning about other cultures can help children accept, and even appreciate, people who are different from them. In today's world, an appreciation for these differences is important.

To Take Care of Themselves

Parents have a responsibility to take care of themselves—both physically and emotionally. Children need all the nurturance they can get. Taking care of themselves is the only way they can take good care of their children.

Adults, like children, need a balanced diet, regular exercise, and plenty of sleep. Parents who do not take these basics for granted are healthier and take better care of their children.

The demands of parenting often result in stress. **Stress** is the tension caused by a condition or situation that demands a mental or physical adjustment. In short, stress is brought on by change.

Because the parenting role is ever-changing, all parents feel stress sometimes. Stress may be only a mild frustration with children. Stress may

1-9 _____
Parents often share traditions with their children that reflect the family's cultural heritage.

also be severe or long-term and can strain the parent's emotional and physical health. Unhealthy parents are unable to provide adequate care.

Parents need to find ways to cope with their stress. Outlets for stress can include time to themselves and time for activities they enjoy and people who can provide emotional support.

A satisfying marriage is a major source of emotional strength, too. Many authorities say parents should view their marriage as their primary relationship and work to keep it strong and healthy. Such a marriage creates positive feelings, and it enhances parent-child relationships, 1-10.

1-10 _____
Parents can be better parents by taking care of themselves. Keeping their marriage strong and healthy is important.

1—Resource:
Responsibilities of Parenting, color transparency CT-1A, TR.

2—Discuss: The marital relationship should be the primary relationship in a family. How can a strong marriage contribute to the development of good parent-child relationships?

3—Resource:
Responsibilities and Rewards of Parenting, Activity D, SAG.

Rewards of Parenting

Why do so many people choose to become parents and accept all these responsibilities? For most parents, parenting has rewards that far outweigh the challenges. No other job offers the satisfaction parenting does. Nothing can compare to the opportunity to watch your children grow and develop.

1—Resource: Rewards of Parenting, color transparency CT-1B, TR.

2—Reflect: What do you think are some special rewards you can look forward to if you become a parent?

Parenting sparks a wide variety of emotions. Parents feel content when they rock a baby to sleep. They feel happy when they hear "mama" or "dada" for the first time. They feel proud when their child learns to read.

Parenting can help people experience new or deeper emotions. They may feel a new tenderness within themselves when they care for a sick child. Parents are often amazed at how much they are able to love their children. Parental love is also a unique kind of love, unlike any other love. After becoming parents, a couple may grow closer and find they love and respect each other even more than before.

Parenting also offers the reward of constant adventure. Every stage of development brings new experiences for both parents and child. Parents learn how to make an infant smile and how to help a baby build a tower of blocks. They learn to answer questions like "Where do stars go during the day?" Later, parents may learn to coach a Little League team or referee a soccer game.

It is impossible to describe all rewards of parenting. They differ from day to day and from child to child, 1-11. Many people feel the special love their children have for them is the best reward of all.

1-11 ───────
Just as all children are different, the rewards of parenthood are many and varied.

Summary

- Parenting can be compared to a career because both require commitment, involve responsibilities, present challenges, and offer rewards.
- **1** Three important qualities that parents need are dedication, flexibility, and nurturance.
- Parenting is fulfilling, but many myths about parenting should be recognized.
- People should understand the responsibilities and rewards of parenting before they become parents.
- Parents must be able to fulfill their legal responsibilities and rights before they become parents.
- Parents must be able to fulfill their children's physical, intellectual, emotional, and social needs.
- Children are first exposed to moral standards as they interact with their parents.
- Parents pass the richness of their family's heritage and cultural traditions to their children.
- Parents can better provide care for their children when they take care of themselves.
- Parenting offers satisfying rewards that cannot be found in any other job.

2
Reviewing Key Points

1. Describe the process of parenting.
2. Briefly describe the importance of dedication, flexibility, and nurturance in parenting.
3. Explain one of the myths about the job of parenting.
4. List the seven responsibilities of parenting.
5. Parents can help their child develop an _____ by teaching him or her about their family's heritage and cultural traditions.
6. Describe two ways parents can help their children develop morals.
7. Explain one reward of parenting.

Learning by Doing

1. Interview a parent about the importance of being a dedicated, flexible, and nurturing parent. Ask if this person always finds it easy to display these qualities. Are there things about being a parent that make it more difficult? What advice would the parent give others about developing dedication, flexibility, and nurturance before they become parents? After?

2. Gather pictures from magazines and newspapers that depict parenting. Working in small groups, sort the pictures according to which of the seven responsibilities of parenting they most represent. Share your group's thoughts about the pictures with the rest of the class.

3. Write a paper describing what your parents have taught you about your heritage and culture. End the paper by writing what you think you will want to teach your children about their heritage and culture.

4. On a piece of paper or the chalkboard, write these two headings: *Responsibilities of Parenting* and *Rewards of Parenting.* Working as a class, create a list for each heading. Do the lists seem to balance, or does one list seem much longer than the other? What conclusions can you draw?

Thinking Critically

1. Do you accept or reject the parenting myths presented in this chapter? Why? What other misconceptions do you think people have about parenting?

2. How does a person know when he or she is ready to have children? Discuss this question in a small group and then share your group's ideas with the rest of the class.

3. Pretend you are a parent. List moral standards you feel are important for your children to develop. Explain why you selected each moral value.

Spending family time with their children is one of the biggest rewards parents receive.

Chapter 2
Parenting:
A Choice

Objectives

After studying this chapter, you will be able to

- describe factors that influence parenting decisions.

- evaluate reasons some people choose parenting and others do not.

- identify factors couples should consider when deciding about parenting.

- describe challenges and risks faced by teen parents.

- demonstrate how people can use the decision-making process to decide about parenting.

Key Terms

goal
short-term goals
long-term goals
time/life line
role
dual-career families
hereditary
infant mortality rate
decision-making process
alternatives
consequences

Becoming a parent is one of the most significant events that can occur in a person's life. Someday, you may discuss marriage with a future spouse. The two of you will want to consider many issues, including the decision to have children. One of the most important issues is parenting. Your decision about parenting will change your lives. Think carefully about this decision, as parenting involves a lifelong commitment.

In years past, almost all married couples had children. Married couples relied solely on biology to determine their family size and spacing. For the most part, married couples did not choose if, or when, they would have children.

Today, more couples decide whether or not they want to have children. If couples choose to have children, they can plan how many children they want and when to have them. This allows couples to postpone having children until they are ready. It also allows couples to decide not to have children.

Parenting decisions can be difficult to make, but they are important. Couples should consider carefully whether they will have children, and when, if ever, they will have them. People should have children only when they want and are ready for them.

In this chapter, you will learn what influences parenting decisions—why some people choose parenting and others do not. You will also learn what factors couples should consider as they make parenting decisions. This chapter also presents a decision-making process couples can use and describes the challenges and risks faced by teen parents.

1—**Vocabulary:** Look up terms in the glossary and discuss their meanings.

2—**Resource:** *The Personal Choice*, Activity A, SAG.

3—**Resource:** *Parenting Views*, Activity B, SAG.

4—**Discuss:** Why do today's couples have more decisions to make about parenting and planning their families?

1—Resource: *Your Feelings About Parenting*, Activity C, SAG.

2—Reflect: Does having a baby enhance or decrease the love a married couple has for one another? Think about examples of how having a baby changed a couple's marital love.

What Influences Parenting Decisions?

Most people spend a large part of their lives as parents. Other people choose not to become parents. For most couples, a variety of factors influence their decisions about parenting. Couples should be careful not to make these decisions for the wrong reasons. Considering why they want, or don't want, to be parents will help them decide if parenthood is for them.

The following sections describe several factors that influence parenting decisions. A factor might affect different couples in different ways. Some people might choose parenting for the same reasons that influence other people not to have children.

Desire to Express Marital Love

Perhaps the best reason that married couples choose parenting is to express their love for one another. When a husband and wife love each other and want to be parents, having children can be a wonderful experience, 2-1. Becoming parents can be a natural extension of a couple's love for one another. Nothing compares to the closeness couples can feel as they share the joys and responsibilities of raising children.

New emotions develop as a man and woman become parents. They feel parental love for the first time. Parental love is based on concern for the well-being of the child. New parents are suddenly responsible for the life of another human being. The idea may be frightening at first. However, most parents soon accept the responsibilities

2-1
Love may be the best reason to have a child.

and look forward to raising their child. New parents face many challenges and have great opportunities for personal growth.

Parental love does not replace other forms of love. In fact, it can enhance other types of love. Parents may discover a new depth in their love for one another. They may grow to respect and admire one another more as each watches the other develop parenting skills.

Couples can express their marital love in other ways than by having a child. A desire to express marital love should not be the only reason a couple chooses to have a child. This is especially true for couples who really do not want to have a child or be parents. Couples who choose not to have children may have more time to spend alone together doing activities they enjoy.

Desire to Be Parents

Another common reason people have children is quite simple—they wish to be parents. A person may feel he or she would be a good parent. This person may strongly desire to nurture a child and raise him or her to adulthood. The person may understand what parenting involves and wish to accept this new responsibility. This focuses on what the parent wants to share with the child, not what the child can offer the parent.

Couples may have children because they wish to add to their families. The marriage of a man and woman creates a family. Many couples, however, wish to add children to their family. They may really enjoy the lifestyle of a family with children. These parents genuinely like children, and enjoy being around children of all ages. They look forward to sharing their lives with their children, 2-2.

Some couples choose parenting out of curiosity. They may wonder what their children would be like. People may be curious whether their children would resemble them in appearance and personality. This curiosity may even motivate people to have children. Curiosity alone may not be a positive reason to have children. It's natural for parents to be curious. It's also important for parents to want their child and be prepared to take care of their new baby.

Prospective parents may be curious about themselves as well. They might wonder if they would be good parents. They may wonder how their parenting skills compare to their own parents' skills. They might ask themselves if they would do a more or less effective job of parenting than their parents did. It's natural to be curious about these things, but curiosity by itself is not a good reason to have children.

Other people do not want to become parents. Parenting may not appeal to them, or they may not enjoy

2-2
Parents enjoy sharing special activities with their children. This father and daughter spend time together fishing.

being around children. These people may feel completely fulfilled by their other roles. Their desire to remain childless may motivate them not to have children.

Expectations About Parenthood

People may decide to become parents based on expectations they have about parenthood. Some people think parenting will be easy. They may mistakenly think parenthood will prove their masculinity or femininity.

Other people believe experiencing parenthood is the only way they will feel completely fulfilled as adults. They might be afraid they would miss out if they didn't become parents. Parenthood can be very rewarding. The thoughts of these rewards might motivate people to become parents.

1—Discuss: What does this mean to have a desire to be a parent? Is this a positive or negative reason to have children?

2—Discuss: How could experiencing parenthood make someone feel more fulfilled as a person?

1—Reflect: What expectations do you have about parenthood? Are they positive or negative?

2—Discuss: How can parenting classes help people develop more realistic expectations about children?

3—Reflect: Is it harmful when parents are "best friends" with their children rather than having a parent-child relationship? Would you want to be best friends with your parents?

Prospective parents may be excited about all the special experiences a child will bring into their lives.

In some cases, people never seriously debate whether to have children. They grow up assuming someday they will be parents. They include parenting in their plans as just another stepping stone—like high school and college graduations, a full-time job, and getting married. Parenting, they may reason, is the natural thing for married couples to do. For these people, the expectation they will be parents is reason enough.

People may choose not to have children if they do not have positive expectations about parenthood. Some people do not look forward to being parents. They may feel they would not be good parents or they wouldn't enjoy parenting.

Expectations About Children

It is not fair to choose parenting based on what you think a child will do for you. This is a selfish reason—it considers what you need and want over what a child needs and wants. People should have children based on what they can give children rather than what they can get from them. Above all, children need effective parents.

Some couples decide to become parents based on expectations they have about children. These expectations may or may not be realistic. People who choose to have children based on realistic expectations about them will be well prepared for parenting. Parents with unrealistic expectations about children will face a more difficult time. They may be very disappointed. Worse yet, their children may suffer if the parents cannot overcome these expectations and become effective parents.

Sometimes people have children because they expect their children will be their friends. Parents may believe if they love their children, the children will love them in return. They may think children will bring love and happiness to their lives. Parents may have children because they are searching for the love their children could give them.

Having a child to gain a friend is not fair to the child. These parents may not have taken time to think realistically about what children need. They may not realize being a parent is a big responsibility. Also, parents will not always be the most important people in their child's life. As children grow, they need to interact with many other people and develop lives of their own. Parents should not expect children to devote all their love and attention to them. If parents expect this, they will likely be disappointed.

Other people have children because they expect their children to be companions for them in their old age. These people may assume their children will take care of them and keep them company. They may believe if they nurture their children now, the children will take care of them when they are old.

People who have children to gain companions for their aging years are not being fair to the children. Having a child does not guarantee the child will take care of the parent once the parent is old. They may not be willing or able to provide this kind of care. Many adult children do care for their aging parents, but there is no guarantee this will be the case. People should prepare for their later years themselves and plan how they will provide for their own care, 2-3.

Couples may also choose not to have children based on their expectations about children. Not all adults wish to be responsible for children. Not all adults enjoy being around children. Some may want to focus more on their other relationships and

2-3
This couple has planned for their aging years. They find companionship in each other, not in their children.

responsibilities. Parenting may not appeal to these couples.

Pressure from Family and Friends

Many people assume when a couple marries, they will have children. This is not necessarily the case. Not all couples have children, and many couples postpone having children for a few years after marriage. Since this assumption is so common, however, newly married couples may feel pressured to have children. This pressure may come from their family, their friends, or both.

Family may be the primary source of this pressure. A couple's family may be excited about their recent marriage.

They may ask the newlyweds about their plans for having children. This may feel like pressure to the new couple. Other times, relatives more directly pressure them to have children. A couple's parents may want to have grandchildren who will carry on the family name. They may also want to become grandparents before becoming too old to spend a lot of time with their grandchildren.

Couples may also experience pressure from their friends to have children. Friends may not understand why a couple would not begin having children right away. Others become parents because it seems like many people their age are having children.

Becoming parents because of this pressure is not a good idea. Raising children involves a lot of hard work. Parents should have children only if they genuinely want them. Family and friends may make parenting sound like the perfect choice. However, they are not the ones who will be responsible for the children's care. This responsibility belongs to the parents, 2-4.

1—Discuss: Cite examples of relatives pressuring a couple to have children. How can the couple respond?

2-4
Parents are the ones with responsibility for raising their children. It can be fun, but it's also hard work.

1—Discuss: How might a person use a pregnancy to trap a partner? What problems might this cause and what might result?

2—Discuss: How might having children affect a marriage that is already shaky?

3—Discuss: Why is it important for couples to make parenting decisions together before they marry? Should a couple marry if they have different parenting goals?

Desire to Influence a Partner

Parenting is a serious commitment that should be based on a couple's mutual desire to have a child. In some dating relationships, one partner may **1** think pregnancy would cause the other to stay in the relationship and marry him or her. This is not a safe assumption. Today, many people would not automatically marry due to an unplanned pregnancy. This is especially true in relationships where the couple was not thinking about marriage before the pregnancy occurred.

It is not fair to use parenting to "trap" a partner. Both you and your partner deserve to be happily married to someone you love and who loves you. Using a pregnancy to influence your partner to marry you is manipulative. It is also unfair to your child. This motivation considers what one partner wants (marriage) instead of the child's needs. Marriages that occur solely because of pregnancy are likely to fail.

For similar reasons, having a child does not strengthen a shaky marriage. Spouses may think having a child will bring them closer together. Research **2** shows this is not true in most cases. If spouses are already drifting apart, adding the pressures of parenting will probably cause even more problems between them. Parents who have a baby as an incentive to stay together don't have much else to keep their relationship going. Being the glue that holds their parents' marriage together is too much pressure for children. This motivation considers the parents' desires first and doesn't ensure if a child was born, he or she would be wanted.

Factors to Consider

In the future, you will probably think about marriage. Before you and your partner marry, you should carefully discuss your views about parenting. You should choose a future spouse who shares your views because these decisions will greatly affect your life together. Before marriage, you and your partner should be able to agree about parenting decisions.

If you and your partner cannot agree whether to have children, think seriously about whether you should marry. When one spouse wants children and the other doesn't, someone **3** will be unhappy no matter which decision they make. When both partners agree about parenting, their marriage will likely be more satisfying.

When the time comes to discuss parenting decisions, you and your potential spouse have several factors to consider. These include your goals, marital relationship, readiness for parenthood, finances, and careers. In each of these areas, you and your spouse will need to carefully consider many questions.

Your Goals

As you approach adulthood, you will begin to set goals for your future. A **goal** is a direction or end toward which you work. Your goals may include further education, such as specialized training or college. You may also have career goals. Many people also hope to marry and become parents someday. Others do not. Only you can decide what goals you want to achieve in your lifetime.

You can set both short-term and long-term goals. **Short-term goals** are goals you hope to accomplish soon, within a few days or months. **Long-term goals** are those you want to accomplish later, perhaps years from now. You and your spouse should talk about your individual and relationship goals as you decide what you want to achieve.

You can use your long-term goals to create a time/life line that represents your married life. A **time/life line** is a graph that represents goals a person or couple plans to reach throughout life. This graph can give you a visual picture of your goals. To make a time/life line, draw a horizontal line that stretches across a piece of paper. Divide the line into five-year segments from age 0 to 90. Fill in the time/life line with the goals both you and your spouse hope to achieve. A sample time/life line is shown in 2-5.

When you are considering marriage, you and your future spouse should talk about your individual goals. Do these two sets of goals fit together? Having compatible goals is important to the success of a marriage. Does either of you plan to continue your education? What career plans and financial goals does each of you have?

In addition to discussing individual goals, you and your future spouse should set goals for your life together.

You will especially need to consider the following questions.

- How do we feel about having children?
- Do we both want children? If so, how many children do we want?
- Have we decided when we want to start a family?
- What kind of child care would we have?
- Would one of us stay home with the children? Who? For how long?
- What are our goals for social life?
- How would our plans for having children change our social life?
- Would we have less time to spend with friends and relatives?
- Do we plan to travel?
- What leisure activities are important to us?
- Would we be willing to give up plans for leisure and travel if we had children?
- What are our plans for retirement?

Considering all these questions at once can seem confusing. Many people find it helpful to write their goals down. Making a written plan can show a couple how certain goals fit together or conflict. For instance, if a couple values travel, leisure activities, and hobbies, these goals may conflict with parenting goals. Some people may choose not to have children for these reasons. Others may decide to

1—**Discuss:** How does the decision to have children affect both short-term and long-term goals? Give examples.

2—**Resource:** *Time/Life Lines,* Activity D, SAG.

3—**Reflect:** Cite goals you should consider as you plot your time/life line. Why is it important to write down these goals?

4—**Example:** A couple has goals that include further education, careers, travel, and hobbies. How might these goals affect their parenting decisions?

Stephen and Sally		0	10	20	30	40	50	60	70	80	90
Student	Stephen										
	Sally										
Full-time worker	Stephen										
	Sally										
Spouse	Stephen										
	Sally										
Parent/Grandparent	Stephen										
	Sally										
Retiree	Stephen										
	Sally										

2-5 Creating a time/life line can help couple set goals for their life together.

compromise their travel desires so they can experience parenting.

Putting plans on paper can help people be more realistic in setting goals. A couple has a better chance of being satisfied with their life together if they have a plan. By setting goals, they know where they are headed and can look to the future with optimism. They can understand the purpose of their hard work and sacrifices. When a couple has goals, they are less likely to be disappointed with the direction their life together has taken.

Your Marital Relationship

When you marry, you and your spouse may begin thinking about whether you are ready to have children. Before bringing children into your lives, take an honest look at your marriage. Asking yourselves the following questions can help.

● *Is our marriage strong and secure?* In a strong and secure marriage, both spouses are content with their roles as husband and wife. Both people truly love one another and are dedicated to their marriage. A

1

solid marital relationship can provide the foundation needed for creating a strong family, 2-6.

● *Are we willing to work to keep our marriage the primary relationship in our lives?* The marital relationship should be the primary relationship within the family. Couples should decide if they are ready to focus much of their attention on parenting. They may decide they need more time to develop their marital relationship. Once children come along, it can be harder for couples to focus on their own relationship. Each partner must make a special effort to keep their marriage strong.

2

● *How well do we communicate?* A weak pattern of communication will likely become even weaker under the stress of parenting. Solid communication skills can help you and your partner make a smoother transition into parenthood. Developing communication skills can help couples strengthen their marital relationship and become better parents.

3

2-6
Being happy in their marriage gives couples a firm foundation for raising children.

● *Do we generally agree or disagree?* Parenting is easier when each parent respects the other's opinions even when they disagree. Couples who usually disagree may spend a lot of time arguing about their children's care and guidance. Couples who argue frequently should also consider whether this is a positive environment for children. Couples can work together to solve problems in their relationship. This will improve their marriage and help them become better parents.

Your Finances

Children are expensive. They put a dent in the family budget even before they are born. This dent grows much deeper after the baby is born. Most parents accept this financial burden without complaint. They are prepared to pay the medical bills (which may be covered by insurance). Shopping for the baby's bed, equipment, toys, and clothes can be fun. Parents often enjoy buying things for their new baby.

Soon, the newness may wear off. Suddenly parents encounter even more bills and expenses, some of which they may not have expected. Parents may wonder how they will pay all these bills and when they will end. Parents may hope that, as children grow, child-related expenses will eventually decrease. However, the opposite is true. Overall, as children grow older, they cost more money. Older children eat more, need more clothes, go more places, and participate in more activities, 2-7. They also need more space, so families may have to move to larger homes. See 2-8 for a summary of the costs involved in raising a child.

Child-related expenses make up a sizable percentage of a family's yearly income. The cost of raising a child through the college years may total tens (or even hundreds) of thousands of dollars. Prospective parents should

2-7 _____
Parents discover their expenses increase as their children grow. Parents must be prepared for expenses such as band instruments.

realize having a child involves huge financial commitments.

Once couples understand how much it costs to raise children, they should evaluate their current and future financial situations. Prospective parents should answer these questions as they decide about parenting. Is their income adequate to pay the costs of raising a child? If both spouses work, will one quit to stay home with the child? If so, can they manage on one salary? If both continue working, can they afford child care costs?

Some people may decide against having children when they discover how large a financial commitment parenting is. They may not be able to afford these high costs. Other people may prefer to spend their money on their own activities and expenses. They may want to have a luxurious lifestyle. Financial reasons influence some couples not to become parents.

Your Career

Before marrying, a man and woman should discuss their feelings about balancing work and child care responsibilities. They should plan in

1—**Resource:** *Couples and Children,* Activity F, SAG.

2—**Resource:** *Costs of Having a Baby,* Activity G, SAG.

3—**Enrich:** Survey parents about how having a child affected their finances.

4—**Resource:** *Parents Spend $ for...,* color transparency CT-2A, TR.

5—**Resource:** *Parents Spend $ for...,* color transparency CT-2B, TR.

6—**Resource:** *Children, Marriage, and Careers,* Activity H, SAG.

2-8

Raising a child is a big financial responsibility. This chart gives some of the costs involved in raising a child. Costs will vary depending on where a family lives.

1—Discuss: Why should the costs of health care, food, clothing, housing, transportation, education, and other expenses be included in the costs of having a child?

2—Discuss: If a couple wants to pay their child's college tuition, how might they start saving early?

3—Enrich: Research the costs of health care for a baby during the first year.

What It Costs to Raise a Child

The total cost to raise a child from birth to age 17 averages $170,500 (2001 figures, USDA). The following categories of household expenses are affected. Percentages of the total dollar amount per category are also shown.

Housing (33 to 37%): Parents and their new baby can live comfortably in a cozy apartment or small house. The family may need more room, however, as the child grows or more children are added to the family. If so, parents face the increased cost of renting or buying a bigger home. Their rent or mortgage will vary depending on how big and expensive their new home is. Housing expenses also include taxes, utilities, furniture, and equipment.

Food (15 to 20%): Food will take a big bite out of the parents' budget. If a baby is breast-fed, the mother will have extra nutritional needs. If a baby is bottle-fed, parents will need to purchase formula. When the baby begins eating solid food, this will add to the family's grocery bill. As they grow older, children eat even more food. Grocery expenses can be quite large, and families may eat many meals in restaurants.

Transportation (14%): Parents will need to buy a stroller and a good car seat for their new baby. If parents work outside the home, they may need to transport their child to and from child care. In cities, parents may use trains or busses. If they don't have a car, parents may decide to buy one, which can be expensive. As their family grows, parents may invest in a second car to meet the family's many transportation needs. Transportation costs also include gasoline, maintenance and repairs, and insurance.

Clothing (6 to 8%): The cost of baby clothes varies, but the cost for diapers adds a substantial amount. Disposable diapers cost at least $750 a year. Babies grow quickly. Parents must replace children's clothing and shoes as often as needed to ensure a proper fit. School-age children and teens grow less quickly than babies. Parents may not have to replace their clothes as often, but their clothing usually costs much more than babies' clothing.

Child Care and Education (7 to 10%): This is the biggest variable. It may include child care tuition and babysitting costs. If children attend private elementary and secondary schools, education costs will be high. Another consideration is whether parents will pay for any education and training their children need after high school, such as college or vocational schooling. (This is not included in the total cost since it occurs after a child is 17.) If parents pay for tuition and books at a state university, expenses for four years will cost at least $20,000. If they pay these expenses at a private university, the cost may be more than $50,000.

Health Care (5 to 7%): During pregnancy and delivery, new parents may suddenly realize the costs involved with bringing a baby into the world. These initial costs of pregnancy and delivery are just the beginning. The American Association of Pediatrics estimates babies visit a pediatrician an average of 10 times during their first two years. Over the next few years, children generally visit the doctor less, but the average child still requires about $600-650 a year for various medical expenses, including dental services. When their children become teens, parents may encounter additional medical expenses, such as braces, contacts, and sports-related injury expenses.

Other Expenses (10 to 13%): Raising a child involves more than providing necessities. Music and sports lessons, camps, toys, books, software, and entertainment for children can be very costly. Regardless of their income level, most parents tend to spend as much as they can on their children's extra activities.

1

2

3

advance how they will handle both parenting and career goals.

Couples may find it difficult to talk about how their parenting goals and career goals mesh (or do not mesh). They may wonder whether parenthood would be compatible with their individual career goals. If a couple wishes to pursue both parenting and careers, they must find an acceptable balance between the two.

In the past, men worked outside the home and women stayed home to care for the children. In most marriages today, both spouses work outside the home, whether for financial reasons, personal fulfillment, or both. In **dual-career families**, both spouses work outside the home.

As couples consider parenting, they should think about child care issues. If both spouses continue working, both will earn money but neither can provide daytime care for their children. If one partner stays home to care for the child, the family will lose the additional income.

Parents must solve this dilemma in the way that works best for them. No single choice is best for every couple. Almost any situation can work if both spouses are happy with the arrangement and genuinely interested in their child's well-being. See 2-9 for a close look at how two couples dealt with this decision.

There are no right or wrong answers when setting career and parenting goals. Each couple must consider its own circumstances and values. A couple may decide against parenting if their careers would not combine well with parenting responsibilities. Careers that require travel, long or irregular work hours, or dangerous job duties may not fit well with parenting tasks. Couples with these careers might choose to devote themselves to their careers rather than becoming parents.

Your Readiness for Parenthood

When considering parenthood, you need to determine whether you are ready to be a parent. Start by asking yourself if you are ready to accept the role of mother or father. A **role** is a set of behaviors related to a certain function you assume in life. You already have several roles such as student, employee, son or daughter, and brother or sister.

Adding the role of parent means more would be expected of you. You would have to fulfill parenting responsibilities in addition to your other responsibilities. Most teens are not ready to accept this additional role and choose to delay parenting until they are more prepared.

Spouses who are ready to have a baby can look forward to parenting as a part of their life together. When a husband and wife commit together to parenting, it may strengthen their feeling of complete sharing. Parenting is most fulfilling for the couple when both spouses are ready for these new roles.

Parents must accept responsibility for another human being's life. They should be mature enough to understand what children need and how to provide for these needs. Parents need to be able to guide their children as the children grow and develop.

Another part of readiness is understanding what you will give up if you choose to have children. Once you have a baby, your life will never be the same. If you say yes to parenting, it may mean saying no to some aspects of your social life. You may not be able to go as many places or participate in as many activities as you once did. You and your spouse cannot be as spontaneous in your plans.

Children change a couple's lifestyle in some very important ways. For instance, a couple without children may spend much of their time alone together. When they have a baby, they will have to spend most of their time taking care of the baby. This can be quite an adjustment for new parents. This adjustment is easier, though, when both people anticipate and accept the changes a baby will bring. Couples can learn to shift their focus to activities they can enjoy within the framework of their expanding family.

1—**Reflect:** Is your family a dual-career family? If so, how do your parents divide tasks and manage multiple roles? If not, what do you think it would be like to have dual-career family?

2—**Resource:** *Two Couples—Two Solutions*, reproducible master 2-2, TR.

3—**Discuss:** Give examples of careers people might have that would not fit well with parenting responsibilities.

4—**Discuss:** Does wanting children mean you are ready to have them? How do people know if they are ready to be parents?

5—**Resource:** *What are Your Role Expectations as a Parent?* reproducible master 2-1, TR.

6—**Resource:** *Couple Profile*, Activity I, SAG.

2-9

This chart offers two examples of ways couples can balance their careers and parenting roles.

Balancing Career and Parenting Roles

Jermaine & Suzanne

Jermaine and Suzanne have been married four years and they want to have a child. They both have good, steady jobs. Two years ago, they bought a small house. Jermaine and Suzanne need both paychecks to pay the mortgage and other living expenses. Therefore, both plan to continue working after the child is born. They realize their situation may be difficult. These are their concerns:

- Jermaine and Suzanne worry they may feel guilty about not spending enough time with their child.
- Finding quality child care may be difficult.
- Even with both paychecks, child care expenses will strain their budget.
- Jermaine and Suzanne may feel stressed by trying to fulfill too many different roles. They will need to remember expecting one another to be loving spouses, caring parents, skilled housekeepers, and valued employees is asking a lot.

Jermaine and Suzanne have identified the following ways they can make the best of their situation:

- Jermaine and Suzanne will need to find satisfaction in their work.
- Both spouses will need to find satisfaction in caring for their child when they are not working.
- Jermaine and Suzanne will need to find quality child care at an affordable price.
- Jermaine and Suzanne must work out alternate plans for times when their child care may not be available, such as holidays and illnesses.
- Jermaine and Suzanne will have to share the responsibilities of child care, running the household, shopping, cooking, cleaning, and doing repair and maintenance chores.

Mike & Angelica

Mike and Angelica have been married two years and want a child. Mike has high goals for his banking career. Angelica enjoys her job as a nurse, but wants to be a full-time homemaker once their child is born. They realize the potential difficulties in this situation. These are their concerns:

- The child may develop a closer relationship with Angelica since she will be at home. This may make Mike feel left out and alienated.
- Mike and Angelica may grow apart if Mike's main interest is work and Angelica's main interest is their child.
- Mike and Angelica may find it difficult to meet their expenses on one paycheck.
- Angelica may be bored and lonely. She liked her previous job, which put her in contact with lots of people.
- Angelica may find it difficult to re-enter the workforce once their child is grown.

Mike and Angelica believe the situation will work if they keep these factors in mind:

- Mike will need to spend much of his time off work developing a close relationship with their child. Angelica will need some time to herself.
- Mike and Angelica will need to keep communicating so their relationship can stay strong. Mike needs to know what is happening at home, and Angelica needs to know what is happening where Mike works.
- Both spouses will need to be satisfied with the division of labor and the roles they have. Angelica will need to find satisfaction in her tasks at home. Mike will need to find satisfaction in his job.
- Mike and Angelica will have to tighten their budget since they will only have one paycheck.
- Mike and Angelica need to realize the benefits gained by having a parent as the primary source of care, nurturance, and guidance for their child.
- Both spouses will need to maintain other interests so they can continue enjoying life even as their lives change.

Another way to assess your readiness for parenthood is to learn more about parenting. Both you and your spouse need to have realistic expectations about parenting. You should understand what responsibilities you would have. Being familiar with basic child development principles helps you know what to expect from children at various ages. As you understand more about parenting, you can better judge if you are ready to be a parent.

You can learn about parenting and child development by taking classes, reading books, and observing parents interact with their children. For example, prospective parents may want to learn about child care, guidance, and discipline. Children need to be encouraged to reach their potential, rewarded when they do well, and disciplined when they misbehave, 2-10. If you become parents, you and your spouse will need to perform these tasks.

2-10
Parents must be prepared to provide child care, guidance, and discipline for their children.

Readiness for parenthood involves many different factors. It is important to carefully consider these factors before having children. If either spouse does not feel ready to have children, the couple should delay parenting until both spouses are ready.

Your Age and Health

Prospective parents need to consider how their age might affect their ability to parent. Biologically, some ages are better than others for women to give birth. The ages of 20 through 32 are considered best for childbearing. Teen women and women over 35 face greater health risks during pregnancy. Their babies are also at greater risk for a variety of health problems.

A teen's body may still be undergoing the changes of adolescence. If her own body has not fully matured, she may have difficulty meeting the physical demands of her developing baby. Also, teens may not be emotionally or intellectually mature enough to be parents.

Infants of mothers age 35 and over are more likely to have Down syndrome. This condition occurs when body cells have 47 chromosomes rather than 46. Down syndrome affects a child's physical and intellectual growth.

People who give birth at much later ages may worry also about how their own aging will affect their children.

Prospective parents also need to consider whether their health would affect their ability to parent. Ideally, both prospective parents should be in excellent health, capable of handling the physical and emotional stress of raising children, 2-11.

When making parenting decisions, you should consider each spouse's genetic background and general health. Certainly, people should think about how any health problems they

1—**Example:** Do you think TV sitcoms give a realistic view of parenthood? Cite examples.

2—**Discuss:** If a couple doesn't want to change their lifestyle, should they postpone parenting? Why or why not?

3—**Enrich:** Ask a doctor to speak about how parents' general health and genetic backgrounds might affect their ability to parent.

1—Reflect: If you know you had a hereditary health problem, how would this affect your decisions about parenting?

2—Discuss: Why do you think so many teens become pregnant each year? What would help lower the teen pregnancy rate?

3—Resource: *Teen Parents: The Risks and Challenges,* Activity J, SAG.

2-11

Couples should consider their health when making parenting decisions. Regular exercise is essential to good health.

have would affect their ability to care for their children. Also, when a couple is trying to conceive, the woman's health is an important consideration. A pregnant woman needs to evaluate her health habits and seek quality prenatal care. This will assure that she and the baby will be in the best health possible. The baby's health is directly related to how the mother cares for herself during pregnancy.

Couples may wish to share any health concerns with their doctor. Many health problems are **hereditary,** or genetically passed from parent to child. Couples should be aware of the statistical odds of their child inheriting a genetic disorder or condition from them.

Couples may decide against having children if it is very likely they would pass a genetic disorder to their child. People with serious health problems may decide not to have children for fear their health would affect their parenting abilities.

Teen Parenthood

People of all ages have many factors to consider before deciding to become parents. Becoming a parent is a big responsibility—one many adults find difficult to accept. Parenting is an even bigger challenge for teens.

In the United States, more than a million teens become pregnant each year. The vast majority of teen pregnancies are unplanned. An unplanned pregnancy can drastically alter the lives of everyone involved, including the child.

Most teens make responsible decisions that allow them to reach their future goals. Other teens are drawn into risk-taking behaviors involving drugs, alcohol, and sexual activity. These behaviors are often linked. For instance, using alcohol and drugs decreases a teen's ability to make responsible decisions concerning sexual activity. Some teens mistakenly think pregnancy can never happen to them. Every year, over a million teens and their partners face the sobering reality that teen pregnancy can, and does, occur.

Becoming pregnant during the teen years creates health risks for both mother and baby. Pregnancy also causes many changes in teens' social relationships. Finally, teen pregnancy can jeopardize young people's educational plans and career goals.

Health Risks

Several health risks threaten pregnant teens and their babies. Teens are still growing and developing. Adding the burden of pregnancy is hard on a young woman's body. Pregnant teens have a higher rate of complications during pregnancy than do women in their twenties.

During pregnancy, women have greater nutritional needs. Many teens have poor eating habits. They cannot sufficiently meet their own nutritional needs, let alone those of pregnancy. If a pregnant teen doesn't eat enough nutrients, she and her baby must compete for the nutrients she does consume. Neither gets an adequate amount of the nutrients that are essential for their health.

Many teens also do not have good general health practices. They may not get the exercise and rest they need. Some teens have harmful habits, such as smoking, drinking, and using drugs, that would seriously harm an unborn baby's health. Pregnant teens are also less likely to receive prenatal care. Fewer than two-thirds of pregnant teens receive early prenatal care. Without this care, developing babies are at much higher risk for many health problems.

Babies of teen mothers face many health risks, 2-12. They are commonly born too early or too small. These problems cause other complications, such as disorders of the brain, heart, liver, and respiratory system. Babies who are born too early have not completed normal growth before birth. Their organs and body systems may not be fully developed or function properly, reducing their chances of survival.

For this reason, infants of teen mothers are more likely to die than infants born to women in their twenties. The **infant mortality rate** indicates the rate of infant death per 1,000 live births. This rate tells the average percent of all births in a year that result in infant death. The infant mortality rate for babies born to teen mothers is 12.5 per 1,000 live births. This means about 13 infants in every 1,000 born to teen mothers die during infancy. The average infant mortality rate for all

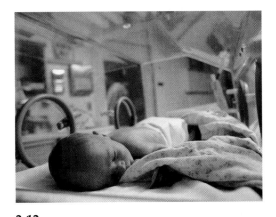

2-12 _____
Babies born to teen mothers are at risk for a number of health problems.

mothers is 7.1 deaths per 1,000 live births.

Teen mothers face even greater health risks if they become pregnant again too soon. After pregnancy, a woman's body needs time to replenish itself and become strong again. If her body doesn't have this time before a second pregnancy, it can affect both her health and her baby's. If a teen's development was interrupted by her first pregnancy, a second pregnancy would tax her body even more.

Social and Emotional Changes

When an unplanned pregnancy occurs, a teen couple will experience many social and emotional changes. They may feel uncertain about the future, the baby, and their relationship. What they do know is that everything is about to change.

A pregnant teen and her partner must make many difficult decisions. About half of all pregnant teens choose to give birth and become parents. Some pregnant teens make this decision alone—their partners end the relationship once the pregnancy is discovered. Other teen fathers stay committed to the relationship and provide whatever emotional and financial support they can.

1—Discuss: Statistics reveal teen marriages are likely to end in divorce. What might cause such a high divorce rate among teens?

2—Reflect: How would your social life change if you were a teen parent?

3—Discuss: Quitting school may lock teen parents into low-paying jobs. How can this impact their future and their child's future?

A teen couple may consider marriage once pregnancy occurs. This is a very important decision. Raising a child is easier when both parents share the responsibilities and support each other emotionally. However, studies show teen marriages are more likely to end in divorce than marriages later in life. The stresses of teen parenting make these marriages more difficult.

If it is their only reason, marrying for the baby's sake may not be a wise decision. Marriage is a lifetime commitment, and it takes work. Teens are still growing and changing. They may not be ready for marriage, or mature enough to make it work. Other teens have strong and long-lasting marriages. They put forth the effort to make the relationship work despite the challenges.

Teen parents may feel isolated from their friends as they realize they will no longer be "just teens." Instead, they must prepare for their soon-to-be roles as parents. Teen parents may also feel trapped by the large responsibilities they now have, 2-13. After the baby is born, they will not have as much freedom as they once did. Instead, the baby will consume much of their time and energy.

2-13
Teen parents may feel overwhelmed by their new parenting responsibilities.

Some teen parents find it hard to adjust to their new roles. They may feel insecure about their parenting skills. Teen parents may not know much about child development. They may not understand their baby's natural needs and demands. Teen parents with unrealistic expectations may easily become impatient and irritable. If they don't have adequate coping skills, frustration may lead them to harm their children physically or emotionally. Learning about child development can help teen parents form more realistic expectations and encourage their children's development.

Teen parents experience major changes in their social lives. Most have little time to spend with friends. If they want to go out, they must find a babysitter. Many teen parents, mothers especially, feel they have less in common with their friends than before becoming parents. Their lives are now very different from their peers' lives. However, teen parents need at least a few close friends they can turn to for support and understanding.

Education and Career Risks

Most teen parents had educational and career goals before pregnancy occurred. Completing high school was probably one of their most important goals. High school graduation is a requirement for many jobs. People seeking further education from universities, community colleges, and other training programs also need a high school diploma.

When teen pregnancy occurs, the young couple may wonder whether they will be able to finish high school. Almost seventy percent of pregnant teens never graduate from high school. Teen fathers may also have to quit school and work to provide financial support. A teen couple's ability to finish school depends largely upon their situation and on their outlook.

Teen mothers may have to leave school if they cannot afford child care and family members cannot provide this care. Some school districts now provide child care programs to help these parents return to school, 2-14.

Going to school while raising a child can be difficult. However, it is the only way teen parents can meet their educational and career goals. Meeting these goals will help teen parents provide for their children financially. If they do not graduate, teen parents may have to settle for low-paying jobs. They may have to abandon their original career goals, which severely limits their lifetime earning potential. These parents may also feel disappointed not to have fulfilled their career goals.

Financial Risks

Couples who plan to have children can plan how to pay the costs of raising a child. In unplanned pregnancies, couples cannot do this kind of planning beforehand. Most teens don't plan to become pregnant and are caught by surprise if pregnancy does occur. Pregnant teens and their partners may have no idea how they will handle the costs associated with pregnancy and parenting.

For most teen parents, the largest expense is housing. If teen parents move into their own home to raise their child, their expenses will soar. If they live with their parents, the added expenses of the new baby may jeopardize the family's financial well-being. The teen parents and their own parents must divide the work and child care responsibilities. Either the teens or their parents will likely have to stay home and provide child care. Anyone who stays home is not earning an income and must be supported by those who do work. This can be stressful for the entire family.

Housing and child care are not the only expenses, however. Children also require food, clothing, medical care, and other items. If the teen father is involved with his child, he can help by providing financial support. Many teen fathers shirk their responsibilities, though, and do not support or care for their children. In these cases, the teen

1—**Discuss:** Find out what options are available to teen parents in your school district who want to stay in school.

2—**Reflect:** How would you manage financially if you were a teen parent?

2-14 ——————
This young mother can stay in school with the help of a special program for teen parents. Child care is provided and she can feed her baby before classes.

1—Resource: *The Parenting Decision*, Activity K, SAG.

2—Resource: *Decision-Making Chain for Marriage and Parenting*, transparency master 2-3, TR.

3—Reflect: Consider this statement: Parenting does not allow you to try out a child. Can learning about parenting help you prepare for it?

4—Discuss: Describe how couples can use the decision-making process to make parenting decisions.

5—Resource: *Decision-Making Chain for Parenting*, transparency master 2-4, TR.

mother may have to raise her child alone.

Single teen mothers are at great risk of being poor throughout their lives. They simply do not have the financial resources to do it all alone. Many must seek help from federal assistance programs. The TANF (Temporary Assistance for Needy Families) program provides food, money, and child care assistance for those who qualify. Families in the Medicaid program receive free or low-cost medical services. Local social service agencies may be able to provide additional help.

Teen parents face many challenges and risks. Teens should consider these challenges and risks before placing themselves in a situation where pregnancy might occur. Teen pregnancy can dramatically alter a teen's life plan. This does not mean, however, that teens cannot be good parents. Teens can be effective parents if they can overcome these hurdles. Some teen parents finish their education and reach their career goals while raising healthy, happy children.

Decision Making

Deciding about parenting may be even more difficult than deciding about marriage. When you consider marriage, you will already know your potential spouse. As you date, you will find out if you are really compatible. If it doesn't work out, you can date someone else.

Parenting is different. You can't try out a child or practice being a parent. You will not meet your child until he or she is born. Once you become a parent, you can't change your mind and decide you don't want to be one

anymore. This decision is irreversible. That's why you need to think about parenting so carefully beforehand. It will change your life forever.

One way to make parenting decisions is by using the decision-making process. The **decision-making process** can help you make careful, responsible, and informed decisions. The decision-making process involves several steps. These include the following:

1. Identify the decision to be made.

2. List all possible alternatives. **Alternatives** are the available options from which you can choose.

3. Evaluate the consequences of each alternative. **Consequences** are the results of each alternative. Some will be good and others will not. Some consequences will affect the present, while others will affect the future.

4. Choose the best alternative. Make your decision based on the evaluation of each alternative.

5. Act on the decision.

6. Evaluate the results.

Following this six-step process can help you make the best decision possible. You will be more satisfied with your decision than if you made a hasty choice. When making parenting decisions, carefully consider how having children would influence every aspect of your life. Think about the consequences and the responsibilities.

When you and your partner begin thinking about marriage, talk honestly about your views about parenting. Perhaps the most important decisions you will make together are those concerning parenting. Any decision you make prior to conception can be reversed. Once a child is born, however, your choice of parenting is irreversible.

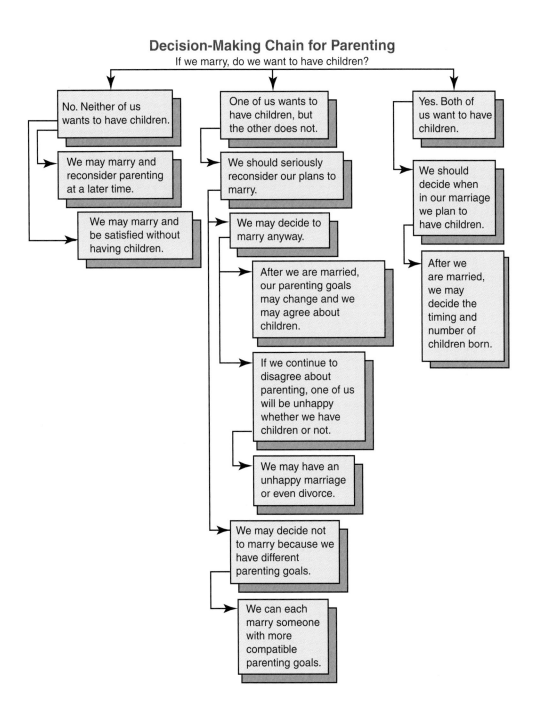

Decision-Making Chain for Parenting

If we marry, do we want to have children?

No. Neither of us wants to have children.

We may marry and reconsider parenting at a later time.

We may marry and be satisfied without having children.

One of us wants to have children, but the other does not.

We should seriously reconsider our plans to marry.

We may decide to marry anyway.

After we are married, our parenting goals may change and we may agree about children.

If we continue to disagree about parenting, one of us will be unhappy whether we have children or not.

We may have an unhappy marriage or even divorce.

We may decide not to marry because we have different parenting goals.

We can each marry someone with more compatible parenting goals.

Yes. Both of us want to have children.

We should decide when in our marriage we plan to have children.

After we are married, we may decide the timing and number of children born.

2-15 _____
Couples can use the decision-making chain to think logically about parenting decisions as they consider marriage.

1—**Resource:**
Role-Playing the Parenting Decision, reproducible master 2-5, TR.

A decision-making chain for parenting is shown in 2-15. This chain may help you identify the available alternatives and the consequences of each. As you study the decision- making chain, assess your feelings about parenting. This may help you decide whether parenting is right for you.

1

Summary

- Today's couples have many important choices regarding parenting.

- Several factors may influence a couple's parenting decisions. These include the following: the desire to express marital love, the desire to be parents, expectations about parenthood, expectations about children, pressure from family and friends, and the desire to influence a partner.

- Some of these influences are positive ones, while others are negative reasons for having children. An influence can affect different couples in different ways.

- When making parenting decisions, a couple should consider their goals, relationship, finances, careers, readiness for parenting, ages, and health.

- By considering these factors, some couples may choose to have children, while others choose to remain childless. No one decision is right for every couple.

- Teens have additional considerations related to parenting. These should be carefully considered before a teen places himself or herself in a situation where pregnancy might occur.

- More than a million teens become pregnant each year. Serious risks threaten the health of pregnant teens and their babies. The social lives of pregnant teens and their partners change dramatically. Teen pregnancy can also jeopardize young people's educational and career goals.

- Couples can use the decision-making process to make responsible decisions about parenting.

Reviewing Key Points

1. What may be the best reason for having a child?
2. Describe two negative reasons for having a child.
3. List four reasons a couple might decide not to have children.
4. Explain two factors a couple should consider when making decisions about parenting.
5. What is the purpose of designing a time/life line?
6. How should a couple's marital relationship relate to their parenting decisions?
7. Does the cost of raising a child increase or decrease as the child grows older? Why?
8. Describe one health risk faced by pregnant teens and one health risk faced by their infants.
9. Explain one other lifestyle change teen parents may experience.
10. List the six steps of the decision-making process.

Learning by Doing

1. On a piece of paper, write these two headings: *What I Like About Children* and *What I Don't Like About Children*. With a partner, discuss how each item listed might affect parenting decisions.

2. Role-play a situation in which one spouse is unhappy about an unplanned pregnancy. Show how feelings of entrapment might eventually affect their marriage and their relationships with their child.

3. Interview the parents of an infant or a toddler about the financial impact their child has had on their lives. Ask them how they expect their child's expenses to change in the coming years.

4. Design a time/life line that shows the goals you have for your life and when you hope to achieve them.

5. Interview a teen parent. Ask questions regarding how he or she coped with the challenges and risks facing teen parents described in this chapter.

Thinking Critically

1. In small groups, discuss the following statement: If you say yes to parenting, you are saying no to other things. Give examples of what people might say no to if they choose parenting.

2. Find newspaper or magazine articles concerning career pressures faced by working parents. Write a paper examining the pros and cons of having a dual-career family. Suggest ways parents in dual-career families can share child care responsibilities.

3. Select one of the factors mentioned in the chapter that people should consider when making parenting decisions. Write a paragraph explaining how you think this factor might affect your future parenting decisions.

4. In small groups, discuss how couples can use the decision-making process to make parenting decisions. Role-play a couple using this process as they decide whether to become parents.

Chapter 3
Families

Objectives

After studying the chapter, you will be able to

● explain ways families may be formed.

● identify the five family structures.

● evaluate the unique characteristics of each structure.

● list the functions of the family.

● summarize ways families have changed over time.

● identify all the roles you may assume in life.

● describe the stages of the family life cycle.

● explain how cultural, lifestyle, community, media, and technological influences can make families unique.

Key Terms

family
adoption
adoptive families
foster family
nuclear family
1 single-parent family
stepfamily
extended family
family life cycle
multicultural
ethnic diversity
cultural bias
prejudice
stereotypes
lifestyle
technology
Internet
e-mail

What makes a family? Do people have to live in the same home to be family? Do they have to have a biolog-
2 ical connection? Does a family need a certain number of people to be called a family? Does everyone in a family have the same last name?

As you answer these questions, compare answers with a classmate. Did your classmate have all the same answers? Your classmate probably sees family a little differently from the way you do. No two families are the same, and people define the word *family* in many different ways.

Basically, a **family** is a group of two or more people who are related by birth, marriage, adoption, or other circumstances. When family is mentioned, many people immediately think of the members of their household. A family also includes relatives who do not live in the same home.

Your *family of origin* includes the family members with whom you lived during your childhood, 3-1. You may
3 have grown up with one or both of your biological parents, adoptive parents, or foster parents. If you have brothers and sisters, they are also included in your family of origin.

How Are Families Formed?

Families can be formed in several different ways. The most obvious way people enter a family is by birth.
4 People also commonly become related to one another by marriage. Adoption is a third way people can add to their families. In addition to these ways, sometimes other circumstances bring people together to form a family.

1—Vocabulary: Look up terms in the glossary and discuss their meanings.

2—Vocabulary: What does the word *family* mean to you?

3—Vocabulary: Define *family of origin.* Who is included in your family of origin?

4—Resource: *How Families Are Formed,* Activity A, SAG.

3-1

These girls' family of origin includes their biological mother and father. Some families of origin include adoptive parents or foster parents.

By Birth

A baby is biologically related to the man and woman who gave him or her life. This man and woman are the baby's *biological parents* or *birthparents*. The baby is also related to members of the biological parents' families, including brothers, sisters, grandparents, aunts, uncles, and cousins.

When you were born, you became a member of your biological parents' families. You will always be related to these parents, even if they are not your family of origin. For instance, children who were adopted will always be related by birth to their birthparents. Their families of origin include their adoptive parents, however, because their adoptive parents raised them.

By Marriage

People also become related to one another by marriage. When a man and woman marry, they create a new family. As husband and wife, they form a family unit separate from, but still connected to, their families of origin. Spouses begin a life together and generally establish their own household. Their marriage is the foundation of their family. The couple may or may not choose to add children to their family by birth or adoption.

Marriage can also create other relationships. Suppose when a man and a woman marry, one spouse has children from a previous relationship. In this case, stepchild-stepparent relationships are formed. The couple's marriage is the foundation for these new family relationships.

By Adoption

Adoption also creates family relationships. **Adoption** is the process of transferring a child's legal guardianship from his or her birthparents to adoptive parents. **Adoptive families** include adoptive parents and one or more adopted children.

People may choose adoption for various reasons, 3-2. Some couples are unable to conceive children. Adoption can allow them to experience parenting. A couple may also adopt if one spouse has a hereditary condition that would likely affect their future biological children. Other couples adopt simply to offer loving homes to children who need them.

Through the adoption process, the child's birthparents transfer their parenting rights and responsibilities to the adoptive parents. After the adoption is final, the adoptive parents, not the birthparents, are legally the child's parents. From that point on, adoptive parents have the same responsibilities and roles as other parents.

3-2 _____
This couple became parents when they adopted several children who needed a loving home.

Many adoption agencies require that prospective adoptive parents be married. It's growing more common for single adults to adopt, however. What is important is that adoptive parents, whether married or single, can provide for their children both physically and emotionally.

Because they have chosen to become parents, adoptive parents are usually very dedicated to parenting. To be accepted by an adoption agency, adoptive parents must meet the agency's criteria and standards. Adoptive parents must then go through an extensive screening process. This process usually includes interviews, criminal background checks, and a home study. In a home study, the agency visits the adoptive parents' home. The purpose of the visit is to ensure they have enough room and a safe environment for raising a child.

After being accepted as adoptive parents, people may wait a long time before being matched with an available child. Many more people wish to adopt children than there are children available for adoption. This is especially true of infants. Many adoptive parents would prefer to adopt an infant so they can be parents from the start of their child's life.

Some adoptive parents choose international adoption. The wait may be much shorter to adopt infants from other countries than to adopt American infants. Many agencies now arrange international adoptions. This can be expensive, especially if the couple must travel to a foreign country to pick up the baby.

People may also choose to adopt older children. The wait is much shorter, and the fees involved may be much lower. Adopting an older child can be fulfilling, but it may involve special challenges. Older children may have lived with their birthparents and may remember them. This can make adjusting to the adoption more difficult for them. They may feel confused about the adoption or sad about losing their birthparents. It may take them time to trust their new parents. If they

1—**Discuss:** Can single adoptive parents provide as good a home as married adoptive parents? Why or why not?

2—**Discuss:** Why are adoptive parents often very dedicated to their roles as parents?

3—**Discuss:** Today fewer babies are available for adoption. Can you think why this is true?

4—**Enrich:** Research the process involved in adopting children from foreign countries. Would you ever consider adopting internationally?

1—Discuss: If a nonrelated adult serves as a child's parent, should the adult and child be considered family? Why or why not? Give examples of situations where this might occur.

2—Activity: Invite a foster care case worker to class to discuss the benefits of foster care for both foster children and foster parents.

3—Enrich: What training is required for foster parents in your state? Who determines which children are matched with which foster families?

felt abandoned by their birthparents, they may fear their adoptive parents will abandon them, too. In time, this fear usually begins to fade as the adoptive parents build trust with their new child.

If the child was adopted as an infant, adoptive parents must decide when and how to tell the child about the adoption. It is important to be honest about how the child joined the family. Experts recommend parents begin telling children about adoption at an early age. Simple explanations the child can understand are best. It is not necessary to give all the details at once. Children will ask more questions as they are ready.

Although they may face a few special challenges, adoptive families function in the same way as other families. Adoptive families are just like other families, except they are formed differently. Members of an adoptive family form lasting bonds and create special family memories. Adoptive families are just as loving as other families.

Other Ways Families Are Formed

Most children enter families by birth or adoption, but sometimes other circumstances create family relationships. Occasionally, children are raised by nonrelated adults who serve as their parents and fulfill the parenting role. For instance, if a child's biological parents die, close adult friends of the family might raise the child. These adults are not biologically related but may feel very close to the child emotionally. They can provide a loving, familiar home for the child. The child would probably consider these adults part of his or her family.

Foster Families

Another circumstance that creates family relationships is foster care. *Foster care* is care provided for a child who needs a loving home temporarily. *Foster parents* are adults who volunteer to provide a temporary home for a child who needs one. Basically, a **foster family** provides a child with a substitute family, 3-3. While the child is in their care, foster parents have the same legal rights and responsibilities as biological parents. Foster parents assume the parenting role. They take care of their foster child as if he or she was their own.

Most children are placed in foster homes because they have been abandoned, abused, or neglected by their biological parents. In other situations, children's biological parents may be temporarily unable to care for them and ask the state for help.

Foster homes are evaluated and licensed according to state requirements. Placements are made by state or county child welfare offices. Foster parents volunteer their time, effort, and love. They are reimbursed for the children's expenses.

Foster care may last a short time or several years. It usually lasts only until a permanent arrangement can be found or the child is eighteen years old. Children will return to their biological parents if the state determines it is safe for them to do so. When this is not possible, the state attempts to place children in adoptive homes.

Foster parenting can be challenging. Many foster children have been abused, neglected, or abandoned. These traumatic experiences often lead to emotional or behavioral problems that can be difficult for foster parents to handle. Foster parents need to be understanding of the child's situation and continue offering the child love and care.

Since foster care is temporary, foster parents must prepare to release foster children to their biological or adoptive parents. It can be difficult for them to let go, especially if the foster

3-3 _____
Foster families
provide loving care
for children who
need an alternate
home temporarily.

child lived with them a long time. Foster parents and their foster children may have developed a special relationship. Some children continue a lifelong relationship with their former foster parents.

No matter how long foster care lasts, it can be rewarding for both foster parents and foster children. Foster parents have the satisfaction of helping children grow and develop. They can experience parenting and contribute to a foster child's life in positive ways. Foster children can gain a loving home and quality care until a permanent arrangement is made.

Family Structures

Another way families differ is by their structures. A family's structure tells how it is organized and how it functions. The structure tells how many people live in a household and how they are related. How many adults are in the family? How are they related to one another? How many children are in the family? How are they related to one another and to the adults in the family? By answering these questions, you can identify the family's structure.

Five basic family structures are common in America today. These are nuclear families, single-parent families, stepfamilies, extended families, and couples without children. Each family structure has advantages and disadvantages.

Each person may prefer one family structure over the others. The family structure that works best for one family may not work well for another. Families in each structure can be loving, nurturing, and strong. A family's well-being depends much less upon the family structure than upon how well the family meets its members' needs.

1—Reflect: Would you ever consider becoming a foster parent? Why or why not?

2—Resource: Family Stuctures, color transparencies CT-3A and CT-3B, TR.

3—Vocabulary: What does family structure mean? What does it tell us?

4—Resource: Parent Panel, Activity B, SAG.

5—Resource: Family Structure Opinions, Activity C, SAG.

1—Discuss: Cite three reasons many people consider the nuclear family the ideal family structure. Do you agree?

2—Discuss: If most people want to maintain a nuclear family, why is this structure becoming less common than in the past?

3—Discuss: What is the difference between a traditional nuclear family and a dual-career nuclear family?

4—Examples: Give examples of various ways single-parent families can be formed. Are single-parent families formed one way any different from single-parent families formed another way? Why or why not?

Nuclear Families

A **nuclear family** includes a husband, wife, and the children they have together, 3-4. These children may be biological or adopted. Many experts think the nuclear family structure is ideal. They believe it provides the most stable and secure setting for raising children. At one time, nearly all American families were nuclear families. Today, the nuclear family is becoming less common.

In nuclear families, spouses share parenting responsibilities, which can make parenting less stressful. Neither parent must carry the entire burden alone. Both parents may have more time and energy to enjoy their children and each other. Living with two parents also gives children both male and female role models. Relationships in a nuclear family may also be less complicated than those in other family structures.

Suppose a man and woman marry. This couple will begin a nuclear family with the birth or adoption of their first child. Most couples hope to maintain this family structure throughout their lives. They hope their marriages will last. Unfortunately, many marriages do not. When a nuclear family dissolves, the family forms a new structure. The number of nuclear families decreases as other family structures become more common.

Many nuclear families are dual-career families. Both parents work outside the home and contribute to the family's income. In some nuclear families, the husband is the only wage earner. The wife stays home, takes care of the children, and manages the housekeeping tasks. This type of family is sometimes called a *traditional nuclear family*. Fewer traditional nuclear families exist today because more wives are choosing to work outside the home.

Many child care options are readily available to nuclear families. With two parents, the husband or wife may elect child care responsibilities while the other parent works. Because of high child care costs and costs of working, such as transportation, clothing, and taxation, this can be a good option. In some dual-career families parents work different shifts and care for children when not working. Child care in centers is also a popular choice of many dual-career families. Among upper-income dual-career families, and especially those with long or variable work schedules, in-home child care is another possible option.

Single-Parent Families

A **single-parent family** includes one parent and his or her biological or adopted children. Single-parent families can be formed in a variety of ways. Many single-parent families consist of a once-married parent and his or her children. The other parent has left the family as a result of death, divorce, desertion, or legal separation. Other single parents have never been married. Today, it is becoming more

3-4 _____

Nuclear families offer two parents who can be role models for their child.

common for never-married adults to give birth or adopt children. These single parents may not have had the opportunity or the desire to marry.

The single-parent family is the fastest growing structure in America. More and more adults are raising children alone. One-fourth of all children in the U.S. will spend at least part of their childhood living with a single parent.

A single parent may have unpleasant feelings about his or her situation. Separation, divorce, the death of a spouse, or unplanned pregnancy can be traumatic. Single parents may not have expected or wanted to raise children alone. A single parent also carries the burden of providing all the care and guidance his or her child needs. This can be overwhelming.

Many single parents have the total responsibility for child care and earning a living. Because they are employed out of the home, they must seek child care. The child care options of an employed single parent often depend on income. For many single-parent families, especially households headed by single women, money problems are common. These parents often have their children cared for by a relative or friend. Sometimes two single parents who have different work hours trade child care tasks. Family child care, which is generally less expensive than center care, is another popular option. Single parent families may afford or qualify for not-for-profit centers, such as those sponsored by their place of work, a religious organization, or a community agency or through federal or state funds. Single parents in higher income groups, especially men- and professional women-headed households, may find center or in-home care the best option.

If their parents were once married, children may find it difficult to adjust to living with just one parent. They may have intense feelings about the separation, divorce, or death of their other parent. Children usually love their other parent and may feel sad about the changes in the family.

Despite these challenges, single-parent families can be happy and successful, 3-5. Having strong relationships with friends and other relatives can help. Both children and adults need relationships with people outside the family. It may help if they know other people in single-parent families. Single parents and their children need to know their situation is not unique.

Children from single-parent families also need role models of both genders. Children who have little or no contact with their father, for instance, need other adult males in their lives. These role models may be relatives, neighbors, teachers, or friends.

Living in a single-parent family may be challenging, but this structure may have certain advantages. For instance, children of single parents are likely to have more and earlier opportunities to become self-reliant. Being

3-5
Members of a single-parent family can feel happy, secure, and loved.

1—Discuss: Can children feel as much love and security in a single-parent family as in a nuclear family? Why or why not?

2—Reflect: If you were a single parent, how could you provide role models of the opposite gender for your child?

1—Discuss: Under what conditions might children be happier and better cared for in a single-parent home than with two parents?

2—Examples: Cite examples of stepfamilies on TV. Do you feel these shows portray stepfamilies realistically?

3—Discuss: Why might the word *complicated* describe stepfamily relationships?

4—Discuss: How can financial concerns affect stepfamilies?

3-6 ─────────────

A stepfamily includes each spouse's children from previous relationships and any children they have together.

raised by a well-adjusted single parent may be better for children than growing up in an unhappy two-parent home. One happy parent may be able to give children more love, guidance, and attention than two parents who argue constantly.

Children in a single-parent family can feel just as much love and security as those living with two parents. They can grow up to be just as intelligent, cooperative, friendly, mature, and responsible as other children. A single-parent family can provide stable, close parent-child relationships.

Stepfamilies

When two people marry, one or both of them may bring children from a previous relationship into the marriage. The new family they create is called a **stepfamily.** In a stepfamily, one or both spouses may have been married before, 3-6.

Stepfamilies are becoming more common as the number of single parents increases. A single parent may meet a new partner and decide to remarry, creating a stepfamily. Each spouse becomes a *stepparent* to the other spouse's children. Stepparents are related to *stepchildren* by marriage instead of biologically. In their new marriage, parents may decide to have a child of their own together. This child is a *half brother* or *half sister* to the other children in the family.

Family relationships may become more complicated in a stepfamily. A nuclear family includes relationships between husband and wife, parents and children, and brothers and sisters. Stepfamilies may include the following relationships: parent and child, stepparent and stepchild, brothers and sisters, half brothers and half sisters, and stepbrothers and stepsisters. Each set of stepchildren also has another parent outside the stepfamily. This parent may or may not be remarried and head a stepfamily of his or her own.

In the beginning, everyone may find it hard to adjust to the new family structure. Each family operated on its own before the marriage, with its own way of doing things and its own space. Then the two families merge, and their lifestyles have to blend into one. Schedules may change as the new family develops a way of doing things that will work for everyone. Family members must also learn to share space, and children may have to share bedrooms.

Parents in a stepfamily must readjust their budgets and set new financial goals. One or both spouses may have to pay alimony and child support. Spouses may have to pay debts left by their former spouses. The larger household of a stepfamily may also cost more to run.

Stepfamilies basically have the same child care options as nuclear families. If several preschool children need care, the total costs of child care can be very expensive. These families might consider these options:

- a stay-at-home or work-at-home mother or father
- in-home care that might be less expensive than out-of-home care for several children
- centers that discount child care costs for families enrolling more than one child

If the family size is large and the income is modest, the family would likely qualify for not-for-profit center programs, too.

Members of a stepfamily must work together to overcome these challenges. A positive attitude and willingness to make the most of the situation are a good start. Family members must learn patience, cooperation, and good communication skills. Life will run more smoothly if they can be understanding toward one another.

Developing a stepfamily takes patience and effort, but it can be a positive experience for everyone involved. As husband and wife form a team, the entire family is strengthened. Spouses can share parenting tasks and responsibilities. Each family member can develop several new relationships, which can be very rewarding. With humor, cooperation, empathy, and creativity, stepfamilies can be happy and strong.

Extended Families

An **extended family** includes all the relatives in a family, such as grandparents, aunts, uncles, and cousins. In contrast, a family of origin, which may also be called an *immediate family*, includes only parents and their children.

In the extended family structure, more relatives than an immediate family live in one home. Any mixture of grandparents, parents, children, aunts, uncles, and cousins may live in one residence. These living arrangements may be temporary or permanent, depending upon the family's situation. The extended family structure is more common in other countries than in the United States. Many American families do share their homes with extended family members, however.

Extended family members may live together for various reasons. Adult children may move back into their parents' homes following college, while they are searching for a job. Newlyweds may live with one spouse's parents until they find a separate living space. Following divorce, a parent and his or her children may move into a relative's home temporarily.

Another type of extended family structure includes aging parents who move in with an adult child's family. Sometimes this arrangement can be very helpful to the family. Grandparents may be able to help with cooking, cleaning, or taking care of younger children while the parents work. Older people may also move in with an adult child if they become unable, for health reasons, to live alone. Many adult children provide care for their aging parents. It can be easier to provide this kind of care when the two live in the same home.

In-home care by a relative is an option in many extended families. However, elderly people living in an extended family may be unable to take care of young children. Some extended families need care for their elderly members during work hours. In a few cities, centers provide both elder care and child care. Some families may find this a good option.

An extended family structure allows members of the extended family to develop closer relationships. Children can learn to respect and appreciate aging members of the family.

1—Reflect: Why do you think some people do not think of married couples without children as families?

2—Resource: *The Shape of Family Structures*, reproducible master 3-2, TR.

3-7
Couples without children are able to develop their relationship and spend more time alone together.

Grandparents can offer advice that might be helpful in raising children.

It can take time to adjust to living with extended family members. If everyone works together, living in an extended family structure can be very successful. This arrangement can meet the needs of extended family members. This is one way family members can help one another in times of need.

Couples Without Children

The fifth family structure includes married couples without children. 1 People may not always think of childless couples as families, but spouses are related to one another by marriage. This makes them a family even if they do not have children.

A married couple may be unable to conceive or may choose to remain childless. Some couples delay parenthood until they have been married several years. They remain in this family structure until they have children and enter the nuclear family structure.

Couples without children may focus more time and energy on their own relationship, 3-7. Each spouse may also become more involved in his or her own career, hobbies, and interests. The couple may develop closer relationships with family and friends. They may also travel or pursue other leisure activities.

Many couples without children find fulfillment in their marital relationships. Their marriage meets their needs for love and companionship. Spouses do not experience role overload. For people who do not wish to become parents, this is the most satisfying family structure. Couples without children can have a strong and happy family life.

Functions of the Family

After learning about how families are formed and structured, you may wonder why people need families. What does a family do? What purposes does it serve? The American family performs three basic functions in society. The family:

● **Provides for the physical needs of all family members.** Parents provide physical care for their children. Families also share economic resources. Employed family members work to provide the family's income. With this income, the family can pay for food, clothing, shelter, and other items it needs. Family member's physical needs also include health and safety needs.

- **Meets the emotional needs of all family members.** All people need to feel their family members love and accept them for who they are. Each person's self-esteem is affected, positively or negatively, by being part of a family. Family members support each other as they cope with the stresses of life.

- **Nurtures the growth of all family members.** Family members help one another grow and develop. Parents guide all aspects of their children's growth and development, including social and intellectual growth. Families also nurture adults' growth, because adults continually grow and change, too. A supportive family encourages every member to grow to his or her fullest potential.

1 All families perform these three functions, but how they perform them differs from family to family. Families from all five structures are able to do these tasks.

Families: Yesterday, Today, and Tomorrow

2 Families are affected by social, economic, and cultural changes in society. As society experiences these changes, families adapt to meet the new challenges and needs created. Meeting these needs and challenges can mean adjusting family lifestyles. How families adapt to these changes reveals their strength and durability.

In early times, society was mainly agricultural. Each family grew crops, hunted, and fished for its food. Families produced the goods they needed to survive or produced surplus crops they

3-8
Working moms may have to take their children to child care centers during working hours.

could trade for needed goods. Children were valuable economic assets because they could help work on the farm. Families with many children had more people who could contribute to the family's financial well-being. Fathers headed families and made most of the important decisions. Mothers raised the children and took care of the home.

3 The Industrial Revolution changed family life forever. Men began working outside the home. Their jobs determined where families lived. As people began taking jobs in factories and manufacturing plants, they became consumers. Families began to depend on others for many of the goods and services they needed. Women continued their roles as homemakers and caregivers.

During World War II, women began working in factories and jobs left vacant by the men fighting in the war. When the war was over, some women continued working. Since the 1950s, the number of women in the workforce has steadily been increasing.

1—**Reflect:** Families perform three basic functions. Can you think of any other functions all families perform?

2—**Resource:** *Families: Yesterday, Today, and Tomorrow,* Activity E, SAG.

3—**Examples:** Give examples that show how families today are different from families 100 years ago.

1—**Discuss:** Families continue to change as society does. What do you think families will be like in the future?

2—**Resource:** *Your Family Roles,* Activity F, SAG.

3—**Reflect:** How does your attitude toward roles affect your ability to be flexible as you add new roles?

In the 1960s, just over a third of all women were in the workforce. By 1990, more than two-thirds of all women were employed.

Women's entry into the workforce has changed family life dramatically. Traditionally women were expected to stay home, take care of the children, and manage the household. As women's roles expanded to include wage earner, parenting roles also changed, 3-8. Most families now hire child care providers to care for their children during working hours. Families today are much smaller than families in the past. Many parents work full-time and do not have the time or the financial resources to have large numbers of children.

In dual-career families, both parents come home from a full day at work to their children and housework. Mothers who work all day may not have time to do all the household tasks alone. Many families now share household tasks and child care responsibilities. Most men today are much more involved in these tasks than in the past. In many families, both spouses work together to head the family and make important decisions.

Family life today is much different from what it was in years past. As society continues to change, families must be flexible and change along with it. Adapting to these changes can be difficult. Family roles must continually be adjusted to meet the needs of all family members. With patience and understanding, families can succeed in meeting and overcoming these challenges.

Imagine what families 100 years ago would think about family life today. In much the same way, no one can predict how families will change in the future. In future years, families may be very different from the way they are today. With dedication and flexibility, however, they can be just as strong.

Your Roles

As a member of a family, you may have many roles. For instance, you are a son or daughter. You are also a grandson or granddaughter. Additionally, you may be a brother or sister, and a niece or nephew. You may even be an aunt or uncle. These family roles help to define who you are as a person and how you fit into your family.

Your family roles are not the only roles you have. In school, you are a student. You may also be a class officer or a member of a sports team. You may already be a wage earner, carrying out specific work roles. In your teen years, you will begin to learn how to balance your many roles. This is an important task because as you get older, you will take on even more roles.

Some of the new roles you assume may replace old ones. For instance, when you graduate from high school or college, you may end your role as a student. At that time, you will likely assume a new role as a full-time employee. You may also assume other roles in different groups or organizations. Some of these roles might be leadership roles, while others may not. For instance, you may become a council member of your city government. One day, you may also become a grandparent, or maybe even a great-grandparent.

Other roles never change. You will always be a son or daughter in your family of origin. This will not change even if you create your own family someday. You may one day take on roles as a spouse and a parent, but you will still be your parents' child. Once you have children, you will always be a parent, even if your child creates his or her own family.

No matter how your roles change or expand throughout your life, you will probably always have multiple roles to manage. Identifying the roles you play can help you think more clearly about how to manage the demands of each one.

In the next section, you will learn how your roles will change during the family life cycle.

The Family Life Cycle

A family grows and changes over the years, just as the individual members do. In most families, these changes occur in a cycle called the **family life cycle**. The family life cycle follows a sequence of expansion and contraction. The stages are formed primarily by decisions concerning parenting.

The family life cycle follows six stages, 3-9. A newly-married couple enters the beginning stage of the family life cycle. When children are born, the couple enters the childbearing stage. The parenting stage includes the growth and development of the couple's children. Once the children begin to leave home, the family contracts, or becomes smaller. This occurs during the launching stage. The couple becomes independent again in the mid-years stage. The aging stage includes the years following retirement.

Each family member's roles change from one stage to another in the family life cycle. As you will see, the number of role positions in the family expands and contracts throughout this cycle.

The Beginning Stage

The first stage of the family life cycle begins with a couple's marriage, which establishes a family unit. The married couple assume their roles as husband and wife. During this stage, their main goal is adjusting to married life. Newlyweds need to become comfortable with each other. Each person must learn to share life with the other while maintaining his or her own individuality.

During the beginning stage, each spouse must adjust to living with another person and consider this person's needs. The couple establishes daily routines and divides household responsibilities. Often in this stage, both spouses have careers. The couple learn to support each other in their work as well as in their marriage.

The length of this stage varies from one couple to another. Some couples shorten this stage and enter the expanding stage right away. Other couples enjoy this stage longer while they postpone parenting. Couples without children remain in this first stage until the aging years.

The Family Life Cycle

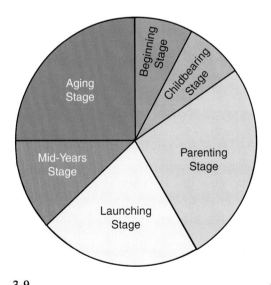

3-9 _____
The family grows larger during the childbearing stage and smaller during the launching stage.

1—Discuss: How can balance be achieved between the husband-wife and parent-child relationships?

2—Activity: List ways parenting might bring a couple closer together and ways it might increase conflict.

3—Discuss: Explain how parents of school-age children can balance needs of individual family members with family goals. Cite the rewards and pressures.

4—Enrich: Invite parents and teens to discuss the challenges and rewards the family experiences when teens assume more independence and responsibility.

5—Discuss: How do family relationships change when children begin leaving home?

The Childbearing Stage

The second stage begins with expectant parenthood. As this stage begins, the couple focuses on the coming birth. As they prepare for the arrival of their first child, the couple realizes nothing will ever be quite the same.

After the first child is born, couples must give their primary attention to their infant's needs. Roles of father and mother are added to the roles of husband and wife. Spouses should be patient with one another as they learn to balance these additional roles. Parents must learn how to manage extra responsibilities and conflicting demands on their time and energy.

Parenting can bring a couple closer together, or it can increase conflicts. If both parents wanted a child and have realistic expectations, parenting can be very fulfilling. If either spouse did not want a child, parenting may be viewed as limiting and confining.

As a couple has additional children, the family experiences new levels of sharing and growing. Each additional child requires more of the parents' time, energy, and money. Children can also bring their parents joy and love.

The Parenting Stage

The main goal in this stage is reorganizing the family to fit the expanding world of school-age children. Parents need to recognize that each child has individual needs. Blending these individual needs with shared family goals can bring joys and pressures.

As children begin school, their circle of friends grows. Life may become more hectic as children become more involved in activities outside the home. Parents may spend much of their time taking children to lessons, activities, events, and parties. Children begin spending more and more time with their friends.

During the teen years, children become more independent. Parents must learn to increase the flexibility of family boundaries, giving young people more freedom and greater responsibility. Parents can find it challenging to offer their teens a balance between freedom and responsibilities. As their children grow into adults, parents realize they must let go and allow them to make important life decisions.

The Launching Stage

During the launching years, children begin to leave the family home. The family contracts as children pursue education and career goals or establish families of their own. The major family goal during the launching stage is to reorganize the family as members leave.

As each child moves away from home, the family feels his or her absence. Parents and younger siblings must adjust to the family member being gone.

The Mid-Years Stage

During this stage, their children may begin establishing families of their own. When their youngest child leaves, parents are alone together again, which can be a big adjustment. Their day-to-day parenting tasks have ended, but parents remain connected to and supportive of their children. Parents have to learn to relate to their sons and daughters as adults. The couple may become grandparents.

During the mid-years stage, husband and wife can begin to refocus on their marriage. With their children gone, parents may have more leisure time to develop new interests. If couples have worked to maintain a strong marriage, they will likely welcome this period of time together. If they have withdrawn from other activities and their relationship, they

3-10
Spending an afternoon in the park is fun for both children and their grandparents. A special bond is often formed between children and their grandparents.

may feel isolated and bored. Couples must work to rebuild their relationship and adjust to this new family stage.

The Aging Stage

When they retire, couples enter the aging stage. Some couples take early retirement, but many continue their careers as long as they are physically able. The retirement years mean breaking away from a person's role as an employee. Since most adults work forty to fifty years before retiring, this can be a big adjustment.

Many people look forward to their retirement. Retirement can give them the opportunity to focus on hobbies and interests. Travel and friendships can add enjoyment in the retirement years.

Grandparents

For many people, grandparenting is one of the most fulfilling parts of the aging stage. When people become grandparents, they accept a new role. Some people think of grandparenting as a fringe benefit of parenting. People can enjoy their grandchildren in a different way from the way they enjoyed their children. They don't have total responsibility for their grandchildren. Grandparenting is a rich and rewarding experience for many older people, 3-10.

1—Examples: Cite examples of how aging couples can focus their lives on new hobbies, interests, and travel. How can you include these as goals in your future?

2—Resource: *Grandparents*, Activity H, SAG.

1—Discuss: Some families seem very close while others lose touch. What can grandparents do to keep a family together?

2—Resource: *Your Family Life Cycle*, Activity G, SAG.

3—Resource: *A Unique Family*, Activity I, SAG.

4—Resource: *Each Family is Unique*, transparency master 3-4, TR.

5—Reflect: How have the cultural or ethnic groups to which your family belongs influenced you?

The relationship between grandparents and their grandchildren is very special. Their time together often includes memorable experiences like baking cookies, feeding ducks in the park, and taking train rides through the zoo. Grandparents often have the time and patience to read a story over and over again or mend broken toys. They also enjoy helping their grandchildren make new discoveries, because they know how important learning is to young minds.

A tricky part of grandparenting is knowing the difference between being lenient with children and spoiling them. Some grandparents boast they have fun spoiling their grandchildren only to send them back home to their parents. Grandparents probably can afford to be a little more generous than parents. If they truly love their grandchildren and want what is best for them, grandparents will respect the parents' wishes and authority. Grandparents can offer love and attention while still enforcing parental rules and limits. They enjoy their grandchildren without upsetting the order of the family.

Grandparents have another important role in families. They serve as the focal point of the wider family of aunts, uncles, and cousins. When families gather for holidays and special events, they often do so at Grandma and Grandpa's house. Even when families live apart, grandparents bind them together emotionally. They help family members remember all they have in common.

Just as parents' roles change, so do grandparents' roles. Today, many grandparents are busy expanding their lives with their own activities, community groups, and hobbies. They may travel great distances to see their grandchildren's school plays, sports tournaments, graduations, and weddings. Some grandparents have the best of both worlds. They have their independence, yet they also have the joy of being connected to their loved ones.

Some grandparents find their roles are changing in a different way. They are becoming more involved in their grandchildren's lives. They may provide care for their grandchildren during the day when parents are at work. This can be challenging but rewarding. Grandparents can help their children grow and develop. The responsibility of providing daily care may be more than some grandparents want. It can limit their freedom to do other things they might enjoy. In these cases, each family has to examine its situation and find the best solution for all concerned.

Grandparenting allows people to continue growing and expanding their lives. It also helps people recognize the continuity of life. The past is linked with the future as grandparents pass their heritage on to their grandchildren.

Each Family Is Unique

Just as no two snowflakes match exactly, no two families are alike. No other family is exactly like yours. Every family has a unique way of interacting with one another and meeting each member's daily needs. As you have learned, families differ in the ways they are formed and in the structures they have. Other factors also influence families in ways that make them even more different from one another. These factors include cultural, lifestyle, community, media, and technological influences.

Cultural Influences

Families are influenced significantly by their ethnic and cultural backgrounds. Some of these effects may seem subtle, but others are more obvious. For instance, it may be easier to identify the influence of cultural holidays and traditions than the influence of cultural beliefs and personal priorities.

Members of a cultural or ethnic group often share attitudes, beliefs, and personal priorities unique to their group. A group's attitudes, beliefs, and personal priorities affect how families in that group perform their family functions. In some cultural groups, the family unit as a whole is considered a priority over the individual as a person. For instance, a family member's personal decisions may be made by the head of the family. Decisions may be based upon what is best for the whole family rather than what is best for one member. In other cultural groups, independence is stressed. These families expect members to make decisions for themselves based upon what is best for them as individuals.

Cultures and ethnic groups also vary in the ways family members relate to one another. For example, in many cultures, extended family relationships are very important, 3-11. The extended family may share responsibility for child care, support, and assistance. The extended family may serve as a resource on which each family can depend. In other families, this is not the case. Each individual family unit may stand alone. If these parents need assistance, they may need to find other resources.

Parenting roles and styles also differ among cultural and ethnic groups. Parents from one group may interact with their children differently from parents from another group. For example, in some groups, children are expected to do as they are told, with little or no discussion. In other cultural groups, children are encouraged to ask questions and express their feelings.

Families are greatly affected by their cultural and ethnic backgrounds. Although many differences exist, no group is better than any other. Each group may have its own way of doing things, but that doesn't make any one group right or wrong. People tend to think their way is the best one. It's important to remember that other people's ideas may work just as well.

Teaching Children About Diversity

The United States is a **multicultural** country, because it includes people from more than one culture. Millions of people from many different countries have made the U.S. their home. In fact, many cultural and ethnic groups live in the United States.

Parents teach children about their own heritage and culture, but teaching them about other cultures is important, too. As they grow, most children come into contact with people of different ethnic groups. In any setting, when people of more than one ethnic group are represented, this is called **ethnic diversity**. When they are taught to respect and appreciate ethnic diversity, children are better able to get along

3-11
Extended family relationships, such as those between granddaughters and grandfather, are important to many cultural and ethnic groups.

1—**Examples:** Give examples of ways parenting styles may differ from one cultural or ethnic group to another.

2—**Discuss:** Do your classroom, school, and community reflect ethnic diversity?

3-12 _____
Getting along with people of other cultures is an important skill children can learn both at home and at school.

1—Discuss: How can cultural bias, prejudice, and stereotypes keep people separate from one another?

with others. Children need this skill to succeed in a multicultural world, 3-12.

In their neighborhoods, child care centers, schools, and communities, children often meet new people. Some people may look like them, but others may look different. Children may be curious and wonder why all people are not the same. They may also be frightened or confused. Parents can help children understand how people are different from one another, and that diversity is positive. They can also encourage children to accept and appreciate people from all cultural and ethnic backgrounds.

Teaching children about diversity can also help them overcome three negative influences—cultural bias, prejudice, and stereotypes. These negative influences can occur when people do not understand or accept people of other cultures. A **cultural bias** is a belief that a person's own cultural or ethnic group is better than any other. Someone with a cultural bias might treat people of other cultures differently from people of his or her own culture.

People may also form prejudices about people who are different from them. **Prejudice** describes forming unfair judgments or opinions about people of another group without getting to know them. Prejudices keep people from knowing what other people are really like.

Stereotypes are widely-held beliefs that all members of a group are alike and share the same characteristics. If children believe stereotypes about an ethnic group, they may think all people from that group are alike. Stereotypes can lead people to form incorrect views about other people.

Parents should teach children that stereotypes usually involve untrue statements or myths. Parents can help children distinguish between myths and the truth about people of other ethnic groups. For instance, statements about an ethnic group that include the words *all, none, always,* or *never* are often stereotypes. These statements make generalizations about an entire group. Statements that include words such as *some* and *sometimes* are more likely to be true.

Read

3-13 _____

Parents can follow these suggestions for teaching their children about ethnic diversity.

Teaching Children About Diversity

- Examine your attitudes and comments about people from other cultural and ethnic groups. Your example is an important influence.

- Learn more about other cultural and ethnic groups. This will increase your own understanding and prepare you to teach your children more about other groups.

- Correct children's negative statements and incorrect ideas about people from other ethnic groups. Use children's conflicts or problems with children of other cultures as learning experiences.

- Encourage children to meet people from other cultures. Include people from various ethnic groups in your life.

- Provide books, toys, games, and movies that reflect ethnic diversity. Children learn through play. Toys and books that represent other cultures can help them understand, accept, and appreciate ethnic diversity.

- Help children find answers to their questions about people from other cultures. Reading books or talking to people from these cultures (if possible) may help.

- Attend events that reflect a cultural or ethnic group different from yours. Cook foods, wear clothes, or celebrate a holiday as people in another culture or ethnic group do.

- Remind children that being different from one another is positive. Everyone has unique strengths and gifts.

show video

Cultural biases, prejudices, and stereotypes are harmful because they keep people from knowing and understanding one another. They divide people instead of encouraging people from different groups to get along. Children may learn these behaviors from other children, but more often they learn them from adults. Parents should be aware of the examples they set. If parents have cultural biases, prejudice, or stereotypes, their children may develop these same attitudes.

Parents may wonder how to begin teaching their children about diversity. The suggestions in 3-13 may be helpful. Most importantly, parents should be willing and available to talk to their children about their concerns regarding diversity issues. Children have many questions or just want their parents to listen to their experiences. Talking to children about diversity issues can be challenging, but it can help them succeed in the multicultural world in which they live.

Lifestyle Influences

Lifestyle can be defined as the typical way of life a person chooses for himself or herself. You may choose a lifestyle that is quite different from someone else's. Today, there are many more lifestyles available than in the past. As society continues to change, families will continue to adapt to these changes.

A major component of lifestyle is where a family lives. Families may live in cities, where their lives may take on a hectic pace. Other families live in smaller towns or suburban areas. Some people live in rural areas, where their activities revolve around a smaller community.

Another factor that reflects lifestyle is how a family spends its leisure time. Some families value time spent together. They may share many family activities. Other families may enjoy participating in sports or athletic events. Traveling to practices, events, and games may be part of their lifestyle.

1—Discuss: What other suggestions could you give parents about teaching their children to appreciate ethnic diversity?

2—Reflect: What have your parents taught you about ethnic diversity? How did they teach you this?

1—Reflect: How do you think your parents' lifestyle has affected you? Will you choose a similar or different lifestyle for your future family?

2—Activity: Research laws and regulations in your community that affect families.

Families may enjoy being involved with community events or volunteer work. How families spend their time influences the lifestyles they lead.

The parents' jobs or careers also affect the family's lifestyle. In some families, both parents work. These families may have a different lifestyle from families with only one wage earner. If one or both parents work at more than one job, this can also affect the lifestyle the family leads. Parents' jobs or careers also determine the family's earning potential. Families with higher-paying jobs may be able to afford a lifestyle different from those with lower-paying jobs.

Children are affected by the lifestyle choices their parents make. Their lives, attitudes, and beliefs will be shaped by the lifestyle of their family of origin. When children leave home, they may choose a lifestyle that is similar to, or quite different from, their parents' lifestyle. Many people adopt the lifestyle of their family of origin because they are familiar with it.

Community Influences

Families are influenced by the communities in which they live. For example, families who live in an urban area have different concerns from families who live in rural areas. People in an urban area may worry about high rates of crime and violence. In a rural area, people may worry about isolation from others.

Each community differs in the amount of resources available to meet its citizens' needs. In larger cities, for instance, many more social service agencies and programs might be offered. Smaller towns may have fewer resources, but their services are sometimes more personalized. A family might already know and trust the people who work in these agencies and programs.

Each community passes regulations and laws that reflect the needs of its members. These laws may affect individuals and families within that community. For instance, a community may determine what schools children must attend, where houses can be built, and what the penalties are for certain offenses. Communities also regulate the activities of their local businesses.

A family's level of involvement with its community can also make a difference. In small communities, people may have more say in local government. Large cities may have more political groups and organizations that people can join. In small towns, every family may know one another. In larger areas, people do not know everyone in their community, but may have a wider variety of acquaintances.

No matter where families live, they will be influenced by their communities. Living in each type of community has advantages and disadvantages. When selecting the community where they will live, parents should weigh these carefully before making a decision.

Media Influences

The media has powerful influences, both positive and negative, on today's families. Families are affected in different ways by the media. Some families are better able than others to use the media in beneficial ways and limit its negative effects. Forms of the media include television, movies, radio, magazines, and newspapers.

The media is an important source of information and a powerful learning tool. Families can learn vast amounts of information about weather, world news, sports, science, nature, and history. Parents can also use TV programs to open family discussions about important societal issues such as

3-14
Children can be exposed to many kinds of harmful programs when they watch TV unsupervised.

AIDS, hunger, poverty, violence, drug abuse, sexuality, and teen pregnancy.

Entertainment is another function of the media. Families may spend time together watching TV, going to the movies, or listening to music. Sharing these activities can make families closer. It can also be a lot of fun. Families need to spend time enjoying one another's company. The entertainment industry provides ways to help them do just that.

When used responsibly, the media can be very useful. Dangers exist, however, when parents do not monitor their children's exposure to the media, 3-14. For example, unsupervised children may watch shows or listen to music that condones violence. Also, TV programs or music with adult language and themes are not suited for children. Children are too young to understand what they see and evaluate its content. These programs and music can send damaging messages to children.

Another danger is overexposure to the media. The average child watches an estimated four hours of TV daily. Time spent viewing TV is time taken away from other activities, such as reading, hobbies, and exercise. Families should balance their viewing time with other activities that will help children grow. Parents who set standards for their children's exposure to the media help their children profit from the positives the media offers while limiting negative effects.

Technological Influences

Technology involves using scientific knowledge for practical purposes. Technology is created in the search for new ways to improve life. Inventing new devices or improving current ones can make tasks easier or faster. In years past, technological advancements included the invention of the lightbulb and the airplane.

Think of the many ways family life is touched by technology. Families have come to depend on electricity and heating and cooling systems in their homes. Many also enjoy having telephones, cable television or satellite dishes, and home entertainment centers.

1—Examples: Give examples of TV programming that is inappropriate for children. What can parents do to counter these influences?

2—Examples: Give examples of how families can use computers to manage household tasks.

1—Discuss: How have cellular phones, voice mail, and pagers changed the ways in which families communicate?

2—Discuss: What are some other drawbacks of technology?

3—Activity: Research places in your community that make the computers available to the general public.

Home appliances speed up cooking, cleaning, and other household tasks that once took a great deal of time. These appliances make it easier for families to manage their homes. Think how each of the following has made family life easier: refrigerators, stoves, dishwashers, vacuum cleaners, trash compactors, and lawn mowers. These time-saving devices also allow families to spend more leisure time together.

Technology has also provided alarm systems that can make homes, businesses, and cars more secure. Smoke detectors and fire alarms also increase a family's safety.

Advancements in computer technology have revolutionized the communication process. Computers can provide access to the **Internet**, a computer linkup of individuals, groups, and organizations, in government, business, and education. Today, many families choose to gain Internet access (also called *going online*) so they can use the Internet for information and entertainment. For instance, families can use online services provided by banks to handle their banking transactions. They can also shop on the Internet, which may be very convenient.

People also use the Internet to send electronic messages called **e-mail** to one another. E-mail has become a widely-used form of communication for both personal and business use. E-mail messages can be sent from one person to another in seconds or across the globe in minutes.

The communication process has also been improved by inventions such as cellular phones, pagers, voice mail, and fax machines. These items make it easier for family members to stay in touch with one another despite their busy schedules.

Technology in the health fields enables doctors to enrich, lengthen, and even save lives. Advancements in laser surgery and organ transplants provide new hope for people with diseases or injuries. Today people live longer, which means family members can spend more time with older relatives. On the other hand, more families must provide care for their older relatives along with their child care responsibilities.

Despite its usefulness, technology does have drawbacks. Relying too heavily on technology can make families dependent upon it. When families adjust to technology, they may find it harder to adapt if it becomes unavailable. Families rely so heavily upon cars, for instance, when cars break down, families cannot function as they normally do. They must make arrangements to go to stores, practices, appointments, school, and work.

Also, it costs families money to have the newest technology. This means technology may not be equally available to everyone because not everyone can afford it. When use of a certain technology becomes fairly common, people who don't have access to the technology are left behind. As more and more families purchase home computers, for example, children whose families don't have one will be at a disadvantage. These children may not develop the same computer skills as children with home computers. People need computer skills to compete in the job market, 3-15. As a result, many public libraries and schools are working to make computers more accessible to the general public.

Technology costs can also strain a family's budget if they do not spend carefully. Families must weigh the advantages of having technology against the costs.

Families must be careful to use communication and entertainment technology in moderation. Spending long hours in front of a TV screen or computer monitor takes time from other activities, such as exercising and spending time with family and friends. Families must balance their time among various activities.

Technology has many benefits for families. It can also have negative effects. Families can invest in the technology they want and can afford, but they should be careful. A family should not rely too heavily upon technology, spend more than they can afford on it, or devote too much time to it. Families who follow these guidelines will benefit greatly from the available technology.

3-15 _____
The computer skills this boy is developing will help him compete in the workplace when he is older.

Summary

- The word *family* has many different meanings, but basically *family* describes two or more people who are related by birth, marriage, adoption, or other circumstances.

- Five basic family structures are common in America today. These are nuclear families, single-parent families, stepfamilies, extended families, and couples without children. Each structure has both advantages and disadvantages.

- Regardless of their structure, all families perform three basic functions. A family's ability to perform these functions is an indication of its strength.

- Throughout its history, the American family has undergone dramatic changes. Many of these changes were in response to social, economic, and cultural changes in society. The family will continue to adapt itself to meet future changes.

- You have many roles, including roles as a member of your family. Thinking about these roles can help you to manage multiple roles now and in the future.

- The family life cycle generally follows five stages, which are influenced by decisions concerning parenting. These stages are the beginning stage, the expanding stage, the developing stage, the launching stage, and the aging stage.

- Each family is unique. Several influences affect families in different ways. These include cultural, lifestyle, community, media, and technological influences.

Reviewing Key Points

1. What is a family of origin?
2. Explain three of the ways a family can be formed.
3. Name two reasons couples might choose to adopt.
4. How do adoptive parents differ from foster parents?
5. Identify the family structures described below.
   A. husband, wife, and their biological or adopted children
   B. an immediate family unit plus other relatives
   C. husband and wife with children from previous relationships
   D. husband and wife
   E. a man or woman raises his or her child or children
6. Give two advantages of the nuclear family structure.
7. What is the fastest growing family structure in the United States?
8. List three adjustments stepfamilies may have to make.
9. Describe the three functions of the family.
10. What roles do you have currently?
11. Briefly describe two stages of the family life cycle.
12. Describe one way grandparents' roles are changing.
13. Explain why it is important to teach children about ethnic diversity.
14. Give two examples that show how lifestyle can influence a family.
15. List two forms of technology that affect the family but were not mentioned in the chapter.

Learning by Doing

1. Research foster care laws in your county or state. Who can become a foster parent and how are children placed in foster homes? Present you findings to the class in an oral report.

2. Interview a parent or parents who head a family structure different from your own. Ask about the roles of family members and the pros and cons of the family structure.

3. Create a collage depicting families in various stages of the family life cycle.

4. Survey grandparents about how they view their grandparenting roles.

5. Interview a teacher from a child care center or preschool that serves children of different cultural or ethnic groups. How does the teacher help children learn about the similarities and differences among them? How does he or she promote ethnic diversity and appreciation for other cultures?

Thinking Critically

1. Write a paragraph describing your family. Tell who the members of your family are and how they are related to one another. Explain which family structure your family represents and whether it has ever had a different structure.

2. Watch a TV program based on family life. Identify the family structure represented and analyze the relationships of the family members. Do you think the program realistically represents that family structure? Discuss your findings with the class.

3. Write a paper identifying programs in your community that promote ethnic diversity and multicultural awareness. If there are no such programs, why do you think this is? What, if anything, should be done to change this?

4. In small groups, discuss how computers, the Internet, and e-mail have influenced families. Are these influences all positive? Why or why not?

Chapter 4
Effective
Parenting

Objectives

After studying this chapter, you will be able to

- identify physical, intellectual, emotional, and social forms of development.

- describe the principles of growth and development.

- distinguish between the influences of heredity and environment on a child's development.

- summarize the influence of the family on a child's development.

- identify characteristics of strong families.

- analyze the influence of effective communication on parent-child relationships.

- describe effective communication techniques that can strengthen family relationships.

- explain how parents can influence their child's self-concept and self-esteem.

- identify sources of parenting support and assistance.

Key Terms

growth
development
maturation
physical development
intellectual development
emotional development
social development
1 heredity
environment
communication
active listening
problem ownership
"I" messages
"you" messages
"we" messages
self-concept
self-esteem
support system
support group

Parents may tell you having a baby is easy, but raising that child is difficult! When a new mother and father cradle their newborn in their arms, they view their baby as a miracle. Suddenly, however, the coos of a newborn change to the incessant, piercing cries of a baby in distress. The soft, warm cheeks of a tiny baby change to the sticky, gooey skin of a toddler eating an ice cream cone. Babies grow up. This is a reality of parenting.

Since you are reading this parenting textbook, you may be interested in a future role as a parent. Reading this 2 book also indicates you are willing to study and learn what is needed to become a good parent.

Good parenting is not all instinct. As with anything worthwhile in life, 3 you have to work at it. This chapter will help you learn how to become an effective parent.

How Children Grow and Develop

Effective parents need to understand how children grow and develop. Each child is unique, but every child's growth follows certain developmental patterns, 4-1. Parents may expect their toddlers to be toilet-trained by eighteen months of age. At this stage of their development, however, most children are not physically or emotionally ready for toilet learning. Parents may wonder why a younger child can't skip like an older one. The younger child may not have refined the coordination needed for skipping that the older one has. As the younger child grows and develops, he or she will be able to skip, too.

Growth is a process that begins at conception and continues through

1—**Vocabulary:** Look up terms in the glossary and discuss their meanings.

2—**Reflect:** Do you think parenting education should be a required course? Why?

3—**Discuss:** Does having a baby mean a person automatically knows how to be an effective parent? Why or why not?

1–Vocabulary: Define *growth, development,* and *maturation.* How do they work together?

2—Discuss: Every child has an inborn blueprint timetable for maturation. In your own words, explain what this means.

3—Vocabulary: Define *physical, intellectual, emotional,* and *social development.*

4—Resource: *Types of Development,* Activity A, SAG.

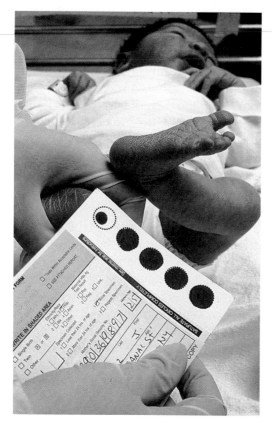

4-1

Each child is unique, but every child's growth follows certain developmental patterns.

adulthood. Growth refers to an increase in size, strength, or ability. Physical growth includes weight (measured in pounds or kilograms) or by height (measured in centimeters).

Development means a change of function as a result of growth. Development refers to progress in skills and abilities. Development is measured in stages, because it occurs in an orderly sequence. Early development involves simple abilities, which lead to increasingly complex abilities. First, a baby crawls. In a few years, the child can perform all sorts of complex maneuvers! Small children have no sense of right or wrong. By the teen years, their developing minds are able to judge behavior in more abstract terms.

Maturation is the overall process of growth and development from infancy to adulthood. Every child has an

inborn timetable and blueprint for maturation. This timetable and blueprint are unique to that child. As the child matures, the blueprint unfolds. Growth and development do not occur because of learning. Instead, they result from maturation, which cannot be stopped or altered under normal circumstances. For instance, the body changes that occur during puberty are a part of normal maturation. These physical changes cannot be speeded up or slowed down.

Types of Development

Parents need to understand how children grow, develop, and mature. This helps them know what to realistically expect from their children. Several types of development exist. These include physical, intellectual, emotional, and social development.

Physical Development

Physical development refers to changes in a person's size, height, or weight. These changes are due to growth of the body's muscle, bone, and tissue. Internal organs grow as well. As growth occurs, children are able to gain more control over their bodies. As the muscular and nervous systems develop, children are able to move their bodies in more complex ways.

Intellectual Development

Intellectual development refers to progress in a person's mental and thinking abilities. This includes the development of a person's abilities in perception, attention, and association. Intellectual development also involves the ability to understand and use spoken and written language. Thinking, reasoning, and problem-solving skills are also included.

During infancy and early childhood, intellectual development occurs at an astonishing pace. Psychologists estimate 50 percent of mature intelligence has developed by age four. In later childhood, intellectual development may be slower, but it is just as important. Communication skills and the ability to think in abstract terms are achieved in these later childhood years.

Emotional Development

Emotional development involves recognizing feelings or emotions such as love, hate, fear, happiness, and anger. Another part of emotional development is learning to express emotions. Children show love with kisses and hugs. They can also show anger and frustration. Learning acceptable ways to express these emotions signifies emotional growth. Emotional development includes learning to control certain responses to emotions.

Emotions or feelings play an important role in personality development. Children learn to experience and express their feelings through their interactions with parents, siblings, and others. All children need to feel loved and wanted. As parents express love for their child, the child learns to respond in the same manner. Parents' child rearing patterns greatly impact a child's emotional health.

Social Development

Social development is the process of learning to relate to other people. The family provides the first model for socialization. Children first learn about relating to others by observing, and interacting with, their parents. A child's social development is also greatly affected by contact, or lack of contact, with other children and adults. Children need to practice relating to others, learning to cooperate, and recognizing others' feelings. They can do this only when they spend time with people outside the family, 4-2.

4-2
Participating in play groups can help children develop social skills.

Patterns of Development

Children around the world are much more alike than different. They share most of the same physical characteristics. Children also develop along the same general patterns. These patterns are often referred to as principles of growth and development. These principles will help guide your study of child growth and development.

Development Proceeds from Head to Foot

Development proceeds, in general, from head to foot. At birth, the baby's head is more highly developed than its legs and feet. Babies remain top-heavy for many months. At about six months, a baby's lower body can finally support him or her in a sitting position. Usually a baby's legs become strong enough to take their first steps by the end of the first year.

Development Proceeds from Trunk Outward

Development also generally proceeds from the trunk of the body outward. A baby's first learned

I—Discuss: Compare and contrast each of the patterns of development.

2—Reflect: Why is it important for parents to remember that each child is unique?

3—Resource: Heredity or Environment, Activity C, SAG.

4—Vocabulary: Define heredity and environment. Give examples of how each contributes to the uniqueness of each child.

movement is to roll over. Rolling over requires control of muscles in the trunk of the body. Later, the baby learns to control muscles in the arms and legs. Still later, a baby gains control of his or her hands and feet. Finally, the baby learns to use his or her fingers and thumbs to pick up small objects.

Development Follows a Sequence

Development follows many predictable patterns. Children sit before they stand, stand before they walk, and walk before they run. Children follow another predictable pattern as they learn to talk. First, they learn to make sounds. Gradually, they build upon that skill and learn to say words. As development continues, children learn to put words together to form sentences.

Rate of Development Varies

The sequence of events in a developmental pattern is the same from child to child. This means all children learn certain skills in the same order. The timing, however, varies with each child. Suppose Cameron and Camille are the same age. Cameron may be just learning to stand, but Camille may have been walking for weeks. However, Cameron might say more words than Camille. Both babies will learn to walk, and both will learn to talk. They will follow the same patterns of development as they learn to walk and talk, but their timetables will differ.

Parents enjoy talking about their children's accomplishments. They like to boast about their children's advances in growth and noticeable achievements. Parents should realize, however, each child's development follows a different timetable. They should not compare their children to other children of the same age. Children may have different abilities at

a certain age and still be growing normally. Also, children develop so rapidly that one or two months can make a big difference in their abilities.

Each Child Is Unique

Since development follows predictable patterns, child development authorities have described how the average child develops. After observing thousands of children, they have written general descriptions of how and when most children develop certain skills. These general descriptions help parents understand children's growth and behavior. They provide a basic idea of when something might occur. It is important, however, for parents to remember: *Each child is a unique individual from the moment of birth.* See 4-3.

Parents cannot expect their children to match every trait listed in child development charts. Instead, parents need to use the charts as a tool to familiarize themselves with the different stages of child development. Then parents can observe their child and respond in ways that are best for their child's level of development.

Effects of Heredity and Environment

What makes each child unique? Differences from one child to another are due to both heredity and environment. **Heredity** includes all the traits passed down from one generation to the next. A person is born with certain inherited traits passed down from his or her parents. These inherited traits affect almost every aspect of a person's appearance. They determine eye, skin, and hair color. They govern height,

4-3 _____
Although children follow predictable patterns of development, parents must keep in mind no two children are exactly alike.

bone structure, and facial features. A person's gender is also determined by inherited genes.

Hereditary traits do not act alone to form the total person. Environment also plays a role. **Environment** consists of everything in a person's surroundings. It includes family and friends, as well as home, community, and life experiences.

Hereditary potential is influenced by the environment. For instance, an inherited physical trait is hair color. Hair color can be changed by exposure to sun or beauty treatments, both of which are parts of the environment. Intellectual abilities are also inherited. A person who doesn't study, however, may not realize his or her intellectual potential. Social and emotional traits are greatly influenced by the environment, especially the family.

The Influence of the Family

Though families have changed over the years, the family remains the foundation upon which most societies are built. Regardless of a family's structure, it has tremendous influence on its members. The family serves as a foundation upon which children build their own lives. The following sections describe the influence of the family. You will also learn some of the characteristics of strong families, 4-4.

The Family Is the Primary Nurturing Unit

Nothing is more important to a child than family. The family is the primary nurturing unit. It is within their families that children first receive love and attention. This love is shown through supportive and caring parenting.

Children have many needs, which are primarily met by the family. For instance, children need loving care, freedom to grow, and steady guidance. They need close family ties to serve as the basis for security and trust.

Children need structure in their lives to help them develop a sense of order and purpose. They need consistency and reasonable limits placed on their behavior. Children need to recognize the consequences of their actions and learn their behavior affects people other than themselves.

1—Discuss: Why are families the foundation of society?

2—Resource: *Needs of Children and Parents*, Activity D, SAG

4-4 —————
Strong families are
the foundation of
society. They
share certain
characteristics.

1—Discuss: How
can parents give their
children more inde-
pendence and still
provide a nurturing
influence?

2—Resource:
*Balancing Needs of
Parents and Their
Children*, Activity E,
SAG.

3—Discuss: Why do
children exhibit inse-
curity if they sense
their parents' relation-
ship is weak? What
behaviors might be
expected?

4—Resource:
*Characteristics of
Strong Families*,
Activity F, SAG.

In the family, children learn to listen and express themselves clearly. They also gain self-esteem by knowing others are willing to listen to them and talk with them. Children learn about developing relationships with others by observing, and interacting with, their family members.

As children grow older, they become more independent. Even so, the family continues to influence their lives in important ways. The nurturing a family provides is continuous. As children reach adulthood, they establish new families. Their families of origin usually continue to be their refuge in times of trouble. As adults become parents, the cycle is repeated. Attitudes held by a family create a lasting influence upon children from one generation to the next.

The Influence of the Marital Relationship on Children

The husband-wife relationship should be the primary relationship in the family. A strong marital relationship supports both spouses and helps them be better parents. A good marriage can provide a solid foundation upon which to build strong parent-child relationships. By nurturing this relationship, parents strengthen the entire family.

Children are greatly influenced by their parents' relationship. Children can also sense if their parents have a weak marital relationship. They may feel threatened by a division that exists between their parents. Children may worry their parents will divorce. Such worries may cause them to do poorly in school. Their own relationships with siblings and peers may suffer.

A strong marital relationship can affect children in positive ways. If a husband and wife love one another and openly show their affection, children can sense their parents' happiness. These children feel free to also love and show affection. They feel safe and secure in their families. This security frees children to grow and pursue their own goals without worrying about the future of their families.

Characteristics of Strong Families

Children who grow up in a strong family may be better prepared than other children to succeed as adults. You might ask what makes a strong family. Strong families pull together and overcome difficulties while others fall apart. Researchers have identified several characteristics commonly found in strong families. Six of these characteristics are explained in the following sections.

Support and Appreciate One Another

1 In strong families, members are dedicated to each person's welfare and happiness. They support each other in good times and bad. Family members show their affection with words, as well as actions. Strong families love one another and don't hesitate to express this love.

Each person has a basic human need to feel appreciated by others. Children thrive and develop healthy personalities when they feel loved and valued. Adults feel worthwhile and successful when they feel appreciated. Strong families also acknowledge each person's contribution to the family.

Strong families recognize each member's needs and goals. Parents understand each child is a unique individual with strengths and weaknesses. Family members recognize one another's individual commitments and goals. They support one another in achieving individual goals, and work together to achieve family goals.

2 In strong families, members show their support by respecting one another. They respect each person's rights, opinions, privacy, property, and decisions. When children learn to respect family members, they learn to respect people outside the family, as well.

3 When family members support one another, they develop an atmosphere of trust. Children learn they can depend upon their parents and look to them for love, support, and nurturance. Children who feel they can't trust their parents find it difficult to trust others outside the family. They will be afraid to love others for fear their love will be betrayed. Likewise, parents who find it hard to trust their children

will have trouble giving them more freedom when they are teens. In families where feelings of trust are strong, this is not as likely to occur. Parents are able to trust their children and give them increasing responsibilities.

Spend Time Together

4-5 Strong families spend time together. One of the lasting memories of childhood should be of time spent together as a family. Family members work together to complete household chores. They eat meals together and share concerns with one another. They spend some of their leisure time together.

It is important family members try to find time to be together. Children need time to be with their parents. Husbands and wives need time together to foster their relationships. Feelings of appreciation, support, trust, and respect develop when family members spend time together.

4 Work demands sometimes interfere with time available for families. Families need to learn how to balance competing demands. They should strive to spend meaningful time (quality time) together rather than large amounts of time (quantity time) together. Strong families realize the time they spend together must be as good as possible.

Strong families have fun together. Humor allows family members to relax after stressful situations and enjoy the pleasures of family life. Children often remember their parents more for the times they played and laughed together than for the times they had to be disciplined.

Communicate with One Another

Communication is a key component to developing strong family relationships. In strong families,

1—Example: Give examples of how family members can show support and appreciation for one another.

2—Discuss: Members of strong families exhibit respect for one another. How does this help children show respect for others outside the family, such as teachers and authority figures?

3—Discuss: How can teens earn their parents' trust by fulfilling basic responsibilities within the family?

4—Discuss: Which is more important, the quality or quantity of time parents spend with their children?

4-5 _____
Strong families
spend time together
sharing activities
they enjoy, such as
having a cookout.

1—Discuss: How
does communication
within a family
promote unity?

2—Example: Cite
examples that show
how family members
can share household
responsibilities.

members feel free to share their joys,
as well as their sorrows. Family
members who communicate feel closer
to one another. By talking and listening
to each other, family members come
to know one another better. This
promotes a sense of family unity.

Good communication is the basis
for solving the problems that occur
within every family. Even strong families have conflicts and misunderstandings. In a strong family, however,
members understand the importance
of communication to help them solve
these problems. Instead of ignoring a
problem, strong families talk about it.
They are open and truthful with each
other about how they feel and what
they think. Members listen to one
another's thoughts and feelings with
respect. This promotes a sense of closeness and understanding, which brings
families closer together. You'll learn
more about communication later in
this chapter.

Manage Resources and Share Responsibilities

Strong families may not have all
the resources they need, but they make
the most of what they have. In a strong
family, members work as a team and
share their resources. If one member
has items or talents the family needs,
he or she shares these with the family.
Members of strong families help one
another in normal circumstances, as
well as in times of need. Family
members work together to find ways to
solve their problems, meet their needs,
and reach their goals.

Members of strong families feel a
sense of devotion to their family. They
also feel a certain responsibility to help
their family. A family needs the effort
of all its members to be strong. In
strong families, members share household responsibilities. One person does
not carry the load. Instead, all family
members pitch in and do their part. As
children grow, they are given more
responsibilities. They learn to contribute to the family and share in meeting
the family's responsibilities.

Share Moral Standards

Strong families share moral standards. These include compassion, respect, justice, honesty, integrity, equality, and responsibility. In strong families, the members share a common sense of what is right and wrong.

For many families, moral standards are an expression of their religious faith. Their religious beliefs direct them to adopt certain moral beliefs and behaviors. Family members act in a way they feel is right, based on their religious ideals.

In other families, moral standards stem from a natural concern for other people and the world in which they live. These families may not have a particular religious affiliation. They still have beliefs about what is morally right or wrong, however. These beliefs guide their behavior.

Moral standards provide families with measures by which they judge behavior. Strong families teach children to differentiate right from wrong. Moral standards children learn from their families influence them as they develop relationships with others.

Share Family Rituals and Traditions

Strong families provide their members with a sense of family. One of the ways to foster a sense of family is through family rituals and traditions. A family's identity is strengthened by its traditions. For instance, children learn very early their family has special ways of doing things. This may be something as simple as serving the same meal on a certain night of the week. It may be a way of celebrating special holidays. Children remember from year to year the little things that make celebrations special. A child is often the first to get out a special family holiday decoration. As the family expands and children marry, new family members share in these traditions as well.

As new families are formed, family members may create their own special traditions. This ties the young family together. At the same time, they will continue to practice many of the traditions of their families of origin. Newlyweds may argue about how to celebrate holidays. Each spouse may want to celebrate the holiday as his or her family of origin did. With communication and flexibility, the couple will reach a solution and establish their own way of celebrating the holiday.

Family members with a strong sense of family may also gather for family reunions. This is another type of family tradition. At such gatherings, children learn about their ancestors as relatives share family stories. Children enjoy hearing about their family's history and heritage. They develop a sense of pride, increasing their own self-esteem.

How can families establish their own rituals and traditions? See 4-6 for some ideas.

Effective Parent-Child Relationships

A key component in effective parenting is developing effective parent-child relationships. For parents to effectively guide their children's behavior, they must first share strong and loving relationships with their children. Parents need to be aware of how they influence their children. They also need to recognize the important role of communication in developing positive parent-child relationships.

1—Reflect: What moral standards do you think children should learn from their parents? How do moral standards help children choose acceptable behavior?

2—Activity: Make a list of family traditions you think help strengthen a family.

3—Discuss: When each spouse has a favorite way to celebrate a certain holiday, how might a couple compromise on choosing its own special traditions?

4—Discuss: How can family rituals give children a sense of security? Name three rituals children might enjoy.

4-6
Building family traditions can strengthen family relationships.

Building Family Strength Through Family Traditions

- **Recognize your family history.** Even a young family has a past. Keep a family history by saving photos and mementos in a special place. Videotapes, photos, and birthday cards allow families to record the family's past. Recognizing past traditions allows you to repeat them. Children love to look at old photos and videos and talk about how their family is special.

- **Take cues from your children.** Children may be quicker than adults to recognize the potential for turning a routine into a tradition. Children often say, "But we always do it this way." Children feel a sense of security when family routines are repeated. Doing something together is an opportunity for a child to bond with his or her family.

Family rituals or traditions also give a child a sense of safety and control.

- **Give your traditions a name.** You may want to designate a traditional family supper, and call it "Spaghetti Monday." A pet rabbit's addition to a family may be designated as "Harvey the Rabbit Day." These special days, even though they are very simple, can be very meaningful. They give your family a distinction that sets it apart from the ordinary.

- **Remain committed to your family rituals.** Let your family know these are special events for your family. Rituals and traditions prompt a sense of "us" or "we" for families. It provides a feeling of connection, and this is important.

1—Activity: Watch a family TV sitcom. Note verbal and nonverbal communication between family members. Does the pattern help or hinder positive balance in the family?

2—Discuss: Children respond to all forms of communication. How can each strengthen the parent-child bond?

The Role of Communication

Communication is vital to all loving and caring relationships. It strengthens family relationships and plays an important role in children's development. **Communication** is any means by which people send and receive messages. Communication has two parts: messages are sent by the sender and messages are received by the receiver.

A sender may send messages verbally using words. Speaking and writing are both forms of verbal communication. Messages are also sent nonverbally. Gestures, facial expressions, and body movements send messages. A person's touch and tone of voice are an important part of communicating.

Receiving is the other half of communication. For communication to be effective, the message sent must be the message received. This means the receiver must understand the message in the same way the sender meant it. This is extremely important, and

it plays a major role in effective communication in the family. When the receiver understands a message differently from the way the speaker intended it, this is called miscommunication. Miscommunication can cause conflict and misunderstandings.

Children are receptive to both verbal and nonverbal communication. They respond to hugs, hand gestures, and facial expressions, as well as spoken words. Parents need to establish good communication patterns with their children at an early age. These patterns help set the stage for good parent-child relationship throughout all stages of the family life cycle.

Children are extremely sensitive to how their parents communicate with them. Small babies sense warmth, caring, and trust in the way parents hold and talk to them. Babies also communicate their needs. From birth, they cry when their basic needs are not met. The piercing wail of a hungry baby usually brings fast results. Babies communicate contentment with coos, gurgles, and smiles.

Small children quickly learn to sense when parents are pleased with what they are doing. They can also sense when parents are upset by their behavior. Small children also have special ways of communicating with their parents. Before a child learns to speak, the child may tug at a parent's clothes to get attention. A child may take a parent's hand and pull the parent to a desired location. If these attempts at communication fail, children may intentionally misbehave. They quickly learn that misbehaving will get their parents' attention, even if it means they will be scolded.

Teens' ability to communicate with their parents often depends on the earlier communication patterns established in the family. In families where communication is strained or nonexistent, teens may resort to drastic measures to ask for help. When they are troubled, teens are more likely to turn to their parents if they already communicate freely with them. If the lines of communication are already open, teens know when and how to seek their parents' advice.

The Importance of Open Communication

Communication involves sending and receiving messages. This sounds simple enough, but it isn't always easy to share your thoughts and feelings with others. People can't always identify how they feel, much less clearly explain these feelings to someone else. Even simple statements are sometimes misinterpreted. How a person says something may give another person the wrong impression. Communication is also restricted when people don't listen to one another.

Many of these problems can be overcome with open communication. In open communication, both people share their thoughts and feelings as best they can without hiding what they really feel. Both people communicate openly and honestly. Each person listens carefully to what the other person is saying. When people are honest and open about their true feelings, it is much easier to reach an understanding. When people are truly honest with one another, they can respond to one another appropriately.

Open communication will not occur if the person receiving the message is not willing to accept the message being sent. For instance, the receiver might think what the sender is saying is silly or wrong. If this happens, the sender will not feel able to openly share thoughts and feelings with the receiver. Has anyone ever made light of your fears by saying "Don't worry about it" or "You're making a big deal out of nothing"? How did this make you feel? You probably didn't say anything else about your fears. You may have decided not to be open after all. If there is no feeling of openness within a family, people will not feel free to share. If family members respect one another, open communication is more likely to occur.

Open communication is necessary if families are going to deal with everyday living. It promotes growth and understanding in a family. Children are not afraid to express their feelings. When they have questions, they know to ask their parents for answers. If parents don't have the answers, they will help their children learn to find them. Open communication promotes understanding, sharing, respect, and trust among family members.

Inhibitors to Open Communication

When family members fail to communicate openly, their relationships will suffer. Family members will feel remote, detached, and afraid to express their feelings or ideas. Small problems between individuals may escalate into major family problems.

1—Discuss: Why might a child misbehave just to be able to communicate with a parent?

2—Discuss: Why might some teens' drug problems actually be a message asking for help from their parents?

3—Resource: *Communication in Families: Communiation Enhancers,* color transparency CT-4A, TR.

1—Discuss: If parents make most of a child's decisions for him or her, what might be the result?

2—Discuss: Describe three ways a parent may use subtle inhibitors that can stop open communication.

3—Resource: *Communication In Families: Communication Inhibitors,* color transparency CT-4B, TR.

4—Resource: *Communication Enhancers and Inhibitors,* Activity G, SAG.

5—Enrich: Role-play situations in which active listening takes place.

6—Resource: *Active Listening...,* transparency master 4-2, TR.

Inhibitors to open communication can be very subtle. Parents who always tell their children what to do will build resentment in their children. Children like to feel they can share in the decision making. Parents who want to make all children's decisions for them eliminate children's chances to learn to make decisions. Children may either become very dependent on the parents' control or rebel against it. A defensive climate in the home will reduce further communication among family members.

When parents assume responsibility for solving all children's problems for them, this inhibits open communication. Parents may immediately take over when their child has a problem. This can give the child the message he or she doesn't know how to handle the problem. Parents need to know when to stand back and support their children by not taking over their problems.

Other, more subtle inhibitors to open communication also exist. Some parents tend to give too much advice to help their children with their problems. They may tell their children how they handled similar problems when they were young. Parents may present their solution as the only possible answer. A well-meaning parent may influence the child to handle the problem in the manner the parent thinks is proper. Other parents may try to help their children by making light of problems. They may try to protect their children by getting them to think about other things. All these communication patterns inhibit open communication between parents and children. Additional behaviors that can inhibit communication are summarized in 4-7.

Effective Communication Techniques

Open communication is important in strengthening family relationships. It helps family members express love and concern and positively resolve conflicts. You may wonder what parents and children can do to communicate more effectively with one another. Several communication techniques have been found to be effective. These include active listening, defining problem ownership, and using "I" and "we" messages.

Active Listening

An important part of communication is listening. Without listening to another person, you cannot understand what he or she is really saying. In **active listening,** the receiver actively participates in the communication process. The listener does not just listen passively, but listens with the eyes as well as the ears. He or she responds to the sender of the message in ways that convey the message is being received.

Active listening involves a lot more than hearing what someone is saying. Active listening:

- encourages the speaker to share.
- makes the speaker feel respected and accepted.
- helps the speaker clarify the meaning of the message.
- minimizes the chance for misinterpretations of ideas.

To be an active listener, you can do the following:

- *Pay attention to the speaker.* Show you are listening to what is being said by giving the speaker your full attention. If you are a parent and your child wants to talk, turn off the TV. Put down your paper or close your book. Stop what you are doing and pay attention, 4-8. This shows children you care about them and what they have to say.
- *Acknowledge what is being said.* Nod your head or repeat simple phrases to indicate you are listening. Don't listen in absolute

Roadblocks to Open Communication

Slow

Ordering

Directing

Demanding

Warning

Caution!

Advising

Giving solutions

Preaching

Moralizing

Threatening

Lecturing

Judging

Criticizing

Blaming

Overpraising

Danger!

Analyzing

Interpreting

Ridiculing

Name-calling

Assuming

Sympathizing

Probing

Questioning

Withdrawal

Distracting

4-7 _____
Keep the lines of communication open by avoiding these roadblocks.

silence. Instead, say something like "I see" or "Uh-huh" to indicate you are listening. Ask questions to help the speaker clarify what he or she is saying. You can also summarize points if they become long and drawn out. This helps the speaker know whether the message was received correctly.

- *Let the speaker do most of the talking.* You can't be a good listener if you do all the talking. You only need to make occasional comments or ask a few questions.

- *Acknowledge feelings.* Show you understand what the speaker has said and how he or she feels. Saying "You must feel very angry" can reflect how the speaker probably feels. Children sometimes do not understand their own feelings. Having a parent acknowledge how the child may feel helps the child deal with these feelings.

1—Discuss: Why is it important to be an active listener, even with very small children?

1

4-8 _____

Giving a child your complete attention as she speaks can make her feel valued and loved.

1—Vocabulary: What is meant by *problem ownership*? Why does it help to know who owns the problem?

2—Discuss: What can happen when parents try to handle all a child's problems? Does anyone win in this situation?

3—Example: How do "I" messages promote better relationships within a family? Give three examples.

4—Discuss: Why does a "you" message place the blame on others and create defensiveness?

Defining Problem Ownership

Families can prevent many misunderstandings by using open communication. Even in families that communicate very well, however, conflicts will still occur from time to time. One way to handle conflicts is to define **problem ownership**. This means determining who owns the problem, or whose problem it is. The person who owns a problem is the person most concerned or upset by it. This person is most likely to seek a solution to the problem, because he or she is most affected by it. For instance, maybe you are upset because your sibling borrows your clothes and doesn't return them. Your favorite shirt wasn't in your closet when you were ready to get dressed for a special date. This made you mad. This is your problem, because you are the one who is upset by the situation. You are the person most interested in solving this problem.

Some parents tend to assume ownership of every problem within the family. This can be a problem in itself. Suppose you looked to your parents to have them solve the situation of the borrowed clothes. If your parents didn't handle matters to your satisfaction, you and your sibling might both become angry. Having your parents solve your problems also fails to teach you to handle them yourself. Parents deprive their children of important learning experiences by not allowing them to handle their own problems.

Parents do need to handle those problems that affect them. For instance, a child misbehaves when his mother is talking on the phone. This is the mother's problem because it affects her behavior and how she feels. She must find a solution.

Sometimes a problem affects more than one person. By defining problem ownership, it may become obvious that the problem is owned by the entire family. Everyone in the family may be affected by the problem, and everyone might benefit from a positive solution. In these cases, family members should work together to solve these problems in a way everyone can accept.

Using "I," "You," or "We," Messages

Communication within the family can be improved by using "I" messages. **"I" messages** describe a thought, feeling, or other experience in the singular, first-person manner. "I" messages give the responsibility for a problem to the person making the statement. The speaker owns the problem. "I" messages allow the speaker to declare how he or she feels without attacking the other person. These statements are less threatening and do not provoke rebellion or resistance.

"I" statements have three parts: a description of the situation, the speaker's feelings, and how the speaker is affected. For example, parents might be upset when toys are left out when the family is getting ready to leave. A parent might say "I get upset when toys are left out when we are ready to leave. We won't be able to go until the toys are put away. This will make us late." Children can easily understand the message, yet do not feel they have been accused of causing the feeling.

"You" messages are a much less effective form of communication. **"You" messages** place all the blame for a problem on others, creating defensiveness and resistance. These statements may cause conflicts instead of improving family relationships. "You" statements tend to create greater distance between people. When parents use "you" statements with their children, they blame or criticize the children for the parents' feelings.

In the above family situation, a "you" statement may create resentment and actually ruin a planned family outing. The parent might say "You always leave your toys all over the room. You will spoil our outing by making us late." Continually hearing "you" messages can make children feel rejected and unloved. It can also make them feel defensive and resistant to changing their behavior.

Another kind of message is the "we" message. **"We" messages** imply that two or more people are jointly involved in a problem situation. "We" statements increase the intimacy, togetherness, and sense of cooperation in a relationship. They create much less defensiveness and resistance than "you" messages.

"We" statements can indicate a whole family is involved in the problem situation. These statements put the responsibility for solving the problem on the family as a group. They do not imply one person has more responsibility than another. "We" statements enhance the togetherness of the family. In today's fast-paced life, many forces pull family members apart. If families can learn to use "we" messages, it may help strengthen the family. "We" statements emphasize the feeling that the family is involved in the situation together.

The use of "I" statements should be encouraged within the family when problems are owned by one person. Broader "we" statements are appropriate when more than one family member is affected by a problem or situation. The use of "you" statements should be avoided if at all possible.

Using active listening techniques, defining problem ownership, and using "I" and "we" statements will improve family communication. Additional tips for good communication in families are listed in 4-9.

Parental Influence on a Child's Self-Concept

When you become a parent, almost everything you do and say will influence your child's development. Your opinions and reactions will have a significant impact on your children. Parents are the most important people in a child's life, so their influence is the greatest. A child's self-concept is especially affected by the his or her relationships with parents, 4-10.

A child's **self-concept** is his or her mental image of himself or herself. This self-concept may be healthy or realistic. It may also be unhealthy or

1—**Activity:** Compare and contrast "I" messages and "you" messages.

2—**Discuss:** How can "we" messages bring a family closer together?

3—**Resource:** *Building a Child's Self-Concept and Self-Esteem,* Activity H, SAG.

Tips for Good Communication in Families

- Recognize feelings of each family member.

- Encourage family members to express good feelings as well as bad feelings.

- When sending messages, make sure the message is received as you intended it to be received. Ask for feedback if you are uncertain.

- When receiving messages, avoid jumping to conclusions.

- Provide feedback to the speaker using both verbal and nonverbal acknowledgement.

- Watch for nonverbal messages and clues.

- Open the door to communication by inviting people to talk to you. Tell them you are interested and concerned about them.

- Pick a good time to begin a discussion.

4-9 ———
Following these guidelines can improve family communication.

4-10 —————
When this mother shows interest in her daughter's school project, both people benefit. Having good relationships with their parents positively influences children's self-concepts.

unrealistic. Children may see themselves as they are, or they may have unrealistic ideas about who they really are.

The way children see themselves guides their behavior and influences their decisions. For instance, a girl who thinks she is awkward and clumsy may not even try out for the basketball team. She may feel it isn't even worth trying. A boy who thinks he doesn't know how to talk to people may stay home alone most of the time. He may be afraid to call someone for fear the person won't want to be his friend.

How Self-Concept Develops

A person's self-concept begins to form almost from birth. It develops as a result of experiences with others. In the early years, most of these experiences involve parents and other family members. Later, as children interact more with people outside the family, teachers, friends, and neighbors help shape the child's self-concept. During the teen years, experiences with peers greatly influence a young person's self-concept.

Self-concept formation begins in infancy as parents react to the infant's constant experimentation. With each new experience, children look to their parents for their reactions. How parents respond influences the child's developing self-concept. Children form their self-concepts based on what they feel their parents think of them and how they treat them. Showing children encouragement, love, and support helps them develop a healthy, realistic self-concept.

A person's self-concept can change. All children go through trying periods as events and circumstances in their lives change. These events may change a person's mental self-image. For instance, if a child develops a serious illness, it may change the way the child sees himself or herself. The child may believe he or she has the same abilities as before, when this is not true. The child might also mistakenly feel he or she has lost certain abilities that are still present.

Parental Influence on a Child's Self-Esteem

1 While self-concept describes a person's perception of himself or herself, **self-esteem** describes how a person *feels* about himself or herself. Children may feel good about themselves. These children are said to have self-esteem. They may feel happy, outgoing, good, helpful, or talented. Children may also feel negatively about themselves. These children lack self-esteem. They may feel worthless, awkward, shy, or stupid.

2 Many people think self-esteem is an either/or situation. They think you either have self-esteem or you don't. You either feel good or bad about yourself. In reality, everyone has ups and downs, as well as secure and insecure moments. People grow from these experiences if they learn from their mistakes as well as their successes. A person's self-esteem fluctuates over time. The amount of self-esteem a person generally has is more important than his or her self-esteem on a given day.

Stressful situations and events may affect a child's self-esteem. For instance, a child may move with his or her family to a new home and have to go to a new school. The events may be very upsetting. The result may be a temporary loss of self-confidence. As the child becomes more comfortable in this new setting, his or her self-confidence will likely return.

4 Parents can have a dramatic influence on their children's self-esteem, 4-11. Parents can build their children's self-esteem by encouraging children to feel good about themselves. Children should feel loved for who they are, not for what they can do or may become. Parents' words, facial expressions, gestures, and reactions give children messages about their worth. Children who receive positive feedback from their parents are more likely to develop self-esteem. Showing genuine concern for children's interests and problems also encourages self-esteem. If children

1—Vocabulary: What is the difference between *self-concept* and *self-esteem*?

2—Reflect: How can the ups and downs of self-esteem help a person become more secure?

3—Reflect: Compare the indicators of persons with self-esteem with those who lack self-esteem. Does either list describe someone you know?

4—Example: Give examples of ways parents can show genuine concern for their children's interests and problems.

Self-Esteem Indicators

3

A person who has self-esteem:	A person who lacks self-esteem:
+ Is not afraid of new situations.	− Lacks initiative.
+ Makes friends easily.	− Depends on others for direction.
+ Tries new ideas and projects.	− Usually asks for permission.
+ Trusts teachers or others in authority.	− Is not spontaneous.
+ Cooperates and follows reasonable rules.	− Enters few new activities.
+ Manages behavior responsibly.	− Prefers to be alone.
+ Is creative and imaginative.	− Does not say much.
+ Talks freely.	− Is possessive.
+ Is an independent worker.	− May respond to threats by being aggressive or withdrawing.
+ Is generally happy.	− Is easily frustrated.

4-11 ——————
These signs can indicate how much self-esteem a person has.

1—Reflect: Compare praise used as manipulation with praise used as encouragement. What are the results of each?

2—Discuss: How can too much praise actually limit a child?

3—Resource: *Parent Helpers*, Activity I, SAG.

are given encouragement, praise, and support, they will feel worthwhile. If they hear constant criticism or feel rejected in their efforts, they may feel worthless.

Using praise and encouragement is one way parents can boost children's self-esteem. How parents praise their children is important, however. Some types of praise are not as helpful as others. Parents should try to use praise in a way that will help their children grow. Sincere, spontaneous reactions, such as "Wow" or "That's terrific" are fine. Praise that is used to manipulate the child's behavior, emphasizing what the adult wants is not good. Praise as manipulation tends to stifle children's natural desire to learn. Encouragement, on the other hand, helps build a child's confidence. It allows the child to own his or her accomplishments. This creates a desire within the child to do his or her best.

Can praise be overused? Children like honest praise, but undeserved praise may lead a child to doubt himself or herself. Children are not fooled by false praise. Lavish praise at home is poor preparation for what children may receive in the real world of friends, school, and work.

Lavish praise can be addictive. Children who are hooked on praise will often repeat behaviors guaranteed to bring them more praise. If they become too concerned with praise, children may become unable to appreciate their own abilities unless others approve. A praise-addicted child may grow afraid to take risks. If children know they will be praised for familiar behaviors, why should they try something new? Unwise praise—too much or too often—doesn't help children grow. It limits them. Overpraised students may only work for gold stars rather than for the joy of learning.

Parents need to use praise and encouragement wisely in helping their children develop self-esteem. They need to keep in mind the danger of overusing praise. The guidelines in 4-12 will help you learn to use praise wisely.

Resources for Parents

Raising children can be a tough job. Though parenting can be one of the most rewarding experiences, it can also be one of the most demanding. No parent can do it all alone.

One of life's realities is that problems and crises will occur. Even the most stable and self-sufficient family may need to ask for help. Maybe parents need someone to care for their children during an emergency. Maybe health care is needed quickly, and no funds are available for a doctor's care. Maybe a parent under stress is beginning to abuse a child. Perhaps children are having trouble adjusting to their parents' divorce. These and many other problems may be too much for parents to handle alone. They may need to seek outside help.

Many services are available to assist families in times of need. Too often, however, parents don't use the services available to them. They may think asking for help is a sign of weakness. Parents may be embarrassed to admit they have problems. They may feel they should be able to solve their problems on their own. Other parents don't realize when they need help, or they may deny a problem exists.

Asking for assistance when it is needed is not a sign of weakness or failure, but a sign of strength. It shows parents truly care about their children and want what is best for them. Good parents know when to seek and accept help from others.

The Do's and Don'ts of Praise

Don't

Don't praise by comparison. It may encourage unnecessary competition or fear of failing the next time. Don't say "You're the best player on the team!"

Don't praise constantly. If everything your child does is wonderful and terrific, you may run out of superlatives, and your child may become immune to praise.

Don't praise indiscriminately. Children know when something they have done is really not so great. Parental praise over average performance can make children cynical.

Don't praise so extravagantly children feel pressured to go on shining. Overenthusiastic applause destroys a good motive for activity (to please oneself) and substitutes a poor one (to please parents).

Don't use backhanded praise. For instance, don't say "It's nice to see you being good for a change." This takes away any earned behavior.

Do

Do be specific. Instead of using words that evaluate, describe the encouragement in concrete terms of what you see. "You caught the ball, threw it, and made the out for your team."

Do describe behavior and its consequences. For instance, "Thanks for putting the dishes away. When we all work together, we can get done faster and have time to spend at the park."

Do focus on the child's effort—not on the end result. "You practiced hard for your piano recital."

Do point out how your child has progressed. "Three cartwheels in a row! You couldn't have done that last year."

Do give control back to the child. Let your child do his or her own thing. Instead of saying "I'm so proud of you," say "You must feel very proud that you did that all by yourself."

4-12 ——————
To be most effective, praise must be used properly.

Parent Support Systems

The people, institutions, and organizations parents turn to in times of need make up their **support system**. Parents' primary support comes from the people they know and trust. These include family members, relatives, friends, neighbors, teachers, and coworkers. A clergy member may also be close to the family. A parent may be able to turn to these people for support.

Many times, family members can solve problems themselves. Relatives can also help. Today, however, families are often scattered across the country and even across the world. People may live far away from relatives who could help them in the midst of a crisis.

Today, more than ever, families depend upon people outside the family. Friends, neighbors, teachers, and colleagues can be important members of a parent's support system. During a difficult time, a parent may just need a good friend who can listen and give advice. Neighbors may be able to provide short-term child care if parents are called away during an emergency. Sometimes coworkers or teachers can offer advice or support. A person's religious organization may offer counseling and referral services.

Today's families also have a wide range of public and private agencies available to provide needed support. These agencies can be an important part of a parent's support system. Some agencies can diagnose and treat health problems. Other agencies can provide financial or legal assistance. There are services for child care and parent education, and even recreation.

You should acquaint yourself with resources for parents in your

1—Enrich: Role-play situations described in this chart. Identify which are proper uses of praise and which are not.

2—Resource: *Building a Parent Support System,* Activity J, SAG.

3—Discuss: Praise should focus on a child's effort—not on the end result. What does this mean?

1—Activity:
Investigate additional
resources for parents
in your community.

community. It may take effort to locate these resources, because they may not be easy to find. These resources exist to help people feel less isolated and frustrated in a crisis. They can also help people solve problems. Throughout this text, you will learn more about various resources available to parents.

Finding Help

When you think of finding help in an emergency situation, your first thought might be to dial 9-1-1. In almost every city in the United States, the 911 telephone number offers quick help in emergencies. If the 911 service is available, parents should teach their children how to use this number in case of emergency.

Toll-free hot lines can also help families in times of crisis. A hot line is a number people can call for information or other assistance with a specific problem. Many hot lines operate 24 hours daily. Persons familiar with the specific crisis will answer the phone, offer guidance, and refer callers to local services. Hot line services may serve victims of domestic violence, sexual assault, or child abuse. Other hot lines are available for people addicted to drugs. Hot lines may also assist those wanting to report missing children or for children who have run away from home. Information hot lines are also available to offer information on AIDS and other STDs. Some of these hot lines may be listed in your phone book. You may be able to find others on brochures, in advertisements, and by asking a doctor, teacher, or counselor.

The Yellow Pages or Blue Pages of your local phone book should list agencies available in your community. City, county, and state government agencies will be listed. Calling one of these agencies may be the first step in solving a problem. If you call the wrong agency, the person you reach may be able to direct you to the appropriate agency. Some cities and counties have general information numbers that can direct you to the agency that provides the services you need. Government agencies can also refer you to volunteer organizations and support groups that provide various types of assistance.

In many cities, the United Way offers a Helpline that links people to appropriate service agencies. Schools, hospitals, and religious organizations can also be helpful in locating services.

Your local public library can be a valuable research center. There, you may be able to locate books and pamphlets on the topic of concern. You can research the names, addresses, and telephone numbers of agencies that might be able to assist you. A librarian can direct you to the most helpful reference books.

Support Groups

Sometimes parents need to add a support group to their support system. A **support group** is a group of people who share a similar problem or concern. Members of a support group hold regular meetings where they discuss their concerns. These meetings may or may not be facilitated by a professional counselor. Support groups are available for victims of abuse. Other support groups serve persons who are addicted to alcohol or drugs, their families, and friends. Support groups are also available for people who are affected by certain illnesses. See 4-13 for a list of support groups that exist in many communities.

In a support group, members find support by talking to one another about their common concern. They can listen as others share their experiences. Members of a support group encourage each other as they learn new ways to cope with their own problems. People might attend a support group for a short period of time, or for many years.

Support Groups for Families

Adult Grief Support Group: for bereaved adults.

AIDS Support Group: for people who have tested positive for HIV.

Al-Anon: for family members and friends of alcoholics.

Alateen: for teens (ages 11-18) affected by another person's alcoholism.

Alcoholics Anonymous: for people who want to stop drinking.

Alliance for the Mentally Ill: for families and friends of persons with severe mental illness.

Alzheimer's Disease Support Group: for family members of people with Alzheimer's Disease.

Battered Women's Support Group: for women who are victims of domestic violence.

Cancer Support Group: for cancer patients and their families.

Child Find: for parents trying to find missing children and teens.

Cocaine Anonymous: for cocaine addicts who still suffer, but are trying to recover.

Diabetes Support Group: for diabetics and their families.

Down Syndrome Parent Support Group: for parents of children who have Down syndrome.

Families Anonymous: for people concerned about drug abuse and behavioral problems of a relative or friend.

Gamblers Anonymous: for people who gamble compulsively.

Make Today Count: for people who face life-threatening illnesses, their families, and friends.

Mended Hearts: for people who have had heart surgery.

Nar-Anon: for family members and friends of drug addicts.

Narcotics Anonymous: for drug addicts who seek to recover from their addiction.

National Center for Missing and Exploited Children: for parents trying to locate missing children or teens.

Parents Anonymous: for the treatment and prevention of child abuse.

Parents Helping Parents: for families who have children with special needs (covers all disabilities).

Parents United: for individuals and families who have experienced child sexual abuse.

Parents Without Partners: for single parents and their children.

Phoenix: for people going through divorce, widowhood, or separation.

Resolve: for infertile couples who are trying to become parents.

Runaway Hotline: for children or teens who have run away from home.

Share: for parents who have lost a newborn through miscarriage, stillbirth, or infant death.

Tough Love: for parents who are going through adjustment/addiction problems with their teenage children.

Visually-impaired Support Group: for the newly blind and those facing blindness.

1

4-13
In many communities, these and other support groups and agencies can help families in times of need.

1—**Enrich:** Consult a telephone directory to find out which of these groups and sources of information are available in your community.

Summary

- Parents need to understand children's physical, intellectual, emotional, and social development as children grow, develop, and mature.

- Although each child is unique, children's growth follows certain basic developmental patterns.

- Development proceeds from head to foot, proceeds from the trunk outward, and follows a predictable sequence. The rate and timing of this development varies from child to child.

- The influence of heredity and environment makes each child unique.

- The family, as the primary nurturing unit, is a tremendous influence on children.

- In strong families, members support one another, spend time with one another, communicate well, and manage their resources. They also share responsibilities, moral values, rituals, and traditions.

- Effective parent-child relationships are aided by open communication, active listening, defining problem ownership, and the use of "I" messages and "we" messages.

- Parents influence a child's self-concept and sense of self-esteem.

- Sometimes parents need help. Building a support system of people, institutions, and organizations can help parents through tough times.

Reviewing Key Points

1. What is the difference between growth and development?
2. Give an example of each of the four types of development.
3. Which principle of development is illustrated in each of the following:
   A. Babies can grasp with their hands before using their fingers.
   B. Babies can sit before they can stand.
   C. When lying on their stomachs, babies can raise their heads and then their chests.
4. Give two examples to illustrate the influences of heredity and environment.
5. Why is communication a key characteristic of strong families?
6. Name the two parts of communication.
7. Give an example of verbal communication and an example of nonverbal communication.
8. List four things an active listener will do.
9. Why is it important to determine who owns a problem?
10. Give an example of an "I" statement. Identify the three parts of this "I" statement.
11. Explain how parents can influence their children's self-esteem.
12. Explain the difference between a support system and a support group.

1

2

Learning by Doing

1. Observe a group of preschool children and cite examples of physical, intellectual, social, and emotional development. Note similarities and differences among the children.

2. Create a bulletin board titled "Each Child Is Unique." Select pictures from magazines that illustrate children's differences.

3. Role-play a person using "I," "you," and "we" messages to talk with a family member about a problem. Discuss the strengths and weaknesses of each type of message.

4. Find newspaper articles featuring family problems. List resources in your community these families might turn to for assistance.

5. Visit your public library. Ask the reference librarian to show you reference materials parents could use to locate needed community resources.

Thinking Critically

1. Write a paragraph explaining whether you think a child's development is influenced more by heredity or environment. Give examples to support your position.

2. Select one of the characteristics of strong families. Explain how you think having this characteristic can make families stronger.

3. Complete the following statement: Parents can improve a child's self-esteem by... Share your responses with the class.

4. Working in a small group, write a case study depicting a problem families might face. Exchange case studies with another group. Identify the problem faced in each case study. Then describe a possible support system for each family.

5. Debate whether seeking support outside the family is a sign of weakness or a sign of strength.

Part Two
The Beginning of Parenthood

Chapter 5
Planning a Family

Chapter 6
Pregnancy

Chapter 7
Prenatal Care

Chapter 8
Childbirth

Chapter 9
Decisions Facing
Parents-to-Be

Chapter 10
New Parents, New Baby

Chapter 5
Planning a Family

Objectives

After studying this chapter, you will be able to

- summarize the advantages of family planning.
- identify factors that influence family planning decisions.
- explain the process of reproduction.
- identify causes of infertility.
- describe options for infertile couples and the implications of these options.

Key Terms

family planning
sperm
egg
testes
vas deferens
ovaries
ovulation
fallopian tubes
uterus
endometrium
menstruation
chromosome
gene
genetic counseling
congenital disorders
infertility
artificial insemination
in vitro fertilization
independent adoption
agency adoption
closed adoption
open adoption

Family planning describes a couple's commitment to making decisions regarding their reproductive capabilities. Included in family planning are decisions about the number, timing, and spacing of any children born. Couples should learn about family planning before deciding to have children. The best time for this is before marriage. Then a couple can begin their marriage with a clear understanding of their parenting goals as a couple. Sharing common parenting goals increases the chance a couple will be happy in their marriage.

Advantages of Family Planning

Family planning has several advantages. First, family planning helps ensure parenthood is by choice rather than by chance. Couples may be more satisfied with becoming parents if they have planned to do so. This helps ensure every child born is wanted, which has great implications for families and society as a whole.

Responsible family planning also allows a couple to achieve the goals they have set for themselves, 5-1. A couple may decide never to have children. They may postpone having children until they have met certain educational and career goals. Couples may want to wait until they are more emotionally and financially prepared. Postponing parenthood until they are ready enables couples to be better parents when they do have children. This benefits children as well as adults.

Another advantage of family planning is that couples can determine what size of family they desire. They can have the number of children they want, spaced over a desired number of years. Couples can decide to stop having children when they feel their

1—Resource:
Planning Considerations, Activity A, SAG.

2—Resource:
Factors to Consider, Activity B, SAG.

3—Discuss: What factors influence parents' decisions about having more children?

5-1 _____
A husband and wife may want to take plenty of time adjusting to their marital roles before starting parenthood.

family is the right size. This can keep families from being overburdened by having more children than they can care for or afford.

Factors That Influence Family Planning Decisions

A common question about family planning is when a couple should have their first child. The simplest answer is when both spouses feel ready. Some experts recommend couples be married at least 18 months before

becoming parents. This will allow them to adjust completely to their marital roles before adding parenting roles.

When couples feel ready to start having children, they have probably already considered many related factors. Some of these factors, such as the security of the marriage, goals, personal readiness, age, and health, were described in Chapter 2.

Ideally, a couple will have discussed parenting goals before they were married. If not, they should do so before having a child. Even if they discussed parenting before marriage, however, they should talk about the subject again. Talking about parenthood as a goal for some future time is different from discussing parenthood as an upcoming reality. A couple's financial situation or readiness may be much different from when they were first married. Their views or opinions may have changed.

After the birth of their first child, many couples make further decisions about family planning. Couples may wish to consider the questions presented in the decision-making chain in 5-2. A couple may decide to have only one child, or they may want more children. They may want to have a second child immediately or wait several years.

Many factors influence parents' decisions about having more children. All the factors that influenced their decision to have their first child must be reconsidered. Several new factors enter into the picture as well.

Emotional factors may influence family planning decisions. If one or both spouses were only children, they may recall how they longed to have a brother or sister. In this case, they may decide to have at least two children. On the other hand, they may have enjoyed being only children and wish the same for their child. Couples from large families may be influenced by their

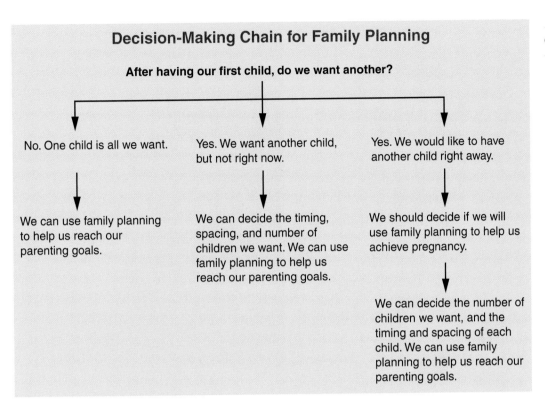

Decision-Making Chain for Family Planning

After having our first child, do we want another?

No. One child is all we want.	Yes. We want another child, but not right now.	Yes. We would like to have another child right away.
We can use family planning to help us reach our parenting goals.	We can decide the timing, spacing, and number of children we want. We can use family planning to help us reach our parenting goals.	We should decide if we will use family planning to help us achieve pregnancy.
		We can decide the number of children we want, and the timing and spacing of each child. We can use family planning to help us reach our parenting goals.

5-2
Couples may ask themselves these questions about family planning after having their first child.

backgrounds, too. Spouses who grew up in large families may want a peaceful home with a small family. They might also choose an action-packed home filled with children.

Financial factors are a necessary part of any family planning decision. More children cost more money. Food, clothing, transportation, entertainment, education, and health care costs keep climbing. They grow with the birth of each child, as well as when each child grows older. Also, as a family grows, they may need a larger, more expensive home.

Couples don't have to delay parenthood until their financial future is absolutely secure. They may never reach that point. In fact, most couples do not feel they have reached total financial security by the time they have children. Couples do need to have some degree of financial security, however. This will ensure adding children to the family will not cause great financial problems.

Decisions about the spacing of children are related to emotional, physical, and financial factors. Most authorities agree about three years between children is best. This amount of time allows each child to achieve a separate status in the family. The older child will be better able to accept and understand having a new brother or sister. There may be less sibling rivalry as a result. See 5-3.

The spacing of children has an effect on the health of the mother. It takes about 18 months for a woman to resume her normal health after the birth of a baby. If there is less time than this between pregnancies, her health and the baby's health may be at risk. The more time there is between pregnancies, the better chance a woman has to maintain her health and strength.

Another consideration for the spacing of children is future educational costs. If children are born three to four years apart, their college years will overlap little if at all. With college expenses rising, this factor is becoming more important.

1—Activity: List financial factors couples should consider when planning a family.

2—Discuss: Why do child development experts recommend spacing children three to four years apart?

5-3 _____
Spacing children three to four years apart allows each child to achieve a separate status in the family. It may also lessen sibling rivalry.

1—Resource: *Human Reproduction,* Activity C, SAG.

2—Resource: *Reproductive Organs,* transparency master 5-2, TR.

3—Enrich: Draw a diagram of the male reproductive system, identifying each of the parts described in the chapter. Write a sentence describing the purpose of each part.

Human Reproduction

A good first step in family planning decisions is understanding human reproduction. Knowing how babies are created helps couples plan pregnancy. Humans reproduce sexually. Two sex cells—the **sperm** from the male and the **egg** from the female—unite to form a fertilized egg. This fertilized egg then divides millions of times to form the new human being. Both men and women have important roles in reproduction.

The Man's Role

The man's role in reproduction is to produce sperm he will then deliver to the woman. A man begins producing sperm at puberty and continues throughout his lifetime. At first, sperm are produced in small numbers. By adulthood, men produce millions of sperm each month.

Sperm are produced in a man's two **testes** or testicles. Next to each testis is a coiled tube called the *epididymis.* Sperm pass through a series of ducts to reach the epididymis. There the sperm mature. Each epididymis is attached to a long, narrow tube called the **vas deferens.** Sperm are carried through the vas deferens up into the man's body. Each vas deferens leads to an *ejaculatory duct.* The two ejaculatory ducts are located side by side and connect to the *urethra.* The urethra extends through the penis. Sperm leave the body through the urethra in the penis.

When sperm first leave the epididymis, they are relatively inactive. They are propelled upward by contractions of the muscular walls of the vas deferens. Secretions from three sets of glands are added to the sperm as they reach the urethra. The secretions and the sperm together are called semen. It is this semen that leaves the man's body through ejaculation during sexual intercourse.

The Woman's Role

1 The woman's role in reproduction is to provide eggs and to carry and nourish a fertilized egg within her body until a baby is born. A woman is born with about 400,000 immature egg cells. Her body does not produce any more eggs after she is born. The eggs are stored in her two **ovaries**. Usually only one egg is released from the ovaries each month, starting at puberty and ending at menopause. Thus, only about 400 eggs are released during an average woman's reproductive years.

An egg is released from the ovaries through a process called **ovulation**. Ovulation happens about once a month. After leaving the ovary, the egg 2 passes into one of two tubes called the **fallopian tubes**. One end of each fallopian tube lies close to an ovary. The other end of each tube attaches to the **uterus**, a hollow muscular organ.

The egg usually spends about three to four days traveling through the fallopian tube to the uterus. This egg is fertile for only about a day after ovulation. Therefore, sperm must meet the egg while it is in the fallopian tube to achieve fertilization. The sperm must pass through the uterus and finally into the fallopian tube. Sperm can survive in a woman's body for as long as 72 hours (three days).

The egg eventually leaves the fallopian tube and enters the uterus. The major purpose of the uterus is to hold and nourish a fertilized egg as it develops into a baby during pregnancy.

The inner lining of the uterus is called the **endometrium**. Each month, it thickens and develops a large network of tiny blood vessels. An unfertilized egg results in the endometrium passing out of the uterus. This bloody discharge leaves the body through the vagina in the process called **menstruation**.

If the egg is fertilized, a different sequence of events takes place. Within hours, the newly fertilized egg begins to divide. By the time it leaves the fallopian tube and enters the uterus, it is a ball of many cells. This ball of cells attaches to the endometrium of the uterus in the process called *implantation*. Cell division will continue as pregnancy progresses.

The Role of Heredity

3 Humans have 23 pairs of chromosomes (46 total) in every cell of their bodies. A **chromosome** is a threadlike structure that contains hereditary information. Each chromosome is made of thousands of genes. A **gene** is the basic unit of heredity. Genes carry all the characteristics that will transfer from parent to child. Genes occur in pairs. In each pair, one gene comes from the mother, and one from the father, 5-4.

4 Each baby's traits are determined by the kinds of genes inherited from each parent. Some genes are dominant and others are recessive. The effect of a recessive gene will be masked by that

1—Activity: Compare and contrast the man's role and woman's role in reproduction.

2—Enrich: Draw a diagram of the female reproductive system, identifying each of the parts described in the chapter. Write a sentence describing the purpose of each part.

3—Vocabulary: Differentiate between a *chromosome* and a *gene*.

4—Vocabulary: Differentiate between *dominant genes* and *recessive genes*. Explain the role each plays in heredity.

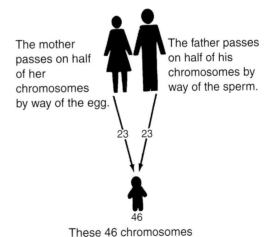

The mother passes on half of her chromosomes by way of the egg.

The father passes on half of his chromosomes by way of the sperm.

23 23

46

These 46 chromosomes determine the total heredity of the child.

5-4 _____

As the chromosomes from the sperm and egg unite, they determine a baby's total heredity.

1—Resource:
The Role of Dominant and Recessive Genes in Heredity, transparency master 5-3, TR.

2—Discuss: Why is genetic counseling so important in making responsible choices concerning family planning?

3—Discuss: Why is it important for a person to know whether he or she is a carrier for any genetic disorders?

4—Reflect: If you knew you might give birth to a child with a congenital disorder, what would you do?

5—Resource: *Family Planning Issues*, color transparency CT-5, TR.

6—Resource: *Family Planning Opinions*, Activity D, SAG.

of a dominant gene. For instance, dark hair is a dominant gene, and blond hair is recessive. A child with two dark-hair genes or one dark-hair gene and one blond-hair gene will have dark hair. A recessive trait will appear only if recessive genes from each parent combine for that particular trait. If the same child received two blond-hair genes, the child would be blond.

Genetic Counseling

Responsible family planning may include genetic counseling. **Genetic counseling** is counseling that offers scientific information and advice about heredity. Couples may seek genetic counseling to learn how likely it is their baby will be born with certain congenital disorders. **Congenital disorders** are disorders a person is born with that result from heredity. See 5-5 for a list of common congenital disorders.

Genetic counselors are usually physicians or genetics specialists. They usually begin their work by asking the prospective parents for complete family medical histories. Next, the parents are given physical exams and blood tests. In some cases, parents' chromosomes may be photographed and analyzed. These procedures can identify people who carry certain genes that cause congenital disorders. A *carrier* is a person who has genes for a disorder without suffering any of its effects. Those genes might be passed along to a carrier's child, however, and the child might inherit the disorder.

Genetic counseling cannot prevent congenital disorders. It can simply tell prospective parents the statistical chances their children will inherit these disorders, 5-6. Counselors can also tell couples how a certain disorder would affect a child and the family.

The best time for a couple to seek genetic counseling is before conception. This way they have a chance to use the information before any children are involved. They can also decide not to have children if the likelihood of a congenital disorder is high.

Some couples seek genetic counseling after pregnancy is confirmed. While genetic counseling can provide helpful information during pregnancy, a baby's life is already involved. If the baby might have a congenital disorder, couples can prepare for parenting a child with disabilities.

Issues of Family Planning

Many complex and emotional issues are involved in family planning. Each couple's decision must be based on religious, family, and personal beliefs. People who view family planning as a responsibility say every child has the right to be wanted.

Family planning decisions should be made jointly by husband and wife. Some people mistakenly believe family planning is only a women's issue because it is women who become pregnant. Both partners are affected by family planning decisions, however, so both should take responsibility for the decision making. As with other decisions, a couple must be informed before they can make the best decision for themselves.

Couples planning for the birth of their children may want to use certain family planning methods. Other couples do not want children or want to delay having children. These couples may use some form of birth control. Birth control, or contraception, is the deliberate prevention of conception or pregnancy by using any of a number of different methods. Information about family planning methods can be obtained from the couple's family physician.

Common Congenital Disorders

Disorder	Symptoms	Cause	Treatment
Cleft lip/palate	A cleft lip occurs when the two sides of the upper lip do not grow together correctly. A cleft palate is an opening that remains in the roof of the mouth. These conditions, visible from birth, interfere with breathing, talking, hearing, and eating.	Variable: often caused by a number of factors working together.	Corrective surgery and speech therapy.
Cystic fibrosis	A chemical failure affects the lungs and pancreas. Thick, sticky mucus forms in the lungs, causing breathing problems. Digestion is affected by reduced amounts of digestive juices. An excess amount of salt is excreted in perspiration.	Recessive gene.	Physical therapy, synthetic digestive hormones, salt tablets, and antibodies can relieve symptoms. No known cure exists. People often have a shorter life span because they are very vulnerable to respiratory diseases.
Diabetes	Metabolic disorders cause high blood sugar, making people feel thirsty, hungry, and weak. Weight loss is common.	A number of factors working together.	Insulin injections, along with careful diet and exercise, can control this disorder. No cure exists.
Down syndrome	Distinct physical features are evident. Common effects are slanting eyes; large, misshapen forehead; oversized tongue; curved fingers; and varying degrees of mental retardation.	Chromosome abnormality. More likely to occur when the mother is over age 35.	Special education, started as soon as possible, can help. Life span may be nearly normal.
Hydrocephalus	Extra fluid is trapped in the brain, making the head larger than normal.	A number of factors working together.	Surgical removal of excess fluid is normal. Without treatment, hydrocephalus is usually fatal.
Muscular dystrophy	A group of disorders which damage muscles, causing progressive weakness that leads to death.	Carried by the chromosomes.	There is no cure, but therapy and braces offer some relief.
Phenylketonuria (PKU)	An enzyme deficiency that makes people unable to digest a certain protein. This protein collects in the bloodstream and harms brain development.	Recessive gene.	A special diet that avoids the indigestible protein. If treated within six weeks after birth, effects of the disease can be avoided.
Sickle-cell anemia	Causes red blood cells to be sickle-shaped rather than round. Sickle cells cannot carry oxygen through the body well. The body attacks these cells, lowering the red-blood-cell count, which can cause organ damage and disability. People with sickle-cell anemia may become pale, tired, and short of breath. They have occasional pain and low resistance to infection.	Recessive gene.	No cure exists. Various treatments may relieve some symptoms. Occasional blood transfusions may be needed. Life span may be shorter than normal.
Spina bifida	Baby's backbone does not close during the prenatal period. Paralysis and problems of the bladder and bowels are common.	Cause is unknown.	May require surgery to repair the spinal column. Prenatal tests can detect spina bifida.
Tay Sachs	No symptoms until about six months of age, when baby stops growing normally. Causes a lack of a blood chemical that breaks down fatty deposits in the brain. Results in blindness and weakening muscles. Nervous system eventually stops working.	Recessive gene.	No known cure or treatment exist for Tay Sachs disease. People with Tay Sachs often die in early childhood.

1

5-5
Congenital disorders are inherited and present from birth. This chart lists the most common congenital disorders.

1—Enrich: Ask a genetic counselor to speak to students about the congenital disorders mentioned in this chart.

1—Discuss:
Compare common
causes of male and
female sterility.

Infertility

Some couples wish to achieve pregnancy, but find they cannot. Couples who cannot conceive are said to be infertile. **Infertility** is defined as the inability to achieve pregnancy despite having intercourse regularly for at least one year. Infertility occurs in as many as ten percent of marriages.

It was once widely believed that infertility was a women's problem. Today, it is understood that both men and women can experience fertility problems. In about one-fourth of all cases, both the man and the woman contribute to the problem. In the remaining three-fourths of cases, about as many men as women experience fertility problems.

Rarely, psychological stress can interfere with a couple's ability to conceive. Much more commonly, the causes of infertility are physical and require some type of medical aid. Many different physical factors can hinder fertility in both the male and the female, 5-7.

In men, most fertility problems result from problems with the sperm or semen. These problems include no sperm production, insufficient sperm production, and the production of weak sperm. Problems with sperm and semen production may be the result of certain diseases, such as the mumps. These problems may also occur after prolonged fever.

Other problems with the sperm may be due to physical or metabolic disorders, some of which may be present from birth. A man's use of alcohol and drugs can lessen his ability to produce healthy sperm. For maximum fertility, a man's entire reproductive system must be healthy and operating properly.

In women, infertility may be caused by a number of factors. First, a woman's body must be able to produce and release mature eggs. Problems with egg production, hormone production, or ovulation account for many cases of female infertility. Secondly, all a woman's reproductive organs,

5-6 _____
Genetic counselors offer factual information about heredity and the risks of congenital disorders.

including her ovaries, fallopian tubes, and uterus, must be in working order. If not, this can interfere with her ability to conceive.

Blocked fallopian tubes are a common fertility problem. The fallopian tubes must be open so eggs and sperm can unite and fertilization can occur. Blockage of the fallopian tubes may be caused by physical abnormalities or by scar tissue left from surgery or diseases. Failure of fertilized eggs to implant in the uterus is another problem couples experience. Implantation problems may be due to a number of factors.

Age is also an issue. Women's fertility begins to slowly decrease after age 30. After age 40, her fertility declines even more. Four percent of women in their twenties experience infertility compared to 21 percent for women over age 35. A man's fertility does not decline as rapidly or as early as a woman's.

If a couple has trouble conceiving, they may wish to consult their doctor. The doctor can help them discover what is causing their problem and advise them about their options. Knowing what the problem is and how they might solve it can greatly reduce the stress associated with fertility problems. Understanding the problem is the first step to solving it.

1 Options for Infertile Couples

If a couple is unable to conceive, they have several options to carefully consider. First, a couple may decide to accept their infertility and pursue goals other than parenting. More often, however, couples may wish to investigate options that could help them reach their parenting goals. Some of these options include fertility drugs, surgery, and assisted reproductive technologies, medical technologies that

1—Resource:
Options for Infertile Couples, Activity G, SAG.

2—Vocabulary:
What are *assisted reproductive technologies?* How do these procedures help couples reach their parenting goals?

Physical Causes of Infertility

In Women:

- Absence, disease, or disability of the ovaries, which prevents egg production or ovulation.

- Failure to ovulate.

- Hormone imbalance that prevents ovulation.

- Absence, disease, disability, or blockage of the fallopian tubes, which prevents the sperm from meeting the egg.

- Absence, disease, or disability of the uterus, which prevents implantation, nourishment, or development of a fertilized egg.

- Disease or disability of the cervix that prevents sperm from reaching the fallopian tubes.

- Disease or disability of the vagina that destroys sperm or blocks its entrance into the cervix.

In Men:

- Absence, disease, injury, or disability of the testes, which interferes with sperm production.

- Absence or blockage of the vas deferens, which interferes with travel of sperm to the ejaculatory duct.

- Blockage, disease, infection, or disability of the urethra, which interferes with ability to release sperm during ejaculation.

- Absence of sperm in semen.

- Insufficient amount or strength of sperm in semen.

- Problem related to erection or ejaculation.

5-7
The physical causes of infertility can be identified, and in many cases, remedied.

1—**Activity:** Collect newspaper and magazine articles about multiple births that result from the use of fertility drugs. How do these multiple births affect the parents?

2—**Enrich:** Research artificial insemination. What legal guidelines apply? When is this method most commonly used?

3—**Enrich:** Research in vitro fertilization. What legal guidelines apply? When is this method most commonly used?

4—**Discuss:** With so many unplanned pregnancies, why do you think there are still too few children available for adoption?

can aid a couple in conceiving a child. Adoption is another alternative for infertile couples.

Fertility Drugs

Fertility drugs can increase a couple's likelihood of conceiving. Doctors sometimes prescribe synthetic hormones to correct hormone imbalances. This can lead to conception. In other cases, doctors prescribe drugs that stimulate or regulate ovulation. Often, the use of fertility drugs may be a couple's first step to achieving pregnancy.

One important consideration with using these drugs, however, is the increased likelihood that couples will experience multiple births. The birth of more than one baby (twins, triplets, or more) is much more likely among mothers using fertility drugs. Couples using these drugs should be prepared to accept this possibility.

In many cases, fertility drugs are successful at solving infertility problems. Otherwise, couples may turn to more involved options, such as surgery or assisted reproduction.

Surgery

Surgery may be used to repair either a man's or a woman's reproductive system, making conception more likely. In particular, surgery can be used to repair the vas deferens and fallopian tubes so eggs and sperm can travel through these pathways. Surgery might also be used to correct problems with a woman's vagina, uterus, or cervix (mouth of the uterus) that prevent fertilization and implantation.

Artificial Insemination

Artificial insemination is one type of assisted reproduction technology. It uses technology to help couples experience pregnancy, birth, and parenthood. In **artificial insemination**, a doctor places semen, which contains sperm, directly in the upper part of a woman's vagina or uterus. This increases the chances for fertilization.

In Vitro Fertilization

In vitro fertilization is another common type of assisted reproduction technology. Couples using in vitro fertilization can experience pregnancy, birth, and parenthood. In **in vitro fertilization**, an egg is removed from a woman's ovary. The egg is then fertilized by a man's sperm in a glass dish (in vitro). After the fertilized egg has begun cell division (in one to two days), it is transferred to the woman's uterus. If the procedure is successful, the fertilized egg will implant in the uterus and develop into a baby.

The first "test-tube baby" (as babies born as a result of in vitro fertilization are sometimes called) was born in 1978. Now, many fertility clinics across the country offer this service. The process is expensive. The success rate for a single attempt is only a little over ten percent.

Adoption

Adopting a child is another way couples can experience parenthood, 5-8. An adopted child will not be biologically related to the adoptive parents. Many couples choose adoption as an alternative to biological parenthood. Decisions about adoption are permanent, however, and should be made carefully.

People wishing to adopt have two options. They can work through an adoption agency or arrange an **independent adoption**. In an independent adoption, adoptive parents do not use an agency. Instead, they may work with a doctor or lawyer to arrange an adoption. In an independent adoption, the birthparents and adoptive parents must find one another, agree to the terms of the adoption, and handle all the legal matters. Independent adoption is legal in most states.

In an **agency adoption**, adoptive parents work with a state-licensed adoption agency that helps them prepare for adoption, matches them

5-8

Adopting their son allowed this married couple to experience the joys of parenthood.

When considering an adoption, the prospective adoptive parents must also decide whether they prefer a closed or open adoption. A **closed adoption** means there is no contact between the birthparents and the adoptive parents. This type of adoption offers more privacy for both families. Before 1970, all adoptions were closed.

An **open adoption** involves some degree of contact between the birthparents and the adoptive family. The birthparents may meet the adoptive parents. They may also send letters, talk by phone, or arrange visits. In some open adoptions, the adoptive parents are present for the baby's birth. Open adoptions vary from situation to situation. Some adoptive parents may prefer to have this contact with their adopted child's birthparents.

If a couple wishes to adopt, they may wish to contact several adoption agencies in their area. They should also research the laws governing adoption in their state. Adoption counseling may help them clarify their options and choose an adoption situation that is best for them.

Choosing an Option

No matter how they attempt to resolve their fertility problems, couples have many factors to consider. Their decision has legal, financial, physical, and emotional implications.

Certain laws apply to adoption, assisted reproductive technologies, and fertility drugs. These laws determine who is eligible to adopt or use other methods. Laws also govern the procedures involved. Couples must learn the legal guidelines that apply in their case.

Most of a couple's options involve a large financial commitment. It takes money to purchase fertility drugs or pay for surgery. Assisted reproductive technologies can cost several thousand dollars for each attempt, with no guarantee pregnancy will result. Couples may not be able to afford

1 with an available child, and handles the legal matters. Agency adoptions are legal in every state.

When considering an agency adoption, couples must decide what type of agency they will use. Public adoption agencies are run by the government. They generally place children who are in the state's custody. These children may have been abandoned or surrendered to the state by their parents. Public adoption agencies place fewer infants, have much lower fees, and may have a much shorter waiting list than private adoption agencies.

Private adoption agencies are operated by organizations other than the government. Some private agencies operate for a profit, and others are associated with religious or church 2 groups. Adoptive parents may be required to pay a larger fee and wait longer to adopt through a private agency. Private adoption agencies place more infants, however.

3

1—Vocabulary: Compare *agency adoptions* and *independent adoptions*. Which would give the adoptive parents and children greater security and why?

2—Vocabulary: Compare and contrast *public* and *private adoption* agencies.

3—Reflect: Imagine you are considering becoming an adoptive parent. Would you prefer a closed adoption? Why?

1—Reflect: Compare tubal ligation and vasectomy. For couples whose families are complete, which mate do you feel should choose a permanent procedure?

5-9

Couples who have overcome a fertility problem are especially happy about the arrival of a healthy baby into their family.

these technologies, or they may go into debt trying to conceive. Adoption also requires a couple be financially stable.

Couples must also consider any risks posed to the woman's physical health. Fertility drugs, surgery, and assisted reproductive technologies may involve side effects or health risks. The couple should be aware of any risks they face and weigh these carefully.

Decisions about infertility are emotional ones. With most of their options come an uncertainty that can be difficult to handle. Even assisted reproductive technologies cannot guarantee a couple can become parents. For the couples who do become parents, however, the emotional rewards are great. They may feel their success is a miracle, 5-9.

Sterilization

Couples who do not ever want more children may choose sterilization. Sterilization is a surgical procedure that permanently prevents pregnancy. A couple might also choose sterilization if pregnancy would threaten the woman's health or their baby might inherit a congenital disorder. Sterilization surgeries are expensive and permanent.

A vasectomy is the surgical procedure of sterilization for men. It is considered permanent, so a man should be sure he does not wish to father any more children before having a vasectomy. Vasectomy can sometimes be reversed with the aid of complicated surgery, but there is no guarantee it will be effective. Only about half of reverse vasectomy surgeries are successful.

During a vasectomy, both of the vas deferens are blocked surgically. Sperm can no longer travel into the penis. Sperm are still produced, but they are absorbed by the body.

Tubal ligation is the surgical procedure of sterilization for women. It is considered permanent, so the woman should be sure she does not want to have any more children before having the surgery.

In tubal ligation, the fallopian tubes are blocked, which prevents the eggs from coming in contact with sperm. The fallopian tubes are cut, clamped with clips, or sealed closed with a laser. The woman's body will continue to release eggs, but they will disintegrate in the body.

Summary

- Responsible family planning has advantages for both parents and children.
- Several factors influence a couple's family planning decisions.
- Understanding human reproduction is an important first step in family planning.
- Responsible family planning may include genetic counseling.
- Infertility may be caused by emotional factors, but most of the causes are physical.
- Couples who cannot conceive have many options that can help them reach their parenting goals.

Reviewing Key Points

1. Name two advantages of responsible family planning.
2. Why do most authorities suggest children be spaced three to four years apart?
3. For each of the descriptions below, identify the reproductive organ described.
   A. inner lining of uterus
   B. organ containing eggs
   C. male sex cell
   D. long, narrow tube carrying sperm from epididymis to ejaculatory duct
   E. fluid containing sperm and secretions from three sets of glands
   F. hollow, muscular organ that holds and nourishes a fertilized egg as it develops
   G. organ in which sperm are produced
   H. lower portion of the uterus
   I. female sex cell
   J. tube connected at one end to the uterus and lying close to an ovary at the other end
   K. coiled tube in which sperm reach maturity
4. Briefly explain the man's role in reproduction and the woman's role in reproduction.
5. Briefly explain the relationship of dominant and recessive genes to a baby's traits.
6. What is genetic counseling?
7. What are congenital disorders? How can they be treated?
8. What does infertility mean?
9. Name two alternatives for couples who cannot conceive.
10. List two ways a couple might adopt a child.
11. Briefly explain the difference between public and private adoption agencies.
12. Name the surgical procedures for male and female sterilization.

Learning by Doing

1. Collect several articles from newspapers and magazines concerning family planning and create a bulletin board featuring these articles.
2. Interview a genetic counselor. Ask the counselor who should seek genetic counseling, when counseling should be sought, what kinds of advice may be given, and what steps a couple can take in response to this advice. Present your findings in a written report.
3. Research the effects of one of the congenital disorders described in the chapter. Can this disorder be detected by genetic counseling and prenatal tests? Is there a cure? How is the disorder treated?
4. Role play an infertile couple discussing the possibility of adopting a child. What factors might they consider?

1—Vocabulary: Compare *agency adoptions* and *independent adoptions*. Which would give the adoptive parents and children greater security?

2—Vocabulary: Compare and contrast *public and private adoption agencies.*

3—Reflect: Imagine you are considering becoming an adoptive parent. Would you prefer open or closed adoption? Why?

Thinking Critically

1. Debate the advantages of family planning as compared to "letting nature take its course."

2. Discuss how decisions about having additional children compare to decisions about having a first child.

3. Debate whether family planning is a shared responsibility. If not, which partner should have more responsibility and why? Do males in your class have different opinions on this issue than females? If so, why do you think this is?

4. In small groups, discuss how genetic counseling can benefit couples with congenital disorders in their family histories.

5. Write an essay that answers the following questions:

   ● If you and your spouse found you could not conceive, how do you think you would feel?

   ● What do you think you would do?

   ● Which options would you consider?

   ● Are there options you would not consider? Why or why not?

   ● What issues would be important to you?

Family planning can help couples become parents when they feel they can meet all the responsibilities of parenting.

Chapter 6
Pregnancy

Objectives

After studying this chapter, you will be able to

- explain the process of conception.
- describe the highlights of month-by-month prenatal development.
- identify signs that may indicate pregnancy.
- describe physical and emotional changes that occur during pregnancy.
- propose ways a husband can be involved during his wife's pregnancy.
- describe possible complications of pregnancy.

Key Terms

trimester
conception
zygote
prenatal development
blastocyst
placenta
umbilical cord
amniotic fluid
embryo
fetus
miscarriage
stillbirth
pregnancy-induced hypertension (PIH)
rubella
Rh factor disorder
sexually transmitted diseases (STDs)
AIDS (acquired immunodeficiency syndrome)
HIV (human immunodeficiency virus)

Many couples find pregnancy to be a fascinating time of life. A baby's development seems magical, yet it follows a set biological sequence. Pregnancy can be a very happy time, but it may bring fear and doubt. The months of pregnancy may seem to go by slowly. When labor finally begins, however, couples may still feel unprepared for the birth of their babies. For many couples, no other time of life is as complex as pregnancy. They may find that no other time is as mysterious, as exciting, as joyful, or as rewarding.

Conception

Pregnancy is the period during which a fertilized egg grows and develops into a human being inside the mother's body. This period lasts approximately nine months, and is divided into three trimesters. A **trimester** is a period of about three months. At the beginning of pregnancy, the mother's egg cell and the father's sperm cell unite to form a fertilized egg. By the end of the third trimester, a newborn baby is delivered into the world, 6-1.

Pregnancy begins with the union of a sperm cell and an egg cell, which is called **conception**. For conception to occur, a sequence of events must happen. Through ovulation, the woman's body released an egg that can be fertilized. The egg is fertile for about a day. If it is not fertilized during this time, it will pass through the woman's body during menstruation.

Through sexual intercourse, the man releases semen, which contains sperm, into the woman's body. A man may release as many as 200 million sperm in a single ejaculation. These sperm swim up the vagina and through the cervix, uterus, and fallopian tubes. In the fallopian tubes, sperm

1—**Vocabulary:** Look up terms in the glossary and discuss their meanings.

2—**Enrich:** Ask parents-to-be to describe how pregnancy has changed their lives.

3—**Discuss:** Describe the process of conception.

1—Resource:
Gender Determination,
color transparency
CT-6, TR.

2—Discuss: Explain it is the father's chromosomes, not the mother's that determine a baby's gender. Note that historically wives could be divorced for failure to produce a son. Was this the wives' fault?

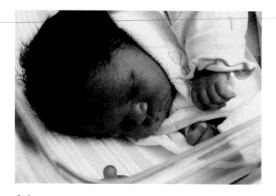

6-1
This baby developed over three trimesters of pregnancy. He started as two separate cells and developed into a human being.

come into contact with the egg. Sperm can live in the female body for as long as three to five days. Conception is likely if sperm are released into a woman's body a few days before, during, or after she ovulates.

Only about 200 sperm ever reach the egg. Those that do reach the egg will try to penetrate its surface. Eventually, one sperm will penetrate the egg. Immediately following the union of the sperm and egg, the egg prevents other sperm from entering. The egg sends out a brief electrical shock that immobilizes any sperm touching the egg. It also produces a hard outer coat that other sperm cannot penetrate. This protects the egg from being fertilized by more than one sperm.

During the next few hours, several important events occur. The nucleus of the egg cell contains the mother's genetic information. The sperm cell's nucleus carries genetic information from the father. These two separate cells join into one cell. This cell, called a **zygote**, is formed when the separate nuclei of sperm and egg combine into one nucleus.

Gender Determination

The single-celled zygote contains all the genetic information needed to

determine the gender of the developing baby. Whether the zygote will become a boy or a girl depends upon the sex chromosomes it has inherited from its parents. Each person possesses two sex chromosomes. One is inherited from the mother, and the other is inherited from the father, 6-2.

Females possess two X chromosomes. Therefore, a mother will always pass an X chromosome to her children. Males possess one X chromosome and one Y chromosome. This means that a father might pass an X chromosome to his child. If so, the child would be a girl because she would have two X chromosomes. Instead, a father might pass a Y chromosome to his child. This child would be a boy because he would have one X chromosome and one Y chromosome.

Every cell of a woman has two X chromosomes.

Every cell of a man has one X chromosome and one Y chromosome.

Every egg has one X chromosome.

Half the sperm have an X chromosome: half have a Y chromosome.

If a sperm with an X chromosome enters the egg, the result is a person with two X chromosomes—a girl.

If a sperm with a Y chromosome enters the egg, the result is a person with one X and one Y chromosome—a boy.

6-2
The sex chromosome from the father's sperm determines what gender a baby will be.

Prenatal Development

The formation of a zygote begins the *pre-embryonic stage*, which lasts from conception until about two weeks later. The pre-embryonic stage is the first stage of prenatal development. **Prenatal development** is all development that occurs between conception and birth. *Prenatal* means before birth.

The single-celled zygote begins to grow rapidly. In about a day, it divides into two cells, each of which grows and divides. This cellular division will continue as the new organism travels down the fallopian tubes and into the uterus. By ten to twelve days after fertilization, the new organism has developed into a hollow ball of cells. This ball of cells, called a **blastocyst**, implants itself into the endometrium (uterus lining). After implantation, the blastocyst will remain in the uterus and continue to grow and develop.

Parts of the blastocyst develop into the placenta. The **placenta** is a special organ that functions as an interchange between the developing baby and its mother. The placenta allows nutrients, oxygen, and water to pass from mother to the baby. It also allows the baby's waste products to pass to the mother to be eliminated. The **umbilical cord** is the flexible cord that contains blood vessels and connects the baby to the placenta, 6-3.

Still other parts of the blastocyst develop into the fetal membranes. These fetal membranes are the outer membrane, or *chorion*, and the inner membrane, or *amnion*. Together, they are called the *amnio-chorionic membrane* or "bag of waters." Inside the amnio-chorionic membrane is **amniotic fluid** that completely surrounds the baby. Amniotic fluid has several important functions. It regulates the baby's

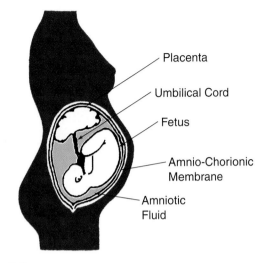

6-3 The female body undergoes many changes to provide nourishment and protection of the fetus growing inside her.

temperature. It cushions the baby against possible injury and allows the baby to move around easily.

The remaining cells of the blastocyst form the embryo. The developing baby is an **embryo** from two weeks after conception until the eighth week of pregnancy. This is called the *embryonic stage* of prenatal development. From the ninth week of pregnancy until birth, the developing baby is called a **fetus**. This is the *fetal stage* of prenatal development.

Month-by-Month Development

It is accurate to describe prenatal development by its stages—the pre-embryonic stage, the embryonic stage, and the fetal stage. This description does not explain much about *how* the baby is developing, though. The fetal period, for example, lasts about thirty-two weeks. It is difficult to easily describe how much a baby grows and changes during these thirty-two weeks.

It is much more helpful to describe prenatal development in smaller segments. For instance, studying this

1—Resource: *Pregnancy Changes,* Activity B, SAG.

2—Discuss: What are the three functions of amniotic fluid?

3—Vocabulary: Describe the difference between an *embryo* and a *fetus.*

4—Resource: *Pregnancy Terms,* Activity C, SAG.

1—Resource:
*Month-by-Month
Development*, Activity
A, SAG.

development month-by-month makes it easier to describe how a baby grows and develops before birth, 6-4.

First Month

The first month of pregnancy begins the first trimester. During this month, the developing baby begins as a zygote. It then grows into a blastocyst, and finally an embryo. Its heart, which resembles a bulging gland, begins to beat and send blood through tiny arteries. The neural tube, which will become the brain and spinal cord, begins to form. A primitive digestive system and lungs are forming. Little limb buds, which will later grow into arms and legs, appear. By the end of the first month, the embryo is about ½ inch long and weighs less than an ounce.

1

6-4
Prenatal development is most easily studied in a month-by-month fashion. Fascinating changes take place in the developing baby during each of the nine months of pregnancy.

Prenatal Development

First Trimester

Second Trimester

First Month	Second Month	Third Month	Fourth Month
• The baby becomes an embryo and is ½ inch long.	• Embryo is now 1 inch long and weighs ⅓ ounce.	• Now called a fetus, the baby is 4 inches long and weighs one ounce.	• The baby is 6 to 7 inches long and weighs about five ounces.
• First signs of the baby's heart, face, arms, legs, and lungs show.	• Arms and legs become longer and take shape.	• Fetus moves often, but cannot be felt by mother yet.	• Fingernails appear.
• The baby's brain, spinal cord, ears, and eyes begin to form.	• Liver and stomach start to work.	• Bones growing.	• The placenta is now formed.
• Tissue that will later form the baby's backbone, skull, ribs, and muscles can be seen on ultrasound.	• Eyes take on color and eyelids form.	• Kidneys working.	• The umbilical cord grows and thickens to carry enough blood and nourishment to baby.
• Heart beats and pumps blood	• Ears, nose, and mouth take shape.	• Fetus can open and close mouth and swallow.	• The baby's airways develop, but are not in use yet.
	• Head makes up nearly half of the embryo.	• Fingerprints appear.	
	• Brain grows quickly and directs the baby's movements.		

1st Month   2nd Month   3rd Month   4th Month   5th Month   6th Month

Second Month

During the second month of pregnancy, all the embryo's major body organs and systems are developing. The arms and legs become longer. Distinct wrists, elbows, hands, knees, and feet are present. Fingers and toes develop. The eyelids start to form, but are still sealed shut. The ears, nose, and mouth take shape. By the end of two months, the embryo is about 1 inch long and still weighs less than an ounce.

Third Month

Beginning with the ninth week of pregnancy, the developing baby is

1—**Activity:** List the highlights of a baby's development during each month.

Second Trimester		**Third Trimester**	
Fifth Month	Sixth Month	Seventh, Eighth, & Ninth Months	
• The baby is about 9 to 12 inches long and weighs about one pound. • Eyelashes, eyebrows, and scalp hair appear. • Blood supply to lungs increases. • Silky body hair and a waxy coating protect baby's skin from its watery surroundings.	• The baby is 12 to 14 inches long and weighs about 1½ pounds. • The baby opens and closes its eyes and can hear sounds. • The baby stretches, kicks, and sucks its thumb.	• The baby still gaining quickly in weight and length. • Bones are developed, but are soft and flexible. • Lungs have matured and can now support the baby outside the uterus.	• The outline of the baby's fist, foot, or head may be seen outside the mother's body when baby moves. • During the ninth month, the baby moves into its final position—usually head down—and stays there until birth.

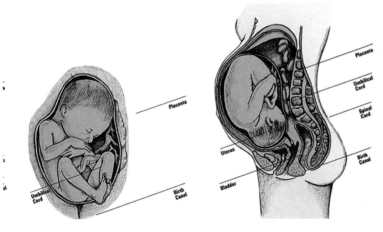

7th, 8th, & 9 Months

called a fetus. Hair starts to grow on the head. The bones are growing, and the kidneys start to work. Tooth sockets and buds for teeth are forming in the jawbones. By the end of this month, all the parts of the body are formed. For the rest of pregnancy, the baby's organs and systems will continue to develop further and grow. By the end of the third month, the fetus is about 4 inches long and weighs just over 1 ounce. This is the end of the first trimester.

Fourth Month

The fourth month begins the second trimester. The heartbeat is strong. The baby moves, kicks, sleeps, and wakes. It can swallow and urinate. The skin is transparent and thin. The placenta is fully formed and the umbilical cord continues to grow. Late in the fourth month, the mother may be able to feel the fetus move. By the end of this month, the fetus is about 6 to 7 inches long and weighs about 5 ounces.

Fifth Month

During the fifth month, eyelashes and eyebrows grow. Fine, downy hair covers the body. The fetus sleeps and wakes in a pattern. It turns from side to side, kicks, and moves a lot. The internal organs continue to grow and develop. At the end of this month, the fetus is 9 to 12 inches long and weighs ½ pound to 1 pound.

Sixth Month

During the sixth month of prenatal development, the baby opens and closes its eyes. It can hear and respond to sounds. The baby stretches, kicks, and sucks its thumb. The skin is red, wrinkled, and oily. Growth speeds up. At the end of this month, the fetus measures 12 to 14 inches and 1 to 1½ pounds. This is the end of the second trimester.

Seventh Month

The seventh month begins the third and final trimester of prenatal development. The baby kicks and stretches to exercise. The skin is still wrinkled, but fatty tissue begins developing under the surface. Covering the fetus is a thick, white protective coating called *vernix*. The bones are starting to harden. The brain, nervous system, and lungs have become much more mature. The baby begins quickly gaining weight and size. About two-thirds of babies born during the seventh month will survive. Babies born this early may have mild, moderate, or severe medical problems or disabilities. By the end of seven months, the fetus measures about 15 inches and 3 pounds.

Eighth Month

During the eighth month, the fetus continues to grow quickly in weight and size. Rapid brain growth continues. The fetus does not have as much room to move around, but it still kicks strongly. The skin is no longer wrinkled, and is now pink instead of red. The baby may position itself head-down in the uterus. At the end of the eighth month, the fetus is about 18 inches long and weighs about 5 pounds.

Ninth Month

In the last month, a fetus gains about half a pound each week. The fine, downy hair that had covered the skin has disappeared. The baby's lungs are mature. The fetus will drop down lower in the mother's abdomen in preparation for birth. By the end of nine months, full term is reached and the baby is ready to be born. The fascinating process of prenatal development is complete. At birth, babies average 19 to 21 inches in length and weigh an average of 6 to 9 pounds.

Signs of Pregnancy

The miraculous process of conception occurs within a woman's body without her even knowing it. Most of **1** the time, a woman does not know she is pregnant until several weeks after conception. In fact, most women initially suspect they are pregnant only after observing certain signs that often indicate pregnancy, 6-5.

Missed menstrual periods are the most common signs of pregnancy. This is because women do not menstruate during pregnancy. When a woman has had intercourse and her period is more than 14 days late, she probably is pregnant. If she misses another period, this probability is even stronger. If a woman's period is lighter or shorter than normal, this may also indicate pregnancy.

A missed menstrual period is not a sure sign of pregnancy. Women may stop menstruating for other reasons. These include emotional stress; changes in climate, diet, and exercise; rapid change in body weight; and chronic diseases such as anemia. A woman should see her doctor to determine the cause of the missed period. The doctor can advise her what, if anything, she can do to make her cycle more regular.

Changes in a woman's breasts may also indicate pregnancy. During pregnancy, the breasts become larger to accommodate breast milk, which will be produced to nourish the baby. A woman's breasts begin changing during the first trimester. Generally, these changes start about the same time the woman misses a menstrual period.

A woman's breasts may swell and enlarge during pregnancy. They may also become quite tender or sore. The *areola*, the pigmented area around the nipple, will become darker and wider. Since many women's breasts become tender or slightly swollen just before a menstrual period, changes in the breasts by themselves are not a sure sign of pregnancy.

Nausea is another common sign of pregnancy. The nausea that occurs during pregnancy is often called **2** "morning sickness." Although it may occur at any time of day, many women experience this nausea upon waking in the morning. About one-third of pregnant women have nausea severe enough to cause vomiting. Another third experience occasional or mild nausea. The remaining third feel no nausea at all.

Morning sickness usually occurs in the first trimester as a woman's body adjusts to being pregnant. Fatigue, a poor diet, or an empty stomach may add to the problem. If a woman experiences nausea during pregnancy, she should be sure to get plenty of sleep and eat nutritious foods. Eating several small meals a day rather than two or three large ones may also help. If the nausea is severe enough to cause routine vomiting, a woman should consult her doctor.

Increased urination is another sign of pregnancy. During the first trimester, the uterus grows and pushes against the bladder. This pressure

---

Signs of Pregnancy

Missed menstrual period

Changes in the breasts

Nausea

Increased urination

Fatigue

6-5
Many signs can indicate pregnancy. No single sign is, by itself, a sure sign of pregnancy.

1—Discuss: Some signs of pregnancy are quite obvious, others less obvious. Distinguish between them.

2—Discuss: If morning sickness occurs, what can a pregnant woman do to ease the problem?

1—Discuss: How do pregnancy tests work? What do they detect?

2—Discuss: Identify reasons for using a home pregnancy test and reasons for using a lab test to detect pregnancy.

3—Reflect: In the future, if you (or your spouse) were pregnant, how do you think you would feel about your (or her) changing body? Why?

on her bladder causes the pregnant woman to urinate more frequently.

Fatigue is another sign of pregnancy. As a woman's body adjusts to pregnancy, she may feel very tired. She may sleep more than usual and need to take naps. For some pregnant women, this fatigue lasts throughout the first trimester. By itself, fatigue is not a sure sign of pregnancy. Fatigue can occur for many other reasons.

Pregnancy Tests

If a woman suspects she is pregnant, she should have a pregnancy test done to confirm she is indeed pregnant. The way a pregnancy test works is fairly simple. A hormone called *HCG* **1** *(Human Chorionic Gonadotropin)* is secreted by the blastocyst as early as a week after conception. Pregnancy tests use antibodies that react to the HCG in a blood or urine sample.

If a woman is pregnant, her body will produce the HCG hormone. The antibodies in the pregnancy test will cause a chemical reaction to any HCG in the blood or urine sample. Observing this reaction confirms the woman has this hormone and is pregnant.

If the reaction does not occur, the woman is probably not pregnant. If she continues having symptoms of pregnancy, she should be tested again in a few days. Sometimes a reaction does not occur because the woman's level of HCG is too low for the test to detect. This means she has taken the test too soon in her pregnancy for the test to confirm her pregnancy. When she is tested again, her level of HCG will have risen if she is pregnant. This second test should indicate whether she is pregnant.

A woman may choose to first use a home pregnancy test. She can buy this test over-the-counter in a grocery or drug store. Home pregnancy tests are fairly inexpensive. They require a sample of the woman's urine. A woman should read the directions and follow them carefully. Some home pregnancy tests can detect pregnancy as early as the first day of a missed menstrual period. The level of accuracy in home pregnancy tests varies from one test to another. Home pregnancy tests are less accurate than lab tests done in a doctor's office.

If a home pregnancy test is positive, the woman should make an appointment with her doctor. The doctor will have a lab test done to confirm the pregnancy. The lab test will **2** require the woman to give a sample of her blood or urine. Also, if she is pregnant, she will need to talk with her doctor about her pregnancy and the medical care she will need. Prenatal care is described in Chapter 7.

Some women do not use a home pregnancy test, but go directly to their doctor's offices for lab tests. These women may worry a home pregnancy test will be inaccurate. They may feel certain they are pregnant and know they will need a doctor's care.

Physical Changes During Pregnancy

A woman's body undergoes dramatic changes during pregnancy. The basic changes are much the same for all women. No two pregnancies are exactly alike, however, even for the same woman.

The most obvious changes during pregnancy are the increased size of a woman's breasts and abdomen, 6-6. Many pregnant women have mixed **3** emotions about their changing body shape. A woman may be very excited

6-6

The most obvious physical change during pregnancy is a woman's body shape. Her breasts and abdomen grow larger as the pregnancy progresses.

when she first notices the tiny bulge in her abdomen. When her pregnancy starts to show, it may begin to seem more real to her. A woman may enjoy the way her body looks as her abdomen grows. She might also feel embarrassed or less attractive. A woman may feel she is growing fat as her size increases. She should remember her shape is changing because the baby is growing inside her, not because she is fat.

As her breasts and abdomen grow, a woman's skin must stretch as well. As her skin stretches, the tissues just below the skin surface may tear. This can cause pink or red marks called *stretch marks* to appear on her skin. After pregnancy, these marks usually fade into faint, silvery lines. A slow, even weight gain within the doctor's recommendations is the best way to prevent stretch marks. Rapidly gaining too much weight will cause more stretching and more stretch marks. Daily massaging with cream or lotion helps keep the skin soft and supple. This may reduce the amount of tearing and stretch marks.

Pregnancy may also affect a woman's digestive system. During the first trimester, she may experience nausea. Toward the end of pregnancy, as the growing fetus exerts more pressure on her stomach and intestines, she may feel heartburn and indigestion. If a woman is bothered by these problems, she should talk with her doctor. Often, changing what she eats can help. Nutritional needs during pregnancy are described in Chapter 7.

Internal pressure also affects the bladder. Early in pregnancy, the growing uterus pushes against the bladder and causes the woman to urinate more often. In the middle months, the fetus moves out of the pelvic region and into the abdomen, which lessens pressure on the bladder. Late in pregnancy, the growing baby again puts pressure on the bladder, causing a need to urinate more frequently. This may be eased when the baby drops lower into the pelvis in preparation for birth.

Emotional Changes During Pregnancy

Emotional changes during pregnancy aren't as obvious as physical ones, but they are just as real. Like the physical changes, they can be described only in generalities. These changes vary widely from woman to

1—**Discuss:** Why do stretch marks sometimes appear? How can they be controlled?

2—**Reflect:** Pregnancy causes many changes in emotions. Why do mood changes vary greatly among different women?

1—Discuss: Husbands, as well as wives, can have emotional changes related to pregnancy. Why might this occur?

2—Discuss: Why is having a baby often a bigger adjustment than getting married?

3—Discuss: Why is it important for each spouse to support the other? How can couples do this?

woman and from pregnancy to pregnancy. An important influence on a woman's emotions is how she feels about being pregnant. Women who are happy about being pregnant usually adjust much easier than women who are unhappy about pregnancy.

Hormones cause many of a woman's emotional changes during pregnancy. A woman's hormone levels change dramatically during pregnancy, which can cause mood swings. Some mood changes are short-lived. A woman may become upset easily or cry for no reason. She may crave foods she has never liked before. A woman may become angry or frustrated more easily than before she was pregnant. She may worry about her emotional health and whether these mood changes are normal.

Other mood changes are more subtle, but long-lasting. Throughout pregnancy, a woman may feel more self-assured and confident. She may be filled with hope and optimism. Another woman may feel more depressed and worry throughout pregnancy. She may be afraid of miscarriage, having a baby with congenital disorders, or having a difficult delivery.

The Husband's Emotions

A man's hormones do not change when his wife is pregnant, but he also experiences emotional changes. He may be upset by his wife's sudden mood changes. He may blame himself, thinking he has somehow made her angry. Other times, he may become angry with his wife for acting so strangely. He may worry she will never regain her prepregnancy behavior and personality.

A husband usually shares many of his wife's worries and doubts. He may worry the baby will not be healthy or his wife will have a difficult delivery. He may feel anxious about driving his wife to the hospital when she is in labor or participating during the delivery. He may wonder whether he will be a good father.

These feelings are normal. Despite any negative feelings, however, most husbands are truly excited about the upcoming birth of their children. A husband may think his wife has never looked so beautiful. He may be happy about becoming a father.

The Couple's Relationship

Pregnancy triggers dramatic changes in each spouse's life, as well as in the couple's married life. It is normal, even healthy, for a couple to wonder what their life will be like after the baby arrives. If this is their first child, the couple must adjust to the idea they are going to be parents. At first, this concept may seem a little hard for them to believe, 6-7. Their family structure will change, and they will enter a new stage of the family life cycle.

Talking about the emotions they are experiencing can bring an expectant couple closer together. It is helpful for each spouse to share both positive and negative emotions. The more a husband and wife communicate, the more they learn about one another. By knowing each other better, they will find it easier to love, support, and understand each other.

When one spouse expresses negative feelings, the other can listen and offer reassurance. Sharing positive feelings with a spouse can lift his or her spirits. Each partner can remind the other they are a team and together they will successfully adjust to becoming parents.

There may be times when one or both spouses wish the pregnancy had never happened. This is normal, even in a happy marriage where both spouses really want a child. Fearing the unknown makes them human. By talking about their feelings, spouses can

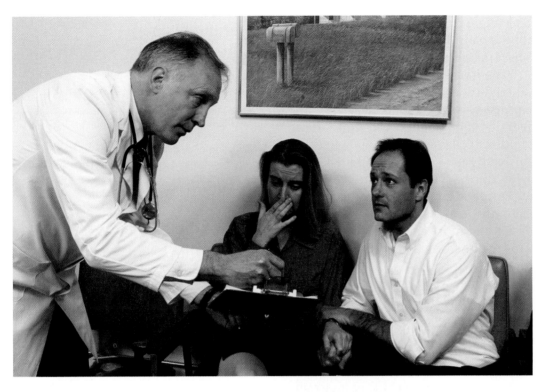

6-7 _____
Couples may have
many reactions to
the news of a preg-
nancy. A combina-
tion of joy, pride,
fear, concern, and
confusion is
normal.

help each other overcome these fears.
Together, they will be able to look
forward to the birth of their baby.

The Expectant Couple as a Team

As a husband and wife share the
emotions and experiences of pregnancy, they may feel closer to one
another. The couple can work together
as they prepare for the birth of their
child. This spirit of teamwork draws
the couple closer together. It also
strengthens their relationship, 6-8.

The husband cannot physically
experience pregnancy, but he can be
actively involved in his wife's pregnancy. There are many ways he can
participate in the pregnancy. Most
importantly, the father-to-be can support and encourage his pregnant wife.
He can encourage her to eat well-
balanced meals and get enough sleep.
He can exercise with her, which will
put both of them in the best possible
shape. The father-to-be can help
his pregnant wife with some of the

6-8 _____
A husband's loving support is the most
important way he can participate in his
wife's pregnancy.

1—Discuss: Propose
ways fathers can be
involved during preg-
nancy. Is it important
for expectant couples
to work as a team?
Why or why not?

housecleaning tasks and child care
tasks (if the couple has other children).

The expectant couple can work
together to prepare for the baby's
arrival. They can shop for the furniture,
clothes, toys, and supplies the baby
will need. The father may enjoy
putting together the baby's crib or

rearranging the house to make room for the baby. A father may want to help select possible names for the baby.

The husband can also go to prenatal medical checkups with his wife. He can listen to the baby's heartbeat and feel its movements. He can attend childbirth classes with his wife. The husband may choose to be with his wife during labor and delivery. His support and coaching during labor and delivery can make the experience easier and more enjoyable for his wife. This way, he can also participate in the birth of their baby.

A father who has been involved throughout the pregnancy is likely to stay involved after the baby is born. He and his wife will probably share the joys and burdens of caring for the newborn. As this sharing continues, it will enrich all aspects of their marriage and their life as a family.

Complications During Pregnancy

Most pregnancies proceed normally. Sometimes, however, complications occur. These complications may be caused by nature or by the lack of proper health care during pregnancy. Some of these complications can be prevented or treated. Others simply run their course.

In many cases, complications are preceded by warning signals. If a pregnant woman notices any of the warning signals listed in 6-9, she should contact her doctor at once. Proper medical attention and care reduce the risk of serious, untreatable complications.

Two of the most common complications that can occur during pregnancy

Warning Signals

Bleeding from the vagina.

Severe or continuing nausea or vomiting.

Continuing or severe headache.

Swelling or puffiness of the face or hands, or marked swelling of the feet and ankles.

Blurring of vision or spots before the eyes.

A marked decrease in the amount of urine passed.

Pain or burning while passing urine.

Chills and fever.

Sharp or continuous abdominal pain.

Sudden gush of liquid from the vagina before the baby is due.

6-9

Reacting promptly to one of these warning signals may help avoid serious complications during pregnancy.

are miscarriage and stillbirth. Other common complications include pregnancy-induced hypertension, rubella, and Rh factor disorder. Sexually transmitted diseases (STDs) may also complicate a woman's pregnancy and affect her baby.

Miscarriage and Stillbirth

Miscarriage refers to the natural ending of a pregnancy before the fifth month. The natural ending of a pregnancy after the fifth month is called a **stillbirth**. Doctors often refer to miscarriage and stillbirth as *spontaneous abortion.*

Miscarriages may occur in as many as one-fourth of pregnancies. Most occur during the first trimester, often before a woman even suspects she is pregnant. Other times, a woman may lose her pregnancy as late as the eighth month.

No single factor explains all miscarriages and stillbirths. The causes may vary. Over 60 percent of miscarriages are due to chromosome problems in the embryo or fetus. If the baby is not developing normally, it may not survive. Miscarriage may occur.

Miscarriage can also be caused when the developing baby is exposed to harmful substances or illnesses. Habits of the mother, such as smoking, drinking, and using drugs, can lead to miscarriage. Some sexually transmitted diseases or other infections can result in death of the fetus.

No matter what the cause, miscarriage or stillbirth can be a tragic event. Emotional trauma may be greatest for the woman. Both partners may feel intense sadness and grief over the loss of the child they were expecting.

Couples who have experienced a miscarriage or stillbirth may worry about their ability to have other children. Fortunately, a miscarriage generally will not prevent a couple from having successful pregnancies in the future. This may be little consolation while the couple is grieving their loss, however.

Many doctors suggest couples wait three to six months after a miscarriage or stillbirth before trying to conceive again. This time will allow the woman's body to recuperate and allow the couple to grieve their loss.

Pregnancy-Induced Hypertension

Pregnancy-induced hypertension (PIH) is a condition that affects a woman's kidneys, heart, or blood circulation. It usually develops gradually during the second half of pregnancy. The symptoms of PIH include an abnormal rise in blood pressure, rapid weight gain, swollen face and fingers, headaches, and blurred vision. If a woman notices these symptoms, she should contact her doctor at once, 6-10.

6-10
A woman's doctor wants her to call if she has any questions or concerns about her pregnancy. Obstetricians handle many such calls every day.

PIH can result from a lack of proper nutrition and health care during pregnancy. Medical authorities are disturbed by an increase of PIH cases. PIH is most common in teen pregnancies. Pregnant teens are the least likely to receive proper medical attention early in pregnancy. They are also less likely to eat well-balanced meals. PIH may also occur in the pregnancies of women who have abnormally low weight gains.

In mild cases, PIH can be treated with a carefully monitored, nutritious diet and bed rest. Severe cases may require hospitalization. If it is not treated, PIH can cause convulsions and the pregnant woman's death.

Rubella

Rubella (also called German measles) is a virus that can cause miscarriage, stillbirth, or serious congenital disorders. Rubella poses the greatest threat during the first trimester of pregnancy.

For the woman, the symptoms are quite mild. She will have a low-grade fever, a rash, and swollen lymph glands in the neck. For the fetus, the effects are much worse. If the baby survives, he or she may have vision,

1—Enrich: Research the causes of miscarriage and stillbirth.

2—Reflect: How do you think you might feel if you and your spouse experienced a miscarriage or stillbirth?

3—Discuss: Why is PIH common in teen pregnancies?

4—Discuss: Research how rubella affects a pregnant woman and her child.

hearing, or heart problems. Mental disability may also occur. A pregnant woman should inform her doctor if she thinks she has been exposed to rubella. Blood tests can determine if she is infected.

Rubella can be prevented by a vaccine. The rubella vaccine should not be confused with the regular measles vaccine. The two vaccinations are different. The best time to be vaccinated is during childhood. Adult women should be vaccinated only if they are sure they are not pregnant. After receiving the shot, women should avoid becoming pregnant for at least three months. The rubella vaccine itself poses a risk to a fetus.

Rh Factor Disorder

Early in pregnancy, a woman's blood is tested for a substance called *Rh factor*. Most people have the Rh factor in their blood. These people are Rh positive (Rh+). In most cases, both mother and baby are Rh+. Only about 15 percent of people do not have the Rh factor in their blood. They are Rh negative (Rh−).

Rh factor disorder occurs when a mother who is Rh− gives birth to a baby who is Rh+. During pregnancy, the mother and baby exchange substances through the placenta. The fetus produces substances that enter the pregnant woman's blood. Some of these substances contain Rh+ cells. These cells are incompatible with the mother's Rh− blood cells.

Once the Rh+ cells are in the woman's bloodstream, her body produces certain antibodies to fight them. These antibodies may cross the placenta and pass into the baby's bloodstream. In the baby's bloodstream, these antibodies will destroy red blood cells. This can cause anemia, brain damage, and even death of the fetus.

Rh factor disorder is not usually a problem in first pregnancies. It takes time for antibodies to develop. In second or future pregnancies, more antibodies are present and the risk to the fetus is much greater.

Rh factor disorder can be easily treated with a vaccine called RhoGAM. This medicine destroys any antibodies the mother may have built up during pregnancy. An Rh− mother should receive this shot during the 28th week of pregnancy and again 72 hours after delivery. She should also receive this shot in every future pregnancy.

Sexually Transmitted Diseases

Sexually transmitted diseases (STDs) are a number of infections and conditions that are passed from one person to another through sexual contact. STDs have serious health consequences. They threaten a person's health, fertility, and in some cases, a

6-11

Avoiding STDs is essential for a healthy pregnancy. Waiting until marriage to begin a sexual relationship is the best way couples can protect themselves from STDs.

person's life. Pregnant women with STDs endanger the health of their unborn children as well as their own health. A couple should keep themselves free of STDs for their own health and the health of their unborn children, 6-11.

Gonorrhea

Gonorrhea is a bacterial STD that affects almost a million people each year. It is asymptomatic, especially in women. In men who do have symptoms, discharge from the penis and painful urination are common. Women may experience an abnormal vaginal discharge or uterine bleeding; painful urination; and infection of the vagina, urethra, and fallopian tubes.

A medical exam and culture can detect gonorrhea. Doctors can prescribe medicine to clear up the infection and cure gonorrhea. If left untreated, gonorrhea can cause arthritis, heart disease, infertility, and eye infections that can cause blindness.

Miscarriage and stillbirth are more common in pregnant women with gonorrhea. A woman can pass gonorrhea to her baby during delivery as the baby passes through the birth canal. Newborns who contract gonorrhea during delivery develop an eye infection that leads to blindness. Since gonorrhea is so common, all newborns are treated with special eyedrops just after birth. These medicated eyedrops can prevent gonorrheal eye infection.

Syphilis

Syphilis is an STD that is carried by a bacterium. The first symptom is a sore, called a *chancre*, that appears 10 and 90 days after contact. The sore heals by itself four to six weeks later, but the disease does not go away.

Untreated syphilis passes through a second stage that includes a fever, rash, headaches, and sore throat. It may also cause wartlike growths, fluid-filled sores, hair loss, and a loss of appetite. These symptoms may also disappear on their own. If syphilis remains untreated, it will damage the person's internal organs. Years later, this damage may cause heart problems, insanity, blindness, paralysis, or even death.

Syphilis can cause serious damage to an unborn child. Pregnant women are usually tested for syphilis early in pregnancy. Treatment during early pregnancy is possible, preventing the disease from affecting the baby. If it is not treated early, syphilis will pass through the placenta to the fetus. Miscarriage or stillbirth may occur. Babies who survive will develop congenital syphilis, which can cause various physical disabilities.

Genital Herpes

Herpes occurs in different forms, and not every form is an STD. The form of herpes that is an STD is called by many different names. It may be called *herpes simplex virus type 2 (HSV-2), herpes II,* or *genital herpes*. Genital herpes is a serious STD that has no cure.

Most people with genital herpes experience symptoms of genital herpes within 2 to 20 days after contact. The most noticeable symptom is blisters or sores that appear on the genitals. Other symptoms may include headaches, fever, aching muscles, and swollen glands.

These symptoms usually disappear in a week or two, but the disease is still present in the body. It may flare up at irregular intervals, causing the symptoms to reappear. Although there is no cure, persons with genital herpes should seek medical attention. They should learn how to prevent these flare-ups and spreading the disease.

Pregnant women with genital herpes may experience miscarriage or stillbirth. A woman with genital herpes may infect her baby during pregnancy.

1—Activity: Prepare a chart describing various STDs, the symptoms, and how the baby can be affected.

2—Resource: *Understanding STDs—Symptoms and Health Risks,* reproducible master 6-2, TR.

3—Discuss: Review which STDs can be treated and which are incurable. Review which of these diseases can cause miscarriage and stillbirth

1—**Note:** Pelvic inflammatory disease is a serious condition that can affect a woman's fertility. It is caused by other untreated infections, such as chlamydia.

2—**Note:** The Centers for Disease Control estimates 40,000 new HIV infections occur each year. What can people do to lower their risk?

Babies can also contract the disease by passing through the birth canal during vaginal delivery. For this reason, doctors often recommend cesarean delivery for pregnant women with genital herpes. Newborns infected with genital herpes may develop a number of congenital disabilities.

Chlamydia

One of the most widespread STDs is *chlamydia*. In many cases, chlamydia is asymptomatic. When symptoms appear, they do so in one to five weeks. Men may notice a discharge from the penis, a burning or itching sensation, and painful urination. Women may notice abnormal discharge or bleeding from the vagina, abdominal or pelvic pain, and painful urination.

Chlamydia is a major cause of urinary tract infections in both men and women. Women may also develop *pelvic inflammatory disease (PID)*, an infection of the female reproductive tract that can lead to infertility. Medical tests can detect chlamydia, and it can be cured with antibiotics.

Pregnant women with chlamydia can pass it to their babies during delivery. Newborns with chlamydia may develop serious eye, ear, and lung infections. In severe cases, these infections may even lead to death of the newborn.

HIV/AIDS

AIDS is one of the biggest health risks of our time. Currently, there is no vaccine to prevent it and there is no cure. **AIDS (acquired immunodeficiency syndrome)** is a disease that breaks down a person's immune system. The immune system fights illness and heals the body. Someone with a weak immune system is more likely to become very sick and less likely to recover.

AIDS is caused by **HIV (human immunodeficiency virus)**. This virus enters a person's body and slowly begins to destroy the immune system, leaving the body vulnerable to diseases a healthy body could easily resist. When a person's immune system can no longer protect him or her from life-threatening illnesses, AIDS develops.

The HIV virus is usually asymptomatic. It can take as long as ten years for a person to notice symptoms of the virus. HIV is primarily transmitted sexually. People can acquire the virus during sexual contact with the blood, semen, or vaginal fluids of infected partners. People with multiple sexual partners are at the greatest risk of acquiring HIV.

The HIV virus can also be contracted by sharing intravenous needles. People may use intravenous needles to inject drugs (usually illegal drugs) into their veins. If a person who has HIV shares a needle with another person, this person could contract HIV.

Before 1985, some people acquired the virus through blood transfusions. All blood now is tested for HIV, so it is very unlikely people can still contract AIDS in this manner. There is no risk of contracting HIV by donating blood. HIV is also not spread through the air, by insects, or through casual contact such as hugging or a handshake.

The HIV virus can also be passed from mother to child during pregnancy, delivery, or breast-feeding. About one-fourth of babies born to HIV-infected mothers contract the virus. A pregnant woman may be unaware she has HIV until her infant shows symptoms of the virus. Most infected babies will eventually develop AIDS and die.

Summary

- Conception is the union of an egg and sperm. It is the beginning of pregnancy.

- Pregnancy can be divided into three stages according to the baby's development. These are the pre-embyonic stage, the embryonic stage, and the fetal stage.

- Prenatal development is the development that occurs between conception and birth. It is most easily studied month-by-month.

- A woman may notice several signs that lead her to suspect she is pregnant. Having a pregnancy test done can confirm whether she is pregnant.

- During the nine months of pregnancy, a woman's body grows and changes to accommodate the growing baby within her. Certain physical changes are common.

- Emotional changes may occur during pregnancy for both the wife and husband. As they share their emotions and experience pregnancy together, their relationship can become stronger.

- Several complications may occur during pregnancy. A pregnant woman should be familiar with these complications so she can watch for warning signs during her pregnancy.

Reviewing Key Points

1. What is a trimester? How many trimesters occur during pregnancy?
2. Identify when during pregnancy the developing baby is called each of the following:
   A. zygote
   B. blastocyst
   C. embryo
   D. fetus
3. Describe the purposes of the placenta and the umbilical cord.
4. What three things does the amniotic fluid do?
5. In which month does each of the following occur?
   A. the baby's eyes open
   B. the baby's heart beats
   C. the baby's lungs are mature
6. Describe how a baby's gender is determined.
7. List three signs of pregnancy.
8. Name the hormone pregnancy tests detect.
9. What can the husband do to stay actively involved throughout the pregnancy? What benefits are likely to result from his involvement?
10. Differentiate between miscarriage and stillbirth.
11. What causes the largest percentage of miscarriages?
12. Describe the symptoms of PIH.
13. True or false. The effects of rubella are much more severe for a pregnant woman than for the fetus she is carrying.
14. Carmen and Consuela are pregnant. Carmen is Rh– and Consuela is Rh+. Which woman will experience Rh factor disorder?
15. Name three STDs and describe the possible effects of each on a newborn baby.

1

2

1—Activity: Review and outline this chapter emphasizing the information you found most useful.

2—Answers: Answers to review questions are located in the front section of this TAE.

Learning by Doing

1. Design a poster that shows month-by-month prenatal development.

2. Interview a woman who has been pregnant about the physical changes she experienced during pregnancy. Which ones were the most uncomfortable? How did the woman adjust to these changes? Share your findings in an oral report.

3. Select one of the complications of pregnancy discussed in the chapter. Research the topic further and prepare a written report.

4. Read a magazine or newspaper article about pregnancy. Discuss your article in a small group discussion.

5. Investigate the resources for pregnancy counseling in your area through the telephone book, school nurse, health clinics, hospitals, etc. Create a pamphlet that describes these counseling resources.

Thinking Critically

1. Write a paragraph explaining the process of conception.

2. Debate whether you think couples should use home pregnancy tests, laboratory tests, or both to confirm pregnancy.

3. In a small group, discuss the emotional changes that occur during pregnancy. Be sure to consider both the wife's and the husband's emotional changes.

4. Write an essay describing how a father should be involved during pregnancy. If you are female, propose ways you would like your husband to be involved in your pregnancy. If you are a male, propose ways you would like to be involved in your wife's pregnancy.

5. In a small group, discuss how you think the complications described in the chapter might affect a couple's experience during pregnancy. How might these complications make them feel? Which ones are especially threatening for the baby? How can couples prevent these complications?

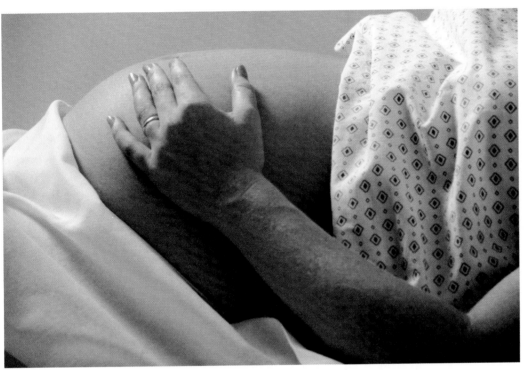

There are many changes during pregnancy, both physical and emotional.

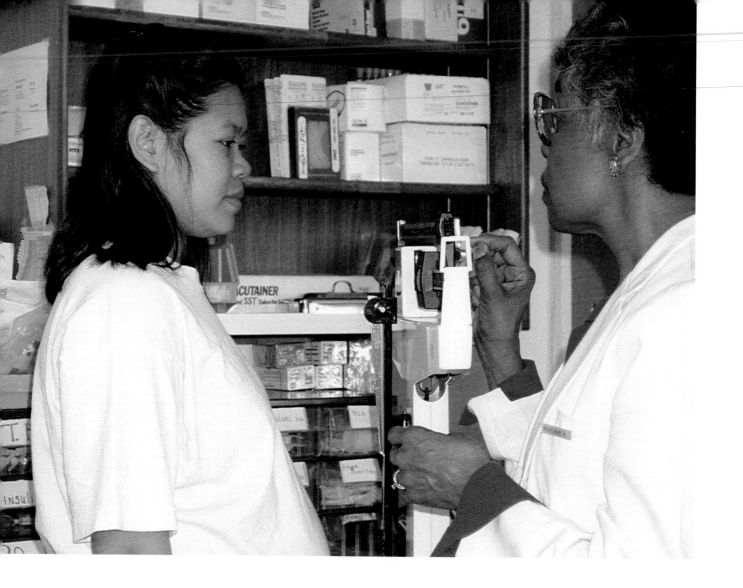

Chapter 7
Prenatal Care

Objectives

After studying this chapter, you will be able to

- summarize the importance of quality prenatal care that begins early in pregnancy.
- describe medical care needed.
- compare and contrast the three types of prenatal tests.
- identify basic nutritional needs during pregnancy.
- plan a daily menu that meets a woman's needs during pregnancy.
- explain why proper weight gain is important.
- summarize the importance of exercise.
- describe various factors that increase health risks to mother and baby.

Key Terms

prenatal care
obstetrician
certified nurse-midwife
ultrasound test
chorionic villi sampling (CVS)
amniocentesis
Food Guide Pyramid
anemia
fetal alcohol syndrome (FAS)
sudden infant death syndrome (SIDS)

Prenatal care is the name for the special care a woman and her developing baby need during pregnancy. When some people mention prenatal care, they may be talking only about the medical care a doctor provides during pregnancy. While medical care is very important, it is only one component of prenatal care. A woman's nutrition, weight gain, and exercise are also included. Another component of prenatal care involves avoiding certain factors that increase health risks to the mother and fetus. All the special considerations that are important during pregnancy are part of prenatal care.

Pregnancy is a special time in a woman's life. The way she cares for herself will greatly affect her baby's health. Babies are more likely to be born healthy if their mothers begin to follow good prenatal care practices early in pregnancy. In fact, if a woman is considering becoming pregnant, she should strive to be in the best health possible *before* her pregnancy, 7-1.

Medical Care During Pregnancy

As soon as a woman notices symptoms of pregnancy, she should visit a doctor for a pregnancy test. Her husband may wish to go with her. The couple may visit their family physician, an obstetrician, or a certified nurse-midwife. An **obstetrician** is a doctor who specializes in providing medical care for pregnant women and delivering babies. A **certified nurse-midwife** is a nurse practitioner who has extensive training and experience delivering babies and providing prenatal care.

1—Vocabulary: Look up terms in the glossary and discuss their meanings.

2—Resource: *Prenatal Health Care*, reproducible master 7-1, TR.

3—Vocabulary: Define *prenatal care*. What is involved in prenatal care?

4—Discuss: Why should a woman strive to be in the best health possible before becoming pregnant?

1—**Discuss:** Why is the first prenatal visit important? What is done at this appointment? Why might a woman's partner wish to go with her?

2—**Resource:** *Ask the Doctor,* Activity A, SAG.

3—**Enrich:** The costs of having a baby vary. Research costs in your area, including doctors' fees, hospital charges, and costs for delivery, use of the birthing room, and nursery services. How are most costs covered?

7-1 _____

Being physically fit is a good way for a woman to prepare her body for a healthy pregnancy.

Most couples are referred to an obstetrician or nurse-midwife by friends or relatives. Other couples call a local hospital or the American Medical Association for a list of obstetricians and nurse-midwives in the area. A couple should choose a doctor or nurse-midwife who helps them feel comfortable, confident, and secure. If they have specific wishes concerning childbirth procedures, they should find a professional who will accept their wishes. A woman should receive a doctor's care as early as possible in pregnancy.

The First Medical Visit

The first medical visit is an important one. The doctor or nurse-midwife will review the couple's medical histories for possible congenital disorders. He or she will also ask the woman what signs of pregnancy she has noticed. The doctor will also want to know about any previous pregnancies and deliveries the woman has had. A woman should tell her doctor or nurse-midwife if she drinks, smokes, or takes any drugs. She should also tell her doctor if she has ever had any STDs.

A lab test will be done to confirm her pregnancy. Next, the woman will be given a thorough physical examination, including a pelvic exam. The woman will be weighed and her blood pressure will be taken.

After pregnancy is confirmed, the doctor will describe what changes the woman should expect and what health guidelines she should follow. He or she will schedule a series of checkups to monitor the health of both the pregnant woman and the developing fetus.

The doctor or nurse-midwife will also answer any questions the couple may have. One of their first questions may be about when the baby will be born. To answer this, the doctor will need to know the date of the first day of the woman's last regular menstrual period. The doctor will then calculate the probable due date using the simple formula shown in 7-2. The average duration of pregnancy is 280 days, which is about 40 weeks or just over nine months.

Another important question may concern the costs involved in prenatal care and delivery. Each doctor or nurse-midwife has different policies about fees. Fees may vary with a couple's specific needs, the location of the office, and other factors.

An expectant couple should review their insurance coverage and discuss payment of the fees with their medical professional. If the couple has insurance, most of the medical care costs during pregnancy may be covered. In some cases, they may have to pay an amount called a co-pay or a deductible for some services. In other cases, all office visits may be covered by a single fee.

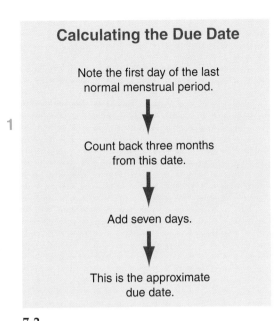

Calculating the Due Date

Note the first day of the last normal menstrual period.

↓

Count back three months from this date.

↓

Add seven days.

↓

This is the approximate due date.

7-2 _____

Counting from the first day of the last regular menstrual period, pregnancy lasts an average of nine months.

If a couple does not have insurance, they should consider their options for paying the medical bills. The topic of money should not, however, cause a woman to delay her first medical visit. It is very important to their baby's survival and health that a woman receive quality medical care early in pregnancy. If they cannot afford this care, they should visit their local social services office or health department to learn what, if any, help they can provide with affordable medical care.

Medical Checkups During Pregnancy

About one month following an expectant mother's first medical visit, she should have another checkup with her doctor or nurse-midwife. For the first seven months of pregnancy, checkups are usually recommended once a month. During the eighth month, visits generally increase to twice a month. By the ninth month, a pregnant woman should have medical checkups once a week until the baby arrives.

During these checkups, the woman's weight gain, blood pressure, and general health will be checked. The doctor will also check the size of the mother's uterus to be sure the pregnancy is proceeding normally. When the baby's heartbeat and movements become obvious, the baby's growth and activity will be charted at each visit, 7-3. Near the end of pregnancy, the doctor or nurse-midwife will examine the cervix to check if it is preparing for labor and delivery.

The Centers for Disease Control recommend women who are in their third trimester of pregnancy during flu season should receive an influenza vaccine. A woman can receive this vaccine during a prenatal checkup in her doctor's office.

Prenatal checkups give the doctor or nurse-midwife a chance to monitor any possible problems. He or she can also advise the expectant mother about what she should or should not do in terms of exercise, nutrition, weight gain, and general health practices.

Many fathers accompany their wives for these medical checkups, 7-4. This way both parents can ask any questions or share any concerns they might have with their medical professional. Fathers, as well as mothers, enjoy learning how their babies are

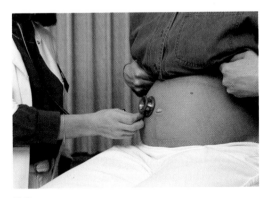

7-3 _____

During later prenatal visits, the doctor uses a stethoscope to listen to the baby's heartbeat. The mother and father can usually listen to the heartbeat, too.

1—**Activity:** Using pretend dates and names, calculate several due dates.

2—**Enrich:** Ask an obstetrician to describe the typical procedures involved in a pregnant woman's checkups.

1

2

7-4 _____
Fathers can be more involved during pregnancy if they accompany their wives to prenatal visits. Fathers often want to ask the doctor questions and learn more about pregnancy and childbirth.

1—Discuss:
Describe how the ultrasound test works. What can this test reveal?

growing and developing. A couple's good relationship with their obstetrician or nurse-midwife helps them have a healthy pregnancy and a healthy baby.

Prenatal Tests

During medical checkups, special prenatal tests may be used to determine the position, size, or development of the fetus. Prenatal tests can also determine if the fetus has a congenital disorder. If tests reveal a possible problem with the pregnancy, the parents can prepare themselves to care for an infant with a disability. Three main prenatal tests are used. These are the ultrasound test, chorionic villi sampling, and amniocentesis.

The **ultrasound test** provides a way to view the position and development of the fetus. This test can show if the mother is carrying more than one fetus. It can also reveal certain physical disabilities the baby might have.

The ultrasound can reveal how far into the pregnancy the woman is and

the baby's probable due date. Later in pregnancy, an ultrasound test can reveal the gender of the baby. Some parents are eager to know whether their baby will be a boy or girl. Others want to be surprised when the baby arrives.

Ultrasound works by using a special machine to bounce high-frequency sound waves off the woman's internal structures. This creates a "map" of the fetus. The outline of its skeletal growth can be viewed on a TV monitor. This picture can also be reproduced as a photograph called a *sonogram.* The parents-to-be can keep this sonogram. Many enjoy putting this picture into their photo albums. It is their first picture of their new baby.

Most experts consider ultrasound safe for the mother and baby. Still, its use is advised only when valid reasons exist. Ultrasound should not be used routinely on all pregnant women.

A second prenatal test is chorionic villi sampling. In **chorionic villi sampling (CVS)**, the doctor inserts a special instrument into the mother's vagina and cervix. With this instrument, a small amount of the tissue from the amino-chorionic membrane is removed and examined. This examination can reveal problems with the developing baby's genes and chromosomes, which can indicate any congenital disorders that might be present.

Chorionic villi sampling can be done as early as the eighth week of pregnancy, but it is commonly done in the tenth week. An advantage of this test is it provides results early in the pregnancy. Some risks to the baby are present with CVS, however. Not all expectant parents will want to have this procedure done. Couples who meet certain conditions are commonly advised to have chorionic villi sampling done, 7-5.

A third prenatal test is amniocentesis. In **amniocentesis**, the doctor inserts a hollow needle through the mother's abdomen and into the uterus. Amniotic fluid is drawn from the amniotic sac that surrounds the fetus. By examining cells in this amniotic fluid, lab technicians can detect chromosomal abnormalities or chemical problems in the genes. When problems are present, it usually means the baby has a congenital disorder.

Amniocentesis can be performed between weeks 14 and 16 of pregnancy. The procedure carries only a slight risk to mother and fetus. It cannot be done as soon as chorionic villi sampling, but it carries a smaller risk. Like CVS, amniocentesis is recommended only if a woman is at risk for giving birth to a baby with congenital disorders.

Nutrition During Pregnancy

When they discover they are pregnant, many women wonder what they should eat (or not eat) to have a healthy pregnancy. Nutrition is an important concern. A woman's interest in a well-balanced diet should begin long before she becomes pregnant, however. Women who eat well are more likely to be healthy and continue good eating and health habits during pregnancy. These advantages can protect women from complications. They will also improve their chances of having healthy babies.

When a woman is properly nourished, her body stores nutrients. Early in pregnancy, the baby's development

1—Discuss: When are prenatal tests recommended?

2—Vocabulary: Compare and contrast *chorionic villi sampling* and *amniocentesis*.

3—Discuss: Why is it important for women to eat well-balanced, nutritious diets before becoming pregnant?

4—Resource: *Prenatal Care*, color transparency CT-7A, TR.

When Prenatal Tests Are Recommended

● When the woman is over 35

● When there is a family history of congenital disorders

● When one spouse is known to be a carrier of a congenital disorder

● When one spouse has been exposed to an infection, such as rubella

● When the mother has been exposed since conception to a substance or substances that might have harmed the developing baby

● When the mother has had previous miscarriages or stillbirths

● When the mother has previously given birth to a baby with a congenital disorder

7-5
In some situations, prenatal tests may be recommended.

1—Discuss: Explain the significance of the saying: A pregnant woman should eat for two.

2—Resource: *Diet During Pregnancy,* Activity B, SAG.

3—Discuss: Review the Food Guide Pyramid. How many servings does a woman need from each group?

4—Resource: *Food Guide Pryamid,* color transparency CT-7B, TR.

depends on these stored nutrients. A woman's nutritional status before pregnancy is also important since most women do not know of their pregnancy for several weeks. During this time, all the baby's major organs and systems are forming. The baby's optimum growth depends on the nutrients provided by the mother. If a woman waits until she knows she is pregnant to eat more healthfully, her baby may have already been deprived of needed nutrients.

The old saying "A pregnant woman should eat for two" is usually misunderstood. A pregnant woman should not eat twice as much food as she did before she was pregnant, 7-6. Instead, the nutrients in the foods she eats must meet the demands of both the fetus and her own body.

If a woman doesn't eat enough nutrients, she and her baby must compete for the nutrients she does consume. Her body will provide the nutrients the fetus needs first, even if this means the woman's nutrient needs will go unmet. In this case, neither baby nor mother will get an adequate amount of the nutrients essential for her health.

Although a pregnant woman doesn't need to eat twice as much, her needs for certain nutrients increase dramatically. She must plan her meals carefully to include all the foods she and her baby need. A variety of healthful foods is essential to a healthy pregnancy.

A woman can plan her meals using the **Food Guide Pyramid**, an outline of what to eat each day. The Food Guide Pyramid is based on national guidelines for healthy eating. The Food Guide Pyramid can help a pregnant woman select the right foods for a balanced diet, 7-7. The following paragraphs explain each group of the Food Guide Pyramid, as well as explaining women's other nutritional needs during pregnancy.

7-6

Eating for two means eating foods that will meet the nutritional needs of both mother and baby. Pregnant women can meet these increased nutritional needs by selecting a variety of healthful foods.

The Bread, Cereal, Rice, and Pasta Group

The bottom segment of the Food Guide Pyramid features the bread, cereal, rice, and pasta group. Foods in this group are made from grains. Whole-grain breads and cereal products are especially rich sources of the B vitamins. They are also good sources of fiber and *carbohydrates* (the body's main source of energy).

A pregnant woman's overall need for energy increases. In the second and third trimesters of pregnancy, a woman requires an extra 300 calories daily. Some of these extra calories should come from the bread, cereal, rice, and pasta group. Pregnant women need 6 to 11 servings from this group each day,

Food Guide Pyramid
A Guide to Daily Food Choices

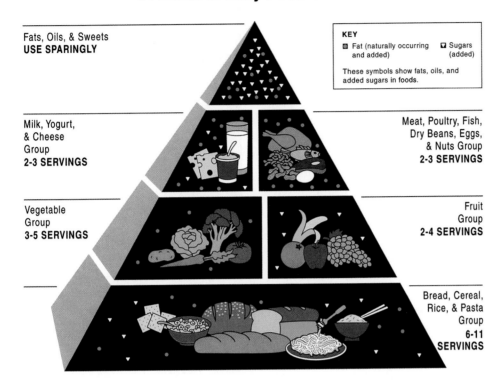

Fats, Oils, & Sweets
USE SPARINGLY

KEY
▨ Fat (naturally occurring and added)   ▨ Sugars (added)
These symbols show fats, oils, and added sugars in foods.

Milk, Yogurt, & Cheese Group
2-3 SERVINGS

Meat, Poultry, Fish, Dry Beans, Eggs, & Nuts Group
2-3 SERVINGS

Vegetable Group
3-5 SERVINGS

Fruit Group
2-4 SERVINGS

Bread, Cereal, Rice, & Pasta Group
6-11 SERVINGS

7-7
Choosing a variety of foods from the Food Guide Pyramid can help an expectant mother get all the nutrients she and her baby need.

depending on their body sizes and activity levels.

The Vegetable Group

One level higher on the left side of the Food Guide Pyramid is the vegetable group. Vegetables, especially those that are dark yellow, orange, or green, are an excellent source of vitamins and minerals. Eating lots of vegetables can help meet a woman's increased need for these vitamins and minerals. Vegetables also provide fiber and carbohydrates. Some of a pregnant woman's extra calorie needs during the second and third trimesters should come from the vegetable group.

During pregnancy, demand grows for the B vitamins and vitamins C, E, and K. Eating certain vegetables can help meet these increased needs.

Green, leafy vegetables are also a rich source of another vitamin, folate, which is essential. Folate aids in the proper development of the baby's *neural tube*, a tube that will develop into the brain and spinal column. For this reason, a woman needs twice as much folate during pregnancy as she did before she was pregnant.

One mineral that women need much more of during pregnancy is iron. Iron is an important part of the blood. A pregnant woman's body produces almost 50 percent more blood. This extra blood is needed to transport nutrients and oxygen to the fetus and carry the fetus' waste products away. The demands of the fetus are in addition to the woman's needs. Her blood must get nutrients to and carry wastes away from all the cells in her own body as well.

1—**Discuss:** Explain why a woman needs to consume more iron during pregnancy.

1—Vocabulary:
What is *anemia*? Why is it dangerous during pregnancy and what can be done to prevent it?

A pregnant woman needs extra iron for all this extra blood. Iron is also needed for the baby's blood and red blood cells. Additionally, the baby builds a supply of iron in its liver, upon which it will rely during the first few months after birth. A woman needs twice as much iron during pregnancy as she did before she was pregnant. Women who lack enough iron in their blood have **anemia**, or iron deficiency. Green vegetables, such as peas and spinach, are a good source of iron.

Increased amounts of other minerals, such as magnesium, iodine, zinc, and selenium, are also needed. The amount of other vitamins and minerals needed may not increase, but it is very important for a pregnant woman to consume the recommended amounts of these nutrients. Expectant mothers can get many of the vitamins and minerals they need from a variety of vegetables and vegetable juices. The Food Guide Pyramid recommends three to five servings of vegetables daily.

The Fruit Group

In the Pyramid, directly to the right of the vegetable group is the fruit group. Fruits are another optimum source of vitamins and minerals women need during pregnancy, 7-8. Fruits also help provide the fiber and carbohydrates pregnant women need.

Oranges, for instance, are a rich source of folate and vitamin C. They also provide some fiber. Apricots are a good source of vitamin A and carbohydrates. Raisins, dates, and prunes are a good source of carbohydrates, iron, and fiber. Including a variety of fresh fruits and fruit juices into her diet can help a pregnant woman meet her nutritional needs. The Food Guide Pyramid recommends two to four servings from the fruit group daily.

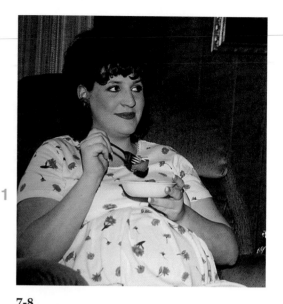

7-8

Snacking on fruits, such as peaches, can help a pregnant woman meet her nutritional needs.

The Milk, Yogurt, and Cheese Group

Moving up another level in the Food Guide Pyramid is the milk, yogurt, and cheese group. Foods in this group provide a variety of the nutrients a pregnant woman and her growing baby need.

Milk and milk products are a rich source of several minerals, such as calcium and phosphorus. A woman does not need additional calcium or phosphorus during pregnancy, but it is important she get the daily recommended amount of these minerals. They help build the baby's bones and teeth.

Milk is also fortified with vitamin D. Like calcium and phosphorus, vitamin D aids in the development of strong bones and teeth. A woman does not need more vitamin D during pregnancy, but she should be certain to consume the recommended amount of vitamin D for women.

Milk and milk products are a good source of protein. They also supply carbohydrates, which provide energy. Some of the extra calories a woman needs during the second and third trimesters of pregnancy can come from this group. The Food Guide Pyramid suggests two to three servings daily from the milk, yogurt, and cheese group for pregnant women.

Pregnant women should keep in mind, however, that many foods from this group are quite high in calories and fat. A woman may want to choose milk and milk products with reduced fat and calories. For example, fat-free milk, reduced-fat cheese, and lowfat yogurt might be good choices.

The Meat, Poultry, Fish, Dry Beans, Eggs, and Nuts Group

Directly to the right of the milk, yogurt, and cheese group in the Food Guide Pyramid is the meat, poultry, fish, dry beans, eggs, and nuts group. Its name suggests the types of food in this group. Most of the foods are rich in *protein*, a nutrient that helps build and repair body tissues.

Protein is vital for prenatal development. It is involved in building the baby's cells, tissues, and organs, as well as the baby's blood. Protein also helps build the expectant mother's extra blood cells and repairs body tissues. For these reasons, a pregnant woman's need for protein increases. However, most women already consume more protein than is required, so a woman may not need to consume extra protein. Each woman should check with her doctor or a registered dietitian about her protein needs.

As you have read, pregnant women need twice as much iron as they did before pregnancy. Foods from the meat, poultry, fish, dry beans, eggs, and nuts group are the very best source of iron. Red meats and organ meats, such as liver, are the richest iron sources.

Foods from this group also provide the B vitamins a woman needs during pregnancy. Some of a pregnant woman's extra calorie needs can come from this group. The Food Guide Pyramid suggests eating two to three servings from the meat, poultry, fish, dry beans, eggs, and nuts group daily.

Pregnant women should keep in mind that many cuts of meat are quite high in calories and fat. A woman may want to choose lean meats, beans, poultry, and fish for the bulk of her servings from this group.

Fats, Oils, and Sweets

Fats, oils, and sweets top the Food Guide Pyramid. These include foods such as butter, margarine, salad dressings, candy, and soft drinks. While fat is an essential nutrient, only a small amount of fat is needed in the diet. Many people consume much more fat than they actually need. Many people also eat foods high in oils and sweets in place of more nutritious food choices.

Fats, oils, and sweets usually have little nutritive value, so a woman should limit the amount of these items she consumes. Limiting fats, oils, and sweets does not have to mean cutting them out completely. However, a woman should be sure the extra calories she needs do not come from fats, oils, or sweets. These calories should come from the five main food groups. The Food Guide Pyramid recommends fats, oils, and sweets should be used sparingly.

1—**Discuss:** What role does protein play in having a healthy baby?

2—**Discuss:** What are the recommendations for fats, oils, and sweets during pregnancy?

1—Discuss: Give the recommendations for water, salt, and dietary supplements during pregnancy.

Other Nutritional Concerns

Consuming the recommended number of servings from each food group is important. See 7-9 for information on what constitutes a serving.

It is equally important that a woman consume enough water, watch her salt intake, and ask her doctor or nurse-midwife before taking any dietary supplements. Following these guidelines will help a woman deliver a healthy baby.

Water

Water is an essential nutrient. During pregnancy, it can be even more important. The human body is over 70 percent water. Water supports fetal development. Drinking enough water will also help the pregnant woman rid her body of waste products, both hers and the baby's. A pregnant woman needs eight glasses of water, juices, and other nonalcoholic, caffeine-free liquids each day.

7-9 ——————
A pregnant woman should pay close attention to her increased nutritional needs.

What Is a Serving?

Food Groups	Number of Servings	Typical Servings	Special Notes
Bread Group	6-11	1 slice bread 1 biscuit, muffin, or roll 1 ounce ready-to-eat cereal 1/2 cup cooked cereal, grits, rice, or pasta	Look for whole-grain or enriched breads and cereals.
Vegetable Group	3-5	1/2 cup cooked or chopped raw vegetables 1 cup raw, leafy vegetables 3/4 cup vegetable juice	Eat at least one good source of vitamins A and C daily. Good sources of vitamin A include dark green and deep yellow vegetables and fruits such as spinach, carrots, sweet potatoes, and cantaloupe. Good sources of vitamin C include citrus fruits, tomatoes, strawberries, broccoli, and brussels sprouts.
Fruit Group	2-4	1/4 cup dried fruit 3/4 cup juice 1/2 large grapefruit 1 medium fruit (apple, orange) 1/2 cup chopped, cooked, or canned fruit	
Milk Group	2-3	1 cup milk To equal the calcium content of 1 cup milk, it would take: 1 cup yogurt 3 inch cube Cheddar cheese 1 1/2 slices American process cheese 2 cups cottage cheese 1 3/4 cups ice cream	Remember 1 3/4 cups ice cream have the same amount of calcium as 1 cup milk, but ice cream has many more calories.
Meat Group	2-3	2-3 ounces cooked lean meat, fish, or poultry 1/2 cup cooked dry beans 1 egg 2 tablespoons peanut butter	Eat a variety of protein foods from both animal and vegetable sources.

Salt

1   Sodium intake can be a concern during pregnancy. Salt used in cooking, at the table, and in processed foods is the main source of sodium in the diet. While sodium is important in a balanced diet, moderation is the key. Too much salt might cause a pregnant woman's ankles, hands, or feet to swell. Salt has also been linked to an increase in blood pressure. A woman should talk with her medical professional or a registered dietitian about whether she needs to reduce her sodium intake. If she is advised to reduce the amount of sodium in her diet, she can cook foods without adding salt. Reading food labels carefully will help her select foods that are lower in sodium.

Dietary Supplements

2   During pregnancy, a woman's need for certain vitamins and minerals increases dramatically. Most of these needs can be met by eating a well-balanced diet. A well-balanced diet includes the recommended number of servings from each of the five food groups. Some women may not have had an adequate diet before pregnancy. Their body stores of these vitamins and minerals may be quite low. Other pregnant women do not consume enough nutrients through their diet. This can be especially true in the first trimester if a woman experiences continued nausea and vomiting.

Many doctors prescribe prenatal vitamin and mineral supplements. A woman should only take supplements prescribed by her doctor. She should also be sure the supplements do not provide more of a vitamin or mineral than she needs. Consuming certain vitamins and minerals in amounts that are much larger than recommended can be dangerous to both mother and baby.

Weight Gain During Pregnancy

3   The average recommended weight gain during pregnancy for a woman of normal weight is 25 to 35 pounds. Women who begin pregnancy underweight for their body frame and height may be advised to gain more weight than this. Women who start pregnancy above their recommended weight may be advised to gain slightly less. A woman should consult her doctor or nurse-midwife about how much weight she should gain.

Women gain an average of 2 to 4 pounds during the first trimester. After the first trimester, a weight gain of 1 pound a week is recommended. It is important a woman gain this weight in a slow, steady pattern. A quick gain or loss may signal a problem the doctor should monitor carefully.

If a woman gains too little weight, she is probably not getting enough nutrients. This can negatively affect her health and the baby's health. Medical

4   research indicates babies born weighing at least 7 pounds have a better survival rate. Babies are more likely to be born at *low birthweights* (weighing less than 5 1/2 pounds at birth) if their mothers do not gain enough weight. They are also at greater risk for congenital disorders and *neonatal* (soon after birth) death.

Gaining more than the recommended amount of weight can strain a woman's body. It can also make labor and delivery more difficult. In addition, the woman will have even more weight to lose once the baby is born.

When a woman gains the recommended amount of weight, most of this weight is created by or associated with

1—Activity: Have students propose ways for women to cut their salt intake during pregnancy.

2—Activity: Have students ask a doctor whether dietary supplements containing vitamins and minerals are important during pregnancy.

3—Discuss: What is the average recommended weight gain during pregnancy? Using 7-10, explain why it is important to gain this much weight during pregnancy.

4—Discuss: What might be the effects of not gaining enough weight during pregnancy? Of gaining too much?

1—Activity: Research exercise classes for pregnant women in your community. Are any classes available? When do they meet? What are the costs and requirements to join?

2—Discuss: What are the guidelines for exercising during pregnancy?

the baby growing inside her, 7-10. Much of this weight gain consists of the baby, placenta, and amniotic fluid. The mother's breasts and uterus also weigh more, and her body produces extra blood and fluid.

Exercise During Pregnancy

Another common question pregnant women have concerns exercise. A woman might be afraid exercise will hurt her baby. Under normal circumstances, however, exercise is good for a pregnant woman. Physical activity helps keep her body in shape, which can help her have an easier pregnancy and delivery.

A pregnant woman should check with her doctor or nurse-midwife regarding any exercise she plans to do. Generally, she should be able to continue most exercises she was doing before she was pregnant. During pregnancy, however, is not the time to introduce new activities. A woman should not begin a new sport or intense workouts after she becomes pregnant. If she did not exercise regularly before pregnancy, she may begin by taking a brisk walk every day.

Walking is the best exercise for pregnant women. Some women join special exercise classes for pregnant women offered by their hospitals, 7-11. These classes are designed to be safe for pregnant women, and they can be a lot of fun.

A pregnant woman should remember to warm up and cool down during each exercise session. Also, she should not exercise at intense levels for more than 15 minutes without cooling down. An expectant mother should also stop exercising immediately and contact her doctor if the notices any of the following warning signs:

- pain
- cramps in the uterus
- blood or fluid coming from the vagina
- dizziness
- shortness of breath
- fatigue

Late in pregnancy, a woman's doctor or nurse-midwife may recommend she stop exercising until after the baby is born. Until then, however, regular exercise can help a woman feel her best.

Sources of Weight Gain During Pregnancy

Baby	7-8 lbs.
Blood volume increase	3 lbs.
Placenta	1 lb.
Tissue fluid	2-6 lbs.
Uterus	2 lbs.
Fat deposits	5 lbs.
Breasts	1 lb.
Amniotic fluid	2-4 lbs.
Tissue fluid	2-6 lbs.
TOTAL	25-35 lbs.

7-10 _____
Gaining the recommended amount of weight during pregnancy is best for both mother and baby.

7-11 _____
Exercising throughout pregnancy helps a woman maintain good health. Exercise classes are a fun way to stay fit.

Factors That Increase Health Risks to Mother and Baby

In addition to getting the nutrients and exercise she needs, a pregnant woman must protect herself and her baby from harmful substances. Anything a pregnant woman puts into her body may pass through the placenta and reach the fetus.

Prescription medications and over-the-counter drugs can harm an unborn child. Taking illegal drugs, drinking alcohol, or smoking cigarettes can have deadly consequences for the baby. Finally, pregnant women should avoid x rays and caffeine, which can also damage their babies' developing bodies.

Medications and Over-the-Counter Drugs

An expectant mother should be sure to check with her doctor or nurse-midwife before taking any medications. Her doctor can advise her which medicines are safe and in what amounts, 7-12. She should not take any medications that her doctor has not prescribed or approved.

A pregnant woman should consult her doctor about continuing to take prescription medicines. For instance, tetracycline, a very common antibiotic, can affect the development of the baby's bones and teeth. A woman's doctor can help her weigh her need for the medicine against the potential damage to her unborn child.

Even common over-the counter remedies may harm a fetus. This includes heartburn medications, pain relievers, and laxatives. Aspirin, for instance, can cause the baby to bleed. Before taking any over-the-counter medication, a woman should consult a doctor or pharmacist.

7-12
Certain medications can harm an unborn baby. A woman's doctor should approve all the medications she takes during pregnancy, whether they are prescriptions or over-the-counter medications.

Illegal Drugs

No one should take illegal drugs, such as marijuana, heroin, cocaine, and hallucinogens. These drugs are dangerous for adults. They have even more deadly consequences for an unborn child.

Pregnant women who are heavy drug users often neglect their own health. This decreases their chances of having a healthy baby. Drug users are more likely to have miscarriages or

1—Resource: *Pregnancy Considerations,* Activity C, SAG.

2—Resource: *Deadly Consequences,* Activity D, SAG.

3—Discuss: Why should a pregnant woman consult her doctor before taking any medications, both prescription and over-the-counter?

1—Enrich: Ask a neonatal nurse to describe the effects of drugs upon babies born to drug-addicted mothers.

2—Vocabulary: Define *fetal alcohol syndrome*. How does alcohol reach a developing baby? What are the symptoms of fetal alcohol syndrome?

3—Discuss: How can smoking affect a pregnant woman and her baby?

premature deliveries (delivering a baby earlier than week 37 of pregnancy), 7-13. Babies born to drug users may also have low birthweights, physical disabilities, brain damage, or respiratory problems.

Another problem with drug use during pregnancy is that babies can be born addicted to the same drugs as their mothers. A pregnant heroin or cocaine user can also addict her baby. The baby will then go through withdrawal from the drug upon birth. Babies born addicted to drugs may not survive this withdrawal.

Infants who do survive withdrawal from drugs may have emotional, visual, and hearing problems as well as mental disabilities. Babies born to mothers who use drugs may never have the chance to develop normally. Giving up drugs will also improve the mothers' health and increase their babies' chances for survival. Addicted women may need to seek help to stop using drugs. They should talk with their doctors or go to a drug counseling center to learn what help is available in their communities.

Alcohol

Alcohol passes through the placenta so quickly a fetus is affected

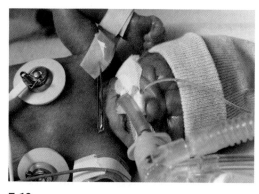

7-13 _____
Avoiding illegal drugs can help mothers carry their pregnancies to term. Premature babies are often born with tremendous health problems and require special medical care.

by an alcoholic beverage almost as quickly as his or her mother. Recent studies indicate even moderate drinking during pregnancy can affect the developing baby. The wisest choice is to avoid all alcoholic beverages (beer, wine, and liquor) during pregnancy. In fact, many doctors now recommend women avoid consuming alcohol if they are planning to become pregnant.

Alcohol use during pregnancy has been linked to miscarriage, stillbirth, and early infant death. A woman who drinks excessively or steadily also risks having a baby with fetal alcohol syndrome. **Fetal alcohol syndrome (FAS)** is a condition that includes physical and mental disabilities common among the babies of mothers who drink heavily during pregnancy, 7-14.

A major symptom of fetal alcohol syndrome is growth deficiency. An affected baby may be abnormally small at birth and never catch up to normal growth. He or she may have a heart problem severe enough to require surgery. A baby with FAS may also have a small head and brain, narrow eyes, a low nasal bridge, and a short upturned nose.

Babies with FAS often have moderate to severe mental disabilities. In later childhood, poor coordination, short attention spans, and behavioral problems are typical of children with this syndrome. A woman can protect her baby from FAS by not drinking during pregnancy.

Smoking

Smoking cigarettes is dangerous to a person's health. When a woman smokes during pregnancy, however, she risks severely harming her baby's health as well as her own. Medical research has shown pregnant women who smoke are more likely to lose their babies to miscarriage or stillbirth than nonsmokers.

The infants of smoking mothers are also at greater risk for premature

Effects of Fetal Alcohol Syndrome

- Prenatal growth deficiencies
- Growth deficiencies after birth
- Damage to brain and nervous system
- Small head and brain size
- Narrow eyes
- Low nasal bridge
- Short, upturned nose
- Mental disabilities
- Irritability
- Behavioral problems
- Academic problems
- Poor coordination
- Short attention spans
- Heart problems

7-14 _____

Mothers should not consume alcohol during pregnancy. Several serious problems can result from fetal alcohol syndrome.

delivery and low birthweight. Being born too early or too small puts babies at a high risk for many other health problems.

Babies whose mothers smoke are also more likely to die in early infancy than babies of normal weight. One common cause of death among the infants of smokers is **sudden infant death syndrome (SIDS).** In SIDS, a seemingly healthy infant dies without warning.

Babies of smoking parents are more likely to develop respiratory infections and problems during their first year. Low-birthweight babies are more likely to later develop learning or behavioral problems.

If a woman is considering becoming pregnant, it is best for her baby if she quits smoking before she conceives. Pregnant women who smoke should quit smoking for the health of their unborn babies. If a woman finds it impossible to quit smoking, she should at least cut back on the amount she smokes. Women can give birth to much healthier infants if they do not smoke.

Caffeine

Caffeine is a substance found in coffee, tea, chocolate, and some soft drinks. Research has not yet determined exactly how dangerous caffeine is during pregnancy. In animal studies, however, consuming caffeine has been shown to cause congenital disorders in a mother's young. For this reason, many doctors recommend pregnant women avoid or severely limit their caffeine intake. The effects of caffeine may be especially dangerous during the first trimester when a baby's organs are forming. A pregnant woman should consult her doctor or a registered dietitian about consuming caffeine. Many coffees, teas, and soft drinks are available in caffeine-free form.

X Rays

Radiation can be harmful to a pregnant woman. The most common source of radiation to which women might be exposed is X rays. Exposure to X rays can cause congenital disabilities in a developing baby. For this reason, dentists now ask a woman to wear a lead apron that will protect her during an X ray even if she does not think she is pregnant. An expectant mother should always tell her doctor or dentist she is pregnant before receiving any X rays. If possible, X rays should be postponed until after the baby is born.

If a pregnant woman works at a hospital or in a doctor's or dentist's office, she should inform her supervisor she is pregnant. She should not work near or operate any X-ray machines during her pregnancy, 7-15.

1—Reflect: What suggestions would you make to a woman who works throughout her pregnancy about getting plenty of rest?

7-15 _____

Some types of medical equipment emit radiation, which is harmful during pregnancy. Women who work in the medical field should not work with any such equipment while they are pregnant.

Rest

During pregnancy, a woman may become tired much more easily. In the first trimester, her body requires a lot of energy as the baby's body is developing. Her body must adjust to being pregnant. Getting enough rest at night will help her feel her best. She may find she needs to take a short nap during the day as well.

During the second trimester, a woman may not feel as tired. By the third trimester, however, carrying the extra weight of the baby can tire the expectant mother. A woman should listen to the signals her body sends her. When she feels tired, she should rest, 7-16. Late in pregnancy, many women need daytime naps besides eight or more hours of sleep every night.

Maternity Clothes

As the expectant mother's abdomen and breasts grow, she will begin to notice her clothes fit differently. Tight or restrictive clothes will soon become uncomfortable. By the fourth month, she may need to start wearing different clothes.

Some women choose to wear maternity clothes, garments especially designed for pregnancy, during much

7-16 _____

Late in pregnancy, a woman may have to stop and rest frequently while on outings. She should listen to her body's signals.

of their pregnancies. A woman should select maternity clothing in her regular size. Other women wear regular clothing in larger sizes.

A pregnant woman's larger, fuller breasts should be supported by a well-fitting bra. She may simply wear a larger-sized bra or choose a special maternity bra. Her growing abdomen should be free from tight waistbands and belts. Loose-fitting clothes are better because they do not restrict blood circulation.

Women who continue working during pregnancy may need to wear professional clothes to work. Maternity specialty stores often offer business clothing that meets a pregnant woman's needs. These clothes may be quite expensive, however. If cost is a factor, borrowing maternity clothes from friends or family members may be an option. Garage sales and other stores may be another alternative.

A woman may find her feet are a size longer or wider during pregnancy. This may be caused by fluid retained in her tissues.

Women should avoid wearing high heels during pregnancy. Shoes with low heels are better because they help the woman maintain good posture and balance. Good posture, in turn, helps her avoid backaches. Whatever a woman chooses to wear, she should remember that comfort is the key.

1—**Enrich:** Research different fabrics and styles often used in maternity clothing.

Summary

- If a woman is planning to become pregnant, it is a good idea for her to be in the best health possible before she becomes pregnant.

- As soon as a woman notices symptoms of pregnancy, she should visit a doctor. Quality prenatal care started early in pregnancy is important to the health of both mother and baby.

- Having regular medical checkups is important. During her first medical visit, the woman will have a complete physical exam and lab tests. The doctor or nurse-midwife will also calculate the baby's due date. Later medical checkups are also important.

- Three useful prenatal tests are the ultrasound test, chorionic villi sampling, and amniocentesis. Women who are over age 35, have family histories of congenital disorders, or have given birth to infants with congenital disorders may be advised to have prenatal tests done.

- A pregnant woman should eat a balanced diet that provides all the nutrients she and her baby need. This can take some planning, but it is very important.

- A pregnant woman should gain the recommended amount of weight during pregnancy to ensure her baby will be born at a healthy weight. Gaining much more or less than recommended can be harmful for both mother and baby.

- Factors that increase health risks to both mother and baby include medications and over-the-counter drugs (unless approved by her doctor), illegal drugs, alcohol, smoking, caffeine, and X rays. A pregnant woman should avoid these substances.

- Getting enough rest is important during pregnancy. Wearing comfortable clothing can help a woman feel and look her best.

Reviewing Key Points

1. What does prenatal care mean? What does it include?
2. What kind of doctor specializes in providing medical care for pregnant women?
3. Calculate the approximate due date of the following women given the first day of their last regular menstrual periods.
   A. Karen—July 5
   B. Natasha—November 17
   C. Sonia—February 12
4. Explain the purposes of the ultrasound test, chorionic villi sampling, and amniocentesis.
5. Identify which nutrients are provided by each of the following groups:
   A. The Bread, Cereal, Rice, and Pasta Group
   B. The Vegetable Group
   C. The Fruit Group
   D. The Milk, Yogurt, and Cheese Group
   E. The Meat, Poultry, Fish, Dry Beans, Eggs, and Nuts Group
6. Give the recommendations for consuming water, salt, and dietary supplements.
7. What is the average total weight gain recommended?
8. What are the recommendations for exercise?
9. Describe the possible symptoms of fetal alcohol syndrome.
10. True or false. Women who smoke are more likely to have miscarriages and premature deliveries than nonsmokers.

11. Is caffeine dangerous during pregnancy?
12. Why are X rays dangerous for pregnant women?

Learning by Doing

1. Interview an obstetrician about medical care during pregnancy. Ask questions about the signs of pregnancy, choosing an obstetrician, and the importance of medical care. Share your findings with the class in an oral report.
2. Plan seven daily menus for a pregnant woman. While preparing the menus, consider a pregnant woman's need for foods from the five main food groups of the Food Guide Pyramid.
3. With a partner, role-play expectant parents talking about the importance of eating right, exercising regularly, and avoiding harmful substances.
4. Working with a small group, create a directory that lists available sources of prenatal medical care in your community. Include phone numbers, addresses, and a brief description of each source.
5. Research one of the factors that increases health risks to mother and baby. Prepare a written report on your findings.

Thinking Critically

1. With a small group, discuss why it is important to receive medical checkups early in pregnancy and to continue having checkups throughout the pregnancy.
2. Pretend you are an expectant parent in your late 30s. This will be the first child for you and your spouse. Would you choose to have prenatal tests done? If so, which test would you have done? If not, why not? Write a short essay explaining your decision. Support your answer with information from the chapter.
3. Role-play a friend who is talking to a pregnant woman who has poor eating habits. The friend should try to convince the woman she should change her eating habits and suggest ways to do this.
4. Debate the following: if a woman drinks alcohol, takes illegal drugs, or smokes cigarettes during pregnancy, do you think this should be considered child abuse? Why or why not? If yes, what should be the penalty?
5. Most of the recommendations for prenatal care involve what a pregnant woman should or should not do to keep herself and her baby healthy. What can expectant fathers do to make sure their babies are as healthy as possible when they are born? Suggest ways a husband can be actively involved in prenatal care.

Chapter 8
Decisions Facing
Parents-to-Be

Objectives

After studying this chapter, you will be able to

● summarize the benefits of taking prepared childbirth classes.

● describe options a couple has when choosing a location for their baby's birth.

● determine which baby supplies are essential for a newborn and which are optional.

● compare breast-feeding and formula feeding.

● explain the benefits of parental leave.

● list child care options for working parents.

● explain factors to consider when selecting a doctor for the baby.

Key Terms

prepared childbirth
birthing room
birth center
colostrum
1 job sharing
parental leave
Family and Medical Leave Act
primary caregiver
pediatrician

When a couple first learns they are expecting a child, they may feel a variety of emotions. They may not believe they are really having a baby. This realization can be overwhelming. As the initial shock and excitement wear off, 2 parents-to-be begin wondering how to prepare for the big event. Actually, the birth of a child is a process rather than a single event. A baby grows for nine months and is born through a series of events that lasts several hours, 8-1.

The good news is expectant parents don't have to be ready in an instant. They have several months to prepare for their new arrival. During the pregnancy, a couple has many decisions to make. They must also take steps to prepare for the birth of their baby.

If this is their first child, the decisions may be more difficult. The pros and cons may seem less obvious since pregnancy, childbirth, and parenting are new experiences. For people who are already parents, many of these decisions will be based on past experience.

Childbirth Preparation Decisions

One way to prepare for childbirth is to learn more about it. Parents-to-be should understand what happens during pregnancy, labor, and delivery. First-time parents may not know much about these processes. Parents who already have children may need to review what to expect.

Most parents learn about birth in a prepared childbirth class. **Prepared childbirth** describes birth in which 3 both parents have been taught about the birth process. In prepared childbirth classes, parents learn techniques to control the woman's pain. These

1—**Vocabulary:** Look up terms in the glossary and discuss their meanings.

2—**Reflect:** If you were a parent-to-be, would you be nervous about all the preparations you and your spouse would have to make before the baby was born?

3—**Resource:** *Childbirth Preparation Class Observation,* Activity A, SAG.

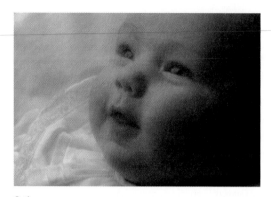

8-1 _____
Parents have plenty of time to prepare for
their new babies—it takes babies nine
months to grow and develop before birth.

methods may differ from class to class,
but often include breathing and relaxation exercises. Couples learn how to
actively participate in their baby's
birth.

In childbirth classes, parents-to-be
can discuss their fears as well as their
expectations about the upcoming birth.
Sharing these feelings may help them
feel more confident and less afraid.
Counselors and trainers provide useful
information for parents-to-be, 8-2.
These professionals can also reassure
couples about their fears.

Many couples take childbirth
classes in the last six weeks of pregnancy. Hospitals and birth centers
usually hold childbirth classes. Some
private and community agencies also
offer classes. Often, a couple's doctor
or nurse-midwife can make recommendations. Friends, family members,
or neighbors might also know of
classes in the area.

Taking a childbirth class has many
benefits. Childbirth classes can do the
following:

- Foster a closer relationship
  between spouses

- Promote the father's involvement
  in pregnancy, labor, and
  delivery, 8-3

- Allow the couple to meet other
  expectant parents

- Answer expectant parents'
  questions

- Teach parents-to-be breathing,
  relaxation, and coaching
  techniques

- Build the confidence of the expectant parents

- Teach both partners how to control
  the woman's pain

- Provide a successful, pleasant, and
  less stressful labor

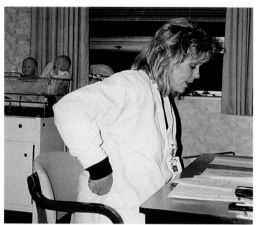

8-2 _____
This childbirth instructor demonstrates
techniques for controlling pain during
labor. She shows expectant couples where
the father can apply pressure to ease the
mother's pain.

8-3 _____
This expectant couple looks at a poster on
electronic fetal monitoring in their prenatal
class. When fathers learn what labor will
be like, they can be more involved in labor
and delivery.

Parents may also take infant care classes. These classes will teach them basic parenting and child care techniques. Classes on parenting or child care are especially helpful for first-time parents. If they are not very familiar with infants, these classes can ease some of their concerns. They can also teach important daily care skills and help the parents-to-be form realistic expectations.

Where Will the Birth Take Place?

An important question parents answer during pregnancy is where their baby will be born. Several options are available, and couples can select the one that best suits them. Most parents-to-be choose to give birth at a hospital. Depending on where they live, there may be several hospitals from which to choose. In many hospitals, couples may select either traditional delivery rooms or birthing rooms. Other couples choose to deliver at birth centers. A few couples have their babies delivered at home by certified nurse-midwives.

A couple may have chosen an obstetrician or nurse-midwife to deliver their baby. If so, they may not have as many options about where the baby is born. Most medical professionals only deliver babies in the places they work, 8-4. For some couples, using a specific location matters more than having a certain doctor. These couples can choose a doctor who works in this location.

Expectant parents may visit several hospitals and birth centers to find one that best meets their needs. It is important for them to find a place they will feel comfortable. They will want to

8-4 ———
This doctor can only deliver babies in the hospital where he works. If a couple wants him to deliver their baby, they must deliver at his hospital.

learn about any special policies and procedures each place has regarding birth. Knowing these policies may help them make their selection.

Hospital Delivery Room

When the parents-to-be visit a hospital, the doctor will explain what they can expect from delivering in that hospital. Expectant parents may visit each hospital in their area. This can help them make a final decision about which hospital to use. It also helps couples know what to expect.

Hospitals often offer expectant parents tours of the labor, delivery, and nursery areas. This can help them visualize what delivery might be like at this hospital. They may be introduced to the maternity ward staff. These are the professionals who would provide medical care for both mother and baby.

If an expectant couple uses a hospital delivery room, they can expect to be moved around quite a bit. They will spend several hours in a labor room. The couple will be moved to a delivery room just before the baby is born. After delivery, the mother will recover for a short time in a special recovery room. Then she will be transferred to the room where she will spend the rest of her hospital stay.

1—Discuss: List advantages and disadvantages of using a hospital birthing room.

A hospital delivery room is used only for delivering babies. It is stocked with all the needed medical equipment. This is the best place for a mother to give birth if her pregnancy is considered high-risk. (This means complications will likely occur during pregnancy or delivery.) Emergencies can be handled with ease in the hospital delivery room.

Hospital Birthing Room

A popular delivery option in many hospitals is a birthing room. A **birthing room** is a special room in a hospital where a woman can labor, deliver, recover, and rest. The entire birth process occurs in just one room.

A birthing room is much more private and homelike than a delivery room, 8-5. In a birthing room, the furniture and decor are comfortable and calming. The room might even include a private bathroom, a radio or stereo, and television.

The birthing room may seem like home, but it is located in the hospital. The room has all the equipment needed for an uncomplicated delivery. A certified nurse-midwife may stay with the couple during labor. Family members are often welcome. The baby's brothers and sisters may even be able to share the birth experience. In some hospitals, children are actually allowed to witness the birth of their new brothers and sisters.

When delivery nears, a doctor, nurses, and other medical staff may be present. They provide the same type of care as in a delivery room. If emergencies arise, the woman can quickly be moved to a traditional delivery room, which is usually close by.

After delivery, both mother and baby rest quietly in this same room. Couples often enjoy this relaxed

8-5 _____
In this hospital birthing room, couples can enjoy a more homelike setting without sacrificing quality medical care.

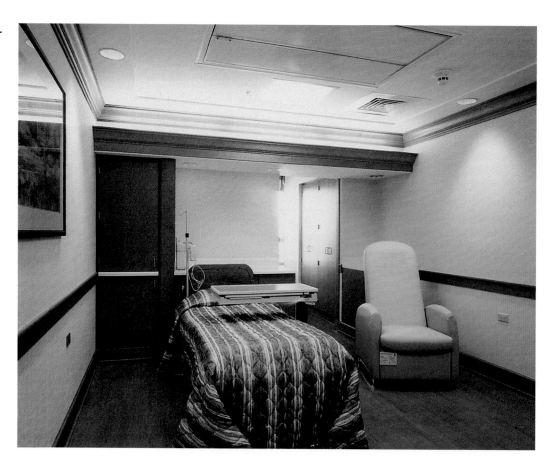

atmosphere. A birthing room is a compromise between delivery rooms and at-home delivery. It is homelike but allows mother or baby to receive emergency care if needed.

Birth Center

1 A couple may consider using a birth center. A **birth center** is a nonhospital facility that provides prenatal care and delivery services. These centers often employ certified nurse-midwives. The rooms are comfortable, much like a person's own bedroom.

Birth centers are not equipped to handle emergencies. If an emergency occurs, an ambulance must be called to take the woman to a hospital. This can be dangerous, even if the hospital is close. For this reason, delivery may be less safe at a birth center than at a hospital.

Most birth centers will not deliver babies in high-risk cases. However, a reputable birth center may be an option in an uncomplicated delivery. If a couple wants to use a birth center, they should check to see if any are available in their area.

At Home

Some parents wish to deliver their babies at home. They may want their newborn to arrive among family and friends in a warm and loving atmosphere. These couples may argue all babies were once born at home before hospital deliveries became the norm. However, maternal and infant death rates were also higher then.

2 Today, home births are not commonly recommended—in some states they are even illegal. Parents-to-be who wish to deliver at home should check to see if their state allows this. They must also choose a qualified doctor or certified nurse-midwife to attend the delivery.

Home deliveries should not be done in high-risk pregnancies. If something goes wrong, emergency services are not close at hand. A couple must be sure an ambulance can transport the mother and baby immediately to a nearby hospital if needed.

What Baby Supplies Will Be Needed?

During pregnancy, parents-to-be must prepare their home for the new baby. Babies need space where they can sleep, bathe, and play. They need clothes to wear and various supplies for their daily care. Some items are essential, while others are optional. Parents should be sure to get all the essential items before splurging for optional ones.

3 When buying baby items, parents-to-be may want to prepare a budget. This will help them avoid overspending and ensure they get the most for their money. For instance, if they spend too much on an elaborate crib, they might not have enough for a stroller. A couple should be realistic about what they can afford. Parents-to-be may be able to borrow many items from family, neighbors, and friends. If expense is a concern, they might consider shopping for used items at garage sales or resale shops. Expectant parents or their family members may be able to make some of these items. For instance, they might build a crib or sew baby clothes for the new little one, 8-6.

4 Comparison shopping is also important. Rather than buying the first item they see, parents should shop around to get the best prices and values. Comparison shopping can also help expectant parents plan a realistic budget.

1—**Enrich:** Research whether there are any birth centers in your area. What services do these provide?

2—**Note:** Having a baby at home can be quite risky. This does not eliminate the need for quality medical care during, and soon after, the birth.

3—**Activity:** Brainstorm ways parents can get the most for their money when purchasing baby supplies.

4—**Resource:** *Nursery Furniture and Equipment,* reproducible master 8-1, TR.

8-6

This grandfather admires the cradle he is building for the new grandchild on the way. Having someone make some items for the baby can lessen the expense.

Relatives, friends, and coworkers may also want to buy items for the baby. This can be a great help for the expectant couple. People may even hold a baby shower for the parents-to-be. At a baby shower, people celebrate the upcoming birth and bring gifts for the baby.

Preparing the baby's living space is an especially exciting task. It can make the upcoming birth seem more real. If they have an extra bedroom, parents may wish to set up a nursery for their baby there. They can decorate, arrange the baby's furniture, and fill the nursery with the supplies the baby will need.

If there isn't an extra room, the baby may share a room with either the parents or an older child. When sharing a room, the baby will still need space of his or her own. Parents can divide a room into sections with a partition or room divider. They can then decorate and arrange the baby's furniture within whatever space is available.

Baby Furniture

A baby's most essential piece of furniture is his or her bed. For the first few weeks, parents may prefer a cradle or small bassinet (basketlike bed). As the baby grows, he or she will need a crib.

When selecting a crib, parents have many guidelines to follow. First, they should not use a crib that was manufactured before 1988. Cribs older than this may not be safe for the baby because they don't meet current safety standards. Older cribs are more likely to have lead-based paint that could chip or peel. Infants, who often chew on their cribs, might get lead poisoning from ingesting this lead-based paint. Lead poisoning can cause severe physical and mental disabilities.

The distance between the tops of the rail and the mattress must measure at least 26 inches. For this measurement, the mattress should be set at its lowest level. If the distance is shorter, older babies might crawl out of the crib and get hurt. The distance between crib slats or bars must be less than $2\,^3/_8$ inches. Slats that are farther apart are dangerous because a baby's head can become stuck between them.

If the crib has drop sides, it must also have a secure locking mechanism. Otherwise, the baby could accidentally trigger the side to drop and could fall out. The top rails should be covered in plastic. This is sometimes called a teething rail. It prevents the baby from chewing directly on the crib.

Finally, the mattress should be firm and fit snugly in the crib. A firm mattress prevents possible suffocation. The space between the mattress and the crib should be no wider than two adult finger-widths. A baby's fingers, arms, legs, or feet could become stuck in a wider space.

Babies may have other furniture besides their cribs. Many parents use a chest of drawers for the baby's clothes. This may be a chest they already have, or one they have bought especially for the baby. Some parents purchase a changing table. A changing table has a flat, padded top on which parents can dress and undress their babies. Many changing tables have storage shelves or drawers. Parents may also want a baby swing or an adult-sized rocking chair for rocking the baby, 8-7.

Diapers

Diapers are a baby's most essential clothing need. Newborns use as many
1   as 90 to 100 diapers a week. Parents can choose between cloth and disposable

8-7

Shopping for baby supplies can be fun. This mother-to-be tries out a rocking chair for her baby's nursery.

diapers for their babies. Each type has advantages and disadvantages.

Many parents use disposable diapers every day. They like the convenience of these single-use diapers. Also, parents who regularly use cloth diapers may keep some disposables on hand. These diapers are handy for traveling and outings.

Disposable diapers are made of paper and plastic with an absorbent inner fiber. These diapers are fitted and have elastic around the legs to protect against leaks. They are fastened with two tabs of tape, one on each side. Disposable diapers come in various sizes according to a baby's weight and age. Some companies offer different diapers for boys and girls. Parents can choose among many available brands of disposable diapers.

Some people object to the use of disposable diapers for environmental reasons. If a newborn uses as many as 100 diapers a week, that's about 400 diapers a month. Imagine multiplying this number by all the infants wearing disposable diapers! You can see how much material this contributes to land-fills and dumps. Also, since they are plastic-coated, these diapers do not decompose over time as much waste does.

Some parents choose not to use disposable diapers because of the expense. Disposable diapers can cost more than $60 a month. This is several hundred dollars a year, more than many parents can afford or want to spend on diapers.

Parents who don't want to use disposable diapers can choose cloth diapers. Cloth diapers are reusable
2   diapers made of absorbent cotton. They are washed after each use. A separate, disposable lining may be used inside cloth diapers. This lining keeps the baby drier and more comfortable. It also prevents soiling and staining of cloth diapers, making it easier to keep them clean.

1—Resource: *Types of Diapers,* Activity C, SAG.

2—Activity: Compare cloth and disposable diapers   in terms of cost, comfort, and convenience.

1—Activity: Bring baby clothing to class and have students examine the labels. What information do the labels contain?

2—Activity: Obtain a typical basic layette from a store that sells baby clothing. Examine the different items and note the number needed for a beginning layette. Evaluate the cost of a basic layette.

In the past, cloth diapers were always sold as flat pieces of fabric. Parents folded each clean diaper before putting it on the baby. Flat cloth diapers are still used. They are fastened with special safety pins. These diapers last several months. They can continue to be used as the baby grows—they must just be folded differently. Flat cloth diapers cost about $70 for a supply of four dozen. This is a one-time expense.

Today prefolded cloth diapers may also be purchased. These diapers are more convenient because the parents do not have to fold them. Some prefolded diapers use hook-and-loop tape fasteners instead of diaper pins. Others feature elastic legs for a better fit. Prefolded diapers are slightly more expensive per dozen than flat cloth diapers. These diapers come in sizes, which means they are not a one-time expense.

Babies must wear something over cloth diapers to protect against leaks. Vinyl or plastic pants can be used. These pants should be soft and flexible. Today, many parents use overwraps or diaper covers, which are more comfortable for the baby. Overwraps close with hook-and-loop tape and wrap around the diaper. Diaper covers pull on over the diaper. Vinyl pants, overwraps, and diaper covers come in various sizes for the growing baby.

Some parents who use cloth diapers use a diaper service. A diaper service takes care of laundering cloth diapers. They come to the parents' home each week to pick up soiled diapers and deliver clean ones. Parents pay a weekly or monthly fee for this service. Diaper services offer convenience, but they may be quite expensive. For parents who can afford or wish to use a diaper service, it can be well worth the money.

Baby Clothes

Expectant parents often have fun buying clothes for their new babies. Parents should keep in mind, however, that newborns spend most of the time sleeping and eating. They don't need extensive wardrobes. Babies grow quickly, so garments that fit at birth will soon be too small. Basic wardrobe items a newborn needs are listed in 8-8.

As parents shop for baby clothes, their main concern should be the baby's comfort. A second concern is ease of care, since baby clothes are laundered often. Babies can get more wear from a few durable items than from many poorly made or hard-to-launder ones. Another important factor is how easy the garment is to put on and take off the baby. The climate, season, style, and price are other factors to consider.

Reading labels is important when shopping for infant clothes. Infant clothing is sized by age, weight, or both. Weight is generally a more accurate guide than age. Babies of the same age may be quite different in size. Labels also list the fiber content and care instructions.

The fabric in baby clothes is also important. It should be comfortable and washable. Cotton is an excellent fiber for baby clothes. It is soft, absorbent, and comfortable. Cotton is also durable and easy to launder. Acrylic is a fiber commonly used in baby sweaters, booties, and blankets. It is soft, comfortable, and washable.

Knitted fabrics are more comfortable than woven ones because they stretch with the baby's movements. Wraparound and snap-on styles are excellent for newborns. Pullover garments should have stretchable necklines. Baby garments should not have any drawstrings around the neck that could strangle the baby. Infant sleepwear must meet government standards for flame resistance.

The Newborn's Wardrobe	
Item	**Quantity and Other Notes**
Diapers	Disposable diapers as needed. 1 dozen disposable or cloth diapers for emergencies if using a diaper service. 4 dozen cloth diapers if laundered at home.
Diaper liners	As needed for use with cloth diapers.
Diaper pins	4–6 for use with cloth diapers. Be sure they have safety heads.
Vinyl pants, overwraps, or diaper covers	4–6 pairs for use with cloth diapers. Replace when they become brittle. They should not be tight around the waist and legs.
Cotton knit shirts	3 or more. Worn to protect the baby from drafts and to absorb persperation
Cotton knit nightgowns	2 or more. For both boys and girls. May have drawstring around the bottom to keep feet warm. Should be long and loose so the baby can move freely.
Stretch garments	3 or more. One-piece or two-piece knit garments with built-in feet for day or night wear. Should be comfortable and loose-fitting. Lightweight, cool fabrics for warm weather; warm, cozy fabrics for cool weather.
Special outfits	1 or 2 cute outfits for special occasions.
Sweaters	2 or more. Choose fabric according to climate. Should fit comfortably without binding.
Caps or hats	1 or more. Worn for warmth and protection from drafts. Choose cotton or silk caps for warm weather; acrylic caps for cool weather.
Mittens and booties	1 or 2 pairs of each. Should have plenty of room for the baby to move fingers and toes.
Blanket sleeper or bunting	1 or more if needed for cold weather.
Cotton receiving blankets	3–6 or more. Used to wrap the baby after bath or when outdoors in warm weather. Used to protect parent's lap during feeding. Used as a lightweight crib blanket in warm weather or as a cozy sheet for the crib in cold weather.
Acrylic or wool blankets	1 or 2. Used in cold weather as a crib blanket or to wrap the baby when outdoors.

1

8-8
Comfort and ease of care are the major considerations when selecting a newborn's wardrobe.

1—Resource: *The Newborn's Wardrobe, Activity D, SAG.*

1—Discuss: What supplies do parents need if they formula-feed? If the baby is breast-fed?

Other Equipment and Supplies

When parents-to-be have obtained baby furniture, diapers, and baby clothes, they have accomplished a great deal. However, there are still many other items they will need for their new baby. Babies require special equipment and supplies for all their major activities, including eating, bathing, sleeping, and traveling.

Mealtime

Whether they are breast-fed or bottle-fed, all newborns need some supplies and equipment for feeding. Babies may need a few bibs to wear during mealtime to keep their clothes clean. The bib should remain on until after the baby has been burped. This cuts down on the number of clothing changes the baby will need.

Bottle-fed infants need at least eight bottles and a continuous supply of formula. Bottle-cleaning brushes, extra bottle nipples and caps, and sterilizing equipment are also needed. Parents can purchase disposable bottles that are prefilled with formula. These are more expensive, but a large supply of regular bottles is not needed. The other bottle equipment is also not needed for use with prefilled bottles.

It might seem breast-fed babies would not need any feeding equipment, but they do. Nursing mothers may use a breast pump to help them express (pump out) breast milk. A nursing mother expresses this milk and stores it in the refrigerator or freezer for later use. If a mother expresses breast milk, she will need bottles to feed it to the baby. Bottles can also be used for water or juice. The mother will also need to wear nursing pads inside her bra to catch any leaks that occur.

Bath Time

When a newborn comes home from the hospital, he or she will need sponge baths. After the stump of the umbilical cord has dried and fallen off, the baby is ready for tub baths. Parents can give these baths in a small plastic tub or dishpan. They may decide to buy a specially made bathtub for infants, 8-9. Eventually the baby will outgrow this plastic tub. When the baby can sit up on his or her own, baths can be given in a regular bathtub.

For bathing their infants, parents need a gentle soap, cotton balls (for wiping around the eyes), washcloths, and towels. If they choose, parents can buy special baby washcloths and hooded towels. They may also wish to use baby lotion, oil, or powder after the bath. Some parents buy toys for their babies to play with during bath time.

Bedtime

The goal of infant bedding is to provide a comfortable, safe sleeping

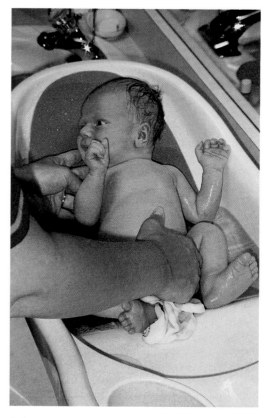

8-9 _____
This baby is a few weeks old—ready for Dad to give him a tub bath.

area. In the crib, the baby's mattress should be covered with a waterproof pad or mattress cover. A fitted crib sheet should be used over this pad or mattress cover. Parents should have more than one set of sheets. They will need to change these often, especially if the baby spits up or has a leaky diaper. To cover the baby, parents can use a few lightweight blankets in summer or a warm crib-sized blanket in winter. Pillows or stuffed animals should not be placed in the crib until the baby is a year old. These items pose a risk of suffocation.

1   A set of bumper pads is also essential for the crib. Bumper pads protect the baby from getting hurt by rolling against the sides of the crib. They also keep the baby from poking his or her arms, legs, or head through the slats and becoming stuck. Bumper pads go along the entire inside of the crib and should be securely fastened.

Travel Time

Among the most important items a baby requires is a car safety seat. Laws require that every baby must always be secured in an approved car safety seat when traveling in a vehicle. In fact, parents must take their infant home from the hospital in an approved car safety seat.

2   Until an infant weighs 20 pounds, parents should use a rear-facing car seat. These infant seats must allow the baby to ride in a reclining position. Children who weigh over 20 pounds must use car seats that allow them to sit up and face forward.

Infants and young children are safer in the back seat of a car. They should not ride in the front seat, especially in vehicles with passenger-side air bags. The force created when an air bag inflates during an accident can kill an infant or small child.

Parents must be sure their baby's car seat meets all current federal safety standards. For more information, they can contact their local highway safety department. They can also call the National Highway Traffic Safety Administration auto safety hot line. As long as the car seat meets safety standards, parents can choose the car seat they like best. Ease of use is an important factor to consider.

In addition to a car seat, parents may need other traveling equipment. Items such as baby carriages and strollers must also meet current safety standards. Parents who travel often may choose a lightweight stroller that folds to transport easily. Other parents may choose a sturdier stroller that holds up well for lots of walking. Some parents buy both types.

Choosing Breast-Feeding or Formula-Feeding

Another decision parents must make is how they will feed their babies. They may choose breast-feeding, formula-feeding, or a combination of both methods. Each method has advantages, 8-10. Since the baby must be fed soon after birth, parents should make this decision during pregnancy. This way, they have time to learn about each method before deciding. They can also make any preparations necessary before the baby arrives.

Parents should talk to their doctor about the advantages and disadvantages of each method. However, their doctor should support them in whatever decision they make. Family and friends also offer advice to the expectant parents. At times, people may try to persuade the couple to choose one

8-10 _____
The choice between breast-feeding and formula-feeding is a personal decision to be made by parents.

1—Discuss: Compare the advantages and disadvantages of breast-feeding and formula-feeding.

2—Resource: *Breast-Feeding or Formula-Feeding,* Activity E, SAG.

3—Enrich: Invite a lactation specialist from a hospital to give a presentation on the benefits of breast milk.

Breast-Feeding or Formula-Feeding

Benefits of Breast-Feeding

The newborn receives colostrum from the breasts for a few days before the milk "comes in."

The breasts adjust the qauntity and rate of milk production to meet the baby's needs.

The baby is less likely to overeat, to have coinstipation or diarrhea, or to have allergic reactions.

Breast milk is always available, sterile, and the right temperature. There is nothing to buy or prepare.

Close physical contact is emotionally satisfying for both baby and mother.

Nursing helps the mother's uterus return more rapidly to its normal size and position.

Benefits of Formula-Feeding

The nutritive value of formula never varies. The milk supply is not affected by what the mother eats or drinks, the medications she takes, or her state of mind.

Several types of formula are available and suitable for most babies. Some formulas require very little preparation.

The quantity of food the baby eats can be measured.

Both father and mother can experience the emotional satisfaction of feeding their baby.

The mother is not tied down by the baby's feeding schedule. She can resume her career or other activities sooner.

method of feeding over the other. However, the parents must feed the baby, so they must make the final decision.

Parents should feed their baby in the way they find most satisfying. If parents enjoy feeding times, they can relax and express their love, warmth, and tenderness to their infant. Feeding is one of the best times for parents and their newborns to be close and share quiet moments together.

Breast-Feeding

Many mothers choose to breast-feed their babies. Experts support breast-feeding as the preferred choice for newborns. The American Academy of Pediatrics says breast milk is the best food for a baby's first year of life.

What makes breast milk such a good choice? Breast milk is nature's food for babies. This milk is produced naturally by hormones in the mother's body. It contains all the essential nutri-

ents babies need, as well as extra antibodies to fight diseases and infections. Breast milk requires no preparation. It is always available and ready at the right temperature. In addition, breast milk is easy for babies to digest, and babies are not allergic to it.

Today, more women are choosing to breast-feed their babies, even if only for a short time, 8-11. Research shows breast-fed babies develop at a faster rate than bottle-fed babies. They also have fewer allergies and are ill less often.

Breast milk is a thin, bluish liquid. It comes into the mother's breasts within a few days after the baby is born. Until that time, the baby gets a special substance called colostrum. **Colostrum** is a thick, yellowish liquid in the mother's breasts that nourishes the baby until the mother's milk supply is established. Colostrum contains special antibodies that are very good for the baby. When the mother's milk comes in, it will replace this colostrum.

8-11 _____
Breast-feeding is a natural way to provide a baby with nutrients. Since it has so many benefits, many mothers today are choosing to breast-feed their infants.

Breast-feeding, which is also called *nursing*, provides a sense of closeness between mother and baby. The skin-to-skin contact promotes this feeling of connection. Holding a baby close makes the baby feel loved. It helps a baby trust that a parent will take care of his or her needs.

Nursing mothers also experience some benefits from breast-feeding. The baby's sucking action stimulates hormones that help the mother's uterus return to normal. The energy required to nurse and produce breast milk speeds a mother's postpartum weight loss.

Mothers may worry about how they will feed their babies when they return to work. Some mothers, especially those whose babies are cared for at the work site, may devise an alternate working arrangement that allows them to breast-feed during work hours. To continue the benefits of breast milk,

many employed mothers use a breast pump to collect the milk. The expressed milk is stored in a refrigerator or ice chest. (Extra milk can be frozen, too.) The baby is fed the expressed milk in a bottle during the work hours and possibly for at-home time, too. If the mother cannot or does not want to breast-feed or use a breast pump during work, she can switch to formula-feeding while at work or for all feedings. Experts agree that even a short period of breast-feeding or some breast milk daily is helpful.

Nursing does have certain disadvantages. Unless a mother uses expressed breast milk or formula in a bottle, the mother is the only person who can feed the baby. She is the one who has to get up to feed the baby at night. Newborns may nurse as often as 8 to 12 times daily and spend 20 to 30 minutes at each feeding. This means the mother nurses every 2 to 4 hours. This may not give her as much flexibility for other activities.

Nursing does not allow the father to feed the baby. Fathers can develop close ties with their babies by being involved in other care activities. For instance, fathers can still dress, diaper, bathe, hold, and play with their infants. This can mean just as much to the baby.

Nursing in public can be inconvenient, and for some people, embarrassing. It does not offer as much modesty as feeding from a bottle. Some women simply do not feel comfortable with the idea of nursing. These women should not feel guilty about their choice.

Formula-Feeding

Despite its advantages, some parents choose not to feed their babies breast milk. Instead, they prefer formula-feeding from a bottle. Formula can be purchased in liquid or powder forms. Most formulas are *concentrated*, which means they must be mixed with

1—**Discuss:** Identify reasons parents might choose to formula-feed despite the advantages of formula-feeding.

water before feeding. Formula is based on skim milk from cows and modified to be as much like breast milk as possible. Babies who are allergic to cow's milk can drink a soy-based formula.

Many couples choose to feed formula or expressed breast milk if the mother plans to return to work soon after the baby is born. This allows the baby's caregiver to feed the baby. Some working mothers prefer to use expressed milk, and other mothers choose to rely on formula-feeding. A few mothers use both breast milk and formula. However, using the combination may confuse the baby because both the sucking and the taste differ.

Some expectant parents prefer formula-feeding because they find nursing unappealing. Bottle-feeding offers more modesty for the mother, especially in public places, 8-12. If a mother does not want to nurse, it is better for her to formula-feed than for her to be unhappy. Babies can pick up on this unhappiness, making feeding times less pleasant for both mother and baby.

8-12
In public places such as restaurants, parents may find it much more convenient to bottle-feed their infants. Bottle-feeding also provides more modesty for the mother.

An advantage of formula-feeding or feeding expressed breast milk is that both mother and father can feed the baby. This can help the father feel close to the baby and relieve some of the strain on the mother. Also, feeding from a bottle is easy and convenient. Parents can measure how much the baby eats, so they can feel reassured the baby is getting enough to eat.

Parents who choose formula-feeding should not feel guilty. Formulas can provide needed nutrients. Holding the baby during feedings fosters closeness and nurturing similar to that of nursing.

A baby should never be fed by propping the bottle on a pillow or other item. Newborns do not have the muscles needed to eat from that position. They cannot stop the flow of milk from the bottle, which creates a potential choking hazard. Babies also need the closeness of being held.

Who Will Share in the Baby's Care?

Expectant parents are often very excited about having a baby. However, preparing for their new baby can also be stressful. Parents-to-be have many issues to settle before their baby arrives. Questions about who will be involved in caring for the baby can be especially difficult. Parents-to-be must determine what impact parenting will have on the jobs they do. They must decide who will provide the daily care for their newborn. Expectant parents must also choose a doctor to care for their baby. These decisions are best made before the baby arrives.

Employment Decisions

When they marry, most couples discuss their goals regarding work. Whether one or both spouses work, the couple has settled into a pattern. When pregnancy occurs, the couple's life changes. Now they have a child to consider. Both spouses must reevaluate their employment decisions. Couples have many options. They must be certain they choose working arrangements that will work best for their new family.

Both spouses may work outside the home after their baby is born. If both husband and wife work the same hours, someone else will need to care for their baby during these hours. If they can arrange it so their working hours alternate, one parent could always be home with the child. However, this would leave very little time for them to spend together as a couple.

If both parents work, the family's income will be higher. The price they pay for child care, however, can put a big dent in their earnings. After paying child care costs, some families find they actually lose money when both parents work. Parents must determine whether the benefits of working outweigh the costs.

The success of these dual-career families depends on how well spouses work together to achieve mutual goals. Parents in dual-career families need to revise their expectations, redefine their roles, and invent creative solutions for their problems, 8-13.

When both parents work, the couple must talk about how they will divide household and parenting tasks. Work affects the family, and family life affects work. Some work-related factors that could affect the family include work schedule, number of hours worked, job location, job responsibilities, health and safety concerns, benefits, and income. Family-related factors that could affect work include child care issues, household tasks and responsibilities, family relationships, and available leisure time.

The advantages and disadvantages must be considered when making this

1—**Discuss:** Identify alternative arrangements parents can make for the baby's care in dual-career families.

8-13 ————
In dual-career families, it helps when Dad shares more of the household responsibilities, like taking the baby grocery shopping with him.

1—Reflect: If you were an expectant parent, what arrangement would you want to make for your baby's care?

decision. Advantages of working might include interacting with adults, feeling satisfied professionally, continuing one's career, and earning money to meet family expenses and goals. Disadvantages might include child care costs, being away from the child, having less time, feeling more stress, and experiencing role strain in meeting the demands of family and work.

In some families, one parent works outside the home, and the other stays home with the baby. Today, fathers, as well as mothers, may choose this option. With a parent providing daily care, both parents can feel confident in the care the baby is receiving.

The family's income may drop dramatically with only one wage earner. However, the money saved in child care costs could be substantial. For this reason, some families compromise. One parent may stay home with the child for a few years. This is often until the child goes to preschool or kindergarten. Then the stay-at-home parent will rejoin the workforce.

Depending upon their situation, parents may be able to plan other work arrangements. Some parents are able to arrange flexible work schedules. For instance, an employer may permit two employees to share a job, each working part-time. This is called **job sharing**. It allows each employee more time to be at home with family, 8-14.

Another option may be having one or both parents work from the home. This may or may not be possible, depending upon the type of work the parents do. Some companies allow an employee to work from home. Modern technology can aid communication between at-home workers and their companies. In other situations, a parent may be self-employed and work from home.

It can be difficult to get work done while caring for a newborn. Babies require a lot of time and attention. Meeting deadlines can be challenging since the parent must juggle child care and work responsibilities. For some families, however, this arrangement can be ideal.

8-14
A mother may be able to use job sharing to spend more time with her family. In job sharing, two workers split the responsibilities for one full-time job.

Parental Leave

No matter what arrangement they choose, new parents soon realize parenting will change every aspect of their lives. They should be patient with themselves as they adjust to their new parenting roles. Taking parental leave from work after the baby is born may help them concentrate on their new roles. **Parental leave** is paid or unpaid leave from work to tend to parenting duties. Parents most often take this leave when they give birth or adopt a child or if their child is seriously ill. Two types of parental leaves are *maternity leave* for mothers and *paternity leave* for fathers.

Many experts advise three to four months of parental leave after the birth or adoption of a child. They believe having this time to concentrate solely on parenting is best for both parents and child, 8-15. By learning more about parenting, new parents may feel more confident in managing their multiple roles. If and when they do return to work, they may feel a little less overwhelmed. Their parenting duties will have already begun to feel familiar.

To support this belief, many companies offer parental leaves as part of their benefits packages. Often, a company will grant a set amount of paid parental leave employees can take after the birth or adoption of a child. This way the new parents can continue to receive their pay while spending some time with their newborn.

Each company differs in the amount of paid parental leave it offers. Some grant extended leaves; others are as short as four to six weeks. Employees who have worked for a company for many years may receive more paid parental leave than newer employees.

After the paid parental leave has ended, the company might offer a period of unpaid leave. During unpaid leave, the person's job is held until he or she returns to work. If their company does not offer paid parental leave, parents might take vacation days, personal days, or unpaid leave to care for a new baby.

According to the **Family and Medical Leave Act**, employees may take up to 12 weeks of unpaid leave in certain circumstances. This law applies to workers in the following circumstances:

- The worker or worker's spouse has just given birth to or adopted a child.
- The worker must provide care for a seriously ill family member.
- The worker has a serious health condition of his or her own.

Under this act, the employee must be allowed up to three months of parental leave. The employer must guarantee the employee can have his or her job (or an equal job) when he or she returns to work. The company must provide health care benefits during this parental leave. It is not required by law that the employee be paid during this leave.

The Family and Medical Leave Act does not cover workers in companies with fewer than 50 employees. Workers can also be denied parental leave if they are among the highest paid 10 percent of a company's salaried employees. Almost half of U.S. workers are covered by this act.

8-15 _____
Taking time away from work to spend with the baby can be valuable for new fathers.

1—Reflect: If you were a new parent, how much parental leave would you take to be home with your baby, and why?

2—Vocabulary: What is a *primary caregiver*?

3—Discuss: What options might parents have regarding the baby's caregiver?

Often, an employee learns the company's policy on parental leaves at the time of hire. This is usually discussed as part of the benefits package. When a couple is expecting a baby, both spouses should check with their employers to be certain what options are available. Then, they can decide what, if any, leave each parent will take. In the case of unpaid leave, they must weigh the benefits with the income they will lose while they are at home with the baby.

Maternity leave is more common than paternity leave. Beyond the bonding benefits, maternity leave allows the mother's body time to rest and recover. Maternity leave promotes her return to good health after the birth. It also allows her to develop a close and special relationship with the baby. For many mothers, even a short maternity leave is important.

As more is learned about the special role fathers play, paternity leaves are becoming more common. Paternity leave allows a father to spend time with his new baby and help care for his recovering wife. Not all companies offer paid paternity leave, but some do. If his company doesn't offer paid leave, a father may be able to take vacation days to be home with his family. Some fathers time their paternity leave to start when the mother returns to work. This make it possible for the baby to be home with at least one parent for a longer period of time.

Choosing a Caregiver

The person who provides the most care for the baby is called the **primary caregiver.** This is the person who spends the most time with the baby. He or she answers the most cries, feeds the most meals, and changes the most diapers. This primary caregiver may be the father, a grandparent, an older sibling, or a babysitter, but it is often the mother.

Many experts believe a baby benefits from the consistent care given by a primary caregiver. This person is a constant in the baby's life. The baby often forms a special attachment to this person. The primary caregiver helps the baby learn to respond to the rest of the world. The baby needs to know this caregiver can be depended on for love, comfort, help, food, and all other needs.

Parents will want to decide who will be this primary caregiver. In addition, they should decide who else will be providing care for the baby. In many families, both parents plan to work outside the home after the baby is born. Finding quality child care is a top priority for these parents. They must carefully select the person or agency who will care for their baby.

During pregnancy, parents may begin to investigate their child care options. They will likely want to decide before the baby arrives. Each family's situation and resources are unique. This makes each family's options slightly different.

8-16 _____
If they're available, grandparents can make excellent caregivers for their grandchildren.

In some families, a grandparent or other relative is willing and able to care for the baby, 8-16. This is a good way for the baby to spend time with extended family members. Parents often trust their family members more than anyone else.

Other times, close friends or neighbors may be able to provide child care. Parents may have to pay for this care, but they would still feel confident in the quality of care provided. They would feel comfortable knowing their baby was in the hands of people they know.

If no one they know and trust can care for their infant, parents will probably have to hire a caregiver. The parents may take the baby to the caregiver's home, or the caregiver may come to the family's home. In the family's home, a caregiver would probably care only for their infant. Caregivers who work from their own homes may care for more than one child at a time.

Another option is to use a child care center. In a child care center, trained staff provide care for infants and children while their parents work. A child care center may be the most expensive option, but it is often very attentive care. A reputable center can make parents feel at ease. Costs for infant care are considerably higher than care for older children. Babies require much more individual care.

The ultimate goal is to provide the best quality care available for the new baby. Their baby's health and safety are important. Parents will want to carefully examine a situation before placing their child in someone's care. Local service agencies can refer parents to reputable caregivers and child care centers. (You will learn more about child care in Chapter 20.) Selecting child care can be one of the most difficult decisions for parents to make. They should choose the care for their child that will make them the most comfortable.

Choosing the Baby's Doctor

Another aspect of caring for a newborn is choosing the baby's doctor. Parents want a capable, caring doctor to provide quality medical care for their baby. They must be able to rely on the doctor's knowledge, skills, and advice.

Choosing their baby's doctor is important. During pregnancy, a couple has time to carefully select their baby's doctor. Since the doctor will examine the baby just after birth, parents should choose the doctor before the baby is born.

A few parents know exactly which doctor they want to care for their baby. Most others have to search for just the right doctor. A couple may want to ask their obstetrician or nurse-midwife to refer them to a trusted doctor. Family and friends may also have suggestions.

Parents must first decide which type of doctor they prefer. They may choose a **pediatrician**, a doctor who specializes in providing medical care for infants and children. The other option is to select a family doctor or clinic.

Using a pediatrician is a sound choice. These doctors are specially trained in children's medical care. After passing certain exams, they are certified by the American Board of Pediatrics. A pediatrician only sees child patients. This makes him or her quite familiar with children's health concerns, 8-17.

Choosing a family doctor or clinic can also be a good choice. In this case, the parents' family doctor may provide care for the entire family. He or she already knows the parents fairly well. Parents might be more likely to trust their family doctor than someone new. If they choose a family doctor, their child won't have to change doctors in the teen years. (Since a pediatrician only sees children, teens usually have

1—Resource: *Choosing the Baby's Doctor*, transparency master 8-2, TR.

2—Vocabulary: How does a *pediatrician* differ from a *family doctor*?

8-17
A pediatrician is specially trained in caring for children. This type of doctor knows how to put children at ease.

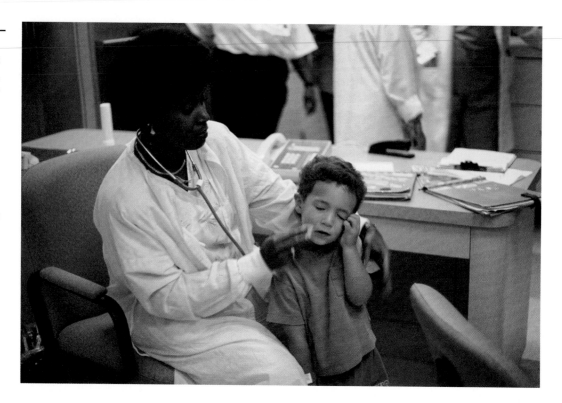

1—Activity: Write a list of questions parents-to-be could ask when selecting a doctor for their baby.

to switch to a family doctor.) If the family doctor has sufficient knowledge and experience with children, he or she would probably be a fine choice.

No matter which type of doctor they choose, expectant parents need to feel comfortable with their decision. Once they decide which type of doctor to use, they can begin their search for the specific doctor. If they have a few doctors in mind, parents can call for an appointment with each one. Visiting prospective doctors can help parents narrow their choice. Most pediatricians welcome parents-to-be for a visit before the baby is born. This can be a time for them to get to know one another. It can also be a good time for the parents to ask questions about parenting and child care.

Important factors in choosing a doctor are the doctor's training and the parents' comfort. A key element is their impression of the doctor. For instance, does the doctor welcome their questions? Does he or she truly seem to care about their baby? Does the doctor explain things in a way parents can understand? Other factors include office location, office hours, emergency and after-hours care, average wait for an appointment, cost of services, and payment arrangements.

Carefully choosing their child's doctor can reassure parents their baby will have quality medical care. The doctor is a valued member of the team who will share in the baby's care.

Summary

● Prepared childbirth can make birth more pleasant for parents-to-be.

1 ● Expectant parents should carefully review their options for the location of the birth. They should make this decision well before the actual delivery.

● Parents-to-be can use the time during pregnancy to gather supplies their new baby will need. Couples need to buy the essential items first and use any money left over for optional items.

● Babies need furniture, diapers, and clothes. They also need special equipment and supplies for mealtime, bath time, bedtime, and travel time. Parents should be aware of safety guidelines for all baby items and purchase those that meet current safety standards.

● Both breast-milk and formula feeding can provide the nutrients a newborn needs. After learning about each method, expectant parents should choose the one that is best for them.

● Making decisions about the baby's care may be very difficult for parents-to-be. They must decide about continuing their employment and taking parental leave. Expectant parents may also need to choose someone to provide daily care and someone to provide medical care for their infant.

Reviewing Key Points

1. What does prepared childbirth mean?

2 2. List three benefits of taking a childbirth class.

3. Briefly describe each of the options parents-to-be may choose for the delivery of their baby.

4. Give four tips that can help parents get the most for their money when buying baby supplies.

5. Why should parents not use a crib that was made before 1988?

6. List two advantages and two disadvantages each for cloth diapers and disposable diapers.

7. List three factors to consider when buying baby clothes.

8. Describe one essential item for each of the following newborn activities:
   A. eating
   B. bathing
   C. sleeping
   D. traveling

9. List two reasons mothers might breast-feed and two reasons parents might formula-feed.

10. List two advantages and two disadvantages of employment for parents of a newborn.

11. What is the purpose of the Family and Medical Leave Act?

12. Why do child development experts advise three to four months of parental leave after the birth or adoption of a child?

13. List four child care options parents of a newborn might have.

14. What is the difference between a pediatrician and a family doctor?

15. Name three factors parents should consider when selecting a doctor for their baby.

Learning by Doing

1. With a small group, research childbirth classes that are available for expectant parents in your community. Give an oral report to your class, briefly describing each class.

2. Create a directory of available birth locations in your area. Include contact information for every hospital and birth center in your community. For each location, describe available services.

3. Interview parents of an infant about the supplies they gathered before their baby's birth. Ask the following questions as well as any others you might have:

   ● Which items did you find essential, and which were optional?

   ● Did baby supplies cost more than you expected?

   ● Which item was the most costly?

   ● What methods did you use to stretch your money?

4. Create a pamphlet for expectant parents to help them decide whether to breast-feed or formula-feed their baby. Use information given in the chapter about each choice.

5. Working with a small group, contact each child care center listed in your local phone book. For each center, ask whether the center accepts infants. If so, what ages of infants does the center accept? Finally, for centers that do provide infant care, ask what it costs per month for full-time care (40 hours a week).

Thinking Critically

1. Form a small group to discuss the following statement: Childbirth is a natural event and should take place in the home.

2. Research diaper services in your area, as well as prices for both cloth diapers and disposable diapers. Based on your findings, if you were the parent of a newborn, would you use cloth diapers or disposable diapers? Why would you choose this type?

3. If you were a parent, would you prefer breast-feeding, formula-feeding, or a combination of the two for your baby? Why would you choose this method? Write a paragraph on this topic, using information from the chapter to support your answer.

4. Refer to the information your group gathered on infant care in your area. Write a brief paper explaining how this information would affect your decisions about child care if you were the parent of a newborn. With this information in mind, what child care arrangement do you think you would choose? Support your answer.

5. Debate whether pediatricians or family doctors are best for a baby's medical care.

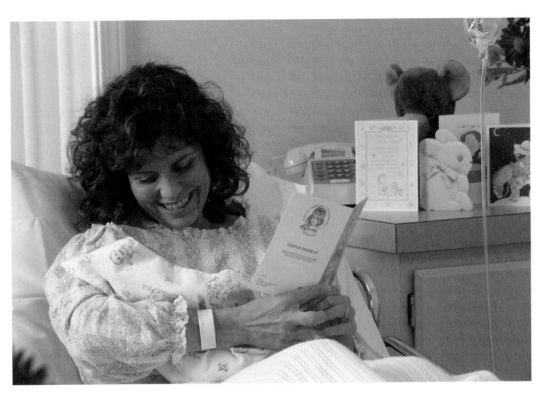

Preparing for the parenting experience can be exciting and joyful.

Chapter 9
Childbirth

Objectives

After studying this chapter, you will be able to

● identify the signs of labor.

● explain common hospital procedures before, during, and after birth.

● describe what types of medications are available during childbirth.

● identify key events in each stage of labor.

● compare different methods of childbirth.

● summarize the importance of bonding.

● describe routine neonatal care.

● explain reasons a newborn might need emergency medical care.

● propose ways new parents can adjust during the postpartum period.

Key Terms

1
contractions
epidural
dilation stage
delivery stage
episiotomy
afterbirth stage
traditional childbirth
family-centered childbirth
Lamaze method
Leboyer method
breech delivery
cesarean delivery
Apgar test
Brazelton scale
circumcision
bonding
postpartum period
postpartum depression

2 The last weeks of pregnancy may be a time of mixed emotions for parents-to-be. A woman may be eager to be relieved of the physical burdens of pregnancy. Both prospective parents may be anxious for the birth so they can meet their new baby. At the same time, they may wish they could have a little more time for the final preparations.

3 As the due date approaches, the expectant mother will have weekly checkups. Her doctor or nurse-midwife will watch closely for signs the baby is ready to be born. The woman should pack a bag with items needed for her hospital stay and for the new baby's trip home. A typical list of these items is given in 9-1. It is wise to pack her bag several weeks before the due date. Babies often arrive earlier than expected. Packing early will reduce the chance she will forget something important.

Signs of Labor

Like symptoms of pregnancy, signs of labor vary from woman to woman and from pregnancy to pregnancy. The very first sign labor is approaching is
4 called *lightening*. This occurs as the baby's head descends into the mother's pelvis. When the baby moves down, it relieves pressure on the mother's abdomen. This can make breathing easier for her. In a woman's first pregnancy, lightening may occur anytime in the final month. In later pregnancies, it may not occur until the week or the day labor actually begins.

A second sign that labor will soon occur is the passage of a small amount of blood-tinged mucus. This is sometimes called the *show*. Labor usually begins within 24 hours of the appearance of the show.

1—Vocabulary: Look up terms in the glossary and discuss their meanings.

2—Discuss: Why might both parents be anxious in the days just before delivery? Cite the concerns of prospective mothers and fathers.

3—Activity: Pretend you and your spouse are expectant parents. What would you pack for the hospital stay of the mother-to-be and the baby?

4—Discuss: Review signs labor is approaching. What is the significance of each sign?

1—Resource: *Signs and Stages of Labor*, Activity A, SAG.

2—Discuss: What are Braxton-Hicks contractions? Why do these occur, and how do they differ from true labor contractions?

3—Discuss: When someone says a pregnant woman's "water has broken," what does this mean?

Mother's Needs

2-4 nightgowns, one for each day she will stay in the hospital. These should be comfortable, opaque, and preferably not full-length.

Robe and bed jacket.

Comfortable, low-heeled slippers.

Nursing bras (if planning to nurse).

Sanitary pads.

Toothbrush and toothpaste.

Comb, brush, rollers, cosmetics (as needed).

Small hand mirror.

Birth announcements, stationary, address book, stamps, pen.

Outfit for trip home.

Baby's Needs

Sleeper, kimono, or "coming home" outfit.

2 diapers.

Diaper pins and vinyl pants (if using cloth diapers).

Receiving blanket.

Bonnet, sweater, bunting, or warm blanket (if needed).

Infant car seat.

9-1 _____

In the last weeks before the baby is born, the mother should pack a bag with the items she and her baby will need while they are in the hospital.

When labor begins, a woman will notice one or both of the following signs:

- regular contractions of the uterus
- passage of liquid from the vagina as the amnio-chorionic membrane ruptures (also referred to as the "water breaking"). Sometimes, however, this doesn't happen until much later in the labor process.

Contractions are pains felt during labor when the muscles of the uterus tense. The uterine muscles contract to open the cervix and push the baby out of the uterus. Once contractions begin, couples should time the contractions. They should record when a contraction occurs and how long it lasts.

Some types of contractions are not actual labor contractions. For instance, *Braxton-Hicks contractions* may begin a month before labor. These muscle contractions happen infrequently, last less than a minute, and stop when the woman changes position. These contractions are sometimes called *prelabor contractions*.

On the other hand, true labor contractions last longer and are closer together. No matter what the woman does, these contractions will not stop. They become progressively more frequent, lengthy, and evenly spaced. Between contractions, the woman is free from pain.

Contractions usually begin as aches that occur infrequently in the small of the back. After a few hours, the pains move to the front. Each contraction begins as a slight twinge, builds in intensity, and reaches a peak. This peak is maintained for a few seconds, and then fades gradually.

Also during labor, the amnio-chorionic membranes will rupture and release amniotic fluid. If contractions have not begun, the breaking of the membranes will signal them to start. Once the membranes have broken, delivery should occur within 24 hours. Amniotic fluid cushions the baby and regulates his or her body temperature. Without this fluid, the baby may be in danger. The baby might also develop an infection if he or she is not born soon. The membranes may not break right away. In some cases, the doctor may have to rupture them just before delivery.

Going to the Hospital

Once a woman notices signs of labor, she should make her final preparations before going to the hospital.

9-4 _____
Using medications to relieve the pain of childbirth is not a new idea.

Medicines and Childbirth

Women have used pain medicine during childbirth since the mid-1800s. Doctors knew the pain women felt during childbirth could be almost overwhelming. Giving medication to take away this pain seemed only logical. No one knew then that substances in a woman's body could cross the placenta and harm the baby.

It was once routine to use general anesthesia for childbirth. When the risks and side effects were learned, it was less commonly used. Today, general anesthesia is only used for emergency deliveries. Other anesthetics and analgesics have almost replaced the use of general anesthesia in childbirth.

In the 1970s, a push began for women to give birth without pain medication. This was known as natural childbirth. Women were encouraged to take childbirth classes to learn more about labor and delivery. Instructors taught them how to manage pain through breathing techniques. The idea was that knowing what to expect might eliminate a woman's need for pain medication.

Currently, there is less emphasis on childbirth without medication. The focus has shifted from natural childbirth to prepared childbirth. Women are still encouraged to take childbirth classes. Instructors still teach techniques to manage pain. Today, childbirth instructors know many of their students will choose some type of pain medication. Some may even teach about the medications available.

1—Discuss: Review the basic types of childbirth medication available. In which category does an epidural belong?

2—Resource: *The Three Stages of Labor*, transparency master 9-1, TR.

can be injected into the spinal cord during labor. The mother is awake, but cannot feel the lower half of her body. Epidural use is growing more common. An epidural can make childbirth easier, but it has drawbacks. Not being able to feel the contractions can make pushing harder. The woman must stay in bed and be continually monitored. Regional anesthesia has some side effects and risks.

Local anesthesia takes away pain in a small area. It is usually given in a shot. Local anesthesia is often used to relieve pain in the vaginal area. It causes few risks and side effects.

Analgesics are another type of medicine used during childbirth. *Analgesics* dull pain but do not take it away entirely. This type of medicine reduces pain to a more tolerable level. Analgesics can be given intravenously or in a shot. They may have fewer side effects and risks than other medications.

Three Stages of Labor

Labor is a series of changes in the mother's body that enables the baby to be born. Delivering a baby is hard work for the mother's body. It requires strength, stamina, and muscle control. Labor can be divided into three stages—the dilation stage, delivery stage, and afterbirth stage. Each part of this process takes longer for a mother's first baby than for later ones.

Dilation Stage

The first stage of labor is the **dilation stage**. The purpose of this stage is to dilate (stretch and expand) the cervix. It must open wide enough that the baby can be pushed out of the uterus and into the birth canal.

1—Discuss: Which is the longest stage of labor? Does the average length of time for this stage vary between first and later pregnancies?

2—Reflect: How might a husband support and encourage his wife during the first stage of labor? Why is it important for him to understand what is happening during this stage?

Normally, the cervix is less than a centimeter wide. During labor, the cervix will dilate to ten centimeters wide.

The dilation stage is the longest stage of labor. It begins with the first true contraction and ends when the cervix has fully dilated. This may take **1** anywhere from 8 to 20 hours for a first baby. For later babies, this stage is usually shorter.

When contractions begin, they don't last long, come often, or hurt much. The woman will probably spend a few hours of this stage at home. She and her partner should try to rest, as well as making any final preparations before leaving for the hospital, 9-5. They should also time her contractions so they will know when to go to the hospital. Until her contractions come

9-5 _____

If a mother-to-be has not packed her bag before labor begins, she should do so when contractions begin. Soon it will be time to go to the hospital.

every 5 to 10 minutes, she will probably not be admitted to the hospital.

Each contraction of the uterus causes the cervix to dilate a little more. During the first stage, contractions grow progressively longer, stronger, and closer together. When the woman goes to the hospital, her blood pressure and other vital signs will be monitored. She will also be examined periodically for her progress. The cervix will be measured for dilation.

When the woman's cervix has dilated about 7 to 8 centimeters, she will enter a phase called *transition*. **2** Transition is often the most painful part of labor. This is the time when the cervix stretches the last little bit before delivery. The contractions are the most powerful during transition, and the time between them is very short. The mother-to-be will feel very tired, uncomfortable, and stressed. Her partner's support is very important at this time.

During transition, the woman may be moved from the labor room to the delivery room. (If she is using a birthing room, she will remain there for the delivery.) The nurses and doctor prepare the woman for delivery. Her husband will need to prepare by washing up and dressing in a sterile gown and mask, 9-6.

By this time, the amnio-chorionic membrane will probably have ruptured. If not, the doctor will rupture it when the cervix is fully expanded. The time has come for the woman to push the baby out of the uterus. This is the end of stage one.

Delivery Stage

The second stage of labor is the **delivery stage**. It begins when the cervix is fully dilated and ends when the baby is born. The delivery stage doesn't last long—the average is about 45 minutes. It is also normal for this stage to last half an hour or two hours.

9-6
A nurse can help the father-to-be dress for the delivery after he washes up. In the delivery room, everyone wears sterile clothing to prevent the spread of germs.

During this stage, the mother is encouraged to begin pushing. The force of the mother's pushing will move the baby out of the uterus and through the birth canal. *Crowning* refers to the moment the baby's head is first seen. This is an exciting time for the couple—soon they will be able to see their new baby. The woman is also relieved because the end of her labor is near.

As crowning occurs, the doctor will decide whether to perform an episiotomy. An **episiotomy** is a small cut made at the opening of the birth canal. This cut makes the vaginal opening wider so the baby has more room to be born. An episiotomy is not necessary in all deliveries. A local anesthetic may be given before making the cut or stitching it closed.

After the baby's head is pushed out of the birth canal, the doctor turns it gently. This allows the shoulders to slide out more easily. The rest of the body follows quickly. After delivery, amniotic fluid is suctioned from the baby's nose and mouth. The umbilical cord is cut, and the baby is cleaned and examined. Unless the baby needs emergency medical care, he or she is then handed to the proud new parents.

Afterbirth Stage

The **afterbirth stage** is the third and final stage of labor. The afterbirth stage usually lasts 10 to 20 minutes. During this stage, the afterbirth is expelled. The *afterbirth* is the name for the placenta and other tissues still inside the mother's body from the pregnancy. These tissues are no longer needed after the baby is born.

Mild contractions continue after the baby is born. These contractions cause the placenta to separate from the wall of the uterus and exit through the vagina. After the placenta is expelled, it is examined carefully. The doctor wants to be sure the placenta has not torn, leaving excess tissue in the uterus. Tissues left in the uterus after birth might cause heavy and uncontrollable bleeding. A nurse may massage the uterus to help it begin to shrink.

Methods of Childbirth

Childbirth is a natural human event, a set biological process. Opinions vary, however, about some of the details surrounding labor and delivery. What preparations should a couple make for labor and delivery? Who besides the mother should be allowed to participate in the delivery?

Differing answers to these questions led to the development of various childbirth methods. Each method reflects a slightly different viewpoint or style. Couples have several options. Generally, they can choose the method they prefer. Other times, their choice is limited by the practices of their hospital and doctor or nurse-midwife. A couple should decide which method

1—Discuss: In traditional childbirth, where is the attention focused?

2—Discuss: What are the advantages of family-centered childbirth? How can birthing rooms enhance the feeling of togetherness?

3—Discuss: Why do most hospitals require expectant parents to attend childbirth classes if they plan to use family-centered childbirth?

they want to use long before the due date. The method they use, however, may change during labor or delivery. This happens when the health of the mother or baby is at risk.

Traditional Childbirth

In **traditional childbirth,** attention is focused on the health of mother and baby. The woman's comfort is also important. The woman is given anesthetics as needed, and the baby's health is monitored. Family members wait in a waiting room. The husband may or may not be allowed to be with his wife during labor. Traditionally, fathers were not allowed in delivery rooms. Today, however, most hospitals allow them to be present for the birth of their children, 9-7.

After a traditional delivery, a woman is moved to a recovery room and then to a room for the rest of her hospital stay. The baby generally stays in the hospital nursery and is brought into the mother's room periodically.

Rules about visitors may be fairly strict. Young children, for instance, may not be allowed to visit their mother or the new baby.

Family-Centered Childbirth

Some hospitals offer a family-centered childbirth program. **Family-centered childbirth** is based on the belief childbirth affects the family as a unit and each family member as an individual, 9-8. The birth of a new baby is important to each family member.

In family-centered childbirth, the father is encouraged to participate in labor and delivery. Other support people (in a few cases, even children) may also be present if the mother so desires and the doctor approves. Labor and delivery generally take place in a birthing room.

Anyone who will be present at the birth must first attend childbirth classes. These classes prepare them for what will take place in the delivery

9-7
Today most hospitals allow men to remain with their wives during labor, even if the woman uses a traditional delivery room.

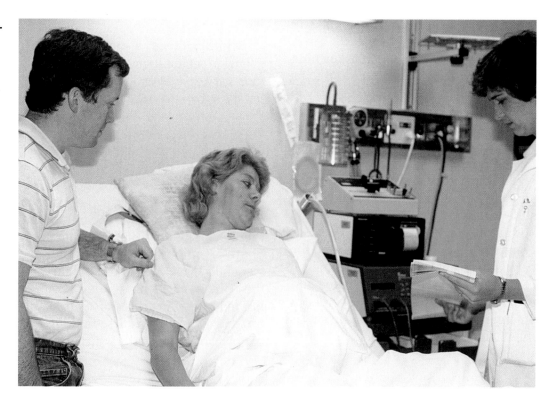

9-8 _____
Family-centered childbirth programs involve the entire family. In some cases, children may learn the basic facts about pregnancy and childbirth.

room. Some hospitals also offer classes for children who are expecting a new brother or sister.

During labor and delivery, an obstetrical nurse or certified nurse-midwife is normally present throughout the labor and delivery. The doctor may attend the delivery or be on-call in case of complications. The medical personnel encourage and support the natural forces of labor, interfering as little as possible. They try to make sure everything goes right while respecting the family's wish to share this important experience.

After the birth, the family may spend as much time together as they wish. Rooming-in is common in family-centered childbirth. _Rooming-in_ means the baby stays in the mother's room instead of in the hospital nursery, 9-9. Brothers and sisters can visit their mother and the new baby.

Lamaze Method

The **Lamaze method** of childbirth is a prepared childbirth method. In this method, parents-to-be prepare themselves for the experience of childbirth. About two months before delivery, they start attending weekly classes. They learn what to expect in the final stages of pregnancy and during labor

and delivery. When they know what to expect, parents are less afraid and more likely to enjoy the childbirth experience.

In Lamaze classes, mothers-to-be learn special breathing and muscle control techniques. Fathers-to-be learn to act as labor coaches. Delivery may take place in a birthing room or in the delivery room, whichever the parents choose.

Using Lamaze techniques helps women maintain control of their bodies during childbirth. A woman's normal response to contractions is to become tense. If she can instead learn to relax, she will feel less pain. Also, if she can concentrate on breathing instead of on the contractions, the pain will seem more tolerable. The father-to-be can help his wife remember and use the techniques they practiced in class. He can comfort her, which can help her through the pain.

9-9 _____
In hospitals where family-centered childbirth is practiced, rooming-in is common.

1—Discuss: Why are breathing exercises and muscle control so important in the Lamaze method of childbirth?

1—Discuss: What are the main differences between Lamaze and the Leboyer childbirth methods? What are the similarities?

2—Discuss: Why do you think a doctor or hospital might not welcome using the Leboyer method?

3—Vocabulary: What is the difference between a *breech presentation* and a *breech delivery*?

4—Discuss: Under what conditions is a cesarean delivery performed?

The goal of Lamaze is to make childbirth a safe, pleasant, and memorable experience for both parents. The woman does not fail if she needs some pain relief. Medication is viewed as a tool to help her relax during childbirth. Other tools include the breathing and muscle control techniques and her partner's coaching.

Leboyer Method

The **Leboyer method** focuses on the baby's birth experience. Its goal is to make birth less shocking and more comfortable for the baby. The medical staff tries to provide a quiet, cozy environment. The lights are dimmed and soft music is played. Immediately after birth, the baby is placed on the mother's warm, soft abdomen. When separated from contact with the mother's skin, the baby is placed in warm water.

Couples who use the Leboyer method often take childbirth classes to prepare for labor and delivery. Doctors and hospitals vary in the extent to which they accept the Leboyer method. Couples who want to use this method should talk to their doctor about their wishes early in pregnancy.

Breech Delivery

A baby's head is often the first part to come down the birth canal. This is generally the first part to leave the mother's body. The baby's head settles into the mother's pelvic bone during lightening. This happens in the last few weeks before birth.

Occasionally, a body part other than the baby's head settles into the mother's pelvic bone. When the baby's rear end or feet do this, the baby is in a *breech position*. Since lightening doesn't occur until the last weeks of pregnancy, babies born very early are often in a breech position.

Sometimes a baby turns itself around to the normal position. Other times, the doctor can help the baby turn around before delivery. In a few cases, the baby will be delivered from this position. This is called a **breech delivery**. It is riskier than a normal head-first delivery. Often, babies in a breech position must be born by cesarean delivery.

Cesarean Delivery

Cesarean delivery is an operation in which a baby is delivered through incisions in the mother's abdomen and uterus. Cesarean deliveries are also commonly called *cesarean sections*, or *C-sections*. Almost 21 percent of births in the U.S. are done by cesarean delivery. This method is used for a number of reasons, including the following:

- labor has been too long or too difficult
- the baby's health is in danger
- the mother's health is in danger
- the baby is in a breech position
- there is a problem with the umbilical cord or placenta
- the woman's pelvis is too small for the baby's head to pass through it
- the mother has an active STD the baby might contract in the birth canal

Doctors may also perform cesarean deliveries for other reasons. In some cases, a cesarean delivery might not actually be necessary. For instance, some doctors perform a cesarean delivery if the mother has had previous cesarean births. Many women can have a vaginal birth after a previous cesarean delivery. The doctor may perform a cesarean for his or her convenience, or the mother's convenience. This alone is not a compelling reason to deliver by cesarean.

Many reasons exist for having a cesarean delivery, but it is not the preferred method under normal conditions. Generally, a cesarean delivery is an emergency procedure. It involves major surgery. Although it can be life-saving, it does carry some health risks. The recovery period is several days longer for cesarean births than for other births.

Neonatal Care

As soon as a baby is born, he or she requires medical care. The doctor or nurse-midwife must cut the umbilical cord that connects the baby to the mother. Fluid must be suctioned from the nose and mouth, allowing the baby to begin breathing. The baby must be washed. Particles of a white coating called *vernix* may still be on the baby's skin. Vernix protects the skin before birth. The *neonate* (name for a baby from birth to one month) is weighed and measured. Bands are placed on the wrist or ankle to identify the baby, 9-10. Prints of the baby's feet may also be made.

The medical staff will be busy providing some routine care. All newborns are tested for conditions such as anemia and PKU. They are also

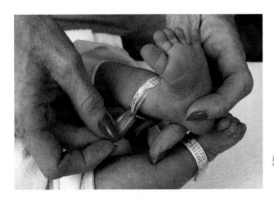

9-10 ———————————————
The identification band placed on the baby's ankles matches the one on the mother's wrist. This helps the hospital know which baby belongs to which mother.

given eyedrops to prevent eye infections caused by any STDs. They are examined for any obvious problems and given assessment tests.

One of these tests is the **Apgar test.** This assessment is used to evaluate a newborn's overall physical condition. It reveals the chance, on a scale of zero to ten, a neonate will survive. This allows the doctor to quickly evaluate the baby's condition. It can also call attention to the need for any emergency steps. More information about the Apgar test is given in 9-11.

Another way to assess newborns is with the Brazelton scale. The **Brazelton scale** identifies problems a baby may have that do not need emergency medical attention. This test is very thorough. It checks the baby's movement, reflexes, responses, and general state.

Emergency Care

Sometimes a neonate might require emergency medical care. This might happen for one of several reasons. Common reasons emergency care is needed include the following:

● *The baby was born prematurely.* Premature babies, or babies born before week 35 of pregnancy, are at risk for numerous health problems. Babies born too early require emergency care much more often than other babies. Commonly, the lungs of premature babies are not fully developed. This means they cannot breathe normally. Premature babies may need to use respiratory support systems until their lungs mature.

● *The baby was born at a low birth-weight.* A low-birthweight baby is one who weighs less than $5 \frac{1}{2}$ pounds at birth. Babies with low birthweights are also usually born prematurely. These babies are at risk for a great many medical problems. They are less likely to

1—Discuss: Why is the recovery period much longer with a cesarean delivery than for other child-birth methods?

2—Discuss: What are the Apgar test and the Brazelton scale? Why are they used?

3—Resource: *Emergency Care,* color transparency CT-9B, TR

4—Discuss: When might a neonate need emergency medical care?

5—Note: Of all births, 7.5 percent are low-birthweight babies. What might be done to lower this number?

9-11 _____
The Apgar test is used to determine a newborn's chance of survival.

1—Reflect: How do you think you would feel if your newborn had to be rushed to an intensive care unit before you could even hold him or her? What would you do?

Apgar Test

Vital Sign	Range from Good to Poor Condition
Coloring	From pink to blue in light-skinned babies or strong color to grayish color in dark-skinned babies (Color is best observed on the lips, palms, and soles.)
Pulse rate	From above 100 beats per minute to below 100 beats per minute
Reflex irritability	From coughing or sneezing in response to a stimulus to making little or no response
Muscle tone	From active movements to little or no movement
Respiration	From healthy crying to slow or irregular breathing

Within one minute after birth, a baby is evaluated according to the Apgar test developed by Dr. Virginia Apgar. A score of 2, 1, or 0 is given for each of the five vital signs listed above. The scores are added together, so a perfect Apgar score is 10. Scores ranging from 7 to 10 indicate the baby is in good condition. Scores of 4, 5, or 6 indicate fair condition, and scores of 3 or below indicate poor condition. A baby who scores less than 7 is evaluated again five minutes later. If the score is still low, the baby may need special medical attention.

survive than normal-weight infants. Generally, babies cannot be released from the hospital until they reach 5¹/₂ pounds. Instead, they remain at the hospital and receive special care.

● _The baby was born addicted to drugs._ Often, babies whose mothers used drugs during pregnancy are born with a drug addiction. Their tiny bodies are not strong enough to fight this addiction. They experience withdrawal symptoms and other medical problems. Drug-addicted babies need the help of medical personnel to overcome their addiction and their other medical problems.

● _The baby scored very low on the Apgar test._ This would probably mean the baby was not breathing, had a low heart rate, or both. A lack of reflex irritability and movement could mean the baby was unresponsive. Problems with coloring would indicate the baby's body was not getting enough oxygen. One or more of these signals might indicate the baby was in immediate danger.

● _The baby has another serious health condition that requires emergency care._ For instance, if the baby has a serious heart condition, this might require surgery immediately after birth. The baby might be rushed from the delivery room to the operating room. After surgery, he or she might require an extended hospital stay to recover.

Newborns who require emergency care may be moved to a special intensive care unit for neonates. They may need a variety of machines and monitors to help them survive. These babies may be placed in special incubators that protect them from germs and air drafts. Neonates in intensive care will be continually watched and treated. Special tubes may allow for feeding through the nose, mouth, or stomach, as needed. In an intensive care unit designed especially for neonates, these babies will receive whatever care is needed to restore their health.

When a baby needs emergency medical care, it can be very frightening for the parents. They may wonder if their baby will be okay, 9-12. Normal emotions include fear, anger, sadness,

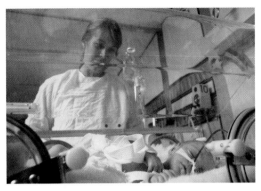

9-12 _____
Parents may worry if their babies need emergency medical care. Visiting the baby in the intensive care unit can help ease their fears.

1—**Discuss:** Why is circumcision less common today than it once was? Should it be done? Why or why not?

2—**Reflect:** Why is bonding so important in the early hours following birth?

and even guilt. Parents need to be reassured the hospital staff is doing everything possible for their infant. The doctors and nurses who provide this care are experienced in working with newborns. They understand the seriousness of these situations and know how to help. Parents should also feel comfortable to ask questions about their baby's care. They have a right to know what is wrong and what is being done to correct the problem.

If the baby must stay at the hospital after the mother goes home, this can also be difficult for parents. They should be allowed to visit the baby whenever they like. Both mother and father can talk lovingly to their baby. If the baby's condition permits, they can touch and massage him or her. This is often possible, even if the baby is in an incubator. Many times a mother can express milk from her breasts to be fed to her infant. This way her baby still gains the benefits breast milk offers. Parents can find ways to be close to their baby until the baby is well enough to come home.

Circumcision

Circumcision is the surgical removal of a male's foreskin. The *foreskin* is a flap of skin that covers the head of the penis. Many parents have their newborn boys circumcised. Some do this for religious reasons. Their beliefs support circumcision of a male infant within a few days after birth.

Other parents have their babies circumcised for health reasons. Removing the foreskin makes it easier to keep the genital area clean. In uncircumcised males, a substance called *smegma* can collect under the foreskin. Washing under the foreskin will remove the smegma and prevent irritation and infection. Cancer of the penis is also far less common in men who have been circumcised.

At one time, the practice of circumcision was very routine. Almost all newborn boys were circumcised. Today, people disagree about whether this procedure is really needed. A man with good hygiene habits can keep himself clean even if he has a foreskin. Some medical experts say there is no medical reason for circumcision. Others disagree. They believe benefits do exist.

Parents may want to ask their pediatrician and religious leader for advice, but the final decision should be theirs. If they choose to have their baby boy circumcised, this can be done before the baby leaves the hospital. The doctor will tell them how to care for the area as it heals.

Bonding

The first moments after birth are full of emotion. It is a time especially suited to **bonding**, the formation of close emotional ties between parents and child. See 9-13.

Most hospitals and doctors encourage bonding. They say that after the normal birth of a healthy baby, the mother and baby need to be together. The baby needs to be comforted after

9-13 _____
This new mother looks at her baby with a mixture of love and curiosity. Having this time to bond will help them feel close.

the difficult passage through the birth canal. The mother needs to relax after the physical strain of labor. She needs a moment to blend her mental image of her future child with the reality of her new baby. The natural reaction of a new mother is to hold her new baby gently. She caresses the baby, touching the tiny facial features, noticing the hands and feet, and stroking the chest and abdomen. As the mother learns about her baby, the baby responds to her touch and voice. These first interactions have a powerful effect on bonding.

If the father has been present throughout labor and delivery, he will bond with the baby, too. A common reaction of new fathers is to be somewhat protective and possessive. Birth has transformed the fetus into a baby, and not just any baby. Suddenly, it has become his son or his daughter—a tiny, fragile being that needs his protection.

The atmosphere in the delivery room or birthing room after the birth of a healthy baby is filled with relief and happiness. The parents claim the baby as their own with pride, happiness, and a sense of awe.

In hospitals where bonding is encouraged, the new family is left alone together as soon as possible, 9-14. In the next few days, the mother spends several hours each day holding,

caressing, and feeding her baby. She assumes responsibility for the care of her baby. The baby may even stay in her room. The nurses are there to care for her needs, answer her questions, and offer help when needed.

Often parents who experienced early bonding tend to spend more time with their babies. They touch, cuddle, and soothe the babies more. They talk more and have more eye contact with their babies. This closer relationship between parents and their children seems to continue throughout infancy into childhood, and perhaps far beyond. In general, bonding seems to help parents be more patient and less demanding. It also helps children feel closer and more trusting of their parents.

This immediate bonding may not be possible in all circumstances. Birth by cesarean delivery is one example. If the mother remains conscious throughout delivery, she will be able to see her new baby. She will be able to touch and maybe even hold the baby for a while. If she is put under general anesthesia, however, she may not be alert for several hours following the delivery. In these cases, the father may be able to hold the baby immediately after delivery even if his wife cannot.

9-14 _____
Bonding can begin soon after birth when the family has a chance to be alone together. Both mothers and fathers develop a special closeness with the new baby.

Another example is premature births. A premature baby's life may depend on immediate treatment. Once the baby is settled in an incubator, the parents are encouraged to spend time with the baby, 9-15. Touching and stroking have been shown to help a baby's development. Gradually, parents become acquainted with their baby. Both the baby and the parents benefit from the bonding that occurs.

If bonding cannot occur immediately after birth, it can still happen later. As soon as the parents and baby are reunited, bonding can occur. Bonding provides the basis for building a close parent-child relationship.

Postpartum Period

The **postpartum period** is the period of time following the delivery of the baby. It begins when the baby is born and lasts about six weeks. During this time, a woman recovers from the exhausting experiences of pregnancy and childbirth.

Following stage three of labor, a woman spends a few hours in

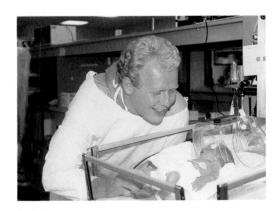

9-15
Even though this newborn needs special medical attention, the father can spend time touching and talking to him.

recovery. During this time, she is watched very closely as her breathing, heart rate, and blood pressure return to normal. Recovery does not end there, however. Throughout her hospital stay, the woman continues to rest and regain her strength. Even when she returns home, she is still recovering as her body slowly returns to its prepregnancy condition.

The Mother's Hospital Stay

Immediately after delivery, a new mother may be extremely tired. Her body has done an incredible amount of work. If the woman gave birth in a delivery room, she will soon be moved to a recovery room. If she used a birthing room, she will likely recover in that same room.

For at least an hour, her condition will be carefully monitored. The medical staff must be sure she is not experiencing complications. They will monitor her vital signs to be sure her body is recovering well. Her body rids itself of any medications taken during labor. She will be encouraged to drink plenty of fluids and possibly even eat a snack. The nurse will encourage her to get up and walk, even if it is only as far as the restroom. (Mothers who had a cesarean delivery may not get out of bed for the first day or so.)

The nurses will continue to massage the mother's uterus. As the uterus shrinks, she may have pains similar to strong menstrual cramps. Heavy bleeding that is similar to a menstrual period will last for a week or more. The area surrounding her episiotomy may be tender and sore.

If the mother is doing well, at this time she will be moved to her hospital room. (If she used a birthing room, she will likely spend her hospital stay in that same room.) She can spend time resting and getting to know her new baby, 9-16. The father and their other

1—Discuss: If a baby is born prematurely, how can bonding be accomplished?

2—Discuss: The postpartum period begins just after the third stage of labor. When does it end?

3—Discuss: What happens during the mother's postpartum hospital stay?

1—Examples:
Obtain photos of
parents bringing their
new babies home
from the hospital.
What emotions are
evident in the
pictures?

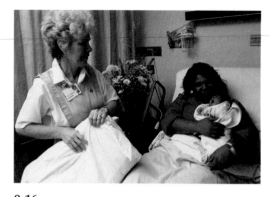

9-16 _____
During her hospital stay, a new mother
can spend lots of time holding and talking
to her baby. She should also spend time
resting and recovering.

children may spend lots of time at the
hospital with mother and baby. Friends
and family members may be eager to
see the new baby. They may visit the
hospital and bring gifts.

During her hospital stay, she
should try to get as much rest as possible. This may mean limiting the
number of visitors or the length of their
stay. Resting will help her rejuvenate
her body. It will prepare her to handle
all she has to do when she goes home.

While she is in the hospital, she can
ask the doctor and nurses any questions she might have. Maternity nurses
are very familiar with the daily care
skills parents will need, 9-17. They can
show parents how to hold, dress,
diaper, bathe, and feed their neonate.
Some hospitals offer classes for new
parents while others teach mainly one-
on-one.

Breast-feeding mothers can ask
their nurses about the proper technique for feeding the baby. Nurses can
tell a mother how to relieve any
discomfort she may have when her
milk comes in. This will happen in two
to three days after birth. She can also
ask how to relieve any discomfort
caused by breast-feeding.

Bottle-feeding mothers are sometimes given hormones to stop the
breasts from producing milk. The

mother may feel some discomfort until
the milk dries up and her breasts
return to normal. A nurse can advise
her how to relieve this discomfort. The
nurse can also tell the parents what
they need to know about bottle-feeding. At first, babies are given water.
Soon they will drink formula.

Going Home from the Hospital

Within one to two days, the mother
will be discharged from the hospital.
(For mothers who have cesarean births,
the hospital stay is several days
longer.) Usually, her baby will be
discharged at the same time. It is an
especially joyous occasion. The father
will probably come to the hospital to
take mother and baby home. They may
take pictures or videotape their journey

9-17 _____
Maternity nurses truly enjoy working with
newborns. They know how to care for
babies and can teach parents some of the
skills they will need.

home from the hospital. Older brothers and sisters may come, too.

Once they return home, however, new parents face many challenges. They must fit their new roles and responsibilities into their old life. Things will change. During this postpartum period, the mother must adapt to the physical changes that continue as her body returns to normal. Both parents must manage emotional changes. The new mother must try to get enough rest as she continues to regain her strength. She may have questions about starting to exercise again.

Adapting to Physical Changes

Even after she returns home, the woman's body will continue to adjust. The uterus will keep shrinking until it returns to its normal size. This process is speeded up by nursing the baby. The mother may continue to have a vaginal discharge, which will slowly subside. She may have some discomfort as her episiotomy heals.

Her breasts will change, whether they are adjusting to breast-feeding or returning to normal if she bottle-feeds. Her abdomen gradually flattens, and she slowly loses the weight she gained during pregnancy. Immediately after birth, she will lose as much as ten pounds. This is the weight of the baby and the placenta. She will lose another five pounds within the first month. The other weight will be harder to lose. Exercise and healthful eating will help. Most women return to their prepregnancy weight within 6 to 12 months.

Handling Emotional Changes

Many mothers feel somewhat depressed shortly after childbirth. This is called **postpartum depression,** but it is commonly called "the baby blues." These feelings vary widely from woman to woman and may be caused by various factors. Hormonal changes in the woman's body may be one such factor. Another factor may be the woman feels a sense of loss when the baby leaves her body. She no longer feels the movements of the fetus inside her.

Some aspects of postpartum depression are shared by the mother and father. Even though parents are happy about their new baby, they may feel a letdown after the excitement of delivery. This tension or stress is caused by the major change in their lives—a new baby! They may worry about all their new responsibilities. They may doubt their ability to care for the baby. They may resent being tied down. The first days at home may be tiring and demanding.

During this time, the husband and wife need to be honest with one another about their feelings. They need each other's understanding and support. Luckily, postpartum depression usually doesn't last long. As the man and woman grow used to their new roles as parents, depression fades away.

Getting Enough Rest

When the new mother returns home, she should continue to get a lot of rest. She should avoid lifting anything but the baby. Also, she should try to limit visitors, except for relatives and close friends who are offering help. These visitors can ease the burden of caring for the new baby.

When newborns are awake (even during the night) they require a parent's full attention. When they are sleeping, parents often try to clean house, wash laundry, or other tasks. If parents do this, however, they will not get enough sleep. The new mother should take advantage of the baby's sleeping schedule. When the baby is asleep, she can rest, too.

1—Discuss: What concerns does a new mother have after going home from the hospital?

2—Vocabulary: Why might *postpartum depression* occur? How can the new mother and father cope with this situation?

3—Discuss: Why shouldn't visitors overwhelm new parents and their baby during the postpartum period?

1—Discuss: Why is the postpartum checkup important?

2—Resource: Childbirth Crossword, Activity D, SAG.

3—Resource: Childbirth Case Studies, Activity F, SAG.

Starting to Exercise Again

Exercise will help a woman regain her prepregnancy weight and shape. A woman should consult her doctor before starting an exercise program. She should begin slowly, especially if she did not exercise much during the pregnancy.

Walking is a safe and effective way to burn calories and rebuild strength. In a few weeks, the mother may decide to add other exercises, such as swimming, bicycling, aerobic dance, or jogging. She may do special toning exercises to flatten her abdomen. Strength training with weights can improve her muscle tone, which will help her burn fat more quickly. Exercise can be a good way to release tension and build self-confidence. It can also help a new mother feel more energetic.

Postpartum Checkup

The mother should be sure to attend her postpartum checkup. This medical checkup is usually scheduled six weeks after delivery. At this visit, the doctor will check her blood pressure and weight, 9-18. A physical examination will reveal if the uterus and cervix are returning to normal. The doctor will look to see if the episiotomy is healing. At her postpartum checkup, a woman can ask questions about any problems or discomforts she is having. She may also talk to the doctor about continued family planning, nutrition, and exercise.

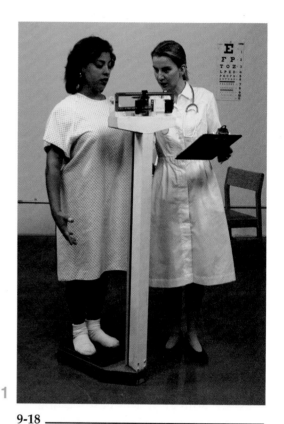

9-18 _____

At the postpartum visit, the doctor will monitor the mother's weight loss and blood pressure. The new mother can also ask the doctor any questions she may have.

Summary

- Signs of labor vary somewhat from woman to woman and from pregnancy to pregnancy.

1 - Most hospitals have the same basic procedures during childbirth. These procedures follow the natural sequence of labor and delivery.

- Several types of pain medication are available for use during childbirth. A woman and her doctor should decide what to use. If a woman needs or wants pain medication, it is not a sign of failure.

- Labor consists of three stages. Each stage plays a unique role in the childbirth process.

- A couple may be able to choose the method of childbirth they will use. The choice may be limited by the practices of the doctor or hospital. A different method might be used if the health of the woman or baby is in danger.

- All newborns must have routine neonatal care, but some require emergency medical care as well. One decision parents must make is whether to have their sons circumcised.

- Bonding often occurs during the first moments after birth. If parents and child must be separated immediately after birth, bonding can occur when they are reunited.

- In the postpartum period, a woman recovers from pregnancy and childbirth. Recovery occurs while she is in the hospital and after she goes home. About six weeks after delivery, the mother should have a postpartum medical checkup. The postpartum period is a critical time to adjust to the new baby, too. A new baby brings both joy and stress. New parents have many adjustments to make.

Reviewing Key Points

1. Name three signs that might indicate labor is approaching.

2 2. What is a contraction?

3. How can a woman distinguish between prelabor contractions and real labor contractions?

4. Why might a couple want to fill out some of the hospital admittance forms before labor begins?

5. Describe what electronic fetal monitoring is and why it is used.

6. Briefly describe two of the four types of medication that may be used during childbirth.

7. Name each stage of labor and identify the key event that happens in each stage.

8. Five childbirth methods were described in the text. Briefly describe two of these methods.

9. Give three reasons a cesarean delivery might be used.

10. What is bonding and why is it important?

11. Name four procedures involved in routine neonatal care.

12. How does the Apgar test differ from the Brazelton scale?

13. Give two reasons a neonate might require emergency medical care.

14. What is the postpartum period and how long does it last?

15. Why is the postpartum checkup important?

Learning by Doing

1. Prepare a pamphlet for expectant parents about the signs and stages of labor.

2. Interview new parents about their first birth. Ask them how they knew labor had begun, what they took with them to the hospital, what method of delivery they used, and what discomforts the mother had after delivery.

1—Activity: Review and outline this chapter emphasizing the information you found most useful.

2—Answers: Answers to review questions are located in the front section of this TAE.

3. Gather information from local hospitals about their policies concerning training for childbirth, methods of childbirth, the care of mother and baby during labor and delivery, and the father's involvement. Ask about the average costs related to the birth of a baby.

4. If possible, visit a neonatal intensive care unit. Talk with the doctors and nurses about what kinds of special care the babies require. Share with your class your reaction to seeing the babies.

5. Research postpartum depression. How common is this, and what can be done to help it go away?

Thinking Critically

1. In a small group, discuss the similarities and differences among the five methods of childbirth described in the text. Which method do you think you would choose? Why?

2. What would you say to a couple in which the father did not want to be present during labor and delivery?

3. Debate the use of medications during childbirth. If you think they should be used, which ones should be chosen and when should they be used? If you think they should not be used, explain why not.

4. Research circumcision. Write a short report explaining reasons couples choose to have their male infants circumcised. Conclude your paper by expressing your opinion. If you were the parent of a male newborn, would you have him circumcised? Why or why not?

5. Propose ten ways new parents can adjust during the postpartum period. What could they do to support the recovery process, adjust to a new baby, and cope with their emotions? How could friends and family help?

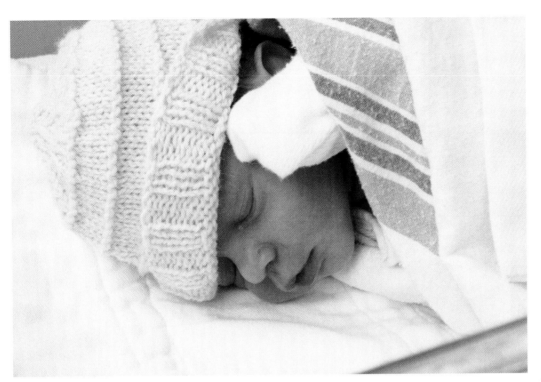

The tiny knit cap and warm blankets help regulate a newborn's body temperature.

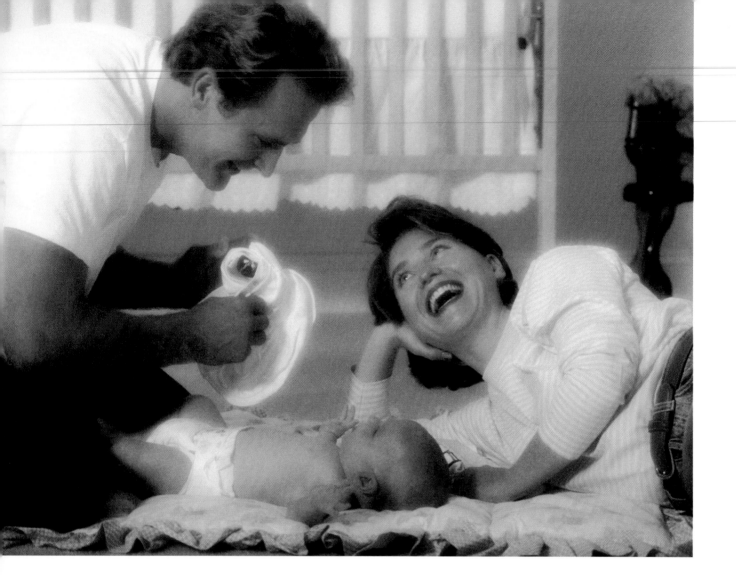

Chapter 10
New Parents,
New Baby

Objectives

After studying this chapter, you will be able to

- explain changes that occur during the first days of parenthood.

- describe the appearance and abilities of a newborn.

- demonstrate proper techniques for holding, feeding, bathing, and dressing a newborn.

- describe a newborn's sleeping habits.

- identify adjustments families with newborns may need to make.

Key Terms

1

fontanel
reflexes
self-demand feeding
cradle cap
diaper rash
colic

2

The birth of a couple's first baby triggers a series of changes. The baby begins living as a separate human being. The woman begins her life as a mother. The man begins his life as a father. New relationships are formed with grandparents, aunts, uncles, and cousins. Previous relationships acquire new dimensions. For instance, husband and wife must learn to relate to each other as parents as well as spouses. Friendships are likely to change. Job schedules may change. Household routines definitely change. All these changes can be linked to the baby's birth. That tiny bundle wrapped in a soft blanket creates lots of powerful changes!

The First Days of Parenthood

3

The first days at home with their baby are exciting but tiring for new parents. Mom and Dad have to adjust to night feedings, diaper changes, and other needs of their baby. They are learning to enjoy their new little one. Their home may be flooded with visits, gifts, and calls from friends and loved ones.

In addition, the mother's body is recovering from labor and delivery. Both she and the new father are catching up on their rest from the past few days of preparation and excitement, 10-1. At the same time, parents are adjusting to their new baby and learning to care for him or her.

4

They may worry about their ability to take care of their new baby. Parents can enjoy this time more if they try not to worry too much. It's true that babies are totally dependent on parents to meet their every need. This dependency can be overwhelming for new parents. Parents can rest assured, however,

1—Vocabulary: Look up terms in the glossary and discuss their meanings.

2—Enrich: Invite a new parent to speak to the class about adjustments new parents have to make.

3—Resource: New Parents, Activity A, SAG.

4—Discuss: Why do new parents often feel babies are very fragile?

10-1
Fathers and newborns need lots of rest in the first few days at home together.

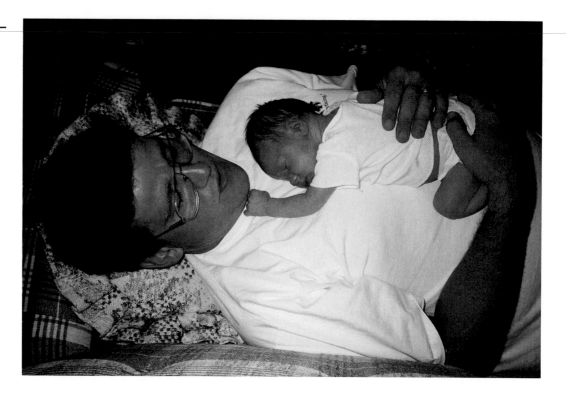

1—Vocabulary: What is the *fontanel?* What purpose does it serve?

2—Resource: *How Newborns Look,* Activity B, SAG.

that the new baby is not as fragile as they might think. Babies don't fall apart at the first problem. Babies need love more than they need worrying. The following paragraphs explain some of the worries parents might have concerning their newborns.

Almost all new babies sound like they have a cold. They sniffle and sneeze a lot. This doesn't mean they are sick. Their breathing organs haven't been used before, so it takes awhile for them to adjust.

For the same reason, most babies look like they are constipated. They strain when they have bowel movements. This is normal, since those organs haven't been used before, either.

Most parents are aware of the soft spot on top of a baby's head, but many are too concerned about it. This soft spot is called the **fontanel**. It does need to be protected from injury, but it will not be damaged by normal, gentle handling. The soft spot allows the baby's head to pass through the birth canal during delivery. The bones in the skull will grow together

during infancy, and the fontanel will disappear.

New parents may wonder whether their baby is normal. Some things their baby does may seem a little strange. If they have questions, they can always ask their pediatrician or read a reputable child development book. An alert, active baby is probably healthy even if some behaviors seem a little odd.

How the Newborn Looks

At birth, the new mother and father see their baby for the first time. Naturally, they notice the obvious features first: boy or girl; lots of hair or none; flat, little nose; tiny fingers. Emotion will sweep over them as they realize, "This is our baby!"

To parents, their newborn looks beautiful. Other people may not agree until a few weeks later. A newborn's physical appearance may not be quite what people expect. Several characteristics of a newborn disappear on their own before long, 10-2.

At birth, a baby's skin is usually blotchy and wrinkled. The head may be misshapen as a result of passing through the birth canal. Soon, however, it will regain its shape. The newborn's ears are pressed to the head. The eyebrows and eyelashes can barely be seen. The cheeks are fat. The nose is flattened, and the chin recedes. These last two features are useful because they prevent the nose and chin from getting in the way during sucking.

A newborn's head seems oversized for the rest of its body. The head accounts for one-fourth of a baby's total length. (Adults' heads account for only one-seventh of their total height.) A newborn's neck is short, with weak muscles. Until the neck muscles strengthen, the baby's head will wobble when he or she is lifted and held. Therefore, it is very important for parents to support the baby's head when they lift and hold him or her.

The newborn's shoulders slope, the chest is narrow, and the abdomen protrudes. The legs usually are bowed because of the position assumed in the uterus. The newborn's heart beats twice as fast as an adult's, and the newborn breathes twice as fast.

The average newborn is 20 to 21 inches in length and weighs 7 to 7 $\frac{1}{2}$ pounds. Boys are often longer and heavier than girls. Babies usually lose weight the first few days after birth. They quickly regain this loss, however, and then continue to grow.

What the Newborn Can Do

The newborn has remarkable abilities, including the use of all five senses: seeing, hearing, smelling, tasting, and feeling. This new human being can breathe, suck, swallow, and get rid of wastes. He or she can also respond to various stimuli with reflex actions.

What the Newborn Can See

At birth, a newborn's eyes are almost always light in color. This is because the baby's eyes have not been exposed to light. If the baby has inherited a darker eye color, this color will begin to show in the weeks to come.

The newborn's eyes function from birth. Both eyes don't always work together right away. The muscles that keep both eyes pointing in the same direction don't work well at first. As a result, the baby's eyes may cross. In a few weeks this should correct itself as the baby's muscles develop. Parents should not worry if their newborn's eyes are crossed. If this problem persists for several months, however, parents may wish to consult an eye doctor.

Newborns' eyes are very sensitive to light. Their pupils adjust to both bright and dim lights. In fact,

1—**Discuss:** Boys are often longer and slightly heavier than girls. Is this always true? What other factors determine the height and weight of babies?

2—**Resource:** *Senses of the Newborn*, Activity C, SAG.

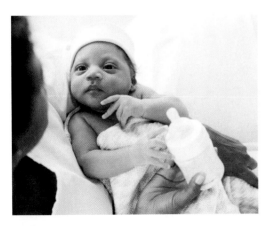

10-2 _____
Newborns have their own distinct appearance. To a parent, the newborn looks beautiful. Others may think older babies are cuter.

1—Discuss: What types of objects can parents provide for newborns to look at?

2—Discuss: At what point do babies like to look at the human face?

3—Reflect: If a woman listens to music during her pregnancy, do you think it will influence her baby to appreciate music?

newborns squeeze their eyes closed when exposed to intense light.

In normal light, the newborn sees patterns of light and dark and can distinguish some shapes. The eyes focus best at a distance of 8 to 12 inches. When a brightly colored object is placed within this range, the newborn becomes alert and tries to focus on it, 10-3. If the object does not move, the newborn will focus on it for only a short time. If the object moves back and forth, the baby will be able to watch the movement. A little later, the baby will be able to follow an up-and-down movement if it is slow.

Newborns like to look at some things more than others. They prefer patterns to plain colors. They prefer stripes and angles to curves and circles. They prefer moving objects to stationary ones. By the age of three weeks, the human face is what babies most like to see.

Parents seem to instinctively behave according to their newborn's needs. When parents talk to their newborn, they usually bring their faces close to the baby's face. This is within the range where the baby's eyes can best focus. Also, as parents talk, they tend to nod and shake their heads. This movement helps the newborn stay attentive.

What the Newborn Can Hear

Hearing develops even before birth. A fetus responds to loud noises while still inside the woman's uterus. At birth, the baby can distinguish between sounds, but does not yet know what these sounds mean.

Newborns will turn toward the source of a sound. If both a man and a woman speak at once, babies will turn toward the female voice. This is because they became used to hearing their mothers' voices during prenatal development.

Babies respond readily to the cries of other babies. When one newborn in a nursery cries, others are likely to start crying, too. Babies also respond well to higher-pitched sounds. This may be

10-3 ————

This newborn tries to focus on brightly colored, moving objects within his short range of vision.

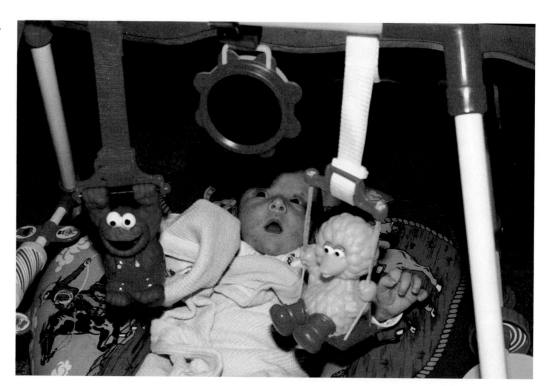

why parents tend to talk to their newborns in high-pitched voices rather than in low-pitched ones.

Human voices and music tend to be a newborn's favorite sounds. They also like soft, rhythmic sounds. In fact, the recorded sound of a human heartbeat can be used to lull babies to sleep. Babies grew used to hearing their mothers' heartbeats before birth, so they may find this sound comforting.

What the Newborn Can Smell and Taste

The senses of smell and taste are well developed at birth. A newborn can distinguish between two smells when both are presented at the same time. A baby soon learns to recognize its mother by her smell. By two to three days after birth, babies will cry and turn their heads away from strong, unpleasant odors.

Babies can tell the difference between flavors within two or three days of birth. They will reject a bitter flavor. Babies prefer sweet flavors. They will start sucking in response to a sweet flavor. They can make faces when sour flavors are placed on their tongues.

What the Newborn Can Feel

Newborns can sense changes in temperature at birth. Most babies dislike being cold. This is why many babies cry when being dressed or undressed. Newborns can also use their sense of touch to distinguish textures. In the first days after birth, they can feel pain.

From birth, newborns are extremely sensitive to being touched. They respond quickly to a light touch on the skin. They stop crying when they are rubbed gently or held closely. Holding and cuddling have been found to enhance a baby's overall development,

10-4. This physical contact also tends to strengthen the emotional bond between parents and baby.

The Newborn's Reflexes

A baby cannot think about a situation, form a plan, and then act on it. Instead, nature has provided babies with **reflexes**, or automatic reactions to certain stimuli. Some reflexes are related to the baby's survival instinct. Other reflexes are related to actions the baby will not be able to do voluntarily until later. A few reflexes seem to exist for no reason at all. These reflexes are replaced in a few months by voluntary movements.

Rooting Reflex

When a baby's cheek or mouth is touched, the baby turns toward the touch and begins rooting to find food. The mouth opens, and the sucking motion begins. The rooting reflex helps a newborn find the nipple of the bottle or breast. This reflex disappears after a few months when the baby learns to use the eyes to look for food.

Being aware of this rooting reflex can help a parent at feeding time. The parent should touch the cheek closest

10-4 _____
Both babies and parents enjoy time spent cuddling. Holding a baby stimulates all areas of the baby's growth and development.

1—**Discuss:** How can parents help their babies use the rooting reflex to find the source of food?

to the breast or bottle, causing the baby to turn toward the nipple. If a parent didn't know about this reflex, he or she might push the baby's head toward the nipple. That would mean touching the other side of the baby's head, causing the baby to turn away.

Grasping Reflex

This reflex is triggered by placing a finger or a long, thin object (like the handle of a rattle) in the palm of a newborn's hand. The newborn will grasp the object and will increase the strength of the grasp if the object is pulled away. A newborn's grasp is very strong. The grasping reflex applies to toes, too. When a finger or object is placed on a newborn's foot, the toes will curl in a grasping motion. The grasping reflex disappears in a few months when the baby learns to voluntarily reach for and grasp objects.

Babinski Reflex

The Babinski reflex also involves the feet, but it has the opposite effect of the grasping reflex. When the outside of the sole of a newborn's foot is stroked, the newborn's toes will extend upward and outward, 10-5. This is the Babinski reflex.

Moro or Startle Reflex

The Moro or startle reflex is seen when the baby is startled. This reflex is seen when the baby's position changes quickly or a loud noise occurs. The baby throws the arms apart, spreads the fingers, extends the legs, arches the back, and throws the head back. Then, the baby brings the arms and legs back toward the body. To calm a startled baby, a parent can hold the baby or apply a light but steady pressure against the baby's body.

Stepping Reflex

When a baby is held in an upright position and the sole of a foot touches a surface, the baby raises the foot. When the baby is tilted slightly from side to side so alternate feet are raised, the baby appears to be walking. This is

10-5
This baby's feet demonstrate the Babinski reflex. When the sole of the foot is stroked, the toes fan out.

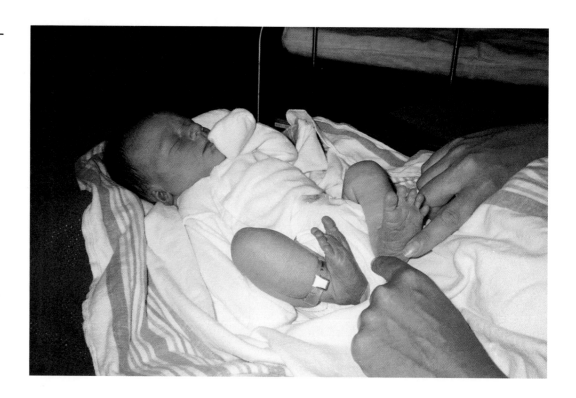

called the stepping reflex. Parents should realize this is only a reflex, not a signal their baby is learning to walk at an amazingly early age. Babies don't learn to walk until many months later. Then, their stepping motion is voluntary, not a reflex action.

How Parents Care for Their Newborns

Parents may feel awkward as they begin caring for their new baby. Even with training, new parents are seldom fully prepared for the first days at home with their baby. By being patient with themselves, however, they can learn how to meet their baby's needs.

There is no doubt caring for a newborn will require many changes in the family's daily routines. If parents view these changes as positive, parenthood won't be just hectic and frustrating. It will also be fulfilling and rewarding.

Help from an experienced parent makes adjusting to life with a baby easier, 10-6. Sometimes one of the new grandparents comes to stay with the family for a short time after the baby arrives. Even if a grandparent or other relative cannot stay, their trusted advice may be only a phone call away.

The new parents' friends and neighbors may also offer some help. In many communities, service agencies offer support groups and parenting classes for new parents. With friendly support and assurance, the couple will more quickly adapt to their new roles as parents.

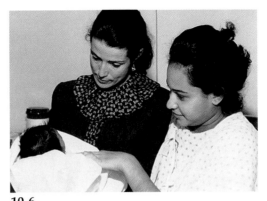

10-6 _____

An experienced parent can offer advice to a new mother, such as how to hold the baby.

Holding the Newborn

Newborns like to be held. It makes them feel safe, secure, and loved. Newborns also like it when people talk to them. When parents hold and talk to their baby, it makes the baby feel good. In addition, this encourages the baby's intellectual and emotional development.

When holding a newborn, parents should be sure to firmly support the newborn's back and head. The baby's neck muscles are weak at birth, so a newborn's head tends to roll about if it is not supported. The neck, spinal cord, and brain are extremely sensitive to uncontrolled movements. Babies can be injured if their heads, necks, and backs are not supported properly.

The Newborn's Sleeping Habits

Newborns spend most of their time sleeping—as much as 18 to 20 hours a day, 10-7. Their longest sleeping period is about five hours. Newborns wake up once or twice during the night to be fed. Therefore, the parents' sleeping patterns are dictated by the newborn's sleeping pattern.

1—Discuss: How are the sleep patterns of the newborn determined?

2—Enrich: Research SIDS. How many infant deaths each year are SIDS-related?

3—Discuss: Compare the techniques for breast-feeding and bottle-feeding. Should parents prop the bottle and leave the baby alone to drink the formula? Why or why not?

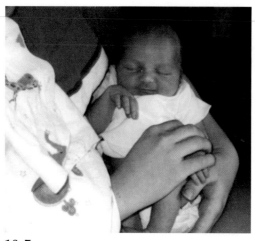

10-7
Newborns need lots of rest. Their bodies are busy growing and developing, which takes a great deal of energy.

Sleeping patterns vary from one newborn to another. A baby's sleep pattern is guided by how much sleep the baby needs and how often he or she is hungry. Some babies need more sleep than others. As babies grow, they sleep for longer periods. By five months of age, many babies sleep through the night.

Parents can lull newborns to sleep by cuddling them and rocking them. Some parents choose to rock their babies until they are sleepy, but not asleep. These parents put their babies to bed awake so they can learn to fall asleep on their own. This may make bedtime easier for everyone as the child grows older.

As they sleep, newborns move their mouths to smile and make faces. They may make sucking motions in their sleep. They breathe irregularly and move their eyes beneath their closed eyelids. Newborns should be warm and dry as they sleep. They should be away from drafts, strong light, and loud noises. Babies do not have to be protected from ordinary household noises, however. Parents do not need to tiptoe and whisper while their babies are asleep. Babies are adaptable and will learn to sleep through ordinary noises.

Sudden Infant Death Syndrome

Sudden infant death syndrome (SIDS) is a condition in which an infant dies suddenly in his or her sleep without warning. In SIDS cases, no illness or accident can be determined as the cause of death. Losing a baby to SIDS can devastate parents. SIDS is a major cause of death among infants ages two weeks to twelve months.

SIDS is not caused by anything parents do or fail to do. However, some risk factors have been determined. Babies of parents who smoke are at greater risk. Infants who sleep on their stomachs also have an increased risk of death from SIDS. For this reason, parents should place babies on their backs to sleep. If a baby is placed on the side, he or she might roll onto the stomach. Firm bedding is recommended. Pillows should not be used, and covers should only reach the baby's shoulders. Parents should talk with their doctors about preventing sudden infant death syndrome.

Feeding the Newborn

Next to sleeping, the newborn's most time-consuming activity is eating. Feeding times provide both nourishment and nurturance. Feeding the baby is a perfect opportunity to enhance parent-child relationships. This is true whether the baby is fed breast milk or formula from a bottle.

If a mother breast-feeds, she will have learned how to do so while she was in the hospital. After the mother leaves the hospital, she can ask her doctor or pediatrician any questions she might have about nursing. A breast-feeding mother should remember the following:

● Every substance that enters her body will affect the breast milk she produces. Nursing mothers should check with their doctors before taking any medications. They should also avoid using illegal drugs, tobacco, or alcohol. These substances can enter breast milk and harm the baby.

● Nursing mothers need 500 more calories a day than they did before they were pregnant. This extra energy is required for producing breast milk. Women can talk to their doctors about their increased nutrient needs. They can meet these needs by choosing healthful foods from the Food Guide Pyramid, 10-8.

● A newborn generally nurses from 8 to 10 times daily. The baby may nurse for 20 to 30 minutes at each feeding. The mother might have the baby begin with the right breast at one feeding and the left breast at the next feeding.

● The mother should position herself and the baby correctly during nursing for best results. A woman can ask her doctor, another nursing mother, or a representative from La Leche League about tips for breast-feeding. *La Leche League* is an organization that supports breast-feeding mothers.

If parents formula feed their baby, they should use the formula recommended by their pediatrician. If they have any problems using this for-

10-8
Eating plenty of healthful foods gives a woman the energy her body needs to produce breast milk.

mula, they should ask the doctor about switching to another one. Keeping the following suggestions in mind will help formula feeding parents:

● Read the label of the formula carefully to be sure the formula is mixed properly. This will ensure the baby's nutritional needs are met.

● Parents do not need to warm the baby's bottle, but they can if they choose. When warming a bottle, place it in a glass or pan of warm water. Bottles should not be warmed in microwave ovens. Microwaves heat unevenly, which can cause hot spots. This means some of the formula might be too hot, even if the bottle feels only slightly warm on the outside. Hot formula can burn the baby's mouth and tongue.

● Hold the baby in a semi-upright position. Hold the bottle so both the neck and nipple of the bottle are always filled. This prevents the baby from swallowing too much air.

● Never prop the bottle or leave the baby alone to drink the formula. Babies need the nurturance and emotional closeness their parents provide by holding them during a feeding, 10-9. Small babies can also choke if left alone with their bottles propped.

● If the baby falls asleep during a feeding, remove the bottle from his or her mouth. Formula will drip from the bottle even if the baby is not sucking. This liquid pools in the mouth and can cause cavities and ear infections.

● Discard any formula left from a feeding. Bacteria could grow in leftover formula and make the baby sick.

Most doctors recommend parents use **self-demand feeding**. This means the parents feed the baby when he or she is hungry. (Parents can tell the baby

1—Discuss:
Compare self-demand and scheduled feeding routines. What are the pros and cons of each routine?

1

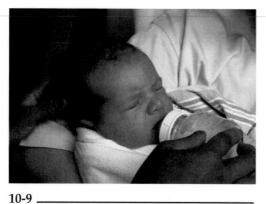

10-9
Like nursing, bottle-feeding can provide physical and emotional closeness between parent and child.

is hungry because the baby will cry.) Self-demand feeding differs from scheduled feedings, in which parents feed their baby on a set schedule, no matter when the baby is hungry. In the past, doctors more commonly recommended scheduled feedings.

If parents try to adhere to a rigid schedule, they may have trouble satisfying the baby's appetite and sleeping needs. If they choose self-demand feedings, the baby decides when to eat and when to sleep based on its natural needs. The baby soon sets a schedule of its own, but this may not always be a convenient schedule for the parents.

Eventually, most babies develop fairly regular hunger patterns. Newborns need six to eight feedings during a 24-hour period. When baby begins sleeping through the night, night feedings are eliminated. The babies will take larger quantities at the remaining feedings. Babies should not be fed solid foods for a few more months because their stomachs cannot yet digest them. Breast milk or formula are sufficient to meet a newborn's nutritional needs.

Whether a baby is nursed or bottle-fed, he or she should be burped once during each feeding and again after each feeding. Parents burp the baby to bring up any air the baby may have swallowed while eating. To do this, a parent should hold the baby upright, either sitting on the parent's lap or lying up against his or her shoulder. (Parents may prefer to lay the baby, stomach down, across their laps.) Then they should pat the baby gently on the back until any air bubbles are released. Sometimes the baby does not burp, and this is okay. He or she may not need to burp every time.

Bathing the Newborn

Bathing their new baby is a skill that may not come easily for new parents. Hospital personnel usually show new parents how to bathe the baby safely before they leave the hospital. It takes practice, however, to feel comfortable bathing a newborn.

Parents can bathe their baby at any time of day, whenever it is convenient. Bath time is a social time for the baby and parents. If the parents are relaxed and talk quietly and soothingly, the baby will learn to enjoy bath time.

The bathing area should be warm and free of drafts. Parents should gather all the bath items, clean diapers, and clean clothes before beginning to bathe the baby. The most important rule to remember is: *never leave a baby alone on a table or in a tub, not even for a few seconds.* An unattended baby can roll off a table or drown in even a few inches of water.

Sponge baths are usually given until the stub of the umbilical cord drops off and the navel heals. To prepare a baby for a bath, undress the baby except for the diaper. Keep the baby wrapped in a blanket while washing the face and head. Further directions for sponge baths are given in 10-10.

After a few weeks, a baby is ready to enjoy tub baths. The temperature of the water should feel warm to the skin. A parent can test the temperature by

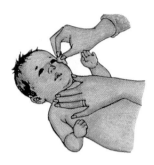 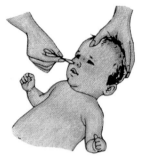 

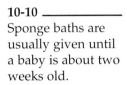
10-10
Sponge baths are usually given until a baby is about two weeks old.

1—EYES Hold the baby's head firmly and wipe each eye with a fresh cotton ball that has been dipped in lukewarm water and squeezed out. Wipe each eye from the inside corner out. Use a fresh cotton ball for each eye.

2—NOSE Moisten a fresh swab with warm water and gently cleanse just inside each nostril. Be careful not to push swab or let water drip into nose. Pat the baby's face dry.

3—EARS Using a soft washcloth, gently wipe the outside of the baby's ear and then clean behind each ear. There is no need to clean inside the ear canal because the ear naturally expels any wax buildup. *Never put anything into the baby's ear canal to try to clean it.*

4—FACE Wrap a wet, squeezed-out washcloth around your hand. Wash face, one side at a time. Pat dry with small, soft towel.

5—HEAD Next, shampoo your baby's scalp. Put your arm under the baby's back and your hand behind his head. If you hold the baby's head back, soap and water will run off at the back, not down his/her face or front. Start by squeezing plain water from the washcloth onto the baby's scalp. Don't be afraid of the soft spot. It's tougher than you think. With free hand, wash head with liquid baby bath, using circular motion. Rinse by squeezing more plain water from the washcloth onto scalp until all suds have been washed away.

6—BODY Remove the diaper. Soap the rest of the baby's body. Remember, avoid wetting the navel area until the cord has completely healed. Rinse away lather with washcloth. Pat dry, being careful to dry all creases and skin folds. Finally, dip cotton ball in baby oil or baby lotion and apply lightly to groin, buttocks, and creases in diaper area. Preparation for dressing is the same as in tub bath under general skin care.

JOHNSON & JOHNSON BABY PRODUCTS CO.

dipping an elbow into the water. It should feel comfortably warm, not hot or cold. Further directions for tub baths are given in 10-11.

Some babies develop **cradle cap,** a condition in which a scaly crust appears on the scalp. Sometimes cradle cap develops on the fontanel, or soft spot. Parents should not be afraid of injuring the baby by touching the fontanel. Gentle handling will do no harm.

The best way to prevent cradle cap is to thoroughly wash and rinse the scalp daily. If the condition does appear, soap should not be used on the scalp for a few days. Instead, a little baby oil should be rubbed gently into the crust. The oil will soften the crust so it can be removed easily with a washcloth. Forceful rubbing should never be used to remove the crust. If treating the area with baby oil treatment does not work, parents should call their doctor for advice.

1—Vocabulary: What is *cradle cap*? What causes it, and how can it be prevented?

10-11

During a tub bath, place a towel inside the tub to keep the baby from slipping.

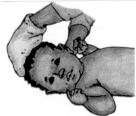

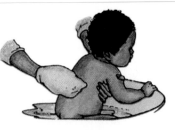

1—ON TABLE Undress the baby except for diaper. Cleanse eyes, nose, ears, and face as in sponge bath. Apply liquid baby bath to head with hand, or use washcloth after about first two months. Note: when the baby is older and has more hair, use a baby liquid shampoo that will not irritate eyes.

2—INTO TUB After removing a baby's diaper, you can place the baby in the tub. Use a safety hold: slip right hand under the baby's shoulder and fingers under right armpit. Support buttocks with left hand, grasping right thigh with thumb and fingers. Lower the baby into tub feet first, keeping head out of water. With left hand rinse head, letting water run well back.

3—BATHING BODY Soap the front of the baby's body, being careful to wash inside all skin folds and creases, then rinse. Reverse your hold to soap and rinse the baby's back. It's not necessary to turn the baby over.

The genital area should be cleansed during the bath, just like the rest of the baby. In the internal folds of a baby girl, a white substance may gather. If it remains after bating—as it may sometimes do—gently wipe it away with a washcloth or with a cotton ball dipped in oil. Be sure to wipe from front to back.

When cleansing a baby boy who has not been circumcised, do not push back the foreskin unless your physician advises you to do so. If your baby has been circumcised, he may be immersed in a tub as soon as thearea has healed, or sooner, on a physician's advice.

1—OUT OF THE TUB Use the same safety hold to lift the baby onto a warm, dry surface. Cover the baby with a towel and pat dry, paying special attention to the fold and the creases.

5—DIAPER AREA CARE To keep the diaper area dry, use baby cornstarch to help prevent chafing, irritation, and redness.

6—GENERAL SKIN CARE Moisten fingers on cotton ball dipped in baby oil or baby lotion. Apply to all tiny creases—around neck, armpits, arms, hands, legs, feet. Use a little baby oil on a cotton ball to help remove cradle cap. Apply baby cream to any irritated part. Sprinkle baby powder on your hand and pat lightly over large areas of body.

JOHNSON & JOHNSON BABY PRODUCTS CO.

1—**Activity:** Using a life-sized baby doll, demonstrate for students how to dress a baby.

Dressing the Newborn

Dressing a baby is another daily care skill parents learn mostly by practice. While dressing the baby is a routine task, parents should make it a time to interact with the baby. Babies enjoy being talked to or sung to while they are being dressed. Parents can turn this into a fun time for themselves and their babies.

The following important tips can help parents when dressing a baby:

● Be gentle.

● Guide the baby's clothes on as quickly as possible.

● Minimize the need to move the baby's body position, arms, and legs. Imagine how you would feel if someone was jerking your body around, adjusting your arms and

1

legs. This may explain why some babies don't like to be dressed and undressed.

- Keep the baby from being cold while dressing and undressing him or her.

- Talk to the baby while you are dressing and undressing him or her. Use an unhurried calm manner. If you seem rushed or anxious, it may upset the baby.

Dressing babies in layers of clothes makes sense. Babies are more sensitive to temperature changes than adults are. They can quickly become too hot or too cold. Parents can check whether their baby is comfortable by feeling the baby's hands and feet. If the hands and feet feel cold or hot, parents can add a sweater or remove a blanket accordingly.

Diapers

A newborn's most important need is diapers. Parents may choose to use either disposable diapers or cloth diapers. Each has advantages and disadvantages. Parents should select the type that will work best for them. In the beginning, newborns use as many as 12 to 15 diapers daily. With all this diaper changing, parents will soon become practiced at how to manage this task, 10-12.

If parents use cloth diapers, they should take extra care in washing the diapers. Thoroughly rinse soiled diapers and place them in a covered plastic diaper pail until they will be washed. The pail should be about half-filled with water, suds, or a borax solution. Cloth diapers should be washed at the hottest water temperature available to kill any bacteria in the diapers. Diapers should be rinsed thoroughly, using an extra rinse, if available. Any soap residue or hard-water film will make diapers stiff, nonabsorbent, and irritating to the baby's skin. Cloth diapers should be

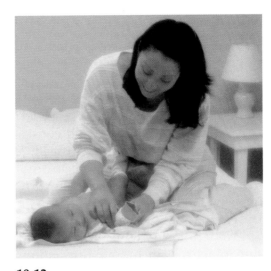

10-12 _____
This mother has become skilled at changing her baby's diapers.

washed separately, instead of with the baby's other clothes.

No matter which type of diapers parents use, they must be careful to prevent diaper rash. **Diaper rash** is a skin rash caused by bacteria that build up on warm, moist skin in a baby's diaper area. Diaper rash can make the skin rough, irritated, and even raw. In mild cases, parents can treat the problem themselves. They can apply a diaper-rash ointment to the affected areas. Parents should also be sure to change the baby's diaper more frequently, clean the diaper area carefully, and avoid using waterproof pants until the rash clears. If diaper rash persists, parents should ask their pediatrician for advice.

Diaper rash is easier to prevent than it is to cure. Cleanliness is the key to preventing diaper rash. Parents should change wet or soiled diapers promptly. They should also cleanse and dry skin in the diaper area thoroughly. It is important to pay special attention to skin folds and creases. This will keep the skin dry and clean, preventing bacteria from growing in the diaper area.

1—Activity: Using a life-sized doll, demonstrate how to diaper a baby using both cloth diapers and disposable diapers.

2—Resource: *Diapering Detail*, color transparency CT-10, TR.

3—Discuss: Review the techniques for washing cloth diapers.

4—Vocabulary: What is *diaper rash?* What causes it? How can it be prevented? How can it be treated?

When the Newborn Cries

Crying is the only way newborns can communicate. They cry whenever they need something. Since newborns' cries are based on their needs, parents should not hesitate to respond. Answering cries promptly and consistently does not spoil babies. Instead, it is a good way for parents to express their love and concern. This, in turn, helps babies learn their parents can be trusted to fulfill their needs.

Moderation is wise in most child care practices, including responding to cries. Generally, parents should respond to their baby's cries promptly and consistently. However, this doesn't mean parents must jump up and answer every whimper right away. Sometimes parents may be too tired or too busy to immediately answer a mild cry for attention. That's okay. Babies build their trust on overall fulfillment of their needs, not on instant answers to each one of their cries.

Babies and their parents gradually refine their communication patterns. Babies vary their cries according to their needs. Parents soon learn to interpret the various types of cries their baby uses. This helps parents know how to respond to the baby.

A hunger cry starts slowly and builds to a loud demand. It usually begins shortly before the baby's feeding time. However, since newborns aren't always regular in their hunger patterns, hunger cries may not come at regular times.

A cry for attention is a fussy, whimpering cry, 10-13. It becomes louder and more insistent if it is ignored. It sounds more forced or less natural than the hunger cry. The cry for attention may stop as soon as a parent appears. At other times, it may continue until the baby is cuddled, carried to a different room, or entertained by the parent.

A cry of pain is an urgent cry that begins as a sudden, shrill scream. The

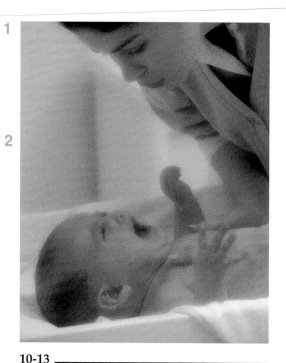

10-13
A whimpering, fussy cry often means the baby just wants attention. This cry indicates the least danger of all the cries.

scream is followed by a brief silence and then several short gasps. The scream-silence-gasps cycle is repeated until the pain is relieved and the baby is calmed. Parents will instinctively respond to this cry faster than the others. This cry can frighten parents. They should assess the situation to determine the cause of the cry. Sometimes the baby is more surprised than hurt. In this case, parents can calm the baby by cuddling, rocking, and using soft, reassuring words or music. Other times, the baby may have a minor injury, such as a scratch, the parent can handle easily. In some cases, a baby may need medical attention. If the parents aren't sure whether the baby needs medical care, they should call their doctor and ask.

A colic cry is particularly disturbing for parents. **Colic** is severe and intermittent abdominal pain. The baby cries because of the pain and is inconsolable until the pain subsides. All babies cry if they get air or gas in their digestive systems, because this causes cramping and pain. Colicky babies react more violently to this air than others. The most comfortable position for a colicky baby may be an upright position against a parent's warm body. Babies who have colic may keep their parents awake at night with their crying. Some doctors offer medication to relieve colic, while others hesitate to do so. A typical case of colic does not last beyond three months and stops on its own.

Parents should try not to become upset when their baby cries. They should respond to the cries and comfort the baby as much as possible. Although it can be frustrating to hear continual crying, their baby is communicating with them in the only way he or she can. When nothing works and the baby's needs have been met, parents should continue to try to comfort the baby. Parents should try to keep the scene in perspective and not become upset. Eventually the crying will stop, 10-14.

The Husband and Wife as Parents

In all the commotion of caring for the new baby, it can be easy for a husband and wife to focus more on the baby than on their relationship. At this time especially, they need to reassure each other their mutual love for the baby will enhance their love for one another. Each parent needs the other's support and reassurance. This is easiest when both parents become involved in caring for their baby.

Personal Adjustments in Family Life

New parents soon learn their lives will never be the same. The dream of becoming parents has come true. The

1—Resource: *Personal Adjustments,* Activity G, SAG.

2—Discuss: New parents take on multiple roles. The transition to handling these roles may cause role overload. How can each parent assist the other in lessening role overload?

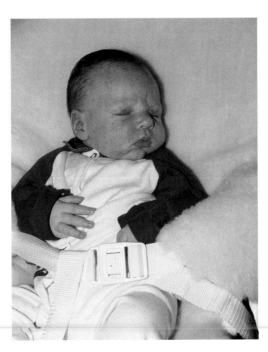

10-14
Hearing their baby cry can make parents uncomfortable. Soon, however, the baby will be sleeping peacefully again.

1—Reflect: If you were the parent of a newborn and older children, what would you do to help older children develop a relationship with the baby?

2—Discuss: Combining family and work is a challenge for new parents. What factors of work can affect the family? What factors of the family can affect work?

3—Enrich: Survey local employers to find out how they help employees balance family and work.

realities of parenthood also quickly become apparent the first night the baby keeps them awake! New parents are often amazed how much one tiny person can change an entire household.

Families face several tasks when a child is born. Roles often need to be modified. If it is their first child, husband and wife each take on new roles as mother and father. New parents should realize they do not have to be "supermom" and "superdad." If they have other children, parents must help them adjust to having a new brother or sister, 10-15. Parents must also try to spend special time with the older children to reassure them they are not being replaced by the baby.

While they are adjusting to their new tasks, parents may have to let some chores go for awhile. It may be impossible to get everything done and they may feel overwhelmed. The most important task is learning to take care of their little one. The family may have to reassign household tasks and chores. The husband or other children may need to take a bigger role in caring for the house.

Schedules and routines will have to be adjusted. Parents may have less time to spend on their own hobbies or friendships. They may also have difficulty planning time for themselves. Each parent still needs time alone.

10-15

Being a big brother takes a little getting used to, but it can be lots of fun.

10-16

New parents need to spend time nurturing their marital relationship. This can keep their marriage strong and help them feel better able to handle the stresses of parenting.

Spouses also need time together to nurture their relationship, 10-16.

Juggling strained finances can also be stressful. Parents must refigure their budget to include this new child's needs. This can mean they have less money to spend on recreational items or activities. They may not be able to spend as much on themselves as they did before the baby came.

The ability to balance family life and work is an issue new parents often face. This is especially true in dual-career families. If both parents work, they must grow used to adding on parenting responsibilities in the evenings.

Parents may find this tiring, at least in the beginning. One parent will have to hurry from work to relieve the child's caregiver. The baby must be fed, bathed, cuddled, played with, changed, and put to bed. Dinner must be made, eaten, and cleaned up. Laundry and other household chores must be done.

By the time the exhausted parents are ready for bed, the baby wakes up for a feeding. He or she must be changed again, fed, and put back to bed. No matter how late the baby keeps them up, parents must be back at work again the next morning. In time, however, most parents adjust to balancing family and work.

Caring for a newborn can be physically and emotionally tiring. Parents may not feel they have much left to share with each other. Even so, parents need to make an effort to keep their own relationship strong. They need to share their thoughts, concerns, dreams, and doubts. This will enable them to grow even closer together. A healthy husband-wife relationship builds a strong foundation for the entire family.

1 Managing Stress

Regardless of your status in your family structure, managing stress is an important task. Life changes can bring about tensions, or stress. Hormones change to respond to this tension. Many people experience physical symptoms related to stress. Some people sleep too much and others can't sleep enough; some become irritable and others withdrawn. These reactions often create more stress. Over a period of time, stress can damage physical and emotional health.

Having a new baby is one of the most happy and exciting times, and yet it is one of the most stressful. Most new mothers leave the hospital within days after delivery. Once out of the hospital, maternal and baby care is no longer available by touching a call button. At this point, parents have truly entered the world of parenting.

Hospital care is too short for getting comfortable with caring for a baby. The mother goes home to an extended postpartum recovery period. The parents may feel overwhelmed with both old and new responsibilities.

The demands of the baby seem to take up every moment. Apart from baby-care tasks, parents must cook, do laundry, and greet guests, all while trying to rest. Many parents have other children who must also have their needs met. For most parents, new baby demands will not lessen before one or both return to work.

Most first-time parents are surprised at how exhausted they become. Managing stress is essential to experiencing the rewards of parenting. These simple tips may help:

- Expect to learn skills as a new parent. Because each baby and parenting situation is unique, all parents require on-the-job training. Knowing developmental stages and parenting skills are helpful.

- Talk to experienced parents and grandparents. They can share many ways to reduce the stress of having a new baby.

- Remember that the baby is going through major adjustments, too. The world is bringing things to see, sounds to hear, and movements and textures to feel. Sometimes the baby is uncomfortable or bored. Body tensions (stress) result in crying. The baby is counting on the parent to help him or her through this stage.

- Realize that most babies fuss. Some babies fuss a great deal. All babies are ill from time to time. This doesn't mean you are doing anything wrong.

- Focus on the joys of having a baby.

If stress seems to be unmanageable and you feel as though you may hurt your baby or yourself, seek immediate help. Sometimes chemical changes due to pregnancy and childbirth require medical treatment. Living situations may need to be changed, too. Stress at this level cannot be managed without help.

1—Reflect: How do you manage your stress?

2—Activity: Have students research the relationship between exercise, endorphins, and stress.

1—Activity: Review and outline this chapter emphasizing the information you found most useful.

2—Answers: Answers to review questions are located in the front section of this TAE.

Summary

- New parents have many adjustments to make. Their schedules change greatly. They must learn daily care skills for feeding, dressing, diapering, bathing, and holding the baby. Although the family's new lifestyle is tiring, it is also exciting.

- Newborns have a distinct appearance as a result of adjusting to life outside the mother's body. A newborn may only seem beautiful to his or her parents. A few weeks after birth, however, babies are much cuter.

- The newborn has remarkable abilities, including the use of all five senses.

- Since babies cannot think and then act, nature has provided them with reflexes, or automatic reactions to certain stimuli.

- Newborns like it when their parents hold and talk to them. When holding a newborn, parents must be sure to firmly support the baby's head, neck, and back.

- The parents' sleeping patterns are dictated by the newborn's sleeping pattern.

- Answering a baby's cries promptly and consistently teaches the baby to trust parents to meet his or her needs.

- Sharing the joys and responsibilities of child care strengthens their marriage, and in turn, their family.

Reviewing Key Points

1. Name two emotions parents may feel in the first few days of parenthood.
2. What is the fontanel? How should it be handled?
3. Briefly describe three characteristics of a newborn's appearance.
4. Give an example to show how a newborn is capable of using each of the five senses.
5. Describe two of the five newborn reflexes.
6. When holding a newborn, why is it important to firmly support the newborn's head, neck, and back?
7. Newborns sleep as much as _____ hours a day. A baby should be placed on his or her _____ to sleep.
8. Why should a parent burp a baby during and after a feeding? How should this be done?
9. What is self-demand feeding?
10. What is the most important rule to remember when bathing a baby?
11. What can parents do to protect their baby from diaper rash?
12. Will answering a baby's cries promptly spoil the baby? Why or why not?
13. What is colic?
14. Identify two adjustments families with newborns may need to make.

Learning by Doing

1. Fill a bulletin board with pictures of newborns. Note the physical characteristics described in the chapter.
2. Visit the nursery of a local hospital and observe newborns. Describe to the class your reaction to seeing real newborns.
3. Using a soft, limp, life-sized doll, demonstrate skills needed to pick up, lay down, hold, feed, burp, bathe, and dress a baby.
4. Create a pamphlet called "Caring for Your Newborn." In this pamphlet illustrate and describe daily care skills parents will need to use with their newborns.
5. Research Sudden Infant Death Syndrome (SIDS). What if anything can parents do to prevent this occurrence?

Thinking Critically

1. Finish this sentence: If and when I become a parent, the most important feeling I will have when I bring my newborn home is...

2. Pretend your aunt and uncle have just brought home a new baby. They already have two older children. Write a letter to your aunt and uncle offering suggestions of how they can help the older children develop relationships with the baby.

3. Debate whether self-demand feedings and sleeping or scheduled feeding and sleep are better for newborns. Identify advantages and disadvantages of each before reaching a conclusion.

4. If you were a new parent and you didn't feel comfortable holding, feeding, bathing, and dressing your baby, what would you do? Where could you go for help? What resources could you access to learn more about infant care?

5. Write a paragraph suggesting ways dual-career families can adjust to having a newborn.

Part Three
Understanding Children's Growth and Development

Chapter 11
Parents and Their Infants

Chapter 12
Parents and Their Toddlers

Chapter 13
Parents and Their Preschoolers

Chapter 14
Parents and Their School-Age Children

Chapter 15
Parents and Their Teens

Chapter 11
Parents and Their Infants

Objectives

After studying this chapter, you will be able to

- describe the physical, intellectual, emotional, and social development of infants.

- differentiate between large motor skills and small motor skills.

- explain how parents can influence their infants' brain development.

- describe how different types of development relate to one another.

- explain how stranger anxiety and separation anxiety affect social and emotional development.

- summarize the importance of parental guidance during a child's first year of life.

- explain why medical checkups are needed during infancy.

Key Terms

infant
large motor skills
small motor skills
mitten grasp
pincer grasp
weaning
object permanence
stranger anxiety
separation anxiety
immunization

Throughout their baby's first year, parents watch the infant grow and develop at amazing rates. (An **infant** is a baby under one year of age.) During these first 12 months, infants triple their birthweight. They grow to $1\frac{1}{2}$ times their birth height (length). Controlled movements replace most of the newborn reflexes. For instance, instead of just grasping objects, infants learn to pick things up, bang them together, and drop them intentionally. Instead of depending on their sucking reflexes, they learn to eat solid foods and drink from a cup.

Parents may think of their newborns as helpless. Twelve months later, *helpless* might be the last word they would use to describe their infants. By that time, infants are busy exploring—crawling, standing, and perhaps even walking.

Infants take giant leaps in developing their senses and comprehension, too. Babies learn to recognize their parents and often greet them with smiles. They learn to understand simple words and react appropriately. They may even say a few words themselves.

As babies approach their first birthdays, their individual personalities become more apparent, 11-1. Their styles of learning differ as do their interests and abilities. Some babies insist on feeding themselves, while others still want to be fed baby foods. Some will be just learning to stand, while others are already walking with confidence. The range of normal behavior is quite broad. Parents should try to resist comparing their baby's achievements with those of other babies.

Infancy is a challenging period for both parents and their infants. Often, however, parents feel surprised and a little disappointed when they suddenly realize their child is no longer an infant. They can hardly believe their tiny, cuddly baby has already become an active toddler.

1—**Vocabulary:** Look up terms in the glossary and discuss their meanings.

2—**Discuss:** Describe changes in height, weight, and reflexes during the first year. Why are these changes so astonishing in such a short period of time?

3—**Reflect:** Think about children you know. In what ways is each child unique?

1—**Example:** Babies grow and change rapidly. Most experts advise parents to make the most of each day. Can you give examples of how this helps?

2—**Resource:** *Large and Small Motor Skills*, Activity A, SAG.

3—**Activity:** Using a life-sized doll, have students demonstrate how to properly support an infant's head and neck.

11-1 —————————————
Each baby has a unique personality. Signs of this personality are evident from birth, but become much more obvious near a baby's first birthday.

Some of the best advice parents give one another is to make the most of each day as it comes. That way, parents can enjoy infancy to the fullest and not be overly sad when it ends. Wise parents accept each stage as special and unique, with its own high and low points. They enjoy all the different stages of their child's development.

Physical Development

In their first year, babies progress rapidly in their physical development. Humans grow and develop more as infants than they will at any time after birth. Only prenatally does physical growth occur faster.

Infants master many new skills and abilities. Parents may keep track of these achievements in a keepsake book. They often want to capture images of these special moments and save them for a lifetime. To achieve this, many parents shoot roll after roll of film or record hours of videotape.

An infant's physical development involves much more than just growing in height and weight. Babies make great strides in muscle control and coordination. They learn to move their bodies and to control and coordinate these movements. As their muscles develop, babies constantly work toward developing motor skills. *Motor skills* are skills that require the movement and control of certain muscles. There are both large motor skills and small motor skills.

Large Motor Skills

Large motor skills involve the use of the large muscles of the body, such as the trunk, neck, arm, and leg muscles. Babies must master the initial steps of motor skill development before moving on to a more complicated skill.

When parents bring their newborns home, the babies spend most of their time lying in the *fetal position* (a curled-up position babies assume inside the uterus). When newborns do move, their movements may look disorganized. These movements are reflex actions rather than voluntary movements. Their whole bodies twitch when they cry, with arms and legs flinging out in all directions.

Voluntary Body Control Develops

As infants grow older, their reflex actions fade. One of their first voluntary movements is using the neck muscles to lift the head. As infants lie on their stomachs, they can lift their heads slightly and turn them from one side to the other. The neck muscles are weak, however. When parents hold their baby, they must remember to support the baby's head. Babies gain more control of their neck muscles. As this happens, they are better able to lift and turn their heads.

As their arm and leg muscles develop, babies begin to cycle their arms and legs more smoothly. With increased coordination, babies can move an arm and a leg on the same side of the body in unison. They can also move both arms or both legs at the same time with some control. Their kicking will become more vigorous.

Parents may suddenly have more difficulty changing diapers and dressing their babies. A baby may wiggle, turn, or thrash his or her arms and legs instead of lying still. Babies enjoy being able to control their movements, and they practice endlessly.

Around the age of four months, babies have good control of their large muscles. They begin moving voluntarily in response to their parents' actions. At the sounds of their parents' voices, babies turn their heads and begin waving their arms and legs in excitement. When lying on their stomachs, babies may playfully rock like an airplane, with their arms and legs extended. They may even enjoy being propped up with pillows in a sitting position for short periods of time. This gives them a new perspective on the world.

Rolling Over

The next new skill for babies is rolling over, 11-2. First, infants roll from side to side when on their stomachs. After some practice, they can roll over from their stomachs to their backs. The first time a baby rolls over, he or she may look pleasantly surprised. Babies practice this skill repeatedly. Before long, they learn to roll over the other way—from their backs to their stomachs.

Parents are proud of their babies' accomplishments. They are also happy to know their babies are now able to change their own positions for comfort. While practicing their rolls, babies also learn to move by rocking, twisting, and kicking against a flat surface.

Sitting, Standing, and Crawling

Babies enjoy being supported in a sitting or standing position. When in a sitting position, their bodies may slowly begin to lean to one side as their trunk muscles tire. When in a standing position, babies move their bodies up and down and stamp their feet as if to say "I'm getting ready to move!"

1—Discuss: Babies' arm and leg motions at first appear disorganized. What are signs an infant is gaining control over these muscles?

2—Discuss: Briefly describe the coordination babies must exhibit in order to roll over. Why is this an important milestone in development?

11-2 _____
The floor or ground is the best place for babies to practice rolling over since they cannot fall.

1—Discuss: How do babies reveal their instinct to achieve an upright position? What problems might they encounter?

2—Vocabulary: What is meant by *cruising*? How does it help babies learn to walk?

3—Example: Have you witnessed a baby learning to stand? Briefly describe a baby's first attempt at standing.

At about six months of age, babies are continuing to develop better muscle control and a sense of balance. They can sit with slight support, as in a high chair. On a flat surface, infants may get up on their hands and knees, only to lunge forward on their noses. Babies this age are surprisingly durable. They bounce back easily from their tumbles. Instead of crying, they simply try again. Babies seem to sense that bumps and falls are part of growing up.

Before long, babies learn to balance themselves on their hands and knees. At first, they may just rock back and forth in this position. When they start crawling, their first attempts may find them traveling backward. Soon they are moving forward and crawling everywhere, 11-3.

Babies seem to have an instinct to achieve an upright position. They work to pull themselves into a flexed, half-standing position with their bottoms out and wavering. Once they achieve this standing position, they discover a new problem—getting back down! At this point, some babies cry for help. Others will simply let go and fall back with a thud to a sitting position. In either case, babies try again and again. Slowly, they will learn to sit from a standing position.

Babies take some time perfecting the motor skills of crawling and pulling themselves to a standing position. With these skills, they are able to explore their surroundings.

Taking Steps

Standing becomes a favorite activity for babies. As their leg muscles strengthen and their balance improves, they become more daring. At first, they may practice stepping sideways. Usually, infants do this while facing and holding onto a low table or couch. This maneuver is called *cruising*. At first, they hold tightly to the furniture as they cruise around it. As their cruising skills improve, they need only to lightly touch the furniture as they take tiny steps around it. At this stage, parents can delight children by holding their hands and helping them take a few wobbly steps.

The next large motor skill babies learn is standing on their own. This differs from their old routine of pulling themselves up by hanging onto something. To stand on their own, babies flex their knees and push off from a squat. They may surprise themselves by standing alone for few seconds. Then, they may not know what to do next.

Walking

Parents should not be overly concerned about how quickly their children learn to walk. The average age for babies to walk alone is 12 to 14 months. The actual time a baby starts walking varies widely from one baby to another. Some may walk earlier, while others may start later.

When a baby is ready to walk, he or she usually begins by taking a few steps, often toward a parent. The baby may totter forward on the toes, take a few steps, and then fall into the parents' waiting arms. Everyone, including the babies, will squeal with delight.

11-3 _____

Crawling is a large motor skill. Each baby develops a unique crawling style.

Walking will be a challenging task for a long time and will demand the babies' total concentration. At first, babies extend their arms high as they walk in order to balance themselves. Slowly, they develop the ability to balance themselves from within their bodies, using their trunk muscles. This is yet another large motor skill.

The Baby's Own Pace

Each baby achieves the same steps in the development of large motor skills, 11-4. However, babies are individuals. Each baby develops at his or her own pace. As they approach their first birthdays, babies may be at different points in their large motor skill development.

Some babies get around by crawling rapidly. They follow their parents from one room to another like a shadow. When placed in a playpen, their desire to explore is so strong they climb out and start roaming.

Other babies are more fascinated by standing. They stand next to furniture, in their high chairs, in bathtubs, in strollers, and in grocery carts. Their

1—Discuss: When babies take their first steps, why do they hold their hands high?

2—Discuss: Briefly describe the pattern babies follow from lying in a fetal position to ultimately walking. All babies follow the same patterned sequence. Do they all follow the same timetable? (Review 11-4 and note each new accomplishment.)

11-4 _____
Babies follow the same general patterns of development although their timetables differ. These steps are some of the highlights of large motor skill development in the first year.

Step 1—Newborns lie curled in the fetal position.

Step 2—As infants gain more control of their neck muscles, they can hold up their heads.

Step 3—Babies can hold their heads higher and for a longer time when they bend their arms for support.

Step 4—Soon, babies can rise their chest, supporting themselves with straightened arms.

Step 5—Babies can keep their backs firm and heads steady when propped up in a sitting position for a short time.

Step 6—With better muscle control and balance, babies can sit with slight support.

(continued)

11-4
(continued)

Step 7—Babies can sit without support.

Step 8—Once babies can crawl, they are ready to explore.

Step 9—Babies' first attempts to pull to a standing position may be shaky.

Step 10—Before long, babies stand whenever possible and cruise around furniture.

Step 11—Stairs are challenging and fun. They can also be dangerous.

Step 12—Babies like to walk holding onto a parent's hand.

Step 13—A baby's first steps alone are wobbly, with hands held high for balance.

Step 14—Eventually, babies learn to walk more steadily.

parents have to keep a close eye on them to protect them from dangerous falls. With practice, babies add squatting and stooping to their standing skills. Babies who are fascinated with standing may be content at this stage. They may wait a few months before starting to take steps.

Still other babies move more quickly through the crawling and standing stages. They seem to be in a great hurry to walk. They practice cruising around furniture for hours. They love to walk, holding their parents' hands. Suddenly (and sometimes by accident) they take their first steps alone. It is a grand occasion, and babies sense they have accomplished something wonderful. Parents can encourage their babies to continue walking by showing their pride and excitement over the baby's accomplishments.

Small Motor Skills

Small motor skills involve the use of smaller muscles in the body, such as those of the eyes, hands, fingers, feet, and toes. Since development proceeds from the trunk outward, babies begin developing their large muscles before they develop smaller ones. They can control the muscles of their trunks, necks, arms, and legs before those of their hands, feet, and fingers. Babies' eye-hand coordination also relates closely to small muscle development. Several highlights in eye-hand coordination and small motor skills during the first year are shown in 11-5.

Newborns have very little control over their small muscles. Their squirming and stretching movements result from reflexes, not small motor skills. For the first couple of months, babies keep their hands fisted or only slightly open. Parents may marvel at how a newborn's tiny fingers curl and grasp an adult's finger. This action is caused by the grasping reflex, not a voluntary movement.

Eyesight Improves

Babies begin exploring their new world with their eyes. They glance at stationary objects and follow moving objects for a brief time. Infants may suddenly stop moving to stare in the direction of a sound they hear. They try to focus on objects that are neither too close nor too far away. Gradually, as babies develop better control of their eye muscles, their vision improves.

Babies like to look at things, so parents should try to provide them a variety of things to see. Mobiles that are attractive from the babies' point of view are good, 11-6. These mobiles should be brightly colored, but they do not have to be fancy. A mobile should be hung within the baby's range of sight. It should be changed often, if possible, so the baby can look at something new.

At age two to three months, mirrors begin to fascinate babies. Parents can place a mirror about seven inches above a baby's eyes to draw the baby's attention. (Mirrors used for babies should not be made of glass.) Since the image in a mirror constantly changes, it will capture the baby's interest for several weeks. Another way to encourage babies' interest in looking is to give them a change of scenery. For instance, a parent might carry the baby from room to room in the home to look at different things.

Voluntary Body Control Develops

During the third month, reflexes fade, and babies begin to practice voluntary body control. This is the time when parents should move crib mobiles and mirrors out of the baby's reach. Parents can replace these objects with a sturdier cradle gym.

With their hands open, babies may try to reach or swipe at objects on the cradle gym. At first, they may be far off target. Babies first notice their hands at

11-5 _____

Hand manipulation skills are dependent upon eye-hand coordination, an important small motor skill.

Hand Manipulation Skills

Step 1—As babies wave their arms, they begin to notice their hands.

Step 2—As babies practice swiping and grabbing, their aim improves.

Step 3—Babies playfully grab their feet with a crude mitten grasp.

Step 4—Babies enjoy handling and mouthing anything they can grasp between the fingers and palms of their hands.

Step 5—With a pincer grasp, babies can pick up a ribbon or string.

Step 6—Improved grasping skills allow babies to feed themselves using their fingers.

1—Discuss: Briefly describe how eye-hand coordination is balanced with development of small muscle development.

2—Enrich: When do babies first notice their hands? What are their first reactions? Why is this an important milestone of development?

about this time. They may spend much time tracking their hand movements. Babies enthusiastically watch and try to control their own movements. Parents often enjoy watching as infants discover more about themselves.

Mitten Grasp Appears

Infants continue developing better control of their hands. They practice grabbing and swiping at objects, gradually improving their aim. They tug and pull at their clothes. They discover and grab at their feet. Babies often hold their feet with a **mitten grasp**, where the palm and fingers oppose the thumb, 11-7. When infants learn to touch their mouths with their fingers, it triggers a whole new way of exploring. Babies stick every object they can grasp, including their fingers and toes, into their mouths.

As their grasp becomes more refined, babies enjoy handling different objects. They can begin lifting pieces of

11-6 _____
Infants spend hours staring at their surroundings. Providing a colorful mobile is one way parents can stimulate baby's mind.

food from their high chair trays to their mouths. If their parents have introduced drinking from a cup, babies may try to grab and hold the cup. They can pick an object up but have not yet developed the coordination needed to release it from their grasp.

1—Discuss:
Compare the mitten grasp with the pincer grasp. How can this refinement give babies greater dexterity and the ability to entertain themselves?

1 Pincer Grasp Develops

With continued practice, an infant's grasping skills continually improve. Eventually, babies can pick up objects between a thumb and index finger. This is called a **pincer grasp**. Mastering this small motor skill is a great achievement. Next, babies learn to transfer an object from one hand to the other. Before long, they can hold two objects,

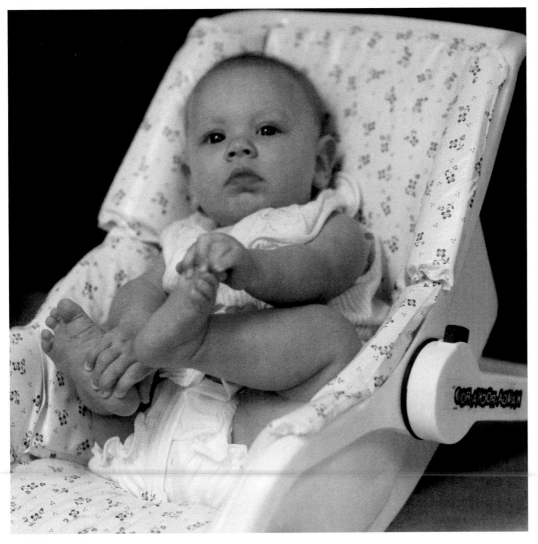

11-7 _____
This baby uses a mitten grasp to grab her feet and toes. This grasp is an important small motor skill.

1—Discuss: What precautions do parents need to take as babies' ability to open containers develops?

2—Resource: *Dangers and Safeguards for Infants*, Activity B, SAG.

3—Discuss: Cite examples where babies have been seriously hurt because of simple household accidents.

4—Resource: *Car safety Seats*, reproducible master 11-1, TR.

5—Discuss: Briefly describe how parents should introduce solid foods to their babies. What techniques can parents use?

one in each hand. Then, they will learn to bang these two objects together to make all kinds of exciting noises.

They can use this advanced grasp to pick up objects and also learn to drop objects they have grasped. Babies still cannot release objects in a controlled motion, however. This skill develops later. With all this practice in grasping and holding, babies also learn to drop things. They seem intrigued by this new ability and may pick up and drop objects at will just to practice. Babies' dropping games may be frustrating for parents, but they help babies develop important skills.

Most babies use both hands equally well throughout the first year. They love to play with a variety of objects and will finger, rattle, mouth, and bang anything they can reach. They also learn hands can do more than grasp. They learn to stroke, pat, and feel different textures. Experimenting with their hands is very exciting for seven-month-olds, who usually have an object in one or both hands. If they crawl, they often carry a toy around with them.

By the ninth month, babies have discovered their index fingers are useful for leading and pointing. They also use these fingers to poke into holes and even into parents' faces. Infants also learn to release grasped objects instead of just dropping them. At this point, they will enjoy playing with any kind of container. Putting large beads in a jar or taking spools out of a box fascinates them. They may also try to empty any drawers or cupboards they can reach.

Another milestone occurs when babies begin using both hands in different ways on the same object. For instance, the baby might hold the object with one hand while manipulating it with the other.

Keeping Babies Safe

Parents must keep a close eye on their infants and remove any potentially harmful objects from their reach. As their small motor skills improve, babies become better at removing the lids from containers. Nothing is safe from a mobile baby unless it is locked or placed totally out of reach. By their first birthdays, babies can be trying, but they are also delightful. Parents can make this first year a safe one by recognizing dangers and following good safety practices. Some of these dangers and safeguards are shown in 11-8.

Introducing Solid Foods

For the first four to six months, mother's milk or formula provides babies with adequate nutrients. Before this time, a baby's digestive system is not mature enough to handle solid foods. When a baby's digestive system becomes a little more mature, however, parents can begin introducing solid foods. Many professionals suggest a sequence like the one shown in chart 11-9. Parents should consult their pediatrician before introducing solid foods. They should follow the doctor's recommendations about when to start giving foods, which foods to offer, and what to do if any food sensitivities appear.

When babies are ready to begin eating solid foods, a small amount of iron-enriched baby cereal may be mixed with milk or formula. Parents should mix the cereal to a smooth and creamy consistency, free of lumps. When parents first introduce cereal, babies don't know what to do with it. They are familiar with liquid foods, and they don't know how to swallow at will.

To help their babies learn how to eat solid food, parents should start by feeding small amounts of food. They

Dangers and Safeguards During Infancy

1

Babies can move by kicking their feet and pushing their bodies. They may fall off a flat surface. When babies are laid on a bed, barriers should be placed around them to prevent them from falling. Their positions should be checked often.

Babies discover open doors and will travel where there might be danger. They also like to close doors and may close them on their fingers. All doors should be closed or doorways blocked with secure barriers.

Slats in cribs and playpens should be no more than 2 3/8 inches (6 cm) apart so a baby's head cannot be caught between the slats. If there is more than a two-finger space between the mattress and the side of the crib, the mattress is too small. An infant could suffocate by wedging his or her head in this gap.

11-8 _____
Safety must be a constant concern of parents.

1—Discuss: Review safety precautions as depicted in each situation. Discuss how dangerous situations can happen and why parents must be alert to prevent them.

2—Resource: *Infant Safety*, reproducible master 11-2, TR.

2   Babies should never be left alone in the bathtub. They can drown in only a small amount of water. They can also scald themselves by turning on the hot water. In fact, parents may want to wrap a washcloth around a hot faucet to prevent babies from burning their waving hands.

When traveling in a car, babies should be securely fastened in a car safety seat that has been approved by the federal goverment. Infant carriers are designed so babies face the back of the car. Babies should always ride in the backseat of a car. (If a baby is placed in the front of any vehicle equipped with a passenger-side airbag, the initial impact of the airbag could lead to serious head injury or death.)

Babies like to pull dangling cords and poke things into electrical sockets. To prevent these dangers, covers should be placed over unused sockets. Unused lamps and appliances should be put away. Cords need to be made inaccessible to a baby's reach.

Babies like to pull themselves up on any available furniture. Unstable tables and chairs should be removed while babies are in this stage.

Bottles should not be propped in bottle holders. Milk may flow too fast and cause choking or digestive problems. Instead, small babies should be held while feeding so the milk flow can be controlled.

11-9
Most doctors rec-
ommend a
sequence like this
one for introducing
solid foods in
baby's diet.

Introducing Solid Foods

Approximate Age Timing	Foods to Be Introduced, One at a Time*
4 to 6 months	Iron-fortified baby cereal mixed with formula or breast milk
5 to 7 months	Strained or pureed vegetables and juices, such as carrots, squash, green beans, peas Strained or pureed fruits and juices, such as applesauce, pears, peaches, and bananas,
6 to 8 months	Soft or strained cheese, yogurt, egg yolk, beans, meat, poultry, and fish
8 to 10 months	Soft table foods
10 to 12 months	Chopped foods, cooked fruits and vegetables, and finely chopped meats
12 months	Whole milk from cows

* Introduce solid foods in very small amounts, one at a time. For instance, when introducing strained fruits, start with just 1 or 2 tablespoons (5 to 10 ml) of one fruit. Wait a few days before introducing another fruit. Then, if baby is sensitive to a food, the problem food can be identified and avoided for a few weeks.

1

1—**Enrich:** Ask a die-
titian or pediatrician to
discuss the sequence
in which foods are
introduced to babies.

2—**Discuss:** When
children want to start
feeding themselves,
parents may have to
accept that mealtimes
may be messy. What
can they do to help
make mealtime more
pleasant?

should use a small spoon with a long handle. Parents should insert the spoon between the baby's lips, so the baby can suck the food from the spoon. Food put on the front of the tongue will dribble out of the mouth. Babies are not practiced at getting the food back into their mouths. Food pushed to the back of the mouth may gag them.

Babies may be fed a variety of foods, but they should be introduced one at a time. They can gradually advance from cereals to fruits and vegetables to egg yolks and meats. Parents may buy commercial baby foods or make their own. Since babies can't chew well and their digestive systems are delicate, their foods must be soft and rather bland.

When babies start eating solid foods, their nutritional needs are still being met by milk or formula. Parents shouldn't worry about how much of the food the baby actually eats. The goals at this stage are for the baby to learn how to swallow at will and to enjoy mealtime.

Babies need several weeks to get used to this new way of eating. Then they will want to start feeding themselves with their hands. They may be a little awkward at first. Parents need to allow their babies to practice this important skill. Given the chance, infants usually do a good job of getting enough food into their mouths. Babies also try to put their spoons into their mouths. A parent's job is to provide nutritious food and clean up the mess afterward.

Parents might as well accept mealtimes at this stage will be messy, 11-10. They should stop an older baby from deliberately throwing food, but dropped food and spills are normal, especially in younger infants. Parents can cope with this stage by putting newspapers or sheets of plastic on their floors and large bibs on their babies. Like adults, babies have food likes and dislikes. Their tastes will change, however, so a food baby rejects once may be introduced again a month or so later.

2

11-10
Mom's job is to clean up the mess baby makes trying to feed himself. Food may seem to go everywhere but in the baby's mouth.

Weaning

Weaning is the phasing out of taking milk from a breast or bottle. Weaning should be a gradual process, like the introduction of solid foods. Mothers may breast-feed their babies as long as their schedules permit and the process is satisfying for both themselves and their babies. Some mothers nurse their babies for more than a year. Others wean their babies from breast to bottle within the first months. Babies usually begin tapering off breast or bottle feedings shortly after solid food is introduced. Weaning is complete when drinking out of a cup becomes more satisfying for them. Most babies will be totally weaned from the breast or bottle by 13 to 15 months of age.

Some parents may continue to give their babies a bottle when they put them to bed at night. This is generally not a good idea. It may encourage a baby to use food for emotional security. Falling asleep with a bottle of milk or juice in the mouth can also cause tooth decay and ear infections. Parents can feed the baby just before bed if the baby needs a feeding before bed. If the baby insists on a bottle at bedtime, it should contain only water. Some parents find substituting a pacifier satisfies the baby's need to suck as he or she falls asleep.

Teething

Babies react differently to the process of teething. One baby will chew, fret, and drool before each tooth erupts (comes through the gums). Another baby will produce new teeth without any fuss at all. In any case, teething does not cause serious health problems. If a baby has a high fever, diarrhea, or vomiting, parents should not assume the problem is caused by teething. Instead, they should consult a doctor.

To ease minor teething discomfort, parents can massage the baby's gums. They can let the baby chew on a frozen bagel, teething biscuits, or a boiled-clean cloth that won't shred. Cold, hard objects feel good in the baby's mouth. Some doctors recommend the use of teething rings and ointments, while others discourage using them. Parents can ask their pediatrician for advice.

Like other aspects of development, teething follows a predictable pattern, but the timing varies. The first two teeth to appear are the lower front teeth, 11-11. The average age for a first tooth is five to nine months. However, some babies are born with a tooth, and others are still toothless on their first birthday. By two years of age, most children have their full set of baby teeth.

Tooth development begins prenatally. The crowns (tops) of the baby teeth form in the gums before the baby is born. This is why the mother's diet

1—Vocabulary: Define *weaning*. What type of weaning schedule may parents try? Is it best to do it suddenly or gradually?

2—Discuss: Should babies be given a bottle at night? What problems may result?

3—Discuss: Cite common problems some babies seem to have during teething. How can minor discomforts be relieved?

1—Discuss: As babies mature, they learn to keep themselves awake. This can create problems at bedtime. How can parents make bedtime less problematic?

2—Example: Why does establishing a bedtime ritual help provide a baby with a pattern and security for bedtime? Cite some examples of rituals parents may use.

11-11
Teething may mean a lot of drooling. Babies cut their lower front teeth first.

during pregnancy is so important. The crowns of permanent teeth begin forming during infancy. Calcium, phosphorus, vitamin D, and fluoride are important nutrients that aid in tooth development.

Dental care is important, even during infancy. Many experts recommend cleaning an infant's teeth with a piece of gauze or a washcloth. Once an infant is used to having his or her teeth cleaned, parents can introduce an infant toothbrush. It should have a small head and soft bristles. Parents should use only a pea-sized amount of toothpaste and discourage the baby from swallowing toothpaste. Parents should brush their infant's teeth regularly, especially if the child eats sweets.

Sleeping Patterns and Problems

For the first few months, babies' bodies dictate their sleeping patterns—babies fall asleep when their bodies

need rest. Only severe hunger or illness can keep them awake. Sometime during the middle to late months of infancy, babies learn to keep themselves awake. As they become more active and more social, they may have trouble settling down to sleep.

Babies may refuse a morning nap and take just one afternoon nap. They may also begin to protest bedtime. Since babies need lots of sleep, parents should handle this issue firmly. Parents can make bedtimes more relaxed by helping babies calm down from the day's activities. Cuddling or reading to babies in a quiet room may help them wind down from daytime activity. Most babies respond well to bedtime rituals that are performed in exactly the same way at about the same time each night. A ritual may include bathing, changing, dressing for bed, rocking, singing a special lullaby, putting the baby in bed, kissing the baby, and turning out the light.

Bedtime rituals don't always work. Once in their cribs, babies may cry or call out for their parents. Parents need to be kind but firm in this matter. They should respond once to reassure the baby they are nearby. After that, parents should let babies know it is bedtime, not playtime. Speaking firmly may help make the message clear. If babies continue to cry, parents should listen to interpret the cries. If the baby uses cries of hunger, pain, or distress, parents should respond to the baby promptly. Otherwise, parents should probably let the baby learn to fall asleep on his or her own.

Intellectual Development

Intellectual development refers to the development of a person's mental and thinking abilities. Parents may hesitate to think of their infants as intellectual beings. Babies can't hold a conversation, think logically, or solve math problems. However, their intellectual growth and development occurs at a rapid rate.

At birth, babies are helpless creatures unable to coordinate their own movements. Twelve months later, most infants are beginning to walk and talk. Developing the skills needed to perform these and other tasks shows great strides in intellectual development during the first year, 11-12.

Intellectual development advances in an orderly way, as outlined in the charts at the end of the chapter. The charts suggest a sequence of development stages; they are not definite timetables. Parents may find these charts useful in identifying and understanding a baby's current stage of development and anticipating future stages.

The Brain Grows and Develops

The first year is the most important year in brain growth and development. At birth, the brain is one-fourth its adult weight. At six months, the brain has grown to half its adult weight.

11-12
This one-year-old is hardly helpless! He uses his large motor skills as well as his mind when playing with this riding toy.

Three-fourths of a person's brain growth is complete by age two.

Much of a person's intellectual ability depends on certain connections between *neurons* (nerve cells) in the brain. These connections activate the neurons. The number and kinds of connections between these neurons determines a person's capacity to learn. By age 10, the brain begins eliminating inactive neurons. After this time, the potential to make new connections is severely limited, if not entirely gone. The first ten years, then, are crucial to brain development.

In addition, brain research has revealed certain skills have a "window of opportunity." This window of opportunity is a critical period in which a person's capacity to develop a certain skill peaks. Before this time, the person is not developmentally able to learn the skill. After this time, learning the skill is difficult, if not impossible. The window of opportunity for many skills begins and ends during early childhood. For instance, birth to four years is the window of opportunity for learning basic motor skills. After this time, people lose their capacity to learn basic motor skills. It may be very difficult or even impossible to master these skills after age four.

Early experiences also influence the brain's ability to grow and function. As a child's brain develops, it is affected by the kind of care the child receives. When parents offer a child constant, loving, and appropriate care, it promotes the connection of neurons in the child's brain. Cuddling and other emotional support stimulates brain development. Parents can also encourage a child to develop skills and abilities during their specific windows of opportunity. In turn, developing these skills forms even more neuron connections in the brain.

Just as positive experiences can promote brain growth, negative ones can hinder it. Infants who are malnourished, for instance, develop smaller

1—Discuss: How does memory development help babies anticipate but wait for their feedings?

brains than those who are adequately fed. Their bodies do not get the nutrients needed to build brain cells or make neuron connections. A lack of nutrients during the first three to four years (when the majority of brain growth occurs) can cause irreversible damage.

Without a nurturing environment, children's brains are not able to develop as many neuron connections. Child abuse and neglect in the first three years can also change a child's brain in ways that can never be repaired. Young children who are abused or neglected develop smaller brains than nonabused children. Also, abusive parents may be less likely to provide their children experiences that will stimulate brain growth. Chronic abuse can also affect the balance of certain chemicals in the brain that further affect its development.

Physical and Intellectual Development Are Related

From birth, babies are constantly learning. Each day, an infant has certain periods in which he or she is quiet and alert. In newborns, these periods may be as short as half an hour, 11-13. By twelve months, an infant may be alert for as long as several hours at a time.

During these alert periods, infants use all their senses (vision, hearing, touch, smell, and taste) to learn more about the world around them. Infants look at objects, particularly patterned objects and human faces. They listen to sounds and voices. Babies may even stop sucking during a feeding to look or listen. They cry when they need assistance, and become calm when they feel secure.

The use of each sense is a physical ability that relates to intellectual development. When a baby's physical ability of sight improves, so does the baby's intellectual development. The baby uses this physical ability to learn more about the world. As vision improves,

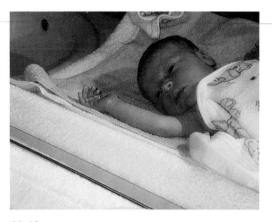

11-13 _____
Newborns have short periods in which they are quiet and alert. This is the time they learn the most.

the baby can focus more clearly and may stare at objects. Soon, he or she will show a preference for people over objects. The baby will learn to associate a person's appearance with the person's voice, smell, and touch. These intellectual advances depend upon the development of a certain physical skill. Many other physical and intellectual developments are related.

Memory Develops

By the third month, parents often sense new skills in their babies. Babies begin to show signs of a developing memory as they wait for an anticipated reward such as feeding. They can even begin to remember a sequence of steps leading to a reward. For instance, the infant may recognize a series of actions parents do to prepare for feeding times. If these actions are done in the expected sequence, babies will wait, realizing they will soon be fed. If the sequence of actions is interrupted, they will become upset and cry. Babies like routines and predictability. This helps them learn what to expect from their environment.

An infant's developing memory helps him or her learn to recognize family members and familiar objects and sounds. Their memories also enable them to become bored with the same visual images. They like a change of scenery. They like to see different objects.

As their memories develop, babies may like to begin playing hiding games with their toys. Peek-a-boo is a memory game babies may begin playing at this stage. Parents hide their faces with their hands and then remove them. Babies soon learn to cover their own faces. Gradually, parents can throw a light cover over their baby's face, and the baby will pull it off with much enthusiasm. The peek-a-boo game is possible when babies have memories of people they love. They can retain those memories and feel secure in the few seconds it takes to reveal the faces again.

Awareness Improves

At about three months, babies begin to become aware of themselves. They play with their hands and feet, studying how they look and move. Babies begin swiping at objects with their hands. As they practice this skill, they learn about distance and depth perception. They also begin learning about cause and effect. They learn that swiping at an object will make the object move.

As babies grow, their alert periods lengthen. They use this quiet, alert time to learn more about themselves and their surroundings. As they play with toys, they start noticing differences in shape, size, and texture. Babies also learn to repeat acts they enjoy, such as shaking a rattle to make noise. Infants at this stage can recognize familiar faces, so they may resent and fear strangers. As this fear of stranger develops, parents may need to provide more comfort and reassurance when the baby is in new situations.

Babies continue to learn about themselves. They learn to recognize and respond to their own names. They smile at themselves in mirrors, 11-14. They put fingers and toys in their mouths, noting how things taste and feel.

By about six months, babies stay alert for as long as two hours at a time. They sit with support and turn their heads in all directions, searching for new things to see. They grab any objects within reach and study them intently. They turn the objects in their hands to see all sides.

Meanwhile, they are learning more about the relationship between their hands and the objects they are handling. Babies this age discover they can look down from their high chairs at objects they have dropped to the floor. They enjoy repeatedly picking up and dropping objects. Often babies see this as a game. Their parents spend much time retrieving the objects, and may be frustrated by picking a spoon off the floor twelve times in a row during lunch. It may help to remember babies use this game as a learning experience. Babies learn about distance and spatial relationships while practicing their small motor skills. Infants also learn objects don't disappear when dropped; they simply fall to the floor.

At about this same time, babies can anticipate a whole object by seeing only part of it. Thus, a simple hide-and-seek game is fun for both babies and their parents.

Associations Are Formed

Almost from birth, babies learn to make simple associations. This skill develops with time. When they hear the refrigerator door open, they expect to be fed. When they hear the front door open, they expect to see a family member enter the room. When looking at books with parents or siblings, they associate the words they hear with the pictures they see. They also begin to show an interest in the relationship between objects. For instance, if they

1—Discuss: Why is a baby's ability to play peek-a-boo a signal for intellectual development?

2—Discuss: What simple actions indicate babies are learning distance and depth perception, as well as cause and effect?

3—Discuss: When babies play picking up and dropping games, what significant lessons are they learning?

11-14 _____
This baby likes to see the baby in the mirror smiling at him. In time, babies learn they are the babies in the mirror.

1—**Example:** Briefly discuss how babies learn simple associations and relationships. Give examples.

2—**Discuss:** How can parents encourage lessons of associations for both interest and safety for their baby?

3—**Discuss:** Describe how babies learn to solve simple problems. Name other actions that indicate babies' ability to solve problems.

4—**Example:** Learning by trial and error is an important achievement. Give some simple examples of how babies learn concepts through this method.

pick up a spoon, they may push it around on a plate. They may even bring the spoon to their lips, although they won't yet be able to feed themselves with a spoon.

Babies gradually learn to make other kinds of associations. When an infant hears the sound of an airplane outside, the baby may learn to point to the sky. Later, a parent may ask "Where is the airplane?" The baby will point to the sky even when there is no airplane sound. Parents can encourage these lessons of association by allowing their babies to watch or participate in their everyday activities. Babies soon learn sponges are used with water, spoons are for stirring, ovens are hot, and refrigerators are cold.

Simple Problems Can Be Solved

As babies make further advances in intellectual development, they learn to solve simple problems. They will pull a string to bring a toy closer to them or shake a bell to make it ring. Through trial and error, babies learn they can make more noise banging on certain objects than others. As babies empty and fill containers, toy boxes, and drawers, they learn the concepts of in, out, one, more than one, and "all gone."

Babies may use trial and error to solve their own problems. Parents can almost see their little minds working as they try to turn lids to open a container or push chairs to use for climbing. Babies work intently until they get nesting toys to fit together. Then they start all over again, feeling good about their achievements and seeking their parents' approval.

In the late months of infancy, many babies show a preference for one hand, most often the right hand. A baby will pick up a toy with the preferred hand, transfer it to the other, and reach for another with the first hand. If the baby wants a third toy, he or she may hesitate for awhile before finding a solution. This might be resting the second toy in

11-15 _____
This baby is showing hand perference when he picks up his toys.

the crook of one arm while reaching for the third toy with the other. Problem-solving skills are signs of advancing intellectual development. See 11-15.

Babies See Similarities and Differences

Babies at this stage begin to recognize similarities between their actions and those of other people. When parents or siblings imitate the babies' actions, the babies watch with fascination. Then the babies will imitate the actions of others. Imitation games can be fun for both parents and infants.

Some babies are able to identify parts of the body. When asked where their noses are, they point to them with big smiles. They love to show off, winning their parents' attention and approval. Identifying body parts helps babies recognize similarities among people. They discover everyone has eyes, ears, and a nose.

Babies also note differences or changes, particularly in familiar environments. If a chair has been moved or a new decoration added, a baby will spot the change immediately. Infants will investigate a coffee mug left on a low table before the parents have a chance to retrieve it. If the mug is dropped, a baby may blink his or her eyes, anticipating the crash before the mug hits the floor. At this age, infants develop a sense of timing as well as an understanding of cause and effect.

Gradually, babies develop a sense of dimension and spatial relationships. They reach for a big beach ball with both hands. They reach for a crayon with just a thumb and finger. Their new understanding of distance is accompanied by new fears. They may gaze fearfully at places where they used to climb with ease.

Object Permanence Appears

By about ten months, most babies have a reliable memory for what is out of sight. At this point, they learn the important concept of **object permanence**. They learn unseen objects have not necessarily disappeared. They will remove an obstacle (such as a blanket) to reach for a toy they can partially see—or even a toy they can't see at all. They can find a toy a parent has hidden—if they saw the parent hide the toy within the past few minutes. They deliberately hide and then find objects. (Siblings' toys are favorite objects for this game.) With their new understanding, babies can also anticipate the return of a person or object that leaves. When they roll a ball to a parent, they are no longer afraid it will disappear.

As their understanding of object permanence develops over the next months, they will become more skillful. They will be able to reach behind their backs for a toy without looking at

1—Vocabulary: Define *object permanence*. Describe how babies apply this concept.

1—Discuss: As babies mature, their memory span lengthens. How does this aid their ability to imitate? Describe simple behaviors babies like to imitate.

2—Discuss: Why is play important to a baby's learning?

3—Activity: Demonstrate some simple exploration games parents can introduce to their babies.

4—Discuss: How do babies communicate from birth even though they are not able to actually talk until much later?

it. They will also learn to search for hidden objects even if they did not see where the objects were hidden. If they remember where they last saw the objects, they will go there to look for them.

Learning by Imitation

As they become more observant, babies become better imitators. This skill also depends on a longer memory span. Babies must be able to remember a behavior they see in order to imitate it. Imitation is an important method of learning, but babies don't want to be pushed. They resist "teaching" efforts of their siblings and parents. They would rather just watch. Later, when they feel ready, they will imitate the behavior they have seen.

Babies seem especially interested in imitating the actions of other babies. They also enjoy imitating their siblings and parents. They may try to feed their parents, just as parents have fed them. They may dab a washcloth on their parents' faces as the parents bathe them. Given some props, they will pretend to dust, sweep, wipe, stir, and do other household tasks along with their parents. Many babies are learning to talk at about this time, and imitation helps them. They imitate the rhythms, tones, and inflections of their parents as they try to make similar sounds.

Playtime Means Learning

Learning and playing go hand-in-hand for babies. They can learn and play by themselves, but their most valuable and fun playtimes are usually shared with others, 11-16. Parents can make the most of playtimes by being observant, patient, and creative.

Observant parents will pick up clues from their baby. They will sense when their baby wants active, tumbling play and when he or she wants quiet, cuddling play. This will vary according to the baby's mood at the time as well as the baby's overall temperament. Each baby is an individual—what is right for one may be wrong for another. By observing their babies' reactions, parents will know how much stimulation the baby needs. Babies need enough stimulation to stay interested and attentive. Too much stimulation, on the other hand, will overwhelm babies and make them withdraw.

Patient parents slow down their actions to match their babies' timing. When they smile at their babies, they wait several seconds, giving their babies time to smile back. When babies are learning new skills, such as reaching and grasping, parents wait patiently for them to respond. This gives the babies time to succeed in new and difficult tasks. When babies crawl after them, patient parents walk slowly so the babies do not feel frustrated and left behind.

Creative parents help their babies learn through exploration. They provide a variety of sights, sounds, smells, textures, and tastes. Their babies learn the sights, sounds, and smells of the outdoors as well as those inside the home. Babies feel the difference between soft sponges and hard building blocks. They learn that spools and balls roll, containers may be big or small, and pots and pans make noises. The time and effort parents put into playtimes are well rewarded by the delighted reactions of their babies.

Language Development

Babies need a few years to learn a specific language, but they can communicate from birth. At first, they express their needs by crying. Human voices and music can comfort infants. Babies make sounds right away, too, but usually these early sounds are natural reactions to physical comfort or discomfort.

Babies make their first deliberate sounds at about three months. They

11-16 _____
Infants learn a lot
from their play.
They love it when
their older sisters
and brothers play
with them.

begin cooing one-syllable, vowel-like sounds, such as *ooh*, *ah*, and *aw*. Soon they practice talking. When they hear a voice, they respond by smiling and making sounds. They imitate the natural rhythm of conversations by pausing, waiting for the other person to speak. They listen until the person stops talking, and then make more sounds. Babies practice this kind of speech even when they are alone. They make sounds, pause, and then make more sounds in a conversational rhythm.

When the first consonant sounds are added (usually *p, b, m,* and *l*), the noises sound more like words. Something like *ma* may be heard, but at this point, the sound is not meant as a name. This repeated vocalizing is called babbling. Soon, it becomes a favorite activity. Babies babble a lot to themselves and even more in response to their parents' words, 11-17. Generally, babies babble when they are happy. When they are upset, they are more likely to cry, wail, whimper, or fuss. Parents can reinforce conversa-

tion as a pleasant social exchange by responding pleasantly to their babies' sounds. Conversations mean the most to babies when parents talk directly to them and make eye contact.

At about five months, babies show an intense interest in watching their parents' mouths move. It may seem they are studying the mechanics of talking. They can recognize people by their voices, and they understand their own names.

Gradually, babies add more consonants to their vocabularies, such as *f, v, th, s, sh, z,* and *d*. They form two-syllable sounds by repeating their one-syllable words. They are excited about their new words and may make each one sound like an exclamation. Babies eventually make sounds like *mama* and *dada*, much to their parents' delight. Parents encourage their babies to repeat these sounds and associate them with mother and father. In a month or so, babies make the association and start using those words as names.

Babies become great imitators of behaviors and sounds. They imitate

1—Discuss: Babies
learn to form two-
syllable sounds by
repeating their one-
syllable sounds. When
they first say mama
and dada, do they
understand the mean-
ings of these words?

11-17

Parents can help their babies learn to communicate by responding to the babies' babbling. This can be a fun game for parents and babies alike.

1—Discuss: When do babies understand the meaning of the word no? What actions do they often add, indicating they understand?

2—Discuss: Babies like labeling words. How can parents improve their babies' understanding by using labeling words?

coughs, tongue clicks, and kisses. They imitate tones of speech and inflections. They "sing" along with songs they hear, whether they are sung by a parent or played on the radio or TV.

Next, babies put together a long series of syllables such as: *ba-ba-ba-ba*. Before long, they will learn to put strings of different syllables together such as: *ba-la-shoo-dee-sa*. This high-level babbling becomes so fluid it sounds like a new language. With different inflections, babies seem to ask questions, state facts, make exclamations, and tell funny stories.

As early as the ninth month, babies learn the meaning of a few specific words, such as *no*. They show their understanding by responding appropriately. Soon, they learn to say a few words and add appropriate gestures. They shake their heads when they say no. They wave their hands when they say bye-bye. They may repeat a word endlessly when they first learn it, making it a response to every question.

Babies try to imitate any sound they hear, so parents will want to watch what they say. Swear words can be repeated just as easily as other words.

Near the end of infancy, babies realize particular sounds or words refer to certain people or objects. Parents can help them learn the meaning of words by using labeling words. Compare these two groups of sentences. Group one: "Where did it go? Here it is. Let's get you dressed." Group two: "Where did the ball go? Here is the ball. Here are Jimmy's socks. Let's put the socks on Jimmy's feet." The sentences in group one are not specific. They have less teaching value for babies than the sentences in group two. The sentences in group two contain labeling words. They help babies learn to associate words with objects and to recognize their own names. Spoken with expression and accompanied with gestures, these sentences help babies learn about language.

Emotional and Social Development

1

Emotional development involves the recognition and expression of feelings and emotions. Social development is the process of learning to relate to other people. These two areas of development are closely related. Together, they influence a person's entire scope of feelings, behaviors, and relationships. Joy, sadness, fear, humor, confidence, pride, trust, friendship, and love are part of emotional and social development. Many parents find their babies' emotional and social development the most enjoyable kind of growth in the first year. The disorganized stares of passive newborns change to the proud smiles of active infants.

2

3

Newborns show their individualism from birth. Each is unique in appearance, activity level, reactions, and preferences. Newborns interact with people by listening to their voices and trying to focus on their faces. They are especially sensitive to touch and will stop crying when they are held.

Within weeks, infants improve their interactions. They become quiet when they see faces and they try to make eye contact. They may smile at faces and voices. Before long, parents and their babies have give-and-take interactions. When babies are in distress, they cry. Parents respond to their needs, and babies are soothed. When content, babies look at parents alertly and directly. Their stares and smiles intrigue parents, who respond by giving them more time and attention. Babies like this attention. They show their delight by putting on performances. They gradually work up to a big smile while cycling their legs with enthusiasm.

Babies at three months are even more responsive. They smile spontaneously when someone plays with them. They experiment with different sounds and facial expressions. When they are pleased, they smile and chuckle with delight. When they are uncertain, infants look puzzled and make questioning sounds.

By this time, most babies have learned how to start social interactions with their parents. First, they look around the room to see if their parents are nearby. Then, they make cooing sounds to capture the parents' attention. Next they fuss until the parents come. Finally they arch their backs and reach out their arms to be held. Even without words, their message is clear.

4

Sometime during the fourth month, both parents and babies find even more pleasure in their social interactions. By now, parents feel more at ease with the family routine. Most babies will have given up their night feeding, so parents can enjoy a full night of sleep. If there are brothers and sisters in the family, they probably have adjusted by this time, too. They may begin participating more in the care and entertainment of the new family member. Infants and their siblings learn to play little games together.

Babies soon start showing a sense of humor. They may giggle while playing with their siblings. They may repeat many times an action that caused their parents to laugh. They will wait for their parents to laugh and then start laughing themselves.

Attachment to Special Objects

A sign babies are becoming more aware of people and objects other than themselves is forming an attachment to one special toy. This attachment is an important step in self-development. Only when babies feel loved and secure can they extend their inter-

1—**Resource:** *Emotional and Social Development*, Activity D, SAG.

2—**Vocabulary:** What is meant by social and emotional development as it concerns babies? Since these two areas are closely related, how do they influence babies' feelings, behaviors, and relationships?

3—**Discuss:** Why does being touched mean so much to babies? If babies are not touched, held, or cuddled, how might this affect their emotional development and brain development?

4—**Discuss:** During the fourth month, babies and parents enjoy much social interaction. Siblings, as well, learn to enjoy the new baby. Cite examples of this.

1—Reflect: Should parents try to discourage their baby's attachment to a special toy? Why or why not?

2—Discuss: How can parents increase their babies' feelings of emotional security by reassuring them when they become frightened by noises or experiences?

3—Discuss: Stranger anxiety increases by the end of the first year. What can parents do to help prepare their babies for new experiences?

4—Discuss: Attachment to a primary caregiver is very strong by the end of the first year. How might babies react when they can't see their primary caregivers?

ests beyond themselves. When they reach out to their special toy, they are taking their first steps away from depending on their parents for comfort. These are also their first steps toward independence, 11-18

New Fears

As infants become more mobile and aware of their surroundings, they may develop new fears. They may be afraid to climb down from chairs where they used to enjoy playing. They may be more easily frightened by loud noises. Parents can increase their babies' feelings of emotional security by reassuring them.

Some babies also suddenly become frightened of the slippery bathtub. Up to this time, they may have enjoyed splashing in the big tub without noticing the potential dangers. Parents may try bathing their babies in another area for a short time while babies regain their confidence.

Appropriate comfort and reinforcement are very important at this stage. Parents who are alert to cues from their babies will know best how to respond and help their babies develop. When babies are startled, a hug may be all they need. If babies are given this reassurance, they may even turn some antics into a game. Babies who suddenly sprawl flat on their noses may repeat the act if their parents laugh.

Stranger Anxiety

Fear of strangers, also called **stranger anxiety**, often begins around five to six months of age. This fear begins when babies become aware of the differences among people. At about this time, babies begin to realize they are separate individuals and their parents are separate from them. With this new awareness, babies can now tell which people are not their parents. The result is they become more sensitive to strangers. Sometimes babies react this way even to other adults they know.

For instance, babies who used to smile at their parents' friends may now turn away from them, fussing and crying. The fear grows throughout infancy, peaking during the last four months.

As a kindness to babies at this stage, parents should try to prepare them for visits to strange places. Babies need time to adjust to a new setting. On arrival, parents should cuddle their babies and let them look at the people and surroundings. Relatives may have to be warned not to approach or look at the babies right away. Eye contact with strangers can frighten babies. Gradually, the babies will relax. Their curiosity may overcome their shyness. They will start looking at people and objects. With encouragement and reassurance from parents, they will become more sociable.

Separation Anxiety

Toward the end of the first year, babies' crawling skills allow them to be very mobile. They learn to crawl away from their parents. An even more frightening realization is their parents can walk away from them! Infants' attachment to their primary caregivers is very strong. Their fear of being abandoned is great. Infants try to stay with

11-18 —————————————————
Babies form attachments to special objects and learn to play independently.

their parents at all times. When they can't see their parents, they may become uneasy or panic-stricken. This fear is called **separation anxiety**.

Separation anxiety can be frustrating for parents. Babies turn away from almost everyone else but their parents. They will crawl wherever the parents go, if at all possible. They interrupt conversations, trying to demand parents' full attention. If the parents hold other babies, their own babies will jealously try to push the other baby away and reclaim their parents' affection.

Almost all parents have to leave their children with someone else at one time or another. During the months of separation anxiety, it is best to leave the children with people they already know. Parents should not sneak away while babies are busy playing. That would just make babies watch them even more closely. Instead, they should warn the babies with a signal phrase such as, "Bye-bye for now." Then they should announce their return with another signal phrase such as, "I'm here again." If babies see their parents putting on their coats to leave, they may start fussing. Rather than scolding, parents should try cuddling their babies. Gentle reassurance the parents will return may calm babies.

From their point of view, babies are not being unreasonable. At this age, babies are unable to see another person's point of view. Their parents are the centers of their worlds. If their parents temporarily disappear, babies feel lost and helpless. They need the security their parents represent. If parents resist babies' attempts to stay nearby, the babies will become more anxious and clingy. The best way to foster independence later is to let babies cling at this stage.

Since separation anxiety is so great at this time, preparations should be made for emergencies. Babies should become used to being cared for by at least one other person. A close friend,

relative, or neighbor is a good choice. In an emergency, the baby would be more comfortable with a familiar face than with a stranger.

Other Emotional Responses

By about ten months, babies' emotional responses are quite specific. Instead of just crying, babies show anger when they are frustrated. They can look hurt, sad, or uncomfortable. More often, they look happy. Their squeals of laughter can delight their entire families.

Babies at this stage grow sensitive to social approval and disapproval. They begin seeking the approval of their parents. At home, they love to show off their accomplishments. They love the reinforcement of approval. Very often, they will not perform these same tricks away from home.

Babies' new walking skills may create emotional tensions. Babies are still closely attached to their parents and fearful of strangers, yet they enjoy the independence walking gives them. This struggle between dependence and independence will continue for many months. With their parents' encouragement, reassurance, and loving care, babies will gradually develop identity and independence.

Babies Learn the Meaning of No

Babies know the difference between being good and being naughty. When they know they have been good, they seek a sign of approval. They look at their parents with a proud grin and expect to be praised for their efforts. They also know when they are being naughty, but often they can't stop themselves.

Just before their first birthdays, babies learn the meaning of the word *no*. They may spend a lot of time shaking

1—Vocabulary: What does separation anxiety mean? How can this create problems for babysitters?

2—Discuss: When parents have to leave their babies, what should they do to reassure them?

3—Discuss: If babies cling at this time, does it mean they will have difficulty learning independence later?

4—Discuss: When babies first learn to walk, how do they display their struggle between dependence and independence? How can parents help them develop their self-identities?

1—**Example:** Give examples of how babies learn what the word no means.

2—**Discuss:** Why is it important to set limits and stick to them, even with small babies? How can parents prevent further naughty behavior?

3—**Discuss:** Should parents let their babies cry it out? Will they ultimately spoil them if they answer their calls for attention?

4—**Discuss:** Are babies capable of considering someone else's point of view? Do parents sometimes interpret this as selfishness?

5—**Discuss:** Why is it important for parents to respond to their baby's attempts at communication? Does this help build trust?

their heads and saying no to everything—even when they mean yes. They may try new tricks that get them into trouble, such as turning on the TV or radio. They learn that a loud blast of sound will bring a parent running. Often they give themselves away by looking at their parents with a guilty expression before they start on some escapade they know is off-limits, 11-19.

When parents are tested, they should resist rewarding the bad behavior by overreacting. A better solution is to try to divert the babies attention. Parents can try to interest the babies in another, more acceptable activity. Parents should avoid having to say no too often. Babies need to explore in order to learn about their world. If the home is as baby-proof as possible, parents won't have to say no too often. When a sharp no is reserved for important times, such as when safety is threatened, babies will be more apt to listen. If the word *no* is overused, babies will tune it out.

Parents need to set limits and stick to them. Babies will test their parents, but parents should help babies learn no means no. After enforcing a no, parents can divert the babies' attention. Babies are easily distracted and eager to seek approval. When parents offer an alternative, such as a game of hide-and-seek, babies may quickly abandon a naughty behavior. If parents do not offer an alternate activity, babies will likely repeat the naughty behavior.

Can Parents Spoil Their Babies?

Parents need not worry about spoiling their babies by answering calls for attention. Social contact is as much a need at this stage as food and sleep. When babies' needs are met reasonably, they seldom feel stress and frustration. Meeting a baby's needs builds in the child a sense of trust and

11-19
When it comes to catching naughty behavior, babies often give themselves away as the culprits.

security. This will help them become more independent and self-sufficient.

Parents may think they should let their babies cry it out, work it out by themselves, or learn to be less selfish and demanding. Babies this age don't have wants—they only have needs. They need social contact to help them grow and develop. Since infants are not capable of using logic or reason to solve their own problems, they need help. Infants need attention, but they really don't mean to be selfish or demanding. They simply are not capable of considering someone else's point of view.

Parents who fulfill their babies' needs as well as they can are not spoiling their babies. Rather, they are helping their babies develop a sense of trust, well-being, and confidence that will lead to independence.

It is important for parents to respond to their babies' attempts at communication. Babies need to learn they can expect people to respond to them. When they can trust people to answer their calls, they tend to be more flexible. On the other hand, babies whose babbling, calls, and cries go unanswered become anxious and more demanding. They cannot build trust in their environment.

Medical Checkups for Infants

The American Academy of Pediatrics recommends infants see their doctors five times during the first year. These visits should be scheduled at 2 to 4 weeks, 2 months, 4 months, 6 months, and 12 months. Medical checkups are important for monitoring the baby's health. The doctor can identify any problems, and these can be treated as early as possible.

During medical checkups, parents can ask any questions they might have about the baby's health, nutrition, sleeping, and growth. The doctor will check the baby's growth by measuring the baby's height (length), weight, and head size. The eyes and ears will also be examined. If there is cause for concern, vision and hearing screenings may be given. The doctor will thoroughly examine the baby's physical condition. Any necessary tests will be done to check the baby's health.

During checkups, the doctor also gives parents an immunization schedule for their child. **Immunizations** are treatments that prevent people from developing certain diseases. A treatment may be given in the form of a vaccination (shot) or an oral medicine. Children need various immunizations from infancy through the school-age years. These treatments protect them from very serious illnesses. A recommended schedule of immunizations is shown in 11-20. Some must be given several times before a person is completely immune, as indicated on the chart. Parents should record each shot given, along with the date. This is an important part of a person's medical records. Children cannot start school without the proper immunizations.

1—**Discuss:** How often should babies have medical checkups? What occurs at these checkups?

2—**Discuss:** Why are immunizations important? When should they be given?

11-20

The American Academy of Pediatrics recommends this immunization schedule for infants and children. Parents should consult their baby's doctor about when to have the child immunized.

Immunization Schedule

Immunization	Age
Hepatitis B	Birth – 2 months 1-4 months 6-18 months
Diphtheria, tetanus, and pertussis (DTaP vaccine) Td	2 months 4 months 6 months 15-18 months 4-6 years After age 7, once every ten years
Measles, mumps, and rubella (MMR vaccine)	12-15 months 4-6 years or before junior high (middle) school
Haemophilus influenzae type b (Hib)	2 months 4 months 6 months 12-15 months
Polio – Inactivated polio virus vaccine (IPV)	2 months 4 months 6-18 months 4-6 years
Varicella (chickenpox vaccine)	12-18 months 11 or older (if recommended by doctor)
Pneumococcal	2 months 4 months 6 months 12-18 months

CHILD DEVELOPMENT

1 Month*

1 Physical Development
Large Motor Skills
Does not control arm and leg movements—movements are still reflexive.
Needs support for head. Without support, head will flop forward and backward.
Lifts head briefly from **2** surface in order to turn head from side to side when lying on tummy.
Twitches whole body when crying.

Small Muscle
Keeps hands fisted or slightly open.
May hold object if placed in open hand but drops it quickly.
Follows moving object with eyes briefly if the object is within the line of vision.

Intellectual Development
General
Learns about the world by using all five senses.
Prefers to look at patterned objects and human faces.
Follows slowly moving object with eyes.
Listens attentively to sounds and voices.
Cries deliberately for assistance.

Language
Cries to express needs.
Is comforted by human voices and music.

Emotional and Social Development
Emotional
Responds positively to comfort and satisfaction; negatively to pain.
Is comforted by cuddling and being swaddled in blanket.

Social
May seem to smile at faces or voices.
May recognize parents' voices.
Is comforted by human faces.

1—**Resource:** *Developmental Highlights for Infants,* transparency master 11-3, TR.

2—**Discuss:** Review the physical, intellectual, and emotional and social development of a month-old child.

3—**Discuss:** How does a two-month-old infant show distress and excitement?

* These charts are not exact timetables. Individuals may perform certain activities earlier or later than indicated in the charts.

2 Months

Physical Development
Large Motor Skills
Can keep head in midposition of body when lying on tummy.
Can hold head up for a few minutes.
Can turn head when lying on back.
Cycles arms and legs smoothly. Movements are still mainly reflexive but becoming voluntary.

Small Muscle
Grasps objects in reflex movements but grasps are becoming voluntary.
May hold object longer but still drops object after a few seconds.
Uses improved vision to look at objects more closely and for a longer time.

Intellectual Development
General
Coordinates eye movements.
Is better able to follow moving objects with eyes.
Shows obvious preference of faces to objects.
Is clearly able to discriminate between voices.
Associates certain behaviors with certain people (such as mother with feeding).

Language
Makes some sounds but most vocalizing is still crying.
Shows interest in sounds and will stop sucking to listen.

Emotional and Social Development
Emotional
Is able to show distress, excitement, **3** contentment, and delight.
Can quiet self by sucking.

Social
Smiles spontaneously and fleetingly to sensory stimulation from parent.
Looks at person alertly and directly.
Quiets in response to being held, seeing human face, or hearing voice.
Shows affection by looking at a person while kicking, waving arms, and smiling.
May perform to get attention.

(continued)

CHILD DEVELOPMENT

1—Discuss:
Compare the development of large motor skills and small motor skills. How does a baby combine the two?

3 Months

Physical Development
Large Motor Skills

Switches from reflexive to voluntary body movements.

Keeps head in midposition so posture is symmetrical when lying on back.

Moves arm and leg on one side of body in unison, then moves the other arm and leg in unison.

Can move arms together or legs together.

Turns head vigorously.

Can hold chest up and keep head erect for a few seconds when lying on tummy.

Can lift head for several minutes.

Can sit briefly with support.

Small Motor Skills

Keeps hands open most of the time. The grasp reflex is fading.

Begins to control arm and hand movements.

Begins to swipe at objects such as a cradle gym. May accidentally hit object with fist.

Intellectual Development
General

Is attentive for as long as 45 minutes at a time.

Shows memory by waiting for anticipated feeding.

Recognizes family members and familiar objects and sounds.

Likes to look at a variety of objects since vision has improved.

Is able to suck and look at the same time (thus doing two controlled actions at once).

Discovers hands and feet as extensions of self.

Searches with eyes for sounds.

Swipes at objects but does not always make contact.

Language

Begins cooing one-syllable, vowel-like sounds—*ooh*, *ah*, *aw*.

Squeals and chuckles.

Practices talking by making sounds, pausing, and making more sounds in a conversational rhythm.

Emotional and Social Development
Emotional

Shows feelings of security when parent holds and talks to him or her.

Senses hands and feet are extensions of self.

Whimpers when hungry, chortles when content.

Social

Communicates with different sounds and facial expressions.

Smiles spontaneously when parent plays with him or her.

Responds with total body to familiar face.

May stop or start crying if a certain person holds him or her.

Tries to attract parents' attention.

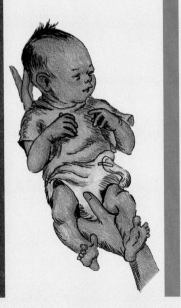

(continued)

CHILD DEVELOPMENT

4 Months

Physical Development

Large Motor Skills

Can bend to touch feet with hands when lying on back.

On tummy, can lift head and chest from surface using arms for support.

Can rock like an airplane on tummy, with arms and legs extended and back arched.

On tummy, may roll from side to side.

Can maintain a sitting position (with head erect and steady) for several minutes if given proper support.

Small Motor Skills

Uses hands more skillfully.

Begins to use mitten grasp for grabbing objects.

Looks from object to hands to object.

Swipes at objects, gradually improving aim.

Intellectual Development

General

Is alert for as long as an hour at a time.

Is aware of different depths and distances.

Likes to repeat enjoyable acts, like shaking a rattle.

Is able to discriminate among faces and may resent a strange face.

Shows interest in details of objects, such as shape, size, and texture.

Enjoys watching hands and feet.

Looks at object, reaches for it, and makes contact with it.

Language

Makes first consonant sounds—*p, b, m, l.*

Is able to babble strings of syllable-like sounds as if talking.

Smiles and coos when parent talks to him or her.

Prefers to babble when parent responds.

Emotional and Social Development

Emotional

May form an early attachment to one special object. (Feels secure enough to extend interest beyond self.)

Still depends on positive stimulation for feelings of security.

Responds to continued warmth and affection.

Social

Shows increased pleasure in social interactions.

Responds to and enjoys being handled and cuddled.

May babble and make sounds to imitate socializing.

Enjoys social aspect of feeding times.

Becomes more sensitive to strangers.

Becomes unresponsive if left alone most of waking hours.

1—Discuss: At four months, babies learn to make noises, which is the beginning of language development. Describe these first attempts by the baby.

(continued)

CHILD DEVELOPMENT

1—Discuss: At five months, most babies are able to roll over from stomach to back. This is a significant development that gives the baby more mobility. How does this also help babies use their small muscles?

5 Months

Physical Development
Large Motor Skills
On back, can lift head and shoulders off surface.

Can roll from tummy to back.

On tummy, lifts head and chest high off surface.

Can rock, twist, roll, and kick to change position on surface while on tummy.

When supported under arms, stands and moves body up and down, stamping feet alternately.

Helps when being pulled to a sitting position.

Can sit supported for 15 to 30 minutes with firm back.

In sitting position, keeps head steady and erect.

Small Motor Skills
Reaches for objects, such as the cradle gym, with good coordination and aim.

Begins to grasp objects with thumb and fingers.

Grasps objects with either hand.

Transfers objects from one hand to the other, dropping objects often.

Can grasp cover to pull it off when face is covered in peek-a-boo game.

Intellectual Development
General
Is alert for as long as an hour and a half at a time.

Can anticipate whole object when only part of object is visible.

May be able to play peek-a-boo and hide-and-seek.

Reaches out for object and may grab it awkwardly.

Recognizes and responds to own name.

Smiles at self in mirror.

Learns to differentiate between self and rest of world by comparing fingers to toys.

Language
Watches parents' mouths as they talk and experiments with own sounds.

Understands own name.

Can recognize people by their voices.

Emotional and Social Development
Emotional
Senses self as being separate from parent.

May show fearful behavior as separateness is felt.

Distinguishes between familiar and unfamiliar adults.

Shows fear, disgust, anger.

Enjoys learning new activities.

Builds trust when cries are answered; grows anxious and demanding when cries are unanswered.

Social
Smiles and babbles to initiate social contact.

May be able to play peek-a-boo game.

Shows anticipation when near people, especially parents.

(continued)

CHILD DEVELOPMENT

6 Months

1—**Discuss:** At six months, babies learn to respond to affection. How does this help initiate further social development?

Physical Development
Large Motor Skills
Rolls from back to tummy.
Turns and twists in all directions when on back or tummy.
On tummy, moves by pushing with legs and reaching with arms (creeping).
Gets up on hands and knees but then may fall forward.
Is able to stand while supported.
Sits with slight support and maintains balance.
Is able to lean forward or to side while in sitting position.
Is able to sit in walker or high chair and use arms to reach for objects.
If unsupported in sitting position, may slump forward on hands for balance.
May be able to sit unsupported for short periods of time.

Small Motor Skills
Is able to rotate wrist to turn and manipulate objects.
Reaches with one arm and grasps object with hand. Then transfers object to other hand. Then reaches for another object.
Holds an object in each hand.
Learns to drop objects at will.
Begins eating with fingers.

Intellectual Development
General
Is alert for as long as two hours at a time.
Reaches out to grab objects with better aim and coordination.
Grabs any and all objects within reach.
Studies objects intently, turning them to see all sides.
Learns that objects do not disappear when they are dropped; they simply fall to the floor.

Language
Makes more consonant sounds.
Repeats sounds to make two-syllable "words."
Reacts appropriately to various tones of voice.
Varies volume, pitch, and rate while babbling.

Emotional and Social Development
Emotional
Senses adults are different from children; enjoys playing with children.
Responds to affection and may initiate signs of affection.
Likes attention and may cry to get it.
May begin clinging to primary caregiver.
Calls parents for help and trusts them to respond.

Social
Laughs when socializing.
Enjoys playing cooperative games with parents and siblings.
Smiles at familiar faces and stares solemnly at strangers.
Desires constant attention from parent.

(continued)

CHILD DEVELOPMENT

7 Months

1—Discuss: At this age, babies begin to make associations and recognize relationships between objects. How does this help babies entertain themselves?

Physical Development
Large Motor Skills

Crawls awkwardly, combining movements on tummy and knees.

When pulled to a standing position, helps by keeping legs straight and supporting own weight.

Likes to bounce when in standing position.

May try to pull self to a standing position.

Is able to sit alone for several minutes or with slight support for longer periods of time.

Can lean over and reach while in sitting position.

In walker, is able to push with legs to move in all directions.

May be able to move from a lying position to a sitting position.

Small Motor Skills

Has mastered grasping by using thumb in opposition to fingers.

Holds an object in each hand.

Brings objects together with banging noises.

Keeps objects in hands much of the time.

Fingers, manipulates, and rattles objects repeatedly.

Intellectual Development
General

Is aware of dimensions; can sort blocks by size.

Begins making simple associations.

Begins to show interest in relationships between objects. **1**

Responds with expectation to repetition of an event.

Enjoys looking through books with familiar pictures.

May begin to imitate an act.

Language

May have favorite, well-defined syllables.

Imitates sounds, tones of speech, and inflections.

"Sings" along with music.

May say *mama* or *dada* but does not connect with parents.

Emotional and Social Development
Emotional

May show more dependence on parents for security.

May fear performing some familiar activities.

Has increase drive for independence but senses frightening situations.

Social

Shows desire to be included in social interactions.

May be responsive to other persons but is clearly attached to parent.

Thoroughly enjoys company of siblings.

Begins to develop sense of humor, teases.

(continued)

CHILD DEVELOPMENT

8 Months

Physical Development
Large Motor Skills
Sits alone steadily for
longer periods of time.
On tummy, pushes up
easily to a crawling
position.
Crawls.
May carry objects in one
hand or both hands
while crawling.
Is able to pull self to a
standing position by
holding onto crib or
furniture.
May need help getting
down from standing
position.
Achieves sitting position
by pushing up with
arms.

Small Motor Skills
Learns pincer grasp,
using just the thumb
and forefinger.
Is able to pick up small
objects and string.

**Intellectual
Development**
General
Learns to solve simple
problems.
Likes to empty and fill
containers, meanwhile
learning concepts
such as in, out, and
"all gone."
Remembers past events
and past actions.
Begins imitating
behaviors.
Notices changes in the
whole scene, such as
a cup left on a table.
Begins to develop a
sense of timing.
Begins to understand
cause and effect.

Language
Begins putting together a
long series of
syllables.
Uses different inflections
when babbling.
May label object in
imitation of its sounds,
such as *choo-choo* for
train.
Begins to recognize
some words.

**Emotional and Social
Development**
Emotional
Exhibits fear of strangers.
May develop separation
anxiety and need
constant reassurance
of parent's presence.
Wants to be held by
parent when with
strangers.
May anticipate being left
and become
disturbed.
Values quick display of
support and love from
parent.
Likes to explore new
spaces but wants to
be able to return to
parent.
Enjoys playing with own
image in mirror.

Social
Definitely prefers parents
to strangers.
Is more aware of social
approval and
disapproval from
family members.
May cling to parent if
taken to a strange
place.
Sustains interest in play,
especially when
playing with family
member.

1—Example: Give
examples of language
development at this
age. If possible, have
someone tape a
baby's first attempts at
language and play
them for the class.

(continued)

CHILD DEVELOPMENT

1—Activity: As a baby's ability move increases, list potential safety problems from which parents should protect the baby.

9 Months

Physical Development
Large Motor Skills
Sits alone.
Develops own crawling style.
Can vary speed while crawling.
May try to crawl up stairs.
May be able to achieve a standing position without holding onto furniture.
Is able to move from a standing position to a sitting position.
May be able to move along furniture, touching it for support (cruising).

Small Motor Skills
Uses index finger to point, lead, and poke.
May be able to build a tower of two blocks.
Waves hands to say goodbye.

Intellectual Development
General
Recognizes dimensions of objects. Approaches small objects with hands, large ones with arms.
May show new fear of height with new understanding of distance.
May show some symbolic thinking.

Language
Responds appropriately to a few specific words.
Says a few words and adds appropriate gestures.
Says *mama* and *dada* as specific names.
May follow simple directions.

Emotional and Social Development
Emotional
May show fear of heights; may be afraid to crawl down from chair.
May show fear of new sounds.
Needs appropriate comfort and reinforcement during this stage.
May begin to protect self and possessions.

Social
Shows interest in play activities of others.
Likes to play games like pat-a-cake with siblings.
Definitely prefers certain people to others, family members are favorites.
Recognizes the social nature of mealtimes.
May be more sensitive to other children.

10 Months

Physical Development
Large Motor Skills
May be able to stand by self without hanging onto furniture.
Varies crawling and standing to achieve goals.
Steps sideways along furniture in cruising motion.
Likes to walk holding on to parents' hands.
Climbs on chairs and other furniture.
Stands with little support.

Small Motor Skills
Can hold an object in one hand and manipulate it with the other.
Carries two small objects in one hand.
Can release grasped object instead of just dropping it.

Intellectual Development
General
Is able to play games involving object permanence.
Will search to find hidden objects.
Likes to open containers and look at their contents.
Imitates behaviors in greater detail.

Language
Learns more words and appropriate gestures.
May repeat one word endlessly.
Likes to listen to familiar words and songs.
Understands and obeys simple words and commands.

Emotional and Social Development
Emotional
Cries less often.
Shows emotions in other, more specific ways.
Expresses delight, happiness, sadness, discomfort, and anger.
May be able to show symbolic thought by giving love to stuffed toy.

Social
Is more aware of and sensitive toward other children.
Likes to play with siblings and understands that "lost" objects may reappear.
Enjoys music and may mimic movement others make to music.
Likes to perform for family audiences; may repeat acts if applauded.
Will not show off in unfamiliar surroundings.

(continued)

CHILD DEVELOPMENT

11 Months

Physical Development
Large Motor Skills
Stands alone.
Can stand against support and wave.
Can stand against support and lean over.
May be able to climb out of crib or playpen.
Is able to squat and stoop.
Is able to stand and pick up objects.
May push chair ahead of self for support while walking.
Likes to climb stairs.
Likes to follow parent; will cruise or crawl fast to reach parent.
Small Motor Skills
Uses hands together and separately.
Likes to grab feeding utensils and cup.
Likes to squish foods in hands.
May carry spoon to mouth in feeding attempt.
Takes off shoes and socks.

Intellectual Development
General
Shows increased individuality in interests and abilities.
Can point to parts of the body.
Learns to make many kinds of associations.
Becomes even more skilled in imitation.
Knows the meaning of the word *no* but may disregard it.
Likes to look at pictures in books.

Language
Still uses babbling, but includes some meaningful words.
Recognizes words as symbols for objects.

Emotional and Social Development
Emotional
May not always want to be cooperative.
Recognizes difference between being good and being naughty.
May say *no* while shaking head, but will continue to do forbidden deed.

Social
Seeks approval and tries to avoid disapproval.
Imitates movements of other children and adults.
Likes to say *no* and shake head to get a response from a parent.
Tests parents to determine limits.
Objects to having his or her enjoyable play stopped.

12 Months

Physical Development
Large Motor Skills
May still prefer crawling to walking for speed but uses both.
May add maneuvers to walking around furniture, backing away, carrying toys, etc.
May take steps to parent, falling into arms when reaching parent.
Climbs in and out of playpen and crib.
Climbs up and down stairs.
In tub, makes swimming movements in water.

Small Motor Skills
Masters pincer grasp.
May show preference for one hand.
May be able to pull off clothing.
Can take lids off containers.

Intellectual Development
General
Solves simple problems.
Sets goal and takes action to achieve goal, as in pushing a chair in place to use for climbing.
Puts nesting toys together correctly.
May search for lost toys in more than one place.
May use a preferred hand.
Learns how to pick up and hold a third object.

Language
Begins to use language as an expression of self.
May have vocabulary of several words.
Says words that imitate sounds of animals and objects, such as *bow-wow*, for a dog.

Emotional and Social Development
Emotional
Senses consequences of new mobility and may have renewed fears.
May reveal an inner determination to walk.
Begins to develop self-identity and independence.
Expresses many emotions and recognizes emotions exhibited by others.
Shows increase negativism.

Social
Is more able to play and enjoy games.
Enjoys playing with siblings.
May react sharply to being separated from primary caregiver, but may know separation is temporary.
Likes to practice communication with adults.
Continues to test parental limits.

Summary

- During the first 12 months of life, infants grow and develop at an amazing rate. An infant's physical development involves much more than just growing in height and weight. Great strides are taken in muscle control and coordination.

- Large motor skills require the use of the large muscles of the body. Small motor require the use of the small muscles.

- When introducing solid foods and weaning their infants, parents should follow their doctor's recommendations.

- Teething follows a predictable pattern among babies, but the timing varies. Dental care is important, even in infancy.

- A baby's brain is growing rapidly during the first three years. Parents can do much to encourage or hinder the child's brain development.

- Babies learn about the world through the use of all five senses: seeing, hearing, feeling, smelling, and tasting.

- Babies learn a great deal through play. Parents can make the most of playtimes by being observant, patient, and creative.

- It takes babies a few years to learn to speak a specific language, but they can communicate from birth.

- As babies develop emotionally and socially, they experience joy, sadness, fear, humor, confidence, pride, trust, friendship, and love.

- Babies need five regular medical checkups during the first year. Immunizations are an important part of a baby's health care.

Reviewing Key Points

1. Fill-in-the-blank. In the first 12 months, infants _____ their birthweight and grow to _____ times their birth height (length).

2. True or false. Infants can control their small muscles before they can control their large muscles.

3. Describe a mitten grasp and a pincer grasp.

4. At about what age should solid food be introduced into a baby's diet? What food is generally introduced first?

5. What is weaning?

6. How can teething pain be relieved?

7. Briefly describe two ways parents can influence their infant's brain development.

8. What skill is needed to play the peek-a-boo game?

9. What do babies learn by playing picking up and dropping games?

10. Why is a baby's attachment to one special object an important step in self-development?

11. Explain the concept of object permanence.

12. Describe the difference between stranger anxiety and separation anxiety.

13. Give an example of one way babies use imitation to learn about what people do and how they act.

14. At what ages should infants receive medical checkups?

15. What are immunizations, and why are they important?

Learning by Doing

1. Ask a mother and father to describe problems they had with their infant when establishing sleep patterns, teething, weaning, stranger anxiety, separation anxiety, and introducing solid foods. How did they solve these problems?

2. Propose ways parents can make the most of their infant's playtimes by being observant, patient, and creative.

3. In a small group, research brain development in infancy. Create a poster based on your research. Present your poster to the rest of the class.

4. Interview a pediatrician about the general sequence of events in the physical, intellectual, emotional, and social development of infants. Ask the pediatrician why it is important to view each infant as a unique individual.

5. Prepare a pamphlet on immunizations for parents of infants. List the immunizations a child should have at each of the following ages: 2 months, 4 months, 6 months, and 12 months.

Thinking Critically

1. Several advances in physical development occur during a baby's first year. Explain how each advance listed below creates new concerns for parents in terms of safety and care.
   A. rolling over
   B. sitting up
   C. crawling
   D. standing
   E. walking

2. Observe several infants to see signs of various stages of physical development. Look for such skills as rolling over, crawling, standing, cruising, walking, swiping at objects, grasping objects, and dropping objects. For each infant you observe, list the age of the baby and which skills have been mastered. Share your findings with the class. Explain why some infants do not match the abilities listed in the charts, while others exceed them.

3. In a small group, discuss how the types of development (physical, intellectual, emotional, and social) are interrelated. What implications does this have for parents?

4. Write a paragraph explaining what you would do as a parent to stimulate your child's brain development, and why this stimulation is important.

5. Do you agree or disagree with the following statement: Parental guidance is important during a child's first year. Give reasons supporting your position.

Chapter 12
Parents and Their Toddlers

Objectives

After studying this chapter, you will be able to

- identify major steps in a toddler's physical, intellectual, emotional, and social development.

- summarize the importance of beginning to learn life skills in the toddler years.

- describe a toddler's competing needs for independence and dependence.

- select appropriate toys and books for toddlers.

- explain how parental guidance can encourage toddlers to develop self-control.

- explain why play is important to a toddler's development.

- explain why routine medical checkups are recommended for toddlers.

Key Terms

toddler
life skills
egocentric
¹ teachable moments
parallel play
cooperative play
temper tantrums

Parents are often amazed at the constant motion of their toddlers. (The
² term **toddler** describes children who are one or two years old.) Each new activity opens up a wonderful world for both the toddlers and their parents. Parents often wonder if they have the energy to keep up with these active little children, 12-1.

In all areas of development, one- and two-year-olds are striving for independence and developing their individuality. Physically, toddlers become more independent as they improve their coordination and motor skills.
³ Intellectually, toddlers' ability to understand the world broadens. They learn to think of themselves as individuals. Socially and emotionally, toddlers try out their independence by pushing away from their parents one minute, only to run back to them the next. This competing drive for independence and dependence is confusing for both parents and toddlers.

1—**Vocabulary:** Look up terms in the glossary and discuss their meanings.

2—**Resource:** *Observing a Toddler,* Activity A, SAG.

3—**Example:** Cite examples of how the improvement in toddlers' physical, intellectual, social, and emotional growth help them achieve independence and individuality.

12-1 _____
Toddlers are bundles of energy. They love to run and jump, both inside and outside.

Parents need to be patient and understanding to cope with the frustrations of toddlerhood. However, the joys of watching toddlers take steps toward independence make it all worthwhile.

Physical Development

One- and two-year-olds grow quickly, but not as quickly as they grew during infancy. The most noticeable physical changes during toddlerhood are in body proportions. A toddler's head may still seem large, but the trunk, arms, and legs are catching up. The legs grow longer and stronger to meet increased walking needs. The backbone often seems to curve forward, and the abdomen protrudes. The "baby fat" of the plump infant begins to disappear, and gradually a leaner, more muscular shape evolves. A toddler's hands and feet are still rather short and stubby, so small motor development still occurs pretty slowly. As children's bodies become more proportionate, their coordination improves.

At age one, children weigh an average of 20 to 22 pounds. They are an average of 28 to 30 inches tall. By age two, toddlers are an average of 33 to 35 inches tall. They weigh about 25 to 28 pounds. By their third birthdays, they are an average of 36 to 38 inches tall and weigh about 31 to 33 pounds.

Large Motor Skills

By their first birthdays, children vary in their levels of large motor development. Some are walking alone. Others hold their parents' hands while taking steps. Some one-year-olds cruise along furniture and stand alone for short periods of time, 12-2. Some enjoy standing but still rely on crawling when they really want to cover distances. Others are

12-2 _____
In early toddlerhood, many children are still cruising around the furniture.

just learning to pull themselves to a standing position.

Parents are eager for their children to begin taking steps. As in other areas of development, however, timetables vary a great deal. Starting to walk early or late does not necessarily indicate a delay in another area of development. Healthy babies will walk when they are ready. When they do take their first steps, they walk with their feet flat and their toes turned inward. They walk with their feet spread apart and their arms held out high at their sides for balance.

Toddlers are almost always in motion. As they become more mobile, they also become more curious about the world around them. They explore every corner of every room. They climb any stairs they see. Dangerous stairs should be blocked, but most toddlers can learn to climb a few stairs safely with supervision. Usually, they back down the stairs, but sometimes they turn around and descend by sitting and bumping on each step.

Toddlers are quite resilient to bumps and falls. They are so intrigued by their walking and climbing skills they pay little attention to these minor inconveniences. When they see their toddlers fall, parents often anticipate painful cries. Often, toddlers jump up, scamper away, and try again.

Once toddlers can walk well, sitting down is the next hurdle to conquer. At first, the only way they can sit is to fall down. Within a few months, they manage to squat and sit down with control.

Toward the middle of the year, toddlers are learning to walk sideways and then backward. They are delighted with these new tricks. They may clap their hands and laugh as they try to 1 achieve each new skill. Eventually, they will be able to stand on either foot alone. They may even try walking on their tiptoes.

By the time they are two, toddlers are walking with more assurance. They can walk more quickly, even sideways or backward with ease. Some are even running stiffly. Toddlers may begin walking up stairs by holding on to a parent's hand. They move with rhythmic responses to music and enjoy bouncing and swaying in simple dancing movements. As the year progresses, toddlers become more coordinated. They put their improved coordination and balance to the test with all kinds of complex movements, 12-3.

Toddlers are proud when they manage to seat themselves in small chairs. They may repeat the process of sitting, getting up, and sitting again several times as they learn this new movement. Sitting in chairs is an 4 2 accomplishment. It requires toddlers to judge distances, back up to chairs, and without looking, sit with controlled muscle movements.

Toddlers struggle for control, and they are determined to do things themselves. The struggle is not theirs alone.

12-3 _____
This toddler shows off his improved balance and coordination as he plays.

Parents struggle to figure out when to help and when to let toddlers do things for themselves. Toddlers are not capable of doing some things they want done. A toddler can't tie his or her shoes. A toddler can't reach a toy on a high shelf. Ideally, parents should give help only when it is needed or requested, and let the toddler do the rest.

The simple act of walking together may create struggles. Toddlers love to walk, but do not learn to walk alongside an adult until about three years of age. Until then, they walk toward whatever interests them—a bit of uneven ground, puddle, or low wall that looks good for climbing. As long as their parents stay nearby, toddlers are happy wandering in any direction. As soon as parents show signs of moving off in a specific direction, toddlers stop walking. They stand in front of their parents with their arms up, asking to be carried. They are not being lazy. They are following their natural instincts, knowing they cannot keep up with the parents. If their parents walk away, they will be lost. Holding toddlers' hands helps only for a few steps. They simply cannot match the pace and direction of an adult's walk. When a toddler is tired, allowing the child to ride in a stroller or on a parent's shoulders may help, 12-4.

1—Discuss: How do toddlers exhibit their improving coordination as they try variations in walking?

2—Discuss: Briefly describe the new skills toddlers learn when they try to sit in a small chair.

3—Discuss: Parents must learn when to offer help to toddlers (and when not to offer it). How can this create a struggle with a determined toddler?

4—Discuss: How do toddlers demonstrate their competing needs for independence and dependence?

Small Motor Skills

One-year-old toddlers can grasp objects almost as well as adults can, but their skills in manipulation still need improvement. Toddlers practice their grasping and manipulating skills by picking up objects and lugging them from one place to another. Daddy's big shoes or Mommy's favorite doorstop may be found almost anyplace in the home. Their pincer grasps improve as they pick up small pieces of cereal or transfer blocks from one container to another. Toddlers also like to look at picture books. Books with stiff cardboard pages or cloth pages are best since they cannot be torn.

With improved walking and grasping skills, toddlers become even better explorers. They can move to any corner of a room and pick up all kinds of objects. One-year-olds gradually improve their ability to pick up and release their hold on an object. This makes them better ball players. These same skills make them less desirable as shopping companions. They try to grab everything within reach. A toddler in a grocery store may fill a parent's cart with unwanted items. Picking up all those colorful boxes and cans can be so much fun.

Advances in small motor development can be seen as toddlers learn to add hand gestures to their new communication skills. They continue to enjoy rummaging through drawers and examining objects. Their curiosity helps them learn about their environment. Most of the lessons are fun, but some are not. For instance, toddlers learn pushing drawers shut without first removing their fingers can be very painful.

Toddlerhood is a time for parents to make regular safety checks of their homes. They should look closely at each room (as well as the basement, garage, and yard) from a toddler's point of view. Parents should keep in mind toddlers like to climb onto and crawl under things. They like to empty and fill containers. Toddlers like to put things in their mouths. Parents should watch for safety pins, nails, razor blades, broken toys, and other hazards. Coins, buttons, earrings, paper clips, and small beads are also dangerous. Toddlers may swallow them or choke on them. All poisons, cleaning agents, and medicines should be stored out of reach. Using locks provides the most protection. Other safety tips are illustrated in 12-5.

Toys and Play in Physical Development

Play helps children develop their physical capabilities. One- and two-year-olds gradually gain greater control over their environment. Active play allows children to develop their

12-4
A ride on Dad's shoulders can relieve tired feet. It can also be lots of fun.

Dangers and Safeguards During Toddlerhood

12-5 _____
Parents must supervise their toddlers' activities to warn them of dangers and prevent accidents.

1

Parents should examine all toys to make sure they are safe. The eyes on dolls and stuffed animals should be securely fastened so a toddler cannot pull them off and swallow them. Tops with pointed ends are dangerous, and no toys should have sharp edges.

Toddlers like to investigate any opening. Parents should close and lock all windows. Toddlers have enough strength to open a window and crawl through it or to slam a window shut on their fingers.

Toddlers should be placed in safety seats in the backseat whenever they ride in cars.

Matches should never be left within reach of young children.

1—Activity: Review each safety hazard in Figure 12-5. List ways parents of toddlers can prevent accidents and what precautions must be taken.

Toddlers like to reach for things on shelves. By grabbing the bottom can on a kitchen shelf, they could cause a dangerous avalanche. Parents should keep lower shelves free of dangerous items.

Handles on all pots and pans should be turned toward the back of the stove to prevent inquisitive toddlers from pulling them down.

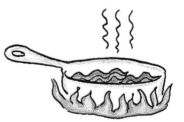

(continued)

12-5

(continued)

Doors should be closed or barricaded to prevent toddlers from gaining access to potentially dangerous areas.

As toddlers' physical skills improve, they may try to climb anything in sight and end up in danger. Parents need to know where their toddlers are and what they are doing at all times.

1—Discuss: A toddler's inability to judge risks of climbing, traffic, pets, and hot stoves may be dangerous. What lessons in safety can parents instill in their toddlers?

Toddlers are not sufficiently aware of the dangers of traffic. They will run after a pet or a rolling ball without thinking about oncoming cars or buses.

Toddlers think all pets are friendly. They should be warned that what they consider a friendly pat or squeeze may cause an animal to scratch or bite.

Toddlers are fascinated by knobs. They may turn stove burners on or off. Children can be warned to stay away from stoves, but parents also need to be aware of what they are doing at all times.

muscles, use their energy, and build stamina. Children love to climb on outdoor play equipment, but coming back down may still be a little frightening. They climb indoors, too. With the help of chairs, they may get into things their parents thought were safely out of reach. They learn to jump off the ground with both feet together, and this broadens their game-playing skills. They also learn to push themselves on riding toys, which gives them a whole new way of traveling.

Small muscle skills improve as toddlers approach their third birthdays. They can turn pages of books, string large beads, and build crude towers of six or more cubes, 12-6. They can turn doorknobs with greater strength, and their scribbles include circles as well as horizontal and vertical lines. Toddlers like to take simple objects apart and put them back together. They have a great feeling of pride when they can put all the parts of a nesting toy or small puzzle together.

Physical play strengthens muscles and refines balance and coordination. The heart and lungs become stronger as children exert physical energy through play activities. Children are more likely to maintain proper body weight if they are active. Active infants and children set a pattern for exercise that will help them maintain good health as they grow. Parents can encourage their children to be physically active by playing with them.

Life Skills

The term **life skills** refers to the eating, dressing, and grooming skills children must learn in order to provide routine care for themselves. Toddlers are eager to improve their life skills, since this helps them gain independence.

Mealtime is a good time to encourage independence. Parents should cut food into small pieces so toddlers can feed themselves. If a food must be eaten with a spoon, parents should help only

12-6
This toddler shows her improved small muscle skills by turning pages in a book.

if the child asks or gestures for help. If parents are asked to help, they should simply load the spoon. The toddler may want to take over from there. If the toddler cannot handle the spoon, parents should be ready to help before the toddler becomes completely frustrated. Toddlers have also mastered the art of drinking from cups, 12-7.

Parents should give their toddlers small amounts of food at mealtimes. They should not fill the toddlers' plates, hoping they will eat more. Toddlers' appetites are rather small, and toddlers can become easily discouraged. Children from one to two years of age usually eat about one-third to one-half of typical adult portions. If they eat more than they want just to please their parents, this can be the start of unhealthy eating habits.

Toddlers can eat just about anything other family members eat. Parents should provide foods that are

1—Discuss: Toddlers love to climb up but may have trouble getting back down. How can parents encourage this curiosity, yet help prevent toddlers from falling?

2—Discuss: How can active play aid toddlers in their physical development?

3—Resource: *Life Skills of Toddlers*, Activity C, SAG.

4—Vocabulary: What does the term *life skills* mean? If parents expect perfection, how might this discourage toddlers from learning simple self-care routines?

5—Discuss: How can parents offer assistance without discouraging toddlers as they learn to feed themselves?

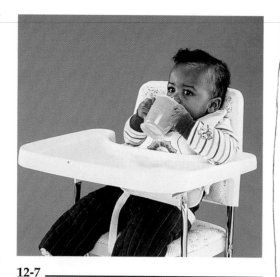

12-7 _____

A toddler is learning life skills, such as feeding himself and drinking from a cup.

low in fat, cholesterol, salt, and sugar. They should offer toddlers nutritious beverages, such as reduced fat or low-fat milk, water, and some fruit and vegetable juices. Soft drinks and other sweet, sugary drinks should be limited or avoided altogether.

Toddlers are ready to share most mealtimes, too, but they have trouble sitting still while everyone finishes eating. Parents may be able to prevent some battles by allowing toddlers to leave the table when they are done eating.

A parent's jobs during mealtime are to provide nutritious food and make mealtimes as enjoyable as possible. Using good table manners is not a reasonable goal for toddlers. They often still find fingers more useful than spoons for feeding themselves. They may prefer to eat their foods in unusual combinations. For instance, they may dip their green beans in their mashed potatoes. If they know pudding is planned for dessert, they may want to eat it along with their meat. As long as they eat nutritious foods and enjoy mealtimes, the primary goals are being met.

Toddlers' eating habits may seem strange to parents. Their appetites and food preferences seem to change from day to day. Parents may start to worry, but they should remember if children are hungry, they will eat. If children don't eat much at a meal, they probably are not hungry. They should not be forced to eat. A toddler is the best judge of how much he or she should eat.

This brings up the question of snacks. A toddler who did not eat much at lunch generally should not eat an afternoon snack. By waiting until dinner, the toddler will be hungry enough to eat a well-balanced meal. On another day, the same toddler may eat a good lunch and still be hungry in the afternoon. A small, nutritious snack of fruit, cheese, or crackers will satisfy this hunger.

Food should not be used as a reward, bribe, or threat. Eating food is a means of satisfying hunger and providing nutrients for the body. A cookie has nothing to do with good behavior. Candy does not lessen the pain of a skinned knee. Linking certain foods, especially sweets, to emotions may set the stage for a lifetime of poor eating habits.

Another life skill is dressing oneself. Toddlers make great progress in this area. At first, they may help by pushing their arms through sleeves. Gradually, they help more and more until they are able to put on and take off simple garments by themselves, 12-8. Toddlers have definite preferences and may want to change clothes several times a day. Parents soon learn there is no sense to having endless battles with their toddlers over these preferences. Providing two outfits and allowing the toddler to choose which one to wear may be a happy compromise. Toddlers react positively to praise when they look good or dress correctly. It will not be until the preschool years, however, that children can dress and undress themselves completely every day.

12-8
A toddler may insist on dressing herself even though she may put her jeans on backward.

Toddlers are also eager to learn simple lessons in cleanliness and grooming. A short stool helps toddlers reach the sink and makes grooming tasks easier. Most toddlers like to wash their hands—a task they view as an experiment with water. When given a small soft toothbrush, they will enjoy brushing their teeth.

Parents need patience to gently guide and encourage their toddlers to master life skills. Children this age want to do things for themselves, but they get frustrated easily. Also, many parents find it difficult to wait patiently while their children perform these skills. Parents can do things for children much faster than the children can do them for themselves, especially at first. Letting toddlers learn these tasks is part of teaching them to care for themselves. Toddlers learn these life skills more quickly if they are encouraged and guided with praise.

Teething

As you learned in Chapter 11, most children begin teething before their first birthday. The amount of teeth children have at age one varies. A few children are still toothless, while most have several teeth.

During toddlerhood, teething continues. The sequence of teething is the same, but timing varies from child to child. The childhood set of 20 baby teeth is usually complete by the age of two-and-one-half years. The sequence of teething is illustrated in 12-9.

If parents did not begin brushing their child's teeth during infancy, they should start to do so in toddlerhood. Teeth should be brushed at least twice a day—after breakfast and before bedtime—to prevent decay. Tooth decay is caused mostly by foods (especially sticky, sugary foods) left on or between the teeth. These foods cause *plaque* (a filmy substance that collects on teeth and contains bacteria). If the plaque is not brushed away, it builds up on the teeth and causes tooth decay.

Toddlers love to copy their parents, and may enjoy brushing along with them. Children should be helped to clean their teeth right from the start. Children can be allowed to brush their teeth, but parents should help them brush thoroughly each time. Children do not have the small motor skills needed to brush well enough by themselves until they reach school-age. Parents may want to give the toddler a toothbrush to hold and use another one to brush the child's teeth. This can keep the child from grabbing the toothbrush while the parents are cleaning the child's teeth.

1—Resource: *Sequence of Teething,* color transparency CT-12A, TR

2—Discuss: Why is it important to maintain good dental hygiene even with baby teeth?

12-9 _____
Teething follows a predictable sequence, but the timing is unpredictable.

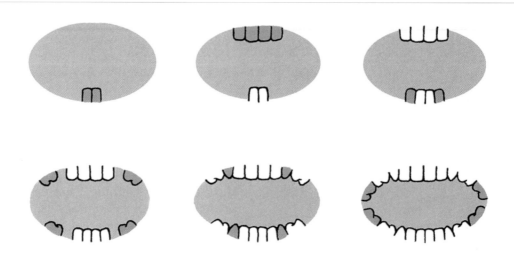

1—Enrich: Ask a dentist to speak to the class about how parents can encourage good dental health. When should dental checkups be given?

2—Discuss: What is the basic rule for parents as they attempt to introduce toilet learning?

Brushing should always be away from the gums (downward over the top teeth and upward over the bottom teeth) to remove trapped particles of food. After this, the teeth should be vigorously brushed to remove plaque. Once a child's full set of baby teeth come in, many experts recommend parents floss the child's teeth once daily.

Baby teeth need to be kept free from decay. A decayed tooth may need to be pulled to prevent infection of the jaw. If a tooth is pulled, the resulting space allows adjacent teeth to grow out of position. This could cause poor alignment of the permanent teeth, which begin to appear at about six years of age.

Parents should take their children for a first dental visit during toddlerhood. Some experts recommend a first visit between ages one and two. Others suggest a first dental visit between ages two and three. This first visit acquaints a child with the dentist. It also gives the dentist a chance to spot any problems. Parents should follow their dentist's recommendations about scheduling regular dental checkups for the child. Many suggest these should occur every six months.

Toilet Learning

Sometime during toddlerhood, children become ready for toilet learning. Mastery of this life skill comes more quickly for some children than for others. The basic rule for parents is to avoid turning toilet learning into a battleground. Children will cooperate when they are ready. If they are not ready, no amount of coaxing will help. Toddlers should not be rushed to achieve this skill.

Learning to use the toilet involves several steps. First, children must be able to understand what parents want them to do. Until this time, diapers have taken care of the process. Children have to learn a new method of handling bodily elimination. Second, children must be able to recognize the sensation of needing to empty the bladder or rectum. Third, children must be able to tighten the sphincter muscles related to the bladder or rectum to prevent immediate elimination. Fourth, they must get to the bathroom, pull down their training pants, and sit on a potty chair. Fifth, they must be able to relax the sphincter muscles so they can empty the bladder or rectum.

Toilet learning usually follows a set pattern. Bowel control is achieved first, followed by daytime bladder control and then nighttime bladder control. Parents should not necessarily expect toilet learning to begin until the child is about two-and-one-half-years-old. Boys often take a little longer at toilet learning than girls.

When toddlers show signs of readiness, toilet learning may begin. An earlier start will not make the process any faster. It will only frustrate both the parents and the children. Once a child is aware of bowel movements, parents can acquaint the child with a potty chair. If children are placed on the potty chair when they show signs of starting a bowel movement, they will soon make the connection. Children should be praised when they are successful. They should not be scolded or punished if they do not succeed, but should be comforted and praised for trying. Toddlers should not be forced to sit on the potty chair for long periods of time.

Once toddlers are fairly successful with the potty chair, training pants may be substituted for diapers. Training pants are thick underpants with elastic bands at the legs for protection against leaks. Bladder control may not be achieved for another two or three months or even longer. Most toddlers urinate every two hours, and the need arises suddenly. Parents have to make many trips to the potty chair to help their toddlers stay dry. Even so, accidents will happen. When they do, children should not be scolded or punished. Most children feel upset about accidents and need consolation rather than punishment. Gradually, toddlers will gain better bladder control. They will also become more skillful in handling their clothes and more independent in their toilet routines.

Intellectual Development

Toddlers gradually realize they are a part of a larger world. With this realization comes the desire to explore that world. Parents play an important role in this phase of toddlers' intellectual development. Parents' enthusiasm can be contagious. Toddlers who see the world as an exciting place full of things to do are more likely to explore. See 12-10.

Many parents become overly anxious if they compare their child's intellectual development to that of other children. Each child is an individual who learns at his or her own pace. Parents cannot control their child's intellectual development, but

1—Discuss: Should toddlers be forced to sit on the potty chair for long periods of time? Should they be punished or scolded if they have an accident?

2—Discuss: When may training pants be substituted for diapers? What extra help should parents provide to achieve toilet learning?

3—Reflect: If you were a parent, how would you contribute to your toddlers' intellectual development?

12-10 _____
A parent with a good sense of humor can delight a toddler with a book and an assortment of animal friends.

1—Vocabulary: Define *egocentric*. How does this control the actions of the toddler?

2—Example: Cite examples of how toddlers learn to understand similarities and differences between objects.

3—Discuss: What role does imitation play in a toddler's intellectual development?

4—Activity: List ways parents can stimulate their children's imagination.

they can encourage it. The best contribution parents can make is to provide stimulating interactions in relaxed settings. When their one-year-old starts searching for a hidden toy, parents can playfully join in the search. Such interactions stimulate the natural growth of the child's brain, intellect, and curiosity.

One-year-olds are beginning to understand more than what they can see, hear, and touch. However, they are still **egocentric** (self-centered), and their activities revolve around their own interests and needs. Toddlers live in the here and now. Their memories are very short, and they are not good at thinking ahead. They may not remember what they were scolded for yesterday. They may not think ahead to the consequences of repeating a forbidden action. Whatever they see, they investigate. Whatever they want, they grab.

As one-year-olds explore their world, they also conduct experiments. When they pick up an object, they try to figure out what to do with it. They may try squeezing, rolling, or dropping it. Through their experiments, toddlers begin to see similarities and differences among objects. Apples and crackers are different, but they are more like each other than like a book. This is the beginning of the ability to form concepts. Gradually, toddlers refine their concepts.

One-year-olds learn a lot by watching how their parents and other people react to events. They demonstrate what they have learned through imitation. They may awkwardly handle a newspaper as if trying to read it. Their imitations will bring many smiles to parents' faces, 12-11.

Toddlers do not think in a logical sequence. They are able to think simple things through by about age 18 months. They remember where certain objects are in their homes, and they may surprise parents by connecting activities with objects. Toddlers who spill dry cereal on the kitchen floor

may head for the closet to get the broom and dustpan.

Eventually, toddlers begin using their imaginations. At first, parents may not notice the changes, but there are differences. By midyear, two-year-olds are not just imitating actions they have seen. They are using original ideas. When they imagine, they use a mental image of a behavior. Then they use their ideas to act out the behavior in a new situation. For instance, they have seen people wearing hats. When playing with an empty saucepan, they find it can be turned over and placed on a head. With imagination, they have invented a hat. Many of toddlers' favorite make-believe activities are based on remembered family events. Toddlers like to share these activities with their parents. For instance, the toddler may imagine parent-child roles are reversed. The child may cover the

12-11 ——————
This toddler imitates her family members as she "calls a friend."

parent with a blanket and say "night-night," imagining it is time for bed.

Imagination and make-believe play offer wonderful learning opportunities for toddlers. Most one-year-olds are egocentric. As two-year-olds, their growing powers of imagination and make-believe allow them to act like others and thus break away somewhat from their egocentric behavior. They slowly begin to realize other people have feelings, too. They may demonstrate their new ability to show empathy by creating make-believe settings. If a brother hurts his finger, the toddler may make believe he or she is a parent. The toddler may then kiss the brother's finger, remembering how a parent has soothed such injuries in the past.

Toddlers are busy little people, and parents are a very important part of their learning. Each day has many **teachable moments,** times when parents have unplanned opportunities to introduce new ideas to their toddlers. Parents also have to act as managers, keeping children's learning environments stimulating but not overwhelming.

Toys and Play in Intellectual Development

A great deal of intellectual development occurs during toddlerhood through experiences with toys and play. Young toddlers are more interested in an activity itself than in any outcome of the activity. They love to empty and fill containers just for the fun of doing it. Older toddlers refine this skill and become more concerned with the precise placement of objects. They enjoy playing with nesting toys, form boards, and simple puzzles.

In a similar way, toddlers' first scribbles are just for the fun of scribbling, 12-12. The first scribbles are just wavy lines drawn without lifting the crayon from the paper. Later, toddlers start drawing single lines—first vertical, then horizontal and circular. (This is also due to their improved ability to grasp the crayon—a small motor skill.) As toddlers approach their third birthdays, they can draw crude pictures. They usually interpret what they have drawn after the pictures are finished. Most toddlers are not yet able to plan what they want to draw and then draw it.

Play is a method of trying out ideas and learning to use objects. Infants and children soon learn the results of their actions when they turn the knobs on a radio—loud noise! Children can use different objects to do many things. They learn simple math lessons as they pile several blocks on top of each other. They learn science lessons as they pour sand from a large pail into a small pail. They invent new play activities as they follow the rules of organized play. Learning can take place with a little imagination and common household objects. For instance, a large dishpan can be a boat, and several oatmeal boxes can be used together to make a train.

Many educational toys are now available that provide a wide variety of structured learning experiences to

12-12

A toddler enjoys scribbling just to see the colors the crayon makes on the paper.

1—**Discuss:** How does the toddler begin to outgrow egocentricity? How might a toddler demonstrate this?

2—**Resource:** *Teachable Moments,* Activity D, SAG.

3—**Example:** Bring examples of toddler's drawings to class. How do their figures of people look? When do toddlers interpret their drawings?

1—Activity: Demonstrate how parents can use simple household objects to teach toddlers the concepts of more versus less and tall versus short.

2—Reflect: Should parents fill their children's free time with planned activities? Why or why not?

3—Resource: Books for Children, Activity H, SAG.

4—Discuss: Describe how a parent would "read" a picture book to a toddler.

challenge young minds. Children learn relationship concepts involved in combining different objects. They learn the meaning of more versus less, tall versus short, and big versus little. They also begin learning numbers, colors, shapes, and names for various objects.

An important aspect of learning through play is the ability to be creative and try new ideas. It is important for parents to provide some unstructured playtime for children to spend as they wish, 12-13. Children need to use their imaginations and creative thinking skills to devise new play activities.

Toddlers should not feel bored, nor should every waking moment of their lives be filled with planned activities. They need balance between new experiences and familiar ones. They need time to play with parents and siblings, and time to play alone. They need chances for active play like running, jumping, and climbing. They also need chances for quiet play like looking at books and working with puzzles. Variety is the key to sound intellectual development.

12-13 ⎯⎯⎯⎯⎯⎯⎯⎯⎯⎯⎯⎯⎯
This toddler's imaginative mind allows him to be the conductor of his toy train.

The Importance of Books

Books are a vital part of a child's intellectual development and enjoyment of learning. By introducing books to their children at early ages, parents can help their children learn to enjoy and value books and reading. Children who learn to enjoy books often develop a fondness for reading that lasts throughout their lives.

Many parents begin by reading books to their infants. Reading books together can continue into toddlerhood. Special family times and routines often involve books. In many homes, reading a book is part of the bedtime routine. Children look forward to picking out a special book they want to read. When reading books to toddlers, parents should find a quiet, comfortable place. Small children may prefer to sit on the parent's lap, 12-14. The floor can a good place for reading a large book, but bedtime stories are usually read in a child's bed.

A child's first books are likely to be picture books. These books may or may not have words. Picture books feature large, colorful illustrations that are familiar to children. Parents can "read" a picture book by talking with the child about each picture in the book. By naming the pictures, parents can help a child prepare to read words later. A parent can involve the child by asking questions, such as "Where is the kitty cat?"

Highly illustrated storybooks are important, too. These allow the child to follow the story being read by looking at the pictures. Young children like stories that rhyme. Children will ask their parents to read the same book repeatedly. While this may seem boring for the parent, the child learns more about the book and the story each time. Soon, a child may know all the words to a favorite story. This can be helpful when the child begins learning to read.

Books can be very entertaining. Children get excited as they become

12-14
This toddler likes it when her sister takes time to read a story.

involved in the story. Books can also provide a restful quiet period in a child's busy day. Toddlers do not sit still for long periods of time, but they can learn to enjoy a little quiet time with a book. Books can help parents occupy children when traveling, when they are ill, or when waiting in the doctor's office for an appointment.

Reading can become a lasting pleasure for children. It is also an excellent way to learn. Parents should read slowly and add explanations as necessary. After the book is read, parents should take time to discuss the story and try to answer any questions the child might have.

Language Development

Early in the toddler stage, most children have vocabularies of fewer than ten words. They gradually build their vocabularies. By the end of this stage, they may have vocabularies of more than 500 words. Toddlerhood is a time of great language development.

Children often use a known word to describe anything that is similar. For instance, the word *dog* may be used to refer to all animals until the child learns differences between animals.

The name *Daddy* may be used for the child's father, but it might mean all other men as well. *No* is the most commonly used word for several months. Toddlers often say no to everything, even when they mean yes.

Some words the toddler uses are distantly related to real words. *Bankie* may mean blanket. *Coocoo* may mean cookie. If the parent understands what the toddler has said, the parent should respond accordingly. After all, the purpose of language is to communicate. If the toddler has made his or her meaning clear, the message should be accepted. Making a toddler repeat a word over and over until the pronunciation is correct would bore and frustrate the child.

A better solution is to accept the toddler's words and respond in adult words. For example, a toddler may say "bankie" with a questioning voice. A parent's response could be "Do you want your blanket? Your blanket is on the chair." This interaction assures the toddler his or her efforts at communication are worthwhile. It also helps the toddler become more familiar with adult language.

Parent-child interactions are important at all stages of language development. When children become toddlers, they need their parents to help them learn new words. Pointing to and naming parts of the body or other objects is a game toddlers like to play repeatedly. This game allows them to use the new words they have learned. As their intellectual development continues, they become better able to understand and respond to language. Most one-and-a-half-year-olds can respond to commands such as "Roll the ball to me."

The rate of language development varies as much, if not more than, any other aspect of development. Parents should not be too worried if their toddlers seem to learn new words at a slow rate. A few months later, the same toddlers may use several new words

1—Discuss: As toddlers learn to put words together, they add their own variations. Should parents be concerned about these instances of incorrect language?

2—Discuss: How can parents learn to accept a toddler's changeable emotions and help the child deal with negative feelings?

each week. If parents are concerned with their toddler's language development, however, they can seek the advice of a doctor or speech therapist. Many communities offer free developmental screenings several times a year. Parents can take their children for testing at these times.

Once toddlers are comfortable using lots of single words, they start combining them in two-word sentences. Toddlers add the second word to make their meaning clearer. They still don't understand correct grammar. As toddlers get better at expressing their thoughts with combinations of words, they gradually lengthen their sentences to three or four words. Toddlers do not just mimic sentences they have heard. They invent sentences to convey their thoughts to others, 12-15.

By the end of the toddler stage, children are aware of certain variations in adult speech. They may begin incorporating these variations in their own speech. For instance, they may begin using pronouns once in a while. *Me* is their favorite as in "Me do" and "Me go." At about the same time, toddlers may start to add an *-ed* ending to verbs in the past tense. They may also add

an *s* to nouns to make them plural. The results may sound strange, as in "Daddy goed" and "See mouses." These are important steps in their overall understanding of language, however.

Emotional and Social Development

The toddler years reveal many changes in emotional and social development. Toddlers' behavior is inconsistent as they struggle for independence. On one hand, toddlers show their desire for independence by trying to do more for themselves. On the other hand, toddlers ask for hugs of security and reassurance. Parents see their toddlers as sweet and lovable one minute and stubborn and willful the next. Meeting their conflicting needs is challenging. Parent-child interactions during the toddler years will be remembered for their many joys as well as their frustrations.

At first, toddlers seem to want to conquer the world. This drive is based on the realization they can control their actions and make things happen. They have an overwhelming urge to try out everything to see what happens. During the toddler years, children have many successful explorations, but they also run into obstacles and frustrations.

Both negative and positive emotions are a normal part of toddlerhood. Parents need to understand it is natural for toddlers to be changeable and intense in expressing all kinds of emotions. Toddlers are learning what it means to have feelings, and how to express them. Many toddlers

12-15 _____

When the need arises, toddlers find ways to communicate with one another!

are happy and pleasant most of the time, 12-16. Sometimes even the happiest toddler has negative feelings. Parents need to help toddlers deal with these feelings and resolve problems.

Once toddlers can walk and talk, their socialization begins in earnest. Their new skills allow them to take a more active role in interactions with others. They feel most comfortable with their family members, and may take plenty of time before becoming friendly with others. Toddlers may even be timid about meeting other children. It is better to let them make the move to be friendly in their own time than to push them into relating with others.

Two-year-olds continue their struggle for independence. Their success depends largely upon how secure they feel in their family interactions. Some toddlers are clingy and hesitant to wander too far from their parents. They may continue to "shadow" their parents well into their preschool years. Toddlers need to feel secure when they first attempt to venture out into the world. They may run from their parents quite easily. They need to feel assured the parents' waiting arms of love and understanding will always be there for them. Parents can help toddlers feel more secure by encouraging, but not pushing, them into new experiences.

A toddler may develop an attachment to a favorite object, such as a blanket, doll, or stuffed toy. The toddler will cling to the object until it is worn almost beyond recognition. Parents may have to search every room of their home to find the tattered blanket or worn stuffed toy in order to soothe their child. This is especially a problem at bedtime. Attachments like this are a normal part of development. Parents should not deprive their children of security objects. Children will gradually abandon them as they grow older and develop a greater sense of security, 12-17.

Toddlers' emotions are quite fragile. They may laugh one minute and cry the next. They have little patience and are easily frustrated. It is important for parents to help their toddlers

1—Discuss: Should parents encourage toddlers to be friendly with other children, or let them make the move on their own?

2—Discuss: Why do some toddlers continue to "shadow" their parents instead of exploring more on their own?

3—Example: Bring examples of items children use as security objects. Should parents deprive their child of a security object?

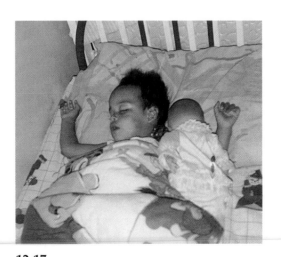

12-16
Toddlers are generally pretty happy people.

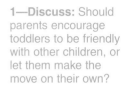

12-17
This little girl needs her favorite doll to go to bed with her every night.

1—Discuss: Play helps toddlers become more aware of themselves and others. How does this help their own self-concept?

2—Enrich: Role-play situations in which toddlers learn give-and-take, sharing, and the concepts of right and wrong.

3—Discuss: Toddlers are very possessive of their toys, but they don't understand why other toddlers feel the same way. How can parents help them learn to share?

4—Discuss: Do toddlers spend lots of time in cooperative play? Why or Why not?

find appropriate ways to express frustration. Physical activities like racing across the yard or pounding with a toy hammer are good emotional outlets.

If parents examine the reasons for their toddlers' frustrations, they may be able to prevent future problems. If toddlers are misusing certain objects in the home, it might be wise to eliminate those objects for a while. Toddlers may be intrigued by pulling the leaves of houseplants. Moving the plants to an inaccessible area may help prevent future temptations. (Parents should be sure any plants in their house are not poisonous—some common houseplants are deadly when eaten.)

Toward the end of toddlerhood, children begin to show more control over their behavior. Parents can help by giving their children approval and praise when their behavior is good. When toddlers behave badly, parents should show love and understanding but use firm guidance, too.

Toys and Play in Emotional and Social Development

Play allows toddlers to experience small successes that can build their self-esteem and confidence. This increased confidence will help them try more difficult activities. At first, toddlers gain confidence in learning to manipulate simple toys. For example, children feel a great deal of accomplishment when they first learn to build a block tower.

Also, as toddlers interact with others during play, they become more aware of themselves and others. This strengthens their own self-concept. Children often expose their concepts of family through their pretend play.

Play also teaches the value of following rules. It helps children learn it is okay to make mistakes and try again

in a play activity. Through play, toddlers begin to learn about give-and-take and sharing. They become more able to respond to another person's feelings. Toddlers learn more about values and what is right and wrong through their play with others.

As they interact in group play, toddlers begin to learn the roles of leader and follower. They learn patience as they wait for another child to go first. Learning to take turns is a valuable lesson in getting along with others.

Types of Play

As toddlers approach three years of age, they become much more interested in relating to others. Their emotional and social growth helps them play near and with others. Most of their play is parallel play. In **parallel play**, two children play separately, but beside one another, in the same activity. For instance, two toddlers might sit side-by-side, each playing with blocks. They may watch one another, grab toys from one another, or completely ignore each other. Their primary interest is in their own play, 12-18.

Toddlers feel very possessive of their own toys, yet they do not understand why other toddlers feel the same way. Toddlers are egocentric—from their eyes, they are the center of the universe. They are incapable of considering someone else's feelings or needs. As a result, parents may have to referee toddlers' parallel play. Since sharing is so difficult, toddlers need to have a few toys that are theirs alone. These favorite toys would not have to be shared. If toddlers are constantly forced to share all their toys, they may become even more possessive. They may need more time than usual to learn to share willingly.

Once in a while, older toddlers may participate in **cooperative play** where they actually play together. Toddlers rarely sustain this kind of play for long

12-18
In parallel play, toddlers play near each other but have little interaction.

periods of time. Their social skills (including the concept of sharing) are not well-developed, so cooperation is difficult.

Separation Anxiety

A significant event in emotional and social development is the ability of toddlers to feel secure when they are separated from their parents. As they begin to feel more secure, they start to overcome the separation anxiety that dominated the last half of the first year.

Separation anxiety often continues well into the toddler years, but it gradually diminishes as a child develops. As toddlers' understanding matures, they realize their primary caregivers have not necessarily disappeared forever if they are not within sight at the moment. Improved memory also helps toddlers handle separation anxiety. They can remember other times their primary caregivers went away and returned. Advances in language skills help, too. Older toddlers can understand when parents explain they must leave for a little while, but will return later.

To help toddlers overcome separation anxiety, parents should try to be understanding and loving. After all, parents are a toddler's security base. Without that base, a toddler feels lost, alone, uneasy, and helpless. If they understand how the toddlers feel, parents may be more willing to offer plenty of love, support, and security. Parents can also help by being truthful. When they must leave, parents should tell their children when they are leaving and when they will return. If parents leave by sneaking out, they will create greater feelings of insecurity in their children.

Before parents feel too guilty about leaving their crying toddlers, they should check with the toddlers' substitute caregivers. Many toddlers possess great acting skills. They sometimes cry to manipulate their parents into staying. They cry for their parents until they realize the parents are truly gone and will not return until later. Then their tears disappear and they turn their attention to their babysitters or child care providers.

1—Discuss: How can object permanence, improved memory, and growing language skills help toddlers overcome separation anxiety?

2—Discuss: Why is it important for parents to offer plenty of love, support, and security to their toddlers?

1—**Discuss:** How can structure provide a feeling of security for children? Give examples.

2—**Vocabulary:** What is meant by *behavioral boundaries*? Give examples.

3—**Enrich:** Role-play situations involving parent-toddler conflict about bedtime.

12-19 ———————————————
When Mom returns, she can see by the messy face that her daughter had fun. Sharing a warm hug makes them forget their sad good-bye when Mom had to leave for a few hours.

Separations between parents and toddlers are unavoidable. Both parents and toddlers have to deal with these times to the best of their abilities. Sharing warm moments when they are reunited can help ease the difficulties of the separations, 12-19.

Guiding the Toddler's Behavior

Children need to learn to follow some established routines. Structure helps young children feel secure. With structure, toddlers learn certain things happen at specific times, and that some routines have a specific sequence. For instance, they may be able to predict a specific bedtime routine that consists of bath time, teeth brushing, bedtime story, and good-night kiss. Toddlers will be less likely to resist bedtime if their routine is followed consistently. It doesn't take long for children to learn routines, and they often are the first to remind parents if a routine is changed.

As toddlers learn to be independent, they must also learn there are limits. This is an important stage for establishing parental control and initiating self-discipline. Children need to be taught behavioral boundaries. If they do not become familiar with these boundaries at this early stage, it will be harder for them to establish limits later in their lives.

Toddlers look to parents to provide guidance. They understand discipline better when it is consistent. This does not mean limits cannot be flexible to meet some particular need or event. There may be times when an extra bedtime story is more important than watching the clock.

Parents often warn other parents about the "terrible twos." Toddlers need many opportunities to assert their growing independence. They also need guidance and direction. Since these needs are so different, conflicts are bound to occur.

Some amount of conflict is healthy. Toddlers need to learn they cannot always have their own way. They must learn how to make and deal with choices and decisions. Toddlers should learn to handle disappointment, frustration, and anger. They also need to experience the positive side of conflict. Toddlers can learn about negotiating, compromising, and finding solutions. They should win some minor conflicts. They should be allowed to feel their ideas and desires are worthwhile. These positive experiences boost their self-esteem.

Although some amount of conflict is healthy, too much can harm family unity. Smart parents think ahead and try to avoid situations that will surely lead to conflict. For instance, smart parents do not offer a choice when there is no choice to be made. They don't ask "Do you want to go to bed now?" Such a question implies there is a choice, while bedtime is actually an inflexible matter. The child would most surely answer with a loud no. His or her choice would go unheard, however, because it was bedtime. Instead, parents should announce in a firm and positive manner it is bedtime. The parent has merely stated a fact. The child has not been offered a choice when none can be made.

Toddlers expect firmness and caring guidance, but they may test parents' patience at times. They may even push their defiance to the limit. Parents have to decide if they will use spanking to guide their children's behavior. Some parents choose slight spankings to reinforce their stands on rare occasions. Other parents choose to rely on psychological approaches. Children should never be physically reprimanded when the parent is in a heightened emotional state. The role of guidance is to achieve results without being abusive. Each child must be treated as an individual. Guidance that is right for one child may be too strong for a more sensitive child.

Firm limits allow toddlers to sense their parents care about them. Even young children comprehend this lesson. They feel more secure when they know their parents establish limits but give them guidelines and freedoms within those limits.

Temper Tantrums

Temper tantrums are violent outbursts of negative behavior. Almost all children between the ages of one and three have temper tantrums. Children in these stages are becoming increasingly aware of all the things they can do without their parents. They are also

12-20
This mother speaks soothingly to her toddler to help prevent a temper tantrum.

aware of, and frustrated by, things they cannot do. They are still very young, but their desire for more freedom and control of their world is evident. As toddlers, children also learn they cannot get their way all the time. This can cause negative feelings the toddler doesn't know how to express. These feelings can lead to temper tantrums.

The best way to deal with temper tantrums is to try to avoid the situations that cause them. When the child, the parent, or both are tired, it may lead to a disagreement that starts a tantrum. By ensuring everyone gets enough rest, these particular tantrums can be avoided. Sometimes parents can detour behaviors that might have led to tantrums into constructive activities. Parents can help their children by meeting their children's reasonable needs. See 12-20.

If prevention fails and a tantrum begins, the parent's first duty is to see the child does not injure anyone, including himself or herself. Once a tantrum has begun, it must run its course. While waiting for the tantrum to pass, the parent should try to analyze what caused it. This may help the parent prevent another similar situation in the future.

1—**Reflect:** If you were a parent, would you use spanking or psychological approaches to teach your children limits?

2—**Resource:** *Helping Toddlers Learn Their Limits*, Activity E, SAG.

3—**Resource:** *Handling Toddler's Behaviors*, Activity F, SAG.

4—**Enrich:** Role-play several situations involving a child's temper tantrum and the parents' reactions. Evaluate how each situation was handled.

After a temper tantrum, children usually need to be soothed and cuddled. They need to know their behavior during the tantrum was not acceptable, but they are still loved. They should not be punished after a tantrum, nor should they be rewarded. Giving into children's demands after tantrums only encourages the children to throw tantrums whenever they do not get what they want.

The Importance of Play to a Child's Overall Development

Play is a powerful tool for learning self-expression, exploration, and satisfaction. Since play is so important to children's growth and development, some experts refer to it as "baby's work." Play such as peek-a-boo or pat-a-cake teaches toddlers about their physical world. As the child grows, play continues to be the tool for learning at all stages of development. The chart in 12-21 gives parents some practical guidelines about playing with their children.

Factors to Consider When Selecting Toys

A multitude of toys are available in today's market for all age groups. Although children may still find a lot of enjoyment in playing with common household items, toys can bring pleasure and be wonderful learning devices. Parents have many factors to consider when selecting toys for their toddlers.

Parents should be realistic and use common sense when selecting toys for their children. When selecting toys, adults should carefully examine the toys for safety and read the label.

The construction of the toy should be considered. Toys with sharp points or edges, long cords, and small pieces should be avoided. These could be dangerous for a young child. Toys should be examined for durability. Items such as wheels, eyes, and knobs must be securely attached so they cannot come off and present a choking hazard. Toys should also be inspected to make sure any noise produced by the toys won't harm hearing. If paint is used on the toy, it should be nontoxic.

Parents should consider the ages and skill levels of children before purchasing toys. Many toys have labels that indicate the suggested age group for whom the toy is targeted. Some parents mistakenly believe purchasing a toy above their children's age group will encourage the child. A toy that is too complicated is more likely to frustrate the child. Parents should also consider whether children need supervision to use a certain toy. Small children who cannot understand how to use a toy can become frustrated, and may even harm themselves if they try to use it without the proper supervision.

Too much of anything is not a good idea, and toys are no exception. Too many toys can overwhelm a child. If a child has too many toys, putting some of them away for awhile might help the child feel less overwhelmed. Many parents find by rotating their children's toys, they can renew their children's interest in their toys. Children often have several favorite toys, and these should remain available at all times. However, sometimes children receive so many toys they cannot actually appreciate them. It is wise to put some of the toys away and gradually reintroduce them one at a time. This helps children to enjoy each toy.

1

Playtime Suggestions for Parents and Their Children

❏ Trust intuition. Parents can intuitively tell when their children are ready for the next step in play.

❏ Pay attention to children's cues. Children will let their parents know they are enjoying a play activity through smiles and actions. Children should not be forced into a play activity that overwhelms them.

❏ Let children take the lead. Children have a natural motivation to play. Parents should let their children initiate and direct their own play.

❏ Recognize the purpose of children's play. Children handle objects to learn about them, and they make movements to initiate the use of that object. Even though children might not use an object as an adult would, the activity can still be a learning experience for the child.

❏ Don't interrupt. Parents learn to use a great deal of patience as they observe their children's play. Parents should allow children to finish exploring before they introduce a new activity.

❏ Recognize children's achievements. Even their simplest successes should be recognized by parents. Dumping things out and putting them back can be a definite learning achievement for small children. When children are aware their parents are delighted with their new ability, they will thrive on this recognition. Saying "You're putting them back" describes what the child has done. This type of praise lets children know what they have achieved. If parents say "You're being good," children might not realize why they were being praised.

❏ Realize children need time to unwind. Children need downtime following an activity. They need time on their own before moving on to another activity.

12-21
Playing with children is one of the most rewarding experiences of parenthood.

Medical Checkups for Toddlers

The American Academy of Pediatrics recommends toddlers see their doctors at ages 1 year, 15 months, 18 months, 2 years, and 3 years. These medical checkups are important for monitoring a toddler's health. The doctor can identify any problems, and these can be treated as early as possible. Routine medical checkups are in addition to any visits due to illness or injury.

2

During medical checkups, parents can ask any questions they might have about their toddler's health, nutrition, and growth. Parents may also want to ask the doctor's advice about sleeping problems, discipline, and toilet learning. The doctor will check the toddler's growth by measuring height, weight, and head size. The toddler's eyes and ears will be examined. If needed, vision and hearing screenings will also be done. The doctor will thoroughly examine the child's physical condition. Any necessary tests will be done to check the toddler's health. Appropriate immunizations will also be given.

1—Activity: Review the playtime suggestions in this chart. Why does toddlers' playtime need to be supervised?

2—Discuss: Why do toddlers need routine medical checkups? How often should these be?

1—Resource:
Developmental Highlights for Toddlers, transparency master 12-2, TR.

2—Discuss: During infancy, physical growth seemed to be the dominant growth. During the toddler years, intellectual development increases rapidly. Describe some improvements during ages 13 to 15 months.

CHILD DEVELOPMENT

13 to 15 Months

1 Physical Development*

Large Motor Skills

May stand erect with only slight support.

May stand alone without support for a short time.

Cruises along furniture.

Takes steps while holding onto parents' hands.

May be able to walk a few steps alone.

Sits by collapsing when first taking steps.

Crawls forward or backward with varying speed.

Crawls over small barriers.

May creep like a bear, with hands and feet in contact with floor.

May climb stairs on hands and knees.

May be able to back down stairs.

Can sit in small chair for a short time.

Climbs on chairs, sofas, and tables.

May climb out of crib, high chair, or stroller.

Small Motor Skills

Has improved grasping skills.

Needs improvement in manipulation skills.

Turns cardboard or cloth pages of picture books.

Enjoys filling and emptying containers with small objects.

Can open small, hinged box.

Builds small towers of blocks.

May try to turn doorknobs.

Uses spoon, spilling little.

2 Intellectual Development

General

Begins to form concepts.

Notices actions of other children and adults. Loves to mimic all actions.

Explores different features of objects as if studying them.

Looks in correct place for toys that roll out of sight.

Experiments with actions never tried before.

Discovers ability to make things happen by own actions.

Has very short memory and almost no forethought.

Likes to look at picture books and pats recognized pictures.

Shows interest in new textures by rubbing fingers over surfaces.

Is able to fit round block into round hole in form board.

Language

Slowly increases vocabulary to four to six words.

May use sounds to indicate specific objects.

Babbles with expression.

Amuses self with vocal play.

May attempt to imitate words others say.

May repeat sounds without understanding the meaning of sounds.

Responds to own name, comes when called.

Follows simple commands, such as give, come, stop, and show me.

Recognizes names of major body parts.

Points to familiar toys or persons on request.

Emotional and Social Development

Emotional

Shows pride in personal accomplishments.

Is more demanding and self-assertive.

Likes to exhibit affection to humans and objects.

Prefers to keep parent or caregiver in sight while exploring environment.

Demands personal attention.

May show fear of strangers.

Shows increased negativism.

May become attached to a special toy.

Social

Enjoys solitary play.

Enjoys play with older siblings or parents.

Shows preference for family members over others.

Shows off for an audience.

Is easily diverted and entertained.

Likes to go for stroller or car rides.

Recognizes self in mirror and may communicate with sounds.

(continued)

These charts are not exact timetables for development. Individuals may perform certain activities earlier or later than indicated in the charts.

CHILD DEVELOPMENT

16 to 18 Months

Physical Development

Large Motor Skills

May be able to walk sideways.

Stands on either foot with support.

Walks fast and runs stiffly.

Walks into ball; is unable to kick the ball.

Squats down smoothly from standing position.

Jumps with both feet.

Improves throwing motion, first using whole body, then using just arm movements.

Pushes and pulls large toys around the floor.

Small Motor Skills

May show hand preference in all activities.

Likes to grab anything and everything.

Adds hand gestures to spoken language.

Begins to scribble.

Continues to enjoy filling and emptying containers.

May turn knobs of radio and TV.

Builds tower of three cubes.

Places round pegs in a pegboard.

Works jigsaw puzzles with 1-2 pieces.

Intellectual Development

General

Gradually refines concepts.

Is very inquisitive about everything.

Remembers where objects belong.

Begins to figure things out through thought process.

Has short attention span.

Tries to imitate the ways parents use objects.

Enjoys working with shapes on form board.

Scribbles more freely but also can imitate strokes in drawing.

Identifies simple pictures in book, such as "ball," "doggie," and so on.

Language

Vocabulary increases to six to ten words.

Uses words instead of gestures to express some wants, such as "up" or "cookie."

Imitates simple sounds on request.

Says "no" more often than any other word.

Obeys command "Give it to me."

Responds to increasing number of verbal directions if combined with actions.

Responds delightedly to children's TV shows.

Understands more words than is capable of saying.

Identifies objects by pointing when requested.

Refers to self by name when asked.

Can point to own body parts on request.

May use two-word phrases.

Emotional and Social Development

Emotional

Is still egocentric.

Responds to parents' emotional expressions by imitating them.

Is emotionally unpredictable and may respond differently at different times.

Hugs favorite toys and may carry them all the time.

May hug pets too hard when wanting to show affection.

Is unable to tolerate frustration.

May be less afraid of strangers.

May reveal negativism and stubbornness.

May exhibit fear of thunder, lightning, large animals, and so on.

Enjoys ability to do things independently.

Social

Is very socially responsive to parents and caregivers.

Demands personal attention from family members.

Hands object to parent and awaits reaction expectantly.

Responds to simple requests.

Realizes different people react in different ways.

Enjoys sociable play before bedtime.

May punch and poke other toddlers as if they were objects.

Will perform for an audience.

Likes to chase and be chased.

Is unable to share.

1—Discuss: In early toddlerhood, children are still egocentric. Their worlds revolve around them. How may this be revealed in their social relationships with parents, siblings, and playmates?

(continued)

CHILD DEVELOPMENT

19 to 21 Months

1—Discuss: By one and one-half years of age, a toddler's large motor skills have improved greatly. Briefly describe how this allows them to move their bodies with more agility.

Physical Development

Large Motor Skills

Walks sideways and backward.

Runs without falling often.

Walks up and down stairs with help.

Responds rhythmically to music with whole body.

Loves to run, jump, and climb.

Jumps forward and in place.

Hangs from bar, grasping with hands.

Can kick large ball without stepping on it.

Squats easily in play.

Sits on floor from standing position quite easily.

Small Motor Skills

Holds two objects in hand easily.

Builds tower of five or six blocks.

Holds container in one hand, puts small objects into it with other hand, then dumps the objects out.

Can fold piece of paper once imitating demonstration.

Uses one hand more than the other.

Intellectual Development

General

Progresses from simple imitation to imaginative play.

Can remember familiar objects without seeing them.

Can obtain familiar objects from different room when asked.

Places circles, triangles, and squares in form board.

Is interested in tiny things such as bugs.

Looks at books for longer periods of time, studying pictures.

Associates tool with function it performs, such as hammer for banging.

Completes simple jigsaw puzzle of two to three pieces.

Likes to make marks on paper with big crayon.

Imitates simple actions on request.

Learns to distinguish different sounds and smells.

Language

Has vocabulary of about 20 words.

Enjoys labeling objects and parts of body.

Responds to speech with speech.

Uses speech to get desired results.

Combines two different words.

Constantly asks "What's that?"

Enjoys hearing nursery rhymes.

Likes to respond to directions.

Understands some personal pronouns such as *me*.

Matches sounds to the animals that make them.

Emotional and Social Development

Emotional

May show increasing need for security object.

May direct anger at person responsible for frustration.

May reveal feelings of jealousy.

May become more possessive of toys, hiding them from others.

Likes to claim things as "mine."

Gives up items that belong to others upon request.

Begins to show sympathy for another child or adult.

Does not yet understand cooperation, but may cooperate some of the time.

Social

Continues to desire personal attention.

Likes to help with simple household tasks.

Indicates awareness of absence of person by saying "bye-bye."

Likes to repeat experiences in simple terms.

Responds less quickly to requests, and may respond in opposite manner.

May enjoy removing clothing and is not embarrassed about being naked.

Enjoys dressing in adult clothing.

May ask for permission to do things.

Reveals a sense of trust in adults.

Plays contentedly alone if near adults.

Likes to play next to other children but does not interact with them.

Tries to imitate play activities of older siblings.

Engages in imaginative play involving daily routines such as eating or going to sleep.

Is able to play some simple interacting games for short periods of time.

(continued)

CHILD DEVELOPMENT

22 to 24 Months

Physical Development
Large Motor Skills

Walks with more coordination and assurance.

Walks sideways and backward with ease.

Bounces and sways in simple dancing movements.

Lacks ability to start efficiently or stop quickly while running.

Likes to walk on low walls and perform other stunts.

Alternates between standing and sitting positions easily.

Can seat self in small chair with ease.

Jumps with both feet off the floor.

Can throw ball into basket.

Throws ball overhead instead of tossing.

Small Motor Skills

Shows increased coordination and smoother hand and finger movements.

Can put several blocks together to make a train or stack them to build a tower.

Likes to play with modeling clay.

Can open screw-type closures.

Snips paper with scissors.

Holds crayon with thumb and fingers.

Intellectual Development
General

Becomes interested in the outcome of activities rather than just the activities themselves.

Becomes interested in the precise placement of objects; enjoys form boards and simple puzzles.

Is curious about objects in environment; feels, squeezes, pulls and pushes objects.

Follows simple directions.

Is able to match familiar objects.

Identifies familiar objects on TV screen.

May distinguish between "one" and "many."

May be able to recall what is lost and where it might be.

Recognizes when picture in book is upside down.

May be able to draw crude pictures and interpret what they are.

Distinguishes between vertical and horizontal lines.

1 *Language*

Has vocabulary of 50 or more words.

Is able to ask for things using simple words.

Continues to ask "What's that?"

Is interested in sound repetition.

Understands more words than is able to use.

Substitutes some words for some physical acts.

Asks for food when hungry and water when thirsty.

Answers questions concerning the names of body parts.

Answers simple questions such as "Where is the doggie?" and "What does kitty say?"

Understands and asks for "another" and "more."

Listens to and enjoys simple stories.

Imitates parents' words and inflections.

Emotional and Social Development
Emotional

Displays signs of love for parents and other favorite people.

May express increased possessive attitude.

Is easily hurt by criticism.

Is afraid of disapproval and rejection.

Becomes frustrated easily.

May show some aggressive tendencies, such as slapping, biting, hitting.

May assume an increasingly self-sufficient attitude.

Has strong positive or negative reactions.

Wants own way in everything.

Recognizes own power to be effective.

May dawdle but desires to please parents.

Social

Is more responsive to, and more demanding of, adults.

Shows genuine interest in other parent-child relationships.

Is occasionally hostile to sibling if frustrated.

Desires approval in social situations.

Still prefers to play alone but likes to be near others.

Enjoys water play.

Likes to "dance" to music.

Engages in imaginative play related to parents' actions.

Uses own name in reference to self when talking with others.

Continually tests the limits set by parents and caregivers.

Likes to control others and give them orders.

1—Discuss: Toddlers' ability to use language to convey their needs and feelings is increasing. Briefly discuss their language abilities and how parents can help them improve their communication skills.

(continued)

CHILD DEVELOPMENT

24 to 30 Months

1—Discuss: Toddlers' small motor skills help them be more agile in handling small objects. Discuss how this makes children better able to entertain themselves. Also, discuss how it may create some safety problems for parents.

Physical Development
Large Motor Skills
Improves motor skills as torso lengthens and baby fat begins to disappear.

Enjoys running but is unable to measure sudden stops. May collide with other people or obstacles.

Climbs everywhere indoors, even in forbidden places.

Climbs on jungle gym with fair amount of ease.

Plays on swings, ladders, and other playground equipment.

Kicks ball forward.

Throws ball overhead but without aiming.

Small Motor Skills
Opens doors by turning knobs.

Can remove wrapping from gum and candy.

Can carefully turn pages of book one page at a time.

Likes to take jar lids off and screw them back on.

Can soap hands and arms easily.

Tears paper and manipulates clay.

Intellectual Development
General
Becomes increasingly interested in children's TV shows.

Understands cause and effect in terms of own behavior.

Is better able to plan a play activity and carry it out.

Is better able to use nearby objects in make-believe games.

Enjoys playing house and imitating family situations.

Likes to listen to tapes and records of stories and songs.

Remembers sequence of stories and may be able to retell them.

Is able to interpret pictures drawn or painted.

Likes to imitate drawings of older children.

Recognizes familiar signs in environment.

Solves problems by imitating past actions.

Distinguishes between *before* and *after*.

Can follow two-step commands.

Language
Vocabulary starts at 200 words and increases to 500 or more in this period.

Uses two-word sentences.

Refers to self by name; then learns to use pronouns.

Enjoys learning names for new objects.

Uses words to make requests.

Understands a few prepositions such as *out, in, on.*

Emotional and Social Development
Emotional
Continues to be self-centered.

May exhibit increasing independence one minute and then run back to security of parents the next.

Likes immediate gratification and finds it difficult to wait.

May exhibit negativism.

Has trouble understanding sharing, but may give back toy that belongs to someone else.

Continues to seek parental approval for behaviors and accomplishments.

Displays jealousy.

May develop fear of dark, needs reassurance.

Social
Likes to play near other children, but is unable to play cooperatively.

May grab desired toys away from other children.

Does not like to share toys.

Has not learned to say please but often desires toys of other children.

Likes to give affection to parents.

May pull hair or bite before giving up prized possession.

(continued)

CHILD DEVELOPMENT

30 to 36 Months

Physical Development
Large Motor Skills
Likes to be in constant motion, running or walking sideways or backward.

Enjoys games involving running.

Goes up stairs by alternating feet, but goes down one foot at a time.

Climbs quickly on jungle gym to reach the top.

Climbs up slide ladder and slides down.

Jumps from any elevated object, sometimes miscalculating height.

Sits in adult chairs and may prefer these to smaller chairs.

Throws ball overhead but aim is still poor.

Catches large ball with arms and hands out straight.

Walks on tiptoe.

Small Motor Skills
Turns doorknobs with greater strength.

Scribbles and draws circles as well as horizontal and vertical lines.

Likes to paint using full arm motions combined with finger motions.

Strings large beads.

Builds towers of six or more blocks.

Takes objects apart and puts them back together.

Makes mud pies and sand castles.

Eats with a fork.

Intellectual Development
General
Begins to classify objects into general categories.

Uses symbolic representation in make-believe play.

Tries out various roles in make-believe play.

Tries new play activities to discover more about how things work.

Becomes more skilled in putting puzzles together.

Reveals intellectual curiosity in reading books and watching TV.

Can remember and follow three-step commands.

Can stack rings in the correct order.

Identifies familiar objects by touch.

Recognizes self in photographs.

Language
Vocabulary starts at about 500 words and increases to 900 or 1000 in this period.

Creates two- to three-word sentences, including verbs.

Starts to use past tense and plurals.

Ask names of objects and repeats them.

May use prepositions.

Connects names and uses of objects.

Understands relative size (big and small).

Uses personal pronouns correctly.

Emotional and Social Development
Emotional
May display negative feelings and occasional temper.

May exhibit aggressiveness.

May dawdle but insists on doing things for self.

Likes to dress self and needs praise and encouragement when correct.

Feels bad when reprimanded for mistakes.

Desires parental approval.

Wants independence but shows fear of new experiences.

May reveal need for clinging to security object.

May exhibit fear and needs reassurance in fearful situations.

Needs an understanding, orderly environment.

May have trouble sleeping if day's events have been emotional.

Social
Continues to feel a strong sense of ownership but may give up toy if offered a substitute.

May learn to say please if prompted.

Has increased desire to play near and with other children.

May begin cooperative play.

Distinguishes between boys and girls.

Likes to be accepted by others.

May continue to show aggressive actions to get own way while playing with others.

Enjoys hiding from others.

Likes to play with adults on one-to-one basis.

Enjoys tumbling play with older siblings and parents.

1

1—Discuss: Toddlers' ability to play with others increases as they develop socially. Discuss the concepts of sharing, cooperative play, and ownership.

1—Activity: Review and outline this chapter emphasizing the information you found most useful.

2—Answers: Answers to review questions are located in the front section of this TAE.

Summary

- In all areas of development, one- and two-year-olds are striving for independence and developing their individuality.

- For toddlers, the most noticeable physical changes are those involving body proportions.

- Through physical play, toddlers strengthen their muscles, as well as refine their balance and coordination.

- Toddlers are eager to learn life skills, but parents must be patient enough to let them practice these skills.

- The rate of teething varies from child to child, but the sequence is always the same.

- Children will cooperate with toilet learning only when they are ready. Parents should not push their children, and should wait until the child shows signs of readiness.

- A great deal of intellectual development occurs during toddlerhood through experiences with toys, play, and books.

- Toddlers gradually build their vocabularies, but they may use a single word to describe similar objects or actions.

- Toddlers' behavior is inconsistent as they struggle for independence. They show their desire for independence by trying to do more things for themselves. At the same time, they ask for hugs of security and reassurance.

- Play can help toddlers gain greater independence and self-esteem. It is also a powerful tool for learning self-expression, exploration, and satisfaction.

- When toddlers begin to overcome separation anxiety, this is a significant event in emotional and social development.

- As toddlers are learning to be independent, they must also learn there are limits. Almost all children ages one to three have occasional temper tantrums as they learn these limits.

- Parents should take their toddlers to routine medical checkups as recommended by their doctors. These checkups are a way to detect and prevent certain health problems.

Reviewing Key Points

1. Describe how a toddler's body proportions change.

2. Sitting down in a small chair is an accomplishment for a toddler. What skills does the toddler need to achieve this accomplishment?

3. Why do toddlers have difficulty walking with adults?

4. Name five tasks toddlers can do with their improved small muscle skills as they approach their third birthdays.

5. Give an example of a life skill toddlers learn.

6. What are a parent's jobs during toddlers' mealtimes?

7. Should parents use food as rewards, bribes, or threats? Why or why not?

8. When should toddlers first visit the dentist? How many times a day should they brush their teeth?

9. Name two of the five steps involved in toilet learning.

10. True or false. Toddlers' interests are usually focused on what is happening to others around them.

11. Give an example of how a toddler may use imagination in his or her play.

12. True or false. Making a toddler repeat a word over and over until the pronunciation is correct is a good way to help the child build his or her vocabulary.

13. True or false. Parents should not deprive their toddler of a security object, such as a blanket or stuffed toy.

14. What is the difference between parallel play and cooperative play? Which type of play is more common among toddlers?

15. List three factors that help toddlers overcome separation anxiety.

16. What is the best way to deal with temper tantrums?

17. How often are routine medical checkups recommended for toddlers?

Learning by Doing

1. Collect pictures of toddlers and their parents. Use them to design a bulletin board with the title "Toddlerhood Opens up a Wonderful World."

2. With improved walking and grasping skills, toddlers become great explorers. Discuss safety practices parents can use to protect their toddlers from danger.

3. Discuss ways parents can encourage their toddlers to learn life skills. Suggest times throughout a typical day's schedule when toddlers could be encouraged to learn new life skills.

4. Interview a child psychologist about separation anxiety, temper tantrums, and other aspects of toddlers' emotional and social development.

5. Interview a child care worker or the parent of a toddler about the separation anxiety toddlers experience. Does it diminish gradually, or suddenly disappear? Are there situations that make the anxiety better or worse? Report your findings to the class.

Thinking Critically

1. As toddlers struggle to gain independence, parents have to decide when they should and should not give their toddlers help. Describe situations when this might occur. Discuss positive and negative parental reactions to these situations.

2. Observe toddlers and look for examples of the following steps in development: walking backward, sitting, climbing, jumping, turning pages of books, putting nesting toys together, feeding themselves, learning to use the toilet, imitating others, using imagination, talking, struggling for independence, playing in parallel play and cooperative play, overcoming separation anxiety, and having temper tantrums. Discuss your observations in class.

3. As a class, make a list of possible teachable moments parents can share with their toddlers.

4. In a small group, discuss the importance of parent-child interactions at all stages of language development.

5. Visit a toy store or bring a toy catalog to class. Make a list of toys that would be appropriate for toddlers and explain why. Make a list of toys that would not be appropriate for toddlers and explain why.

Chapter 13
Parents and Their Preschoolers

Objectives

After studying this chapter, you will be able to

- identify steps in the physical, intellectual, emotional, and social development of preschoolers.

- propose ways parents can help their children develop life skills.

- explain why enuresis occurs and how parents can help children overcome it.

- identify special language problems common among preschoolers.

- list ways parents can encourage the development of reading skills, math skills, and gender roles.

- explain the importance of play in the preschool years.

- explain ways parents can encourage their preschoolers' development.

Key Terms

preschooler
enuresis
stuttering
1 lisping
gender role
alternate play behavior
imaginative play

2 Parents can't help describing their preschoolers as charmers. (A **pre-schooler** is a child from ages three to five years.) Preschoolers are interested in everything. They are outgoing, and full of questions. These years can be great fun for parents and their children. Parents enjoy watching their pre-schoolers' delight in discovering their ever-expanding worlds, 13-1.

Within any group of preschoolers, different levels of physical, intellectual, emotional, and social development can be seen. Each child is an individual, and each has different opportunities for learning new skills. Each child is surrounded by a unique group of family members and caregivers. Although each child's development is unique, certain patterns of development are common among preschoolers. In this chapter, typical highlights in the development of three-, four-, and five-year-olds will be described.

Physical Development

Although preschoolers don't grow as fast as infants and toddlers, they take big steps in physical development. During the preschool period, children grow out of babyhood.

During the ages of three, four, and five, children grow taller, leaner, and better-coordinated. At the beginning of the preschool period, an average child is 37 inches tall and weighs 33 pounds. At the end of this period, an average child is 46 inches tall and weighs 44 pounds.

The proportion and shape of the child's body continue to change during the preschool years. The baby fat disappears, and the body assumes a 3 more adult shape. The legs become longer and straighter. The abdomen remains large, and the chest becomes broader.

1—**Vocabulary:** Look up terms in the glossary and discuss their meanings.

2—**Resource:** *Observing a Preschooler*, Activity A, SAG.

3—**Discuss:** During the preschool years, baby fat disappears and the body assumes a more adult shape. Briefly describe these physical changes.

13-1 _____
Preschoolers are fascinated with nature—even when it's raining!

1—Discuss: How do these changes help refine and improve preschoolers' body control?

2—Discuss: How can parents encourage large motor skill development? When preschoolers' accomplish a small success, should parents encourage them to try something more difficult?

During the toddler years, children were busy learning new motor skills like walking, running, and jumping. During the preschool years, children learn more advanced motor skills like hopping and skipping. They also refine their skills as their movements become smooth, controlled, and efficient.

Preschoolers need lots of active play to exercise their growing muscles, 13-2. They put a lot of energy into their play, so they tire quickly. They recover just as quickly and are soon ready to go again. Preschoolers' bones and joints are still somewhat soft and flexible. Parents need to keep an eye on children's activities since strenuous pulling and pushing could be harmful.

Large Motor Skills

Preschoolers are just starting to hop, skip, climb, and ride tricycles and bicycles. They enjoy practicing, for these newly-learned skills are challenging. As they practice these skills, they take great strides in developing large motor skills. Children at this stage also thrive on repeating a newly-acquired

13-2 _____
Active play is good for preschoolers, and it paves the way for future healthy exercise habits.

antic. When one playmate tries something new, all the children soon follow suit, repeating the stunt over and over again. This is how they learn new skills and refine and improve their body control.

Providing for Active Play

Parents can encourage their preschoolers' large muscle development in several ways. They can make sure their children have plenty of running room in safe and supervised areas. They can take their children to parks to play on swings, jungle gyms, and other play equipment. They can watch for signs their children are ready to try a new skill and then help them. For instance, a child may climb on a tricycle and then be frustrated if it doesn't move. A parent can show the child how to move the pedals so the tricycle will go.

Another way parents can encourage their preschoolers' development is to be generous with praise. Preschoolers are eager to please. They like to show off their new skills to an appreciative audience. They seek approval from adults. When they get it, they will happily repeat a stunt they have just mastered. They might even try a new, more challenging stunt.

Three-year-olds delight in active play that challenges their developing motor skills. For instance, they like to add swerving to their running style. Instead of running in a straight line, they swerve from one side to the other while keeping their balance. In addition, they like to stop suddenly and change direction. They can hop on both feet and jump from a height of 18 inches without help. They may try walking on their tiptoes for a change of pace. They now use alternate feet going up stairs, but still place both feet on each step coming down.

The ball-playing skills of three-year-olds show slight improvement. Children at this stage throw a ball by pushing it with their arms and shoulders. Their motions are rather awkward, and their aim is wild. They try to catch a ball by holding their arms straight out in front of them. If the thrower is skillful enough to land the ball in their arms, they can usually hold on to it. Luckily, preschoolers are not discouraged by their clumsiness. They love to play games that challenge their physical skills. All this practice eventually pays off—they gain coordination and improved skills.

By the time they are four, children are becoming more adventuresome. They add their own new challenges to their activities. They test their improved balance by whirling around, turning somersaults, and hanging upside-down, 13-3. They enjoy riding pedal toys, gaining speed as they grow stronger. They can hop several times in a row and may even combine running and hopping in a "long jump."

Parents may witness some hair-raising stunts by their four-year-olds. They love to climb up slides instead of using the ladders. They race to scramble to the top of the jungle-gym. They jump off the porch instead of walking down the steps. Bumps and tumbles are inevitable, but preschoolers are usually so busy they do not stop long for sympathy.

By five, preschoolers perform more gracefully with less wasted motion.

13-3 _____
Preschoolers stop their parents' hearts with their acrobatic stunts.

1—Discuss: Why is adult supervision important when preschoolers perform these activities?

2—Discuss: Briefly describe the ball-playing skills of preschool children. Do preschoolers discourage easily?

3—Reflect: Do you think parents can discourage creativity by being too protective?

1—Reflect: Can you remember the sense of accomplishment and confidence you felt when you first learned to ride a bike?

2—Discuss: Scissors fascinate four-year-olds. Why must parents carefully control what type of scissors is available to their children?

3—Resource: *Introducing Safety to Preschoolers,* color transparency CT-13, TR.

They run, swerve, and turn corners with even greater speed and smoothness. Their running turns to racing anytime a parent or a friend will accept their challenge. They enjoy competitive games of all kinds and may even set up their own simple obstacle courses.

Five-year-olds can separate control over different parts of their bodies. This can be seen in the way they throw and catch balls. By five, they draw their arms back and use their body weight to project the ball. When catching the ball, their elbows are now held at their sides. With improved body control, five-year-olds can hop on alternate feet. This ability allows them to add skipping to their list of motor skills. Skipping rope becomes a favorite activity.

Most five-year-olds are ready to try riding bicycles with training wheels. Learning this new skill is exciting for both parents and children, 13-4. Once children take off and feel comfortable with this new kind of balance, they enjoy praise for their accomplishment.

Small Motor Skills

Three-year-olds are still emerging from the baby stage of handling things. Their pincer grasp has long been refined, but the way they use their hands is still rather clumsy. They can build towers of blocks, placing each block with much concentration, but most of their towers are crooked. They can recognize shapes and positions on a form board, but they have trouble fitting objects in the board. Rather than turning an object to the correct position, they may try to force it.

Three-year-olds hold pencils much like adults. They can draw circles, crosses, rectangles, and triangles. They like to tell stories about these drawings, some of which may crudely resemble people.

Four-year-olds are much more precise with their small muscle skills.

13-4 _____
Bicycle safety is important, especially when first learning how to ride.

When building block towers, they try to place the blocks neatly. In fact, they may become so interested in a straight-sided tower they upset the blocks they had already stacked. Their drawing skills improve, but many of the figures they draw look like tadpoles with very large heads. They may start adding small lines to these shapes to represent arms and legs. Four-year-olds are fascinated with scissors. They may try to use any scissors they find, sometimes cutting whatever is in sight with disastrous results. Parents need to give preschoolers rounded-end scissors and keep sharp-pointed ones out of reach.

Five-year-olds expand their manipulative skills a great deal. With improved eye-hand coordination, they have much better control of their hands and fingers. They are no longer content with towers. Now their construction projects include bridges, houses, and churches with steeples. Some five-year-olds show an interest in working with tools. If they show this interest, parents would be wise to provide them their own child-sized tools. Adult-sized tools are often safety hazards. Other safety tips are illustrated in 13-5.

Dangers and Safeguards During the Preschool Years

13-5 _____
Preschoolers have the curiosity and motor skills to get themselves into trouble. Parents should try to constantly be aware of where their preschoolers are and what they are doing.

Preschoolers may want to use power tools just as their parents do. When not in use, power tools should be unplugged and kept well out of reach of children.

When playing near any body of water, children should wear safety approved life jackets.

Small swimming pools are fun, but preschoolers may slip, fall, even drown in a small amount of water. Parents should keep an eye on their children's water play.

Preschoolers like to run fast; they do not stop to think about rugs that slip. Some parents simply remove rugs during this period. Others make certain areas of the home "off limits."

1—Activity: Review each of the typical dangers and safeguards. Why must parents pay attention to where their preschoolers are and what they are doing at all times?

2—Discuss: Why should medications be kept out of reach of preschoolers?

Supervision is necessary when preschoolers play in public park areas. High slides, swinging swings, and moving merry-go-rounds may injure a child who is too excited to be cautious.

Preschoolers may mistake vitamins, asprins, or other medications for candy and eat them. All bottles should have safety lids, but more importantly, none should be left within the reach of children.

1—Discuss: What should parents do if a child shows a preference for using the left hand?

2—Resource: Life Skills of Preschoolers, Activity C, SAG.

3—Discuss: Why should parents encourage their children to practice life skills, even though parents can do these tasks for their children faster?

4—Reflect: Recall mealtimes in your childhood. What do you remember the most about them?

Handedness

Most children begin to show a preference for using one hand rather than the other sometime around their first birthdays. The preference is usually definite by age three. Most children are right-handed, but children who show a preference for using their left hands should be allowed to do so. Trying to force children to use their right hands will only frustrate them. Most schools allow a child to use his or her preferred hand. Parents can help by showing a left-handed child how to do various tasks in the most comfortable way. For instance, writing is more comfortable when the paper is positioned with the lower left-hand corner of the paper nearest the body.

Left-handed children may have some problems fitting into a right-handed world, but they can be encouraged to adapt. They may have to think ahead to take a left-handed desk or use left-handed scissors, but these are minor adjustments. Parents should not try to force their children to be right-handed. Instead, parents should watch for signs of hand preference. Then they should encourage their children to refine their hand coordination using whichever hand they prefer.

Life Skills

Parents are encouraged by the improving life skills of their preschoolers. During the preschool period, children learn to handle most of their eating, dressing, and grooming tasks themselves. These achievements please both preschoolers and their parents, but life skills are not achieved without effort. Children need lots of practice to refine their large and small motor skills. Parents need lots of patience to help and encourage their children without pushing them too far. As in all parent-child interactions, love, understanding, cooperation, and clear guidelines lead to success.

Eating

By the time children reach the preschool stage, they are ready to begin learning table manners. They will follow the examples set by their parents and siblings. If they see mealtimes as pleasant, sharing family experiences, they are likely to behave well. The mood and atmosphere can enhance or upset children's appetites. Regular mealtimes help preschoolers develop good eating habits. Snacks may be allowed as long as they do not interfere with children's appetites for regular meals. Nutritious snack items, such as fresh fruit or whole-grain crackers, are preferred. Sweet snacks may be eaten occasionally, and in moderation.

Preschoolers can generally eat the same food as the rest of the family. Parents should not have to prepare special foods for them if they may not like what is being served. Hungry preschoolers can learn to eat what is on the table or wait until the next meal.

On the other hand, parents should accept the fact preschoolers are well-known for their food fads. They may suddenly refuse a food they used to like. They may ask for a certain food, like breakfast cereal, for both breakfast and lunch several days in a row. The fads will pass with time as long as they are not blown out of proportion. A parent may be willing to serve bowl after bowl of breakfast cereal. That same parent may refuse to prepare a cheese soufflé three meals in a row. Common sense is a parent's best guideline.

Introducing new foods to preschoolers is sometimes difficult. Success is more likely if just a small amount of the new food is served along with other foods the children like. Also, preschoolers are more willing to try a new food if they have seen a friend or favorite relative eat it.

Children may have fewer problems at mealtimes if they are involved with shopping and preparing food. Preschoolers who learn about how food looks and smells and how it is cooked are likely to have fewer food dislikes. At the grocery store, parents may want to point out certain foods, explain how they are grown or manufactured, and describe how they are prepared and served. When children help pick out fruits and vegetables, they may enjoy eating them more. Children who help make peanut butter sandwiches are more likely to eat them. Children may drink more milk if they are allowed to pour it from a small lightweight pitcher into a sturdy plastic mug. See 13-6.

Dressing

Children are individuals. This simple fact is obvious in all areas of development, including dressing skills. Some children advance quickly in small motor skill development. They learn to work buttons and zippers earlier than other children. Some children learn dressing skills more slowly. Still other children are so determined to be independent they insist on dressing themselves at early ages.

13-6

Children enjoy helping with meal preparation and can learn to set the table.

Wise parents learn to watch for teachable moments. When children show an interest in dressing skills, parents can be ready to help them learn those skills. Children's first attempts at getting dressed are slow and clumsy. (This is true even though children may have been undressing quite easily for months.) Pants may go on backward, and shoes may end up on the wrong feet. Parents must try to remain calm, patient, and encouraging. Trying to hurry children only makes them feel discouraged and frustrated. Laughing at their efforts hurts their tender feelings. Making negative comments lessens their desire to learn.

It takes tact to help a child without pushing or interfering. Patience and encouragement are the keys. When a child has trouble buttoning a shirt, a parent may want to take over. The shirt would end up in place, but the child would have lost a chance to learn. A better solution would be to calmly explain how to do it, and reassure the child he or she can do it. When the child succeeds, his or her efforts should be praised. If the child becomes frustrated after trying for a reasonable time, the parent can then offer assistance.

Difficult tasks like tying shoelaces may be broken down into simple steps. As each step is mastered, children gain confidence, 13-7.

By the end of the preschool years, most children can dress by themselves. They can handle buttons, zippers, and shoelaces. They are ready to go to school, and will need little, if any, help in dressing from their teachers.

Grooming

Preschoolers still need guidance and assistance in some grooming tasks. They need help and guidance to brush their teeth thoroughly. They need help shampooing their hair and cutting their fingernails and toenails. They can

1—**Discuss:** How can allowing children to help shop for and prepare food help them have fewer problems at mealtime?

2—**Discuss:** How can parents encourage their children to become interested in dressing skills?

3—**Activity:** Bring a child's shoe to class and practice how you, as a parent, would teach your child to tie a shoe.

4—**Discuss:** What types of guidance and assistance do preschoolers need from parents regarding grooming tasks?

1—Vocabulary: Define *enuresis*. When is this most likely to be a problem for children? What may cause the problem? When might medical attention be necessary?

2—Discuss: How should parents handle the "Why?" questions of preschoolers?

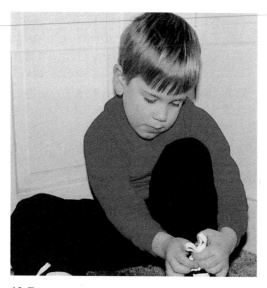

13-7
Five-year-olds may be able to tie their shoelaces if they have been shown how to do it in a step-by-step process.

handle most other tasks, such as washing their face and hands, by themselves. If they have a simple hairstyle, they enjoy combing their hair while watching themselves in a mirror.

At the beginning of the preschool period, children may still need some help using the toilet. If they can recognize the need to use the bathroom, they have taken a big step. Clothes that are easy to remove help preschoolers become more independent. By the time they are five, most children can use the toilet and get dressed again by themselves. These skills are necessary for children who will be entering kindergarten.

Enuresis

Enuresis, or bed-wetting, is a problem that affects some children during the preschool or early school-age years. Almost every child has an occasional accident at night. If the child is reassured, rather than punished, the problem has a better chance of disappearing.

Incomplete toilet learning may be the cause of enuresis in a young child. If the problem is disappearing gradually, parents may just need to be patient and reassuring. If it continues, a pediatrician may be able to advise parents how to help their child learn to use the toilet.

Enuresis may also be caused by physical or psychological factors. Possible physical causes include improper functioning of the bladder, the sphincter muscles, or the urinary tract. These factors can be checked with a medical exam. If the exam shows no physical cause, the problem can best be treated with additional emotional reassurance.

A common psychological cause of enuresis is a new stress in the child's life. If bed-wetting is treated as a distress signal, parents will realize their child may need more comfort and reassurance. Then the problem is more likely to disappear. Parents who punish and belittle a child for wetting the bed may make the problem worse. A cycle may develop. The child is upset and wets the bed. The parents become angry. Then the child is more upset and wets the bed more often. If the parents become even more angry, the situation will get even worse. Parents who realize the cause of enuresis can help their child find a solution.

Intellectual Development

Children's intellectual development progresses in an orderly way. Children construct their own concepts; they do not simply accept ready-made concepts and principles. Preschoolers still find it hard to look at things from another person's point of view. Their favorite question is "Why?" They need to understand before they are ready to believe. Parents sometimes say they can almost see their preschoolers thinking.

Preschoolers are most interested in their immediate surroundings and what is happening at the moment. They are keenly aware of the environment and study it with all five senses, 13-8. This makes them delightful companions on family outings and vacations. They smell odors and hear sounds adults would not notice on their own.

Three-year-olds are intent upon finding out about the size and shape of everything, what purpose each thing serves, and how it works. They use what they learn to classify objects. Their increased knowledge about the world helps them enjoy humorous situations. They laugh at silly ideas such as hiding a giraffe under a table or teaching a fish to fly.

Parents find they can begin to reason with their three-year-olds. Children at this age have the language skills to listen and the intellectual skills to understand. They are beginning to learn the concept of cause and effect. They may carry this to extremes, want-ing to know the cause of everything that happens. They constantly ask "Why?" Their questions may irritate adults, but children need answers to their questions in order to learn about the world. Without explanations from adults, children often draw incorrect conclusions about what they see and hear.

Three-year-olds have vivid imaginations. They are not always sure where reality ends and fantasy begins. They love adventure stories and will connect many stories with themselves. They may say "I chased a lion," or "I'm going to climb higher than Jack in the beanstalk!" Parents should not confuse children's tall tales with lies, for children at this stage do not intend to lie. Sometimes parents may want to play along with the children's stories. Parents may add to the stories, making them so silly children end up laughing. At other times, parents may want to help their children sort fact from fiction. They may listen attentively and then ask "But you didn't really see a monster in the garage, did you?"

Four-year-olds are aware of their growing abilities. They may even remind their parents they are not babies anymore. As their reasoning matures, they arrive at logical conclusions that often amaze parents.

The line between fact and fantasy is still hazy for four-year-olds. They have great imaginations and love to tell tall tales. At the same time, their memories and language skills have improved. They can repeat factual stories with accurate details. Parents have to stay alert to know which stories to believe.

Most four-year-olds like to answer the telephone. The messages they take are usually, but not always, reliable. Preschoolers may be so fascinated with the telephone they pick it up even when it has not rung. Some are content to listen to the dial tone. Others may try dialing or pushing buttons until they find someone who will talk to them. (Depending on whom they

13-8 _____
Preschoolers learn by doing. By planting seeds and then watering them, they learn how plants grow.

1—Resource: *Reasoning with Preschoolers*, Activity B, SAG.

2—Discuss: How can parents help their three-year-olds sort fact from fiction without discouraging their imaginations?

3—Discuss: How can parents teach preschoolers firm limits and discipline in using the telephone?

1—**Activity:** Outline several ways parents can help their preschoolers understand the concept of time.

2—**Discuss:** Why do parents need to establish rules for five-year-olds?

3—**Discuss:** How does symbolism help five-year-olds express creativity in their play?

4—**Resource:** *Intellectual Development Concepts*, Activity D, SAG.

reach, this can be expensive.) Parents can use this opportunity to talk with their children about what they can and cannot do. Firm limits and consistent discipline help children learn to control their behavior.

Time is a difficult concept for preschoolers to understand. Most preschoolers relate the word *yesterday* with anytime in the past, from several hours ago to several days ago. They recognize the word *tomorrow* as a time to come, but they do not know how far away that time is, 13-9.

Five-year-olds appreciate humor and unusual situations. They may become engrossed in television programs and roll on the floor, laughing at funny episodes. Their attention span is lengthening. They are ready for the somewhat structured learning environments of kindergarten.

Five-year-olds are ready to learn about right and wrong. A year or two earlier, they could not understand why they could scribble on paper but not on walls. By five, they are well aware some things are right and others are wrong. They know there are some

13-9
Preschoolers do not have a good concept of time. Parents should be understanding when their children grow tired of waiting even a few minutes.

things they are not allowed to do. They begin to understand rules, even though they may not understand the principles behind the rules. Children this age learn if they disobey rules they will be punished. This is an age when parents can help their children learn to control their own behavior. Parents can show children their behavior produces results that affect other people.

The development of symbolic thinking during the preschool period allows children to use materials around them in a variety of interesting ways. Preschoolers play with a lot of imagination. Parents are often amazed at their abilities to express creativity through symbolism. A stuffed bear becomes a baby they can cuddle or scold. Small pieces of paper become tickets they can use to ride a train they have constructed from boxes. Plastic cups become telephones simply by putting them up to their ears. Big, empty boxes have lots of possibilities.

The kinds of learning experiences preschoolers have affect their overall intellectual development. The neurons in the brain can still make lots of new connections if they are stimulated to do so. Alert parents can help this happen by making the most of teachable moments that occur. Preschoolers are inquisitive, and they want to figure things out. Learning games during these years can provide valuable intellectual growth opportunities. They can also promote a positive attitude toward the desire to learn.

Many three- and four-year-olds attend preschools or child care centers, while many five-year-olds enter kindergarten. For these children, this is a first experience with schooling. In fact, it is often a child's first experience with adults other than friends or relatives. For many preschoolers, it is also the first time they spend much time with their peers.

Preschools, child-care centers, and kindergartens can help children learn,

13-10. The teachers provide instruction that boosts intellectual development. Children read stories, play indoors and outdoors, sing, dance, do art projects, and work on prereading and prewriting skills. Spending time with other children helps preschoolers develop their social and emotional skills, as well.

Language Development

The preschool period is a time of great advances in language skills. Children learn to express their feelings and thoughts more clearly. They learn to consistently add an *-ed* ending to verbs when speaking in the past tense. For instance, they may bring a broken toy to a parent and say "It breaked." Although the grammar is incorrect, they are learning to talk about things that happened in the past.

During the preschool period, children's speaking vocabularies will grow from about 900 words to about 2200 words. Their sentences lengthen to several words. Eventually, they will add conjunctions like *and* or *but* to form even longer sentences. This also shows they can connect two related facts such as "I fell down and hurt my knee."

Preschoolers use language to ask questions, talk about imaginary situations, and exchange ideas with others, 13-11. They use language to label and classify things. They love to repeat new words that identify objects in their environment. When they see the moon, they may say "The moon is up, up and it looks like a big ball." Preschoolers also use language to get things they want and control the behavior of others. They may say "Gimme a cookie" when they are hungry or "No, that's mine" when a playmate tries to take a toy.

1—Discuss: When children add *-ed* to their verbs, what does this indicate about their concept of time?

2—Activity: Listen to audiotapes of preschoolers talking. Although they do not always use correct grammar, do they still seem to get their message across?

13-10 _____
Preschools, child-care centers, and kindergartens can provide an excellent learning environment for three-, four-, and five-year-olds.

13-11 _____
This preschooler points to boats in the water. He has the language to tell his father what he has seen.

1—Discuss: Why is it important for parents to watch their own use of slang language and exaggerations?

2—Enrich: Invite a speech therapist to discuss how parents can deal with problems such as stuttering. How can parents guide children's overall language development?

3—Discuss: Why is it important to detect speech problems early?

Although their vocabularies are growing, preschoolers still understand many more words than they actually use in conversation. Parents should keep this in mind. Any conversation within a preschooler's hearing range is likely to be understood, or at least the child will try to understand it. Misinterpretations and misunderstandings are common among preschoolers. Children may worry when they overhear adult conversations with phrases like "I could have kicked her," "I almost died when," and "I thought he'd never come home." Children are learning the literal meanings of words. They do not yet understand exaggerations or slang expressions.

As with any other area of development, parents may worry about some apparent language problems of their preschool children. Many of these concerns are so common authorities believe they really aren't problems at all. Still, they may cause concern for some parents.

Stuttering may appear in some children's speech patterns during the preschool years. In most cases, the problem is really one of learning how to express themselves. Preschoolers' thoughts are more advanced than their vocabularies and speaking skills. As a result, they may inject long pauses in their sentences. They may stop in the middle of a sentence and then start again, or they may repeat one sound or phrase. Preschoolers may say "I g-g-g-go outside," or "Let-let-let me have a cookie." Usually stuttering is temporary, and parents should not be overly concerned. The less attention parents focus on temporary problems, the sooner they will stop.

Some preschoolers may begin stuttering to get attention. Other children who hear a playmate stutter may try to imitate the sounds. Parents who command children to finish what they are saying or to stop stuttering may increase the problem. Allowing enough time for a child to talk, without calling attention to the problem, may help. Parents should not try to push or speed the flow of speech of their preschoolers. That kind of pressure tends to create more serious stuttering problems.

Lisping may occur because preschoolers still have difficulty pronouncing some sounds, such as s sounds. Most lisping problems are not serious and are quickly self-corrected. Parents who are concerned should discuss this with their pediatrician or family doctor. If the child seems to have a problem, a checkup with a speech therapist may be recommen-ded. The earlier a problem is detected and treated, the easier it is to correct.

Most parents experience their preschoolers' fascination with "toilet talk." Using toilet talk is one way preschoolers can be sure to get laughs from their peers. They sense it is forbidden, and they are thrilled by the reactions of their parents or caregivers. Calling someone a "pee-pee-poo-poo" is sure to get attention from adults and giggles from friends.

Parents cannot stop all toilet talk. Preschoolers use it when they play together. However, parents do not have to allow such language in their presence. If parents explain those words are not to be used around them or other adults, children will get the message. Parents should try to be calm and firm about this, not outraged and emotional. (If children find out certain words truly upset their parents, they may use them just to frustrate them.) Some parents solve the problem by suggesting substitute expressions that are not so offensive. "Goodness sakes" is an adult expression children like to use.

Some children may still use baby talk even after they are capable of using correct language. When they are tired, they may resort to expressions that worked when they were smaller such as "Bobby up." Parents can help by gently encouraging children to talk in a more appropriate way. Parents should not encourage these baby expressions because they are cute. As children associate with others, they may have trouble making themselves understood, and other children may make fun of them.

In some homes, two languages are spoken. This may have both positive and negative effects on preschoolers. On the positive side, children can learn a second language more easily when they are young, 13-12. The window of opportunity for learning a second language is from one to five years. The ability to speak two languages is valuable. On the nega-tive side, some children who grow up in bilingual homes may have trouble learning the fine points of either language. Parents need to decide which will be the primary language used in the home. Parents should think about which language will be most useful for the children throughout their lives. This should be the primary language, although both can be spoken.

Reading and Math Skills

A good way to enhance children's language development and further their reading skills is to read to them. Parents can introduce their preschoolers to letters by reading books about the alphabet. Another way is to help them become aware of the use of letters in the things they see around them. Many parents teach their children to recite the alphabet. There is nothing wrong with this. However, children learn more about letters and their sounds when they connect the letters with the symbols that represent them and the words in which they are used.

Reading to children gives parents opportunities to expand their children's curiosity and awareness. It also gives children a greater incentive to want to learn to read by themselves, 13-13. Story time can be a wonderful, cuddly time for sharing. It is the basis for many treasured memories of both parents and children.

Most preschoolers learn to recite numbers long before they can actually count. Reciting the numbers from one to ten does not indicate an understanding of what numbers represent. Preschoolers may point to different blocks as they recite numbers one to ten. They may touch one block several times and look confused when there are some blocks left after they have said ten.

13-12 _____

In this young girl's home, two languages are spoken. If her parents guide and encourage her, she will become fluent in both languages.

1—Discuss: What do you think are the advantages and disadvantages of growing up in a bilingual home?

2—Discuss: Why is reading to children important during the preschool years?

3—Resource: *Read Me a Story*, reproducible master 13-1, TR

4—Discuss: How can parents help their preschoolers develop math skills?

1—**Example:** Three-year-olds enjoy doing things for their parents. Cite examples of simple tasks parents can ask their three-year-olds to do.

13-13 _____
Parents can inspire their children to read on their own.

Holding up fingers to answer the question "How old are you?" is one of the first lessons in what numbers really mean. Children know, for instance, after their birthday, they may hold up one more finger.

Preschoolers gradually sense quantitative thinking. Most five-year-olds know six blocks are "more than" four blocks. They know taking three cookies is more than taking just one. Eventually, they learn more number concepts. When they can follow instructions to take two toy cars outside, eat five bites of apple, and build a tower of seven blocks, parents will know they understand numbers. If parents are enthusiastic about these basic math concepts, they may help set the stage for their children's success in future math challenges.

Emotional and Social Development

Preschoolers' advances in physical and intellectual development directly affect their social and emotional development. They use their new physical skills to play and interact with parents, siblings, and peers. They feel more confident of their hand movements and coordination. Their improved language skills allow them to express their thoughts and feelings to others, 13-14. If children are surrounded with love and under-standing, their self-esteem grows stronger. They learn to become more

13-14 _____
As preschoolers gain self-confidence, they are more willing to share their talents.

self-reliant. They are still egocentric, but they begin to sense other people are individuals, too, with their own needs and feelings.

Three-year-olds usually have sunny and cooperative personalities. Their frustrations lessen as their physical skills improve. Three-year-olds still seek comfort and security from par-ents, especially when they are hungry or tired. They are rela-tively agreeable to parental requests. In fact, they enjoy doing things for their parents, and love the approval and praise they receive in return. They are learning to take turns and practice give-and-take. Parents find they can begin to reason with their three-year-olds.

Three-year-olds make friends easily. They prefer cooperative play (play involving interactions among playmates) to parallel play (play beside playmates). They may express a prefer-ence for one friend over another. For instance, they may tell a friend "You can come to my birthday party, but Johnny can't."

As preschoolers become more mature, they display their anger verbally instead of physically. Shouting

13-15 _____
Preschoolers are generally happy people, and they make friends easily.

"I don't like you," is an improvement over their previous hitting and kicking routines. Three-year-olds, however, are happy much more often than they are angry, 13-15. They like others to be happy, too. They often try to comfort playmates who are hurt or upset.

Three-year-olds may reveal new fears of the dark or monsters. They may also be afraid of animals and thunderstorms. Children at this age have vivid imaginations. They often invent frightening creatures in their minds. Parents should never encour-age these fears with threats of the boogeyman or with scary stories. Instead, parents should be ready to offer love and reassurance to calm their children's fears.

Four-year-olds experience many advances emotionally. Some of these changes may make children this age seem a little less pleasant as they were at three. Four-year-olds are learning more about how to express their emotions verbally, which takes time and effort. Often, their emotions seem less controlled. They may seem moody, or feel upset longer as they try to deal with their feelings, 13-16. As their language skills develop, they may argue and quarrel more with playmates. (In the past, they were more likely to fight with playmates physically.)

Four-year-olds are more inde-pendent, and want to do things for themselves. When a child cannot do something alone, he or she may be really frustrated, and impatient for an adult's help. Another time, if an adult offers the same help, the child may feel he or she is being treated like a baby. Parents need to respect a four-year-old's desire to do more things alone.

Four-year-olds show an increased interest in friends, but they are still bound to their homes and families. As they play together, they may boast about who has the biggest house, the strongest dad, or the smartest mom. A four-year-old needs to feel he or she

1—Discuss: How do preschoolers of vari-ous ages handle conflict?

2—Reflect: Can you remember fears you had as a preschooler?

13-16
Four-year-olds work at expressing their emotions verbally, and in appropriate ways. They may seem moody, but they're often just thinking about how to communicate their feelings.

occupies a special place in the family—one nobody else can occupy. Four-year-olds often ask their parents for approval, as if they are trying to prove to themselves they are worthy of their parents' love.

Four-year-olds like cooperative play. They are learning to ask for things instead of just grabbing whatever they want. They may even offer to share their possessions with a special friend. On the other hand, cooperative play does not always work with four-year-olds. Sometimes they are too bossy or inconsiderate. For example, they may suggest taking turns but run ahead of their playmates instead. They may try to prevent a child from joining their group, 13-17.

Some four-year-olds resent being told how to do things. These children like to think they know it all and can do it all. They may refuse to accept responsibility for mistakes or misdeeds

13-17
Four-year-olds are sometimes inconsiderate. They may refuse to allow another child to play with them.

by blaming someone else, often an imaginary companion.

Around a child's fifth birthday, the child may seem more peaceful and cooperative. At this age, preschoolers' emotions are more settled. They have grown more used to handling their feelings. Five-year-olds are often more patient, generous, and conscientious. They are more reasonable in a quarrel, for they have developed a sense of fairness. They have become more realistic and practical.

Five-year-olds continue to depend on parents for emotional support and approval. They ask permission before beginning new activities. They are very proud of their parents and delight in helping them. When they are asked to perform small chores, they feel really good about themselves. They may reveal a protective nature toward younger brothers and sisters. They may even volunteer to entertain younger siblings for short periods of time, 13-18.

Five-year-olds are very social and talkative. They seem to prefer friends of their own age and gender. This friendliness attracts playmates. Preschoolers may develop strong friendships, and even pick a best friend. Five-year-olds are more respectful of the property rights of their playmates, so there is less quarreling. When they are angry, they are more likely to call names than to strike blows.

Developing Gender Roles

Preschoolers are great mimics. They love to model other people's behavior. Most children, by the end of this period, have developed a clear sense of being male or female. They learn to distinguish a man from a woman, or a boy from a girl based on visual clues.

Children also begin to form their gender roles during the preschool period. A person's **gender role** includes his or her behaviors, attitudes, and beliefs about men and women. Preschoolers' gender roles are conditioned by what they see in their homes. They model their behavior and attitudes after those of their parents and family members. Their parents may have traditional or nontraditional gender roles. For instance, one child's family may feel a woman's role is to stay at home with the children. This child's idea of women might be very different from another child whose mother is a firefighter.

In the preschool years, children are developing their sense of how men should act and how women should act. Parents should keep this in mind, and help their children develop a healthy picture of both men and women. Often, children express their ideas about men and women through pretend play, such as house. Parents can learn a lot about what their children are thinking by simply watching them play.

13-18 _____
"Reading" to his younger sister helps this preschooler feel he has an important role in his family. It also gives him a chance to show off his growing vocabulary.

1—Enrich: Observe a group of five-year-olds and describe their social interactions.

2—Example: Children develop gender roles from examples set by parents. Give examples of healthy roles mothers and fathers can exhibit.

1

2

1—Resource:
Children's Play,
Activity E, SAG.

2—Vocabulary:
Explain what *alternate play behavior* means and why it is an important learning activity.

3—Reflect: Did your parents ever reprimand you in front of your peers? If so, how did it make you feel?

The Importance of Play

Children learn as they play, and they play as they learn. To children, learning and playing are the same. They do not think of them as separate activities.

Children need to play, just as they need to eat and sleep. They need active play for their physical development. It helps them achieve large muscle skills as well as coordination and balance. See 13-19. Children need to play with a variety of objects to further their intellectual development. Through play, they learn to think, reason, and expand their curiosity. Toys that can be pushed, pulled, rolled, or thrown help them learn basic scientific concepts. Household objects can help them learn some of the basic concepts of arithmetic—more, less, empty, full, bigger, smaller. Play with other children encourages emotional and social development. They learn how to get along with others, express their feelings, take turns, and share.

Play does not have to be planned and structured to be valuable. Parents can help their children make games out of everyday experiences. Drawing on a chalkboard in the corner of the kitchen while parents are preparing dinner may be a lot of fun. Stacking plastic bowls and sorting canned goods are other types of play. Children may enjoy fluffing pillows and helping to make beds. Serving a cup of tea to their parents as they are playing house delights children. It also shows children their parents are interested in their activities.

Preschoolers typically reveal **alternate play behavior**. They do something and then wait for a response from their playmates. They will then repeat the activity again and again, waiting each time for a response before continuing.

Many preschoolers spend quite a bit of time in solitary play. When alone,

13-19
Active play helps this child's physical development.

they use their imagination to think of play activities. They are very social by nature, however, so they may often prefer to play where they can interact with their parents.

Playing with siblings or peers is fun and educational for preschoolers, but disagreements are bound to happen. Most of the time children can settle their own differences. An adult should watch the situation and step in, if needed, to settle serious disputes.

Children's self-esteem is strongly influenced by their peers' reactions. If they are accepted by their playmates, they tend to be pleasant and cooperative. If their playmates reject them, they are more likely to be disruptive and uncooperative. Parents should try to avoid reprimanding a preschooler in the presence of his or her friends. Later, the friends might make fun of the child for getting into trouble. This can hurt a child's self-esteem.

Preschoolers are competitive in their play activities. Each tries to outdo

13-20
Preschoolers use imagination as they dress up and experiment with different roles and behaviors.

the others. In their games, they like to win prizes. This competitive spirit may be encouraging for some. The child who never wins, however, may feel hurt and develop a damaged self-image. Parents need to be aware of competitive games that create damaging images. Games in which everyone has a chance to succeed may be better in some situations.

Imaginative Play

Play involving fantasy or imagination is important for preschoolers. In **imaginative play**, children pretend to be persons or objects other than themselves. For instance, a box becomes a race car, and the child becomes its driver. Imaginative play allows children to try things out mentally. See 13-20. Acting out an experience helps children sort out their thoughts and feelings. When children play house, they often act out family situations they have experienced or they would like to have. Imaginative play is also an excellent way for parents to introduce a new experience children will encounter in the near future. If a trip to the zoo is planned, for instance, parents may act out how they will walk around the grounds and describe animals they will see.

Nightmares

Children have dreams, but they are usually unable to tell their parents about them. Bad dreams or nightmares may frighten both the child and the parent. This is especially true if the child is in a state of distress, or who is half awake and half asleep. Many nightmares are directly related to fears aroused by some creature or crisis in the child's life. Any threat the child feels during the day may be revealed dramatically at night.

A child who cries out at night can usually be calmed with some cuddling and a few soothing words. A parent may want to stay in the room until the child is asleep again. Turning on a small night-light or leaving the door open a little may ease a child's fears. Preschoolers often express fear of something in the closet or under the bed. In this case, a parent may want to "chase" the fearful object away with a broom. Telling a child there is nothing to fear is not nearly as reassuring as accepting his or her concern and physically doing something about it. As children mature, their fears are likely to disappear, and their sleeping patterns will become more stable.

1—Discuss: Can competitive play be damaging to children who never seem to win? What can parents and care-givers do to help these children find some successes?

2—Discuss: How can parents use imaginative play to introduce a new experience to their children?

3—Discuss: How can parents help their children deal with nightmares? What might cause nightmares?

13-21

Routine medical checkups help ensure preschoolers are healthy and growing as they should.

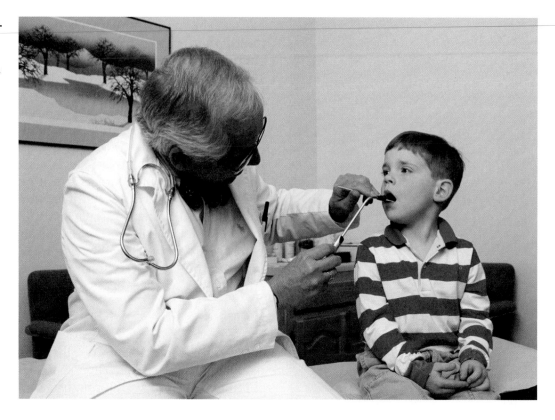

Medical Checkups for Preschoolers

During the preschool years, fewer routine medical checkups are needed than before. The American Academy of Pediatrics recommends one checkup each at ages three, four, and five years. These medical checkups are important for monitoring children's health. They allow the doctor to detect any problems, and treat them as early as possible. Routine medical checkups are in addition to any doctor visits needed for illness or injury.

During medical checkups, parents can ask any questions they might have about their preschooler's health, nutrition, and growth. Parents may also want to ask the doctor's advice about any sleep problems, bed-wetting, or discipline. The doctor will check the preschooler's growth by measuring height and weight. The child's blood pressure and physical condition will be noted, 13-21. Any necessary tests will be done to check the child's health. Appropriate immunizations will also be given.

During the preschool years, children should also visit their dentists and eye doctors regularly. A child's first vision and hearing screenings are recommended between the ages of three and four. (Some children will have these screenings earlier if problems are suspected.)

Children can also be given a developmental screening, such as the *Denver Developmental Screening Test*. This test assesses a child's skills on a number of items. It measures the child's skills for those items, as compared to the skills of other children the same age for those same items. This test can identify if the child has a *developmental delay* (skill level that is substantially below that of more than half of children the same age as the child) in social, language, large motor, and small motor areas. Many doctors, early childhood educators, and other child-development specialists administer the Denver Developmental Screening Test.

Preschoolers are very social and may develop strong friendships.

CHILD DEVELOPMENT

1—Resource:
Developmental Highlights for Preschoolers, transparency master 13-2, TR.

2—Discuss:
Compare the large and small motor skills of preschoolers of various ages. How do these types of development help children adapt to their world and refine their skills?

3 Years

Physical Development*
Large Motor Skills

Improves overall coordination.

Walks with good posture.

Still has protruding abdomen but body is lengthening.

Likes to run. Can stop suddenly and change direction.

Adds swerving to running style. Can maintain balance.

Can walk across balance beam.

Walks on tiptoes.

Hops on both feet; may begin to hop on one foot.

Jumps from height of 18 inches (46 cm) without assistance.

Likes to try jumping from greater heights if assistance is given.

Goes up stairs using alternate feet.

May continue to use both feet on each step coming down stairs.

Enjoys galloping, jumping, and walking to music.

Is able to dance to fast music.

Is able to use pedal toys.

Can throw ball underhand and retain balance, but aim is wild.

Can catch ball if it is thrown to land in arms; holds arms stationary in front of body and will not move them to reach ball.

Can pound with hammer.

Small Motor Skills

Has well-refined pincer grasp but hand manipulation is still clumsy.

Builds crooked block towers.

Uses spoon to feed self.

Can pour liquid from small pitcher with little spilling.

Copies a circle and draws a straight line.

Draws crosses, rectangles, and triangles.

Strings large beads.

Makes crude shapes with modeling clay.

Is able to brush teeth but may need assistance.

Is able to unbutton buttons and pull up large zippers.

Intellectual Development

Studies the environment with all five senses.

Remembers relationships and is able to form concepts about them.

Can remember objects and compare them to other objects.

Has a vivid imagination but is not always sure where reality ends and fantasy begins.

Tells tall tales.

Wants to find out about size and shape of everything.

Asks questions about how things work.

Constantly asks "Why?" Tries to understand cause and effect.

Begins to understand when parents try to reason with him or her.

Connects adventures with self and may inject self into adventure stories.

Likes to listen to stories read by parents.

Can enjoy humorous situations.

Has vocabulary of 900 to 1000 words.

Speaks in two to five word sentences.

May understand more of adult conversation than adults realize.

Can hold up fingers to indicate age.

Can count two or more objects.

Can count by rote to ten.

Emotional and Social Development

Personality

Is usually cooperative, happy, and agreeable.

Feels less frustration because motor skills have improved.

Is learning to share and take turns.

Follows directions and takes pride in doing things for others.

Learns more socially acceptable ways of displaying feelings.

May substitute language for primitive displays of feelings.

May show fear of dark, animals, stories, and monsters.

May feel jealous.

Family

May still seek comfort from parents when tired or hungry.

May act in a certain way to please parents.

Seeks praise and affection from parents.

Friends

Seeks status among peers.

May attempt to comfort and remove cause of distress of playmates or siblings.

Makes friends easily.

Seeks friends on own initiative.

Begins to be choosy about companions, preferring one over another.

Uses language to make friends and alienate others.

Prefers cooperative play to parallel play.

(continued)

*These charts are not exact timetables for development. Individuals may perform certain activities earlier or later than indicated in the charts.

CHILD DEVELOPMENT

4 Years

1—Discuss:
Preschoolers' emotional and social development improves their abilities to play, get along with peers, and become cooperative family members.

Physical Development
Large Motor Skills
Further refines balance and coordination.
Likes to whirl around, hang upside-down, turn somersaults.
Likes to run, turning corners quickly.
Can hop several times in a row.
Goes up and down stairs using alternate feet.
Likes to jump, sometimes from dangerous heights.
Is able to execute standing and running long jumps.
Rides pedal toys, gaining speed with increased strength.
May be able to ride bicycle with training wheels.
Climbs jungle gym with greater speed and confidence.
Plays on playground equipment such as slide and seesaw.
Throws ball overhand and may be able to catch ball with hands.
Is able to dress self more easily.

Small Motor Skills
Further refines dexterity of hands and fingers.
Builds straight towers of blocks with steady hands, but may knock down existing tower.
Uses spoon, fork, and knife to eat.
Laces shoes and wants to learn to make knots.
Cuts on line with round-end scissors.
When drawing, adds lines to body shapes to represent arms and legs.
Brushes teeth, combs hair, and washes hands.
Is able to follow finger plays and do them with assistance.
Makes crude shapes with modeling clay.
Enjoys finger painting.

Intellectual Development
Is aware of intellectual advances and may remind parents "I'm not a baby anymore."
Continues to ask "Why?" and "How?"
Improves reasoning abilities and can form logical conclusions.
May still confuse fact and fantasy.
Likes to try new games and test ability to play them.
Has only a vague concept of time; relates the word *yesterday* with the past and *tomorrow* with the future.
Memory is continually enhanced by growing language skills.
Has vocabulary of 1500 words.
Answers telephone and takes simple messages, but may not always be reliable.
Likes to use silly names and words and enjoys play on words.
Can retell a story following the correct sequence of events.
Loves to tell tall tales.
Likes rhyming poems.
Realizes power of words and often begins statements with "You know what?"
Speech may be rapid, disconnected, and repetitious.
May exhibit mild stuttering because thinking is faster than ability to talk.
Can begin to identify opposites.
Identifies some colors by name.
Identifies use of objects in pictures.

Emotional and Social Development
Personality
May seem less pleasant than at age three.
May be more moody, tries to express emotions verbally.
Strives for independence; resents being treated as a baby.
May be stubborn and quarrelsome.
Resents directions; may think he or she knows it all and can do it all.
Learns to ask for things instead of snatching things from others.
Is increasingly aware of attitudes and asks for approval.

Family
Needs and seeks parental approval often.
Has strong sense of family and home.
May quote parents and boast about parents to friends.

Friends   1
Becomes more interested in friends than in adults.
Shares possessions and toys, especially with special friends.
Suggests taking turns but may be unable to wait for his or her own turn.
Likes to play with friends in cooperative play activities.

(continued)

1—Discuss: How do the new intellectual achievements of preschoolers contribute to their total personality development?

CHILD DEVELOPMENT

5 Years

Physical Development
Large Motor Skills
Performs physical activities more gracefully and with less wasted motion.

Likes to climb and play on jungle gym and other outdoor play equipment.

Can run faster, turning corners with ease and stopping suddenly.

Can hop on alternate feet in skipping motion.

Can skip and may be able to jump rope.

Enjoys competitive physical games.

Enjoys racing with other children or with parents.

May design simple obstacle courses.

Rides bicycle with training wheels.

Can walk along a straight line drawn on the ground.

Can descend ladder, alternating feet easily.

Can throw a ball overhand using body weight to project the ball; aim is improving.

Can catch a ball.

Small Motor Skills
Shows improved eye-hand coordination.

Builds buildings and bridges in addition to towers.

Places small toys, such as soldiers or animals, in position with precision.

Laces shoes and may be able to tie shoes.

Decides what to draw and then draws it.

Completes simple puzzles.

Does simple finger plays.

Can fasten large buttons and work large zippers.

Is able to copy designs and numbers.

May enjoy playing with child-sized tools.

Has definitely established handedness.

Can print own name.

Intellectual Development
Seeks information and serious answers to questions.

Learns about right and wrong.

Accepts that there are rules, even though unable to understand reasoning behind rules.

Has developed symbolic thinking, uses materials in a variety of ways.

Appreciates humor and unusual situations.

Enjoys routines and is aware of daily routines.

Has increased attention span and improved concentration skills.

Likes to look at books and listen to the same stories over and over. Will correct anyone who makes mistakes reading the stories.

Understands number concepts; can follow instructions involving numbers.

Understands quantitative thinking in terms of "more than."

Has vocabulary of 2000 to 2200 words.

May not know the meaning of all words used.

Speaks with grammatical construction comparable with adults in the home.

Emotional and Social Development
Personality
Shows increased willingness to cooperate.

Is more patient, generous, and conscientious.

Expresses anger verbally rather than physically.

Is more reasonable when in a quarrel.

Develops a sense of fairness.

Becomes more practical.

Family
Likes supervision, accepts instructions, and asks permission.

Has strong desire to please parents and other adults.

Still depends on parents for emotional support and approval.

Is proud of mother and father.

Delights in helping parents.

May act protective of younger siblings.

Shapes ideas of gender roles by watching parents' behavior.

Friends
Is increasingly social and talkative. Is eager to make friends and may develop strong friendships.

May pick a best friend.

Prefers cooperative play in small groups.

Prefers friends of same age and gender.

Stays with play groups as long as interest holds.

Learns to respect the property of friends.

Summary

- Within any group of preschoolers, different levels of physical, intellectual, emotional, and social development can be seen.

- During the ages of three, four, and five children grow taller, leaner, and better coordinated. Preschoolers practice such large motor skills as hopping, skipping, climbing, and riding pedal toys. Their small motor skills also become much more precise.

- During the preschool period, children learn to handle most of their eating, dressing, and grooming tasks by themselves. At this time, they may experience some problems with enuresis.

- Preschoolers are most interested in their immediate surroundings and what is happening at the moment. They are keenly aware of the environment and study it with all their senses.

- The preschool period is a time of great advances in language skills. This helps children express their feelings and thoughts more clearly.

- A good way to enhance children's language and reading skills is to read to them. Helping children connect numbers with their meaning promotes the development of math skills.

- Preschoolers' advances in physical and intellectual development are the most important factors in their social and emotional development.

- Children begin forming their gender roles during the preschool period.

- Children learn as they play, and they play as they learn.

Reviewing Key Points

1. What changes occur in the proportion and shape of a child's body during the preschool years?

2. List three ways parents can encourage their preschoolers' large motor skill development.

3. Explain how a three-year-old builds a tower of blocks. Then, explain how building skills change at ages four and five as small motor skills continue to develop.

4. True or false. A child who shows a preference for the left hand should be encouraged to change and use the right hand.

5. What might parents try if they want their children to have fewer problems at mealtimes and fewer food dislikes?

6. What is a common psychological cause of enuresis? How should parents react?

7. What two specific developments make it possible for parents to reason with their three-year-olds?

8. Explain why parents should not consider their preschoolers' tall tales a form of lying.

9. True or false. By the age of five, children can understand some things are right and some are wrong; they begin to understand rules.

10. Give two examples of how preschoolers use symbolic thinking in their play.

11. List five advances in language skills that occur during the preschool years.

12. How should parents react when their preschoolers reveal new fears?

13. Why do preschool children need to play?

14. Describe alternate play behavior.

15. What is the Denver Developmental Screening Test? What does it measure?

1—**Activity:** Review and outline this chapter emphasizing the information you found most useful.

2—**Answers:** Answers to review questions are located in the front section of this TAE.

Learning by Doing

1. Visit a preschool and watch for signs of progress in large and small motor skills as the children run, jump, skip, climb, ride pedal toys, throw and catch a ball, build towers of blocks, draw, and use scissors. Discuss your observations in class.

2. Interview a pediatrician about the problems of enuresis, stuttering, lisping, and nightmares. Ask questions about causes and solutions for these problems.

3. Collect stories about preschoolers from newspapers and magazines. Post several of them on a bulletin board.

4. Role-play a parent explaining to a preschooler the concepts of time: past, present, future, minutes, hours, days, weeks, and so on.

5. Create a pamphlet for parents about helping their preschoolers develop life skills.

Thinking Critically

1. Discuss the increasing intellectual skills preschoolers display as they learn about cause and effect, fact and fantasy, right and wrong, and time.

2. Ages three, four, and five are called the preschool years, meaning "before school." Yet today, many children in this age group attend preschools, child-care centers, and kindergartens. If you were a parent, would your preschooler go to one of these learning centers? Why or why not?

3. Write a paper that explains what you would want your preschooler to know about gender roles if you were a parent.

4. Form small groups and discuss the importance of play in preschoolers' lives. Make a list of the many different kinds of play experiences that can be created in the home to encourage physical, intellectual, emotional, and social development. Discuss your group's findings with the rest of the class.

5. How can parents encourage their children to be competitive without overemphasizing winning?

Preshoolers continue to depend on their parents.

Chapter 14
Parents and Their School-Age Children

Objectives

After studying this chapter, you will be able to

- identify steps in the physical, intellectual, emotional, and social development of school-age children.
- explain the importance of parental guidance and encouragement in the school-age years.
- describe guidelines parents can use for their school-age children's involvement in sports.
- propose ways parents can help their children adjust to new roles as students.
- explain how friendships change over the school-age years.
- identify some of the causes and symptoms of stress among school-age children.
- propose ways parents can help their children deal with stress.
- summarize the importance of regular medical checkups and physical exams for school-age children.

Key Terms

school-age years
multiple classification
seriation
conservation
reversibility
self-care children

2   The first day of school is a great event for both parents and children. To parents, this day seems to come quickly. They may be surprised to realize their children are now grown up enough to start school. For children, 3   going to school opens up a whole new world outside the family, 14-1.

Physical growth is obvious throughout the **school-age years**, the time when children are between ages six and twelve. Children in this stage grow taller and slimmer as they develop a more adult physique. Parents are well aware of their children's rapid growth because they must 4   continually replace their children's outgrown clothes.

School-age children are interested in learning. Parents are often amazed by the curiosity and intellectual progress their children reveal. The school-age period can be a wonderful, sharing time for intellectual development. During these years, parents can help lay the groundwork for continued interest in education and self-development.

Early in the school-age period, children's emotional expressions may still seem somewhat babyish. Their moods change often. They are cooperative for a while and then suddenly act stubborn. Gradually, their emotions stabilize, and their social skills improve. Near the end of the period, parents sense their children are too old to be treated wholly as children. Yet, they are not ready for all the decisions, privileges, and responsibilities of adolescence and adulthood.

During the school-age years, parents should remember each child is unique. Each child has individual needs, concerns, and challenges. With good communication, parents can help a child through the transitional period of the school-age years.

1—**Vocabulary:** Look up terms in the glossary and discuss their meanings.

2—**Resource:** *School-Age Children*, Activity A, SAG.

3—**Reflect:** Can you remember your first day of school? What emotions may parents and children experience on this day?

4—**Activity:** Brainstorm ways parents may be able to keep clothing expenses within the family budget.

14-1

When children go to school, they learn about the world around them.

1—Discuss: How do children indicate they are ready to go to school?

2—Discuss: What should parents be sure their children know before they enter school? What life skills must they be capable of handling on their own?

Readiness for School

As children approach school age, parents may wonder if they are really ready for school. There is no single measure that can identify a child's readiness for school. Each child must be considered individually. Parents must take all areas of their children's development into account in deciding when to first enroll them in school.

Most states have laws regarding enrollment in school, and school districts may have additional policies. Some states set a cutoff date to determine who can enroll in school. Children whose sixth birthday falls after the cutoff must wait until the next fall to start school. This ensures all the children in one grade level are roughly the same age.

Parents can help their children a great deal by making sure they are intellectually prepared for school.

Pressuring children to learn is not a good idea. Helping children discover the fun and excitement of learning is much more helpful, 14-2.

Parents can also make sure their children have certain important skills and knowledge before they start school. Children should be able to say their full names and addresses correctly. They should recognize their names when they see them printed. They should also know the names of their parents or guardians. Children should be able to ask to use the toilet when necessary, using language everyone understands. They should be able to go to the bathroom by themselves. This means being able to undress and dress themselves, flush the toilet, and use the faucet. Children should be able to manipulate ordinary buttons, zippers, and shoelaces. They should be able to manage their coats, hats, mittens, and boots with a minimum of help.

Most children are eager to start kindergarten. If they have attended any type of preschool, they will probably

14-2
Parents can use teachable moments, such as picking flowers, to show their children the wonder of nature. This fuels children's desire to learn.

adjust to school quite easily. Still, it is natural for them to have some worries. Parents can help ease children's minds by showing them as much of the school environment as possible beforehand. If children will walk to school, parents can walk the route with them several times beforehand so it becomes familiar. They might also accompany the child on a tour of the school building and the classroom. Most schools have orientation programs for this purpose, but extra visits may be helpful to some children.

The school-age period is an important time in a child's life. Ideally, children enter school with a feeling of confidence and security, as well as a sense of excitement.

Physical Development

In the beginning of the school-age period, boys and girls develop physically at much the same rate. They grow about 2 to 3 inches taller and 4 to 5 pounds heavier each year.

Six-year-olds are constantly active. They have trouble sitting still for any length of time. If given a choice, they will almost always run rather than walk. Their coordination is improving, but they suffer countless scrapes and tumbles. This is the age when baby teeth begin to fall out and are replaced by the first permanent teeth.

1—**Activity:** Check with elementary schools in your area to see if they offer an orientation before children enter school.

2—**Discuss:** School-age children are very active, and their coordination is improving. Why do they still seem to suffer from countless scrapes and tumbles?

Seven- and eight-year-olds continue to grow at a steady rate. Some children may look lanky because of their thin bodies and long arms and legs. In spite of their rather awkward appearance, their coordination is improving, and they are capable of smoother movements. Bicycling, skipping, and jumping rope are popular activities. Children also like other sports and activities. See 14-3.

By ages nine and ten, children may begin narrowing their interests. If they enjoy sports, they are now ready to learn the proper techniques of organized games. They can run, kick, throw, catch, and hit better because of their improved coordination, timing, and balance, 14-4. Their small motor skills are also greatly improved, so some children become interested in building models or learning crafts.

Near the end of the school-age period, girls and boys have marked differences in their physical development. At ages nine and ten, girls begin to grow faster in height and weight than boys their age. They may actually

14-4 _____
By age nine, many children are ready for organized sports.

14-3 _____
Improving coordination allows eight-year-olds to learn to ski.

grow taller than the boys in their classes. At age twelve, girls begin a major growth spurt. Boys' growth begins to pick up at about ages 12 and 13. This is just before they begin their own major growth spurt at about age 14. These growth spurts start a child's transition into adulthood. These changes are described in more detail in the next chapter.

During the school-age period, children may begin to approach physical activity in different ways. Some children are very active, and they like competitive team sports. Many boys and girls are keenly interested in their physical strength and increasing motor abilities. Other children seem to prefer individual sports, 14-5. These boys and girls may be less competitive, or may enjoy the opportunity to be alone. Still other children are not really interested in sports. They may prefer other, less active interests. While children don't have a definite need to play sports, they do need physical exercise. Parents should encourage their children to get plenty of exercise. Some children need little encouragement; others need a lot.

It may help if parents exercise with the child.

Physical Fitness and Competitive Sports

Children's health and physical fitness is important. School-age children who eat nutritious foods and get plenty of sleep and exercise are usually healthy and physically fit.

Although growth is slowing through much of the school-age years, children need a well-balanced diet for growth and energy. Height is the usual way to calculate needed calories. For example, six-year-olds need 39 calories per inch and by 10 years of age, children will need 46 calories per inch. When the growth spurt occurs, children will need more.

The Food Guide Pyramid for Adults (shown in Figure 7-7) is a good guide. Some experts recommend another serving from both the dairy and meat groups. Food choices are the main concern during this age. Children's food choices are greatly influenced by peers and advertisements. School breakfast

1—Discuss: Compare the advantages and disadvantages of participating in competitive sports during the school years.

14-5
Some children prefer physical activities they can do alone over team sports. This girl enjoys in-line skating.

14-6 ——————
Athletics can offer children fun as well as valuable lessons in physical fitness, respect, and cooperation. Sports can also pose risks.

1—Resource:
Children and Sports,
Activity B, SAG.

2—Discuss:
Brainstorm the psychological risks that may be involved in school-age sports activities. How can parents minimize these risks?

and lunch programs determine up to one-half of the daily intake.

Children's diets are often too high in sugar and fat content. This is particularly true if parents buy convenience foods or eat out of the home often. Such a diet often leads to dental caries, heart problems, diabetes, and unhealthy weight gains, especially when this diet is coupled with little exercise.

School-age children enjoy activities that involve the use of their motor skills. They also enjoy the competition and camaraderie that exist in team sports. Children participate in team sports in physical education classes, during recesses, and in community programs. Combining physical play with healthy competition can aid children's development in all areas. Through athletics, children can learn to appreciate physical fitness, respect authority, and cooperate with others, 14-6.

Children should have a physical exam before joining any competitive teams. Some children are born with conditions that make them especially susceptible to injury. Even healthy children may risk injury to their developing bones and muscles. In a few cases, prolonged exertion may cause heart

damage. Some children, if pressured to win, may develop high blood pressure.

Participation in sports can also have some negative psychological effects. Children who are pushed into sports against their wishes may develop a negative attitude toward exercise and physical fitness. Children who see their parents and coaches argue with umpires and referees may fail to learn respect for authority. Children who try to impress others with their individual achievements may develop conceit rather than a spirit of cooperation. Other children may feel like losers if they cannot match the athletic success of a parent or older sibling. Still other children who seldom, if ever, win may suffer a loss of self-esteem. They may feel humiliated and think of themselves as failures. After a while, they may not even want to try to participate.

With all the risks, parents may wonder if and when their children should begin sports. The most basic rule is to let children decide for themselves. Children who are physically and psychologically ready are usually eager to begin. The National Association for Sports and Physical

Education gives some additional advice. (These guidelines are for healthy children who are developing at a normal rate for their ages.)

1

- Competitive sports for children under six years of age are of questionable value.
- Children between ages six and eight should participate only in noncontact sports such as swimming, tennis, and running.
- Contact sports such as soccer, baseball, basketball, and wrestling are recommended for children over eight years old.
- Tackle football and other collision sports should not be played until age 10.

By following these age-related guidelines, parents can help reduce the risks involved in their children's sports. They can take other precautions, too. Parents should make sure their children play in a safe environment. The facilities for practices and games should be in good condition. A first-aid kit should be kept nearby, and the coach should know how to use it. Any child who is injured or in pain should be removed from the game and given prompt attention. Protective equipment, if needed for the sport, should be used regularly. It should be in good shape and fit well. If parents are unfamiliar with this equipment, they can take it to a sporting goods store and ask for an opinion.

Coaches are often the keys to positive sports experiences. Good coaches place more emphasis on the children's welfare than on winning. Their approach is encouraging and supportive, not tough and degrading. They teach the basic skills and strategies of a sport. Their goal is to help children learn a sport, not to boost their own egos with winning records. Good coaches give all children a chance to play. Most young athletes would rather play and lose than sit, game after game,

14-7
Parents can help their children develop a positive attitude about sports. They should encourage and support their children without pushing or criticizing.

2

1—Enrich: Review the guidelines recommended by the National Association for Sports and Physical Education. Do you agree or disagree?

2—Discuss: How can parents set good examples when their children are competing? What might happen if parents become too emotionally involved in their children's sports events?

watching their teammates win. On the other hand, good coaches do not pretend winning doesn't matter. Honest competition in the pursuit of victory is the essence of all sports.

Parents' attitudes are a major factor in the satisfaction children receive from sports, 14-7. Parents need to encourage their children without pushing them. They need to show their children they are loved regardless of how they played in the last game. Children should not fear their parents will reject or punish them if they strike out or drop a crucial pass. Rather than criticism for mistakes, parents should offer praise for any effort or improvement. They need to emphasize the importance of fair play, honest effort, and cooperation.

Perhaps the most important role for parents is to set a good example. Parents should act like adults when they watch

14-8
School-age children are sometimes too eager, active, and curious for their own good. Parents need to alert them to possible dangers and inform them of safety procedures.

Dangers and Safeguards During the School-Age Years

School-age children enjoy riding bicycles. Parents need to be sure their children are aware of bicycle safety rules and traffic laws.

Medicines still fascinate children in the school-age period. These should be stored where children cannot reach them, preferably in a locked cabinet.

More and more children are using household appliances without knowing the possible dangers. This child is unaware using a knife to dislodge a piece of bread in a toaster may lead to a scary and painful electrical shock. Children need to be taught how to use household appliances safely.

School-age children are generally friendly and may be easily influenced by strangers. Parents should warn their children about accepting any favors, including rides in a car, from strangers.

"Block houses" are safe places where children can go if they need help as they walk to and from school.

1—Discuss: Review the precautions concerning bicycle safety. How would you explain these to school-age children?

2—Activity: Many children use home appliances incorrectly. Review the proper operating methods and cite possible dangers associated with using a toaster, microwave, electric mixer, and range.

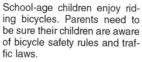

games. They should respect the calls of the officials. They should let the coaches do the coaching and the players do the playing. As spectators, their role is to watch the game with enjoyment. They should maintain a positive attitude in both victory and defeat. Parents can help children realize trying hard, playing well, and enjoying the game are also signs of success. There is more to the game than winning or losing.

Physical Safety

As children reach the school years, they will be moving into new environments and experiencing new situations. They will have many new opportunities to explore and to become more self-reliant. They will also face new dangers. Parents can do much to improve their children's awareness of potential dangers and options for safety. Several safety tips for parents of school-age children are illustrated in 14-8.

Traffic presents many dangers to children. Statistics show accidents often occur on the way to or from school. Using traffic safety techniques is the most important way to prevent accidents. If their children walk to school, parents should instruct them to use intersections where crossing guards can help them. If no crossing guard is available, children should use marked crosswalks and corners with pedestrian signals. Since young children are so small, they cannot clearly view the movement of traffic. As they grow older, they may be easily distracted by games or running races. These children usually know the correct way to cross a street, but they may try to be more daring. They may try to "beat" the light or avoid other safety measures.

Children using other means of transportation must also be careful. Accidents happen regardless of the means of transportation—walking, biking, taking a bus, or riding in a car pool. If children ride bicycles, they should be aware of and follow all traffic rules. Children also need to be taught to watch for traffic as they step out of a bus or car.

School-age children should be warned about kidnapping. Unfortunately, each year, many children are abducted. Children are naive and are easily taken in with offers of candy or other favors. Children should be warned about talking to strangers. They should also be told not to go anywhere with any adult without parental permission. Many schools and community organizations have programs to discuss such situations with children. Some communities also encourage parents to have their children's fingerprints taken. Fingerprint records could provide the key to finding a missing child.

Parents should also inform their children about the dangers of sexual abuse. They should talk to their kids about what are good touches and what are bad touches. Parents should invite their children to talk to them if the children don't like how someone touches them. Children should also be told they have the right to determine who can and cannot touch their bodies. They need to know they have permission to say no. Parents need to talk openly with children about the dangers of sexual abuse. They should also warn them of behaviors that seem harmless but can lead to sexual abuse.

Many communities have established "safe houses" or "block houses." These are designated houses where children can seek help as they walk to

14-9 _____
When shopping, parents should stay close to their school-age children. They shouldn't let the children wander off because they might get lost or be abducted.

1—**Activity:** On the chalkboard, diagram a typical street. Show traffic situations that are dangerous for school-age children. How can parents and school personnel help children recognize these dangers?

2—**Enrich:** Investigate the laws regarding school buses. What background checks are make on potential bus drivers.

3—**Enrich:** Role-play a typical scene where a child is being approached by a stranger. What should parents instruct their children to in this situation?

4—**Discuss:** What can schools, communities, and neighborhoods do to help provide a safe environment for children?

1—Discuss:
Shopping malls and
public parks are
common areas from
which children are
abducted. What can
parents do to warn
their children?

2—Example: Bring
children's drawings to
class. Based upon
these drawings, how
do you believe these
children see their
world?

and from school. If their neighborhood has such a house, parents should be sure their children can recognize it.

In stores and shopping malls, parents should keep their eyes on their children at all times, 14-9. Parents should warn children about running off and talking with strangers. Parents should also warn their school-age children against hitchhiking or accepting rides from anyone.

Another area of danger concerns household accidents. School-age children often begin to take on some household chores. In some homes, they 1 may do these chores unsupervised. A potential for danger exists if a child operates electrical equipment or other dangerous devices without proper supervision or knowledge.

A study by Whirlpool Corporation revealed in many homes, children ages seven, eight, and nine were given some responsibility for cooking and cleaning. Children ages seven, eight, and nine operated appliances such as the refrigerator, toaster, clothes dryer, washing machine, stove, hair dryer, and microwave oven. In many cases, children were not given proper instructions for using these appliances. They simply learned by watching adults. As a result, accidents often happen. Children are injured, and even killed, by using improper operating procedures with home appliances.

Due to the study's findings, appliance manufacturers are now writing their directions with children in mind. Parents have the responsibility to share this information with their children. Anyone using an appliance should know how to operate it and be familiar with safety precautions.

14-10
Early in the school-age years, children's artwork reflects their positive outlook on life.

Intellectual Development

Parents notice the simple "Why?" questions of their preschoolers are gradually replaced by more complex questions as the children enter the school-age years. Children are still full of questions about the world around them, and they like more detailed answers. Generally, children look at 2 their world from a positive point of view. This attitude can be seen in the drawings and paintings they create in the early school years. Young school-age children often draw landscapes with flowers, birds, and smiling suns, 14-10.

Seeing a glimmer of understanding in their child's eyes can be fulfilling for parents. Parents can share their child's excitement about grasping a concept, solving a math problem, or figuring out a play on words.

At the beginning of the school-age period, children's attention spans are lengthening. Children can spend longer periods of time at an activity. Their concept of time also improves, so they can plan ahead for special events. Children in the early school-age years recognize rules and understand some rules exist for their safety. They like to do their own special chores at home, and they willingly help their teachers at school. They favor reality in their play activities, so fairy tales have less appeal. Animal stories are the favorites of many children. Space-age games and stories are popular, too. They are more realistic than fairy tales, but call for imagination and lots of action.

Nine- and ten-year-olds like to act in a more adult manner. Their vocabularies have grown to about 5400 words, and their conversation skills have improved. They enjoy quizzing parents and may astound them with facts they have learned. They like games that involve mental competition. They may challenge parents or grandparents to word games or dominoes, and they may win! They prefer winning, but they also are willing to keep playing a game with the hope of finally winning.

In this age group, avid readers may read constantly, but other children may want to pursue different interests. Parents should encourage their children to enjoy reading. They can take their children to libraries to pick out their own books. Often, children will pick out books about their other interests. Mysteries, adventure stories, biographies of famous persons, and science fiction tales are other favorites of older school-age children.

By ages eleven and twelve, children can solve a problem by remembering past experiences. If something is off-

14-11 _____

Building and testing a model rocket together helps this father encourage his son's interest in science.

schedule, they can often pinpoint the problem. They may even work out a better schedule to avoid the same mistake or delay. Eleven- and twelve-year-olds like active learning experiences such as reading aloud, reciting, doing science projects, and working on the computer, 14-11. They can grasp math concepts and apply them to their own lives. For instance, they recognize the significance of money. They will ask for an increase in their allowance when they hear school lunch prices have gone up. If they have savings accounts, they can understand how interest makes the account balance grow.

By the end of the school-age period, children can converse well. Their vocabularies average 7200 words. Many are increasingly interested in talking. They may enjoy lengthy conversations with grandparents or teachers who sense their enthusiasm for discussion. Some children talk all the time at this age. Others spend long periods of time in quiet meditation or concentrated work on models. In every aspect of development, children are individuals.

1—**Activity:** List some examples of rules school-age children should recognize.

2—**Example:** Bring to class examples of games that appeal to school-age children. Why do you suppose they like these games?

Advances in Thinking Patterns

Children achieve so many little triumphs in learning parents may not notice each new level of intellectual development. However, children make several significant intellectual gains during the school-age years.

Multiple Classification

In the preschool years, children classify objects into single categories such as cars, trucks, cats, dogs, red, blue, squares, and circles. During the school-age years, children begin to classify objects in more complex ways. One of these is **multiple classification,** the ability to understand that an object may fit into more than one category. School-age children know a cat is a cat whether it is black or gray. When given several squares, circles, and triangles of different colors, they can pick out all the red squares. They won't be confused by red circles or blue squares.

School-age children refine their classifying skills by collecting and identifying things. Children of this age are famous for their collections, ranging from rocks or bugs to stamps or baseball cards. Older children within this age group are quick to notice small differences between similar objects. On car trips, they can often identify different makes and models of cars much more quickly and accurately than adults.

Seriation

Another learning development school-age children master is **seriation.** This is the ability to order groups of things by size, weight, age, or any common property. Children may arrange beads on a bracelet from small to large or from light colors to dark colors. They may arrange coins from oldest to newest. Seriation also helps children recognize relationships within

14-12 _____
Children understand conservation when they realize pouring water from a tall, narrow container to a small, wide container does not change the amount of the water.

their families. They can understand different generations represented by children, parents, and grandparents.

Conservation

Conservation is a learning achievement identified by Jean Piaget. (Piaget's theories are described in more detail in Chapter 16.) **Conservation** is the understanding that certain properties (number, substance, weight, and volume) remain the same (are conserved) even if they change in shape or appearance. See 14-12. For example, when two rows of eight blocks are laid side by side, children will see both rows contain the same number of blocks. When one row of blocks is spread out so it is longer, a younger child will assume it contains more blocks. A child who has grasped the concept of conservation will realize the number of blocks has not changed.

Other examples of conservation can be demonstrated with sheets of paper, balls of clay, and glasses of water. When a sheet of paper is crumpled into a ball, a child who understands conservation will realize it has not increased or decreased in substance. When a ball of clay is rolled into the shape of a cylinder, the child will realize the amount of clay has not changed. When water is poured from a short, wide glass into a tall, narrow glass, the child will realize the volume of water is still the same.

Reversibility

Reversibility is the concept that things can return to their original condition after they have been changed. Reversibility is closely related to conservation. School-age children who have mastered conservation will prove their ideas are correct by reversing the changes. They will push the blocks back together. They will smooth out the crumpled ball of paper until it is flat. They will roll the cylinder of clay back into the shape of a ball, and they will pour the water back into the short glass.

School Adjustments

Most school-age children are ready and eager to attend school. Middle childhood is an age of activity and investigation. During these school years, children gather much information and acquire skills in solving problems. Memory improves, and thinking becomes more abstract.

Most children adjust to their school environments and schedules fairly easily. It may take a week or more to get used to going to school, but soon school is just part of a child's routine, 14-13. Parents should talk with their child about what changes will occur,

14-13 _____
Going to school can be quite an adjustment, but soon children are used to their school-day routines.

what to expect, and what feelings are normal during this time. Children may face a similar but shorter transition at the beginning of each school year. If a child has significant problems adjusting to school, parents may want to seek counseling for the child.

Children soon learn they must eat breakfast and lunch at set times. If they dawdle or refuse to eat at mealtimes, they will get hungry later, perhaps when they are sitting in class. Even more than adults, children need an adequate breakfast to fuel their active lifestyles. Whether lunch is offered at school or brought from home, the food should be nutritious. Well-balanced meals with foods from the major food groups help children feel and think better. Well-fed children

1—**Example:** What are some simple experiments displaying reversibility? Do smaller children sometimes practice this concept without realizing it?

2—**Resource:** *School Adjustments*, Activity F, SAG.

3—**Activity:** List some suggestions of how parents can help meet the nutritional needs of their children.

1—Reflect: Do you remember your first day of mid-level school? Were you nervous? Why or why not?

2—Activity: Compare the phonics method and the whole-word method of teaching children to read.

3—Discuss: How can parents help children learn to write?

4—Discuss: Give some simple examples of how parents can teach math skills using common household items.

are unquestionably more alert and ready for activities throughout the school day.

Adjusting to elementary school takes time. Adjusting to middle, intermediate, or junior high school may be even harder for many school-age children. In elementary school, most children have one teacher and stay in the same classroom throughout the day. In middle, intermediate, or junior high schools, students shift to having several teachers in different classrooms. They must adjust from being the biggest kids at the elementary school to being the youngest at their new school. Students are asked to take on additional responsibilities, such as keeping their books in a locker, finding their classes, and arriving on time. A parent's understanding and encouragement is also helpful at this time. Taking the child on a visit to the mid-level school he or she will attend can be very helpful.

Schoolwork and Homework

Each day in school, children learn valuable skills they can use throughout life. They learn how to read, write, count, figure, investigate, and problem-solve. Children learn about the world around them. Maybe most importantly, they learn how to learn.

Reading is one of the most important skills children learn at school. Success or failure in reading affects other areas of learning. Today, many schools combine different methods of teaching children to read. Most teach both the alphabet and phonics, so the letters and their sounds are learned. These letters and sounds are put together to form words. Another method teaches children to recognize a whole word at a time. Parents can help their children learn to read by encouraging them to read and practice their lessons learned in school.

14-14
Writing is a skill that must be learned. Teachers guide children as they learn to write letters and numbers.

Children first learn to print letters and words; then they learn cursive writing. (Cursive writing is writing in flowing strokes, with letters joined together.) They use these skills to write short stories and reports. The teachers' role is to present the correct methods of printing and writing as well as the basic rules of grammar and composition, 14-14. Parents can help by encouraging their children to practice printing and writing and praising them for neatness. Another way for parents to help is to show interest in the stories and reports their children write.

Parents can also help their school-age children learn to add, subtract, multiply, and divide. Multiplication tables still need to be memorized, even though schools also teach students to use calculators. Children are also introduced to computers at an early age. Parents can help their children develop their math skills by alerting them to uses of math in daily living. Examples include using a tape measure while sewing, measuring ingredients while cooking, keeping score on a computer game, drawing a simple floor plan of a child's room, and making a graph of a child's changing height and weight. These are only some of the ways parents can help their children enjoy learning math skills.

Children's natural curiosity opens the door to their interest in science. School lessons lay the foundations for problem-solving and discovery in science. Parents can help their children build upon these foundations by exploring nature, discussing modern discoveries, and dreaming of future discoveries. Some easy scientific experiments, like planting a seed and watching it grow, are easy to do at home. Other science lessons develop informally during family outings and vacations. Children may also learn about science by watching educational television programs and playing educational science computer games.

Art, drama, and music activities provide children with expressive outlets for their emotions. These activities may help children communicate with others about experiences they have had, fears they have faced, and joys they have felt. Parents who recognize the value of these expressions develop a greater understanding of their children's feelings. These subjects also help students be creative, 14-15.

Children's interest in schoolwork is often affected by their peer relationships. Children whose friends display initiative and industry are more likely to try hard and do well in school. If children have friends with negative attitudes toward school, their schoolwork may suffer. Parents should monitor their child's school performance carefully and watch for any slips in their achievement levels. If they notice any problems, they should investigate the reasons for the changes in their children's work. By showing loving concern and support (not pressure), parents may help renew children's interest in school.

School-age children spend their days in school, but their tasks in learning are not complete. Homework becomes high on the list of a student's responsibilities. Homework serves as an opportunity to polish skills learned throughout the day. It also helps students learn to think and problem-solve on their own, away from the school setting.

It is important for parents to understand that homework is the child's responsibility. A parent's responsibility is to offer support, structure, small amounts of help (when needed), and a quiet time and place for the child to study.

Parents can help their child meet his or her homework responsibilities. These responsibilities include the following:

- *Knowing what the assignment is.* The child must pay attention to the details of the assignments. Recording assignments in an assignment notebook or other organized manner helps.

- *Bringing home the materials needed to do the work.* When school ends, students may get side-tracked talking with friends and run to the bus, forgetting their homework. They must make homework a priority, however, and remember to gather everything they need.

14-15 —
This boy shows his creativity through his music. He can also use this talent to express himself.

1—**Example:** Many simple science projects can be done at home. Give some examples.

2—**Discuss:** Why is it important for parents to be alert to any changes involving their children's schoolwork?

3—**Discuss:** What can parents do to help their child meet homework responsibilities?

1—Discuss: Six-year-olds want to be right and win. Upon what do they base their sense of right or wrong?

14-16 _____
Parents should not do their children's homework for them. Instead, they should provide some help, encouragement, and a quiet time and place for the child to study.

- *Having a specific time and place for homework.* A parent's job is to provide a quiet time and place for students to work. They should also monitor the work and encourage the child, 14-16. To help children focus, parents may need to set limits on other activities and distractions. Limits might include the following: television, computer, music, phone, and play with friends. Doing homework right after school is often a good practice. Then it's finished early, and children can enjoy other activities.

- *Being organized enough to get all assignments done and returned to school.* Children must learn to prioritize their assignments, manage their time, and plan ahead. They must also take responsibility for getting their homework and books back to school each day. Packing their backpacks the night before may help. Then, everything is ready to grab the next morning.

- *Turning in all assignments on time.* One of a student's biggest responsibilities is turning all work into the teacher on time. This is a critical skill for students to learn. If a student misses a day of class, it is also up to the student to arrange to do make-up work.

Parents can talk with the child's teacher to be sure children are doing satisfactory work and not falling behind on homework assignments. Children should not spend all their time studying, however. Having a balance between work, rest, exercise, and recreation is important.

Emotional and Social Development

As parents watch their children grow in the school-age years, the biggest changes they see are in emotional and social development. Until this time, children have remained rather immature in these areas. As toddlers and preschoolers, children often rely on their parents to introduce them to new social situations and playmates. During the school years, children become more socially independent. They choose their own friends, and friendships gain importance to them, 14-17. Sibling jealousies may lessen as interests outside the home grow.

Six-year-olds are ready for anything new. They are full of energy and charge ahead to new challenges. They are often

14-17 _____
Friendships take on a new significance in the school-age years. These friendships encourage a child to grow socially and emotionally.

demanding and want all of everything. Choosing between alternatives, such as different flavors of ice cream, is difficult for them. Six-year-olds want desperately to be right and to win. Their sense of right and wrong is based on what parents or teachers tell them to do or not to do. Tattling is a common way to check with an adult to find out if a playmate's actions are really wrong. Children at this age become interested in group activities, but they are still too egocentric to cooperate fully. They have a hard time waiting in line and taking turns.

By age seven, most children have calmed down. In fact, they may seem withdrawn and moody at times. They like to spend time alone or at least in the background. Meanwhile, they are busy thinking, watching, and listening. They may feel everyone, including parents, teachers, and peers, is against them. At the same time, seven-year-olds want and need the approval of adults and peers. Children at this age are often very conscientious and strive to please. Their sensitive feelings are hurt by criticism.

At about age eight, children believe they can do just about anything, and they are willing to try. If they feel they have failed, they may turn to tears and self-criticism, saying "I always do it wrong." Their failures won't stop them from trying again the next day, however.

Generally, eight-year-olds like school and make new friends easily. They enjoy group projects and peer competition. They are becoming aware of other people's points of view. They are concerned about what others do and what they may be thinking. The children are interested not only in how they are treated, but also in how they treat others. This is the start of two-way relationships.

Group activities among children of the same gender are popular throughout the school-age years. It is common to see three or four girls walk across the playground with their arms entwined, 14-18. This same-gender group interest reaches a peak at eight years of age and lasts through the teen years. It seems to be stronger among boys than girls.

1—Discuss: Why is belonging so important to school-age children?

14-18 ———
School-age children, like to form same-gender social groups. Belonging to a group makes people feel special.

14-19 _____
Joining scouting groups and similar organizations promote children's intellectual, emotional, and social development.

Belonging is also extremely important to school-age children. Not only do they want to belong, they also want to look like and act like their peers. Especially when they enter junior high school, children may feel immense pressure to "fit in" with others.

Throughout the school-age years, the desire for group activities can be met in part by organizations such as scouting groups and 4-H clubs. These groups provide learning experiences and fill some of children's emotional and social needs. See 14-19. In these organizations, parents can also share in the activities and meet their children's peers.

Children are also likely to form their own social groups at school or in their neighborhoods. Secret clubs with lots of rules are especially popular. Once school-age children understand the reason for rules and the concept of **1** fairness, they are eager to make their own rules. They want no help from adults as they start their secret clubs. The secret is of little importance. These secrets serve as a way for club members to band together and exclude others. This may sound crude to adults, who are used to other ways of organizing and influencing people. Children use these clubs to learn about boundaries and belonging. Generally, the lessons children learn in these clubs are positive. Such lessons will help them prepare for active roles in community organizations as adults.

As their interest in friends expands, school-age children often single out best friends. Best friends provide important lessons in sharing, give-and-take, trust, and even jealousy. Loyalty at this age may be weak. Children may change best friends often. As friendships change, children may be shunned, excluded, or dropped as a best friend. This is quite common in the **2** friendships of school-age children. Luckily, such harsh treatment rarely lasts long. A child who is shunned one day usually has a new best friend the next day. If parents or teachers sense a child is shunned continually, they should help the child learn to make and keep friends. This will help protect the child's self-esteem.

Most nine-year-olds are relatively quiet. They are individualists with definite likes and dislikes. They resent being bossed by their parents. A new **3** drive for independence begins. Interest in friends grows as family interest declines. Belonging to a group is no longer enough. Now children are concerned about what the group members do together. The group's interests and activities are important. Some children abandon their own interests in favor of the group's interests to remain in the group. (Parents need to keep an eye open for such changes. If children's personal priorities are being negatively influenced by a group, parents may need to step in and take action.) Other children move **4** from group to group until they find one that matches their interests.

Nine-year-olds are well-known for their worrying. They worry about school grades, friendships, the health of their family members, and their own development. They complain about everything that displeases them. When faced with disappointment or defeat, it is hard for them to accept. By this age, most children know right from wrong. They will accept blame if they know they have done something wrong (and if the blame cannot be passed to a sibling). However, they are quick to offer excuses for the wrongdoing.

According to many parents, ten is a child's ideal age. Ten-year-olds are happy with life in general. They like school and their teachers. They like their parents and even their brothers and sisters. They obey adults willingly. They accept responsibility and are fairly dependable if they are given encouragement and praise, 14-20. If differences arise among friends, they are willing to work them out so everyone is happy. Ten-year-olds are nice and friendly, and they expect others to be that way, too.

14-20
Ten-year-olds are learning to be responsible. They can help with family chores, such as washing the dishes.

Group acceptance is still important to most ten-year-olds. On the other hand, some children have gained enough self-assurance to move away from the group. Generally girls are ahead of boys in this area. At ten, girls seem likely to be more loyal to a best friend than a group. Boys this age may start talking about special friends, but are still mainly interested in their groups.

During the late years of the school-age period, many children's emotions may change as their bodies do. (Puberty is described more in Chapter 15.) Both girls and boys may become very moody. Girls begin these changes about two years ahead of boys. These important changes begin at different times for different children. They can create unsettling emotions. Quarrels become more frequent. Feelings are easily hurt in social interactions. Boy-girl socializing may be starting, usually initiated by girls. Both boys and girls may feel awkward about these exchanges.

By the end of the school-age period, many children are less self-centered and reach out to others for friendship. They like to plan group activities and take roles in carrying out their plans. They are also more patient and friendly with younger children. Children at this stage begin to see themselves and others more objectively. They express more concern, compassion, and empathy for others.

The ease with which children develop feelings of security and confidence in these areas depends a great deal on their family environments. Parents can do much to help their children. Love, understanding, and a genuine interest in children at every stage of their lives go far in helping children feel good about themselves.

Parents and Friends

Parents can encourage their children to develop worthwhile friendships. They can also be alert to certain friendships that may create problems.

1—Resource: *Facts About School-Age Children*, Activity D, SAG.

2—Discuss: Both boys and girls will begin changes indicating puberty. Is the timing identical?

3—Resource: *Observing a School-Age Child*, Activity E, SAG.

1—Discuss: Why do parents need to be aware of the friendships their children are forming?

2—Discuss: Should parents allow their children to bring friends home? Why?

3—Discuss: If school-age children form healthy friendships with people of both genders, how will this affect their abilities to form healthy relationships later in life?

Parents who care about their children are also interested in their children's friends.

Friends play an important role in children's development. Children often adopt the attitudes displayed by their friends. They "borrow" some aspects of their friends' personalities for a short time and test them out. By experimenting with a variety of different personality traits, children find the traits with which they are most comfortable. They will eventually include these in their own developing personalities.

Since friends are so important to children, parents need to be aware of the friendships their children are forming. Healthy, positive friendships **1** during the school years can enrich a child's life. They can provide a network that offers stability, trust, cooperation, and a capacity for growth that cannot be found in any other way.

When possible, parents should allow children to invite their friends **2** home. This gives children a valuable sense of security. It also gives parents a chance to meet their children's friends. When children do invite their friends home, parents should treat them as guests. After all, they are important people in the lives of their children. Parents should act friendly and hospitable. They should serve foods, snacks, and beverages that appeal to the children.

Parents may also want to volunteer to chaperone school events. Then they can see for themselves how their children interact with others. This requires some tact and a positive, friendly, noninterfering attitude. Children resent parents butting into their lives with demands concerning their selection of friends. On the other hand, children like the security of knowing their parents can help if they need some advice about their friendships.

14-21

Friendships teach children important lessons about relationships that will influence them throughout their lives.

Conformity

In the school-age years, children begin rapidly conforming to their friends' standards, behaviors, and attitudes. Friendships also allow children **3** to explore ways of establishing and maintaining relationships with people of both genders. The friendships children have during the school-age years will influence the relationships they will establish later in life. See 14-21.

During the school-age years, ties with parents begin to loosen. Children are striving for greater independence from their families. Since most children their age are also striving for independence from parents, children are naturally attracted to their peers. They feel comfortable with one another, and enjoy trying new things together. If one child wears a certain brand of jeans to school, they all may decide to wear only that brand. If one child uses a slang expression, parents may soon notice their child using the same phrase. School-age children usually share the same favorite music groups, movies, and computer and video games. These signs of conformity seem natural. Parents usually see nothing wrong with these behaviors, and they may not seem harmful.

As children near the end of the school-age period, their intense desire for conformity may begin to upset their parents. Parents may object to some of the "in" ways of dressing, behaving, and speaking their children display. Parents should try not to overreact. If they are too critical, their children may feel defensive. They may then adopt even more of the popular styles or behaviors to rebel against parents and prove their loyalty to their peers.

Parents should try to understand as people mature from childhood to adulthood, they need to feel separate from their parents. Their unusual actions are often nothing more than small tokens of independence. As they conform to their friends, they pick and choose different behaviors or styles of dress. Eventually, they sort out what is right for them and establish their individuality. Parents who can be patient usually fare best. Parents need to realize this is a normal part of human development and it will eventually pass.

This stage may be difficult for parents and their children. Parents want to protect their children from hurt feelings, group pressures, and physical dangers. Children want to learn about life through firsthand experience. Common sense and instinct will tell parents if their children are going too far from their family's values. Until then, parents are probably wise to express interest, loving concern, and mild disapproval rather than scorn, disgust, and ridicule. Children who are given the chance to choose from all life has to offer are most likely to choose values and lifestyles similar to those from their own backgrounds.

Parents and their children in the late school-age years should strive to avoid major conflicts and resolve minor ones. Resolving conflicts and differences of opinion will prepare parents and their children for the further struggles of independence during the teen years.

Self-Care Children

Today, more and more children come home after school to empty houses and apartments. These **self-care children** have to tend to their own needs until their parents return home, 14-22. Self-care children are also sometimes called *latchkey children*.

14-22
Self-care children come home after school to an empty house or apartment. They may feel frightened and lonely until their parents return from work.

1—Activity: Prepare a pamphlet for children in self-care. Include safety tips and precautions.

2—Enrich: Research local school-age child care programs. What services are provided? Is this a better alternative than self-care? Why?

3—Discuss: How can stress be positive? Can large amounts of positive stress be hard to handle?

There are several reasons for the growing number of children in self-care. More parents are working than ever before. Many school-age children live in either dual-career families or single-parent families. This means a parent is not available to be home with the child after school. Some parents cannot locate or afford quality after-school child care. Others have confidence their children can care for themselves for the short time the parent will be away.

Self-care children need to be trained in the skills of self-sufficiency. Parents need to establish guidelines concerning the use of the telephone, appliances, and equipment. Safety precautions and emergency procedures should be discussed. The child needs to be able to follow instructions and understand what he or she is and is not allowed to do while the parent is away.

Support for self-care children is growing. Telephone hot lines provide sources of reassurance for children who are home alone. Children can call for help in emergencies, to report problems, or just to talk. These programs have names like Phone Friend, Kidsline, Chatters, and Contact-a-Friend. Unless their employers forbid personal calls, self-care children's parents should also be just a phone call away.

Parents should exercise caution when deciding if their children can care for themselves. Self-care is not an appropriate arrangement for all, or even most, school-age children. Many states have laws that state children under a certain age may not be left home alone. Parents must check to be sure their child is legally old enough to care for himself or herself.

If the child is old enough, the parent must assess whether the child is mature enough in all developmental areas to be left alone, even for a short time. The parent should talk with the child and assess whether he or she would be comfortable at home alone. If a child is not up to this responsibility, it is the parent's obligation to make other arrangements. After-school programs are offered by many schools, churches, community organizations, and child care centers. These programs may be low-cost or free of charge. Parents can also ask for referrals for child care providers.

Children and Stress

Most parents cling to the idea that childhood is a time of constant happiness. Parents want to protect their children from discomfort and worry. They don't want their children to be unhappy or anxious. This is not only impossible, but it is generally not in their children's best interest.

Parents cannot eliminate stress from children's lives. Having some stress in life is good. It offers the child a challenge to do his or her best. It also teaches the child how to deal with change and adapt to stressful situations.

Stress can be both positive and negative. It can be a reaction to exciting events, such as winning a contest or scoring high on a test. The stress felt in these situations can challenge a person to do his or her best. In small or moderate amounts, this kind of stress is necessary and positive.

Another kind of stress, also known as *distress*, is negative. Distress can include feelings of fear, hopelessness, worry, anxiety, and doubt. These emotions can be overpowering. They require the person to change or adapt his or her method of coping. Mild to moderate feelings of distress once in a while are healthy and normal. Intense or lasting feelings of distress can be more problematic. These feelings can interfere with a person's ability to function normally. People may need professional help to deal with this kind of stress.

While children may not experience as much stress as adults, they do experience stress at times. Parents should remember children cannot always verbalize how they feel. They may talk about feelings of sadness or anger rather than stress. Parents need to allow their children to work through these feelings, rather than pretending everything is okay.

Many situations and events can cause stress in a child's life. Conflicts with others may cause emotional stress. Most of the conflicts children have with others are short-lived and fairly minor by adult standards. To a child, however, they may seem monumental. It is important to recognize stress from the child's viewpoint, not the parents'.

Poor health or unhealthy habits can create stress. For instance, if a child doesn't eat, sleep, and exercise regularly, he or she may be tired, less able to think clearly, and less healthy. This can cause the child to perform poorly in school, which creates anxiety and stress. Having trouble keeping up with school work or performing poorly can cause great anxiety.

Having a schedule that is overly full can also be stressful. If children do not have time to play and to relax, they tire more easily and grow irritable and anxious. Children may also feel overwhelmed by all they are supposed to do. If a child is involved in too many activities, he or she may not be able to keep up with any of them. The child may feel helpless and out of control. On the other hand, an empty schedule can cause boredom, which can also be stressful. Children need a balance between stimulation and free time, 14-23.

Major life changes are the most serious causes of stress. Divorce, death or illness of a family member, and moving to a new place are common stressors children experience. Others may include parents' separation or remarriage. Parents can encourage their children to talk, draw, or write about their feelings associated with these events. Expressing their feelings helps children and parents understand the problem more clearly. Parents can also be more understanding and empathetic at times of great change. They may need to reassure the child everything will eventually work out.

It is important for parents to watch for signs of stress in their children. Children commonly exhibit certain signs they are under stress. A child will probably not show all of these signs, and there may be other, more individual signs. Parents should be alert to the following signs:

- loss of interest in previously enjoyed activities
- explosive crying or screaming
- verbal or physical aggressiveness
- cruelty to pets and playmates
- physical symptoms, such as rapid heartbeat, headaches, fatigue, restlessness, upset stomach, and neck pain

14-23 ——————————————
Even children need time to relax and unwind. Too much activity can be stressful.

1—Discuss: What situations can you identify that might be stressful for school-age children?

2—Resource: Children and Stress, Activity H, SAG.

1—Discuss: What other signs might indicate stress in school-age children?

2—Discuss: What other suggestions can you recommend for parents in helping their children deal with stress?

- loss of humor or sense of joy
- nightmares, sleep-walking, or teeth-grinding in sleep
- hair twisting, nail-biting, stuttering, excessive fidgeting
- threats of harming someone or destroying property
- behaviors of escape—immersion in the computer, e-mail, TV
- prolonged display of temper
- increased behaviors of acting out
- jumpiness or fear of sudden sounds

1

When stress interferes with a child's normal functioning, parents need to step in and offer help. Children need to be taken seriously. They need their parents to assure them their feelings are valid. Parents also need to teach their children to deal with stress effectively. This skill will help children as they become adults. Chart 14-24 lists suggestions for parents on helping children deal with stress.

14-24

Parents can follow these guidelines to help their children manage stress.

Helping Your Child Deal with Stress

Parents can use the following tips to help their children handle stress:

- Observe your child closely. Look for hidden signs of stress.

- Listen to your child carefully and empathize. Be as accessible as possible to listen to your child's concerns.

- Acknowledge and accept your child's negative feelings. Let your child know you understand what is being said.

- Reevaluate your expectations for your child. Are they realistic? Are your child's expectations of himself or herself realistic?

2

- Evaluate your own system of coping with stress. Are you setting a good example? Do you use healthy, stress-relieving techniques, or do you cope in unhealthy ways?

- Eliminate unnecessary sources of stress from your own life and your child's life. Prioritize activities, and practice time-management skills. Does your family (and your child) have too many responsibilities or activities?

- Help your child see some stress can be positive. Help the child identify ways to handle stress (relax, play music, write in a journal, draw pictures, run, etc.). Children need to develop ways to relieve stress.

- Guide your child to think of a solution on his or her own. Children need help to learn to solve their own problems. Offer minimal advice only if the child requests it.

- Engage the help of teachers, counselors, and religious leaders. Seek professional help when necessary. It is a sign of love for your child.

Medical Checkups for School-Age Children

Routine medical visits are needed less frequently in the school-age years than in early childhood. The American Academy of Pediatrics recommends school-age children have medical checkups at ages 6, 8, 10, and 12. These medical checkups are important for monitoring children's health. They allow the doctor to detect any problems, and treat them as early as possible.

During these medical checkups, parents can ask any questions they might have about their child's health, nutrition, and growth. The doctor will check and chart the child's growth by measuring height and weight. Blood pressure will be measured, and the doctor will thoroughly examine the child's physical condition. Any necessary tests will be done to check the child's health.

Routine medical checkups are in addition to doctor visits when the child is ill or injured. They may also be in addition to other physical exams children may need. Some schools require a complete health exam before the child can enroll in school. Participation in sports is another reason children might need a physical exam. Most teams or coaches require a physical before each sports season starts. Even if a physical is not required, parents may want their child to have an exam before entering school or starting a sport.

Nearly all school districts require children to have certain immunizations before starting school. Parents can contact their local school district to find out what shots (and what records of those shots) are required. If their child lacks the necessary immunizations, parents should consult the child's doctor about getting these immunizations, 14-25.

During the school-age years, children should also visit their dentists and eye doctors regularly. These visits are important for identifying any vision or hearing problems that may exist. Correcting these problems as soon as possible may keep them from getting worse. If a child has an undetected vision or hearing problem, it could affect the child's ability to learn. Good vision and hearing help a child succeed in elementary school.

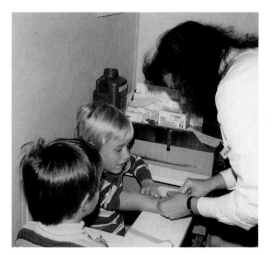

14-25 ———————————
Children need medical checkups and immunizations before they start school.

CHILD DEVELOPMENT

6 Years*

1
2 Physical Development

Body becomes more slender with longer arms and legs; babyhood physique continues to disappear.

Loses baby teeth, which are replaced by the first permanent teeth.

Is constantly active.

Prefers running over walking.

May have frequent minor tumbles and scrapes.

Needs proper rest and nutrition to fuel busy mind and body.

Dances to music.

Throws ball with opposite arm and leg forward.

Ties own shoelaces.

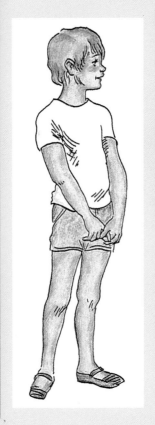

Intellectual Development

Asks more complex questions than just "Why?" Wants detailed answers.

3

Concentrates on doing one activity for longer period of time.

Has improved memory.

Has better understanding of the concept of time.

Is inquisitive and eager to learn in school.

May begin to understand concepts of seriation, conservation, reversibility, and multiple classification.

Begins reading, writing, and arithmetic at school.

Learns constantly.

Can print numbers 1-5.

Can count by rote to 30.

Can correctly use all parts of speech.

Adds and subtracts numbers 1-5.

Locates days of week on a calendar.

Can tell his or her home address and cross the street safely.

Emotional and Social Development

Becomes more socially independent; chooses own friends.

May feel less jealous of siblings as outside interests become more important.

Is still egocentric, but is becoming interested in group activities.

May still have a hard time waiting and taking turns.

Wants desperately to be right and to win.

Tattles often to check sense of right and wrong.

Is full of energy and ready for new challenges.

Wants all of everything; making choices is difficult.

May have nightmares.

May need reassurance as adjusts to new demands of school.

(continued)

These charts are not exact timetables for development. Individuals may perform certain activities earlier or later than indicated in the charts.

CHILD DEVELOPMENT

7 to 8 Years

Physical Development

May look lanky due to thin body and long arms and legs.

Becomes better coordinated; movements become more fluid and graceful.

Develops improved sense of balance and timing.

Enjoys sports, especially boisterous games.

Enjoys rollerskating, skipping, and jumping rope.

Proper rest, nutrition, and exercise are important.

Intellectual Development

Accepts idea of rules and knows harm might result if rules are not followed.

Understands concept of time.

Has longer attention span.

Understands value of money and may be ready for an allowance.

Favors reality; is less interested in fairy tales.

Begins to show interest in collecting certain objects.

Likes to help the teacher.

Enjoys reading animal stories and space-age stories.

May show interest in stories about children of other countries.

Refines concepts of seriation, conservation, reversibility, and multiple classification.

Emotional and Social Development

7 Years

May seem withdrawn and moody.

Likes to spend time alone or in the background.

May feel everyone is against him or her.

Wants and needs approval of adults and peers.

Is very conscientious; strives hard to please.

Is sensitive and hurt by criticism.

8 Years

Shows more spirit; is willing to try just about anything.

May turn to tears and self-criticism upon failure, but recovers quickly.

Is able to get along well with others.

Chooses companions of same gender and age.

Is very sensitive to what others think.

Shows intense interest in groups.

Wants to look like and act like peers.

Enjoys group activities in organizations and in own secret clubs.

Chooses a best friend but may change best friends often.

1—Discuss:
Compare seven-year-olds and eight-year-olds in terms of emotional and social development.

(continued)

CHILD DEVELOPMENT

9 to 10 Years

1—Discuss: Ten-year-olds are beginning to choose best friends and become more interested in joining a group. What positive benefits may result? Are there any problems that might occur?

Physical Development

Continues to improve coordination.
Improves sense of balance and timing.
May develop particular physical skills.
Enjoys organized games.
Can run, kick, throw, catch, and hit.
Further refines small motor skills.
Is able to use hands skillfully in building models, learning handcrafts, or using tools.
Enjoys drawing.
Proper rest, nutrition, and exercise are important.

Intellectual Development

Is able to consider more than one conclusion to problems or choices.
Understands more about truth and honesty.
Likes to act in a more adult manner.
Is still enthusiastic about learning.
Likes games that involve mental competition.
Enjoys quizzing parents and impressing them with new facts.
Shows increasing capacity for self-evaluation.
Enjoys mysteries and secrets.
May show less interest in TV programs.
May continue to show interest in collecting certain objects.
Has vocabulary of about 5400 words.
Has better use of language and is able to converse well with adults.

Emotional and Social Development

9 Years

Is relatively quiet.
Worries about everything.
Complains a lot.
Has definite likes and dislikes.
Begins a new drive for independence; resents being "bossed" by parents.
Knows right from wrong; will accept blame when necessary, but offers excuses.
Shows increased interest in friends and decreased interest in family.
Is interested in group's activities and concerns.

10 Years

Is happy with life in general.
Likes people and is liked by others.
Is dependable and cooperative.
Obeys adults easily and naturally.
Likes to accept responsibility and tries to do things well.
Likes praise and encouragement.
Still has strong group spirit, but it may be diminishing.
May begin to show more loyalty to a best friend than to the group, especially girls.
May enjoy being part of a team.

(continued)

CHILD DEVELOPMENT

11 to 12 Years

1—Discuss: How might the changes that occur during puberty affect children's self-esteem?

Physical Development
May grow little in height (male).
May experience growth spurt (female).
Enjoys sharing activities with friends of same gender.
May like to test strength and daring.
Becomes very conscious of clothes and overall appearance.
Body may begin to change into that of an adult.
Proper rest, nutrition, and exercise are important.

Intellectual Development
Is able to detect problems in daily situations and work out solutions.
Grasps math concepts and applies them to daily activities.
May like group projects and classes based on cooperative effort.
Likes active learning— reading aloud, reciting, science projects, and working on the computer.
Likes to recite in front of class if self-esteem is secure.
May allow peer relationships to affect schoolwork.
Has vocabulary of about 7200 words.
May enjoy lengthy conversations with grandparents or teachers.
May enjoy long periods of solitude to think or to work on projects like building models.
May show interest in reading; mysteries, adventure stories, and biographies are favorites.
Understands concepts of seriation, conservation, reversibility, and multiple classification.

Emotional and Social Development
Is less self-centered.
May express great enthusiasm.
Likes to plan and execute plans for the group.
Is willing to reach out to others for friendship.
Has improved social skills.
May show more tact, especially with friends.
Is patient and friendly with younger children.
May become moody about body changes.
1 May show signs of emotional turmoil as body changes.
Has strong desire to conform to peers' ways of dressing and behaving.

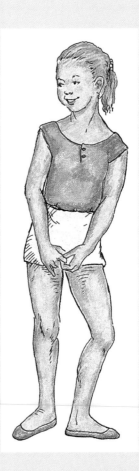

1—**Activity:** Review and outline this chapter emphasizing the information you found most useful.

2—**Answers:** Answers to review questions are located in the front section of this TAE.

Summary

- In determining a child's readiness for school, his or her physical, intellectual, emotional, and social development must be considered. Parents should also check with their school district and state admittance policies.

- Parents can help ease children's minds by showing them as much of the school environment as possible before the first day of school.

- Children who eat well-balanced diets, get plenty of sleep, and participate in normally active play are usually healthy and physically fit.

- Through athletics, children can learn to appreciate physical fitness, respect law and authority, and cooperate with others. However, sports have the potential for both physical and psychological damage.

- Parents can do much to improve their children's awareness of potential dangers and options for safety.

- Children make several significant intellectual gains during the school years. Concepts such as multiple classification, seriation, conservation, and reversibility are usually mastered during this time.

- During the school years, children accumulate much information and acquire skills in solving problems. Memory improves, and thinking becomes more abstract.

- During the school years, children become more socially independent from their parents. They find their own friends, and friendships take on new importance.

- Group activities among children of the same gender are popular throughout the school-age years.

- Parents can show interest in their children by getting to know their children's friends. Children begin to conform more to their friends' attitudes, behaviors, and standards during the school-age years.

- Parents need to recognize symptoms of stress in their children. They should also help their children learn to cope with stressful situations.

- Parents whose children are in self-care should establish guidelines and train their children in the skills of self-sufficiency.

- School-age children need routine medical checkups every other year. They may also need physicals before entering school or beginning a new sport.

Reviewing Key Points

1. List five ways parents can help their children achieve readiness for school.

2. Name an advantage, a physical risk, and a psychological risk of athletics for school-age children.

3. What is the basic rule for parents to follow in deciding if and when their children should begin sports?

4. Define the following intellectual achievements of the school-age years: multiple classification, conservation, seriation, reversibility.

5. What can make the transition from elementary to intermediate, middle, or junior high school so difficult for children?

6. Explain how parents can help their children learn to read, write, use math skills, and understand concepts of science.

7. Children's interest in schoolwork is often affected by their _____ relationships.

8. Propose four ways parents can help their children adjust to schoolwork and homework.

9. Why is tattling a common behavior among six-year-olds?

10. At what age does this same-gender group interest peak? Is it stronger among boys or girls?

11. Why are secret clubs with lots of rules popular among school-age children?

12. Why do many parents consider ten to be a child's ideal age?

13. Why should parents try not to overreact as their school-age children conform to some of the "in" ways of dressing, behaving, and speaking?

14. List two ways parents can know if their child is old enough to stay home alone.

15. Identify three causes and three symptoms of stress among school-age children.

16. At what ages should children receive regular medical checkups during the school-age years?

Learning by Doing

1. Attend a sporting event involving school-age children, such as a Little League game. Take mental notes about the children's ages, coaches' attitudes, parents' involvement, condition of the facilities, and the use of protective equipment.

2. Working in a small group, write directions for using common home appliances. Keep in mind these directions would be used by children as well as adults. Give a demonstration using the directions you wrote. Decide if they are clear enough for school-age children.

3. Write a handbook giving suggestions to students as they leave elementary school and enter middle, intermediate, or junior high school.

4. With a small group, demonstrate the concepts of multiple classification, seriation, conservation, and reversibility for the class, using an original approach. Compare the reaction of a person who understands this concept to that of a person who does not.

5. Observe the social patterns of a class of school-age children. Pay special attention to same-gender group interest, secret clubs, best friends, interest in a group's activities, and conformity. Report your findings to the class.

Thinking Critically

1. If you were a parent, how would you know if your child was ready to start school? What skills would you need to teach the child before he or she entered school?

2. Reflect on your own transition from elementary school to a mid-level school. What do you think helped you make this transition? What problems arose? Write a paragraph explaining your answers.

3. Discuss the importance of reading for children. Explain how parents can help their children enjoy reading. Research the sources of reading materials available for children in your community.

4. Discuss the importance of friends to school-age children. What can parents do to encourage healthy friendships? What can they do if they are concerned about the friends their children choose?

5. Propose seven strategies for parents to use when helping their school-age children deal with stress. (Do not give examples listed in the chapter.) Present these strategies to the class in an oral report.

Chapter 15
Parents and
Their Teens

Objectives

After studying this chapter, you will be able to

- identify steps in the physical, intellectual, emotional, and social development of teens.
- differentiate between primary and secondary sex characteristics.
- describe the dangers teens face related to eating disorders; tobacco, alcohol, and drug use; and sexual behavior.
- describe the importance of decision making during the teen years.
- explain the role parents can play in helping their teens establish healthy friendships and dating relationships.
- propose ways parents can help their teens develop healthy self-concepts and self-esteems.
- summarize the importance of medical checkups during the teen years.

Key Terms

adolescence
puberty
primary sex characteristics
secondary sex characteristics
eating disorder
anorexia nervosa
bulimia nervosa
binge eating disorder
abstinence

Many parents reflect with satisfaction on the guiding and protecting roles they have played in the lives of their young children. These same parents may brace themselves for battle as their children reach the teen years. Unfortunately, our society tends to focus on the rebellious aspect of teenage behavior. In reality, most teens slowly and steadily gain their independence in ways that are socially acceptable.

Adolescence is a transitional time during which people graduate from the dependency of childhood to the independence of adulthood. It includes changes in every area of development. Adolescence has no specific beginning or end, nor can it be described in specific terms that apply to every teen.

The teen years are years of change. Teens are striving toward maturity and self-sufficiency, 15-1. The quality of relationships within the family greatly influences how a teen will meet these changes. If the family relationships are strong, teens can more easily adjust to their changing bodies. Teens with less positive family relationships may face a more difficult transition. Conflicts that were already present may escalate. If parents and their teens love and respect each other, however, they may find the teen years are a time for enjoying family life and renewing the basis for family trust.

For most people, the teen years are positive and without major difficulty. One of the most troublesome aspects of adolescence is many people do not fully understand this period of development. With so many physical and emotional changes occurring so quickly, both parents and teens may become confused. By learning more about this period, parents and teens can cope with the changes more successfully.

1—**Vocabulary:** Look up terms in the glossary and discuss their meanings.

2—**Discuss:** Teens are often portrayed as rebellious. Is this an accurate picture of most teens today, or would you challenge this assumption?

3—**Enrich:** In some cultures, young people take on adult roles at a specific time or signify this transition with a certain custom. Research these customs.

1—**Vocabulary:** What is the difference between *primary sex characteristics* and *secondary sex characteristics*?

2—**Discuss:** It can be frustrating for teens that each person develops at a different time and rate. How can parents reassure their teens?

3—**Discuss:** Describe the effect growth spurts can have upon a teen's wardrobe.

15-1

During the teen years, people grow and develop in many ways. After the teen years, most will become mature and self-sufficient adults.

Physical Development

The most dramatic changes in physical development that occur during adolescence are those related to puberty. **Puberty** is the process through which the body becomes capable of reproduction. During puberty, boys and girls reach physical maturity. They are no longer children, and they will soon become men and women.

Girls and boys experience different kinds of changes during puberty. These changes are called *sex characteristics*. The two types of sex characteristics are called primary and secondary. Hormones from the pituitary gland in the brain control

both types. **Primary sex characteristics** are physical chan-ges related to the development of the reproductive organs. **Secondary sex characteristics** are all other physical changes related to puberty. Secondary sex characteristics include growth of facial hair and change of voice in boys. For girls, breast development and widening of hips are secondary sex characteristics.

Puberty generally begins earlier in girls than in boys. The average age for girls to start their growth spurt is 11. The growth spurt for boys generally starts two years later. Since girls have a head start, they are taller and heavier than boys for a few years. In the early teen years, boys catch up. They soon pass girls in height and weight, a difference that will remain throughout adulthood.

Just as in other areas and stages of development, each person is unique. All boys will experience the same changes, but the timing of these may vary from one boy to another. The same is true of girls. Often, dramatic differences can be seen within a group of peers. Close friends of the same gender may be quite different in size. Teens have a great desire for conformity. They may worry a great deal about such differences. If one teen develops quite a bit earlier or later than peers, this can cause a great deal of anxiety. Parents need to reassure their teens differences in timing are normal.

Although the timing may vary from one person to another, the sequence of these changes is the same. After a period of very little growth, the growth spurt occurs. This growth spurt may come as a surprise for both parents and teens. Teens may be upset as their favorite clothes soon become too small. Parents may complain about having to continually buy new, larger clothes for their teens. If parents and children can laugh together over these incidents, it can help.

Different parts of the body grow and mature at different rates. Teens may feel awkward and out of proportion at times. They may occasionally act rather clumsy and are very self-conscious about their behavior. Parents can help by overlooking their clumsiness rather than focusing on it.

Parents and teens should keep in mind adolescence is a transitional stage. It is a time of change from the childhood of the past to the adulthood of the future. Knowing this, the physical changes of adolescence are easier to accept. The changes occur in every teen's life, although teens react to the changes differently. Parents can add to their teens' worries or offer reassurances, 15-2. Parents who provide helpful information and counsel along with a sense of humor help their teens take giant steps toward maturity.

Puberty involves many physical changes in addition to the growth spurt. The skull grows larger. The jaw lengthens, the chin becomes more pointed, and the nose increases in size.

These changes result in a longer, less-childlike profile. Other changes affect the reproductive system. The testes (in boys) and the ovaries (in girls) increase the production of sex hormones.

Physical Changes in Boys

During puberty, a boy's neck thickens, his shoulders widen, and his waist narrows. His muscles develop rapidly and double in strength. His voice drops to a lower pitch. Hair appears on his face, under his arms, and in the pubic area. His reproductive organs increase in size. He may start to have nocturnal emissions (wet dreams). These may be upsetting, especially if his parents have not told him about them. Parents need to be frank in these discussions and use proper terminology. When a young man's parents talk openly with him, this can help him cope with all these changes. They can reassure him all boys go through the same changes related to puberty.

1—Discuss: Physical changes create new worries for teens. How can parents' comments or criticisms relieve or add to their teens' worries?

2—Discuss: Describe the physical changes boys experience during puberty.

3—Discuss: How can parents help their sons cope with the changes brought on by puberty?

15-2 _____
Parents can often support their teens by offering reassurances.

1—Discuss: Describe the physical changes girls experience during puberty.

2—Discuss: How can parents help their daughters cope with the changes brought on by puberty?

3—Discuss: Who is most likely to develop an eating disorder? Why do you think this is?

4—Enrich: Invite a doctor, nurse, or dietitian to talk to the class about eating disorders. Ask the speaker to describe the symptoms and effects of these disorders.

Physical Changes in Girls

A girl also undergoes a number of physical changes related to puberty. Her breasts develop, her hips widen, and pubic hair appears. She experiences menarche, her first menstrual period. This usually happens at about age 12 or 13, although anytime between age 9 and 17 is normal. Her menstrual periods may be scanty and irregular until her reproductive system matures. Parents can relieve a girl's anxiety about these changes by giving her accurate information about her developing reproductive system. She needs to know all girls experience these changes.

Eating Disorders

An **eating disorder** is an abnormal eating pattern that causes mental and physical health risks. People with eating disorders can be adults or teens, and males or females. It is most commonly young women who suffer from eating disorders. The likelihood of developing such a disorder increases in the teen years. Teens may be vulnerable since many physical, emotional, and social changes are occurring in their lives. Children who lack self-esteem or have serious social and emotional problems are more likely to develop eating disorders. The teen years can be an especially turbulent time for these children.

Anorexia nervosa is an eating disorder in which people are seriously afraid of gaining weight. This fear leads them to voluntarily starve themselves. Anorexics have distorted body images. They see themselves as fat no matter how thin they really are.

A teen may feel pressured to be thin like the celebrities promoted by the media. When people focus on how the body looks rather than on how healthy it is, there is a potential for unhealthy eating habits to develop. An anorexic will starve himself or herself to reach unrealistic weight goals in an effort to be thin. This person abandons eating healthy foods the body needs for fear of gaining weight. As anorexia nervosa continues, persons become severely underweight.

Bulimia nervosa is an eating disorder that is sometimes called the "binge-purge" syndrome. Bulimics binge, or eat huge amounts of food uncontrollably. Next they purge, or rid the body of the food they have eaten. Purging can consist of vomiting or taking laxatives or diuretics (products that induce urination). A bulimic may be of average weight, underweight, or overweight.

Binge eating disorder is a disorder in which persons rapidly and routinely overeat. Their eating behavior is not controllable, and the foods they select are often unhealthy. Unlike bulimics, however, binge eaters do not purge themselves of their food afterward. People with this disorder are commonly overweight.

A person with an eating disorder can develop various physical symptoms, such as weight loss in anorexia nervosa or weight gain in binge eating. When the body becomes malnourished, it cannot function properly. Muscles and organs begin to deteriorate. Body systems begin to shut down. Once an eating disorder develops, it can be difficult to cure. Medical help may be necessary. Treatment must also focus on the causes and triggers of the disorder as well as the person's emotional health and behaviors. If they are not treated, the effects of an eating disorder can become life threatening. Eventually the disorder can lead to death.

Parents should be aware of these eating disorders and their symptoms. If teens show symptoms, their parents should step in and find help for them. Waiting will only make the problem worse. Parents can consult a family doctor, counselor, or registered dietitian for help.

Parents cannot prevent the possibility their teen will develop an eating disorder. They can reduce the likelihood, however. From the time a child is very young, parents can provide healthy foods. They can also promote healthy eating and exercise habits, 15-3. Boosting a child's self-esteem can make a child more resistant to developing disordered eating patterns. Parents should also be supportive rather than critical of a child's body. Children can be very sensitive to comments parents and peers make about their appearance. Nurturing a child's positive feelings about his or her body is also extremely helpful.

Health Risks of Tobacco

The health risks associated with tobacco are well documented. These products are addictive and can cause

15-3

Exercise is a healthy way to maintain a proper body weight. Parents can help their children develop good exercise habits early in life.

many serious health problems. In the teen years, peer pressure on teens to start smoking or using smokeless tobacco may increase. Teens who are especially vulnerable to peer pressure may take up these habits to please peers.

Since tobacco use is so dangerous, responsible parents should discourage their children from smoking or using smokeless tobacco. They should let their teens know they do not approve of tobacco use. Parents must also be aware of the mixed messages they send if they smoke or use smokeless tobacco themselves. Parents may decide to quit using tobacco to set a positive example for their children. Quitting smoking will also greatly improve their own health.

Teens are often more health conscious than adults. They may be more likely to heed parents' warnings if parents can share factual material with them. Parents may want to obtain written information from the American Cancer Society about cancer, emphysema, heart disease, and other health risks related to tobacco use.

Health Risks of Drinking

An increasing number of teens in America are developing drinking problems. The number of alcohol-related deaths among teens is also rising. These facts cause many parents to worry about their teens' use of alcohol as they begin to establish friendships and patterns of social behavior.

Studies show that teens' drinking patterns are often similar to those of their parents, friends, and other people in their communities. Parents are very important role models for their children. Teens are likely to imitate the drinking behaviors they see at home. This seems to be true whether parents avoid all alcohol, drink in moderation, or have drinking problems. Peers are another important influence.

1—Discuss: Why should teens be aware of the legal consequences of drinking?

2—Resource: Drug Abuse, Activity C, SAG.

3—Enrich: Role-play situations in which teens might be tempted to use drugs. Discuss how parents can discourage drug use among teens.

4—Resource: Communication About Sexuality, Activity D, SAG.

Parents need to give their teens factual information about alcohol. Teens need to know alcohol acts as a depressant and may gradually damage the heart, liver, and judgment center of the brain. Parents should explain the laws related to alcohol use as well as the consequences of buying or using alcohol for persons under the legal age.

Parents also need to let teens know how they feel about the use of alcohol, 15-4. They can help their teens by setting clear standards for drinking that are in line with the family's personal priorities. Parents should set a good example for their teens concerning decisions about alcohol. Talking to teens about how to turn down an offer to drink, avoid situations involving alcohol, or get out of an uncomfortable situation is more helpful than telling them to "just say no."

Health Risks of Drug Abuse

Drugs can pose great health risks to teens. Parents should talk with their children about the dangers of illegal drug use. They should also explain the dangers of abusing legal drugs such as over-the-counter and prescription drugs. With accurate knowledge of the effects of drugs, teens are more likely to avoid drug use and abuse.

15-4

Parents need to talk to their teens about the facts related to alcohol use. They should also explain their feelings and beliefs about alcohol use.

Teens most often experiment with drugs in a social setting where they want to fit in with friends. Parents can prepare teens to overcome this peer pressure. They can discuss situations in which drugs might be introduced and ways teens can say no.

Any drug, legal or illegal, may be harmful if used improperly or in excess. The effects of a particular drug differ from person to person. If drug misuse or abuse continues, the health risks increase. Many drugs can cause death.

Parents who suspect their teen uses drugs should try not to overreact. Instead, they should try to focus on the immediate dangers facing their child. These dangers include legal and health problems. Emotional and social problems are also common among persons who abuse drugs. Professional help should be sought if needed. The teen needs to know his or her parents are concerned and have his or her best interests at heart. By providing guidance and support, parents send the message they care about their teen.

Sexual Health and Teens

The dramatic hormonal and physical changes of adolescence may bring with them new feelings about sexuality. Teens of both genders may experience these sexual feelings, but may not know how to react to them. Sexual feelings are a healthy part of adolescence. A teen's responsibility is to learn to express these feelings in a healthy and appropriate ways.

Most teens control their new feelings well. They wait to enter sexual relationships until they are mature enough to deal with the resulting emotions and responsibilities. They choose behaviors that eliminate or reduce the risks associated with sexual behavior. These teens are better prepared to deal with relationships and sexual issues in adulthood.

Some teens choose unhealthy or inappropriate ways of expressing their sexual feelings. These teens have more permissive sexual attitudes. They may enter sexual relationships for which they are not ready. The results can change their lives. Sexual activity has consequences that can be costly, traumatic, and even deadly.

Many medical experts believe the biggest health issue facing teens today is teen pregnancy. Nearly one million teens become pregnant each year. Eighty percent of these pregnant teens are unmarried; almost half are younger than 17. Pregnancy has serious social, emotional, and physical effects for the teen, her unborn child, and her family. Teen pregnancy and parenthood also affect the teen father and his family.

Another serious health risk related to sexual behavior is that of sexually transmitted diseases. These diseases can cause serious health problems, including death. STDs can also complicate the futures of teens and of those with whom they form relationships.

The best way to avoid teen pregnancy or STDs is abstinence. **Abstinence** means not having sexual intercourse. Abstaining from sex until marriage also gives teens time to grow socially and emotionally mature. Mature people are better able to handle the responsibilities of sexual relationships with their marriage partners.

Ideally, parents and their teens should be able to talk openly about sex. Parents need to listen when teens are ready to talk. They need to be open to answering a teen's questions honestly. Teens need guidance and support from their parents in order to understand sexual issues. They also need factual information about their physical and sexual maturity. Parents should give their teens the necessary facts about sexual behavior. They can also direct teens to factual sources of information.

Many schools, community organizations, and religious groups provide educational sessions about sexuality. Parents and teens may be able to attend these sessions together. This can allow the teen to learn about sexuality within the context of his or her family and religious beliefs.

Intellectual Development

During the teen years, students enter high school. They must adjust to different schedules, new teachers, and many more classmates. These changes may be unsettling for teens. Parents can find many ways to help teens adjust. They can attend orientation programs with their teens. Teens need their parents to express interest in their school experiences, classes, and extracurricular activities. Parents should also monitor their teens' progress. Most importantly, parents can make sure their home is a comfortable place where teens feel safe and secure.

Children grow tremendously in their thinking abilities during the teen years. Teens' increased intellectual skills allow them to think better, both generally and abstractly. Instead of thinking in terms of a single situation, teens learn to take what they know and generalize about a similar unknown situation. They form general theories and then test them. Abstract thinking, or nonconcrete thinking, goes a step further. Teens learn to understand matters that exist only as concepts, thoughts, or rules, without being tangible.

Much of teens' intellectual development occurs at school. In high school, many teens are able to select classes that fit their individual needs and goals. Teens may select elective classes on subjects that interest them. Many teens are preparing for college.

1—Discuss: Why is it important for parents and teens to be able to talk to each other openly about sexuality?

2—Discuss: Is information teens obtain from other teens about sex always factual? Where can teens obtain factual information about sex?

3—Discuss: How can parents help their teens adjust to high school?

15-5 _____

By being supportive of their schoolwork, parents can help their teens develop positive attitudes about school.

Some will enter trade schools or vocational/technical schools. Others will enter the workforce directly.

Parents play an important role in their teens' intellectual development. When parents are enthusiastic about education, children are more likely develop positive attitudes about school. See 15-5. These teens are more likely to enjoy their classes, develop good study habits, and do well in school. When they do well in school, it will encourage them to learn more, study harder, and do better. Parents can also help their teens as they make decisions about what to do with their futures.

Decision-Making Skills

Many parents begin teaching their children to make small decisions at early ages. This helps children become familiar with the decision-making process. Young children can make simple choices about which outfit to wear, which activity to do, or which color of backpack they want.

As children grow older, their decisions become more difficult. The consequences of their decisions also become more important. In the teen years, children face many tough choices that will affect the rest of their lives. Developing decision-making skills is an important aspect of teens' intellectual development.

The decision-making process includes six steps. (The decision-making process was described in Chapter 2. You may wish to refer to these steps.) Each step serves a purpose, and no step should be skipped. When teens first use the decision-making process, they may want to write each step on paper. This helps them learn to use the entire process correctly.

No one is ever locked into a decision. If a person is displeased with the results of a decision, he or she can often make a change. Simply "sticking it out" won't make a bad decision any better. Even if a new decision is made, however, consequences of the previous decision may still apply.

The basic decision-making process is adaptable. It can be used as a guide when making any kind of decision. Ideally, teens should learn about the process by using it to make relatively easy decisions. Then they will know how to use it when faced with difficult decisions.

Parents can help their teens develop decision-making skills. They can teach teens the decision-making process. They can encourage teens to make their own decisions and accept responsibility for the consequences. Teens who accept these challenges learn they are in control of their futures.

Emotional and Social Development

Teens spend a lot of time thinking about the future. They consider their many options and recognize their chances for success and failure. The future is both exciting and frightening.

Teens often feel insecure as they face the future's many options. Insecurity may grow as teens desire more independence and pull away from the security of their families. At the same time, teens may feel even more pressure to perform well socially among their peers and adults.

Most teens overcome this pressure and take more time to prepare themselves for adult responsibilities. They remain single while continuing their education. They set goals for their future and work to achieve these. Other teens feel unprepared for adult roles and confused about their futures. They may spend a time trying to "find themselves" and prepare for adult responsibilities. Some teens rush to accept adult roles. They look for jobs, get married, and have children. If they are unprepared to meet these responsibilities, this may create additional challenges, 15-6.

Like every other stage of life, adolescence can be stressful. Parents may feel they are not prepared to handle their teens' normal emotional ups and downs. Teens may feel they have to display a more decisive, independent air around their families. These feelings are common, but they should not prevent parents and teens from maintaining loving, caring relationships.

Most teens maintain good family relationships. They slowly and steadily establish independence while keeping family ties intact. Other teens break away from their parents and cut all family ties. In some families, parents remain overprotective and do not want their children to grow up. During the teen years, conflicts are inevitable in these families.

Teens' emotional development is greatly affected by the emotional climate within their homes. With improved intellectual skills, teens may want to talk more with their parents about everything from world politics to family policies. In an atmosphere of mutual respect, such discussions can be interesting and helpful. If teens fail to respect their parents, or parents fail to respect their teens, these discussions may turn into hostile arguments. If parents do not show respect for

15-6 _____
Teens who work too many hours may have trouble forming their identities. A teen must be careful to balance a part-time job with his or her other activities.

1—Discuss: Why is it important for parents to set rules and guidelines for their teen's behavior? What do you think these rules should include?

2—Discuss: How do a teen's many activities affect family routines? If conflicts develop, how can they be settled?

3—Resource: *Friendships and Dating,* Activity E, SAG.

themselves or other adults, they may have a hard time getting their children to respect them.

As their children become teens, parents should revise their rules and guidelines for behavior. Young children need more limits and guidelines than teens. They are less mature, cannot recognize dangers easily, and cannot make decisions for themselves. Teens need some rules and guidelines as they gradually develop self-discipline and become more responsible. They are preparing for adulthood, however, and must be given some flexibility and freedom.

Parents may struggle over how to balance an increased amount of freedom with necessary guidance and control. Parents should not feel guilty about setting needed guidelines for a teen's behavior. Guidelines keep children safe and help them learn about right and wrong. Parents should weigh the importance of the rules and guidelines they set. They should eliminate unnecessary rules and gradually give their teens more freedom and responsibility.

During adolescence, teens often adopt a more active lifestyle. They may participate in several extracurricular activities, 15-7. Some teens have jobs; others spend more time with their friends. The changes in a teen's lifestyle affect his or her family's lifestyle as well. Teens may begin coming home later at night. Activities might interfere with the family's normal mealtime. Busy teens may not have enough time to do their share of household chores. Parents and younger siblings may become upset. These conflicts will have to be settled in ways that seem fair to everyone. These are times that call for calm discussion, understanding, and cooperation.

The teen years may be eye-opening for teens as well as their parents. For the first time, teens may recognize their parents as human beings who

15-7 ————————————

High school students are often involved in many extracurricular activities, such as cheerleading, sports, band, and clubs. These activities enhance a person's overall development.

sometimes make mistakes. Meanwhile, parents may experience their own stresses. Along with the teen-related changes in family life, parents may face career challenges, the reality of reaching middle age, and other adult pressures.

Friendships

During adolescence, children's interest in friends continues to grow. Friendships are of great importance to teens. Friends are often major influences on a teen's behavior. These influences are often positive. Having a group of close friends interested in his or her well-being can foster a teen's emotional and social growth. Friendships in the teen years are the basis for developing adult friendships, 15-8.

Friends can also be a negative influence, however, when they are involved in undesirable activities.

15-8 ——————————
Teens' friendships serve a very important role. They set the stage for their future adult relationships.

Teens are often exposed to large amounts of peer pressure. Friends may persuade them to use alcohol, tobacco, or other drugs. Teens may be pressured to engage in risky behaviors, such as reckless driving, criminal activities, and sexual behavior. If teens succumb to this peer pressure, there can be heavy prices to pay. Teens can be punished, arrested, harmed, or even killed by going along with the unwise actions of their peers.

Parents are often concerned with their children's selection of friends. They do not want their children to fall in with a "bad crowd." Parents hope their teens will find friends who encourage and uplift them. They do not want their children's friends to sabotage their children's chances for success. Parents cannot pick their teens' friends, but they can talk with their teens about their fears. If teens sense their parents are genuinely concerned about their choice of friends, they are more likely to choose different ones.

Parents can also teach their children to resist peer pressure. They can help their teens plan what to say in difficult situations. For instance, when teens are pressured to do something wrong, they can avoid the situation by falling back on their parents' rules. They can say "I'd be grounded for the rest of the year if my parents caught me. I guess I'd better not."

In the teen years, children learn much about interpersonal relationships. They learn how to get along with others in a mature way. They also have many conflicts and disagreements. Parents need to be sensitive to a teen's friendships. If their teen seems distressed over a problem with friends, parents should not make light of his or her troubled feelings. Instead, they can help by offering love, support, and understanding. Parents should try to understand if their child seems to need time alone or more of their attention. Both responses are normal, even from the same teen. A teen may ask a parent's advice about problems in a friendship. Often, parents can guide the teen to decide what to do on his or her own.

Teen friendships do not have to exist at the expense of the relationships between teens and their parents, however. Teens are often comforted by knowing their parents are interested in them and their friends. Parents can learn to share special times with their children and the children's friends. They must also understand teens will often want to spend time alone with their friends.

Dating

Teens begin to attend social functions, first in group situations and then on individual dates, at different ages. Parents and teens need to talk about what to expect from dating experiences. Dating practices are usually defined by cultural norms. In addition to these norms, parents may set their own rules and standards regarding dating. For

1—Discuss: What should parents do if they disapprove of their teen's friends?

2—Reflect: If you were a parent, how would you show interest in your teen's friends without becoming overinvolved?

3—Enrich: Role-play situations between teens and parents trying to establish dating rules.

1—Enrich: Invite a panel of parents to discuss dating practices when they were teens. How do those practices differ from dating today?

2—Discuss: How can parents help their teens cope with the breakup of a dating relationship?

instance, some parents allow group dating to begin at age 14 and individual dating to begin at age 16.

In many cases, school functions offer the first opportunities for dating, 15-9. Teens may come and leave in groups, pairing off occasionally during the evening. After a while, one girl and boy may start developing a closer friendship. They may begin to go on individual dates. They might also continue to attend group activities with other teen pairs.

During high school, the peer pressure to date is strong. Many teens feel their social success depends on their dating relationships. These teens might accept or request dates just to conform to the expectations of their peers. Other teens are not swayed by this pressure. They may postpone dating while pursuing other activities.

Sometimes a boy and girl may date one another and no one else. Some couples become serious and talk of

marriage. Other teens date different people every weekend. Most find a happy medium, 15-10. Parents may worry more about couples who seem to be too serious too soon. They need to let their teens know about their concerns. If they can talk with their teens in a trusting and caring way, teens are more likely to resolve the situations in a respectful manner.

Parents need to be understanding and supportive as their teens experience their first feelings of romantic love. Whether it is simply friendship or true love, these relationships help teens learn about themselves while preparing for later relationships.

Parents also need to be understanding and supportive as their teens' relationships break up. During these times, parents may need to comfort, advise, caution, or encourage their teens. Teens may even ask their parents to reminisce about their own teen years.

15-9 _____
Dating often begins during the teen years at school events, such as homecoming parades. Soon couples may go on dates alone.

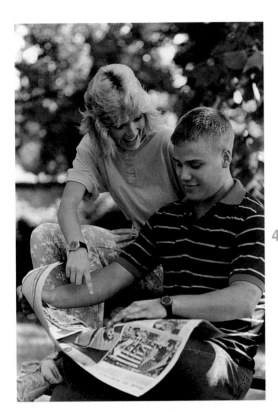

15-10 _____
Achieving a healthy balance is important in teens' dating relationships. Teens should strive not to be too serious too soon.

Self-Concept and Self-Esteem

A person's mental image of himself or herself is called his or her self-concept. People's self-concepts change throughout their lives. As teens, people may begin to notice a difference between who they think they are and who they think they should be or would like to be. This is why many teens ask themselves "Who am I?" and "Where am I going?"

A major developmental task of adolescence is for teens to see themselves as separate from and independent of other people. Each person must accept himself or herself as an individual. Each individual must accept responsibility for his or her life. To accomplish this, teens must do some *self-analysis*, or serious thinking about themselves, 15-11. Through self-analysis, teens may examine various aspects of their personalities from different points of view.

Another major developmental task is for teens to bring these ideas about themselves together in a unified self-concept. As teens form this self-concept, they learn who they are, how they feel, what they think, and what they want. They realize each person has a unique identity.

A person's level of self-esteem describes how he or she feels about himself or herself. A person with self-esteem sees his or her value as a person. People with high amounts of self-esteem accept both the positive and negative aspects of themselves. They try to concentrate on the positive. A person who lacks self-esteem does not think he or she is a valuable person. People who lack self-esteem see only the negative aspects of themselves. They more often focus on their shortcomings.

15-11 _____
Teens spend a lot of time thinking about themselves and their futures.

1—**Resource:** *Building a Positive Self-Concept and Self-Esteem*, Activity G, SAG.

2—**Discuss:** Why is it difficult for teens to understand who they are and what responsibilities they have?

3—**Discuss:** Why is it important for teens to do self-analysis? How can they do this?

4—**Discuss:** How is a teen's self-concept related to his or her self-esteem? Why are these important?

1—Resource: *You, the Parent of a Teen,* reproducible master 15-1, TR.

2—Discuss: Are medical checkups more or less important in the teen years as compared to earlier years?

Most teens fall somewhere in the middle. They may judge themselves as excellent or good in some areas and as average or poor in other areas. By watching others react to them, teens learn how their friends and family members see them. These judgments, as well as their own feelings of success and failure, help teens develop self-esteem. Successes build their self-esteem; failures lower it. See 15-12. A teen's self-esteem may fluctuate between positive and negative views, depending on the day's events. Over time, however, teens learn to form a more stable self-esteem.

Parents can help build their teen's self-esteem by expressing genuine interest in their teen's life. They can accept their teen's faults without excessive criticism and praise the teen's successes.

Medical Checkups for Teens

The American Academy of Pediatrics recommends checkups for teens at ages 14, 16, and 18. These checkups are a good time for teens to talk to their doctors about the changes that occur during puberty. The doctor can explain what the teen should expect and reassure the teen he or she is developing normally.

Teens should also talk to their doctors about reproductive health care. Beginning at age 18, females need an annual checkup of their reproductive organs. Young men can ask their doctors what reproductive health checkups they may need. Both men and women can learn about examining themselves (breasts for women and testes for men) for cancer.

The doctor will check the teen's height, weight, and blood pressure. He or she may also discuss the importance of adopting good health habits and avoiding unhealthy ones. A doctor can advise teens about healthy eating and exercise. Teens may also need to visit the doctor for health exams before participating in sports. If the teen is sick or injured, more doctor visits will be needed.

Teens should also visit their eye doctors and dentists regularly. Routine vision and dental care are important components of overall well-being. If teens notice any problems with their eyes or teeth between checkups, they should report these to their parents.

15-12 _____

By taking part in various activities, teens have many chances to succeed and build their self-esteems.

CHILD DEVELOPMENT

13 to 18 Years

1

2

3

Physical Development*
General
Period of little growth is followed by growth spurt. At first, teens may look awkward and lanky, but as growth continues, body proportions will equalize.
Skull grows larger.
Jaw lengthens.
Chin becomes more pointed.
Nose increases in size.
Profile becomes longer and less childlike.
Acne may develop.

Females
Ovaries increase production of sex hormones.
Hormones add a layer of fat on buttocks, thighs, and arms.
Breasts become fuller.
Hips widen.
Pubic hair appears.
Menstruation begins.
Ovulation begins.

Males
Testes increase production of sex hormones.
Reproductive organs mature.
Muscles develop rapidly and double in strength.
Shoulders widen.
Waist narrows.
Neck thickens.
Voice drops to a lower pitch.
Hair appears on face, under arms, and in pubic area.
Sperm production begins.
Ejaculations may occur.

Intellectual Development
Learns to think better generally and abstractly.
Learns to use the decision-making process.
Can solve problems mentally without having to work with concrete objects.
Can consider several ideas and concepts at one time.
Achieves a new awareness of people and issues.
May think more often about the future.
May speculate about what might be instead of what actually is.
May debate more with adults and parents.
Learns to weigh the relative consequences of an action for the individual and for society.
Can evaluate self and make necessary corrections to get back on the right track.
May think about and compare moral values.
May insist upon fairness.
May believe individuals are justified in breaking an unjust rule.

Emotional and Social Development
Strives to establish a sense of personal identity.
May become preoccupied with self-doubt.
May feel lonely and isolated.
May have dramatic mood swings.
May assert independence and autonomy while fighting feelings of insecurity.
May wonder about the future, which is both exciting and frightening.
May judge self according to perceived opinions of others.
May be preoccupied with own thoughts and forget reality.
May experience role confusion while considering all available options.
Seeks independence from parents; some conflict may result, but overall the relationship with parents is likely to be positive.
Sees parents as human beings who sometimes make mistakes.
Seeks emotional support from parents or peers.
Is generally influenced by both parents and peers.
May show tendency to conform to peers in early teen years, but later may resist peer pressure.
Tries out different social roles.
Learns to interact with an increasing number of people from home, school, and community.
Is capable of forming close relationships with peers of either sex. May begin dating.

1—Resource: *Developmental Highlights for Teens,* transparency master 15-2, TR.

2—Activity: List ways parents can help their teens cope with the changes described in this chart.

3—Resource: *Parents and Teens,* Activity H, SAG.

*These charts are not exact timetables for development. Individuals may perform certain activities earlier or later than indicated in the charts.

1—Activity: Review and outline this chapter emphasizing the information you found most useful.

2—Answers: Answers to review questions are located in the front section of this TAE.

Summary

- Adolescence is a transitional time during which people graduate from the dependency of childhood to the independence of adulthood. 1

- The most dramatic changes in physical development that occur during adolescence are those related to puberty.

- Parents must be aware of and help their children avoid eating disorders, tobacco, alcohol, and drug abuse, and the risks associated with sexual behavior.

- Developing decision-making skills is an important aspect of teens' intellectual development.

- Teens' emotional development is greatly affected by the emotional climate within their homes.

- Friendships are of great importance to teens, and friends are often major influences on teens' behavior.

- Parents need to talk to their teens about what to expect from dating experiences.

- Parents can help build their teen's self-esteem by expressing genuine interest in their teen's life.

- Teens need to visit their doctors and dentists regularly.

Reviewing Key Points

1. _____ refers to the process through which the body becomes capable of reproduction. 2

2. True or false. For the first few years of adolescence, girls in general are heavier and taller than boys.

3. Describe how the skull, jaw, chin, and nose change during puberty.

4. For each of the following physical changes, indicate whether it is a primary or secondary sex characteristic:
   A. menstruation
   B. growth of pubic hair
   C. breast development
   D. voice deepening
   E. growth of reproductive organs
   F. growth of facial hair
   G. nocturnal emissions

5. For each of the following, describe the eating patterns of persons with the disorder.
   A. anorexia nervosa
   B. bulimia nervosa
   C. binge eating disorder

6. Why are eating disorders dangerous?

7. What can parents do to discourage their teens from smoking or using smokeless tobacco?

8. True or false. Teens are likely to adopt the behavior and attitudes of their parents regarding alcohol use.

9. Why should parents tell their teens about drug use and abuse?

10. List three reasons teens should find healthy and appropriate ways to express their sexual feelings.

11. What role can parents play in their teens' intellectual development?

12. When teens can understand matters that exist only as thoughts or rules, they have developed what kind of thinking?

13. How do teens benefit from the rules and guidelines set by their parents?

14. How can parents help their teens build self-esteem and form positive self-concepts?

Learning by Doing

1. Research physical changes during puberty for either boys or girls. Write a paper explaining what you have learned.

2. Interview a doctor about the occurrence of eating disorders during the teen years. Ask questions about the potential consequences if these disorders go untreated.

3. Investigate resources in your community that can offer help to teens with two of the following problems: eating disorders, tobacco use, alcohol use, drug abuse, sexual health problems, teen pregnancy, and lack of self-esteem. Present your findings to the class.

4. Create a pamphlet for parents on helping their children through the teen years. Use the information from the chapter as a basis for your recommendations.

5. Role-play a parent talking to a teen about problems the teen has with a friend. Show how the parent can help the teen reach his or her own solution.

Thinking Critically

1. How would you feel if you were the parent of a teen confronted with decisions about tobacco, alcohol, drugs, and sexuality?

2. Select a typical decision that teens face. Apply the decision-making process to this decision. Write out each of the steps as you work through them.

3. As a class, devise a code of conduct that seems workable for teens today. Discuss the role parents should play in setting limits. Also discuss how parents' positive or negative attitudes affect teens' attitudes toward the parental limits.

4. Discuss the importance of a good emotional climate within the home. List ways a teen's lifestyle can change family life and ways families can cope with this. Is mutual respect important during this time?

5. Experts say having a positive self-concept and high amounts of self-esteem can help people overcome many problems faced in the teen years. What do you think parents can do to build their children's self-esteem? When should they start?

Part Four
The Challenges of Parenting

Chapter 16
Theories and Guidelines

Chapter 17
Guiding Healthy Development

Chapter 18
Family Concerns

Chapter 19
Family Crises

Chapter 20
A Look at Child Care Options

Chapter 21
Children's Education and Health

Chapter 22
The Challenge of a Child and Family Services Career

Chapter 16
Theories and
Guidelines

Objectives

After studying the chapter, you will be able to

- describe each stage of Piaget's theory of intellectual development.

- identify both positive and negative outcomes for each stage of Erikson's theory of personality development.

- describe each aspect of human functioning identified by Freud.

- differentiate among levels of human need as identified by Maslow.

- explain each level of development in Kohlberg's theory of moral development.

- identify ways parents can access information about child development, parenting, and parenting strategies.

- assess how child development theories and guidelines help parents establish good parent-child relationships.

- summarize the importance of an overall view of child development.

Key Terms

Piaget's theory of intellectual development

Erikson's theory of personality development

Freud's theory of personality development

Maslow's hierarchy of human needs

Kohlberg's theory of moral development

Caring parents want to raise their children in the best way possible. However, there is no magic formula for successful parenting. Perhaps one smart plan for parents might be to study the works of well-known child specialists, 16-1. Parents can use those ideas as guidance. They can combine this guidance with their own intuition and common sense.

Child development experts study how children grow and develop. From their research, they form ideas. They test these ideas for their ability to apply to all people. Once an idea has been well-proven and accepted by others in the field, it is called a *theory*. In this chapter, you will learn several of the most well-known theories of child development.

Piaget's Theory of Intellectual Development

Jean Piaget was a Swiss psychologist and educator. He studied child development extensively. According to **Piaget's theory of intellectual development**, people pass through four distinct stages as they develop intellectually. These four stages always occur in the same order. Each stage builds on the one before it. A person must complete one stage before moving on to another.

Piaget's theory gives a general age range for each stage. However, each person is an individual who develops at his or her own rate. A person may reach these stages a little earlier or later than the ages given. A very large delay may signal a problem. If parents notice such a delay, they should talk with their child's doctor.

1—**Vocabulary:** Look up terms in the glossary and discuss their meanings.

2—**Resource:** *Piaget*, Activity A, SAG.

1—Discuss: During the first stage of intellectual development, Piaget describes infants' use of senses and body movements as a learning activity. Briefly describe this.

2—Discuss: By the end of the sensorimotor stage, children learn to experiment mentally as well as physically. Briefly describe some examples of this.

16-1 _____
Parents can learn much about child development by reading the well-known theories of the experts. They can balance this reading with their own beliefs and instincts.

Sensorimotor Stage

Piaget called the first stage of intellectual development the *sensorimotor stage*. In this stage, children learn about the world through their senses and body movements, 16-2. This stage lasts from birth to age one and one-half or two years. The sensorimotor stage may be further divided into six steps:

- *Step one.* At birth, infants are concerned only with themselves. They are not selfish, but are simply unaware of anything other than themselves.

- *Step two.* From about one to four months of age, babies are learning to perform two separate actions. For instance, babies may wave their fists and then bring them to their mouths.

- *Step three.* The next step occurs between ages four and eight months. Babies learn to turn away from movements centered on themselves. They begin to respond to some other stimuli. They develop new response patterns and repeat actions they may have done accidentally. If a baby bumps a rattle and it makes noise, the baby may try to bump it again.

- *Step four.* Intentional behavior begins to appear at eight to twelve months. Babies learn certain actions lead to certain results. They also learn to follow objects with their eyes until the objects can no longer be seen. A game of peek-a-boo delights babies now because they can expect the hidden object to reappear.

- *Step five.* The next stage occurs from 12 to 18 months of age. Children begin experimenting with trial and error to see what will happen. For instance, a toddler may push a cracker off a high chair tray and watch it fall to the floor. The parent may not appreciate the messy results, but the baby learns from this process.

- *Step six.* The final step in the sensorimotor stage occurs between ages 18 and 24 months. Children in this step begin to experiment mentally as well as physically. They think about how they would do something without actually doing it until they reach a satisfactory solution. Children can now use not only physical but also mental ways of learning. Piaget used the term *operations* to describe mental processing of

16-2 _____
As this newborn progresses through the sensorimotor stage, she will learn about the world through her senses and body movements.

information. The sensorimotor period ends when children begin to perform some basic operations.

Preoperational Stage

The *preoperational stage* is the second stage. It extends from ages two to seven. Basic mental operations start replacing sensorimotor activities as the primary way to learn. In this stage, children learn mostly by using language and mental images. See 16-3.

At this stage, make-believe play contributes to a child's intellectual growth. Children use pretend play to create and express all kinds of mental images. Imitation is also useful in the preoperational stage. Children extend this pretend play to help them adjust to new experiences in their lives. When children start school, school often becomes the subject of their pretend play at home.

16-3 _____

During the preoperational stage, children can learn about their world by dressing up and acting out parts in a play.

Children in the preoperational stage are still egocentric. They think mostly from their own point of view. They have trouble putting themselves in other people's places. At this stage, children often describe events in terms of their own lives. For instance, a child may think the sun follows her from place to place. She may think the sun goes to bed when she does. This explanation does not include a universal or scientific reason for the rising and setting of the sun.

Near the end of this stage, children begin to learn about such concepts as seriation and multiple classification. They do not completely understand these concepts for a few more years, however. (Multiple classification and seriation were described in Chapter 14.) The preoperational stage ends when children begin achieving more advanced operations.

Concrete Operational Stage

The third stage of Piaget's theory is the *concrete operational stage.* It begins at age 6 or 7 and continues until about age 11. In this stage, children learn to solve more complex problems and use basic logic. They begin to think more like adults. However, children in this stage still think only in concrete terms—using actual people, objects, events, and situations. They do not have the skills to think about abstract concepts, people, or situations. These skills will develop in the last stage.

Understanding conservation is a major achievement in concrete operations. Conservation means a given amount of anything remains the same (is conserved) even if its shape changes. For instance, imagine that a boy pours water from a tall, narrow glass into a short, wide glass. The amount of water remains the same even though it may look different in its new container. The water looks different, so it takes thought to realize

1—**Discuss:** Explain how children use language and make-believe play in the preoperational stage. How might they describe events in relation to their own lives?

2—**Discuss:** During the concrete operational stage, children can solve more complex problems and use basic logic. Briefly describe some of the concepts they can understand.

the amount of water is the same. Children in this stage have developed these needed thinking skills. They also perfect their understanding of concepts such as reversibility, multiple classification, and seriation. (These concepts were described in Chapter 14.)

Formal Operational Stage

The last stage of intellectual development is the *formal operational stage*. It begins at age 11 or 12 and extends into adulthood. People in this stage can think about abstract ideas like loyalty and freedom, 16-4. They can think through very complex problems, find several solutions, and choose the most logical one. They can reason about ideas and events of the past, present, or future.

People in the formal operational stage have achieved an adult style of thinking. It takes many years, however, to practice and perfect the skills learned in this stage. For most, it is a 1 lifelong process. People continue to grow in their thinking abilities well into late adulthood.

Erikson's Theory of Personality Development

Erik Erikson studied social and emotional development over the lifespan. **Erikson's theory of personality development** divides the lifespan into eight basic stages. In each stage, a person faces certain conflicts and challenges. People are greatly influenced by the way they resolve these conflicts and challenges. In each stage, people must modify their personalities in order to adjust successfully to their social environments.

16-4 _____
During the formal operational stage, teens enjoy discussing abstract ideas, complex problems, and issues of the world.

These stages begin in childhood. Children are greatly influenced by their parents' attitudes and actions. A child's success at resolving conflicts in the early stages depends largely upon his or her parents. If the parents are supportive, it helps children succeed. Parents are not the only people who influence personality development. Other people's actions may also play a role.

According to Erikson, personality development is an ongoing process. This development is never final—people continually adjust their personalities at each stage of the life cycle. These adjustments are not irreversible, but they do influence an individual's overall personality.

If a person successfully meets the challenge of one stage, he or she is ready to meet challenges of the next stage. This person is fairly likely to have a stable personality. If a person does not succeed at one challenge, it **1** can affect his or her ability to meet future challenges. This person is more likely to have an unstable personality. **2** Chart 16-5 shows the stages of Erikson's theory of personality development.

Stage I: Trust Versus Mistrust

Erikson described establishing a sense of basic trust as the important task of the first years of life. Infants are challenged to develop trust that others will meet their needs. This forms the foundation for a stable personality. If parents are usually quick to respond to their child, the child learns to trust the parents to take care of him or her. Parents can also foster this sense of trust by bonding with their infants—holding, cuddling, playing, and talking to them. Infants who are loved and cared for likely establish a sense of trust, 16-6. They grow to see the world as a safe place and other people as helpful and dependable.

On the other hand, not all infants can develop this sense of trust. Some infants receive inconsistent care and little love and attention. These infants are likely to establish a sense of mistrust. They may develop fear and suspicion toward the world and everyone in it. Infants who are mistrustful have a weak foundation upon which to build their personalities.

1—Discuss: Explain how Erikson's theory of personality development is an ongoing process, one stage building on another. What is the ultimate goal of this progression of the stages?

2—Discuss: What might happen if a baby learns to mistrust others?

Erikson's Theory of Personality Development

Stage	Approximate Age	Step Toward Stable Personality	Step Toward Unstable Personality
1	birth to age 2	trust	mistrust
2	ages 2 and 3	autonomy	shame and doubt
3	ages 4 and 5	initiative	guilt
4	ages 6 to 11	industry	inferiority
5	ages 12 to 18	identity	role confusion
6	early adulthood	intimacy	isolation
7	middle age	generativity	stagnation
8	late adulthood	integrity	despair

16-5 According to Erikson, personality development is an ongoing process throughout eight stages of the life cycle.

1—Resource:
Toddler's Developing Autonomy,
reproducible master 16-1, TR.

2—Discuss: How do children exhibit a sense of autonomy? How is autonomy affected by the sense of trust established in the first stage?

3—Discuss: How do increased motor skills help children develop autonomy?

4—Reflect: As a child, how did you feel when you were criticized or scolded for spilling or breaking things?

5—Discuss: What role can parents play in supporting the creative efforts of their children?

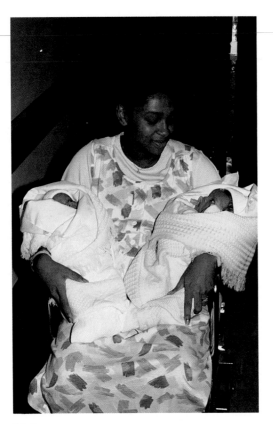

16-6

Even from birth, babies learn whether they can trust their parents to meet their needs.

Stage II: Autonomy Versus Shame

Erikson's second stage, autonomy versus shame, generally occurs from two to three years of age. Children in this stage are striving to develop a sense of *autonomy*, or independence. They go from being totally helpless creatures to having some control over their feelings and actions.

As children gain feelings of autonomy, they begin to develop minds of their own. Children might begin to say no and make choices. Children who mistrust their parents do not feel secure in exploring the world around them. They fear their parents will abandon them. Children who do trust their parents feel confident to explore. They do not worry, because they know their parents will be there for them. Trust allows children to become more independent and establish a sense of autonomy. See 16-7.

Autonomy is possible, in part, because of children's improving motor skills. Children take pride in their new skills and want to do everything themselves. Parents can promote autonomy by allowing children to practice life skills and make simple choices. This gives children a sense they can control their own behavior and their environment. It also helps them build confidence.

When children are not allowed to do things for themselves, they learn to doubt their own abilities. If parents always criticize or scold children for not being perfect, the children develop a sense of shame. They question their worth and their abilities to control themselves and their world.

If children leave this stage with a sense of autonomy, their self-esteem grows. They look forward to meeting greater challenges. If children feel discouraged about their own abilities, they will view themselves and the world with shame and doubt.

Stage III: Initiative Versus Guilt

Erikson's third stage is initiative versus guilt. It includes four- and five-year-olds. In this stage, children succeed if they start showing *initiative*, or ambition. Children in this age group often initiate activities. They spend time imagining what they want to do. Then they think of ways to do those things. Creativity also shows in their motor activities and language skills.

Parents can do much to foster initiative. They can respond positively to their children's ideas. See 16-8. Children need chances to create play ideas and put them into action. Parents can teach children to ask questions, find answers, and form concepts. This promotes intellectual initiative. Finally, parents can offer their approval and

16-7 _____
These children are asserting their indpendence by sliding down the slide on their own.

16-8 _____
When a child decides to build a snowman and then does so, he is showing initiative.

encouragement. Children need to know their ideas, questions, and concepts matter to others.

Other times, children have little chance to develop initiative. Their parents don't encourage but scold them. These parents don't praise children's play ideas. Instead, they belittle and ridicule them. Parents may even punish children for trying to act on their ideas. These parents don't

encourage their children to think or be creative.

In this sort of environment, it is easy for a child to develop a sense of guilt. Parents have given the child the message the child and his or her ideas are not valuable or worthwhile. If parents punish rather than reward the child's attempts at initiative, soon the child will stop trying. The child will begin to feel less confident and may develop a less stable personality.

Stage IV: Industry Versus Inferiority

Stage four is industry versus inferiority. It lasts from ages age six to eleven. During this stage, children become capable of deductive reasoning. They also learn to follow rules. Children this age also become interested in how things are made, how they work, and what they do. The main focus of this stage is developing a sense of *industry*, or capacity to make a productive effort, 16-9.

1—Vocabulary: What does *industry* mean? Give some examples.

1—Discuss: If parents discourage children from doing and making things, how can this affect the children's feelings of industry?

2—Discuss: Can the school environment affect children's sense of industry? Describe ways this might occur.

Parents can promote industry by encouraging their children to do, make, or build projects. They can also stress the importance of seeing a task through to completion. Parents can also strengthen children's sense of industry by praising and rewarding them for their efforts.

Some children don't successfully develop a sense of industry. Instead, they develop a sense of inferiority. They feel they are incapable of succeeding in their efforts. They feel they are less worthwhile and valuable. Parents shouldn't discourage their children from doing and making things on their own. Also, if parents do not praise children for their accomplishments, children may feel they can't do anything right. Deep feelings of inferiority may dominate their personalities. They may passively accept their unsuccessful roles in life, or may misbehave to compensate for their lack of achievement. If they can't get praise for doing things right, they may seek criticism for doing things wrong. Then they are at least being recognized for something.

16-9
This child's parents have strengthened his sense of industry. He feels the importance of making a productive effort.

Children in this age group have contact with other people besides their parents. They attend school and spend time with friends. From this stage on, parents are not the only important outside force on children's personality development. The actions and attitudes of teachers and friends are also a major influence.

Children's school atmospheres can also affect their sense of industry. If the school environment discourages children's desire to succeed, it may lead to academic failures and create feelings of inferiority. On the other hand, school can be a positive force in helping children recognize their potential. Even students who were discouraged at home can have their sense of industry revitalized by a sensitive and committed teacher.

Stage V: Identity Versus Role Confusion

Erikson's fifth stage is identity versus role confusion. It occurs during adolescence, roughly between ages 12 and 18. During this stage, the main challenge is for teens to develop healthy personal identities. They need to learn to see themselves as individuals. They should learn more about who they really are, and what kind of adults they want to become.

Parents have an indirect influence during this stage. Success is more likely if parents have helped their children meet the challenges of previous stages. Achieving a healthy personal identity is easier when parents have provided loving care and concern from the start.

At this stage, teens form images of themselves based on all the roles they play. Teens are young men, young women, sons, daughters, brothers, sisters, students, employees, and citizens. If they can fit these different images together well, they will feel good about themselves and all their roles. These teens know who they are and where they want to go. They have confidence they are in control of their lives. See 16-10.

If teens are unable to form their identities during this period, this is called *role confusion*. This means they have not successfully seen themselves as separate and worthwhile persons. Teens may be confused about what is expected of them in their various roles. They may feel unsure how to merge demands and settle conflicts among these roles. Teens may be confused about who they really are and who they wish to become.

Young people who have not successfully resolved the conflicts of earlier stages are more likely to experience role confusion. Teens with feelings of mistrust, shame, doubt, guilt, and inferiority are less prepared to meet this challenge. They do not feel confident in finding out who they are.

16-10

This teen knows she wants to work with horses. She has achieved an identity.

This can be dangerous. If teens do not form their own identities, they may rely too much on others' perception of them. If they don't know who they want to become, they may become what others want them to be. They may conform to identities promoted by others instead of following their own ideas.

If teens do not establish healthy personal identities during the teen years, there is still time when they become adults. It takes longer for some people than others. Life is full of changes. As people continue to grow, they may develop healthier senses of identity. This type of delay may interfere with people's continued development for a time. It does not, however, guarantee the person will never move ahead.

Stage VI: Intimacy Versus Isolation

The sixth stage is intimacy versus isolation. It begins in late adolescence and extends into middle age. This is a time for forming stable relationships with others. *Intimacy* describes a special closeness between two people that does not compromise either person's sense of identity. Love relationships and close friendships are intimate relationships. See 16-11.

During this period, many people move from their parents' homes. They begin to live on their own. Parental influence at this stage is more indirect. Much of parents' influence in this stage consists of how they have raised their children. People take with them lessons they have learned from their parents. These lessons can affect how well prepared a person is to form intimate relationships. People who have met challenges of the previous stages are also more likely to succeed at this stage.

To establish intimacy with someone else, a person must feel secure

1—Discuss: How can parents help their teens achieve healthy personal identities?

2—Vocabulary: What does *intimacy* mean? How can people develop this?

1—Discuss: Describe the qualities of people who have achieved a sense of generativity. Suggest ways they can contribute to society.

2—Discuss: Integrity versus despair is the final stage of personality development. Describe a person who experiences integrity and one who feels despair.

16-11 _____
Many teens start to form couple relationships. They are learning to build intimacy.

with who he or she is. Role confusion makes it difficult to form intimate relationships. So do unresolved conflicts from the past. People with role confusion or unresolved issues may feel isolated and alone. Isolation may lead to unstable personality development.

Stage VII: Generativity Versus Stagnation

Erikson's seventh stage is generativity versus stagnation. It occurs in middle adulthood. In this stage, people become concerned about their contributions to the world. *Generativity* means showing concern for future generations and for the conditions of society. People who work to make the world a better place for future generations meet the challenge of this stage.

Parenting is the main way people establish a sense of generativity, 16-12. Many adults feel they contribute to the world by raising children. Raising responsible children is one way parents can feel they have contributed something valuable to society. Parents also feel a certain sense of wonder as they think about what their children will become. Each child has the potential to do great things. Parents share joy in their children's accomplishments.

Adults who are not parents can also experience generativity. Often they do so through their work or other good deeds. People whose jobs make the world a better place feel useful. They feel satisfied in their accomplishments and know they are making a difference. Others give through volunteer work or donating to good causes.

Persons who do not achieve a sense of generativity think they do not matter. They see themselves as having done nothing worthwhile for the world. They feel bored and do not feel they are continuing to grow. This feeling is called a sense of *stagnation*.

Stage VIII: Integrity Versus Despair

The last stage of personality development occurs in late adulthood, when a person's major efforts are nearing completion. The goal of this last stage is integrity. *Integrity* means a sense of satisfaction and peace a person has with himself or herself. A person who has achieved integrity can look back with pride on the life he or she has lived. For many, this is a time to enjoy being with family, 16-13. It may also

16-12 _____
Being parents can create feelings of generativity for many adults.

16-13
People who can look back on their lives with pride have achieved a sense of integrity. At this stage, people often enjoy spending time with family.

be a time to pursue hobbies and friendships.

Instead of integrity, some people look back over their lives with a sense of despair. They feel they would like to live life differently, but realize it is too late. These people see their lives as a series of missed opportunities and wasted time. They feel unhappy and wonder about what might have been.

Freud's Theory of Personality Development

Sigmund Freud founded *psychoanalysis*. This is a method to treat a person's problems by studying his or her past, especially the childhood years. Freud reasoned early experiences affect people's personalities in important ways. To treat problems in an adult, a trained psychologist should talk with the person about his or her early experiences.

Freud developed many psychological theories, some of which are controversial. One of his most well-known theories is **Freud's theory of personality development**. It is based on three aspects of human functioning. Freud labeled these the id, the ego, and the superego.

The Id

According to Freud, the *id* is the source of psychological and physical tension. It is also the source of a person's instincts related to sexual behavior and aggression. The id doesn't think or reason. It demands immediate satisfaction of its wants and needs. An example of the id is the hunger cry of an infant, 16-14. Infants do not think about being hungry. When they feel hungry, they cry. They want their hunger satisfied immediately and usually do not stop crying until they are fed.

The Ego

The *ego* is the part of the personality that deals with logic and controlled behaviors. For example, babies learn their hunger is not always satisfied immediately. They learn to deal with this reality. They will look around and play while waiting to be fed. Learning to wait is part of the socialization process.

Dealing with anxiety is an important function of the ego. Babies need to be comforted when they are anxious. As they grow, children learn to cope with their anxieties. Children develop the ability to deal with their own feelings of anxiety. See 16-15.

1—**Resource:** *Freud*, Activity C, SAG.

2—**Discuss:** Describe how children develop strategies to deal with their own feelings of anxiety.

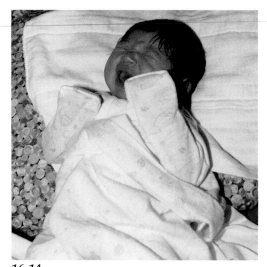

16-14

When babies cry, they are revealing the id aspect of their personalities. The id demands to be satisfied immediately.

16-15

As the ego aspect of personality grows, children learn to cope with their own anxieties.

The Superego

The *superego* is a person's moral code. This part of the personality helps people tell the difference between right and wrong. It is the part that counters the id's irrational desires. The superego has two parts: the conscience and the ego ideal. The *conscience* helps people decide what is right and wrong. When children know they have done something wrong, they feel guilty. The ability to have feelings of guilt rather than just fearing punishment is a sign of a well-developed conscience. The *ego ideal* sets standards toward which people can strive. Children who do not live up to their own high standards may feel shame or lose self-esteem.

Maslow's Hierarchy of Human Needs

Every person has certain basic needs. All humans share these needs, but each person fulfills them in a unique way. For instance, all people need food, but each person chooses different foods to satisfy his or her hunger. People in two cultures may eat very different food. The ways people fulfill their needs affect their thoughts, behaviors, and personalities.

Abraham Maslow, a noted psychologist, devised a system for studying human needs. His theory stated that people have different types of needs, each with its own priority. Some needs are more important than others. Maslow arranged human needs in order of priority as shown in 16-16. This arrangement is called **Maslow's hierarchy of human needs**. His theory helps explain how human needs influence personality development. Realizing all one's needs can make a person feel complete.

Human Needs

- Self-Actualization
- Esteem
- Love and Acceptance
- Safety and Security
- Physical Needs

16-16
According to Maslow's theory, all needs have a certain priority. Needs of one level must be at least partially fulfilled before a person can realize higher needs.

Physical Needs

According to Maslow, physical needs have the first priority. *Physical needs* include food, water, shelter, and clothing. These items are essential for good health, well-being, and the continuation of life. Physical needs must be at least partially met before a person can even be aware of other needs. If a person is starving, he or she has little energy to pay attention to higher needs.

Safety and Security Needs

Once his or her physical needs have been met, a person can recognize needs for *safety and security*. People need to feel safe from physical danger. They need to feel secure in daily routines so they know what to expect from life. In addition, people need to know they are protected from financial troubles.

People who fulfill their needs for safety and security can focus on even higher needs. They will have the energy and courage to experience all life has to offer. On the other hand, people whose lives center on protecting themselves have little chance to develop further.

Love and Acceptance Needs

Everyone needs to be needed. This is the basis for Maslow's third level of human needs, *love and acceptance needs*. People need to feel they are accepted by others. They need to feel secure in their relationships with family members and friends. Praise, support, encouragement, and personal warmth will help fulfill these needs. People who feel loved are also capable of loving others. People who feel accepted are more capable of accepting others.

Esteem Needs

In addition to love and acceptance, people have *esteem* (respect and admiration) *needs*. Self-esteem must be established first. Persons must respect themselves before they can expect others to respect them. Family members can help one another build self-esteem. They can help each other feel they are worthwhile. Friends are also important. Belonging to a group or sharing a special friendship can help meet esteem needs.

When people have self-esteem and the esteem of others, they have the potential for further personality development. They have the confidence they need to strive for achievement and independence.

Self-Actualization Needs

Self-actualization is the realization of a person's full potential. To reach this level, all other levels of need must be at least partially fulfilled. At this level, a person combines concern for self with concern for others and concern for society as a whole. People strive to become the best they can be. For instance, a person who is talented in art might

1—Enrich: Cite ways your community helps meet physical needs (food, water, shelter, and clothing) through government programs, and volunteer groups.

2—Discuss: Discuss how a community can assure its citizens of safety and security.

3—Discuss: Why do people need love and acceptance throughout their lives?

4—Discuss: Is self-esteem something that is given to you or something you have to develop?

1—Vocabulary: What does *self-actualization* mean? When people reach this level, are they finished growing? Why or why not?

2—Resource: *Kohlberg*, Activity E, SAG.

3—Discuss: Why is it important for children to learn which behaviors are inappropriate?

strive to become the best artist possible. A person with skills in auto mechanics might strive to become the best mechanic possible.

People who reach self-actualization believe in themselves. They have the confidence to express personal beliefs and offer support to others. Their personalities are fully developed. However, this does not mean they quit learning or their personalities stop changing. Actually, they are even more interested in improving themselves. They continue to strive to become better people. People who reach self-actualization also strive to fulfill needs for beauty, order, and balance in their lives. These needs have no end point.

Kohlberg's Theory of Moral Development

Moral development is the gradual process of learning to behave in ways that reflect an understanding of the difference between right and wrong. This lifelong process begins in childhood. Many factors influence a person's moral development, but parental influence is perhaps the greatest.

Many psychologists have researched the moral development of children and teens. One researcher, Lawrence Kohlberg, has done some of the most thorough studies of moral development among children. **Kohlberg's theory of moral development** divides moral development into three levels. These are the preconventional, conventional, and postconventional levels. See 6-17.

Preconventional Level

Young children in the preconventional level behave in ways that allow them to avoid punishment or gain rewards. Children are guided in their behavior by these obvious outcomes. If they please parents, they receive rewards. These rewards might be attention, verbal expressions, or material objects such as toys. In this stage, children also learn punishment is a result of unacceptable behavior. If they behave poorly, they may be sent to their rooms or not allowed to go outside to play. Getting into trouble is an unpleasant feeling, so children try to avoid it.

Young children do not think of their behavior as right or wrong. They simply know certain behaviors lead to rewards from their parents, while others lead to punishment, 6-18. Young children try to behave in ways that will help them earn rewards or escape punishment.

Conventional Level

As children grow older, they move into the conventional level. At this level of development, children's deci-

16-17 ———
Kohlberg's theory states that moral development occurs in three levels. Each of these levels can be further broken down into stages.

Kohlberg's Stages of Moral Development

Preconventional Level: *Moral decisions are based on punishment and rewards.*	Conventional Level: *Moral decisions are based on social rules and expectations.*	Postconventional Level: *Moral decisions are based on personal values about what is morally right.*
Stage One: Threat of punishment influences decisions.	Stage Three: Opinions of others influence decisions.	Stage Five: Personal values concerning individual human rights influence decisions.
Stage Two: Desire for rewards influences decisions.	Stage Four: Respect for law and order guides behavior.	Stage Six: Self-chosen ethical principles guide decisions.

16-18
This infant does not like to be scolded. In young children, behavior is guided by the desire to earn rewards and avoid punishment.

sions are shaped by approval or disapproval from others. Children in this stage do not necessarily have to be punished to stop their behavior. They may also stop their behavior if they feel their parents or friends disapprove of what they are doing. Disapproval feels like rejection to a child in this stage. Avoiding rejection is a strong motivator for children in the conventional level. If parents of friends approve of children's actions, their feelings of self-esteem increase. Children will alter their behavior in order to conform. This stage is often experienced in late childhood or early adolescence.

To whom the young person looks for approval during this stage is very important. Some teens may be so anxious to seek peer approval they let others make decisions for them. Peers may influence teens to imitate behaviors that risk their health (such as using alcohol, tobacco, or drugs).

Children also begin to accept the concept of law and order at the conventional level. They learn to obey laws that protect the rights of individuals. They understand the importance of having laws and rules to regulate behavior.

Postconventional Level

Ideally, a person will advance to the final stage—the postconventional level. At this level, behaviors are based on more abstract principles of right and wrong. A person develops his or her own set of morals upon which decisions are based. This does not usually occur until adulthood. Not all adults reach this level. Some remain at the conventional level throughout their lives.

1   Parents play an important role in their children's moral development. From an early age, a child's moral development is shaped by rewards, punishments, approval, and disapproval from parents. Parents can also encourage children to develop moral codes that are consistent with those of the family.

Other Child Development Theories

Bookstores and libraries are full of books about parenting and children. Some are written by qualified psychologists, child development experts, and doctors. Some are written by experienced parents. Others are written by people who see the opportunity to make money by expressing their own opinions about parenting. These people may not be qualified or know anything about parenting or children. Parents should read the section of the book that gives the authors credentials, if such a section is provided. Persons who have studied child development and parenting are often the most reliable sources of parenting information.

2   Parents and prospective parents can gain valuable knowledge from books.

1—**Discuss:** Why is it important for parents to guide children's moral development?

2—**Reflect:** React to this statement: Parenting is instinctive, so you don't need to study books about children.

They should remember, however, to read with a critical eye. They will need to adapt what they read to their own situations and their own children. No author knows a child as well as his or her parents do. Also, parents who try to raise their child exactly as recommended by a book may never pause long enough to relax and enjoy their parenting roles.

In spite of valid cautions, parents should read all the reputable child development information they can. Parents who understand how children grow and develop have more confidence in themselves as parents. They know what behaviors to expect and how to deal with them. Such parents are likely to enjoy parenthood.

Parents can find sections of books on parenting, family life, and children in most major bookstores. They can also purchase such books online or check them out from local libraries. Parents may be unsure which books to choose. Often, they may ask others for recommendations. Doctors, teachers, counselors, religious leaders, and other parents may offer advice about books they have read. Parents may also be able to read reviews of popular parenting books in magazines, newspapers, or on the Internet.

Parenting Strategies

Another type of professional advice can be found in well-known parenting strategies. These strategies are parenting methods devised by psychologists, counselors, educators, and doctors. Each strategy comes from a different perspective, and each has a unique focus. Parents can use these strategies to improve their parenting. They can also learn valuable techniques for interacting with their children.

If a parent wants to learn about well-known parenting strategies, they have a few options. First, parents can read books about these strategies. Second, they could attend workshops or parenting classes on a specific method. They might also ask their doctors, teachers, or counselors what strategies they recommend. A few of the most popular strategies are described in 16-19.

An Overall View of Development

Theories aid people's understanding, but it is important to remember one key point. Developmental theories are just that—theories. Although they are well researched, they are only ideas. What applies to one set of research subjects may not apply to everyone else. Also, ideas and theories change with the times. As new information becomes available, theories may have to be revised or abandoned altogether. New theories are created in their place. Parents must use a critical eye as they look at these theories.

It is also good to remember most theories focus only on one area of development. No one theory fits all areas of development and all stages of

Parenting Strategies

Program	Author/Founder	Highlights
Active Parenting	**Michael H. Popkin**	The goal of Active Parenting is to present the theories of Adler and Dreikurs (see below) in a format that can be easily learned and practiced by parents. It is a video-based program presented in a classroom setting. Group interaction is encouraged. The democratic parenting model presented encourages the active participation of the parent. Parents learn to take a leadership role in the family, "acting" rather than "reacting" when a child misbehaves.
Dreikurs' Doctrine	**Rudolf Dreikurs of the Alfred Adler Institute in Chicago**	States that a misbehaving child is a discouraged child. Identifies four goals of misbehavior: to get attention, to show power, to seek revenge, and to display inadequacy. Describes parents' role as that of blocking children's misguided efforts and encouraging more constructive ones: cooperation, responsible behavior, and a respect for order and the rights of all individuals. Suggests that families should be democratic. Sets up a system of natural and logical consequences.
P.E.T. (Parent Effectiveness Training)	**Thomas Gordon**	Based on the premise parents should give up, absolutely and forever, the use of power, which is damaging to people and relationships. Promotes active listening. Also promotes "I" messages rather than "you" messages. Suggests a "no-lose" method of resolving conflicts.
P.I.P. (Parent Involvement Program)	**William Glasser**	Promotes friendly relations between parents and children which, in turn, depend on involvement and communication. Suggests that irresponsible behavior is common among children who see themselves as failures. If these children can be convinced someone cares about and believes in them, they will be able to improve their self-concept. Their behavior is likely to improve as well. Provides a seven-step approach to help children evaluate and improve their own behavior. Encourages praising successes rather than punishing failures.
Responsive Parenting	**Saf Lerman**	Group sessions provide parents with information and practical techniques to help make parenting more satisfying and effective. The program emphasizes a positive approach to parenting focusing on open communication. It is geared especially to parents of babies and young children.

(continued)

16-19
Many different parenting strategies are available to offer various kinds of help, support, and training.

1—Enrich: Arrange for the class to view Popkin's video on *Active Parenting.* Have students write summaries of the video after viewing it.

2—Discuss: Gordon's *Parent Effectiveness Training* program advocates parents giving up the use of power when they deal with children. Explain what this means.

16-19
(continued)

Parenting Strategies		
Program	**Author/Founder**	**Highlights**
S.T.E.P. (Systematic Training for Effective Parenting)	**Don Dinkmeyer and Gary D. McKay**	S.T.E.P. suggests methods of discipline and communication that lead to practical solutions for a variety of parenting problems. The teen program shows parents how to help their teenage children develop responsibility. This will help them become more self-reliant and able to handle more of their own problems. The stepfamily program offers information, advice, and encouragement for members of families created by remarriage.
Toughlove	**Phyllis and David York**	Emphasizes the establishment of parental authority through firmness and discipline. Encourages parents to establish reasonable limits for their children's behavior as well as consequences or punishments for violations of those limits. Parents meet together and support each other during crises.

1

1—Enrich: Have students research *Toughlove.* Then role-play parents using this method with their children.

life. There is a tendency to divide parenting concerns into bits and pieces. However, the main goal is the healthy development of the whole person. Parents may want to rely on more than one theory or use bits of information from each. They should use only what makes sense and works for them.

Parents should try to remember there is a wholeness to their child's development. The cries and smiles, laughter and groans, sweetness and stubbornness all contribute to this wholeness. When a child seems a little weak or especially strong in one aspect of development, parents need to remember this is just one portion of a whole. They need to keep the child's overall development and well-being in mind.

Summary

- Parents can study theories of well-known child specialists and current parenting strategies to gain insight into ways of raising their children.

1

- Jean Piaget's theory of intellectual development states that people pass through four distinct stages as they develop intellectually.

- Erik Erikson's theory of personality development divides the lifespan into eight basic stages. In each stage, a person faces specific conflicts and challenges that require the person to modify his or her personality.

- Sigmund Freud's theory of personality development is based on three aspects of human functioning that impact the personality.

- Abraham Maslow's theory explains the influence of human needs on personality.

- Lawrence Kohlberg divided moral development into three levels.

- Parents and prospective parents can gain valuable knowledge from books, but they should read with a critical eye, adapting what they read to their own situations.

- Parenting strategies may offer valuable information for people who want to change their approach to parenting and improve their parenting skills.

- Theorists tend to divide parenting concerns into bits and pieces. However, the overall goal is the healthy development of the whole child.

Reviewing Key Points

2

1. What is a theory?
2. List and briefly describe Piaget's stages of intellectual development.

3. For each letter, give the name of the stage from Erikson's theory of personality development that is described.
   A. Infants grow to see the world as a safe place and people as helpful and dependable.
   B. Children begin to think of and initiate activities of their own.
   C. A person learns to develop a special closeness with another person that does not compromise either person's sense of identity.
   D. A person looks back on his or her life with a sense of pride.
   E. Teens form images of themselves based upon all the roles they play.
   F. A person becomes concerned about his or her contributions to the world.
   G. Children strive to develop a sense of independence.
   H. Children develop the capacity and desire to make a productive effort.
4. Does development at each stage of Erikson's theory affect later stages?
5. Name and describe each of the three aspects of human functioning according to Freud.
6. True or false. According to Maslow, the need for love is a more immediate need than the need for esteem.
7. Maslow called the desire for self-fulfillment _____.
8. Name the three levels of moral development identified by Lawrence Kohlberg.
9. List three ways parents can learn more about other child development theories and parenting strategies.
10. What is meant by an overall view of development?

1—Activity: Review and outline this chapter emphasizing the information you found most useful.

2—Answers: Answers to review questions are located in the front section of this TAE.

Learning by Doing

1. Using the information in the chapter, create a set of 10 flash cards on Piaget's theory of intellectual development. On the front of each card, write a key phrase about the theory from the chapter. On the back of each card, write the name of the corresponding stage of intellectual development. Use the flash cards to quiz a classmate.

2. Create a pamphlet or poster for parents that illustrates the importance of learning about child development.

3. Design a bulletin board using pictures that illustrate the three aspects of human functioning according to Freud.

4. Select one of the theorists from this chapter. Research the person's life and prepare a biographical report for the class.

5. Working with a group, select one of the parenting strategies listed in Figure 16-19. Investigate places parents in your community can locate information about this strategy. You might do research in the library and on the Internet, and contact local parenting organizations, doctors, counselors, and educators. Give a report to the class and compile a file with your findings.

Thinking Critically

1. Debate whether parents should be encouraged to read about child development. How do you think parents should use these theories to help them as they parent?

2. For each of Piaget's stages of intellectual development, give two examples of actions performed by children that demonstrate abilities gained in this stage. How does each stage build on previous stages? What roles do parents play in each stage of development?

3. Describe both positive and negative outcomes that can occur at each stage of Erikson's theory of personality development. Cite parents' roles in influencing these results.

4. Select your favorite theory from this chapter. Write a short paper explaining why you like this theory best. Explain how the information in this theory would help you if you became a parent.

5. Working with a small group, choose one of the parenting strategies listed in Figure 16-19. (Use a different strategy from the one your group researched for question 5 in the previous section.) Identify two groups of parents for whom you think this program would be very helpful and one group for whom it would not. Explain the reasons for your selections.

Being affectionate with a sibling is one way to fulfill love and acceptance needs.

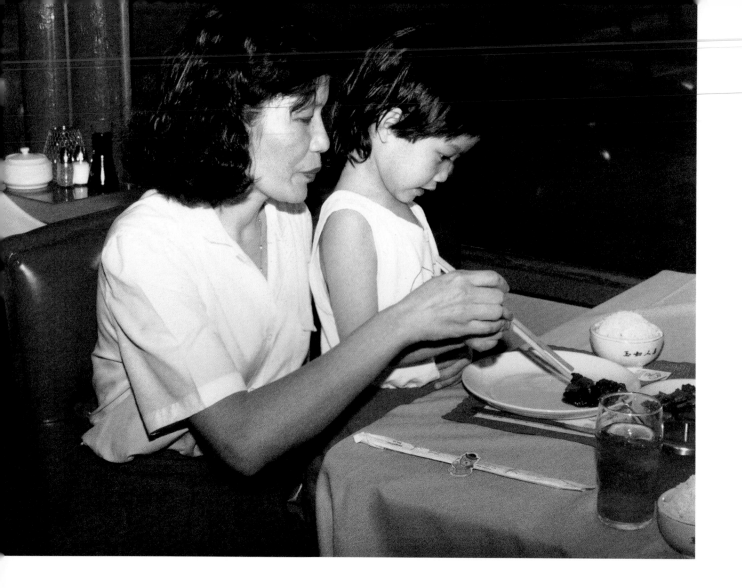

Chapter 17
Guiding Healthy
Development

Objectives

After studying this chapter, you will be able to

- describe the vital role parents play in their children's development.
- explain how children learn behavior patterns.
- describe three styles of parenting.
- explain effective methods of discipline and punishment.
- analyze the experiences provided by sibling relationships.
- evaluate methods of helping children develop responsibility, honesty, and healthy sexuality.
- summarize the influence of the media upon children.

Key Terms

positive behavior
guidance
self-control
discipline
punishment
imitation
identification
trial and error
positive reinforcement
negative reinforcement
authoritarian
permissive
authoritative
natural consequences
logical consequences
time-out
siblings
responsibility
chat room

People should not approach parenting as an exercise in perfection. It may seem strange to include this statement in a parenting book. Experts have much to say about parenting, but this can sometimes undermine the confidence of young parents. Successful parenting takes work, but it also involves lots of happiness. Parents who worry too much about raising their children according to experts may never truly experience the pleasures of parenting.

Parents play a vital role in every area of their children's development. Children are dependent upon their parents for a long period of time. During this time, parents have many responsibilities and make many sacrifices. However, the parent-child relationship is very rewarding. It usually brings just as many joys as anxious hours, 17-1.

Most children think their parents are the most wonderful people in the world. No one can answer a child's questions quite like a parent. No one else can steady those first faltering moments of balancing on a bicycle quite as well. No one else's arms feel quite so comforting. No one else can share the anxiety of a first date or a first job with as much understanding. Children need their parents' love, support, and encouragement to become responsible, independent adults.

Guiding Children's Behavior

An essential part of parenting is guiding children's behavior. Parents must help their children learn positive behavior. **Positive behavior** is behavior that is acceptable, healthy, and satisfying for the child and those

1—**Vocabulary:** Look up terms in the glossary and discuss their meanings.

2—**Resource:** *Memo,* reproducible master 17-2, TR.

3—**Discuss:** Brainstorm the vital roles parents play in their children's lives. Have these roles expanded or been reduced in the last 20 years?

4—**Resource:** *Little Eyes Are Watching,* reproducible master 17-2, TR.

17-1 _____
Being a parent has many tender moments, such as taking your child on special outings.

around him or her. Children feel best about themselves when they use positive behavior. Positive behavior promotes harmony between the child and his or her family and society.

Parents have two main ways to enforce positive behavior in their children. They can use guidance and discipline. Although these two terms are similar, they are not exactly the same. **Guidance** means directing, supervising, and influencing a child's behavior. Guidance can be direct or indirect. In fact, parents may be unaware of all the ways in which they guide their children. For instance, parents guide by allowing certain behaviors while forbidding others. This supervising function regulates a child's behavior until the child can do so for himself or herself.

Positive behavior is one goal of guidance. Guidance also teaches children **self-control**, or the ability to govern their own actions, impulses, and desires. As they grow, children need to learn self-control so they can regulate

their own behavior. Self-control also helps people make responsible decisions for themselves.

Discipline is the process of intentionally teaching and training a child to behave in appropriate ways. It includes all the conscious efforts parents make to help their children learn positive behavior. When they learn which behaviors are right and which are wrong, children have the chance to choose correct behavior. In this way, discipline leads children to develop self-control and form a conscience.

Discipline and guidance should not be confused with punishment. **Punishment** is being subjected to a penalty for something a person has done wrong. It is an assertion of parental control on a child. Punishment is a consequence for inappropriate behavior. Parents hope punishment guides children to choose better future behavior.

New parents often think they will naturally know how to guide, discipline, and possibly punish children when the time comes. They may not even think about these topics until the child misbehaves. Understanding how to guide and discipline children ahead of time is a better approach. This will lead to a more effective parenting role.

How Children Learn Behavior

In order to guide children's behavior, parents need to understand how children learn behaviors. Then, parents can more effectively guide their children to choose acceptable behaviors. As children grow, they must learn which behaviors will enable them to interact effectively with others.

Direct Teaching

Children learn much through the direct teaching of parents and other adults. Direct teaching means an adult deliberately instructs a child how to do something, 17-2. Parents use direct teaching to teach their children about proper ways to behave. The adult explains why the child should act a certain way. Direct teaching begins at an early age and continues into adulthood.

Imitation

When children intentionally copy the behavior of others, they are learning by **imitation**. Children constantly observe their parents and others. They then wait for a chance to experiment for themselves. Little boys who watch their dads shave may try to put shaving cream all over their faces—and every place else!

Similarly, children learn by imitating the negative behaviors of their parents. Parents should be aware of the example they are setting. If their actions conflict with their direct teaching, children will often imitate the behavior rather than follow the direct teaching.

17-2

This mother is explaining how to make deviled eggs and allowing her daughter to practice. She is using direct teaching.

Identification

Identification is another way children learn behavior. **Identification** means children unconsciously adopt the behavior patterns of people they like and admire. Behavior patterns are internalized. The child actually "feels like" the other person. He or she may begin to look and act like the person admired.

Trial and Error

Children also learn by trial and error. **Trial and error** means choosing behaviors through a process of testing. Children keep trying new ways of doing something until they find one that works. They learn from their mistakes. If they try a behavior that doesn't work well, they abandon this behavior and try another. When they find a behavior that works, they will repeat it.

Reinforcement

Behavior learned through trial and error is likely to be repeated if it is reinforced. Reinforcement is a response to a behavior that encourages or discourages a person to use the behavior again. There are two types of reinforcement—positive and negative.

Positive reinforcement describes a response that makes repeating a behavior more likely. A simple word for positive reinforcement is *reward*. Praise and attention are forms of positive reinforcement, 17-3. When children are rewarded for their behavior, they are likely to repeat it. Behavior that does not receive this positive response is less likely to continue. Suppose a boy cleans his room and his mother responds with praise. This praise encourages him to clean his room again. If he is not praised, he may be less likely to clean his room again.

Negative reinforcement describes a response that makes repeating a behavior less likely. Punishment is one

1—Enrich: Role-play ways parents can offer reinforcement or reward to encourage positive behavior.

17-3 _____

Showing affection with a hug is one of the most helpful kinds of positive reinforcement.

form of negative reinforcement. When children receive a negative response to their behavior, they are less likely to repeat it. Suppose a boy was asked to clean his room, but he did not. His mother may respond with disapproval, and assign consequences for not following her directions. This response will discourage him from using this negative behavior (not listening, not cleaning his room) again.

How Parents Guide Behavior

Parents can use a variety of methods and techniques to guide their children's behavior. Researchers have divided these methods into three main parenting styles: authoritarian, permissive, and authoritative.

Authoritarian

Parents who choose the **authoritarian** style value obedience as a virtue. They favor punishment to correct children's behavior. Authoritarian discipline is based on rule by authority rather than by reason. Parents are in control and have the power. Children must learn to respect this authority. Parents offer little or no explanation when they give directions. They expect children to accept and follow the rules without question. They seldom reward their children for fear of spoiling them.

When children misbehave in an authoritarian household, physical punishment is likely to occur. Authoritarian parents think such discipline will produce "good" children. Children are afraid to misbehave for fear of what will happen to them. These children aren't told why they should behave. Authoritarian parents don't teach children to make their own decisions. Instead, they teach the children to rely on their parents for instruction. As a result, these children are more likely to misbehave when their parents are not around.

Authoritarian methods do not encourage self-control. Instead, such methods may cause children to rebel because they want freedom in making choices. This parenting style was used more in previous generations. It is widely considered inappropriate in today's society, but is still used in some homes.

Permissive

The **permissive** style of parenting allows children almost complete freedom in regulating their own behavior. It is at the opposite extreme of the authoritarian style of parenting. Parents establish few rules, little order, and no routine. Children are allowed to "do their own thing" and make their own decisions.

Permissive parents want their children to be happy. They think giving their children complete freedom will make them happy. Instead, children are likely to feel insecure because they have no boundaries. They do not learn about appropriate or inappropriate behavior. Instead, they are likely to become self-centered and uncooperative. Since they have had few restrictions, they will face difficulty as adults whose behavior is regulated by laws, policies, and social conventions.

Authoritative

The **authoritative** style of parenting provides freedom within limits. Parents establish rules, but they explain what the rules mean and why they exist. Rules and limits give children a sense of security, stability, and consistency. Parents explain to their children the reasons for expected behavior, 17-4. Children are encouraged to ask questions and find answers. As a result, children know what their parents expect of them and why.

Although authoritative parents teach their children how to behave, they let the children choose their own behavior and make some of their own decisions. This way, they allow their children to develop decision-making

17-4 _____
When a parent uses an authoritative style of parenting, children know what is expected of them and why.

skills and independence. If the children choose poor behavior, however, consequences do apply. Parents hold the child accountable for his or her choices.

When children misbehave, they are given a chance to explain their behavior. They may also offer their input as the parents set consequences or punishment. Authoritative parents use positive reinforcement to promote the growth of self-control. Experts recommend this style of parenting as the preferred style. Research indicates authoritative parenting has the best outcomes for children.

Effective Discipline

The goal of parental discipline is to build a child's senses of self-control and self-discipline. Through discipline, parents also try to encourage positive behavior and discourage negative behavior, 17-5. To accomplish these goals however, discipline must be effective. The following are guidelines for effective discipline.

Set Reasonable Limits

All children need limits set by their parents. These limits are often communicated as rules. Some rules must be made to keep children safe. For instance, a child who is just learning to ride a bike may not be allowed to ride in the street. Other rules may be made to help children learn appropriate social behavior.

Parents should strive to set limits that are reasonable. These should be appropriate to the child's age. Parents should also set the lowest level of limits needed by the child. They should not attempt to be overly restrictive. Instead, parents should choose the limits that are most important for the child's well-being. They should clearly explain these limits and the reasons for them to the child. Simply saying "because I said so" is not fair to the child.

1—Example: Tommy's parents have given him no rules. They feel children can regulate their own behavior. Tommy feels insecure and wonders if his parents really care about him. What style of guidance is this?

2—Discuss: What is the main goal of the authoritative style? What are some strengths of this style?

3—Discuss: How can parents set limits for their children? Why do limits provide security for children?

17-5

An effective way of discouraging negative behavior might be to have the child sit alone for a few minutes.

Parents do not make rules to be mean. They make rules to protect and guide their children. If parents don't place any limits on a child's behavior, this communicates a lack of love and concern.

Use Positive Reinforcement

Positive reinforcements increase the likelihood a behavior will be repeated. Children are more likely to use positive behavior if this behavior is rewarded. Children need to know when parents are pleased with their behavior. Praise and simple gestures of caring are most effective in helping children learn desired behaviors.

Be Consistent

Parents must consistently enforce the limits they have set. If not, children will be confused and not know what is expected of them. If a rule is enforced one day but not the next, the child's behavior will also be inconsistent, 17-6.

If only one parent enforces the rules, children soon learn what they can and can't do with each parent. When limits are consistent, children are more likely to respect them.

When a Child Misbehaves

Despite a parent's best efforts, children misbehave. Children experiment with both positive and negative behaviors as they learn how to behave. Misbehavior can be parents' best chance to guide and direct their children. Parents can be so upset by misbehavior, however, they do not take advantage of this opportunity. How parents handle such situations will influence how children feel about themselves.

Children need to know their parents still love them even when they disapprove of the children's behavior. If children must be punished, they should understand it is only their behavior that is unacceptable. Parents must reassure children they will

17-6
If this child's parents aren't consistent with their rule not to play on the playground unsupervised, she may not pay this rule much attention.

always love them. Parents should never threaten to withdraw their love to get their children to behave.

Parents should try to determine why a child is misbehaving before dealing with the problem. For instance, children may misbehave to receive attention. These children may feel misbehaving is the only way to get their parents' attention. They would rather be punished than feel ignored by their parents. These children desperately want to be loved. When good behavior goes unrecognized, they misbehave to get the attention they seek.

If parents feel a child misbehaves to get attention, they should ignore the misbehavior if possible. If the misbehavior is not reinforced, it is less likely to be repeated. The parents should try to give extra attention to the child when he or she is using positive behavior. This will encourage the child to repeat the desired behavior.

Sometimes misbehavior can be handled by offering alternate activities. Rather than telling children they can't do something, parents can suggest another activity instead. For instance, if two children fight over the same toy, a parent might invite them to join him or her in a game. If children get rowdy indoors, parents might suggest an outside activity.

Punishment

Sometimes parents may decide punishment is necessary. Punishment should only be used for willful misbehavior. If children do not know they are doing something wrong, punishment should not be used. Parents need to make this distinction when deciding whether to use punishment. Children should be given a chance to explain their behavior. This will reveal if they misbehaved due to a lack of understanding or too little knowledge.

Parents should choose a punishment that fits the misbehavior. If it is a minor offense, the punishment should also be minor. If it is a first offense, only a warning may be needed. Punishment should not be too harsh for the misbehavior.

To be effective, punishment should be immediate. The child should clearly understand what he or she did wrong. If a period of time passes between the misdeed and the punishment, the child may not remember the misbehavior.

Several forms of punishment can be used. One of the most effective is for children to experience the **natural consequences,** or common results, of their misbehavior. When children make choices about how to behave,

1—**Discuss:** When parents do not recognize good behavior in their children, what might the children do to get attention? Should misbehavior be recognized? How?

2—**Discuss:** If parents must punish their children, what factors should apply?

3—**Vocabulary:** What is meant by a *natural consequence*? Give an example.

1—Discuss: How should time-out be used as a punishment? Where should the child go for a time-out? Do you think this is effective?

2—Discuss: Why is physical punishment the least effective method for changing behavior? What might be the result if this is used?

3—Resource: *Sibling Relationships*, Activity B, SAG.

they should experience the natural results of their decisions. With natural consequences, a child very quickly learns the appropriate behavior. For instance, if a child does not eat at dinner, he or she must wait until the next meal. Hunger between meals is a natural consequence of not eating.

In some cases, parents may use logical consequences to discourage misbehavior. **Logical consequences** are those set by parents to show what will logically happen following certain forms of misbehavior. For instance, parents may decide not to pick up or wash clothes left in children's rooms or under their beds. The logical consequence for children who leave their clothes in their rooms is that they will have no clean clothes to wear.

Another effective form of punishment is a time-out. During a **time-out**, children are removed from the presence of others. They may be placed in a room alone for a short period of time. If a room is not available, children may be asked to sit in a chair during the time-out period. This form of punishment is often used when a child is not playing well with others. It is also effective when a child becomes overly excited and needs to calm down. Five minutes of time-out may be all a child needs to correct his or her behavior.

These forms of punishment should be effective in handling most instances of misbehavior. Physical punishment is sometimes used, but it is the least effective method for changing behavior. Children who are physically punished often feel hurt, rejected, humiliated, and angry. They are not likely to remember what they did wrong after they are punished. Instead, resentment begins to build within them. What they do learn is that hitting is an acceptable form of behavior. Physical punishment is more likely to lead to child abuse. It may also lead the child to use physical violence to settle his or her own disputes.

Parents as Positive Role Models

Parents are their children's primary role models. Children learn values from observing others. They imitate and identify with their parents' use of language, behaviors, and emotions. Parents have an opportunity to influence their children in either a positive or negative way. The choice is theirs.

Children will imitate and adopt many of their parents' values and behaviors. It is important for parents to be aware of the examples they are setting. If parents guide their children in a caring and loving way, children tend to relate to others in the same manner. When a child's parents care about other people's feelings, children will likely model this behavior in their own relationships. When parents follow rules and laws, children are more likely to do the same.

If parents are positive role models, they will help children build an inner voice that helps the children choose positive behavior. Most parents try hard to set a good example, one they hope their children will follow.

Sibling Relationships

A shared childhood with **siblings**, or brothers or sisters, can be a rich and rewarding experience, 17-7. Children without siblings, sometimes called only children, do not have this experience. They may, however, have other advantages and form special relationships with other people in their lives.

Each family member has a unique set of family relationships. These relationships change each time a new person enters the family. Thus, each sibling experiences the family in a

17-7
Brothers and sisters can share many new experiences together as they grow up.

different way. A child's birth order also influences the family relationships the child will have. *Birth order* refers to the child's placement in the family. Does the child have older or younger siblings? How many of each? Who was born first, second, third, and so on?

Birth order affects children's personalities as well as their family relationships. Studies show firstborns tend to be more independent and self-confident. They are often less outwardly affectionate than other siblings. Firstborn children are usually given more responsibility and tend to grow up quickly. Parents may pin higher expectations on their firstborns, so firstborns usually have strong desires to achieve.

A second child who becomes a middle child may feel the pressure of that position. A middle child never has the advantage of being the oldest. He or she is the youngest for only a short time. Middle children tend to be good all-around students. They may put forth extra effort to excel in a special skill. Parents usually are less strict and demanding of middle children than of oldest children. Middle children often act as the peacemakers within the family. As adults, they tend to be calm, even-tempered marriage partners and parents.

Youngest children draw a lot of attention. Generally, receiving attention is good. However, youngest children also have all their family members telling them what to do. In some families, the youngest child is expected to grow up faster. On the other hand, the youngest may be more pampered and less independent. As an adult, a youngest child may seek a marriage partner who is capable of taking charge.

Regardless of the number of children in a family, each child has a unique personality. Parents will notice differences among their children, but they should try not to make comparisons. Instead, they should concentrate on the strengths of each child as an individual. It is unrealistic to expect parents to interact with each child in exactly the same way. Sometimes parents will seem to show preferences for one child over another. They should be careful not to do this. If parents try to emphasize each child's special qualities, balance will be achieved.

Sibling Rivalry

Parents should expect some rivalry among brothers and sisters. Children's first experience with competition usually occurs within the home. This competition may lead to feelings of rivalry. Sibling rivalry is a natural part of childhood. Each child feels the need to compete for a parent's love and attention.

1—**Discuss:** Why is sibling rivalry less likely to occur when there are at least three years between children?

2—**Resource:** *Sibling Rivalry*, Activity C, SAG.

Rivalry tends to be greatest when children are closer than three years apart in age. When a child is at least three years older than a sibling, he or she holds the secure position of older brother or sister. The child may feel less threatened since the new baby is not robbing him or her of the family's "baby" position. Also, parents can prepare older children to accept a new baby before he or she arrives.

Even so, accepting a new brother or sister may be painful for a child. Parents need to be understanding. How they handle the introduction of the new baby will determine to a large extent whether serious rivalry develops. Each parent should also try to spend special time alone with each child as often as possible. This makes each child feel important and it may help the family maintain a feeling of harmony.

At home, brothers and sisters tend to bicker and tattle quite a bit, especially if they are close in age. When they are away from home, however, siblings often protect one another from criticism, 17-8. As they grow older, siblings may appreciate one another more and place more importance on family unity.

Sibling relationships are a part of life for most people. The extent to which these relationships are maintained during adulthood depends on the people involved. Some siblings maintain a close relationship, while others are more distant. This may depend largely upon the distance between the siblings' homes. However, even across miles and continents, sibling relationships may continue to offer warmth and support throughout life.

17-8
Siblings may bicker at home, but they are usually protective of one another in the outside world.

Developing Responsibility

It is important for parents to guide their children toward responsibility. **Responsibility** means accepting and meeting obligations without reminder or direction. Children learn this value from their parents, schools, peers, and society. Children begin to develop a sense of responsibility at young ages. Developing responsibility is an ongoing process.

One part of responsibility is being able to recognize and choose appropriate actions. A responsible person knows the difference between right and wrong. This person seeks to use positive behavior. He or she avoids negative behaviors, and tries to stay out of trouble.

Responsibility also implies reliability and accountability. *Accountability* means a person is able to answer for his or her own actions. Responsible people own up to their actions and answer for them. It's easy to take credit for successes, but much harder to admit mistakes. Too often, people are not accountable for their actions. Instead, they blame others for their mistakes.

Parents can guide their children to develop responsibility. They can offer children chances to feel the satisfaction of a job well done. Enthusiasm helps, too. Children are likely to have stronger work values if they hear parents say "Let's see what we can do," more often than "It's no use; we can't do that."

As children grow, parents need to let them accept more responsibility for their own care. Each step toward mastering life skills brings a child one step closer to becoming a responsible person. In addition, taking these steps gives children the satisfaction of feeling self-reliant. One day children will be adults, with total responsibility for

themselves. If parents encourage their children to assume this responsibility gradually, the children's transition to adulthood will be much easier.

Part of being responsible for oneself is meeting daily time schedules. As soon as children are able, they should be encouraged to get themselves up, dressed, and to school on time. Many children are also responsible for walking home from school within a certain amount of time. The minute they arrive home, they are supposed to call a parent at work.

Another way for children to build their sense of responsibility is by doing daily chores. See 17-9. Ideally, parents should demonstrate a task and then allow the child to do it himself or herself. Children may enjoy the work more if they can choose from a number of chores. They receive more satisfaction from the work if they believe their tasks are important to the family.

Some parents set such high standards children can never produce satisfactory results. Eventually, children may think of themselves as failures. In such cases, parents may have to try to

1—**Discuss:** Give examples that show how parents can teach their children responsibility.

2—**Activity:** Draw a chart on the board listing chores you think children ages four, six, and eight can do. How can performing chores teach children responsibility?

17-9 _____
During the summer, the children in this family must pick the fruits and vegetables that are ripe every day from their garden.

1—Discuss: How can parents help children who constantly seek perfection and approval?

2—Resource: *Volunteer Work*, Activity D, SAG.

3—Enrich: Research needs in your community and make a list of volunteer projects children would be able to do.

4—Discuss: How can parents help their children learn the role of a volunteer? What important lesson is learned by children who enjoy volunteering?

5—Resource: *Volunteering Pays Off*, color transparency CT-12B, TR.

lower their standards. They might also ask their children to do other tasks they are able to do well. Then the children can accept responsibility for doing tasks and feel satisfied when the tasks are done well.

At the other extreme are children who are obsessed with perfection. They work endlessly but are never satisfied with their results. These children desperately want approval, and believe the only way to win approval is through their achievements. Therefore, they are constantly striving to achieve. Parents can help by showing appreciation for the tasks their children do well. This will help build the children's confidence and self-esteem. Parents can also help by guiding their children toward other ways of winning approval.

Volunteer Work

Children can learn roles of responsibility by doing volunteer work. The idea of children doing volunteer work may seem strange. Children are often unofficial volunteers when they help at church fairs and community events. Children also have a lot to offer their communities as official volunteers. In return, children can gain much from volunteering.

Children can do volunteer work as individuals, as partners (with another child, sibling, or parent), or in groups. They can work on one-time or long-term projects.

Children can work in parks, fire stations, museums, nursing homes, and hospitals. They can give tours, tutor students, deliver mail, lead games, serve refreshments, and make cheerful decorations.

Choosing projects for volunteer work takes careful thought. The projects should seem interesting and worthwhile to the children. When children choose their own volunteer projects, they can learn a basic democratic

principle. In a democracy, a citizen of any age can identify a need or problem and help to solve it. Thus, children should be encouraged to volunteer for a cause that concerns them. By volunteering, they can prove to themselves they have the power to make a difference.

Children have a great deal to gain by doing volunteer work, 17-10. They can have fun and learn valuable lessons while serving their communities. They can become more familiar with their neighbors and learn the meaning of responsibility. They can develop a wide range of skills and interests. They can feel the fulfillment of helping others. In addition, they learn life involves giving as well as taking.

As children become teens, they will be able to apply the valuable lessons they have learned through volunteer work. The lessons of responsibility will help them get and keep paying jobs. Volunteer work allows children to show initiative, be dependable, work with others, and complete tasks. These skills are valuable assets in the job

17-10 _____
This young boy learns about responsibility as he volunteers to rake a neighbor's lawn.

market. Employers will be more likely to give teens with these kinds of experiences the chance to accept larger responsibilities.

Allowances

Children learn quickly that money plays an important role in life. In fact, they learn about money much earlier than many parents realize. Research indicates children have already acquired knowledge, attitudes, and motives about their consumer roles before entering the classroom. Parents are a child's most important source of learning about money. Children learn about finances through intentional teaching, positive reinforcement, and parental example.

During school-age years, children have many chances to handle money. Parents can help them learn to use money wisely during these formative years. They can talk with their children about how money is earned, used, and saved. Parents can also teach their children how to handle money at an early age. They can allow children to have experiences with borrowing and sharing money as well.

Many authorities feel giving children allowances is the best method of teaching them about the value of money. An *allowance* is a set amount of money given regularly by parents to children for their personal needs and wants. The object of an allowance is to help the children learn how to use money wisely.

Parents have to consider several factors when deciding how large an allowance to give. The child's needs are the most important factor. Depending on the situation, an allowance may be expected to cover such expenses as the child's bus rides, lunches, and school supplies. For older children, this amount may also cover clothing expenses, as well as fees and equipment for extracurricular events.

Parents should include a small amount in addition to what is actually needed. This extra amount, called *discretionary money*, gives children the most valuable lessons in handling money. Children use their discretionary money in various ways. Some children spend it frivolously. Others give it away. Still others hoard it. Most children eventually learn they can have what they need and want if they manage their extra money wisely. Once children learn this lesson, they have taken a giant step toward setting and achieving goals. See 17-11.

Other factors that affect the amount of an allowance are the needs of other family members and the income level of the family. This is an important lesson for children to learn. They need to realize they are members of a family and everyone in the family has needs. The allowance parents give cannot present a hardship to the family budget.

Still another factor to consider is the amount other children of the same age receive as an allowance. Children who live in the same community often have similar needs and wants. However, this factor is not as important as others.

17-11 _____
An allowance should cover the child's needs plus a small amount of discretionary money.

1—**Reflect:** Have you ever done volunteer work? If so, what did you learn from it?

2—**Resource:** *An Allowance*, Activity E, SAG.

3—**Discuss:** Why should discretionary money be included in an allowance? How might children use this amount? What can children learn from having an allowance?

4—**Discuss:** Why is it important for children to realize other family members' needs affect their allowance? If older children get more, how can parents handle this?

Parents should not be pressured into giving larger allowances than they can afford.

Most parents pay allowances once a week. Allowances should be paid regularly. Under normal circumstances, they should not be withheld as punishment. If a child's misbehavior had nothing to do with money, neither should the punishment. Likewise, allowances should not be given in advance under normal circumstances. If children spend or lose all their money, they will have to learn to live with the consequences.

Not all parents use an allowance system. Some use a "pay-by-the-job" system. They place a monetary value on every task that needs to be done, and then allow children to sign up for the jobs they want to do.

Parents who like the "pay-by-the-job" system believe it teaches children the value of work and the value of money. Opponents believe it places a price on tasks that should be done as a part of family duties. They say it teaches children to work only when they want money. In addition, they say the system tends to be unfair. Certain siblings do all the work to earn lots of money while other siblings do very little. Those who don't work may learn to do without much money, or they may beat the system. They may be given everything they need while their brothers and sisters have to work for the things they need.

Many parents use a combination of systems. They set up a basic allowance and hold children responsible for certain household tasks. Other special tasks are assigned monetary values, and children may earn extra money by doing them. In this way, children are taught that family members need to cooperate and share responsibilities, yet they have the chance to earn more with extra effort.

Some parents simply give their children money when they need it. These parents believe this method promotes good communication. In families without open communication, children may not always tell their parents when they need money. If children are constantly criticized for asking for money, they may choose not to ask.

Educating children about money helps them understand the meaning behind the saying "money doesn't grow on trees." Children learn that financial success depends on the production and wise use of money. Taking children to a bank to open a savings account also helps children learn the value of money. Parents need to make an effort to help their children understand money, for this is an important part of their overall education. It is never too early for children to begin to learn the functions of money and its impact on family lifestyles.

Part-Time Jobs

As children become teens, they can find many ways to apply the lessons of responsibility they have learned. One way is through employment outside the home. Teens who have had chances to succeed in small tasks are likely to be ready to accept more and larger responsibilities.

Many teens are eager to move into the world of work. In fact, many high school students work outside the home, and others say they would if they could. Some students hold school-supervised jobs. In this way, they can earn both school credit and money while gaining work experience, 17-12.

Since so many teens have jobs, some parents are concerned about the overall effects of teen employment. This issue has no easy answer—every teen's situation is unique. One crucial factor is the amount of time spent working. Teens who work more than 15 or 20 hours a week are likely to feel more of work's negative effects.

17-12 _____
Teens with school-supervised jobs can earn both money and school credits. They gain valuable job skills.

School performance is one standard that can be used to measure the effects of a part-time job. If a teen works too much, his or her school performance may suffer. This has important implications. School success is an important step toward accomplishing many life goals, including career goals in adulthood.

Some working students are caught in a *self-destructive,* or self-harming cycle. They become absorbed in their work. Long hours of work prevent them from taking part in extracurricular activities. Since they are less involved in school, they lose interest and spend less time on their studies. The end results for these students may be lower grades and negative attitudes about school.

Parents may notice changes in the attitudes of their working teens. Due to their busy schedules, teens may also have less time for family activities and household tasks.

The quality of teens' work experiences is another concern of parents. Although the process of work itself is important in developing responsibility, work experiences are most valuable when they are challenging. Unfortunately, many teens do not have challenging jobs. If teens do not find

their jobs meaningful, it can lead them to develop negative attitudes about their work.

The effects of part-time jobs are not all negative; many are positive. Students can gain valuable work experience in part-time jobs. This experience helps them find full-time jobs after high school graduation. It also teaches students something they cannot learn in classrooms— how to survive in today's working world, 17-13.

Teens can learn many practical lessons on the job. They can learn about time management, business operations, consumer arithmetic, and money management. They can also gain social skills as they learn to deal with other people.

An obvious advantage of jobs is they provide young people with sources of income. Some teens save part of their earnings to help pay for

17-13 _____
This teen is learning good customer service skills that will help her in her future career.

1—**Discuss:** What negative factors may result if teens work too much?

2—**Reflect:** Why is it important for parents to be aware of changes in school and work attitudes when their teens work?

3—**Discuss:** If you work, describe your job activities. Do they challenge you to grow and learn?

4—**Discuss:** Cite positive factors teens can gain from working. Can these lessons be applied in future work experiences?

1—**Resource:** *Children and Money,* color transparency CT-17A, TR.

2—**Discuss:** How can parents help teens manage money? Cite some ways banks and other resources may help?

3—**Resource:** *Encouraging Honesty,* Activity I, SAG.

4—**Activity:** Draw eight columns on the board. Label these ages 3 through 10. Underneath each age, record ways children may tell tall tales. Compare how they change as they grow older.

5—**Example:** Give examples of how children may lie to seek their parents' approval.

6—**Discuss:** How might parents set examples of lying that children may imitate?

long-range goals such as a college education. More often, however, young people spend much of what they earn on clothes, stereos, gifts, and other material goods.

Parents may question the spending patterns of their employed teens. They may want to talk with their teens about the advantages of saving. They can also help their teens set up a money management plan. This could be one of the most valuable lessons teens can learn while working.

Parents and teens should communicate openly about the pros and cons of working. If parents become concerned, they should let their teens know. Young people need to keep a proper balance between school and work to ensure their health and optimum development. Teens need the skills acquired in classrooms to succeed in the next stage of their lives, whether they attend college or begin careers. If working drains them of valuable health and time resources, the overall effects of their jobs should be reevaluated.

Developing Honesty

All children lie occasionally. It is a part of normal development. How parents respond to these lies helps children accept honesty as a value in their lives. Parents are an important influence on their children's development of honesty.

The tall tales three-year-olds tell are a positive sign of their creative development. By the age of four, children love to brag and tell tall tales. They are striving to identify with the world around them. At five, children use tall tales to purposefully fool or deceive others. Their tales are usually designed to protect themselves or reveal unfulfilled wishes. Children who are five and six years old may blame siblings or inanimate objects for their mistakes. Children at this age are poor losers, so they may cheat to win when playing games.

By the age of seven, children are developing a moral sense of right and wrong. They are becoming aware of attitudes as well as actions. They are bothered when friends tell lies or cheat. Most eight-year-olds are basically truthful, but they may exaggerate a story to impress an audience. The words *honesty* and *truth* have become a part of nine-year-olds' vocabularies. Even when they exaggerate, they quickly set the record straight by saying "Oh, Mom, you know that isn't real." By the age of ten, children have developed moral standards. They may be very exacting of themselves and others.

Children have a strong desire to please their parents. For this reason, parents need to let their children know when they are pleased or when the children have done something right. Some parents fail to remember how important this is for their children.

If children are hungry for their parents' approval, they may lie to get it. For instance, a parent may ask "Did you make your bed?" The child answers yes, knowing that is what the parent wants to hear. The child does not stop to think that when the bedroom door is opened, the parent will see the unmade bed. The child's only thought is winning the parent's approval. The result is a parent who is doubly disappointed because of the unmade bed and the lie.

Children learn persoanl priorities by obser-ving their parents. Therefore, parents should be careful about any "little lies" they tell. When adults use false excuses to decline invitations or end phone conversations, children may try to imitate them. They do not understand why adults can tell lies, but children may not.

Parents can help their children learn to value honesty by rewarding them when they tell the truth. The best rewards are not material goods but increased trust and more privileges. Parents should help their children accept that all people make mistakes. They should let children know they will not be severely punished for making mistakes. In fact, parents should realize punishment may backfire. Children may become skillful liars if they find they can escape punishment by telling lies.

Honesty is a value children may or may not develop as they mature, 17-14. Those who find that being honest contributes to their well-being are more likely to be honest. Parents are an important influence on whether their children accept honesty as a moral they value.

Stealing

Early in life, a child needs to learn some things belong to him or her and other things belong to other people. A child should be allowed to have a special toy that is his or hers alone. A child should not have to share everything. Sharing is a lesson to learn, but there is also a lesson to learn about property rights.

Children must learn to distinguish between what is theirs and what belongs to others. Parents who bring their children to the supermarket know how many temptations there are for children. Children have to learn they cannot have everything they want, even when it is within reach. This lesson is difficult but necessary. Children must learn there are many things in life they cannot have.

If parents notice strange toys or objects in their home, they should make sure the objects are returned to their owners. Parents should not

1—Discuss: If parents punish children for making mistakes, why might children become even more skillful liars to escape punishment?

2—Reflect: What does honesty mean to you? Is it an important value for children to learn?

3—Discuss: Why should a child be allowed to have a special toy that is his or hers alone?

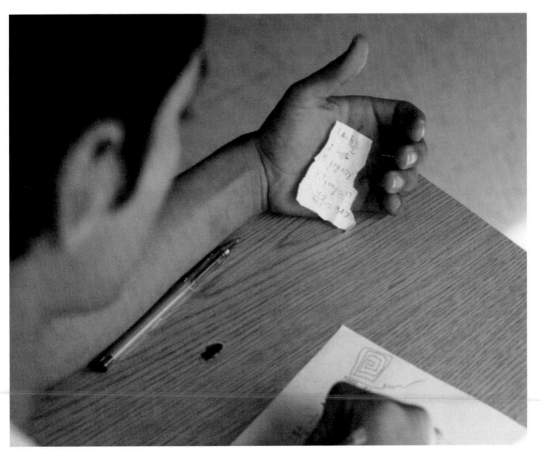

17-14 _____
Although parents want their children to be honest, some cheat or act dishonestly if they think they can get away with it.

1—Discuss: If parents suspect their children are stealing, how should they handle the situation?

2—Enrich: Invite a police officer to discuss the consequences of shoplifting.

3—Discuss: Cite reasons why teens may shoplift. What can teens do to help a friend keep from shoplifting?

4—Enrich: Research state and local shoplifting laws. What are the legal consequences if a teen is caught shoplifting?

overreact with anger, embarrassment, or sermons; nor should parents try to trap a child by asking "Where did you get this toy?" Such a question might encourage the child to be dishonest a second time by lying. By this time, the child will realize the wrong, but will go to great lengths to avoid the parents' disapproval.

A better approach for parents is to act firmly and calmly. They may say "We see a toy that is not yours. Let's take it back to the store." In this way, the child is confronted with the truth and can correct the misdeed. The child needs to learn things that are stolen must be returned. If the child senses parents know the truth and want to help him or her return the item, it will help. The child also learns parents will offer support even when he or she has done something wrong.

Shoplifting

In the teen years, some children become tempted to *shoplift*, or steal from a store. Many teen shoplifters develop a pattern of stealing during their childhood. Others shoplift in response to new pressures they feel. See 17-15.

For some teens, shoplifting is a compulsive act. They steal for the thrill of taking something. They do not need the item, but they may want to act on a dare. Others shoplift because their friends are doing it. Some shoplift as a sign of rebellion against authority or as an expression of revenge. Still others shoplift because they feel they need items they cannot afford.

Teens who have jobs may be tempted to steal from their employers. The frequency of in-house shoplifting has risen dramatically in recent years. Many young people say they become caught up in taking things because they see others doing it. The temptation is great. If they give in to the pressure of trying to impress their

17-15 _____
Shoplifting may become a compulsive habit that begins in the teen years. Continuing this illegal act can lead to adverse consequences.

friends, they may fall into the trap of shoplifting.

Shoplifting is illegal. This crime has both short- and long-term consequences. A person who steals can be faced with legal consequences. People with a history of dishonesty may have trouble finding and keeping jobs.

Laws forbidding shoplifting exist in every city and state. Businesses have set up controls and devices for detecting this crime. They have also hired security personnel in an effort to catch offenders. If a minor is caught shoplifting, his or her parents are notified. The police may or may not be called. Businesses are often firm but cooperative in working with families to solve the problem.

Parents need to be alert and aware of their children's behavior at all ages. If parents see their children with unfamiliar objects, they need to talk with the children. They need to work with their children in a firm but caring way to prevent further acts of shoplifting or stealing.

Media Influences

Most children are influenced by television viewing. Parents need to judge the effects of TV on their children. TV is capable of both positive and negative influences. Television is only one source of media exposure that affects a child's life. Parents play an important role in protecting their children from harmful media influences. They can also aid their children in gaining the benefits these forms of media have to offer.

Television

On the positive side, television offers many educational and entertaining programs. It is a window to the world. Since TV's invention, people have viewed many important moments in history, such as flights into space. On TV, people can see places, people, and sights they might never see otherwise. When used in moderation and with adult guidance, TV can be a positive learning tool.

Parents have several concerns about TV for children, however. First and foremost is the amount of time children spend watching TV. The average American child views 21 to 23 hours of television per week. When children spend so much time watching TV, they are giving up other important activities.

Television viewing should not be a substitute for other types of play and learning activities. Physical and intellectual growth may be stifled if children spend too much time watching TV. Parents and caregivers are responsible for stimulating children with a variety of other play and learning activities.

Although TV is often blamed for children's lack of interest in reading, this is debatable. If parents begin reading to their children when they are young, children are likely to develop an interest in books. As these children grow older, they may choose to spend their time reading rather than watching TV.

Television is also blamed for children's lack of interest in homework. Homework problems can be prevented if parents are aware of their children's assignments and help them learn to manage their time. Parents should encourage their children to develop good study habits and time management skills. Then children will be able to set priorities for homework, TV viewing, and other activities.

Another fear parents have is the content of the programs children watch. Parents are concerned about what their children see and how they interpret it. One of the most serious concerns about content is violence. Even in Saturday morning cartoons, children witness an average of 15 to 25 violent acts per hour. This has alarming implications, since cartoons are often the least violent viewing options. Shows meant for adults often focus on murders and other crimes.

Parents also worry about how different the world TV presents is from the real world. Children may not be able to distinguish between reality and fantasy. Stunt people and special effects may confuse them. Also, some TV shows present smoking, drinking, using drugs, and having irresponsible sex as normal behavior. See 17-16.

The effects of TV viewing on children are another consideration. Experts have identified several negative effects of TV violence on children. Children may become less sensitive to the pain and suffering of others. They may become more fearful and show more aggressive behavior. Children who have been exposed to much TV violence are more likely to hit their playmates, argue, disobey class rules, and leave tasks unfinished.

1—Resource: *Television Influences,* Activity J, SAG.

2—Example: Give examples of TV shows you would and would not allow your children to watch and explain why.

3—Discuss: Why is it difficult for children to distinguish between fantasy and reality? What role does TV play in this confusion?

1—Example: Bring videotaped TV commercials to class. Determine if the commercials are targeted at children. What effect can these commercials have on children?

2—Discuss: How can parents moderate the negative effects of TV violence?

3—Discuss: How would you, as a future parent, control the types of programs your children watch?

4—Resource: *TV Guidelines*, color transparency CT-17C, TR.

5—Discuss: TV is a part of our lives. How can parents help make TV a positive influence on their children?

17-16 _____

Parents need to set time limits on their children's TV viewing and monitor the programs their children watch.

TV commercials are also powerful influences. Young children may be deceived by commercials for toys. When children hear their favorite TV personalities tell them to ask their parents to buy certain toys, they do what they are told. If their parents refuse to buy these toys, children may be upset and confused. Children's eating preferences may be influenced by commercials for sugared food products. Adult commercials often exploit sexuality, promote drinking, and encourage people to be materialistic.

Parents can counter some of the media's negative influences. Most importantly, they should be aware of what their children are viewing. If the TV is used as a babysitter, children may sit for hours and watch anything that is aired. Many TV programs are not appropriate for children.

Parents can set limits for their children's television exposure. A few parents choose to eliminate TV viewing altogether. They may promote the use of this time for hobbies, reading, and family conversation. Most parents limit children's viewing time or hours. This ensures a balance between TV and other activities. Experts suggest no more than one hour for preschoolers and two hours for school-age children daily. Parents should discuss TV viewing rules with their older children. Together they may set weekly limits, choose acceptable programs, and select certain acceptable viewing times.

Parents can also monitor the programs their children watch. This way, they can be sure their children are exposed to appropriate programming. Other parents screen programs and movies before allowing their children to watch them. For instance, they might watch a show alone one week to determine if it is suitable for their children.

Experts advise parents to watch TV with their children whenever possible. This way, parents and children can talk about what they have seen. This allows parents to explain whether what they are seeing is realistic. They can explain that most TV violence is "faked." Parents can explain the motivation behind the characters' actions. They can also discuss whether the program is similar to, or different from, the family's values. This will help children put what they see in perspective.

Television is a part of American culture. All children are exposed to television. These are facts parents cannot ignore. Parents should do what they can to make TV a positive influence on their children. They can join other parents and teachers in an effort to convince local stations and national networks to improve the content of programs. They can help their children learn critical viewing skills so they can distinguish fact from fantasy and good from bad. Parents should monitor their children's viewing and help their children develop responsible TV viewing habits.

Music

Music is another part of the mass media. Children are exposed to music from a young age. In the school-age years, children spend a great deal of time with their peers. They may listen to popular music on the radio or CDs. School-age children also like to watch music videos on TV.

Unfortunately, as with TV, much of the music and many of the music videos available are not suitable for children. Many contain messages that suggest sexual activity, violence, and immoral behavior. These messages can be harmful for children, who are very impressionable.

In response to this concern, many parent groups have formed to persuade music companies and video channels to make this music and these videos less available to teens. These parent groups have expressed their concerns and offered their suggestions. As a result, many producers now label CDs that contain explicit language with parental advisories. This way, parents can identify these CDs before buying them. Parents may also want to listen to a CD before purchasing it for their children. They should be aware of what their children are hearing and watching.

Computer Software and the Internet

With any advance in technology comes advantages and disadvantages. The computer revolution, as it has been called, is no exception. Personal computers are a wonderful tool. They have given people new options in communication and learning. Educational games and software can help students learn more about subjects such as reading, math, science, history, art, and music, 17-17. These games can also help students learn to master computer skills. These skills will be very valuable to students as they prepare to enter the workforce.

The Internet has also changed the way people gather and pass on information. It is estimated almost 10 million

1—Discuss: Cite some of the effects music and music videos can have on children. How can parents counter those effects?

2—Discuss: List advantages of computer technology. How have computers made life easier? In what ways have they improved learning?

17-17 _____
Children can learn valuable skills, such as reading, from computer software programs. Educational games are a way to build computer skills, too.

1—Discuss: What chat rooms might be entertaining and designed for children's use? Which ones might be harmful for children because they are designed for adult use?

2—Discuss: Why does children's use of computer software and the Internet concern parents?

3—Discuss: What dangers does e-mail present for children? How can parents counter these dangers?

4—Activity: Research laws in your state regarding children and the Internet.

children use the Internet. If a person's home computer is linked to the Internet, the person can send e-mail messages. With e-mail, a person can write and send messages to people around the globe in a matter of minutes. This technology is useful for staying in touch with friends and relatives who live far away.

In addition to e-mail, many Web pages exist. These pages have different functions, such as entertainment, education, information, and buying and selling goods and services. From their homes, people can access a variety of information. They can research topics of interest. People can even read many major newspapers online by contacting their Web sites. Much of the information people can access online is accurate and helpful.

Chat rooms are another type of communication on the Internet. A **chat room** is a forum through which several people can communicate at the same time. Chat rooms are accessed through a Web site and open to the public. Each person logs onto the Web site and enters the chat room through his or her own computer. People can chat by typing in responses to what others have already written. The dialogue continues via scrolling text. Up to 24 people can participate in most chat rooms at one time. People can enter and exit at any time. Chat rooms can be a way to get to know new people without actually meeting them. Some people have a lot of fun visiting the same chat room routinely.

Each of these forms of technology has disadvantages for children, however. One of parents' main concerns about computers is that children will spend too much time on them. Children still need time in active play and other activities. Parents may need to help their children set priorities and manage their time wisely.

Parents are also concerned about the content of the software programs and games their children use. Many of these games feature violence. These games can be disturbing for children. They have much the same impact as TV violence does. Other software programs and games are not meant for children's use. These programs may have adult themes and language.

Parents should check the suggested age level on any computer software or game before allowing their children to use it. They should also monitor what their children are doing on the computer. For this reason, experts recommend that parents place the family computer in an open area where they can observe the children on the computer.

E-mail also has certain downfalls. Parents may want to closely monitor the messages a child sends and receives by e-mail. Some Web sites routinely offer prizes and other rewards to children who share their names, ages, and family information with them. These Web sites may use this information to market their products or for other purposes. Some companies send children e-mail in the guise of cartoon characters luring children to visit a certain Web site. Jokes are also often transmitted to e-mail users. Many of these jokes are sexual or profane in nature. They are not meant for children. These are just a few of the problems associated with children's use of e-mail. Parents need to help their children use e-mail responsibly.

Some states have passed laws regulating online material, such as Web sites and home pages. These laws relate to the content of the material. Some states have outlawed the use of pornography on Web sites operated from that state. Others have passed laws against online scams and fraud. Unfortunately, many of these state laws are not well enforced.

More laws are being passed now regarding soliciting children over the Internet. Child molesters sometimes talk to children in chat rooms. These criminals may pretend to be children in their online conversations. They may try to persuade children to meet them in person somewhere. Children are told this is to be a private meeting, secret from any adults. When the children go to meet their online "friends," they are instead abducted by the child molester. Parents should warn their children about this danger. They can insist their children never meet an online friend in person without a parent present.

The government, software companies, and Internet service providers are working to help parents protect their children from viewing certain inappropriate Web sites. This software can filter out access to Web sites on certain topics, such as sex, drugs, and alcohol. Parents can choose which subjects they want to block and install this filtering software on the hard drive of their computers. Research is underway for even more effective ways to protect children from harmful information on the Internet.

A parent should be the one to monitor what his or her children view on the Internet. Parents can help their children learn valuable computer skills in a safe environment. They can protect their children from harmful information and abduction attempts. Further suggestions for guiding a child's computer use are listed in 17-18.

Developing a Healthy Sexuality

Sexuality, or everything associated with maleness and femaleness, develops gradually throughout a person's lifetime. Children begin to sense how they feel about themselves as boys and girls while they are very young. They sense how their parents act toward each other and toward others. From this foundation, children learn to function as complete, unique human beings.

Teaching children about sexuality is not easy. It is a responsibility that evolves out of love for the children and the honest desire for them to live abundant and happy lives. Parents should consider a child's age and needs when offering information about sexuality.

At birth, a child's gender is announced. During each day that follows, parents help their child develop as a warm human being. Parents begin teaching their child about being male or female. Learning about one's masculinity or femininity is a lifelong process that begins almost from birth, 17-19.

Some parents may wonder if they will ever be able to teach their children

1—Discuss: What additional guidelines can you recommend?

2—Note: Clarify for students what the term *sexuality* encompasses. Point out that it is more than just sexual behavior. It includes all aspects of being male or female.

Guiding Your Child's Use of the Computer

- Always be aware of what software programs your children are using on the computer and what they are viewing on the Internet.

- Investigate filtering programs that allow your children to use Web sites only with your supervision. These programs can also restrict certain sites.

- Place the computer in a common room and supervise your children as they use the computer.

- Tell your children not to give any personal information online, such as real names or your telephone, address, and credit card numbers.

- Instruct your children never to meet an online friend in person without an adult present.

17-18 ——————
Parents should follow these guidelines in protecting their children from some of the dangers of computer use.

17-19

This young girl will learn much about becoming a woman from her mother and father.

about sexuality. The issue is not *whether* they should teach their children about sex, but *how and when* they should teach them. These parents should relax. There will not be "one day" when they have to teach their children everything they need to know about sexuality. They actually teach their children much about sexuality through routine acts, such as providing physical care and emotional support.

Questions Children Ask

Children are naturally curious and full of questions. It is normal for them to ask questions about sex. When they do, parents should remain calm and give simple answers. Young children are not ready for detailed information. The answers should be frank and truthful so nothing will have to be unlearned later. The most important message for parents to convey is that children have the right to ask questions and receive answers.

Children have their own timetables for curiosity, but psychologists can generally forecast the sequence of their questions. Children's first real curiosity about their own sexual anatomy occurs around two or three years of age. By then, children notice boys' and girls' bodies are different. They want to know why. Parents do not need to give detailed explanations. They should simply acknowledge the differences— little boys have penises while little girls have vaginas. (When teaching children names for parts of the body, parents should use correct terms.)

The next question usually is "Where do babies come from?" Children are not ready for a full lesson in reproduction, but the best answer is the truth. "Babies grow inside their mothers" is usually all children really want to know at the time, 17-20.

17-20

When children ask where babies come from, they should be told the truth, but in very simple terms. They are not ready for a full lesson in reproduction.

Parents should not put the explanation off by saying "We can't talk about that now." It is important for parents not to suppress their children's curiosity about sexuality or to respond in a guarded, negative way. This is a time that beginnings can be made in open, truthful communication.

Sometime around age four, children may want to know more. If parents have handled their previous questions well, children will feel free to ask more questions. They may ask "How does the baby get out?" Again, a simple answer, "There is a special opening for the baby to come through," will satisfy them for the time. They think a lot about all these things, and they may ask for more details about birth. They make little connection between the size of a pregnant woman and the presence of a baby.

By this age, children will have been exposed to other sources of sex information—television and stories from their friends. Parents who have had open, truthful communication with their children will have less anxiety about their children receiving incorrect information from others about sex. If children know they can ask their parents about sex, they are less likely to ask others.

Five-year-olds are generally more interested in the baby itself than in the baby's origin. The relative quietness about sex at this age vanishes at six or seven. Then they begin to wonder again how a baby comes through the special opening at birth. They may also ask how a baby starts to grow inside the mother. A parent can use a simple answer like "When a father and mother want to have a baby, a cell from the father meets with another inside the mother, and this is how a baby begins."

If nine-year-olds are not satisfied with the answers their parents have given them about reproduction, they may ask their friends. Once they are satisfied, their interest in reproduction may fade. They may tell their parents they would like a baby brother or sister. They may also begin to think of themselves as parents as they care for dolls or small children.

Gender Roles

Much has been said about how social conditioning affects the gender roles children adopt. Parents have an important influence on a child's gender role development. They can support a child's expressions as he or she creates a personal image of masculinity or femininity. This is the most helpful approach they can take.

On the other hand, parents may unknowingly add extra pressures. They may expect little girls or little boys to act in certain ways. They may ridicule a boy for showing tenderness toward a doll, or call a girl a tomboy if she plays aggressively on the jungle gym. This approach can interfere with a child's natural expressions of masculinity or femininity.

Preschool children are observant. They notice how their parents act and often act out roles they have seen their parents perform. Gender role options may be less defined now than in the past. Adults have many different roles today. Both men and women work outside the home, and many parents share household tasks, 17-21.

Consider this example from a preschool. A little girl was busy at the play sink "washing dishes." A little boy came in, put his arm around her shoulders, and said, "I know you are tired, so you sit down. I'll wash the dishes tonight." He evidently had seen his father act this way. It seemed natural to him to adopt that role.

By the age of seven, children are becoming even more aware of and interested in gender roles. At this age, boys and girls seem to stop playing together in mixed-gender activities.

1—Discuss: How can parents help establish open and honest discussions about sexuality?

2—Reflect: As a child, how were you told about where babies come from? Do you feel the explanation was handled correctly?

3—Discuss: Do parents pressure boys and girls to act in different ways? Can this be damaging? Cite ways parents inflict gender bias on their small children.

4—Discuss: How can parents give their children positive examples of sharing roles?

1—Discuss: How many children acquire confusing messages about gender roles in society?

2—Discuss: If you were a parent, how would you establish open honest communication about sexuality with your teen daughter or son?

3—Note: Research indicates teens who have accurate information about sex and feel they can talk openly with their parents are more likely to demonstrate responsible behavior.

4—Resource: *Talking to Your Children About AIDS*, reproducible master 17-4, TR.

5—Discuss: If parents are uneasy about discussing sexuality with their children, what can they do to find other reliable sources?

17-21 —————————————————

Today, as gender roles continue to expand, more fathers help with tasks such as preparing meals for their children.

Instead, they form same-gender play groups. By age eight, boys and girls tend to play separately.

Masculine and feminine roles are still changing in our society. Children are influenced most by the gender roles they see their parents portray in their homes. Children are also influenced by their school environments, where they see less discrimination in role assignments. The changes in gender roles are helpful for the most part, but they may cause some confusion.

People must feel their own masculinity or femininity as they grow. A person's sense of his or her sexuality affects the way the person adopts gender roles. Male roles include being a boy, man, husband, and father. Female roles include being a girl, woman, wife, and mother. If parents guide a child's development of healthy gender roles, the child will grow up feeling comfortable about his or her individual sexuality.

Teens and Sexuality

The teen years pose new demands in many areas of development—social, emotional, intellectual, physical, and sexual. Hormonal and bodily changes create new sexual feelings. It is at this stage the personality may be at its shakiest. Although each teen must find his or her own way through this transition, parents can help by providing a base of security.

Teens should feel free to discuss their attitudes, opinions, and questions with their parents. Parents who have spoken openly about sex with their children will have established open and honest communication. Now, they should be able to talk with their teens in ways that are relevant to their new intellectual, emotional, and physical maturity. See 17-22.

Parents are the first sex educators of their children. They should continue to talk with their children about sex during the teen years. Parents should be sure their teens have accurate information about human sexuality and reproduction. Teens with accurate knowledge about sex are likely to demonstrate responsible sexual behavior and postpone sexual activity.

Teens have many difficult decisions to make regarding sexuality. If they live in an atmosphere of loving concern and open communication, they will find it much easier to make these decisions. They will be able to base their decisions on morals transmitted by their families. They will not have to make decisions out of fear or conform to peer pressure.

Parents may feel uneasy about discussing sexuality with their teens. If so, they may want to seek help from professional resources or training groups. Many groups offer courses

17-22
Although he feels a little reluctant, this teen knows he can ask his dad questions because they have established open communication.

shared by parents and their teens. Many schools also encourage parents to participate in family life education classes.

Since the mass media exploits sexuality, many teens receive the wrong message about the role of sexual expressions in their lives. Parents can help their teens by talking with them about these mixed messages. They can also set a positive example in their own lives. Most teens can learn from their parents what the proper role of sexuality is in a loving, lasting relationship. A good example helps teens realize both the positive and negative aspects of sexual behavior.

Parents can help their teens sense their role of responsibility in sexuality.

Parents need to help their sons and daughters realize young people who become involved in sexual relationships must be ready to accept adult responsibilities. Every teen must understand any act of sexual intercourse can result in pregnancy, an STD, or other negative consequences.

Teens do not want their parents to be their "pals," especially when they are making important decisions about their lives. They also don't want their parents to make decisions for them. What they do value is their parents' loving concern and guidance. A teen's relationship with his or her parents helps determine how that teen makes the transition into mature sexual adulthood.

1—Discuss: How can the media give misleading messages to teens? Cite examples of shows and advertising that give negative messages.

2—Discuss: The basic lesson of self-responsibility in sexuality is one every teen must understand. Are teens accepting this responsibility?

1—Activity: Review and outline this chapter emphasizing the information you found most useful.

2—Answers: Answers to review questions are located in the front section of this TAE.

Summary

1

- Children need their parents' love, support, and encouragement to become responsible, independent adults.

- Parents can use guidance and discipline to enforce positive behavior in their children.

- As children mature, they must learn the kinds of behavior that will enable them to interact effectively in the world. They do this learning in several different ways.

- How parents handle children's misbehavior influences the children's feelings about themselves.

- Punishment means that a person receives a penalty for something he or she did that was wrong or unsatisfactory to others. Many forms of punishment exist.

- Parents are a child's primary role models. The example they set for their children is very important. Children are likely to follow their parents' example.

- Birth order affects children's personalities as well as their relationships with family members. Sibling relationships are also important.

- As children grow, parents need to let them accept more responsibility for themselves. Parents can promote the development of responsibility in many ways.

- Most authorities feel giving children allowances is the best method of teaching them about the value of money.

- Parents and teens should communicate openly about the pros and cons of working at a part-time job in the teen years.

- How parents respond to children's lies teaches children the importance of honesty as a value in

their lives. Parents can help their children learn to value honesty by rewarding them when they tell the truth. They can also set a good example.

- Parents must work with their children in a firm but caring way to prevent acts of shoplifting or stealing.

- Parents should monitor their children's exposure to the media. Parents can help their children have positive experiences (and avoid negative ones) with the media in many ways.

- Parents have an important role in helping their children develop a healthy sense of their own sexuality.

Reviewing Key Points

2

1. What is positive behavior?
2. What is the difference between guidance and discipline?
3. List three ways children learn behavior.
4. Describe the three styles of parenting.
5. Why is it important to set reasonable limits on children's behavior?
6. List two forms of punishment parents may use.
7. True or false. Sibling rivalry tends to be greatest when children are less than three years apart in age.
8. Name two ways children can develop a sense of responsibility.
9. What four factors should parents consider when deciding how large an allowance to give their children?
10. List three negative effects and three positive effects of part-time jobs.
11. How can parents help their children learn to value honesty?

12. What lessons does a child learn when parents bring the child to a store to return an item the child stole?

13. List four reasons teens give for shoplifting.

14. What effects may viewing violence on TV have on children?

15. What dangers exist when children respond to strangers on the Internet without their parents' permission?

16. Why do experts believe parents should be sure their teens have accurate information about human sexuality and reproduction?

Learning by Doing

1. List two examples for each of the ways in which children learn behavior.

2. Parents are the primary role models for children. Role-play several instances in which parents are not being very good role models. Then role-play the same situations, demonstrating how parents can be better role models for their children.

3. Interview a security guard or store manager from a local department store about shoplifting. Ask questions about the store's policy concerning shoplifters and the legal consequences of shoplifting.

4. List several ways parents can control their child's TV viewing.

5. Research ways parents can protect their children from negative influences when using computer software, the Internet, e-mail, and chat rooms. Give an oral report on your findings.

Thinking Critically

1. In a buzz group, discuss the best ways for parents to discipline young children. How can parents teach their children self-control?

2. Ask class members to list both positive and negative aspects of sibling relationships. Discuss ways of resolving sibling rivalry. Discuss how sibling relationships within a family may change as the siblings grow older.

3. Identify ways not described in the chapter in which parents can help their children develop responsibility.

4. Working with a partner, pretend you are parents. Refer to a listing of TV programs and identify those programs that are shown during children's typical viewing hours. Discuss with your partner and decide which programs would be appropriate or inappropriate for your children to watch.

5. In small groups, discuss appropriate ways for parents to talk with their children about sexuality. Discuss the importance of openness and honesty in parent-child communication.

Chapter 18
Family Concerns

Objectives

After studying this chapter, you will be able to

- describe common parenting concerns including balancing work and family roles, divorce, remarriage, serious illness, death, and family moves.
- identify skills and knowledge parents need to handle these concerns.
- propose ways parents can help their children adjust to these concerns.
- summarize community resources available for parents facing these concerns.

Key Terms

regression behavior
custody
1 visitation rights
child support payments

Parenting brings many joys, but it also brings challenges. Along the way, parents may have concerns about their family life. At times, difficult situations may arise. It takes extra effort for a person to adjust to these situations. A sign of successful parenting is the ability to cope with both the predictable and unpredictable events of family life. Parents have to help their children adjust, but they also must take care of their own needs, 18-1. Dealing with family concerns can be difficult, but a little understanding goes a long way. In this chapter, you will read about several common family concerns and how parents can help their children through these difficult situations.

Balancing Family and Work Roles

2

Family and work roles, though different, must balance one another together. Most parents have to work to supply income to meet their families'
3 needs. For most, working is not an option but a necessity. In single-parent and dual-career families, managing the responsibilities of family and career can be challenging.

In single-parent families, one parent must take on all the responsibilities for the family. The parent's job is
4 often the family's only source of income. This parent is also the only adult responsible for providing care for the home and children. Single parents can find all this responsibility stressful. They do the best they can to balance their roles of parent and worker. Single parents may have to ask for help from family or friends. When they work, they hire a caregiver for their children. At home, they may have to ask older

1—**Vocabulary:** Look up terms in the glossary and discuss their meanings.

2—**Resource:** *Balancing Family and Work,* color transparency CT-18, TR.

3—**Resource:** *Dual-Career Households,* Activity A, SAG.

4—**Discuss:** How can being a single parent increase the need to balance multiple roles?

18-1 _____

Even when concerns arise, parents must take care of themselves. A few minutes alone to exercise or collect her thoughts helps this mother deal with family concerns.

children to take on more of the family's chores.

In dual-career families, two parents share the family's responsibilities. Both parents work outside the home and manage the household and child care tasks. Although the partners divide the responsibilities, each parent still has multiple roles that must be balanced— worker, spouse, and parent. Dual-career families must juggle two sets of job schedules and demands. Spouses must blend their schedules and those of their children in a way that meet everyone's needs. This can be an enormous task.

Balancing these multiple demands can be difficult. With determination, effort, and planning, most parents can effectively manage all their roles.

Reasons Parents Work

Most people work for one main reason. They need an income to financially support themselves and their families. Workers provide needed services for their employers. In return, they can earn money to pay for housing, clothing, food, and transportation for their families.

With only one income, it may be difficult to support an entire family. Many two-parent families find it necessary for both parents to work. Having two incomes makes it easier to meet the family's financial needs and purchase some of their wants, 18-2. Couples may have financial goals, such as purchasing a home or saving for the children's education. The additional income makes it possible to meet these goals.

Parents work for other reasons, too. People often gain personal satisfaction from their jobs. For many, the work

18-2 _____

Even in two-parent families, it is often necessary for both parents to work. These parents work so they can provide for their son.

they do is an important part of their identity. A person feels fulfilled knowing he or she is doing a good job. It is satisfying to feel the work a person does is valuable. Working can provide opportunities for self-expression, satisfying relationships with other workers, and personal growth. It allows a person to develop new skills and meet new people. Many adults work almost as much for personal reasons as for financial ones.

1 Options to Consider

The continuing increase in the number of working parents has affected the workplace. The demands of parenting spill over into job performance. If employees must take time off to tend sick children, their work may suffer. If parents are not satisfied with their child care arrangements, they may not be able to concentrate on their jobs. Instead parents may worry about how their children are doing while they are away. For most parents family comes first, but they need their jobs in order to support their families. This situation can create conflicting demands that may jeopardize a parent's career.

Businesses are beginning to recognize the strain these conflicting demands place on working parents. Employers can help relieve rather than add to the pressure created by multiple roles. They can do this by implementing family-friendly programs and policies. Employers with family-friendly policies soon notice the difference in their employees. Workers who are satisfied with their roles, hours, and demands are more productive and cooperative. They miss fewer work days and can concentrate better on their jobs. They are happier and feel less stressed. The company, employee, and employee's family all benefit from these policies and programs.

Family-friendly policies and programs include flexible working hours or job sharing. These options give employees more time to be with their families. Other family-friendly policies involve maternity and paternity leaves, and policies about caring for sick family members. Some businesses let their employees work from home. An employee might stay in touch with his or her company by phone, fax, mail, or e-mail. Other companies offer on-site child care centers, which can alleviate worries over child care, 18-3. This can also allow parents to spend lunch or breaks with their children.

In some jobs and companies, these options may not be available. Parents can talk with their employers about possibilities for making their jobs more family-friendly. If parents and employers can agree on a more workable solution, both will benefit.

Managing Dual Work Roles

2 In a dual-career family, spouses must balance their career, marriage, and parenting roles. It is not easy to balance these multiple roles, but many couples are finding ways to make it

18-3
This young girl experiments with sand at an on-site child care center. Her parents feel secure she is receiving quality care. They can also share lunch and breaks with her.

1—**Activity:** For each option listed, have students list advantages and disadvantages. After considering all the options, which one would students choose if they were parents?

2—**Enrich:** Interview a dual-career family. Ask them how they manage their time and set priorities.

1—Discuss: Do children of dual-career parents tend to be more independent and achievement-oriented than other children?

2—Enrich: Role-play situations where tensions between personal life and careers arise. Evaluate how each situation was handled.

work. How they manage their many responsibilities varies from one household to the next. How well they succeed often depends on the attitude of both partners toward the dual-career arrangement. If one mate does not want his or her spouse to work, continuous friction may cause problems in the marriage.

In most dual-career families, men and women divide the household and child care tasks. Women are still often expected to make more adjustments for family responsibilities than men are. Most women take on a larger percentage of household and child care tasks than their spouses. In other families, husbands are more willing to adjust their work schedules to care for the children, 18-4. Work schedules can sometimes be arranged so one parent is home with the children at all times. Another option is for one spouse to set up a business from home. This way the parent can work and still be with the children.

18-4

Husbands and wives often share child care responsibilities in a dual-career family.

Many differing opinions exist on the effect of dual-career families on children. However, most studies have found few harmful effects for children in dual-career families. In fact, there are even some benefits for children with working parents. Research indicates the following:

● Children of dual-career families tend to be more independent and achievement oriented.

● Stay-at-home parents may be more likely to stifle their children's attempts at independence. 1

● Children of dual-career families are often more social.

Dual-career families must also find ways to manage other tasks and still have time for relaxation. Families have to learn to manage their time. Both husbands and wives often feel there is not enough time within a twenty-four-hour day. The couple needs to establish priorities and make their choices accordingly. Some couples make a list of need-to-do tasks versus want-to-do items. Sometimes they are able to swap one for the other. For instance, a family may need to clean the garage. They may also want to go to a neighborhood ball game on the same Saturday morning. They may decide that relaxing at the ball game will allow them to tackle the garage with more determination when they return.

Many parents designate time in advance for the family to be together. They find this makes them more likely to fulfill these plans, 18-5. They also make the most of family time and work hard when they are on the job. This helps alleviate feelings of guilt that might occur in either area.

Tensions between personal life and career will probably occur no matter how dedicated couples are toward 2 making it work. Spouses can help one another by adjusting to times of increased job pressures. Mates can recognize when their spouses are in

18-5
A dual-career family may need to set aside a definite time to do things together as a family.

difficult times. Taking over more of a spouse's household duties at this time can help ease the pressure. It also keeps the house running smoothly. Open communication, including asking for help, allows couples to work through temporary situations.

Many couples find they have poor managerial skills. They lack the ability to make wise decisions in certain areas that may further complicate their already busy lives. Financial problems may occur even though the couple is making more money. Since both spouses are so busy, they may fail to develop a spending plan. They may find themselves short of cash with no idea where their money went. If couples are unable to create a budget for themselves, they may need to consult a financial adviser.

Other managerial skills may also need to be improved. Laundry, house-cleaning, shopping, and driving children to various places all require time. Working couples often find they need to plan more carefully in order to accomplish all these tasks. Family members may need to talk about how they can reassign tasks so everything gets done. They might need to consider obtaining outside help, if possible.

Otherwise they may simply have to accept that some things must be left undone. Housekeeping standards may have to be altered. Some activities may have to be missed.

There are more pressures in a dual-career family, but most families agree there are also many rewards. Financial goals can be reached sooner with two incomes. Couples who enjoy their multiple roles have a positive attitude toward the additional pressures they face. Job success can benefit family members emotionally and financially. On the other hand, a supportive and happy family can give added energy for meeting on-the-job demands.

Divorce

When a husband and wife decide to divorce, it is never easy. If they are parents, it is even more difficult. Ending the marital relationship will deeply affect their lives and the lives of their children. The couple views divorce as the only way to resolve their unsatisfying marriage. Children are more likely to view divorce as the

1—Discuss: How can open communication help families through pressures?

2—Enrich: Ask a dual-career couple how they use managerial skills to help them manage their daily lives.

3—Discuss: Describe some of the pressures and rewards in dual-career families.

breakup of their family. In a child's eyes, divorce may seem like the end of the world, 18-6.

The possibility their parents will divorce is very frightening for children. Parents should wait to tell their children until they have made a final decision. This way they can avoid alarming the children unnecessarily. Also, if the parents decide not to divorce, their children might live in constant anxiety. They might fear every slight problem would lead to their parents' separation. This kind of constant worry is not healthy for children.

Once the decision to divorce is final, however, parents should tell their children right away. This will protect the children against hearing the news from someone else. It also allows them to begin adjusting to the change. Children do not need all the unpleasant details of their parents' failed relationship. They deserve a brief explanation of why the divorce is happening.

18-6 _____

Divorce is painful for children. Children should be assured that both parents will continue to love and care for them.

This explanation should be age-appropriate and sensitive to each child's feelings. Parents need to truthfully explain what will happen as a result of the divorce.

How children are told about divorce may be even more important than what parents say. The environment should be friendly, not hostile. It may be difficult, but both parents need to sit down together with the children to explain the divorce. A joint explanation reduces confusion. Children only hear one, not two, stories about the reasons for the divorce. Another advantage of the joint explanation is it makes children feel less like they have to choose sides. It also shows the children both parents still care about them and can work together as parents.

Parents should remember the truth is always best. They should not lie to the children about why one parent is leaving the home. For instance, a couple might tell their children that one parent was just leaving for vacation or a business trip. Later, when the children learn the truth, they will be even more hurt because their parents lied to them.

It may seem difficult to find the right words to say. Parents can ask their counselors, religious leaders, or pediatricians for guidance. They can also seek advice from other divorced parents. It's also a good idea for parents to read about divorce. Many reputable books describe the questions children often ask about divorce and helpful answers parents can give. These books can also describe how children often react to divorce and how parents can help them adjust. Children's books about divorce can also be helpful. These books explain the situation to a child at his or her level. They also help the child feel he or she is not the only child to go through divorce.

Parents also need to reassure their children they have considered everything carefully and their decision to divorce is final. Children often hope their parents will reunite. Letting go of these hopes is difficult for a child. Parents can help by not giving their children any false hopes of reconciliation.

Children need to be reassured both parents still love them very much. Parents need to tell children the divorce is not the children's fault. Children also need to know their parents will still meet their daily needs and give them loving care and attention.

Children's Reactions to Divorce

Each family, situation, and child are unique. This explains why children have different reactions when their parents divorce. This section will describe common reactions children have.

Some children try to deny the fact their parents are divorced. They pretend nothing has happened by creating their own fantasies. They keep the divorce a secret from their friends. These children tell themselves their parents will soon reunite. They may even devise schemes to get their parents back together.

Another common response to divorce is regression behavior. **Regression behavior** means a child reverts to a past behavior he or she has since outgrown. For instance, a child may go back to thumb-sucking, whining, or babyish language. A child who has stayed dry at night for years may suddenly wet the bed. These were behaviors of the past, before the child moved on to more mature behavior. In the face of a major life change, however, these behaviors often resurface. Regression behaviors are a child's unconscious way of saying "I'm just a little child. Don't leave me."

Some children react to divorce with hostility and anger. Others become silent, depressed, and withdrawn. They are grieving the loss of their family as they knew it. They are scared about what the future will hold. All these feelings are normal. Parents should try to be very understanding and supportive as children resolve these feelings. Counseling may help the child deal with his or her feelings about the divorce.

Many children believe they caused their parents' divorce. Younger children especially are very egocentric. They believe everything that happens in the world revolves around them. They believe their misbehavior caused their parents to divorce. In their experience, bad things usually happen to them when they are naughty or do something wrong. They assume they have not been good enough to please their parents. This feeling may be reinforced if children have heard their parents arguing about them. The children may believe they have caused their parents to fight and be angry with one another. As a result, they feel guilty and unhappy, 18-7. They may tearfully approach their parents saying "I'll be good. I promise I won't ever be naughty again."

Experts believe children's adjustments to divorce vary with age. Older children are at a different point in their development than younger children. They understand things differently, and have developed different ways to cope with change. While each child is unique, many children in the same age group adjust in a similar pattern.

Infants and Toddlers

Infants and toddlers often have little memory of their family as it was before the divorce. For this reason, they have few adjustments to the change in family structure. If both parents remain

1—Reflect: Cite various reactions children might have to divorce. Have you or any or your friends experienced these or any other reactions?

1—Discuss: How might it affect an infant or toddler if either parent suddenly drops out of his or her life?

2—Discuss: Describe the feelings and reactive behaviors of preschoolers toward divorce.

3—Discuss: Discuss the effects of divorce upon school-age children.

18-7 _____
Young children may be quite upset if they believe they caused their parents' divorce. Parents should explain problems in their marriage, not the children, were to blame.

involved with their care, infants and toddlers will likely adjust quite well. Toddlers had more time with both parents and may miss the absent parent. They may temporarily show regression behaviors, especially in toilet learning. Once they feel secure in their new situation, these behaviors usually stop.

If either parent drops out of the child's life, however, an infant or toddler will sense the loss. As the child grows, he or she may long for the missing parent. The child may idealize the missing parent as perfect. This will make it difficult to accept a stepparent if the other parent should remarry. It can also interfere with the child's attempt to form intimate relationships as an adult.

Preschoolers

Preschoolers are often quite upset by divorce. Their concept of a family is concrete and inflexible. To them a family includes a mother, father, and children who live together and love and care for one another. When divorce occurs, this concept is shattered. Preschoolers are old enough to fully feel the loss, but too young to fully understand it. Children in this age group cannot understand how a parent

can love a child and yet leave the family.

Children in this age group are still egocentric. They think they caused the parents' divorce. They may try to bargain with their parents to stay together or reunite. Preschoolers also experience the divorce solely from their own point of view. They are not yet capable of understanding others' feelings about the situation.

Preschoolers are likely to react with helplessness, grief, and fear. They may show regression behaviors such as bed-wetting, thumb-sucking, and whining. These behaviors express the feelings a child cannot yet effectively put into words. Since these behaviors are a normal part of children's adjustment process, a child should not be punished for them.

Preschoolers slowly adjust to their new family structure. They do best when both parents remain involved in their lives. Children this age actively grieve an absent parent. This is a painful loss for children. Preschoolers may remember their parents as more human. They are not as likely to idealize a missing parent. In time, preschoolers can adjust to the divorce, even if only one parent is still active in their care.

School-Age Children

School-age children have moved beyond being egocentric. They can begin to look at situations from other persons' points of view. Thus, they may be better able to understand their parents' explanations about divorce. Still they are usually upset. They may try to deny the divorce is real to relieve their grief and avoid embarrassment with friends.

School-age children are more likely than younger children to want to talk about the divorce with their parents. This may be hard for the parents, who are going through their own adjustment. Parents should try to be as available as possible to listen to their children and answer their questions.

Like their younger siblings, school-age children may blame themselves for the breakup. They may think their good behavior will bring their parents back together. In other cases, children this age may choose sides during and after the divorce, pitting one parent against the other.

Teens

Teens may show more obvious reactions to pain than children of other ages. Divorce challenges teens' ideas about love, marriage, and family. It may also damage their self-esteem if they feel their parents no longer love them. Teens' reactions to divorce vary widely. Some teens try to push their parents to reconcile. Others team up with one parent to fight against the other parent. Some teens are embarrassed and try to keep their peers from knowing the truth, 18-8. Some withdraw, using the time alone to work through their feelings. Others rebel with bad behavior such as skipping school, stealing, drinking, or using drugs.

Legal Proceedings

To be legally divorced, one or both spouses must file a divorce petition in their county's civil court. A court date will be set for the divorce hearing. At the divorce hearing, one or both spouses goes before the judge and explains why they want to divorce. The judge may ask about how the couple will split their property.

In addition to these issues, the couple must resolve custody of their children. **Custody** means the right to raise a child and make decisions about the child's care, upbringing, and overall welfare. Sometimes the court awards *joint custody*, which means both parents keep their parenting rights and responsibilities. Joint custody works best when the couple can demonstrate the ability to work together in making decisions regarding their children.

In joint custody cases, the parents and the court must determine with which parent the child will live. In many cases, the child will live permanently with one parent. The other

1—**Discuss:** Describe how divorce may affect teens' overall view of love, marriage, and family. How may it affect their self-esteem?

2—**Activity:** Invite a divorce attorney to class to explain the legal proceedings involved in a divorce.

18-8
Spending time with friends may help teens get their minds off problems at home. In fact, teens may try to hide their parents' divorce from friends.

1—Discuss: Many parents who are ordered to pay child support never do so. What effect might this have on the children's well-being?

2—Discuss: Following a divorce, how can parents maintain as much continuity as possible in their children's lives?

parent will have **visitation rights**, or the right to visit the child during certain specified times and conditions. In other joint custody situations, the child may live with each parent for a specified amount of time each year. The children live with one parent and have visitation with the other as ordered by the court. This allows parents to better share parenting responsibilities.

In other cases, only one parent is awarded custody. This is called *sole custody*. Generally, a judge grants sole custody when it has been determined joint custody would produce further conflict or one parent is determined to be unfit to raise the child. In sole custody cases, the parent with custody lives with the child and makes all the decisions about the child's care. The other parent may or may not be granted visitation rights as determined by the court.

Even after a divorce, both parents have an obligation to financially support their children. This is true no matter who has custody. In almost all custody cases, the judge will decide about **child support payments**. These are payments one parent makes to the other parent to meet the children's financial needs. The parent with whom the children are living is the one who receives child support payments.

When parents agree on custody, visitation, and child support, the divorce proceedings will go rather well. The judge may be able to finalize the divorce at the initial hearing. In fact, parents should try to reach an agreement on these issues before going to court. This will make the entire legal process quicker and more agreeable for everyone.

When the parents cannot agree on the terms for custody, visitation, and child support, the judge must decide these issues for them. In this case, each person must tell his or her side of the story. Each person must state what terms he or she would like and support these with valid reasons. The judge must then decide what is in the child's best interest. These cases can be the most upsetting for divorcing couples. They may drag out indefinitely, requiring several court appearances. This type of divorce can also be upsetting for the children. Children should not be used as weapons in the battle between their parents.

Throughout the legal proceedings, parents should be truthful and treat each other with respect. They should not magnify each other's faults or tell lies about one another. Appearing in court is not easy for either of the adults. They should try not to focus on themselves, however. Their goal should be to work together with the judge to decide what will be best for the children.

After the Divorce

After the divorce is final, parents need to work together to maintain as much continuity as possible in their children's lives. Children feel more secure when their housing arrangements, daily routines, and discipline measures stay much the same.

Young children may need extra care to feel secure. As a result of the divorce, one parent moved out of the home. This may make children scared of being abandoned by the other parent. Young children may become frightened if they must stay temporarily with another caregiver, such as a child care provider, 18-9. They may be afraid the parent will not return.

Children need as much love and support as possible from each parent after a divorce. Parents should try to be sensitive to their children's feelings and make special efforts to keep lines of communication open. They should try not to argue with one another, especially in front of the children. Even when they are no longer married, the mother and father are still parents. Ideally, they should work together as a team to continue parenting their children. It is in this type of environment children will adjust best to a divorce.

18-9
This father must reassure his young children he will return soon.

Remarriage and Stepfamilies

Following divorce or the death of a spouse, adults are single once again. As their lives continue, they may begin new relationships. In time, they may remarry. People who remarry are usually excited about finding new life partners. They look forward to building a permanent relationship together.

Quite often, however, these people have children from their previous relationships. When they remarry, it will mean the merging of two families. This new family structure will be a stepfamily. Becoming a stepfamily can take some getting used to, especially for the children.

Children may find it difficult to let go of the hope their own parents will remarry. They may resent their new stepparents. This is especially true if they feel the stepparent is trying to replace their biological parent. Children also feel a sense of loyalty to their biological parent. They may feel they would betray this parent by loving the stepparent. Parents need to reassure children their feelings for a stepparent in no way affect their feelings toward their biological parent. Everyone should remember it takes time to build new relationships.

Stepfamilies face unique challenges, but many are successful. Stepfamilies can create many new relationships for children. Children in stepfamilies may have four parent figures, eight grandparents, and a variety of siblings, half-siblings, and stepsiblings. Money may have to be spread among more people to care for the larger stepfamily. This can sometimes lead to stress and conflict. Focusing on the family's strengths can bring the family closer together. Children seem to adjust well to their new family structure over time. Parents can help facilitate this adjustment. See 18-10.

18-10
Cooperation and respect for one another can bring members of stepfamilies closer together.

1—Resource: *Stepfamilies*, Activity C, SAG.

2—Discuss: If children love their new stepparent, are they taking away from the love for their biological parents? What do you think?

3—Discuss: How are the relationships in a stepfamily more complicated than those in a nuclear family?

1—Resource: *An Illness in the Family*, Activity D, SAG.

2—Discuss: Suggest ways a family can deal with the emotional, physical, and financial burden of the serious illness of a family member.

3—Reflect: How would you feel if a serious illness struck your family? Would you feel cheated? Would it bring your family closer together?

Serious Illness

Serious illness can result from a gradual decline in health caused by chronic illness, such as heart disease. It may also result from a sudden detection of a life-threatening condition, such as cancer or AIDS. Sometimes an accident results in the disability of a family member.

The serious illness of a family member can place a heavy burden on the entire family. Medical bills can put added pressure on the family budget. There is no way, however, to anticipate the emotional or physical burdens a serious illness can place on a family. Some family members may feel cheated because of the burden. Other family members make the best of an undesirable situation and grow closer together.

When a parent is seriously ill, the loss of a wage earner places an extra burden on the family. All family members need to be cooperative and flexible. Family members should be able to talk about the pressures they face and work together to deal with the situation. Family members can adapt to the situation and be flexible in meeting one another's needs.

During the serious illness of a family member, children should not be shut out or ignored. They should be encouraged to share their fears and ask questions. These questions should be answered simply and truthfully, 18-11. When a parent is ill, children should be allowed to keep in contact with the parent as much as possible. If hospital visits are not possible, even a short phone call can reassure children the parent still loves them. When children are ill, parents can reassure them by answering any questions honestly and simply. By finding out about hospital procedures in advance, parents can prepare their children for what may happen.

Serious illness can be devastating, both emotionally and financially. Ideally, families should look ahead and provide financial security through insurance or savings for emergencies. Many social services are also available

18-11
When a parent is seriously ill, it can cause financial and emotional concerns in the family. Telling the children the truth about their mother's condition will help them understand the situation.

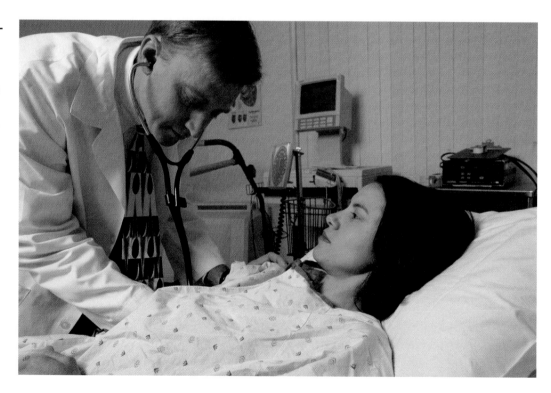

to help families in times of need. Relatives, friends, and neighbors can often lessen the pressure created by a serious illness in the family.

Explaining Death to Children

Most children are far more aware of death than their parents realize. Many parents avoid talking about death, perhaps because of their own fears. Death is a painful reality that touches young and old, but it is a part of life. Parents should treat it as such.

Children form different concepts about death as they grow and develop. Children who are three years old or younger have little or no understanding of death. Four-year-olds are familiar with the word *death*, but it does not mean much to them.

Five-year-olds often associate death with the temporary inability to move. They think people can return to life after being dead just by starting to move again. These ideas are reinforced by television cartoons. Characters are often run over or blown up one minute and spring back to life the next.

Around the age of six, children's ideas about death become more realistic. They cannot yet conceive of their own death, but they can see the possibility of other, older people dying. They may worry about the death of their parents. If so, they need to be reassured their parents probably will not die for a long time.

At seven, children begin to suspect they will die someday. They may talk about funerals and cemeteries. By the age of eight, children accept the reality of their own eventual death. They may talk about the process of dying, such as how people stop breathing when they die. By nine or ten years of age, children accept death as a natural biological process.

Most teens think about death a great deal. They are philosophically reviewing all aspects of life. Teens are also more able to see situations from many perspectives. They may wonder what changes occur in a family when loved ones die. They may wonder what will happen when their parents die. Teens even imagine what would happen if they themselves died. If they are experiencing frustrations, teens are more likely than usual to think about death. At this stage, they tend to compare what their current lives are like to what death would be like.

A Death in the Family

When a family experiences a death, parents should not shut out the children. Children want to be included in all family matters. They sense when their parents are upset, and they want to share this with them. See 18-12.

18-12 _____
When a death occurs in the family, children should be allowed to grieve. Their questions should be answered simply and honestly.

1—Resource: *Explaining Death to Children*, Activity E, SAG.

2—Resource: *Helping Children Grieve*, reproducible master 18-1, TR.

3—Activity: Draw a chart on the board, list children's ages 3 to 10, and record a brief description of how children react to death.

4—Reflect: What does the concept of death mean to you?

1—**Reflect:** Do you recall the death of a pet? How was this treated in your family? How did you and your parents react?

2—**Discuss:** How do adult's reactions to death compare to children's reactions?

3—**Enrich:** Role-play situations of parents explaining death to children. Evaluate the various explanations.

4—**Resource:** *New in Town*, Activity F, SAG.

As with other emotional topics, parents can teach children about the facts of death in natural settings. Children will learn the most about death and grieving when they are exposed to it. For instance, the death of a pet provides a natural opportunity to discuss the concept of death. Children should be allowed to grieve the loss of a pet. Grieving is a natural part of adjusting to death. It is not recommended that parents immediately replace a dead pet with another one. Doing so could interfere with the necessary grieving and adjusting process.

Parents need to realize young children's reactions to death are quite different from those of adults. Adults often withdraw and become depressed. Children are more likely to act out their feelings with hostile and aggressive behaviors. Young children cannot express their feelings with words, but their actions show how upset they are.

Parents should be truthful when telling their children about death. They should not say "Grandma has gone on a long trip." Children will eventually learn this explanation was a lie. In the meantime, they may be afraid that anyone leaving on a trip will not return. Parents should not say "Grandpa has gone to the hospital." That explanation could lead children to believe that when people (including the children themselves) go to hospitals, they may never come back. The statement "Grandma died because she was sick" is another wrong approach. Children may fear all sicknesses will lead to death.

Parents may wonder whether they should take their children to grieving rituals, such as funerals and wakes. The loving support and concern shared among family members could be helpful for the children to see. Experts advise that parents should consider the child's age, personality, and maturity level. Generally, children over age seven can handle these events. A parent should ask an older child if he or she would like to go. The parent should explain what will happen and what it means. The parent should accept the child's decision.

Some younger children may also be mature enough to attend funerals and wakes. The same guidelines apply. Other children are too sensitive or cannot yet really understand what a funeral is. In this case, the parent should use his or her judgment. Even if the child does not attend the services, the parent should talk to him or her about the death.

Suppressing grief over the death of a loved one may have a devastating effect on anyone, especially a child. A child needs to be allowed to complete the task of grieving over the death of a loved one. Otherwise, he or she may be overwhelmed by feelings of unresolved grief at a later time.

Family Moves

You live in a very mobile society. You may have lived in the same neighborhood for most of your life. On the other hand, you may have lived in several different places.

Families may have to move to another town or city for various reasons. Sometimes a move is necessary due to a job transfer, death in the family, divorce, or unemployment. Parents may look forward to a move if it means an advancement in their careers and beginning a new life. Children, on the other hand, may have quite a different view. They may be upset if the move means they will be leaving special friends. It is difficult for children to realize they can make friends in a new area. Teens often resent being asked to leave their

1 friends, special activities, and the chance to graduate from the school they enjoy.

Parents can encourage their older children to write letters or send e-mail messages to their old friends. If it is possible, parents may help their children arrange phone calls and visits with old friends. Parents should be sensitive to a child's feelings about the move.

Moves are usually best made when children do not have to be uprooted during the school year. In some cases, however, it is not possible to wait for the end of the school year. Parents should talk with both the child's old teacher and new teacher about how to make the school transition as smooth as possible. Parents should find out whether the child's new class is ahead of his or her old one. If this is the case, parents may have to work with their children at home to help them catch up to the other students.

A positive attitude can ease the moving experience. Parents can present the move as a new adventure. 2 Children should be encouraged to become involved in the planning, packing, and arranging of their rooms in the new house, 18-13.

It may be a good idea for parents or teens to gather information about the new school and community. A subscription to the newspaper from the new location could help the family 3 learn about the community. The new community may also have a Web site the family could visit. Learning about their new community can help make the transition smoother.

18-13
Helping to decorate his bedroom in the new home can make the move a little easier for this boy.

Summary

- A sign of successful parenting is the ability to cope with both the predictable and unpredictable events of family life.

1

- Balancing family and work roles can be challenging, but with determination, effort, and planning, it is possible.

- Businesses are recognizing the pressures dual-career families face. In response, many offer alternative working arrangements that are more family-friendly.

- When parents divorce, they should reassure their children they will still receive loving care and attention and their daily needs will be met.

- If members of a stepfamily focus on their family's strengths, it can give bring them closer together.

- The serious illness of a family member can be devastating to a family, both emotionally and financially.

- Death is a painful reality that touches young and old, but it is a part of life. Parents should treat it as such.

- A positive attitude can make a family move easier, especially if the move is viewed as an adventure.

Reviewing Key Points

1. List two reasons parents work.
2. How can family-friendly programs help each of the following?
   2
   A. businesses
   B. working parents
   C. children of working parents
3. When should parents tell their children about a divorce?
4. Who should tell the children about the divorce? Why?
5. After divorce, how can parents help their children feel secure?
6. True or false. Good relationships between children and stepparents often take time to develop.
7. When there is a serious illness in the family, how should children's questions be answered?
8. According to authorities, should parents immediately replace a dead pet with a new pet? Why or why not?
9. True or false. Parents help their children accept death by using oversimplified explanations of death.
10. Propose three ways parents can involve their children when the family is moving to a new community.

Learning by Doing

1. Role-play a discussion in which a family discusses ways to resolve problems with their multiple roles.

2. Interview an employee from the human resources department in a company in your area. Ask what family-friendly programs and policies the company offers its employees. If any are offered, are these options popular with employees?

3. In your own words, write a paragraph explaining the meanings of the terms *custody, visitation rights,* and *child support payments* as they relate to children and divorce.

4. Visit your local public library. Check out a children's book on any one of the concerns listed in this chapter. Read the book and write a summary. Present your book and report to the class.

5. Create a poster or pamphlet for parents about one of the family concerns described in this chapter. Propose ways parents can help their children adjust to this situation.

Thinking Critically

1. Interview three to five working parents and pose a list of questions revealing how they divide the tasks in their household. Who is primarily responsible for child care? Who takes off work when a child is ill? How are the couples different and how are they similar?

2. Set up a panel discussion with two female and two male students. Discuss the pros and cons of dual-career marriages.

3. Select one of the concerns presented in this chapter. Write a paper explaining how you, as a parent, would help your child deal with this situation.

4. With a partner, discuss appropriate ways for parents to talk with their children about death. Discuss the importance of openness and truthfulness in parent-child communication.

5. Working with a small group, select one of the family concerns described in the chapter. Investigate resources in your community that could help families in this situation. Contact the agencies or people you identify as possible sources of help. Recommend the three most helpful places you have found that a parent could turn for help with this situation.

Chapter 19
Family Crises

Objectives

After studying this chapter, you will be able to

● describe common family crises, such as substance abuse, unemployment and financial crises, child abuse and neglect, missing children, domestic violence, and suicide.

● identify possible causes for these crises.

● assess the knowledge and skills parents need to handle these crises.

● summarize community resources available for parents facing these crises.

Key Terms

crisis
dysfunctional family
alcoholism
drug abuse
child abuse
1 child neglect
physical abuse
emotional abuse
sexual abuse
incest
physical neglect
emotional neglect
Shaken Baby Syndrome (SBS)
domestic violence
peer violence
bullying
gangs

You might think good marriages and happy families have no problems or conflict. In reality, problems and conflict occur in every relationship and family. The most important factor is how the family handles the problems, whether they recognize conflict, and how they manage it.

Most problems and conflicts within a family are minor. A family's normal method of coping with everyday problems is important. With good coping skills, a strong family can easily overcome small problems. This is good practice for handling larger problems, such as a family crisis.

What Is a Crisis?

A **crisis** is an unforeseen situation that demands adjustment by all members of a family. A crisis might consist of a single event such as the loss of a job. Other crises are long-term situations that require a family to cope. These might include substance abuse, child abuse, or domestic violence. A crisis requires that family members adapt and change. Crises occur at one time or another in every family.

Strong, healthy families can weather a crisis, 19-1. Members pull 2 together to help each other meet their needs and cope with change. These families can even become stronger and closer after helping one another deal with a crisis.

Some families do not adapt well to crisis. In response to a crisis, these families might become dysfunctional. A **dysfunctional family** is one that cannot function properly because of certain overwhelming problems. These 3 problems prevent the parents from being able to care for and nurture their children. In a dysfunctional family, the needs of all family members are not being met. Interactions between the members are not healthy.

1—Vocabulary: Look up terms in the glossary and discuss their meanings.

2—Vocabulary: What is a *crisis*? How can a crisis challenge families and how can it make them stronger?

3—Vocabulary: Cite examples of situations that could make a family dysfunctional.

19-1

In strong families, members support and help one another through good times and bad.

In this chapter, you will learn about several family crises and the adjustments they demand from family members. You will also learn about community resources available to assist families in times of crisis.

Unemployment and Financial Crises

Parents have the responsibility to provide financially for their children. They work to earn an income for the family. Parents may plan and budget carefully to get the most from their money. They can set financial goals for the family and work to meet them.

Families with good economic standing must be careful not to let their spending get out of balance with their income. A family shouldn't increase its standard of living beyond what is financially wise. Families who save and invest more will be protected in times of emergency. They will also have money to meet their financial goals, such as buying a house, paying for the children's education, or saving for retirement. Families who earn more but also spend more may find themselves with no financial security in times of financial crisis.

Unfortunately, a family's financial situation can change rapidly. As the economy changes, there is often a focus on new technologies. Companies may have to let certain workers go. This creates job loss in one area and openings in other areas. Unemployment can create a family crisis. If a parent loses his or her job, it can cause a great deal of stress in a family.

First and foremost, the parent temporarily loses his or her way to support the family. The family may experience financial crisis as the parent seeks another job. They may not be able to pay their bills. The family may not be able to buy essentials such as food. This can be frustrating and scary. It can also affect the parent's self-esteem. His or her identity as a provider may suffer.

Family members can become closer as they focus on adjusting to the situation. They need to be supportive as the unemployed person seeks new work. In some cases, a person may seek a job in a different field. A new job may require concentrated training or study. The other spouse may have to take on the role of sole wage earner temporarily.

Sometimes parents try to shield their children from knowing about a financial crisis. They may worry it will upset the children. However, children need to be aware of the financial changes in their families, 19-2. Children feel better when they are treated as part of the team. This way they can better understand why their parents are upset and concerned. It will also help them understand why they have to do without certain things and why spending may be limited to essentials. Children can also learn from their families' financial problems. It is important for parents to instill in their children the values of wise spending, budgeting, and saving.

During a financial crisis, a family must assess their obligations and assets. They should set up a budget to balance these. Teens may be able to find part-time work to help ease the financial burden. One or both parents may temporarily take a second job to earn more money. Extended family members may help out.

Community resources are also available to help families in financial need. These can include social service programs that provide food, shelter, and other necessities. Families may also wish to seek the services of financial planning experts. These are often

listed in the phone book under *Financial Planning Consultants, Debt Counseling Services,* and *Credit Counseling Services.*

Most often, financial crises are temporary. They require the adjustment and cooperation of all family members. If the couple plans carefully, the family can often manage until the unemployed parent is working again.

Alcoholism and Other Drug Abuse

When a family member abuses alcohol or other drugs, it can devastate the entire family. **Alcoholism** is a condition in which a person's drinking causes the person to hurt himself or herself and others. An alcoholic continues to drink despite the problems it causes. Almost every time an alcoholic drinks, he or she becomes drunk. This

1—**Resource:** *Dealing with Substance Abuse Problems,* Activity B, SAG.

19-2 ────────
Parents can include their children in talks about finances. They can teach children to budget, set financial goals, and save.

1—Discuss: In what way does alcohol abuse impact a person's ability to make rational and responsible decisions? How might this affect other areas of a person's life?

2—Discuss: When teens or children are involved with alcohol or drugs, how might it affect their lives? What are some reasons teens become involved with drugs?

is what separates an alcoholic from a responsible drinker.

Drug abuse is the use of a drug for any reason that is not medical, 19-3. People can abuse both illegal and legal drugs. Illegal drugs include heroin, cocaine, and marijuana. Legal drugs include prescriptions and over-the-counter medications.

Unfortunately, the crises of alcoholism and drug abuse affect many families. For instance, researchers estimate 1 in 10 children has an alcoholic parent. *Substance abuse* (the combined name for the abuse of drugs and alcohol) interferes with a person's ability to function as he or she normally would. The chemicals in alcohol and other drugs alter the mind's ability to work properly.

While using alcohol or drugs, a person's behavior and ability to think clearly are altered. The person is unable to make rational judgments. 1 This can result in dangerous risk-taking behavior. For instance, people under the influence may combine drugs with alcohol, which can result in death. Many of these risk-taking behaviors, such as drunk driving, are illegal. People can face stiff legal penalties related to their use of alcohol and other drugs.

Alcohol and other drugs can also damage the body, especially when they are used heavily. For instance, these chemicals can kill brain cells and

19-3 _____
Drug abuse is a family crisis. It not only affects the person who is abusing drugs, but his or her entire family.

damage the liver. People who are addicted to drugs and alcohol often neglect to care for their bodies as they should. They focus more on using the substance than on eating, sleeping, and exercising.

A person's addiction can invade every aspect of his or her life. Addicts concentrate on little else than using the substance to which they are addicted. Thoughts of using the substance consume the person's time and energy. Alcoholics and drug addicts often sacrifice their jobs, financial well-being, and relationships to use the substance. Addicts often mistreat their family members and loved ones.

People may use a substance in an attempt to cope with their problems. When they are under the influence of alcohol or drugs, it may seem they have escaped their problems. Once the effects of the substance wear off, the person realizes the problems are still there. They have not gone away. Actually, abusing alcohol and other drugs only multiplies the person's problems, 19-4.

Alcoholism and drug abuse affect people of all ages. These crises usually begin in the teen years. Teens may use alcohol or drugs to go along with their 2 friends. They may start using a substance to make themselves look good in front of peers. Children and teens may also be following the example of parents who abuse drugs or alcohol. For many, this is the start of an addiction that will affect them for life.

Dealing with Substance Abuse

When one family member has a substance abuse problem, it affects the entire family. The person who uses the substance can no longer interact in a healthy way with family members. He or she may act in a hurtful way when under the influence of the substance. When not using the substance, the

19-4 ———————————————
Instead of alleviating problems, substance abuse can cause even more problems. People who abuse substances may need help to put their lives back in order.

person may not remember how he or she acted.

When friends and family members mention the problem, an alcoholic or drug abuser will deny a problem exists. He or she may even offer a very convincing explanation about why there isn't a problem. This leads family members to cover up the substance abuse or try to ignore it. This is a mistake. The problems will not go away. Instead, they often worsen when they are covered up or ignored.

Instead, families must face the problems of alcoholism and drug abuse. Many will need professional help. The entire family may need counseling. They must learn new ways to interact with one another and with the substance abuser.

The substance abuser will need help as well. He or she must decide to stop using the substance. Addictions do not have a cure; the person must work daily to avoid using the substance. It may take treatment and professional counseling to learn to master an addiction. Many organizations provide services for substance abusers and their families. A few of these are listed in Chapter 4 of this text. Others can be found in the phone book under *Alcoholism Information and* *Treatment, Drug Abuse Information and Treatment,* and *Drug Addiction Information and Treatment.*

Child Abuse and Neglect

Abuse and neglect pose serious risks to today's children. Incidents of child abuse and neglect are reported at alarming rates across the country. The National Committee for Prevention of Child Abuse (NCPCA) uses the following definition of child abuse. "**Child abuse** is a nonaccidental injury or pattern of injuries to a child. It is damage to a child for which there is no reasonable explanation. It includes nonaccidental physical, sexual, and emotional abuse." **Child neglect** means failing to provide a child's basic needs.

Types of Child Abuse and Neglect

Several types of child abuse and neglect exist. In some families, only one type of abuse or neglect is present. In others, more than one occur. The severity of abuse also differs from one case to the next.

● **Physical abuse** is the intentional infliction of physical injury upon a child. Physical abuse can include hitting, biting, beating, shaking, pushing, and kicking. The adult uses physical force to punish or hurt the child. In some cases, physical abuse can be easily identified by marks left on the child's body. In others, it is not so easy.

● **Emotional abuse** is the use of words to belittle, threaten, or exert control over another person. This may include humiliation, name-calling, and other belittling

1—**Discuss:** Should families cover up a family member's substance abuse problem and try to handle it themselves?

2—**Vocabulary:** Review the different types of child abuse. Have students define each type and give examples.

1—Vocabulary: What is *Shaken Baby Syndrome?* How is it caused and what are the symptoms?

remarks. These remarks are intended to hurt the victim's self-esteem. Other people may notice the abuser talking to the child in an abusive way. Many times, however, abusers do not talk this way to their children in front of potential witnesses.

- **Sexual abuse** means forcing a child to engage in or witness sexual activities. One type of child sexual abuse is **incest**, sexual activity between people who are closely related. It occurs most often between fathers and daughters. Incest often begins when a child is very young. The child regards the acts as a sign of affection. He or she does not know that what is happening is wrong. When incest leads to greater sexual involvement, the child may become confused. Children usually only seek help when they are old enough to understand why incest is wrong.

- **Physical neglect** is the failure to provide sufficient food, clothing, shelter, medical care, education, guidance, and supervision for a child. The parent or caregiver has not met his or her responsibility to provide for the child's well-being. Physical neglect can often be observed. If a child is not dressed in clothing that fits properly and is appropriate for the weather, this can be a sign of physical neglect. Physical neglect can also mean failure to protect a child from abuse.

- **Emotional neglect** is the failure to provide children with love and affection. Children may receive good physical care and still be emotionally neglected. For instance, if a parent never holds his or her newborn, it can be a sign of emotional neglect. Children need to be loved and held, 19-5. It stimulates their brain growth. Emotional neglect is often difficult to prove, but it does occur.

19-5
Children need to be held and cuddled. Nurturing a child stimulates growth and development. Failure to nurture a child is called emotional neglect.

Shaken Baby Syndrome (SBS)

Shaken Baby Syndrome (SBS) describes symptoms that occur when an infant or small child is violently shaken. SBS is a form of physical abuse. It has serious consequences for a child, and can result in death. About one in five victims of SBS die within a few days after the injury occurs. SBS usually occurs before age one, but it can happen in children as old as five years.

Abusers give infant crying as the major reason SBS occurs. Even when a baby's needs are met, the baby may cry. Most adults have good coping skills, and find ways to handle this crying. Some adults may not feel able to tolerate the crying. They become frustrated and desperate, and may shake the baby. The adult does not intend to hurt the child, but may not understand the damage he or she can do.

In infancy, neck muscles are not fully developed. When the baby is shaken roughly, the head jerks back and forth, causing whiplash. The brain is repeatedly jarred against the skull. Tiny veins between the brain and skull break and spill blood. This blood pools between the brain and skull, causing pressure and swelling of the brain. In severe cases, this affects the brain's ability to control vital body functions, such as breathing and heartbeat. Death can occur.

SBS can also cause paralysis, seizures, cerebral palsy, hearing loss, speech difficulties, and mental disabilities. Damage to the retina of the eye is one of the most common injuries. This can cause blindness or vision problems. Even in the most mild SBS cases, irritability, lethargy, tremors, vomiting, and learning and behavioral disorders can occur.

It is not known exactly how much force creates SBS, or how many instances of shaking can happen before damage occurs. For these reasons, parents are strongly cautioned to *never* shake their babies. Many experts tell parents not to even play roughly with their infants, as rough play might lead to an accidental injury.

Over half the abusers are males. Most commonly, it is the mother's boyfriend or husband (often the baby's father or stepfather). Female child care providers account for about one-fifth of all cases. Mothers have been found to cause SBS in just over ten percent of cases.

The key to preventing Shaken Baby Syndrome is to educate parents about the dangers of shaking a child. Another step is to teach parents to cope with their baby's crying. Several suggestions are given in 19-6. If a parent feels he or she is losing control, crisis hot lines are available to listen and offer

Ways to Cope with Crying

- Make sure the baby's needs are met (the baby is not hungry, thirsty, wet, dirty, cold, hot, ill, or in pain.)
- Offer a pacifier, toy, or other distraction.
- Rock the baby gently or walk with the baby in your arms or an infant carrier.
- Take the baby for a walk or car ride.
- Play soft music, sing, or speak soft and comforting words to the baby.
- Ask someone to relieve you for a few minutes or hours.
- If you are tense, don't hold the baby until you can relax. The baby will sense the tension in your body and cry harder.
- If all else fails, put the baby in bed for a few minutes, go in the other room, and take a short break. Relax. Continue to check on the baby every few minutes.
- Call a trusted friend or a crisis hot line to talk about your frustration.
- Remember an infant's crying is not a sign of bad parenting. Crying is the only way babies can communicate.

19-6

Every year babies die from Shaken Baby Syndrome (SBS). Parents must find nonabusive ways to deal with their frustration when their babies won't stop crying.

suggestions. Counseling may also be needed.

Child Abusers

You may wonder how to spot a child abuser. You may ask what kind of people abuse children. The answers are not simple. Most child abusers are ordinary adults caught up in situations they do not know how to handle. You cannot distinguish a child abuser from other people. Reports of child abuse cross economic, social, and ethnic boundaries. The person most likely to abuse a child is his or her own parent. Sometimes, however, substitute caregivers abuse children in their care.

For many parents who abuse their children, this is a learned behavior. Many child abusers were abused themselves as children. Their own parents

1—Discuss: What can parents do to prevent SBS? Who most often causes SBS?

2—Discuss: Is it possible to give one description of a child abuser that will cover all cases? Briefly discuss some factors that may contribute to child abuse.

3—Discuss: What factors might lead parents to child abuse?

1—**Reflect:** In view of the many child abuse cases, do you think parenting classes should be mandatory in high schools?

2—**Discuss:** How can parents know what happens to their children in substitute care situations? What signs might lead parents to suspect something is wrong?

modeled parenting behavior that included abuse. They grew up with abuse. Parents who were abused as children think of abuse as an appropriate parenting technique. They may not know their behavior is wrong. Abusive parents also may not know other, more acceptable parenting behaviors.

Being abused as children does not *excuse* a parent's abusive behavior, but it may *explain* it. Every person is fully responsible for his or her own actions. A person does not automatically become an abuser in response to childhood abuse. Each person must decide for himself or herself whether to continue the pattern of abuse or break free from it. It is up to each abuser to seek help.

Parental stress is another risk factor for child abuse. In families where the stress level is high, abuse is much more common. These parents may love their children, but in times of stress, they strike out at whoever is closest. This is often their own children. Parents may have family problems, financial stresses, or addictions to alcohol or drugs. In addition, stay-at-home parents may feel isolated from the rest of the adult world. They begin to feel trapped, unable to get away. The day-to-day pressures of parenting may build up and lead these parents to abusive behavior.

Another factor common in child abuse cases is the parents have limited knowledge of child development. These parents do not know what they can realistically expect of their children. They may feel a child is purposely misbehaving, when in fact, the child is acting appropriately for his or her development. For instance, suppose a toddler has a toileting accident. People who understand child development know children cannot be expected to master toilet learning before three years of age. Even then, children will have occasional accidents.

This parent would be understanding and comfort the child. A parent without this knowledge is likely to be angry at the accident. Parents who do not understand the developmental stages and needs of their children cannot feel empathy. They can only feel frustration.

People may wonder why, in a two-parent family, the other parent may witness the abuse and do nothing. There are many reasons this might occur. First and foremost, the other parent is often being abused, too. He or she may fear the abuser. In some cases, the parent may not know the abuse is occurring. Other parents may be in denial about the abuse. A person may know that speaking out about the abuse will break up his or her family. A parent may also doubt his or her ability to provide financially for the children alone. Luckily, many spouses of child abusers do speak out. They take their children out of the abusive situation. They realize their right to live a life free of abuse.

Child Care Staff as Abusers

As more children are enrolled in child care, more cases of abuse by these caregivers occur. Most of these cases involve severe punishment and damaging emotional abuse. They sometimes include sexual abuse as well. In many cases, the abuse continues over a long period of time. Children are often too frightened to tell anyone what is happening. The caregivers usually convince them not to tell with threats of more punishment or the withdrawal of food and comfort.

Continual abuse by a child care staff member harms children in many ways. First, they must endure the day-to-day physical, emotional, or sexual abuse. Second, they develop psychological scars they will carry all their lives. These children's concept of the world is distorted; their sense of trust is broken.

The rest of the family can help a child who is abused in child care. Parents should take the time to observe interactions between caregivers and their children. They should be alert to changes in the appearance or attitude of their children. They should listen to their children describe daily events, paying attention to any verbal or nonverbal clues the children give. Children generally do not lie about caregivers. If parents have any suspicions, they should follow up on them. This is important, but it is not always easy. If children have been threatened about "telling secrets" of abuse, parents may need to seek professional help to uncover the problem.

Stopping Child Abuse

Child abuse is usually a pattern of behavior, not a single act. Breaking this kind of behavior pattern is not easy, but it must happen. The longer the abuse continues, the more serious the consequences become. Child abuse has potentially deadly consequences for the child. It also has serious legal consequences for the abuser.

Every state has laws that require certain persons to report suspected cases of child abuse. These persons are called *mandated reporters*. In every state, physicians are legally obligated to report child abuse to the authorities. Other groups of mandated reporters vary from state to state. Teachers, nurses, and counselors are often mandated reporters, 19-7. Each state has an agency that receives and investigates reports of suspected child abuse. In addition, many states maintain central registers of known and suspected cases of child abuse or neglect. In these states, any new report is cross-checked against the central register for previous incidents.

Although only certain persons are required by law to report suspected cases of child abuse, any citizen may

19-7

In many states, nurses and other medical personnel are mandated reporters of child abuse. They are required to report any suspected or known cases of child abuse to the proper authorities.

file a report. A person who reports a suspected case of child abuse in good faith is granted immunity from civil and criminal liability.

Reporting suspected cases of child abuse is a step in the right direction, but reports alone will not end child abuse. If children, families, and society are to benefit, supportive programs are needed. The public must be educated about child abuse. Abusers need rehabilitation programs to help them choose new and healthier behaviors. These programs can be attended voluntarily or by court order. Potential abusers need to know programs exist for the prevention of child abuse.

Most cities have several helpful agencies and programs. Examples are Children's Protective Services, Escape

1—**Resource:** *Child Abuse Laws and Programs*, Activity C, SAG.

2—**Discuss:** How can society help end child abuse?

Centers, Family Outreach Centers, Parents Anonymous, and Children's Resource and Information Services (CRIS).

Some programs are designed to help children avoid further abuse and alert them to possible abusive behavior. One such program is called We Help Ourselves (WHO). The program does not instruct children to talk back to their parents. It does encourage children to say no to sexual advances made toward them and to ask for help if they are abused. The program helps children recognize abnormal acts of affection and teaches them to state their feelings. Children learn to tell others about problems and avoid dangerous situations. Adult leaders use puppet shows and other child-oriented teaching techniques to help children learn these important lessons.

What You Can Do

Before you have children, you should take time to consider your own potential to be a loving and caring parent. By reading books, taking child development and parenting classes, and caring for other people's children, you can gain insight into your possible future role as a parent, 19-8. Also, understanding child development makes you less likely to have unrealistic expectations of children.

As you consider parenthood, examine how you react to stress and anxiety. If you show patterns of aggression when you are frustrated, you need to learn other, more positive ways of handling your emotions. Before getting married or having children, you should consider seeking counseling. This will help you become better able to deal with your feelings and less likely to abuse your future spouse and children. You can also develop your problem-solving and decision-making skills. These skills will help you handle the daily routines and unpredictable events of parenting.

Even if you don't plan to become a parent, you can get involved. Report any instances of child abuse you witness. Serve as a volunteer for an agency that works with abused children. Help educate others about the dangers of child abuse. Find ways you can make a difference and help keep children safe.

19-8
Taking child development and parenting classes can help people understand child development. This understanding may even prevent some instances of child abuse.

Domestic Violence

Domestic violence is any physical, emotional, or sexual behavior intended to harm a family member. Child abuse is a form of domestic violence. Other types of domestic violence include spouse abuse, sibling abuse, and elder abuse. Domestic violence involves people of every racial, religious, educational, and economic background. Both men and women can be abusers.

Abusive people seek power. They want to be in control, but are unable to solve problems in a logical manner. They may hurt and humiliate their family members to assert their own power and control.

Every family has stress that can lead to conflict. Some families are not able to calmly work problems out in a constructive manner. When conflicts arise, an abuser may lose control of his or her emotions. The abuser may choose violent forms of behavior to seek compliance.

As with child abuse, physical, emotional, and sexual abuse can occur. *Battering* is a term often used to describe physical acts of violence. Emotional abuse may take different forms. Making unreasonable demands, withholding love and affection, or criticizing or belittling someone are types of emotional abuse. Forcing family members to observe or engage in unwanted sexual activities is sexual abuse.

Victims of domestic violence often feel helpless, afraid, embarrassed, and guilty. They may hope or believe the abuse won't happen again. However, abuse usually follows a predictable three-phase cycle. See 19-9.

The *cycle of violence* begins with phase one. Tension builds in the relationship. The couple may have increasing arguments. The abused partner generally knows a violent incident is

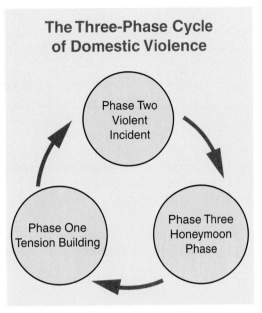

The Three-Phase Cycle of Domestic Violence

Phase Two
Violent
Incident

Phase One
Tension Building

Phase Three
Honeymoon
Phase

19-9

The cycle of domestic violence continues until one partner seeks help to stop it.

coming. He or she may be very careful not to arouse the abuser's anger.

Eventually, however, a violent incident occurs. The abuser may batter his or her partner. He or she might also sexually or emotionally abuse the partner. The abuser has total responsibility for his or her behavior. No one deserves to be abused for any reason. It is the abuser who is in the wrong. The violent incident is stage two of the cycle of violence.

Immediately after the violent incident is stage three, the honeymoon phase. During this phase, the abuser expresses remorse for his or her actions. The abuser promises it will never happen again. Gifts, romantic dates, and other signs of goodwill are evident. Over time, this remorse will fade. The tension builds again and is eventually relieved by another act of violence.

The cycle of violence will continue until either the abuser or the abused person seeks help. Generally the abuser does not admit he or she has a problem. For this reason, the victim is often the person who can break the cycle. He or she can do this by seeking

1—Vocabulary: Define *domestic violence.*

2—Discuss: Why do victims of domestic abuse often feel helpless, afraid, embarrassed, and guilty?

3—Resource: *The Domestic Violence Cycle,* Activity D, SAG.

4—Resource: *The Three-Phase Cycle of Domestic Violence,* color transparency CT-19, TR.

1—Enrich: Invite a police officer to class to speak about domestic violence. Why must the police sometimes intervene when domestic violence occurs? Ask the speaker to describe police involvement in these types of cases.

2—Resource: *Gangs, Bullies, and Peer Violence*, Activity E, SAG.

3—Discuss: What characteristics are common in victims of bullies and gangs? Why? Suggest ways parents can help their children deal with bullies and gangs.

4—Discuss: If children are confronted by bullies or gang members, should they fight back? Why or why not?

help and refusing to continue being a victim. Most often this means the victim must leave the abusive relationship.

Sometimes police intervention may be necessary in coping with domestic violence situations. The abuser may be arrested, and restraining orders may be issued. Both the abuser and the abused family members should seek counseling. Communication, decision making, and conflict resolution are important skills for families to develop. Professional help may be needed to accomplish this. Sources of help are listed in Chapter 4 of this text. Other possible sources can be found within communities through religious groups, hospitals, and law enforcement agencies.

Gangs, Bullies, and Peer Violence

Peer violence is violence directed at a person by someone in the same peer group. Peer violence among children is a major concern of parents. **Bullying** means one or more people inflict physical, verbal, or emotional abuse on another person. **Gangs** are groups of bullies who seek to inflict power through physical means. They set up territorial restrictions and codes often identified by graffiti. They often wear identifiable clothing to designate membership in a certain gang.

Bullies and gang members may seem strong, but they actually need help. Studies show their behavior indicates they are not receiving enough caring and love, discipline, and structure at home. Bullies and gang members may be abused and neglected by their parents. Young children and teens seeking structure and discipline

in their lives are often attracted to gangs. Bullies and gangs come from every ethnic and economic group. Both boys and girls join gangs. They believe that by acting tough and inflicting power over others, they will be regarded as important. They lack problem-solving skills and seek to resolve conflicts with force. Unless stopped, they are likely to face legal consequences.

Anyone can be a victim of gangs or bullies. Children who appear weaker or smaller are often targeted. Parents need to communicate openly with their children about gangs and bullies. They also need to know what their children are doing, where they are, and who their friends are. Parents should also be aware of signs that may indicate their children are victims. See 19-10.

What Can Parents and Children Do?

Parents can help prevent their children from becoming victims of peer violence. They can watch for changes in their children's behavior that might indicate violence is occurring. They can also tell their children what to do when confronted by a gang or bully.

Children should be encouraged *not* to fight back. Fighting back only encourages bullies, and unnecessary physical harm could result. If children do not think they can handle a confrontation, parents and authorities should step in. Often, bullies warn children not to tell. Children should be encouraged to report any threatening incidents. Parents must reassure their children they will not be tattling by reporting bullies or gang activity.

When confronted by a bully, children and teens should be encouraged to say "Stop it now. I don't want to fight you." They should practice taking a stand. There is also safety in numbers, and teens and children should walk to places together.

Signs of Peer Violence

Parents should watch for signs their children are possibly being victimized.

Victims of bullying or gangs usually...

- Act moody, sullen, quiet; withdraw from family interaction
- Become depressed; lack self-esteem
- Lose interest in schoolwork and activities; grades usually drop
- Become loners; shy away from friends
- Change in normal appetite
- Wait to use the restroom until they arrive home
- Arrive home with torn clothes and unexplained bruises
- Display anxiety about going to school, taking school trips, or participating in extracurricular activities
- Ask for extra money for school lunch or supplies, and extra allowance
- Refuse to go to school
- Avoid going to certain areas in school and in town
- Have trouble sleeping
- Begin to carry self-protection weapons, such as a pocketknife

19-10 ————————
If their child shows these signs, parents may suspect the child is a victim of peer violence.

19-11 ————————
These students must pass through a metal detector each morning as they enter school. In schools where peer violence is a problem, stricter security measures are enforced to protect students.

1—Discuss: What can parents and communities do to stop the rising tide of bullying and gang problems? What is meant by "zero tolerance"?

Children and teens should stay away from areas frequented by gangs. They should not wear clothing that resembles known gang symbols or colors. They should avoid wearing clothing that may call attention to themselves, such as popular sport shoes or jackets.

In many communities, parents and children are creating youth forums to rid their communities of gang activity. Schools and communities are establishing clear, strict codes of behavior that prohibit bullying and gang activity, 19-11. They are developing programs to educate teachers, parents, and community leaders about behavioral management. Community organizations are taking a stand and sending the message to gangs and bullies they will not tolerate peer violence.

School Violence

In the past few years, peer violence has tragically escalated into school violence. Certain groups of students and school staff members have been targeted, but random people are also victims. School violence has occurred at all school levels. It can happen anywhere.

Although experts do not totally understand school violence, they do know how to lessen the chances. Violence prevention requires collaborative efforts that include the school staff and children and their parents, as well as law enforcement and emergency response personnel.

Parents have a major responsibility in preventing violence and protecting their children. Parents can

- use positive household rules and behavior expectations

- value individual differences in others and model appropriate behaviors

- monitor children's viewing of or interactions with violent content in television programs, movies, music, video games, and Internet sites

- help organize after-school activities and school-age child care programs

- help their children learn to avoid and cope with negative peer pressure

The most important thing parents can do is listen to their children's feelings and concerns about themselves and their friends. If these feelings or concerns seem unhealthy, parents need to take immediate action.

Missing Children

One of the worst fears parents have is their child will disappear. Each year more than 100,000 children are victims of attempted abductions. An attempted abduction is one in which a person tries to abduct a child but does not succeed. Another 5,000 children are actually abducted yearly. Almost 140,000 more are classified as lost, injured, or otherwise missing. Many of the children in this category are victims of abduction. In these cases, there may be no proof a kidnapping has actually occurred.

Parents and other caregivers must be alert to the dangers of abduction. They should do what they can to prevent their children from being abducted. The following tips are important:

- Know where your child is at all times. *Never* leave your child alone in the car, yard, store, or other public place.

- Teach your child to use the telephone. Make sure the child knows your home number and area code. Also make sure the child knows how to call the police in an emergency. Teach the child to place a collect call to home from a pay phone.

- Do not write your child's name on his or her clothes or books. Abductors could see it and begin talking to the child on a first-name basis.

- Choose a secret code word you and your child can use for identification in case of an emergency. Tell your child never to go with anyone who does not know the code word.

- Teach your child not to get involved with strangers in any way. Be sure the child understands the meaning of the word *stranger*.

- Ask the school to notify you at once if your child does not report to school.

- Fingerprint your child. Keep a copy of the prints on hand for identification purposes.

- Cooperate with your neighbors. Let children know which homes are "safe homes." Also ask neighbors to keep an eye on children when they play outside.

Runaways

While many children are abducted each year, many more run away from home. Over 450,000 teens run away from home each year. Reasons for running away may vary. Many times teens leave home because of problems in their families. Some teens run away to leave abusive home lives. Others simply do not get along well with their parents. Still more teens think running away will make them independent. Runaways may mistakenly think leaving home will solve their problems. Instead, most find it creates many more problems.

In most families, teens feel unhappy at times, and parents are sometimes disappointed. When problems occur, family members need to make special efforts to listen to each other. If necessary, they may have to seek professional help. These steps may be difficult, but they are better than the complete alienation that results from running away.

The families of runaways live in constant fear. They have no way to know what happened to their children. Reports of other runaways who have been

19-12

Teens who have run away can call a toll-free hot line to ask for help in returning to their families.

molested or killed add to their fears.

Teens who run away often do not find the independence they seek. When they run away, most quit school. Because they did not finish school, they are not qualified for many jobs. They have little or no money. Runaways are often homeless and living on the streets. Many turn to crime to support themselves. Runaways often, but not always, find the life they left behind is better than the one they have found.

Some runaways return to their families. If so, they must readjust to living by the family's rules. They must also work with their parents to resolve the problems that lead them to leave. Counseling may help. Teen runaways who return home and go back to school have a good chance of preparing to live on their own as adults. Not finishing school may lead to even greater dependence on their families. Then, they would have to rely on their families for housing and other kinds of support. Their years of dependency become lengthened.

Several local and national agencies are available to help runaways, 9-12. Runaways and their families can find these agencies in the telephone book. They are listed under such headings as *Runaway Hotline, Operation Peace of Mind,* and *National Runaway Switchboard.*

Suicide

Suicide is the ninth leading cause of death in the United States. People from ages 10 to 45 are the most likely to commit suicide. They may view this action as an end to their problems. When a person takes his or her life, the person leaves behind the family and friends who love him or her. The suicide of a friend or family member is a crisis, 19-13. It is a sudden and unexpected

1—Enrich: Cite statistics for teen suicide in America.

2—Resource: *Myths and Truths About Teen Suicide*, reproducible master 19-1, TR.

3—Discuss: Review factors that might lead to suicide. Are there others that are not listed? What can parents do to help teens overcome these factors?

19-13

When a friend or family member commits suicide, it can be hard to understand. Feelings of sadness, grief, and anger are common. In time, these feelings will fade.

event that requires huge adjustments by those involved. Family and friends of a suicide victim have deep feelings of shock, anger, sadness, fear, and uncertainty. They must work through these feelings, plus resolve the grief of losing a loved one.

The suicide rate among people ages 15 to 24 is especially high. Suicide is currently the third leading cause of death in this age group. (The top cause of death is unintentional injury. Homicide is the second.)

Each year in the United States, the families of over 2,000 teens must face the shocking reality their sons and daughters have taken their lives. For every person who commits suicide, as many as 25 others may have attempted it.

Friends and family members of a suicide victim may need counseling to help them cope with this crisis. They may ask why the person killed himself or herself. It is a question that usually goes unanswered. In time, friends and family members must come to terms with what has happened. They must work through their grief and resume living their own lives. Counseling can help.

Factors Leading to Suicide

What drives people to consider such a drastic step as suicide? That question has no simple answer. Several different factors may lead people to attempt suicide. The reasons are complex.

Attempting suicide is often a person's way of expressing severe and overwhelming distress. A person may feel unable to cope with life's problems. Attempting suicide is a very unhealthy way to express these feelings. A person who considers suicide is so distressed and overwhelmed, he or she may feel suicide is the only way to relieve these feelings.

What causes this kind of distress in a person's life? In many cases, emotional health or substance abuse problems are involved. Being emotionally healthy means knowing and using appropriate expressions of one's feelings. People who are emotionally unhealthy do not know how to handle their feelings in appropriate ways. They are much more likely to abuse drugs and alcohol as they try to cope with their feelings. Substance addiction can cause a person to feel hopeless and trapped. This, too, increases the risk of suicide.

Emotional changes during the teen years may be one reason suicide is more likely at this age. Additionally, teens are still growing in all aspects of development. Emotionally unhealthy teens may not have the maturity to choose more effective problem-solving methods. High rates of alcohol and drug use during the teen years may be another contributing factor.

Most people of all ages find better ways than suicide to handle their problems. People with strong support systems and high levels of self-esteem are less likely to attempt suicide. They are less likely to feel isolated and hopeless—two main risk factors for suicide.

People who feel isolated are much more likely to consider suicide. They may think no one will understand them or their problems. These people may not feel anyone cares what happens to them. They need to be able to talk to someone who will understand them, and help them sort things out.

Several other factors can increase the risk of suicide. These are listed in 19-14. People who attempt or commit suicide often have one or more of these factors. Each case is different, however. Many people with risk factors never attempt suicide. Also, a person who attempts suicide may have few, if any, of these factors.

Signals That Warn of Possible Suicide

People who are thinking about suicide often send signals to friends and loved ones. These signals may be a cry for help. A person considering suicide may be seeking a solution for the unbearable pain he or she feels. The person may not really want to die, but he or she may see it as the only way out.

These signals may be quite subtle and indirect. People should be aware of these signals. This way they can identify

1—**Discuss:** What signals are sometimes given that a person is considering suicide? What can others do to help?

Risk Factors for Suicide

- Emotional health problems
- Substance abuse problems
- Feeling isolated or hopeless
- Family violence
- Family history of suicide, emotional health problems, or substance abuse
- Depression
- Change in personal well-being or loss of self-esteem
- Loss of an important relationship through separation, divorce, or moves
- Death of a loved one

19-14 _____
Understanding the risk factors of suicide is an important step in preventing it.

Signals of Possible Suicide

- Depression—Signs of severe depression can indicate a person is thinking of suicide. A person can also be depressed for many other reasons. It is important to find out what is causing the depression. Symptoms of severe depression include:

  withdrawing from friends and family

  extreme distress, sadness, and hopelessness

  sudden changes in eating, sleeping, and grooming habits

  sudden changes in behavior or activity level
- Rapid decline in performance on the job or at school
- Making more negative comments about himself or herself than usual
- Having suicidal thoughts and fantasies; talking, writing, or hinting about suicide
- Having previous suicide attempts—This may indicate a person is more likely to seriously consider suicide
- Sudden swing from extreme depression to being at peace—This may indicate the person has decided to commit suicide and is relieved about having made the decision
- Arranging personal affairs—A person may give away personal belongings, write a will, and settle unresolved issues in relationship to give closure to his or her life. This can be a sign a person is seriously considering suicide and has a plan.

19-15 _____
If someone you know shows any of these signs, talk to the person. If the person is considering suicide, help him or her seek professional help.

them if they occur. Common signals that may indicate a possible suicide are listed in 19-15.

A person who is considering suicide may exhibit all, some, or none of these signals. These behaviors can also indicate problems other than suicide. If a person exhibits these signals, it is important to find out why. When a person sends these signals, loved ones should reach out to him or her. They can help the person find the help he or she needs.

Preventing Suicide

Signals of possible suicide should not be taken lightly. When family members or friends see these signals, they should act quickly. They should not sit back and wait for the person to "snap out of this bad mood." The desperation people feel when considering suicide is more than a passing mood. Nor should they think people who talk about suicide will never really do it. That is a myth. People who

19-16 _____
Children and teens greatly benefit from talking to their family members. This can make them feel loved and secure.

threaten to commit suicide are likely to do it unless they receive help from people who care.

If a person exhibits warning signs of suicide, friends and family members should talk to the person about his or her feelings. This will reduce the person's feelings of isolation. Knowing someone cares may make the person feel life is less hopeless. Parents especially need to be available to talk and listen to their children. This can make an incredible difference in a child's life, 19-16.

The most important step family members and friends can take is to listen to what the person is saying or trying to say. The person may feel awkward discussing his or her problems. Friends and family members can help by being patient and helping the person clarify what he or she is saying.

Friends and family members must also realize their loved one will need professional help to overcome the distress he or she feels. They should not take all the responsibility upon themselves. Friends and family members are not trained counselors. They can help best by seeking the services of a trained professional for their loved one. With counseling, a person has the best chance possible to break away from his or her destructive thoughts.

Across the country, private and group counseling services can help people cope with suicidal thoughts. These services are often listed in the telephone book under *Crisis Hot Line, Crisis Intervention, Suicide,* or *Suicide Prevention*. In an emergency, friends and family members can call the police or the emergency room of a local hospital.

Summary

1

- A dysfunctional family is one that cannot function properly because it has overwhelming problems that prevent the parents from being able to care for and nurture their children.

- Unemployment can cause financial crisis in a family. If the family plans carefully, however, they can often manage until the unemployed parent is working again.

- Alcoholism and drug abuse create devastating health problems and legal consequences for the substance abuser. They also interfere with the person's relationships, job performance, and well-being.

- Most child abusers are ordinary adults caught up in situations they do not know how to handle. Child abusers are often parents who abuse their own children.

- Domestic violence is the fault of the abuser. It can have devastating effects on all family members. Children who witness or experience abuse are more likely to become abusive in their future relationships.

- Parents have an important role in protecting their children from peer violence, bullying, and gang activity.

- Collaborative efforts among school staff members and children and their parents can lessen the chances of school violence.

- Every year thousands of children are reported missing. Parents and caregivers must be alert and do what they can to prevent child abduction. They must also help teens realize running away is not an option to solving their problems.

2

- Suicide is the ninth leading cause of death in the United States. Many factors lead people to consider suicide. By recognizing the warning signals and offering help, some suicides can be prevented.

Reviewing Key Points

1. What is a crisis?
2. Describe three differences between a strong, healthy family and a dysfunctional family when each is faced with crisis.
3. List four ways unemployment can affect members of a family.
4. Why is it not a good idea for families to cover up or ignore alcohol and drug abuse problems within the family?
5. Describe three types of child abuse.
6. List four possible effects of Shaken Baby Syndrome (SBS).
7. Briefly describe each phase of the cycle of violence.
8. What effects can domestic violence have upon children who witness it?
9. List five signs that might alert parents their children are victims of bullies or gangs.
10. List five tips parents can use to prevent their children from being abducted.
11. Why are runaways who return home usually forced to become even more dependent on their families?
12. List five warning signals that a person may send when considering suicide.
13. True or false. The most important thing parents can do to prevent the suicide of their child is to listen to what their child is saying or trying to say.

1—Activity: Review and outline this chapter emphasizing the information you found most useful.

2—Answers: Answers to review questions are located in the front section of this TAE.

Learning by Doing

1. Research laws in your state about mandated reporters of child abuse. Who is required by law to report suspected cases of child abuse? How do they make such a report?

2. Create a poster warning parents about the dangers of shaking a baby. On the poster, list tips for helping parents cope with an infant's crying.

3. Interview someone who works at a domestic violence shelter. Ask the person about how domestic violence can affect a family and ways it can be prevented.

4. Design a bulletin board concerning missing children. Post recent newspaper articles, lists of parental precautions, and resources available to parents should this crisis occur.

5. Compile a directory of local sources of help for people facing the various crises described in this chapter.

Thinking Critically

1. Working in a small group, choose one of the crises described in this chapter. Set up a role-play in which a dysfunctional family tries to cope. Set up a second role-play in which the family successfully copes. Show the family researching and using community resources.

2. Debate the following: What should the punishment be for causing Shaken Baby Syndrome? Should child care providers suffer stiffer penalties than parents and relatives?

3. Write a paragraph explaining what you would do if you, a friend, or a family member were ever a victim of domestic violence.

4. Find out what steps have been taken in your community to help prevent the abduction of children. Discuss what further steps could be taken.

5. Collect articles from magazines and newspapers that address suicide. Discuss the factors that may lead someone to commit suicide and warning signals a person may send when thinking about suicide. Make a list of suggestions for preventing suicide attempts.

Family crises can be lessened when all family members share the load.

Chapter 20
A Look at Child
Care Options

Objectives

After studying the chapter, you will be able to

- identify the different types of child care available.
- list factors to consider when selecting child care.
- evaluate options related to child care.
- describe common concerns of parents who use child care.

Key Terms

child care
nanny
au pair
cooperative child care
play groups

During the first few years of life, children need constant supervision and care. Infants are helpless—they depend on adults to meet all their needs. Toddlers need guidance, discipline, and support as they learn to perform life skills and interact with others. Preschoolers can meet more of their own needs. However, they still aren't mature enough to provide total care for themselves. School-age children attend school during the day, but they need supervision and care when they are not in school.

Parents are responsible for making sure their children receive the care they need. In fact, many experts believe the ideal care for a young child is provided in the home by a loving and caring parent. These experts recommend having one parent be the child's primary caregiver for at least the first three years of life. They say the other parent should also be closely involved in the child's care. Other family members and friends can help by caring for the child occasionally to give the parents some time to themselves. This is the type of care most parents would like to provide for their children, 20-1.

Not all parents can care for their young children 24 hours a day, however. Many parents must work outside the home. If this is the case, parents must make alternate arrangements for the child's care when they work. Care that is provided by a caregiver other than parents is called **child care**. This type of care has become increasingly common as more parents enter the workforce.

1—**Vocabulary:** Look up terms in the glossary and discuss their meanings.

2—**Reflect:** What do you believe is the ideal child care situation for young children?

3—**Activity:** List reasons many parents are unable to be the primary caregivers for their children.

4—**Vocabulary:** The term *child care* may mean different things to different people. What does it mean to you?

20-1 _____

Most parents want to stay home with their young children. They would prefer to be the ones to provide the care their children need.

Deciding Whether to Use Child Care

Couples should discuss their attitudes about child care when they discuss other family planning issues. Ideally, couples should talk about this topic before they marry. Both prospective parents should agree on whether they would want to use child care. This way, they will discover any difference of opinion before they marry and have children.

After a couple marries, they still face decisions about child care. Once they plan to have a child, they should look realistically at their child care options. This may influence if and when they have children. When pregnancy occurs, a couple should focus on deciding who will provide the daily care their child will need.

Each situation is different. It is the parents who must decide what, if any, child care their child will receive. When making this decision, parents should carefully weigh the pros and cons of each option. Parents also need to review their parenting and career goals. They need to investigate alternatives that will help them meet those goals. They also want to choose an option that is consistent with their personal priorities, attitudes, and beliefs. Most importantly, parents want to choose what will be best for their children and family.

Child care is a major family expense. Families may spend between 10 and 25 percent of their income on child care. The costs of child care are associated with quality. Because labor is the most expensive aspect of child care, having highly qualified caregivers increases quality and costs.

Child care programs are made more affordable because the government, religious groups, and businesses pick up some of the costs. Parents need to search for quality programs. When comparing costs, parents need to consider transportation, program services such as education and special activities, and hours of operation. Discounts may be given based on income, additional children enrolled, and services given to the program.

This can be a difficult decision for parents to make. In the end, many parents choose to use child care. Some do not. The most important factor seems to be quality of care, no matter who provides it. Most studies show no major differences between children who receive child care and those who do not. Either option is viable, as long as a child receives the care he or she needs at all times.

Parents who choose child care should carefully weigh their options before choosing a caregiver. Once they have all the facts, they can make a wise and informed decision about which type of child care and which child care provider is best for their children.

Types of Child Care

Choosing child care requires careful consideration. Children are affected by everything and everyone around them. Their physical and emotional health is influenced by the care and attention they receive.

Many types of child care exist. Several of them will be described in this chapter. Parents should keep in mind that no one type is all good or bad. Within each type, there is also a great deal of variation. Each type should be evaluated by how well it meets the family's needs.

Child Care in the Child's Home

Many consider the most desirable type of child care to be care given in the child's own home, 20-2. Having a caregiver come into the family's home may be the most convenient. The parents don't have to worry about transporting their children to and from child care. Parents can hire a caregiver whose availability matches their needs. Children can remain in their homes with familiar surroundings. They also benefit from constant one-to-one interaction with the caregiver.

The most common type of child care in the child's home is babysitting. Most parents hire someone to care for their children in their home occasionally. This type of care might be needed for special events, or just for parents to have some adult time to themselves. It generally lasts a few hours at most. Parents often have one or more persons they can call for this type of child care.

Many parents have more regular child care needs. They may need someone to watch their children on a daily

20-2

Having a caregiver come to the family's home is convenient for parents and comfortable for the children.

basis while they are working. In this situation, the ideal caregiver is an intelligent, experienced person whose values are much like those of the parents. He or she is a warm and loving person who enjoys children. This person is capable of making decisions and enforcing parental rules. Children can develop a very close attachment to their in-home caregivers.

Daily child care in the family's home can be fairly expensive. This is especially true for families with just one or two children. For families with several children, this type of care may be more economical.

The wages for the caregiver depend to a great extent on training and experience and the services expected. Other costs may not be so obvious but must be considered. For example, costs are higher if the caregiver needs a car to transport children

1—**Enrich:** Research child care facilities available in your area. Note the type of care provided, ages of children accepted, rates, and facilities. Compile a file to keep in the classroom or in the school library.

2—**Resource:** *Home-Based Child Care*, Activity A, SAG.

3—**Discuss:** Child care provided in the child's home has advantages and disadvantages. Discuss these.

1—Enrich: Role-play parents interviewing a potential caregiver. Evaluate the types of questions asked and the answers provided.

2—Discuss: Describe what parents can do to help their children adjust to a caregiver.

3—Discuss: List the advantages and disadvantages to child care in the caregiver's home.

to school and to their activities, lives with the family, or even eats one or two meals with the children each day. Employers must also pay FICA taxes, adhere to federal and state tax laws, and possibly carry liability insurance. Because caregivers get some leave time, other child care arrangements must be added to the costs.

Some families have even greater child care needs. They may need someone to be available to provide care 24 hours a day. This type of round-the-clock care may be needed if a parent's job requires travel, unpredictable scheduling, or long hours. It might also be very convenient in a dual-career family. For these families, live-in help may be an option. It is very expensive, but it may be a good option for couples who need and can afford this type of care.

A **nanny** is a specially trained child-care provider who may or may not live in the family's home. Nannies provide child care and do housework for the family. The family pays the nanny a salary and provides him or her with room and board. Nannies are on-call 24 hours a day, but have scheduled days off and vacations.

An **au pair** is a young person who comes from another country to live with a family. The family provides room and board, as well as transportation. Au pairs provide child care and do housework for the family. Like nannies, they are on-call 24 hours a day but have scheduled days off. An au pair may not have as much education and training as a nanny. He or she also may not be fluent in the family's language. If parents plan to employ someone who is not a U.S. citizen, they should be sure the person has the correct paperwork needed to work in this country.

Hiring a person (other than a relative) to work in a family's home requires caution. Parents should request and check references carefully. They should ask about the person's methods of discipline and theories about caring for children. Parents should also see if the person interacts well with their child or children.

When a caregiver is hired, everyone will need a period of adjustment. It takes time for the caregiver and the family to become familiar with one another. Soon, however, everyone should feel comfortable. The caregiver should not feel anxious or frustrated. The child should not complain endlessly. The parents should not have uneasy feelings about the situation. If any of these bad feelings exist, the parents should find a new caregiver. They should observe the situation and trust their instincts. While changing caregivers too often may upset a child's sense of security, parents should *never* leave their children in an unacceptable child care situation.

The government does not license or regulate the care children receive in their own homes. Therefore, parents should carefully investigate any person they intend to hire. Parents are responsible for seeing all their children's needs are met no matter which arrangement they choose.

Child Care in the Caregiver's Home

Another common type of child care is care provided in the home of the caregiver. This type of care is often available in the child's own neighborhood. Another advantage is that the number of children is limited in size as compared to a child care center. This may be the best option for a shy child. He or she can learn to interact with a few children in a familiar home setting. This type of care may also be good for children who need individual attention.

Caregivers who provide child care in their homes are often parents themselves. While they stay at home with their own children, they also care for other children. The best caregivers in these situations are those who are comfortable with children and truly enjoy them. They follow a daily schedule but can be flexible when necessary. They maintain discipline and guide in a gentle but firm manner. They are loving, patient, and calm in emergencies. These ideal caregivers have been educated in child development, and they have experience working with children.

When parents consider placing their child in a caregiver's home, they should visit the home a few times, preferably on short notice. See 20-3. Such visits allow them to see the interactions between the caregiver and the children. They can see how the caregiver solves problems that arise. Parents can learn a lot by watching the other children. They should think of these children as potential future playmates of their child. They can note whether the children seem comfortable and content. Parents can also bring their children to the caregiver's home and watch how their children interact with the other children.

Before making a final decision, parents should ask the caregiver about his or her theories on caring for children. They should ask about the caregiver's rules and how they are enforced. Parents should also ask for references and check them thoroughly.

Child care in the caregiver's home is often less expensive than care in a center. These caregivers keep costs down by using their own homes and by seldom hiring others to help with children. Activities are more homelike for the most part; these caregivers do not purchase as much special equipment and supplies as centers do, which also lessens their costs. Families considering this child care option need to realize they will have to pay for another child care arrangement for days the caregiver is not able to provide services. Furthermore, families often pay the entire cost for this option. Only a few of these caregivers are associated with businesses, charities, or government agencies that pick up some or all of the child care costs.

In most states, child care homes are registered but not licensed. Certain restrictions exist, such as limits on the number of children allowed in each home. However, child care homes are not inspected on a routine basis. Ultimately, parents must judge for themselves the care their children receive. If they are not satisfied, they should look for another home. If serious problems occur in the child care situation, parents should register their complaints with appropriate authorities to protect other children.

Government-Sponsored Child Care

Head Start, Home Start, and entitlement programs are child care programs sponsored by the government. These programs are available to parents in financial need. They offer child care, education, meals, health care, and social services. The services are paid for by a combination of government and local monies. (For example, 80 percent of Head Start funds come from the federal government and 20 percent is from local monies and services.)

1—**Resource:** *Child Care Centers*, Activity B, SAG.

20-3
Parents can learn a lot about a child care situation by dropping in unannounced. This way they can see what the situation is really like.

1—Enrich: Interview different businesses in your community about whether they offer child-care benefits to their employees. Describe the programs that are offered.

These programs must comply with the guidelines set up by the funding agency and with the state's licensing agency.

Children in these programs usually receive good care. These programs have a strong educational component. They also offer lots of time for exploration and play.

Church-Linked Child Care

Some parents rely on church programs for child care. Generally, church-linked child care programs operate on a part-time basis. Most of these programs have high standards and are run by well-qualified staff members. These programs may or may not offer religious teaching as part of their child-care services. Some programs link a church member who can provide care with a family in his or her church who needs it. These types of programs may be more like babysitting in nature, 20-4. Fees may be charged, but these are usually low.

Church-linked child care seeks to provide a service to families rather than to make a profit. Fees may also be kept low because parents or members of the church may volunteer services or donate goods. Parents who need full-time child care may find two or more part-time arrangements rather expensive.

20-4

This woman provides child care for children who go to her church. The family knows her and she shares their religious beliefs.

Employer-Sponsored Child Care

Business managers know many of their employees are parents. They understand that these employees are concerned about their children's welfare. As a result, businesses are becoming more involved in child care.

Some businesses provide on-site child care for their employees' children. This allows parents to be close at hand if their children need them. It also allows parents and children to spend time together while traveling to and from the job site and perhaps during the lunch hour.

Not all employers can offer on-site child care. Some offer a "voucher system" instead. In this system, a parent is given coupons or vouchers which can be redeemed at whatever child care facility the parent chooses. This means the employer is paying for a portion of the child care costs.

Other employers offer a "cafeteria style" package of benefits. Employees may choose any of several different kinds of benefits. Parents may choose company-paid child care. Adults without children may choose dental insurance. Older employees may prefer a pension plan. The options vary from one employer to another.

Regardless of the form of employer-sponsored child care, fees charged to parents are rather low. On-site child care is not operated to make a profit, and if vouchers are used, businesses pay part of the costs for the parents. Families using the "cafeteria style" package for these benefits need to realize that child care costs are reduced but often at the expense of other needed benefits, such as pension plans.

University-Linked Child Care

Many colleges and universities operate child care programs. They offer care for the children of faculty, students, and the general public. They also offer educational opportunities for university students studying child development. Since the caregivers are university students and teachers, the children receive excellent care and guidance. The children are exposed to all kinds of educational equipment and techniques. These programs often have long waiting lists because they are quite popular among parents. See 20-5.

Much like employer-sponsored child care, university-linked child care is not operated as a money making business but as a service for families of students and faculty and staff members. Fees are kept low by using campus housing and by receiving funds from various sources. Therefore, families do not pay the full costs of child care. Child development programs operated for research and training purposes can be more expensive than university-linked child care. However, scholarships may be awarded to some families to cover part or all of the fees.

Cooperative Child Care

Cooperative child care centers have been started by groups of parents who want low-cost, high-quality child care. With **cooperative child care**, parents provide many of the services needed to operate their child care center. For instance, parents may provide building maintenance at "work parties" or on an assigned basis. Parents may also handle the business operations of the center.

Fees are low. Cooperative child care programs are not operated as a money making business. Parents pay for some of the costs through their services.

In cooperative child care centers, parents usually hire one preschool teacher. The parents also take turns participating in the center itself. Parents usually work at the center one day a week for each child they have in the center. Parents with special skills or talents share them with the children. This allows parents to be a part of their children's child care experience. It also helps them become acquainted with other parents in the community.

1—Enrich: Is there a university, community college, or other training facility in your area that offers child care services? Describe what these programs may offer parents and their children. What they offer students studying child development?

20-5
University-linked child care programs offer educational opportunities for the children who attend, as well as for the university students who work there.

20-6

This mother takes her children's play group for an afternoon swim. It's a fun time for the children, and the other mothers get to take a break.

Play Groups

Parents of small children may organize **play groups** to provide social activities for their children, 20-6. These play groups give parents the chance to exchange child-care services. They also allow parents to interact and learn from one another.

Play groups must be small in size, not only because of space, but for manageability. Most groups use a system of tokens or time-exchange records to make sure the exchange of babysitting services is fair. The success of play groups depends on the cooperation of parents.

Privately Owned Child Care Centers

Privately owned child care centers are as different as the people who own them. Some are simply "play schools" where caregivers are little more than babysitters. Other centers have excellent educational programs run by well-qualified staff members. Good centers have plenty of safe play equipment and a variety of supervised activities.

Privately owned child care centers are operated as businesses. Their fees are higher so they can cover expenses and make a profit. Costs vary with the quantity and quality of services offered. For example, privately owned programs that provide an educational program are often more expensive than those that primarily care for children. In addition to education, some very expensive centers provide special programs, such as music, gymnastics, dance, and foreign languages for children. As a general rule, privately owned centers charge more for infants and toddlers, part-time children, and children with disabilities. Overtime can also be very expensive in centers. Because these centers do not have other sources of funding, parents pay the full costs of care. Parents must keep these factors in mind as they compare centers and make a decision.

Nationally Franchised Child Care Centers

Child care centers that belong to a national chain often offer uniformity in child care. See 20-7. The equipment and overall programming are much the same from center to center. There are, of course, some differences from one center to the next. These centers usually have lots of good, safe equipment. They offer well-developed programs that are designed and supervised by trained personnel. Meals and snacks are usually available. Extended hours allow flexibility in parents' schedules.

Nationally franchised child care centers are money-making businesses. The fees are in the medium price range for dependable child care. These franchised centers keep costs a little lower than many privately owned centers because they buy in quantity and have a *centralized administration* (staff members who perform services for the entire franchise). Parents, however, must pay the entire cost of child care.

Drop-In Child Care Centers

Many stores and shopping malls have drop-in child care centers that provide occasional part-time care for preschoolers. This type of care may also be available in community centers, churches, or schools. Drop-in centers are often the first step toward entering children in a continuing child care program.

Many child care options do not offer drop-in care, but a few centers, such as those in shopping areas, are designed for drop-in care. The costs of drop-in care depends on sponsorship. Centers designed to offer a service to families charge less than centers planned as a business. Because part-time care is calculated by the hour, it is generally more expensive than full-time care.

School-Age Child Care

During weekdays, school-age children attend school. They need adult supervision both before and after school, however. Schools usually dismiss their students before their parents leave work. For this reason, many working parents seek school-age child care programs for their children. These programs may be offered before school, after school, or both. They are designed especially for school-age children.

Some schools are helping families cope with the after-school time gap. They provide extended day programs so children can stay at school until their parents can take them home. In these programs, a few teachers or child care workers provide activities for the children until their parents come. Children can make new friends, do homework, and learn new things at such a program.

School-age child care programs may also be offered in schools, homes, churches, or community centers. These programs provide the opportunity for rest and recreation children need after school. They may also offer classes, group activities, or tutoring. Many child care centers for younger children also expand their afternoon programs to include school-age children.

Different types of school-age programs may be offered from one community to another. Parents can ask their child's teacher or other parents to

20-7

Nationally franchised child care centers usually offer well-developed programs, lots of safe play equipment, and trained personnel.

recommend a program in their area. They should also see that anyone providing care in such a program is qualified to do so.

As you have read, parents pay almost as much for part-time care of a school-age child as they do for a younger child's full-time care. The costs of school-age child care depend to a great extent on sponsorship. For example, often privately owned centers charge more than school-based programs. Although the cost per hour is rather expensive, certainly safety for the child and work productivity for the parent are seen by many families as worth the cost.

Selecting Child Care

Parents who are thinking about child care may want to contact local child-related organizations for information. They may also contact city and state licensing agencies, elementary school teachers, friends, neighbors, and coworkers. They need accurate information about the types of child care available in order to make wise decisions.

If parents choose child care for their children, they should put some time and effort into their selections. People shop long and hard for clothes, furniture, houses, and cars. Parents should put even more effort into choosing care for their children. Children's development is greatly influenced by their environment and caregivers.

Some parents consider their own needs to be the main factors in choosing child care. They will accept any center that is in a convenient location and has low fees. Fortunately, most parents consider their children's needs as well as their own. Several factors worth considering are listed in 20-8.

When selecting child care, parents should have realistic expectations. They should expect good care for their children. They should not expect caregivers to fulfill their roles as parents, however. If children are upset by something that happened at home, parents should not expect caregivers to comfort the children. They should calm and comfort the children before leaving them with other caregivers. Also, parents should not take a sick child to a child care facility. This could endanger the well-being of the sick child and the other children.

As parents study their options for child care, they need to consider many factors. Five major factors are the physical setting, program, adult-child ratio, characteristics of the caregivers, and consistency.

The Physical Setting

A desirable setting for child care is one with a welcoming, homelike atmosphere. The decor is colorful and interesting. The entry or lobby gives parents space to interact with their children as they come and go. Windows are at children's eye level. Movable walls can provide either open spaces or secluded areas. Lighting is incandescent rather than fluorescent. Eating areas are small so small groups of children may be served in a homelike atmosphere. Small tables and chairs help children feel comfortable and bring adults down to the children's level.

The Program

No single type of program can meet the needs of all children. Parents must look for the type of program that is best suited for their children. In play groups, simple babysitting is all that is expected or needed. In preschools, programs are carefully designed to offer many learning experiences, 20-9. In any case, the program should be completely supportive of parents and families as well as helpful to children.

Checklist for Choosing Child Care

- Does the care facility meet state, county, and city licensing requirements? Is it checked regularly by authorities to see that certain standards are maintained?

- Does the care facility have a good reputation?

- Is the care facility in a convenient location?

- What is the cost for each child?

- Are alternative schedules available to meet various needs for hours per day and days per week?

- Does the setting have a warm, homelike atmosphere?

- Are the rooms and play areas designed and decorated with children in mind?

- Is the care facility equipped with a variety of safe play equipment and arranged with safety in mind?

- What precautions are taken to prevent children from wandering away and to prevent strangers from entering the premises?

- Are the restrooms clean, easy for children to use, and in good repair?

- Do the children have a comfortable and quiet place for naps?

- Is there an isolated place for an ill child?

- Is good emergency care available for the children if the need arises?

- Is the food nutritious, well prepared, and suited to the age of the children?

- Are the children grouped according to age? Are suitable activities planned for each age group?

- Are children allowed to choose some of their own activities? Are they allowed time for quiet, individual play as well as active, group play?

- Is each child respected as an individual?

- Are the needs of the parents recognized by the caregivers?

- What is the adult-child ratio?

- Are all areas of the care facility supervised at all times?

- If a child needs individual attention at times, would this be available?

- Are the caregivers well trained and experienced?

- Are interactions between caregivers and children pleasant?

- Do the caregivers encourage the physical, intellectual, emotional, and social development of the children?

- Do the caregivers attend promptly to children's needs?

- Are the caregivers calm, gentle, and fair to the children? Do they have a good sense of humor?

- Do the caregivers discipline the children without the use of harsh punishment?

- Do the children seem happy?

1

20-8 _____
Parents should consider these factors before selecting child care for their children.

1—Enrich: Take a field trip to several child care centers. Evaluate them using this checklist.

The Adult-Child Ratio

Children need personalized care. An adult can provide adequate care for only a small number of children. Generally, one caregiver is needed for every two or three infants. For toddlers, the ratio is one caregiver for every four toddlers. One caregiver can provide care for eight preschoolers.

Parents want to be sure their children will receive enough attention and assistance from the caregiver.

Characteristics of the Caregivers

Well-trained and experienced caregivers are keys to good child care. Parents should evaluate the characteristics

1—Note: At any one time, an adult can provide care for more older children than younger children. Why is this? Does this explain why infant care costs more?

2—Discuss: Why are the characteristics of the caregiver an important element in finding the best child care for a child?

20-9 ———————————
Playing at a sand table is one of the many educational activities children at a preschool might have.

of prospective caregivers. One way to do this is to visit the child care site, preferably unannounced. Just before lunch is a good time to visit. This is a time when children tend to be the most restless. If the children seem to be fairly content at this time, they probably are happy most of the time. Parents should pay attention to the noise level, too. A pleasant hum of activity is a good sign. Loud noises and reckless running may be warning signals.

Another way for parents to pick up clues is to notice how caregivers interact with the children. Good caregivers have many positive characteristics. A good caregiver does most of the following:

● Transmits positive feelings about himself or herself and the job.

● Spends most of his or her time interacting with or observing the children.

● Knows the various stages of child development and helps children realize their potential.

● Attends promptly to children's physical, emotional, and social needs.

● Exhibits a calm and gentle demeanor.

● Demonstrates flexibility and a sense of humor.

● Encourages healthy curiosity.

● Uses fairness to settle disputes.

● Tells children what they can do and set limits on what they cannot do in a positive manner.

● Believes in discipline but not in harsh punishment.

Consistency

Consistency is one of the most important qualities in child care. Most children do not adjust well to being moved from caregiver to caregiver. This is why it is so important for parents to consider all the pros and cons when first selecting care. This increases the chance they will pick the best situation the first time.

Consistency within a child care situation is also important. Children need to know they can depend upon their child care routine. They should be able to expect a similar schedule from day to day. The rules should remain the same and be consistently enforced. This gives children a sense of security. Parents can watch for consistency by visiting the child care setting on more than one occasion. They can also ask what the daily schedule is and what rules are enforced.

Evaluating Child Care

Selecting the right child care situation for children can be tough. A parent's responsibility does not end there. Parents must also continually evaluate the care their children receive. They must monitor how well their choice is working for the entire family, especially their children. As they evaluate their decisions, parents may rely heavily on their instincts.

Parents can tell a great deal about the care their children receive by watching the children's reactions. If children complain daily about going to child care and they seem tense and unhappy when they return, parents should find out why. If parents have uneasy feelings, they should trust their instincts and take action. On the other hand, if parents have positive feelings, they should be pleased with the care their children receive. Instinct and common sense can tell parents a lot about the well-being of their children. See 20-10.

Concerns of Parents

Parents using child care may have a number of concerns. To reassure themselves, they can reevaluate their choice. This may not settle all their worries, however. Other, intangible concerns may upset parents. One fearful thought for a parent is "What will happen to my relationship with my child?"

Children in child care must adjust to their caregivers and being separated from their parents. In most cases, children also have to adjust to new environments and other children. In time, they grow used to their new situations. They may even develop friendships with their peers and a special attachment to their caregivers. These feelings may affect the parent-child relationship, but they should not jeopardize it.

From the first day of care, parents learn to share their children with their new caregivers. Mothers and fathers have to accept they are no longer the only special people in their children's lives. This may be an unsettling realization.

In many cases, caregivers spend more time with children and comfort them more often than the parents. In these cases, children may become more closely attached to their caregivers

1—Discuss: If parents notice their children complain or are upset and tense about going to a child care situation, what should they do?

2—Activity: Pretend you are a parent. List concerns you might have regarding child care for your children.

20-10
Parents can tell by children's faces whether they are enjoying themselves in their child care situations.

1—Discuss: Parents may feel jealous if their children seek caregivers instead of them. How can parents feel reassured when this happens?

2—Discuss: What are effective ways of dealing with separation anxiety?

3—Discuss: If the caregiver's ideas differ from those of the parents, what should the parents do?

4—Enrich: Ask a professional from a local emergency room to describe the procedures and forms needed to treat a child whose parents are not present.

than to their parents. In fact, sometimes injured children who need help call out for their caregivers rather than their parents.

Parents may feel pangs of jealousy regarding their children's relationships with their caregivers. These feelings are normal, and parents can learn to handle them. Instead of feeling jealous, parents can feel reassured their children are receiving good emotional support. They should be happy the child is so happy and well-cared for in the child care arrangement. This is one of the prices parents pay when they use child care, 20-11.

Parents also have to struggle with feelings of guilt. Regardless of why they use child care, they will feel guilty at times. There will be days when their children cling to them and beg them not

20-11 _____
This mother may feel jealous when her daughter doesn't want to leave the caregiver's arms. She should take this as a sign her daughter is receiving good care.

to leave. These times are just as difficult for parents as they are for children.

Parents may be able to make parting easier by reassuring their children they will return. Young children quickly figure out they cannot return home unless their parents come and get them. They may worry "Will Mommy and Daddy come and get me, or will they forget me?" Parents should try to be on time so their children do not have to wait for them. Watching other children and parents greet each other increases children's feelings of anxiety.

Another concern parents may have is about the quality of care their children receive. Parents may ask "Are other people really caring for our children the way we would?" Caregivers' ideas may differ from those of parents on simple things, such as asking children to eat everything on their plates. If parents have special concerns, they should talk with the caregivers to ease their minds.

Parents may also be concerned if their children act very differently in the child care environment from the way they do at home. Children may react differently in different situations, just as adults do. Children often behave quite differently from the way they do in the presence of their parents when their parents are out of sight. Parents are often surprised to learn their children are capable of leading separate and distinct lives.

Another concern parents may have regards possible illnesses or medical emergencies. Parents may worry what would happen if their children needed immediate medical care. First, parents should check whether their caregivers are certified in first aid and CPR procedures. Second, parents and caregivers should agree on a plan of action in the event of an emergency. Third, parents should fill out a medical consent form, 20-12. A medical consent form is a form that gives the caregiver permission to make decisions regarding the child's medical care in the event of an emergency.

Many hospitals, private hospitals in particular, will not administer care without the consent of a parent or legal guardian. Exceptions are made only for life-threatening emergencies. The threat of malpractice suits makes hospitals cautious. A hospital may spend hours searching for parents before treating a child whose life is not in danger. Parents can prevent problems and ensure their children will receive prompt medical care by signing medical consent forms. Each person who provides care for a child should have one of these forms.

Managing the Child Care Experience

Using child care can be stressful or fulfilling for parents. Parents can lessen stress and make child care easier by learning how to manage the child care experience. These tips may help:

- If the child care program has written policies for parents, as many centers do, read these carefully and follow them. If the program does not have written policies, discuss procedures with the director or caregiver.

- Complete all forms before leaving your child even for the first day. Review these forms regularly and make changes as needed.

- Keep a list of needed supplies and pack these, if possible, by the evening before they are needed.

- Label all supplies and toys with your child's name.

- Carry a suitable bag for staff to place things to go home each day. In some centers, this bag is placed in the child's cubbie and is filled throughout the day. A folder for

1—Activity: Ask a child care program for samples of forms that must be filled out. Go over the forms in class.

1

STATE OF TEXAS

COUNTY OF

The undersigned parent of _____

does hereby empower _____

to authorize any doctor, hospital, or other medical facility to give medical

care to the said minor as may be necessary.

Dated _____, _____.

_____
Parent's signature

20-12
A medical consent form looks like this. Parents need to fill one out for each of their children's caregivers.

1—Discuss: Why is it so important to keep communication open between parents and caregivers? Can you give additional suggestions for communicating with caregivers?

carrying older children's work and written communication between the home and the program is also a good idea.

- If sending money for special events or projects, put the exact amount and a note about what it is for in a sealed envelope with the child's name on the front.

- Before arrival each day, write any needed messages for the caregivers. Caregivers need to know any family situation that may affect the child's health or behavior. A professional will keep information confidential.

- Keep a log on medications given, accident/illness reports, behavioral problems, and periodic developmental progress reports.

- When parents want a conference, they should set up a specific time. Generally speaking, conferences should not be held in front of children or other adults. Share concerns before they become major problems.

- Read all individual and group messages daily. (Individual messages are often put with the child's supplies, but group messages may be posted at the center or put on a Web site.)

- Attend parent meetings.

The most important aspect of managing child care is to keep the lines of communication open between the family and the caregiver. Parents must also watch for signs of stress in their child and act quickly if something seems wrong.

Summary

1

- Child care is becoming more common as more parents enter the workforce.

- Parents may choose child care for a variety of reasons. Other parents may decide against using child care. Either option is viable as long as the child receives the care he or she needs at all times.

- Choosing child care requires careful consideration. Children's physical and emotional health is influenced by the care and attention they receive.

- Since there are many types of child care, parents should consider how well each type would meet the family's needs before making their decision. Each type has advantages and disadvantages.

- As parents study their options for child care, they need to consider many factors. Each factor may be more important to some parents than others.

- Parents using child care may have a number of concerns. These may include feelings about the child's relationships with others, worries over the child's actions in the child care environment, and concerns over the possibility emergency medical care will be needed while the child is with the caregiver.

Reviewing Key Points

2

1. According to many experts, what is the ideal child care situation for a young child?

2. List three sources of information about child care.

3. What is the difference between a *nanny* and an *au pair*?

4. List two reasons child care in a caregiver's home might be desirable.

5. True or false. The government licenses all types of child care services.

6. Describe three ways employers can help parents acquire child care.

7. Identify two advantages of cooperative child care programs.

8. List five characteristics of nationally franchised child care centers.

9. Why is school-age child care needed?

10. Name the five major factors parents need to consider when selecting child care.

11. Suggested adult-child ratios in child care settings are one caregiver for every _____ or _____ infants, one caregiver for every _____ toddlers, and one caregiver for every _____ preschoolers.

12. List 10 characteristics of good caregivers.

13. Once parents have selected a child care program, what is their continuing responsibility?

14. Why might a parent who uses child care have feelings of jealousy toward his or her child's caregiver?

15. Explain why each person who provides care for a child should have a medical consent form signed by a parent.

1—**Activity:** Review and outline this chapter emphasizing the infomation you found most useful.

2—**Answers:** Aswers to review questions are located in the front section of this TAE.

Learning by Doing

1. Role-play an engaged couple discussing whether they will use child care after they are married and have children. Why can this be a sensitive topic in a relationship?

2. Research nanny and au pair programs in your area. Create a list of advantages and disadvantages for each.

3. Research child-care programs that are available in your community for school-age children. Give a brief description of each. Explain the services provided, hours available, location, transportation, and cost.

4. Design a bulletin board to show the various types of child care options available in your community. Post addresses, photos of the facilities, descriptions of the programs, and fees.

5. Interview parents who use child care. Ask them about what concerns they have for their children and themselves. Ask them how they deal with these concerns. Report the results of your interviews to your class.

Thinking Critically

1. Write a paper explaining whether you would choose child care for your child if you were a parent. Why or why not?

2. Debate this statement: For the first three years, the ideal child care situation for a child is in the home with one parent as a primary caregiver.

3. Pretend you are married. You and your spouse have children, and both of you work. Staying home with your children is not an option. Which kind of child care would you choose? Why?

4. Working in a small group, identify advantages and disadvantages of each type of child care.

5. Can a well-qualified, caring, and understanding person give children the same quality of care as the parents? Write a paragraph supporting your opinion.

Child care centers offer some structured activities such as games. They also provide time for free play and outdoor play.

Chapter 21
Children's
Education and
Health

Objectives

After studying this chapter, you will be able to

- describe parents' roles in their children's education, both at home and at school.
- propose ways parents can increase their children's desire to learn.
- identify the special needs of children with learning disabilities, mental disabilities, physical disabilities, emotional disorders, and giftedness.
- summarize the benefits of inclusion for children with special needs and average learners.
- describe parents' roles in their children's health care.
- list common symptoms of childhood illness.
- explain how to care for a sick child.

Key Terms

children with special needs
mental disability
mental retardation
1 Individualized Educational Plan (IEP)
physical disability
learning disability
attention deficit/hyperactivity
    disorder (ADHD)
hyperactive
emotional disorder
gifted
inclusion

The task of parenting extends beyond the home. Parents must also be involved in their child's education. School and home are separate, but both 2 influence a child's development. They also affect one another greatly. For this reason, parents and schools should work together for the best interest of children's well-being and learning.

The school is affected by children's family lives. Children's readiness for school begins at home, 21-1. Also, family life influences children's ability to succeed in schoolwork. School, in 3 turn, affects family life. A child's school experience affects his or her personality. For instance, success in school can build a child's self-esteem. A child also learns to interact with others at school. These lessons, in addition to academic learning, influence a child and his or her family.

21-1 ⸺⸺⸺⸺⸺⸺⸺⸺⸺⸺⸺⸺⸺⸺
This mother helps prepare her daughter for school by reading to her daily. Parents can promote school readiness at home.

1—**Vocabulary:** Look up terms in the glossary and discuss their meanings.

2—**Reflect:** Why is it important for parents and schools to work together to provide what is best for children?

3—**Resource:** *Education Survey,* reproducible master 21-1, TR.

Parents of children with special needs may have additional concerns about their child's well-being and education. They must work even more closely with their child's school to ensure their child's educational needs are being met. This chapter describes the parenting issues they face.

In addition to education, parents must take an active role in their children's health care. Parents should know signs of illness in children. They should be alert to these symptoms and call their children's doctor if these symptoms occur.

Parents' Roles in Their Children's Education

School-age children must relate to two sets of adults—parents and teachers. A parent-child relationship and a teacher-child relationship are alike in some ways. In other ways, they are quite different.

The parent-child relationship is based on heredity. The teacher-child relationship is based on authority granted by the state. In the close environment of the home, parents soon become familiar with the individual characteristics of each of their children. Teachers deal with many children at once, so they do not become as familiar with children individually. However, teachers see children in group settings. They may learn more than parents about children's social characteristics.

During the early school-age years, children usually have closer relationships with their parents than with their teachers. Good teachers try to provide a wholesome, warm classroom atmosphere.

As a result, the bond between a particular teacher and child may be very strong. In some cases, a child may feel closer to a particular teacher than to his or her parents.

Both parents and teachers need to keep a sense of humor when working with children. When adults are too anxious or serious, it can take the fun out of learning. Parents and teachers should treat each child as an individual. Each child needs the best possible environment in which to grow and develop.

Parents' Involvement at Home

Children are greatly influenced by their parents' attitudes about education. Parents' views on competition, success, responsibility, and discipline also matter. Children model their views after those of their parents.

When they build their children's interest in learning, parents give children a priceless treasure. Parents need to encourage and support their children without pushing them. They can help children learn to think critically. Parents can explain how children can apply the lessons they learn in school to real-life situations.

Parents don't need to buy every educational toy on the market to help children learn. Actually, the way parents interact with their children matters much more than how many toys they buy. Parents need only to make use of what is available to them. They can use household objects to teach their children about size, sequence, numbers, and colors. For example, empty boxes, an assortment of buttons, and kitchen items can serve as teaching tools. Games involving beads, puzzles, words, numbers, and maps can indirectly help a child with schoolwork. See 21-2.

21-2

Stacking these blocks on these rings improves small motor skills. It also teaches this little boy about colors, shapes, and amounts.

Teachable Moments

Parents have a unique role in the informal education of their children. They can seize teachable moments and expand children's natural curiosity. Children can learn without formal programs and rigid standards for achievement. Parents can take the lead from their children. If children seem to enjoy an activity, it can be continued or repeated. If they seem bored, parents can move on to something else. Parents who maximize teachable moments encourage their children to become eager learners. These children think learning is fun.

Parents who fail to appreciate children's curiosity let teachable moments slip by. If they say "don't bother me" too often, children will stop being curious. They will not see the fun in learning and they will stop trying.

Other parents try to be alert to what interests their children. Children can even learn from events in their own neighborhoods. When a house is being built down the street, for instance, children can learn about phases of construction. Visits to museums, parks, and beaches can also be valuable learning experiences. Parents can even use time spent traveling in the car to play fun verbal games or sing songs. Vacations that include visits to national parks or landmarks broaden children's knowledge. In looking back on childhood, many adults have fond memories of family times that were both fun and educational.

In choosing these activities, parents should be careful. They need to consider their child's age and readiness for each activity. A day-long tour of historical buildings might fascinate a school-age child, but it would overwhelm a preschooler. Parents need to consider their children's levels of development. They should offer plenty of learning opportunities without pushing.

Encouragement

Children learn in many different ways. Their favorite way to learn is by doing. Children often ask if they can help. Some parents may not allow a child to help with tasks they can do better and faster themselves. The message this sends is the child is not able or skilled enough to do things for himself or herself. Other parents step in and take over a task if their children are struggling with it. This also discourages children, because it deprives them of a chance to learn.

Parents need to encourage their children to help whenever they can. When children are able to help, they gain self-esteem. Children feel important when they contribute to the family. They also feel pride in their accomplishments, even small ones. In addition, children learn not only about the task itself, but about sharing and cooperating.

1—Resource: *Using Teachable Moments,* Activity A, SAG.

2—Discuss: How can taking advantage of teachable moments help children realize learning is fun?

3—Reflect: Describe some teachable moments you remember as you were growing up. Where did they occur, and why do you remember them?

4—Discuss: In what ways can parents allow children to be "helpers"?

Adjustments to School

Starting school is a big adjustment for children. This is when most children begin leaving home without their parents for the first time. Each child adjusts differently. Some seem adventurous and eager to try a new activity. Others are fearful or uncertain. Still other children are shy and withdrawn.

Parents can do much to ease their child's transition into school. They can talk with the child about his or her feelings. Parents can tell a child what to expect. They can also help the child find ways to settle into the new routine. Offering emotional support and listening are other good ways for parents to help.

Other factors in the adjustment to school are the parents' attitudes toward education and the child's past learning experiences. Children tend to mimic the attitudes of their parents. If parents express a positive attitude toward education, their children will have a head start in school. Success in one area tends to lead to success in other areas. If children have had successful experiences at home, they will be eager for more, 21-3. They will look forward to learning in school.

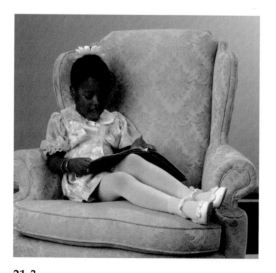

21-3 _____

At home, this young girl has experienced the joy of reading. She is also more likely to enjoy reading at school.

Before children start school, parents may take them to visit the school to meet their future teachers and classmates. On the first day, some children may want their parents to go with them. Six-year-olds usually look forward to first grade, especially if their previous learning experiences have been positive. The relationship between home and school is important to children at this age. They take many things from home for the "show-and-tell" period at school. Their parents' responses to their school experiences mean a great deal to them. After-school or bedtime chats give six-year-olds the chance to talk about themselves and their experiences at school.

For many children age seven or older, home and school are two different worlds. Children are now used to leaving home and going to school each day. Older children still face adjustments at school, however. Every year the child will have a new teacher and new classmates. As children reach junior high school, this can be a large adjustment. Parents can help their child adjust to new and uncomfortable situations. This will help children maximize their learning potential.

Homework

Another role parents have is to provide a good environment for their children to study and do homework. Structure and routines at home can set the stage for good work habits in school. A family's lifestyle should provide time to eat, sleep, play, work, study, and relax. Children who come from homes with clear structure, shared responsibilities, and routines usually develop good study habits. They often do better in school than children from more permissive homes. In these homes, family members do whatever they want when they want to do it.

Homework is an issue every family must face. Children's attitudes toward homework are largely affected by their parents' attitudes. Parents should make it clear they expect their children to meet all school responsibilities including homework.

When children know they must do their homework, they learn to set priorities. They learn to manage their time. This way children can accomplish tasks and still have time to do what they want to do.

If parents find their children are not doing their homework, they should express their disappointment. This shows their concern for the children's failure to meet responsibilities. Parents should ask their children if they prefer being reminded of their homework or allowed to handle it themselves. Some children depend on parental controls, while others prefer the independence of being responsible for their own work.

Parents may use positive reinforcement when children practice good study habits and do well in school. Usually, rewards such as praise or increased privileges work better than money or material goods. Parents should praise children when they have done their schoolwork well. Each child in a family has different abilities, so their accomplishments will vary. Still, every child benefits from praise for work done to the best of his or her ability, 21-4.

Although children must do their own studying, parents may be able to make the work a little easier. Parents can make sure children have a suitable place to study. This does not mean every child needs a separate desk in a private room. It does mean each child needs a well-lit, quiet place to spread out books and papers.

Children need to know their parents are available for consultation. Parents should never do the children's work for them. Instead, children can talk with their parents about homework, especially special projects.

21-4
Children should receive recognition for their accomplishments.

Parents can suggest helpful resources such as a knowledgeable neighbor, current magazines, or pamphlets that are available through the mail. Parents can guide their children while helping them develop their own resources for problem solving.

Parents' Involvement with Schools

Parents should be involved with their children's education at school as well as at home. Schools need input from parents. School administrators, teachers, and parents can work together to ensure quality education for children.

School board members are elected officials. Parents are members of the community, so they vote for school board members. Their votes help decide who serves on the board and

1—Resource: *Education Crossword*, Activity D, SAG.

2—Resource: *Children with Special Needs*, Activity E, SAG.

3—Discuss: How should parents interact with a child who has special needs?

4—Discuss: What unique problems might be faced by parents who have both disabled and nondisabled children?

what policies they set. Parents can also sit on committees and join parent-teacher associations.

Parents should also interact with their children's teachers. Parent-teacher conferences are a good chance for parents to talk individually with teachers. Many schools schedule time for conferences during the school year. These are usually held during both day and evening hours. If a parent has a question or concern, however, he or she should not wait for a parent-teacher conference. He or she should contact the teacher by phone, e-mail, letter, or in person. Parents can make appointments to meet with their children's teachers to discuss these concerns.

Another way for parents to be involved is to volunteer in their child's classroom. Some parents offer to bring or serve refreshments for classroom parties. Other parents might chaperone a class field trip. Parents can also show interest in their children's school by attending athletic events, concerts, plays, and other school-sponsored events.

The goal of education is to stimulate and challenge children at each stage of their development. At home, parents can sense when children are interested in and challenged by their schoolwork. They can also sense when children are bored or frustrated. At school, teachers can see how well children pay attention in class and complete assignments. They can also see how children interact with one another. It is in the best interest of the children when parents and teachers work together, sharing concerns and suggestions. Both have much to contribute to children's education.

Children with Special Needs

Each child is an individual with unique needs. An *average child* displays typical growth and development for his or her age. Children have a disability if their development or abilities are far below average in one or more areas. Children are gifted if their development or abilities are far above average in one or more areas. Children with disabilities and gifted children are often called **children with special needs.** They may need more or different care and guidance than average children. Children who have disabilities or are gifted may need extra support, instruction, or guidance.

As much as possible, parents should treat a child with special needs just like other children. This is especially true in the areas of love and discipline. Children with special needs usually want to be treated like everyone else.

This can be a challenge in a family with both disabled and nondisabled children. Nondisabled children sometimes feel resentful when the family has to make special arrangements for the disabled child. Parents can help by explaining the nature of the disability. They should try to balance the disabled child's needs with those of other family members. Children of all abilities deserve to have their needs met. Counseling can help families adjust to having a child with special needs. Many families find having a child with special needs can be a blessing rather than a burden.

The following sections of this chapter describe groups of children with special needs. These include children with various types of disabilities, as well as gifted children.

Children with Mental Disabilities

1 A **mental disability** refers to limitations in the way a person's mind functions. A mentally disabled person's brain cannot work exactly like an average person's brain. People with mental disabilities have limited intellectual function, daily living skills, or both. Some mental disabilities may be caused by congenital disorders, such as Down syndrome, 21-5. Others may be caused by conditions during the mother's pregnancy, such as drug use or infection. Mental disabilities can also result from accidents or illnesses.

Mental disabilities range from mild to severe. Educators group children with mental disabilities by their IQ test scores and the levels at which they function. Children with mild mental disabilities function at higher levels and have higher IQ scores. Other children may be moderately or severely disabled as indicated by their IQ scores and level of functioning.

The term *mental retardation* does not refer to all mentally disabled people. Many people with mild mental disabilities do not have mental retardation. The American Association on Mental Retardation says **mental retardation** includes the following:

- intellectual functioning at a level that is significantly below average
- deficits in adaptive skills behavior (*Adaptive skills behavior* describes skills needed for self-care and independent living.)
- it occurs before the person is 18 years of age

2 Mental retardation can be measured in two ways. Educators can test a child's IQ and observe his or her adaptive skills behavior. Persons with moderate or severe mental disabilities often have some mental retardation.

Schools must work with families of children with disabilities to set a plan for their education. Federal law states

1—Vocabulary: Compare terms *mental disability* and *mental retardation.* What are the differences between these terms?

2—Discuss: What specific measures are used to determine if a person has mental retardation?

21-5 _____
Down syndrome is a common cause of mental and physical disabilities. Many people with Down syndrome have mild mental disabilities.

1—Vocabulary: What is an *Individualized Educational Plan (IEP)?* Who is involved with this process and what is the result?

2—Discuss: Point out that not all people with mental disabilities function on the same level. Some are more able than others to live independently.

3—Enrich: Have students research what is involved when parents provide care for a child with severe mental disabilities at home.

each child with disabilities must have an **Individualized Educational Plan (IEP)**. This is a written agreement that sets educational goals for a student with disabilities. Parents, teachers, school officials, and other professionals 1 meet to assess the childs abilities and needs. Working together, they create an IEP that meets those needs and focuses on the child's abilities. Once the plan is made, it must be followed. No changes can be made without another meeting to revise the IEP.

It may take more time to teach children with mental disabilities than children of average mental ability. It may also take more effort from both teacher and student. However, children with mild mental disabilities can learn both academic and daily living skills. Most of these children live at home with their parents and attend public schools. They may need some special education classes, but they also often attend classes with average learners. With adequate training and guidance, mildly mentally disabled children can learn to live independently in society as adults.

Children at the next level have moderate mental limitations. They can still learn some academic and daily living skills, however. Many children with moderate mental disabilities live at home with their parents. Community agencies that serve mentally disabled children and their families can help. These agencies offer support, guidance, and counseling for the child and family.

Other children with moderate mental disabilities live in assisted living centers. These centers provide care and supervised living for people with disabilities. The staff are trained to work with persons with mental disabilities.

Some children who are moderately mentally disabled attend public schools.

If so, they may attend mostly special education classes. Others may not function well enough to attend school.

As adults, persons with moderate mental disabilities often enter the workforce. They usually work in supervised settings, such as work- shops in centers for the developmen- 2 tally disabled. They may assemble products or do other supervised tasks. Persons with moderate disabili- ties can live full lives. However, they have more limitations than persons with mild mental disabilities. They are often also less able to live on their own.

Children with severe mental disabilities usually have very limited abilities. These limits occur both in intellectual functioning and daily living skills. Most people with severe mental disabilities have low IQ test scores and function at low levels. They may require almost complete care and supervision. They may not be able to feed, dress, or groom them- selves. Persons with severe mental disabilities may not be able to make decisions or keep themselves safe.

Parents of a child with severe mental disabilities may not be able to provide the care their child needs. Most children who are severely mentally disabled live in centers for disabled persons. If their child lives in such a center, parents can still be very involved in the child's life. They can visit the center regularly and make decisions about the child's care.

A few families do provide care for a child who is severely mentally ill. In these families, the child lives at home with the family. Family members will 3 provide almost constant care for the person throughout his or her life. In these families, parents can reach out to community resources for support and guidance.

Children with Physical Disabilities

A **physical disability** refers to a limitation of a person's body or its function. Some people with physical disabilities have limited mobility. They may use crutches, braces, artificial limbs, walkers, or wheelchairs to aid their movement. Other people have limited vision, hearing, or speech abilities. They may use glasses, braille, hearing aids, or sign language to gather information about the world around them, 21-6.

Physical disabilities can be present at birth. They can also occur after birth after an illness or accident. The causes of a physical disability may be hereditary or environmental.

Many types of physical disabilities exist. Each disability is unique in terms of the needs it creates. For instance,

people who use wheelchairs may have very different needs from people who cannot hear. Even when two people have the same disability, each may experience it differently. One factor may be the degree of severity of the disability. People with low vision may not experience their disabilities in the same way as people who are blind.

Parents should work closely with health care providers to ensure their children receive adequate medical care. They will want to research their child's disability and learn what treatments, if any, exist. This way, they know whether their children are getting the care they need.

Learning about their child's disabilities also prepares parents to give the child the proper care at home. Parents must know how to help their child reach his or her potential. For instance, if a child cannot speak or hear, parents may learn sign language and teach it to the child. This will help the child communicate with his or her family members, 21-7. If the child uses a hearing aid, parents should know how it is used.

Parents must share information about their child's disability with the child's other caregivers and teachers. This will allow others to provide proper care and assistance for the child. It will also help them understand the child's special needs.

Most children with physical disabilities attend school under an IEP. While some children with physical disabilities attend special schools, most attend public schools. A teacher may have to adapt some lessons to suit students' abilities. A student with limited movement may not be able to do a chemistry experiment in the same way as other students. The student's teacher can modify the experiment to make it possible for him or her to participate.

Schools also have to make adjustments for students with physical

21-6
People who are blind may use braille, a system of raised dots, to learn to read.

21-7 _____
Sign language can
help people with-
out hearing
communicate with
others.

disabilities. For example, the facilities must be accessible for students with disabilities, 21-8. This might include braille elevator panels and room number markers. The school might also need to install elevators and widen doorways for students using wheel-chairs, walkers, or braces. Schools can make books or worksheets printed in braille or recorded on audiotape avail-able for students who are blind. A school can find many ways to make learning more accessible for students with physical disabilities.

Children with Learning Disabilities

A **learning disability** is a limitation in the way a person's brain sorts and uses information. It is not the same as a mental disability, which is a limitation in overall brain function. A learning disability is a specific limitation in acquiring certain types of information. People with learning disabilities have varying abilities in other areas.

Some learning disabilities involve a person's reading skills. A person with *dyslexia* often sees letters or words in an order other than they actually appear. This person's brain does not sort the information (words on a page) in a way it can be used (words in the right order). As a result, the person has difficulty reading and grasping the meaning of what is read.

Other learning disabilities involve a person's math skills. A person might not be able to understand math concepts. This person's brain might not process numerical data in a way the person can use it. The person might not understand what it means when two numbers appear with an addition sign. Learners without this disability would easily see they are to add these numbers to get a larger number.

Still other learning disabilities affect the way the brain processes other types of information. There are many kinds of learning disabilities. They can occur singly or in any combi-nation. A learning disability may be hereditary, biological, or environmental.

21-8
By adapting their facilities, such as the playground, schools can become more welcoming for children with physical disabilities.

Parents usually sense when their children have difficulty in early learning experiences. If they suspect a learning disability, they should take action right away. A child's doctor or a learning specialist may be able to identify and treat a learning disability. Ideally, this should happen before the child goes to school.

Diagnosing a learning disability is the first step. After that, parents can find a learning specialist to work with their child. This is a person trained to help people with learning disabilities. Some learning disabilities can be treated. In other cases, children must learn to compensate for the disability. Each situation must be considered individually. See 21-9.

If teachers suspect a learning disability, they may suggest an academic evaluation as part of setting an IEP. This would give parents and school officials an idea of the child's learning abilities. This evaluation can also reveal how children view themselves and their behavior in the world around them. Children, parents, and schools can work together when each clearly understands the child's needs.

Some children with learning disabilities benefit from behavior modification training. Parents and teachers try to modify the child's observable behavior. They offer rewards and reinforcements to motivate the child's behavior.

Other times, perceptual motor programs can help children with learning disabilities. In these programs, the child's brain is trained to process information in a more usable way. In some cases, children with dyslexia can be trained to see words on a page as they really are.

Attention Deficit/Hyperactivity Disorder

Attention deficit/hyperactivity disorder (ADHD) is a learning disorder that causes children to have shorter-than-average attention spans. This means they are less able to focus on an activity for a long period of time. They are easily distracted by other people and activities. Children with

1—**Discuss:** If parents sense their children are having difficulty in early learning experiences, what might they do?

2—**Discuss:** Some learning disabilities have a physical source. What resources can be used to check for these causes and treat them?

3—**Discuss:** What is an academic evaluation? What would it reveal? How might an academic evaluation help in setting an IEP?

4—**Enrich:** Research ADHD. What is known about this disability, and why are the findings controversial?

21-9 _____
Parents should request an academic evaluation if they suspect their child might have a learning disability.

1—Vocabulary: What does *hyperactive* mean? Stress that hyperactivity refers to a pattern of behavior, not a single episode of overactivity.

ADHD may move from activity to activity quickly without finishing projects. ADHD can prevent children from performing well in school. It can also disrupt families' home lives.

ADHD often appears before age six. It affects children of all abilities. ADHD may be identified in infancy, but the symptoms may vary with a child's age.

Children with ADHD may be **hyperactive,** which means they are overly and uncontrollably active. A hyperactive child, for instance, might be unable to sit still and be calm. Instead, the child might fidget constantly. He or she might get up often and run around. This would happen even if a teacher told the child to remain seated and work on an assignment.

Parents are often the ones who initially suspect there is a problem. They should seek help when they sense their child might have ADHD. Only a doctor can diagnose this condition. The doctor can also work with the family to treat this disorder. Researchers now think ADHD is a lifelong condition. It cannot be cured, but it can be treated.

Behavior training may be recommended for children with ADHD. Some children benefit from being trained to control their behaviors. Other children with ADHD may benefit from drug therapy. Certain drugs can decrease hyperactivity and calm a child. This can lengthen the child's attention span and improve concentration. The child can focus longer on tasks and is better able to learn.

Parenting a child with ADHD takes patience and understanding. Parents should accept their child even when they dislike his or her hyperactive behavior. They should work closely with their child, doctor, and school. With teamwork, they can ensure their child has the best possible chance to learn.

Children with Emotional Disorders

An **emotional disorder** is a limitation in the way a person functions emotionally and socially. It may be present at birth or develop later. Some of these disorders are hereditary. Others can be caused by life events, such as a crisis. An emotional disorder may be temporary or lifelong. It is a disability if it affects the person's ability to function regularly.

Emotional disorders can limit a person's ability to feel and handle emotions in an age-appropriate way. A person with an emotional disorder may not express feelings in acceptable ways for someone his or her age. Some ways to express emotion are dangerous or illegal. People with some emotional disorders cannot control their tempers. They respond to negative feelings in violent ways, such as hurting others. Other persons may be severely depressed. They may feel hopeless and seek to end their lives. In both situations, such a response would be both dangerous and illegal.

An emotional disorder can also affect a person's ability to interact with others. For instance, a person may not relate to others in acceptable ways for his or her age. Social skills are an important part of life. Lacking social skills can make life harder. Certain disorders can limit a person's ability to relate to others at all. People with these disorders may be withdrawn and uncomfortable around others. Everyone needs at least a few good relationships. Otherwise, life can be lonely.

Many times, emotional disorders are hard to identify. Parents may sense that something is wrong with their child, but they may not know exactly what it is. They may also attribute the child's emotional problems to his or her temperament. Parents may assume their child acts as he or she does by choice rather than because of a disorder.

An untreated emotional disorder can affect all areas of a person's life. These disorders do not go away on their own. They do not improve over time without treatment. Actually, they often get much worse. An emotional disorder can limit a child's ability to concentrate. This can affect school performance and future job opportunities.

Often, parents or teachers first suspect a child has an emotional disorder. They may note problems in the child's emotional or social behavior. If so, they should seek help at once. Generally, only a doctor or mental health professional can diagnose an emotional disorder. After a diagnosis is made, parents and schools can create an IEP for the child.

Doctors and mental health professionals can also recommend therapy or treatment. Counseling can often help children with emotional disorders. It can also help their families. Behavioral training may also be needed. Medications may be prescribed for certain disorders. With the help they need, people with emotional disorders can improve or maintain their social and emotional functioning. This can help them lead active, satisfying lives.

Gifted Children

The term **gifted** describes a child with outstanding skills in either a general sense or a specific ability. Many gifted children have intellectual skills that are above average for their ages. Others possess extraordinary talent in areas such as art, music, or athletics, 21-10. Gifted students may excel in more than one area. Students with disabilities may also be gifted.

1—**Vocabulary:** What is an *emotional disorder*? What does this type of disorder affect?

2—**Activity:** List various causes of emotional disorders of children.

3—**Example:** Provide specific examples of ways an emotional disorder can limit a person's emotional and social functioning.

4—**Discuss:** Can emotional disorders that are not treated during childhood create severe problems during teen and adult years?

21-10 _____
Gifted children may excel in a general sense, or they may have special talents in specific areas, such as music or athletics.

1—Discuss: Describe a gifted child. How can parents and schools recognize these children and challenge them?

2—Discuss: How can parents be alerted to signs of giftedness? Cite characteristics parents might notice in their children.

3—Discuss: Cite some problems gifted children might face.

No single description fits every gifted child. Consider a child who is gifted in sports and one who is gifted in math. Both may need special help to maximize their talents, but the kinds of help they need may be quite different.

Alert parents are usually the first to see signs of giftedness in their children. Chart 21-11 lists common traits of gifted children. Some of these signs may be evident from infancy. At birth, gifted children may be more alert and sleep less than other infants. From an early age, they may be more independent and show amazing strength of will. Gifted children may also possess more originality, logic skills, common sense, ambition, and talent than their peers. Gifted children are often very curious, so parents and teachers should help them find answers to their many questions.

Parents are often quite pleased to learn their child is gifted. Providing the right kinds of stimulation for a gifted child can be difficult, however. Parents may not have enough energy to continually encourage or challenge their child. They may not understand the child's special needs or know how to be helpful. On the other hand, some parents expect more from gifted children than from other children. They may push gifted children too hard. Some parents exploit their children's talents or embarrass their children by constantly boasting to others about them.

Gifted children often have problems when parents and teachers do not challenge them to develop their special gifts. They may soon become bored with schoolwork that is too easy or that does not stimulate them to learn more. When gifted children are underchallenged, they may develop behavior problems.

Another problem gifted children have is feeling they don't fit in with other children. Gifted children are sometimes labeled and ridiculed by their classmates. As a result, some gifted children hide their talents, which then become underdeveloped.

Until children reach school age, parents are the best observers of their

Characteristics of Gifted Children

- **Early development**—Most gifted children talk early. Their vocabularies are more advanced and descriptive than those of their peers. About half learn to read before they start school, usually teaching themselves.

- **Long attention span**—The child's concentration may be so intense that it resists interruption, or the child may appear to daydream. Gifted children tend to be persistent, know what they want, and refuse to be distracted from reaching their goals.

- **Superb observational skills**— An alert toddler might remember which of ten blocks is missing. A creative child might observe the fried egg on his or her plate looks like Alaska.

- **Advanced reasoning skills**—The gifted child understands complex concepts and relationships. For example, a disagreement about simple household chores may drag on as the child gives logical explanations of why he or she did not do the assigned chores.

- **Questioning mind**—A gifted child usually asks penetrating questions and demands responses. Many questions reflect an intense curiosity: If you can feel the wind, why can't you see it? Why do people have to grow old?

- **Interest in structure and order**—Gifted children may like objects or ideas that are consistent like number systems, clocks, and calendars. Gifted children may be highly skilled at taking things apart and putting them together.

- **Imagination**—A gifted child may be the leader in pretend games. He or she is likely to have an imaginary playmate and see toy cars alternately as football players, mountain climbers, or superheroes.

- **High energy and restlessness**—The child's mind will not stop, even when the body needs to sleep.

- **Unusual talents**—Children gifted in specific areas generally display their talents and interests early.

21-11 Parents are usually the first people to notice many of these characteristics in their gifted children.

children's special talents. Some parents may have their children tested to determine their skills. Others simply trust their instincts and provide children with enriching hobbies or lessons in areas where they seem to excel. Preschools that offer individualized learning opportunities may provide just the stimulation young gifted children need. There, children are allowed to proceed at their own accelerated pace.

Teachers and counselors can do much to guide gifted children. First, children may be tested to pinpoint areas in which they excel. Traditional IQ tests can measure logical thinking skills. Other tests may measure creative thinking or skills in such subjects as math and science. Talents in the arts and athletics are usually judged by experts in those areas. Children who test well may be identified as gifted and receive special school services.

Schools vary in their approaches to meeting the special needs of gifted students. For students who are intellectually gifted, one idea is *acceleration*. This means a school allows gifted students to move to a higher grade level where the work is more challenging.

Acceleration has drawbacks, however. Even gifted students may be average or below average in emotional and social development. Placing them in a class with older students can affect these areas of development. Also, leaving behind one's same-age peers can be upsetting. Many experts advise parents to allow students to skip no more than one grade early in their schooling. Others do not favor acceleration at all.

Another option is placing gifted children in a special school for the

1—Discuss: What are the advantages and disadvantages of acceleration programs?

1—Enrich: Are there enrichment programs in your school? If so, describe them. How do they challenge children?

2—Vocabulary: What is meant by *inclusion*?

gifted. Schools exist for persons who are talented in the fine and performing arts, music, athletics, or academics. Some experts promote these schools, especially for older children with gifts in the performing arts.

A third way to meet the needs of gifted children is through *enrichment programs.* These are programs within a school designed to meet the needs of gifted students. These programs vary from one school to the next. In one school, separate accelerated or honors classes might be offered. Students might study subjects at a more advanced level than in classes for average learners. In another school, students may be in integrated classrooms with opportunities for enrichment provided. Here, teachers might assign special projects for gifted students or allow them to do some independent study. This can be a compromise if schools cannot afford separate classrooms but wish to meet their gifted students' special needs. Parents of a gifted student should work closely with their school to make sure the child's special needs are being met.

Inclusion

In the past, children were often placed into classrooms based on their varying abilities. Children with disabilities were usually separated from nondisabled students. Children with special needs were educated in their own classrooms. They did not interact with other students, except maybe during recess or lunch. It was believed this was best for everyone—students with special needs, average students, and teachers. Teachers for nondisabled students were not trained or experienced in teaching disabled students.

Today research has revealed most children with special needs benefit more in an integrated environment. They do well in classes with average learners. This has prompted educators to focus on inclusion. **Inclusion** means placing students of varying abilities in the same class, 21-12. Inclusion was once called *mainstreaming.* Children with special needs may be placed in integrated classes for part or all of the school day.

21-12 ⎯⎯⎯⎯⎯
Inclusion means students of all abilities share a classroom. The children in this class may have physical, mental, emotional, and learning disabilities. They may also be gifted or average learners.

Experts say inclusion prepares children with special needs to adapt to society at large. In an integrated classroom, disabled and nondisabled learners can interact with one another. Nondisabled students can be role models. They can also help their disabled peers learn. Interacting with disabled students can help nondisabled students appreciate diversity. It can also teach them acceptance and teamwork.

Teaching a class with students of varying abilities can be challenging. Teachers may have to adapt a single lesson in many ways to meet the needs of all learners. A teacher might teach a lesson at one level and make an assignment for average learners. He or she might assign the same work at a lower level for students with learning or mental disabilities. The teacher might also alter the assignment for students with physical disabilities. For gifted students, a teacher might offer an enrichment project to accompany a lesson.

The major goal of inclusion is to place students in the least restrictive environment possible. No student should be restricted from participating in a class in which he or she would learn and benefit. Separate classrooms for disabled students are restrictive if a student does not need the level of services they provide.

Separate classrooms for children with special needs can serve a purpose. Some students cannot learn and benefit in a regular classroom. They may need intensive one-on-one instruction. This may not be available in an integrated classroom. Other students may need training in life skills or social skills. In these cases, students may gain more in separate classes for all or part of the day. A student's IEP will specify whether he or she will be in integrated or separate classrooms.

Parents' Roles in Their Children's Health Care

The promotion of good health is a major responsibility of parents and other adults who care for children. What are the characteristics of a healthy child? Signs of physical, mental, emotional, and social health are seen if a child

- is growing at proper rate
- is developing firm muscles
- has good posture
- has straight and clean teeth that are free of cavities
- has pink and firm gums
- plays vigorously
- is rested and alert
- is developing large-motor control and eye-hand coordination
- has an increasing attention span
- is cheerful and tolerates some stress
- enjoys other children and adults
- is becoming more and more cooperative with others
- shows more and more self-control
- adapts to new situations and people

Parents and other adults should note the age/stage aspects of growth and development. They should also consider the child's nutrition, freedom from diseases and accidents, and the degree of stress in evaluating health.

All children inevitably become ill many times during their childhood years. Parents can keep a child's disease resistance at a high level, however. They can do this by helping their children learn and use good health practices. These include eating a well-balanced

1—**Activity:** List ways inclusion can be beneficial for each of the following: average learners, children with disabilities, gifted children, and teachers.

2—**Resource:** *The Child Who Is Ill*, Activity F, SAG.

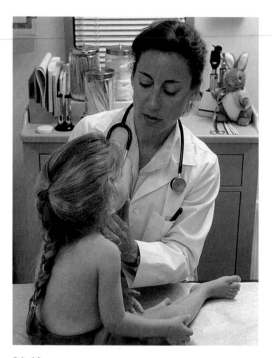

21-13 ——————————
Children should see a doctor on a regular basis to identify illnesses that might cause serious health problems.

diet, getting adequate rest and exercise, maintaining good hygiene, and having routine medical checkups.

Routine medical checkups give doctors a chance to detect any health problems early, 21-13. They are also a good way for the doctor to follow a child's growth and development. The American Academy of Pediatrics recommends children visit their doctors five times during the first year. Yearly visits are recommended for toddlers and preschoolers. School-age children and teens should visit their doctors at least once every two years.

Even with routine preventative health care, children will still become ill at times. If children attend group child care, they encounter many other children and become ill more often, 21-14. Colds and flu are the most common illnesses. These occur frequently during the early years. It is important for parents to recognize symptoms of illness. If their child shows these symptoms, parents can then call their child's doctor and begin treating the illness

right away. When a child is ill, he or she may do some or all of the following:

- exhibit behavior changes (for instance, a normally active child is very quiet)
- fall asleep frequently
- be irritable and easily upset
- refuse to eat
- feel chilled (often a sign of fever)
- vomit or have diarrhea (watery stools)
- complain of aching muscles, ears, head, or stomach
- have difficulty breathing, standing, or seeing regularly

These symptoms indicate a cold, flu, or other temporary condition. They may also signal the onset of a childhood disease. Parents should talk with their child's doctor regarding any symptoms. The doctor may want to examine the child to rule out serious illnesses. Parents should become familiar with the main symptoms of common childhood diseases, 21-15. They should call the child's doctor right away if they suspect their child has one of these diseases.

21-14 ——————————
Children in child care facilities should be taught to wash their hands frequently to prevent the spread of infections.

Many of these diseases can be prevented by immunizations. Parents should make sure they follow their children's immunization schedule to protect their children from these diseases. For the others, vaccines have not yet been developed.

Caring for a Sick Child at Home

When children are ill or injured, they need extra attention. Sick children should not attend school or child care facilities where there are other children. If an illness is contagious, it will spread rapidly among the children and staff. Also, children who are sick need to rest and follow their doctor's instructions so they can restore their health quickly. Parents may have to take time off work or make other special arrangements to care for a sick child.

Parents should not be afraid of spoiling an ill or injured child. The extra attention makes children feel nurtured. They can recuperate much faster if they sense someone cares about their condition. Most babies and young children want to be held and rocked constantly when they are sick. Older children enjoy quiet games, books, television, records or tapes, and coloring materials to pass the time. Rest is important, but the child may not need to remain in bed at all times. If the child has a fever, he or she will sleep much of the time. Once the fever breaks, the child may want to get up and play. Parents can offer fun activities that are not too tiring for these children.

When children are sick, the doctor may recommend a change in the child's diet. Parents should not force children to eat when they are ill. When their health returns, so will their appetites. Parents should encourage them to drink liquids, however. Water, milk, juices, and soft drinks are usually appropriate. If the child is vomiting, he or she shouldn't have anything to eat or drink for one hour. Then parents give can give

the child an ounce of a sweet juice or soft drink. If there is no further vomiting, the child can have more liquid every fifteen minutes. If vomiting resumes, however, parents should wait another hour before giving any liquids.

If the doctor prescribes a medication, parents should be sure to give the child the medicine as directed. Young children should not be allowed to administer their own medication. With detailed instructions, older children may be capable of this. Parents should use an accurate measuring device for liquid medicines. A medically defined teaspoon contains exactly 5 cc of liquid. A household teaspoon may contain anywhere from 2.4 cc to 7.5 cc of liquid. Parents can buy an inexpensive measuring device for dispensing medication. These can usually be purchased from a pharmacy.

Children experience episodes of illness and possible injury frequently, but they are very resilient and usually recover quickly, 21-16. An alert and caring parent will recognize the symptoms of illness and provide the proper care for a sick child. Patience and understanding are needed as the child regains his or her health.

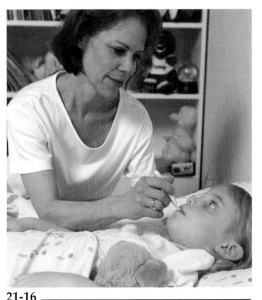

21-16 _____
Parents shouldn't worry too much over a child's minor illness—soon the child will be back to health.

Childhood Diseases

Disease	Symptoms	Care
Chicken Pox	Irritating rash spreading over body. Begins as small, pink dots that change to blisters and then form scabs. Mild fever.	Bed rest is advised. Dress the child in loose-fitting clothes to limit discomfort. Apply talcum powder or water and baking soda solution to soothe irritation. Instruct child not to scratch to avoid spreading the rash.
Common Cold	Nasal congestion, runny nose, sneezing, sore throat, headache, weakness, and fever.	Child needs rest to restore body strength. Give child plenty of liquids to avoid dehydration from fever.
Diphtheria	Nasal discharge, inflammation of mucous membranes, sore throat, and fever.	Consult doctor to obtain proper medication for child. Keep child home to prevent spreading the disease.
Impetigo	Round, crusted sores, usually on face, also common on hands.	Avoid contact with others. Keep infected areas clean. Consult doctor for treatment.
Influenza (Flu)	Weakness and aches of the body, fever, and coughing.	Child needs rest to restore body strength. Give child plenty of liquids to avoid dehydration from fever.
Mumps	Fever, swelling, and aching of the salivary glands and glands near ears and jawline. May also affect the testicles or ovaries.	Keep child in bed. Give liquids and other easy-to-swallow foods. Consult doctor for proper medication to reduce swelling and pain.
Rubella (German Measles)	Onset similar to cold; irritated eyes, mild fever. Red rash on face and neck area. Swollen lymph nodes.	Consult doctor to obtain proper medication for child. Keep child home to prevent spreading the disease.
Streptococcal Infections (Scarlet Fever, Strep Throat)	Sudden infection; severe sore throat, headache, fever, swollen glands. Scarlet fever causes a bright red rash during time of infection.	Keep child in bed to prevent spreading the disease. Consult doctor to obtain proper medication.
Whooping Cough (Pertussis)	Onset mild with slight fever and light cough. Cough worsens and leads to difficulty in breathing and vomiting.	Child needs rest and nourishment that will not irritate the throat. Consult doctor for proper medication and breathing exercises.

1

2

1—**Activity:** Review
the childhood
diseases, indicating
the symptoms and the
care needed for each
disease.

2—**Reflect:** Which of
these diseases have
you had? How did you
feel? Describe the
care you required.

Summary

1

- Parents' roles in their children's education involve roles at home as well as involvement with their children's school. Parents and schools should work together for the best interest of children's well-being and learning.

- Children are greatly influenced by their parents' attitudes about education and related concepts such as competition, success, failure, responsibility, and discipline.

- Children whose development and abilities are far above or below average are often called children with special needs. Children with disabilities and children who are gifted are two groups of children with special needs.

- Inclusion means placing students of varying abilities in the same classroom. Children with special needs may be in integrated classrooms for part or all of the school day.

- Parents can keep a child's disease resistance at a high level by teaching their children good health practices. They should recognize symptoms of illness and call the doctor right away if their child shows these symptoms.

- When children are ill or injured, they need extra care and attention. Parents may have to take time off work or make other special arrangements to care for a sick child.

Reviewing Key Points

2

1. Give three examples of how parents can take advantage of teachable moments to help their children see learning as fun.

2. True or false. Children's favorite way of learning is by watching someone else give a demonstration.

3. Propose three ways parents can increase their children's desire to learn, other than those given in the chapter.

4. In what ways can parents help their children develop good study habits?

5. Describe the difference between mental retardation and a mental disability.

6. What is an IEP? What is it used for?

7. Name three ways schools and teachers can make education more accessible for children with physical disabilities.

8. What is a learning disorder? Give two examples.

9. Describe how ADHD can interfere with a person's ability to learn.

10. An emotional disorder is a limitation in the way a person functions _____ and _____.

11. What is an enrichment program? Give two examples.

12. List three benefits of inclusion.

13. For each of the following ages, indicate how often a child should be seen by a doctor.
    A. school-age
    B. infant
    C. preschooler
    D. teen
    E. toddler

14. Describe three behavior changes that might indicate a child is ill.

15. Should parents worry about spoiling a sick child? Why or why not?

Learning by Doing

1. Create a poster for parents about their roles in their children's education. Use the poster to encourage parents' involvement both at home and at school.

1—Activity: Review and outline this chapter emphasizing the information you found most useful.

2—Answers: Answers to review questions are located in the front section of this TAE.

2. Work in a small group. Select one of the groups of children with special needs described in the chapter. Create a directory of community services and agencies available to help parents of children in this group. Provide the following information for each agency: name of agency, address and telephone number, contact person, services, and fees.

3. Read a newspaper or magazine article about ADHD. Summarize the article in an oral report to the class.

4. Using the Internet, research one of the childhood illnesses from Chart 21-11. Prepare a written report on your findings. Ask your teacher how to cite your references.

5. Investigate options available in your community for working parents with a sick child. Are there any programs for sick child care in your area? Present your findings to the class.

Thinking Critically

1. With a small group, discuss ways parents can help or hinder their children's learning in the home setting. Make two lists: what parents should do and what they should not do. Present the lists for class discussion.

2. What are some ways for parents to become involved in the functioning of your school? How effective are programs that involve parents? Do parents need to be more involved? If you were a parent, how involved would you want to be in your children's education?

3. Write an essay about how you think you would react if you discovered your child had a disability. Explain what you as a parent would do and how you would feel.

4. Research colleges and universities in your state. Which ones offer programs for teachers of special needs students? What are the requirements for graduation at each school? Report to class.

5. Interview two teachers: one who works in a separate classroom for children with special needs and one who works in an integrated classroom. Ask each teacher what are the advantages and disadvantages of teaching in his or her classroom. Ask what each sees as advantages and disadvantages of teaching in the other type of class. Ask what each thinks are the rewards and frustrations of his or her job.

Well-fed children are more alert and ready for activities throughout the day.

Chapter 22
The Challenge of a Child and Family Services Career

Objectives

After studying this chapter, you will be able to

- identify career opportunities in child and family services.
- do a self-assessment of your interests, aptitudes, and abilities.
- explain the personal qualifications needed for a child and family services career.
- describe the general professional qualifications for a child and family services career.
- develop a career plan.
- describe trends that affect careers in child and family services.
- describe how to find and secure employment.

Key Terms

job
career
entry-level job
professional
paraprofessional
entrepreneurship
interests
aptitudes
abilities
career plan
parliamentary procedure
leadership
teamwork
nonverbal communication
resume
references

Parents are not the only people who are involved with children. Many other people interact with children every day. These people include teachers, caregivers, and health care professionals. Children also benefit from the work of many other people. Some examples are the creators of children's books, television shows, computer software, and toys. Other careers include being involved with other family members, such as parents. In this chapter, you will learn about several jobs and careers in child and family services, 22-1.

A difference exists between a job and a career. A **job** is work a person does to earn money. A job is one work experience. A **career**, on the other hand, is a series of related jobs and work experiences. Developing a career is a lifelong process that includes many small goals. To have a career, a person might first need to learn several related jobs. The person might also need specific education and training in his or her chosen field.

22-1
Being a child care worker is a rewarding career in a child-related area.

1—Vocabulary: Look up terms in the glossary and discuss their meanings.

2—Vocabulary: Have students explain the difference between a *job* and a *career*.

One way to divide jobs is by the level of training and education a person needs to do them. For instance, an **entry-level job** requires little or no education and training after high school. Examples of entry-level jobs are child care aides, teachers' aides, and bus drivers. An entry-level job might be your goal, or it might be the first step to meeting a larger goal, such as being a teacher.

Being a teacher is a professional position. A **professional** has advanced training and education in a specific area. Professionals have at least bachelor's degrees from four-year colleges or technical schools. Many professions require master's or doctor's degrees.

Another level exists between entry-level workers and professionals. A **paraprofessional** has education and training beyond high school to prepare for his or her work. Paraprofessionals often have associate degrees from two-year colleges or technical schools.

As you look to the future, you may want to work with, or on the behalf of, children and families. Many jobs and careers are available in child and family services. You must decide which one is right for you. Setting career goals is an important task. It requires much thought. A good first step is to learn what jobs are available in a career field. After you decide which job or career to pursue, you can identify steps that can help you meet that goal.

Working Directly with Children and Families

Many people enjoy being with children. These people might want to be actively involved in the care, education, and training of children. If you are one of these people, you might want to choose a career working directly with children. Such careers include child care providers, teachers, librarians, youth and recreation leaders, social workers, and health care providers.

Child Care Personnel

Child care personnel work very closely with children every day. These workers perform many tasks. Some of these tasks include supervising children's play, teaching games and songs, feeding and diapering young children, and providing needed guidance and care.

Many places of employment exist for child care providers. These include private homes, child care centers, preschools, church and private schools, government agencies, and hospitals. Child care workers can also work in corporate child care centers.

The main entry-level job in child care is a child care aide. This job requires little education and training beyond high school. Many child care aids have taken child development courses in high schools or community colleges. They might have also spent time babysitting or volunteering with children.

The *Child Development Associate (CDA) Credential* program is a national program that certifies child care workers. Applicants must have experience in child care and receive some related classroom training. A CDA council representative assesses each applicant's skills in working with young children. The representative then decides whether the candidate qualifies for the CDA Credential.

To teach in a child care center, a person should have either a two-year or a four-year college degree. Jobs as director or supervisor of a child care center are filled by professionals. These positions require a bachelor's degree from a four-year college or university.

Nannies

Another job opportunity in the child care field is that of nannies. Nannies provide families with quality care for young children in their homes. This meets the needs of growing numbers of working parents for consistent child care. Live-in nannies receive room and board plus a salary.

Training programs for nannies vary in length from four hours to one year. An accredited program of study in a nanny school must include 200 classroom hours and 50 hours of on-the-job training. Most schools require students to do an internship with a family. Certification is granted after a person successfully completes the program.

Teachers

Teaching is a satisfying profession for many people who enjoy interacting with children. Teachers of young children may work in preschool, kindergarten, or elementary school settings, 22-2. Positions are available for teachers at the middle school, junior high, and high school levels as well. The schools may be private or public. Some programs that employ teachers are government sponsored.

Teachers are professionals. All teachers are required to have at least a bachelor's degree from a four-year college or university. They must also receive a license to teach in the state where they are employed.

Paraprofessional positions are available in teaching. For example, assistant teachers might work with teachers in the classroom. Paraprofessionals usually have a degree from a two-year college. They often work under the supervision of the teacher.

Entry-level jobs in teaching may include teachers' aide positions. For these positions, a person might not have a degree beyond high school. A teacher's aide might have some community college courses related to children and teaching. He or she would work under the supervision of the teacher and assistant teacher.

1—Enrich: Investigate an accredited program for nanny training. Compare this training with an entry-level child care worker.

2—Enrich: Investigate the requirements for a teaching certificate at each level of school—early childhood education, elementary, middle school, and high school.

3—Activity: Prepare a career ladder showing the different levels in the teaching field. Identify careers at the various levels within the teaching field.

22-2 _____
Teachers have an important influence on children's lives. To be an elementary school teacher, you would need at least a bachelor's degree in education.

1—Enrich: Talk to a children's librarian. Ask about the educational requirements for this career.

2—Enrich: Investigate the requirements for filling certain recreational positions.

Children's Librarians

If you enjoy books and want to share the joy of reading with children, you might consider a career as a children's librarian. Librarians may work in a school library or in the children's section of a public or private library, 22-3. They design programs to stimulate reading and improve reading skills. Librarians teach children how to use the library. They may initiate story hours and read to groups of children. Children's librarians also spend many hours evaluating new books to add to the library.

In most cases, a librarian must have a bachelor's degree in library science. A position as a children's library assistant may not require a degree. Someone who has taken college courses in children's literature may have an advantage when applying for this position.

Youth and Recreation Leaders

Youth and recreation leaders feel they have the best of two worlds. They combine their enjoyment of recreational activities with the challenge of working with children.

Persons who choose this career may work with children in specific areas such as sports, recreation, fitness, arts, and crafts. They may help children learn new hobbies. Some examples are youth counselors for youth in civic, church, and camp programs.

A coach for children's sports may be hired as a recreation leader, 22-4. Recreation workers may also be employed by city parks and recreation departments. Other employment settings include theme parks, tourist attractions, campgrounds, and recreation areas. Some recreation positions are filled by high school graduates. Other positions require an associate degree in parks and recreation or social work. A recreation supervisor must have a bachelor's degree. The degree might be in parks and recreation management, leisure studies, physical education, or other related fields.

Social Workers

Social workers help children in need. Many social workers are involved in child welfare and family services. Their role is to ensure the well-being of children. They may counsel parents who need help with their children, or

22-3

A children's librarian can help children select books to read. The librarian also selects, orders, and maintains the books in the library's collection.

22-4

As a recreation leader, this man combines his love of children with his love of sports.

youth who need guidance. They may find homes for neglected or abandoned children. Social workers may also be involved in child protective services. They may investigate reported cases of child abuse and neglect. These workers may be called on to decide what steps are necessary to protect the children. Some social workers are involved in placing children into foster care or adoptive homes.

Many social workers are employed by government agencies. Others are employed by social service agencies, community and religious organizations, and hospitals. A bachelor's degree in social work is the minimum requirement for most positions in this field. Advanced degrees are often preferred for social workers.

Health Services

As researchers learn more about health and well-being, children's health services become more important. The demand for children's health care providers continues to grow, 22-5. The following list includes some of the professionals who provide health care for children:

- pediatricians
- pediatric dentists
- pediatric nurses and school nurses
- dietitians
- child psychologists and psychiatrists
- physical therapists
- *ophthalmologists* (Doctors who specialize in structure, function, and diseases of the eye)
- *optometrists* (Licensed specialists who examine eyes and prescribe corrective lenses)

Each of these health care specialists must have at least a bachelor's degree, if not more advanced degrees and internships. Paraprofessional positions include dental hygienists, nurses' aides, and doctors' assistants.

22-5 _____
School nurses are professionals who provide health care for students during the school day. To be a school nurse, you would need special training.

Working on Behalf of Children and Families

Many people work in careers that affect children indirectly. They may not have direct contact with children, but children benefit from their work. Such careers include family life educators, child development teachers, teacher educators, researchers, and consultants, 22-6.

Family life educators are professionals who educate others about effective family living. They might conduct seminars and training sessions for parents. These programs might be sponsored by churches, businesses, or

1—Reflect: If you were a social worker, would you find it difficult not to become emotionally involved in your cases?

2—Reflect: Review the list of professionals who provide specialized health care for children. Do any of these careers appeal to you?

3—Discuss: Many careers are available for people who want to work on behalf of children and families. Brainstorm possible careers available.

1—Enrich: Investigate the requirements for a career as a parent educator. How are they different from those of a child development teacher?

2—Vocabulary: Have students explain the difference between a *researcher* and a *consultant*.

22-6 ——————
This consultant may not have direct contact with children, but she can advise businesses about children's needs.

civic organizations. Family life educators might also teach in high schools, community colleges, and universities. Their work benefits children by improving the quality of family life.

Parent educators are people who teach parenting or child development to parents-to-be and parents. Some parent educators teach in group settings, and others work on a one-on-one basis with a parent, often in the parent's home. Some professionals have the title *parent educator* and do only parent education activities. These activities may be done directly with parents. Workshops may be conducted for the training of other professionals who then work with parents.

Some professionals are parent educators on a full-time basis. Many other professionals in child development, family life, or education do parent education as one aspect of their job. For example, early childhood teachers, who work directly with children, often hold meetings or conduct workshops for parents of children in their class or program. They also have individual parent-teacher conferences with each of their children's parents.

Child development teachers also work indirectly for the benefit of children. These professionals teach the principles of child development and the care and guidance of children. They teach child development and parenting classes to students ranging from junior high to college level. These teachers may supervise child development laboratory classes. They may teach students to work with children in child care settings. A child development teacher must have at least a bachelor's degree.

A teacher educator works at the college level to prepare family life educators and child development teachers for their positions. A teacher educator must have at least a master's degree.

Researchers search for answers in one area concerning children and families. For example, a researcher may be employed by a research hospital or laboratory and do research on one disease seen in children. Another researcher associated with a university may study one aspect of child development, such as how children learn or the roots of childhood violence. Researchers have years of specialized education and experience in their field of research. They also have experience in conducting and analyzing research.

Consultants are closely connected to researchers. Consultants take research data and share this knowledge with those in other child and family services careers. Like parent educators, some consultants are full-time while others consult as part of their career work. For example, a legislative aide may work for a government agency, a specialized committee or program, or a senator or representative. These full-time consultants locate research studies and other data, summarize, and report information needed in handling issues concerning children and their families. Sometimes they prepare reports and present findings before boards or committees. More professionals do consultant work as part of their jobs, such as a college professor who may consult with local school systems or social service agencies.

Creating and Selling Products and Services for Children

You might like to create or sell a child-related product, such as children's clothes, toys, or books. You might enjoy a career in the children's entertainment field. Let's take a closer look at some of these child-related careers.

Designing and Selling Children's Products

Creative people are needed to design or improve products for children. These items include children's clothes, furniture, toys, and games. These items are designed with a child's basic needs, as well as learning and safety needs, in mind. Items must be carefully designed and researched for their appeal.

Even when a product has existed for many years, it can always be improved. For instance, the design of the baby bottle has changed several times since it was created. The design and materials used in diapers are continually being improved. New textile products are created to make children's clothing safer, easier to care for, and more comfortable. New toys are constantly developed. These are just a few examples of the many products designed especially for children.

People who design such products need to understand children's needs. They also need creative talent and design skills. Companies that produce such items also employ people who know how to market and sell these items to parents and their children. They offer entry-level jobs in the factories where these items are created. These

22-7 _____

It may not seem like these workers have child-related careers, but they do. Their work gets these tricycles from the manufacturer to the stores that will sell them.

companies hire entry-level workers to create, pack, and ship their goods, 22-7.

Writers, Artists, and Entertainers

Many of the books written especially for children have become classics. Thousands of new children's books are also being published every year. A career as a writer or illustrator of children's books can be rewarding.

Children's writers must be able to capture children's interest on paper. They must be able to visualize their stories through the eyes of children. An illustrator of children's books must be able to interpret stories using whimsical or realistic drawings, 22-8.

Children's books have been educating and entertaining children for hundreds of years. Books are not the only form of communication used to entertain children. Almost every household has a television, for example. The average child watches 21 to 23 hours of TV each week. Many programs are designed especially for children. Movies and live shows for children are also being produced. Writers, entertainers, directors, and producers are needed to create these programs. People in this field must understand the intellectual, emotional, and social needs of children.

1—Activity: Children's products represent a large market. As you watch TV, list the number of products that focus on children.

2—Activity: Pretend you are a designer of children's products. Describe a toy, children's clothing item, or other object you would like to design.

3—Activity: Writers of children's books often focus on a simple concept for a child. Write a short paragraph on an idea for a book you think a child would like.

22-8 _____
An artist illustrates children's books with vivid and realistic drawings.

Entrepreneurship

An **entrepreneurship** is a business that is owned and operated by one person. Many opportunities exist for entrepreneurships in child-related areas. For instance, a hobby or special talent may form the basis for self-employment. A part-time or full-time job may give you an idea and the experience necessary to start your own business.

Many entrepreneurships exist in the child care field. For instance, many parents who wish to be with their own children operate in-home child care facilities. They may provide care for several children in their own homes. Many child care centers are owned and operated by one person.

Other entrepreneurships have formed in the child-related field. For instance, a person might design and sell his or her own line of children's clothes. A person might go into business selling a new toy or game he or she invented. Some entrepreneurs plan and carry out children's parties, 22-9. Others entertain at special children's events. These include clowns, magicians, and artists. These are just a few of the many options available to entrepreneurs in child-related areas.

Having an idea for starting a business is only the beginning. It is wise to consider both the pros and cons of business ownership before investing your time and money. Many people like the idea of doing something they enjoy in surroundings of their own choosing. They like being their own bosses. It is possible to make a good income. On the other hand, it is also possible to lose a great deal of money. You might have the freedom to set your own hours, but you may have to work long hours to stay in business. There are no company benefits except those you provide for yourself.

If self-employment appeals to you, be sure you are prepared to handle all segments of the business. You will need training in child development, but you will also need to take courses in accounting, business management, and business

22-9 _____
This entrepreneur helped these children create their own masks for a "Royal Ball Party."

law. With the proper training and a willingness to work hard, the rewards of a profitable business can be yours, 22-10.

Know Your Interests, Aptitudes, and Abilities

Finding a career that brings happiness and a sense of fulfillment as a productive person requires a knowledge of yourself—especially your interests, aptitudes, and abilities.

As you approach the time for serious career planning, you should do a careful inventory of your own unique assets. This is called a *self-assessment*. In doing a self-assessment for career planning, you should carefully consider the answers to three questions.

Interests

What are your interests? **Interests** are activities that appeal to a person over a period of time. Interests can often be determined by how you use your time because more time is given to things that interest you.

Interests are developmental in nature. Some interests are mainly age or stage related. These interests often disappear in time. Other interests are more individual, and some of these grow with time. Studies show that interests become more stable around 20 years of age.

You may want to think about family interests in connection with your own. Family life influences the formation and development of interests. You may also want to think about the interests of others who have touched your life, such as teachers and youth leaders. What interests did they share with you?

Some of your interests may become hobbies and simply bring you pleasure and relaxation. Others may be used in careers. Interests have a great deal to do with your motivation to achieve. They are highly connected to career learning and job satisfaction. For this reason, interest inventories are sometimes given to those ready to plan careers.

Aptitudes

What are your aptitudes? **Aptitudes** are your natural talents. For example, a person may have aptitudes in one or more of these areas: motor performance, music, art, verbal, mathematics, and interpersonal (people-oriented) relations, 22-11. Aptitudes come in various degrees, too. Sometimes you recognize your aptitudes as something you can do easily. Other times, aptitudes are discovered through testing or by someone else pointing them out.

Career learning can be difficult. A person's best chance to achieve without too much stress comes in areas in which he or she has an aptitude. Going into a career for which you have an aptitude is simply putting your talents to work.

Abilities

What are your present abilities and what abilities can you develop? **Abilities** are skills that have been learned or developed. Some abilities

1—**Resource:**
Interests, Aptitudes, and Abilities,
Activity C, SAG.

22-10
This entrepreneur is a music teacher. People hire her to teach their children to play the piano.

22-11
People may have aptitudes in various areas, such as music.

are important for many careers, such as communication skills. These general abilities are often learned to a great extent before one graduates from high school. Career-specific skills are learned through specialized training and experiences. Both types of abilities should continue to develop throughout the working years.

Considering a Career in Child and Family Services

The ideal work situation is when your interests, aptitudes, and abilities match your career. Your aptitudes and experiences often determine your interests, which will lead you to develop abilities needed for a career.

The careers discussed in this chapter are in the area of child and family services. Variety is a key feature of careers in child and family services professions. For example, some careers are in hospitality and recreation, such as youth recreation directors. Other careers are in community services, which provide prevention, intervention, and treatment services to children and family members. Examples of these careers are teachers, parent educators, health professionals, and social workers. Some are in personal consumer areas, such as designing and selling products and providing services like entertainment.

Personal Qualifications for a Child and Family Services Career

Personal qualifications are traits that are not learned through career-specific training. These traits are highly important for careers, especially those in which people are involved. Often these traits can make a difference between success or failure even for a well-trained professional.

Personal Characteristics Needed to Work with Children

People need certain professional qualifications to obtain jobs in a child-related area. These have been described in the previous sections. In addition, you would need certain personal characteristics to succeed in a job working with children.

Do you like children? If you can answer yes to this question with no reservations, then you possess the most important characteristic, 22-12. You must enjoy being with children no matter what the circumstances might be.

Liking children means you are concerned about their welfare. A recreation leader, for instance, should not get upset if one child doesn't contribute to a winning team. Children need to be recognized for their efforts as well as their successes.

You must be able to laugh with children. Humor often helps children achieve. Children need to feel they are loved. They like to be physically close to adults. You would need to be comfortable with this closeness. You would need to listen to children and communicate openly with them.

Children can be unpredictable. You must be able to adapt to changing circumstances. Adults need to define limits to provide needed guidance, but children need to know they can make choices within those limits.

Working with children requires patience. Children are usually very anxious to learn anything new, yet their movements are often slow and deliberate. Since their large and small motor skills are not fully developed, children need more time to accomplish tasks. You should not lose patience and take over tasks for them. This might interfere with their growth and development. The bright smile that crosses a child's face when he or she finally completes a task will more than repay you for any lost time.

Personal Characteristics Needed to Work with Adult Family Members

A common characteristic shared by professionals who work with adults in family services is concern for people's problems and a desire to help. Leadership and organizational duties are primary tasks of these men and women.

22-12
Liking children is an essential quality for those who work directly with children. Coaches enjoy teaching children the skills they need in order to play sports.

1—Resource: *Personal Characteristics,* Activity D, SAG.

2—Discuss: Why is patience an important personal characteristic for someone who works with children?

Some specific personal characteristics needed to work with adults include
- sensitivity to others' needs
- patience
- trustworthiness
- composure during a crisis
- leadership skills
- creative thinking
- communication skills

People choosing these careers must have the personal traits needed to work directly with families and with the staff of agencies and organizations that provide services.

Professional Qualifications for a Child and Family Services Career

Just as careers vary in the child and family services profession, so do professional qualifications. Entry-level jobs and paraprofessional careers in this profession require a high school diploma. Many other careers require a bachelor's degree. A few careers require advanced degrees.

In the cases of some careers, people enter from various backgrounds or a broad-based college background. For example, a state's protective service agency may hire people with degrees in

1—Reflect: Is it easier to determine your short-term career goals or your long-term career goals? Why?

human ecology, child and family life education, or social work. Training for the specific program, such as child abuse prevention and intervention, will be given by the agency itself. Other careers, such as teaching or health services, often require very specific education and training, which is governed by state laws.

Developing a Career Plan

Once you have completed a self-assessment and found a career that interests you, it is time to make a career plan. A **career plan** is a list of steps you need to take to reach your career goal—employment within a career.

Career plans have two parts. *Short-term goals* are goals you can achieve immediately or in the near future. They are steps you take toward the career while in high school (and possibly during the early years of college). These short-term goals should be achieved within a year.

Long-term goals are end goals. In career plans, long-term goals describe the experiences required to enter the profession. These include preparation and education. You will also earn credentials, or proof of your abilities.

Because long-term goals determine the steps to take along the path, they need to be written first. Then, the first year of short-term goals should be written. See 22-13 for an example of a career plan for a senior in high school who wants to be a child care worker.

Trends Affecting Child and Family Services Careers

For some time, children and families have been able to rely on support and assistance in caring for children. Child care has helped provide optimal

22-13
A career plan helps people stay focused on the steps toward their career goals

Career Plan for a Child Care Worker	
Short-Term Goals	
Education and Training	Take child development and parenting courses. Select topic in parenting for senior paper.
Extracurricular Activities	In FCCLA, serve on a committee pertaining to children.
Work and Volunteer Experiences	Work at the local Head Start after school each day. Babysit on weekends.
Long-Term Goals	
Education and Training	Get an associate degree at the local community college. Work on Child Development Associate Competencies as soon as I'm hired.
Extracurricular Activities	Join the college chapters of AAFCS and NAEYC.
Work and Volunteer Experiences	Volunteer for 20 hours a week at the Head Start center.

care and encourage development in the interests of children and families as a whole. Today, the need for child care is growing. This has implications for careers in child and family services.

More Entry-Level Child Care Career Openings

The child care field is expanding rapidly. As more parents enter the work force, the demand for child care providers increases, 22-14. This has many implications for careers in the child care field.

Since the demand for child care providers is so high, there are many entry-level openings in the child care field. People interested in providing child care can often start in entry level positions on high school graduation. While they are in high school, taking courses in child development or family life education can teach them about children's needs. It also makes them better qualified to provide care. Experience with children, such as babysitting, is also helpful. Even in entry-level positions, applicants may find some competition over job openings. Credentials such as the CDA Credential are becoming even more important. If employers recognize and value these credentials, they are more likely to hire job applicants who have them than those who do not.

In paraprofessional or professional child care jobs, competition may also be a factor. A worker's skills, knowledge, and experience are very important to potential employers. As the field expands, the number of people wanting to enter the field grows. More college programs are being offered to train future child care workers. As a result, these programs are attracting more workers to the field. Graduating from a child development program at a two-year or four-year college is a good foundation for a child care career.

22-14 ———————————————

Today, more children than ever receive child care for at least part of the day. These children deserve excellent care from qualified caregivers.

Need for More Accredited Child Care Programs

Another trend is the growing emphasis parents are placing on the quality of care their children receive. This emphasis has led both centers and family-based child care homes to seek accreditation. An accredited child care center or home is one officially recognized and approved by a leading agency in its field. For instance, the National Academy of Early Childhood Programs has an accreditation program for center-based care. To apply for accreditation, a center's staff and parents must write a report about how well the center meets the Academy's criteria for accredited programs. These reports are verified by Academy personnel who visit the center. Finally, an Academy commission decides whether to accredit the program based on both reports.

The National Association for Family Child Care is the organization that accredits family child care homes. Family child care providers must complete an application and a self-study packet. They must prove they have at least 18 months experience, are licensed by the state, and have 65 hours of child development requirements. To

1—Discuss: What opportunities are there for early childhood teachers with specialized training? What types of training are in high demand right now?

2—Activity: Brainstorm less conventional settings in which child care workers may be hired today.

be accredited, family child care providers must also be observed by the association in their child care setting.

Parents can inquire whether their child care facility is accredited. This would assure them the facility meets the standards of professional organizations in the child care field.

Expanding Education Programs for Young Children

Today, parents are also placing more emphasis on early childhood education. They want their children to spend most of their time in child care learning. In response, more educational centers for young children are emerging. This provides more openings for early childhood education teachers. Early childhood teachers develop a curriculum for their classes, 22-15. They try to provide a balance between lessons and time for free play. Today's preschool classrooms are often equipped with computers. Computers help teachers manage their classrooms better. They also give children a head start on learning the computer skills they will need in the future.

Many school districts have more positions for early childhood teachers with specialized training than they can fill. This is especially true for teachers of early childhood special education. Federal law now mandates public special education for children with disabilities who are ages three to five years. This has increased the demand for early childhood special education teachers. Training in a second language is another specialization that is in demand for child care workers in many areas of the country.

New Settings for Child Care

Child care workers may also find jobs in less conventional settings, such as corporate child care centers, early Head

22-15 _____

Early childhood teachers provide educational lessons in addition to free playtime.

Start programs, and in hospitals. As more businesses provide on-site child care for employees, job openings are created in these centers. As funding for early Head Start programs increases, the need for teachers in these centers also grows. In many hospitals, child life specialists are hired to work with hospitalized children. These workers help children adjust to their illnesses and being hospitalized. They also provide learning activities for the children in their care.

Growing Child and Family Services Career Demands

More and more parents work long hours outside the home in today's society. Mobility has increased. The number of extended families and even nuclear families has decreased. Many families are headed by only one parent. Economic problems and lack of education have left some families living in poverty.

More than ever before families are needing support, prevention, intervention, and treatment services. As a result, careers in child and family services are expanding and becoming more specialized.

These careers involve working directly with and on the behalf of children and families. The profession is looking for people with creative ideas, strong leadership skills, the ability to collaborate through team efforts, and good communication skills.

Employees Must Prepare

With the expansion of child care field, changes will continue to occur. People entering the field must stay informed about the demands and opportunities in child care careers. Joining student or professional organizations can help. Attending continuing education classes and conferences is another way to stay connected to the field. Reading magazines and journals about child care can also be beneficial. As the field continues to change, workers must change along with it.

Preparing for Tomorrow's Challenges Today

In this chapter, you have learned about several child-related careers. Maybe you want to pursue a career working with children. If so, you may wonder how to start preparing for this career while you are still in high school.

You have several options. You can take classes in child development and family life. You can also join student organizations. These organizations can help you develop your interpersonal skills. They may also help you develop leadership and teamwork skills. Another option is to seek part-time employment while you are still in school, 22-16.

Joining Student Organizations

In your high school, there may be many organizations you can join. Every club needs members who are willing to work for the good of the organization. Members can attend meetings, serve on committees, and participate in club activities. They can find fellowship and work to fulfill the group's mission.

Joining a student organization lets you see the workings of a group. Most groups conduct their meetings by parliamentary procedure. **Parliamentary procedure** is an orderly method of conducting business in a group setting. This method helps meetings proceed in a timely manner. It ensures members handle all important business during the meeting. Parliamentary procedure is used in most adult groups. Learning these procedures now will help you feel more comfortable in meetings you will attend as an adult.

Most teens enjoy being part of a group. Communicating in a group can give you chances for individual expression and group sharing. You will develop interpersonal skills as you learn to work for mutual goals. You will also learn to work with a variety of people in different settings. Learning to work effectively in a group will help you in your future roles. Make the most of the chances for group participation while you are in high school, both as a member and as a leader.

22-16
Finding part-time employment with a child care center is a good way to prepare for a child and family services career.

1—Resource: *Developing Leadership Skills*, Activity F, SAG.

2—Reflect: What opportunities do you have to develop leadership skills?

3—Reflect: Identify leadership skills you believe you possess. Identify leadership skills you want to develop.

4—Discuss: How do good leaders help groups reach their goals?

Developing Your Leadership Skills

Leadership is the ability to direct and influence others. Young people can prepare to fill leadership roles in the years ahead. Schools, businesses, and organizations depend on leaders. Local, state, and national governing bodies cannot function without them.

Leadership skills can help you succeed in school and on the job. They help build your confidence. Being a leader makes you feel good about yourself and what you can accomplish. Leadership skills can also encourage you to set and achieve goals.

You have many chances to develop leadership skills in high school activities. Classmates might elect you to hold an office. You might be an officer or chair a committee in an organization, 22-17. You may take a leading role in a game of softball at a school picnic. Organizing a group of classmates to help with a project can also involve leadership. These are just a few ways you can start developing leadership skills now.

No matter what their position, good leaders share similar characteristics. First, they are considerate. Leaders recognize the needs of all group members.

Good leaders can communicate their ideas clearly and effectively. Their enthusiasm is invigorating. Leaders show a willingness to do their share of the work, but also know how to delegate authority.

Leaders provide structure for their groups. They make sure all group members know what is expected of them and what they can expect of their leaders. Structure helps groups reach their goals.

A good leader is flexible. Leaders can accept change, and help group members accept it as well. Leaders are open to fresh ideas. They are good problem-solvers, but they know when to seek outside help. In a crisis, they are confident and optimistic.

Leadership skills are well worth developing. Groups, companies, and communities need good leaders to help them achieve their goals.

Becoming an Effective Team Member

Teamwork involves working with other people to achieve common goals. Teamwork is vital in almost every career. Teamwork also helps in family living and other life settings.

Careers in child and family services are characterized by teamwork. For example, in most child care programs and in many educational settings, the teaching is done by a team rather than by an individual. These teams have a lead teacher, assistant teachers, and volunteers such as parents or students in child development classes.

Parent involvement is a mark of quality in all child-related careers. Professional workers must create a partnership with parents for effective results.

Teamwork is also required between child care program administrators and their boards or funding agencies. Professionals who organize services for children and families are involved in constant team efforts. They work as teams to secure, deliver, coordinate, and evaluate the impact of their services.

22-17 _____

Leaders in a student group might achieve awards that will help them learn for their later careers.

Good teams allow each person to use his or her own talents to enhance the team effort. Teamwork always begins with a full review of the needs and ideas of all involved. It involves problem solving and decision making.

Teamwork has advantages over individual work. Decisions are often better or more creative due to pooling of ideas. Because all members take responsibilities for decisions, much effort is most often put into making correct decisions. People tend to support group decisions more than individual ones. *Morale*, or enthusiasm in a group, is important for teamwork. Morale is higher when each person contributes, and competition between people is lessened.

You can develop teamwork skills by joining school teams or organizations or by engaging in group tasks in the classroom or in organizations. Through teamwork experience, you can learn to clarify goals, manage conflict, find group solutions, and put ideas into action with others, 22-18. Many communication skills are developed through teamwork, too.

Developing Your Communication Skills

Communication is central to your success in a child and family services career. Communication is vital to

22-18
Experience is gained through teamwork, where students learn how to accomplish tasks together.

relationships, and relationships are the focus of child and family services.

Careers in these fields require communication with children, parents, coworkers, administrators, support agencies staff, community members, and suppliers and distributors of goods. The purposes of communication are many and varied.

All communication should be clear and accurate. They expect positive facial and body messages to accompany face-to-face communication. They also expect employees to have basic electronic communication skills for jobs in today's workplaces.

Active listening is a very important skill. When you listen, be very involved in what the other person is saying. Encourage the other person to express his or her thoughts. If you understand the message, acknowledge what the person has said by restating the central message or by responding. If you do not understand, ask questions or request more explanations.

When verbally communicating, you try to be positive. When you speak, always watch the listener for comprehension and emotional reactions. In this way, you can adjust your communication.

Verbal communication is often accompanied by nonverbal communication. **Nonverbal communication** is any means of sending messages without using words. You want to appear interested and open to the person speaking. Looking around the room shows a lack of interest. Folding your arms, avoiding eye contact, or turning away from another person says you are not open to his or her ideas.

Your posture should be relaxed, but not slouching. Be sure not to stand too close to people when talking. They may become uncomfortable if you enter their personal space.

Written communication must be especially accurate and clear because it is not a two-way communication. Avoid grammar or spelling errors. As a

1—Reflect:
Do you think working with a group is a more organized way to accomplish tasks than working individually? Why or why not?

2—Discuss:
Why is developing communication skills important in terms of your future career?

3—Activity:
Role-play to demonstrate communication skills such as active listening, verbal communication, and nonverbal communication.

writer, you must imagine your reader. Ask yourself questions, such as: Will this person understand? What will be his or her emotional response?

Electronic communication skills are career assets. You should have basic word processing and keyboarding skills. You should know how to write business letters, office memos, and e-mail messages. Being able to use computers to create graphics, spreadsheets, and multimedia presentations is a real career bonus. Electronic communication should be written with the same care and courtesy as other written forms. You must also remember that business computers are for business and not personal use, and your written communication can be monitored.

Finding Part-Time Employment

Many students prepare for their future by working part-time while they are in school. They gain valuable work experience while they are still in high school. You may be able to obtain an entry-level job in the career field you hope to enter after you graduate.

If you enjoy children, you may have been babysitting for some time. This experience is very important if you want a career working with children.

There are other part-time jobs you might be able to have while you are in high school. You might find a job with a park district, school, or church. You might find a job working in the children's section of a library. Some child care centers employ high school students, 22-19. There are also many summer jobs available for young people at camps, recreation areas, theme parks, and tourist attractions.

To find out about job openings, you can contact a business or agency directly to ask if they have positions open. You can also talk to family members, friends, and neighbors. They may know of job leads. The want ads in a local newspaper are another option. Also watch for "help wanted" signs in businesses and notices on community bulletin boards.

When you learn of a position that interests you, contact the employer. You may do so by telephone, by letter, or in person. Express your interest in the position and ask if the job is still open.

22-19 —————
These high school students work in their school's preschool lab. The skills they are learning will help them to gain a job after graduation.

If it is, ask for an interview. Be positive, confident, and polite. Your initial contact must make a good impression. This is true whether that contact be by phone, letter, or in person.

Interviewing for a Job

You can do several things to prepare for a job interview. First, you can create a resume. A **resume** is a document that contains detailed information about your education, work experience, and qualifications for employment. See 22-20 for a description of what you should include on your resume. You can use this resume as your guide when you fill out a job application form. You can also leave it with the potential employer if appropriate.

Include the names and addresses of references. **References** are persons other than relatives whom employers can call to discuss your job qualifications. Former employers, club advisers, teachers, or religious leaders often serve as references. Before listing a reference, ask the person's permission. Some people do not wish to serve as references.

Another way to prepare for a job interview is to learn about the agency or business. Also learn about the position itself. Write down questions you may have. Employers want to hire people who are interested in their companies.

Carefully choose what you will wear to the interview. Your grooming and clothes will make an impression. Be sure it is a good one. Wear clothes that are one step more formal than what you

3

4

1—Resource: *Your Resume Worksheet*, Activity G, SAG.

2—Note: It is acceptable to list references on your resume. It is also acceptable to list them on a separate page and include "References provided on request" on your resume.

3—Discuss: Why is it important to ask your references for their permission before listing them on your resume or job applications?

4—Note: Remind students it is more polite for them to ask "Will you serve as a reference for me?" than "Can I use you as a reference?"

1

2

Your Name	
Address:	**Phone:**
Education:	Name and location of each school (most recent first)
	Dates of attendance
	Major courses of study
	Degrees earned
	Honors or awards received
Work Experience:	Name and address of each employer (most recent first)
	Dates of employment
	Job title
	Major duties and responsibilities
	Names of supervisors
Special Skills:	Abilities related to work
	Hobbies and interests
Activities:	Community and school organizations to which you belong
	Leadership positions held in these organizations
	Volunteer activities
References:	Name, title, address, and phone number for each of the three references

22-20 —————
A resume can serve as a handy reference for you. It also provides a potential employer the basic information about your qualifications for employment.

would wear on the job. For instance, if you interview for a child care position, casual clothes are appropriate. Jeans might be out of place.

Think about questions the interviewer might ask you. Have possible responses in mind. Some questions may be general, such as "Tell me about yourself." Others may be more specific. You might be asked to describe previous work experience. You might want to practice the interview with a family member or in front of a mirror. This will give you more confidence and help you feel more relaxed.

Know where you are going for your interview. Many businesses have personnel departments in separate buildings. Verify the time and date of the interview. Know the name of the person you are to see. Write the name on a note card to carry with you. Allow plenty of time for travel. Plan to arrive a few minutes early. Take your resume and a pen to fill out an application form. Do not take anyone with you.

Before starting the interview, you may be asked to fill out a job application form. Employers often use these forms to compare the qualifications of job applicants. Complete the form accurately. Look over the entire form before you begin. Follow all instructions and place the requested information in the correct spaces. Try not to leave blank spaces. If a question does not apply to you, draw a line through the space or write "does not apply." Print neatly and legibly. Use correct spelling and grammar.

Begin the interview with a firm handshake and a friendly greeting. Do not sit until asked to do so. Sit up straight. Look directly at the interviewer. Listen carefully to the questions you are asked. Respond positively, concisely, and honestly. Show you are enthusiastic about the position. Speak slowly and clearly, using good grammar. Answer questions verbally rather than merely nodding your head.

When the interviewer asks if you have any questions, the interview is nearing an end. This is your time to ask questions. A thoughtful question about the company or the position can indicate your interest. Questions about wages are not appropriate until you have been offered the job.

After answering your questions, the interviewer may offer you the job. In most cases, the interviewer needs time to decide. The interviewer may indicate that you will be called, or you should call by a certain date. If not, ask when you may inquire about the job. Before you leave, thank the interviewer for taking time to meet with you.

If you receive a job offer, let the employer know as soon as possible whether you will accept the position. Thank the employer for offering you the position. This is true even if you decide not to accept the job.

Don't be discouraged if you do not get the job. Instead, review the interview mentally and note where you can improve. This will prepare you for the next interview. Eventually, you will find the right job.

Developing Your Employability Skills

Finding a job is just the beginning. Put as much effort into succeeding on the job as you did into your job search. Read the characteristics of a good employee listed in 22-21. People with these qualities most often find their careers a rewarding part of life.

Courtesy, respect for others, and patience describe some of the most important qualities people need for all aspects of their life including their work. Manners affect your relationships with your employer, coworkers, and clients or customers.

Dependability, honesty, and loyalty are qualities desired in the workplace. Being dependable means being at work when you are scheduled to be there. It means giving your best for the entire work time. It includes coming on time, working except for normal breaks, and staying through your scheduled time.

Being honest is more than not lying or not stealing. Honest people give their best skills or abilities to their job tasks. They separate their personal lives from their business tasks. They do not take care of personal matters during work hours or use work property.

A loyal person is supportive of the goals of the business. Sometimes this means keeping certain matters private. Even when problems arise, the loyal employee works to resolve them without undue hurt or stress.

A good employee is enthusiastic and shows initiative. Enthusiastic people are eager to learn, and others are eager to teach them, 22-22. *Drive* is another word for showing initiative. A person who shows initiative can work without being told to do each task and without constant supervision. Most importantly, initiative

makes a difference between average and high performance. Even gifted people can and do fail in careers unless they work hard.

When you accept a job, you are agreeing to follow rules and regulations. By following directions, you avoid confusing others and wasting time and resources. Accepting criticism is a way of learning. A mature person can accept criticism without becoming angry or defensive.

Your interpersonal skills with your coworkers and clients or customers will help you succeed. Your willingness to help others and be cooperative make you a true member of your workplace family.

Try your best to develop these qualities. Each position you successfully fill will bring you one step closer to reaching your career goals.

Careers are ever-changing. By adapting and changing to new conditions, you further your career opportunities and your own development. Invest in your career by trying new experiences and getting additional training and education.

1—Reflect: Review these qualities of a good employee. Which three do you feel are the most important?

Qualities of a Good Employee

- Courteous and friendly
- Respectful of others
- Patient
- Dependable
- Honest
- Loyal
- Enthusiastic
- Shows initiative
- Follows rules and regulations
- Follows directions
- Accepts criticism
- Willing to help others
- Clean, neat appearance
- Cooperative
- Adaptable
- Invests in career

1

22-21 ————————————————
A good employee will try to develop these qualities.

22-22 ————————————————
Employees who are enthusiastic on the job are more likely to perform tasks well.

Summary

1

- Many work opportunities exist in child and family services. There are exciting careers working directly and working on behalf of children and families.
- Some careers involve creating or selling child-related products. Others exist in the children's entertainment field. Still other people work as entrepreneurs.
- Knowing your interests, aptitudes, and abilities is essential before making career plans.
- People who enter a child and family services career must have certain personal characteristics and professional qualifications.
- Developing a career plan can help you determine goals and begin to work toward them.
- Many of the trends in the child and family services careers are related to the growing number of children in child care and the need for more family services.
- You can prepare for future roles now by joining student organizations; developing leadership, teamwork, and communications skills; finding part-time jobs in child and family services; and developing employability skills.

Reviewing Key Points

2

1. What is the difference between a job and a career?
2. Briefly describe the differences among entry-level, paraprofessional, and professional positions.
3. Briefly describe the procedure for receiving the Child Development Associate (CDA) Credential.
4. List at least three positions social workers might fill if they are involved in child welfare and family services.
5. Briefly describe three careers in which people work on behalf of children and families.
6. Describe two pros and two cons of operating your own business.
7. Explain why your interests, aptitudes, and abilities should be considered in career planning.
8. Briefly explain what is involved in writing a career plan.
9. Why are child care workers in such demand today?
10. What is an accredited child care program?
11. Name three expanding job opportunities in child and family services.
12. Why is it beneficial for teens to learn parliamentary procedure?
13. List five qualities of a good leader.
14. List three part-time jobs working with children you might be able to obtain now.
15. How can you find out about job openings?
16. What types of information are included on a resume?
17. What items should you take with you on a job interview?

Learning by Doing

1. Scan a newspaper's classified ads section and list job opportunities in child-related areas.
2. Contact community colleges and universities in your area. Research child-related course offerings.
3. Create a brochure for parents on selecting an accredited child care program.
4. Conduct a mock meeting in your classroom using parliamentary procedure.
5. Role-play a job interview. Videotape and evaluate the interview.

Thinking Critically

1. In a small group, brainstorm ideas for child-related entrepreneur-ships. Choose one idea and discuss how you could start this business.

2. Research organizations and activities in your school and community in which you can develop leadership skills.

3. Write an essay entitled "What I Am Doing Now to Prepare for My Future."

Glossary

A

abilities. Skills that have been learned or developed. (22)

abstinence. Refraining from sexual intercourse. (15)

active listening. Listening style in which the receiver actively participates in the communication process. (4)

adolescence. A transitional time during which people graduate from the dependency of childhood to the independence of adulthood. (15)

adoption. The process of transferring a child's legal guardianship from his or her birthparents to adoptive parents. (3)

adoptive families. Families that include adoptive parents and one or more adopted children. (3)

afterbirth stage. Third stage of labor when the placenta, or afterbirth, is delivered. (9)

agency adoption. Type of adoption in which adoptive parents work with a state-licensed adoption agency. (5)

AIDS (acquired immunodeficiency syndrome). A disease that breaks down the immune system leaving the body vulnerable to diseases that a healthy body could easily resist. AIDS is caused by the HIV virus and is often transmitted sexually. (6)

alcoholism. A condition in which a person's drinking causes the person to hurt himself or herself and others. (19)

alternate play behavior. Behavior during which a child does something and waits for a response from playmates, thus encouraging the repetition of the activity. (13)

alternatives. The various options available from which to choose. (2)

amniocentesis. Prenatal test usually given during weeks 14 to 16 in pregnancy in which a sample of amniotic fluid is drawn and tested for possible congenital disorders. (7)

amniotic fluid. Fluid inside the amnio-chorionic membrane that regulates the baby's temperature, cushions the baby against injury, and allows the baby to move around easily. (6)

anemia. Iron deficiency. (7)

anorexia nervosa. An eating disorder in which people voluntarily starve themselves for fear they will gain weight. (15)

Apgar test. A test that is used at birth (and again five to ten minutes later) to evaluate a baby's overall physical condition. (9)

aptitudes. Talents that come naturally to a person. (22)

artificial insemination. Assisted reproductive technology that involves inserting sperm into the upper part of the vagina or the uterus, making conception more likely. (5)

attention deficit/hyperactivity disorder (ADHD). A learning disorder that causes children to have shorter-than-average attention spans. (21)

au pair. A young person who comes from another country to live with and provide child care for a family. (20)

authoritarian. Style of parenting in which punishment and control are used frequently. Power and authority are the main means of guiding and disciplining the child. (17)

authoritative. Style of parenting in which parents use set limits but allow freedom within those limits. Communication is the main means to guide and discipline the child. (17)

B

binge eating disorder. An eating disorder in which people uncontrollably consume large quantities of food but do not purge afterward. (15)

birth center. A nonhospital facility that provides prenatal care and delivery services. (8)

birthing room. A special room in a hospital where a woman can labor, deliver, recover, and rest. (8)

blastocyst. A hollow ball of cells that implants itself in the uterus; name for a developing baby from after the zygote stage until the embryo stage. (6)

bonding. Formation of close emotional ties between parent and child. (9)

Brazelton scale. An assessment for newborns that can identify problems not requiring emergency medical attention. This scale checks the baby's movement, reflexes, responses, and general state. (9)

breech delivery. Delivery in which the baby's rear end or feet are delivered first. (9)

bulimia nervosa. An eating disorder, sometimes called the "binge-purge syndrome," in which persons uncontrollably eat large quantities of food, and then purge themselves of the food by vomiting or taking laxatives or diuretics. (15)

bullying. The infliction of physical, verbal, or emotional abuse on a person by one or more people. (19)

C

career. A series of related jobs and work experiences. (22)

career plan. The path you take toward reaching your goal—employment within a career. (22)

certified nurse-midwife. A nurse-practitioner who has had extensive training and experience delivering babies and providing prenatal care. (7)

cesarean delivery. An operation in which a baby is delivered through incisions in the mother's abdomen and uterus. (9)

chat room. A feature of the Internet that provides a forum for several people to communicate at the same time. (17)

child abuse. A nonaccidental injury or pattern of injuries to a child. It is damage to a child for which there is no reasonable explanation. (19)

child care. Child care provided by a caregiver other than a child's parents. (20)

child neglect. Failure to provide a child's basic needs. (19)

child support payments. Payments one parent makes to another to provide financial support for their children following a divorce; usually court-ordered. (18)

children with special needs. Term often used to describe both children with disabilities and gifted children. (21)

chorionic villi sampling (CVS). Prenatal test, usually given the tenth week of pregnancy, that involves removing a sample of fetal tissue studied for congenital disorders.(7)

chromosome. A threadlike structure that carries the hereditary information of genes. Humans have 23 pairs of chromosomes in every cell of their bodies. (5)

circumcision. Surgical removal of the foreskin of the head of the penis. (9)

closed adoption. Adoption in which no contact occurs between the birthparents and the adoptive family. (5)

colic. Severe and intermittent abdominal pain caused by air or gas in a baby's digestive system. (10)

colostrum. A thick, yellowish liquid in a mother's breasts that nourishes the baby until the mother's milk supply is established. Colostrum contains many important substances and antibodies. (8)

communication. Any means by which people send or receive messages. (4)

conception. The union of a sperm and egg cell. Conception is the beginning of pregnancy. (6)

congenital disorders. Disorders a person is born with that result from heredity. (5)

consequences. The positive and negative results of each available alternative. (2)

conservation. The understanding that certain properties remain the same even if they change in shape or appearance. (14)

contractions. Pains felt during labor when the muscles of the uterus tense in order to open the cervix and push the baby out of the uterus. (9)

cooperative child care. Child care centers where parents provide many of the services needed to operate the center. (20)

cooperative play. Playing with others in a play activity. (12)

cradle cap. A condition in which a scaly crust appears on a baby's scalp. (10)

crisis. An unforeseen situation that demands adjustment by all members of a family. (19)

cultural bias. Belief that a person's own cultural or ethnic group is better than any other group. (3)

cultural traditions. A set of beliefs, customs, and behaviors shared by members of a cultural or ethnic group. (1)

custody. The rights and responsibilities of raising a child and making decisions about the child's care, upbringing, and overall welfare; often determined by the court in a divorce case. (18)

D

decision-making process. A six-step process that can help you make careful, responsible, and informed decisions. (2)

dedication. A deep level of commitment; one of the qualities needed for effective parenting. (1)

delivery stage. Second stage of labor, which begins when the cervix is fully dilated and ends when the baby is born. (9)

development. A change of function as a result of growth. (4)

diaper rash. Skin rash caused by bacteria that build up on the warm moist skin in a baby's diaper area. (10)

dilation stage. The first stage of labor when the cervix dilates so the baby can be pushed out of the uterus. (9)

discipline. The process of intentionally teaching and training a child to behave in appropriate ways. (17)

domestic violence. Any physical, emotional, or sexual behavior intended to harm a family member. (19)

drug abuse. The use of a drug for a reason that is not medical. (19)

dual-career family. A family in which both spouses work outside the home. (2)

dysfunctional family. A family that cannot function properly because of certain overwhelming problems. (19)

E

eating disorder. An abnormal eating pattern that causes mental and physical health risks. (15)

egg. Female sex cell that carries 23 chromosomes from the mother and will unite with a sperm to create a baby. (5)

egocentric. Self-centeredness of young children whose main concern is themselves. (12)

e-mail. The feature of the Internet that allows people to send electronic messages to one another. (3)

embryo. Name for the developing baby from the second to the eighth weeks of pregnancy. (6)

emotional abuse. The use of words to belittle, threaten, or exert control over another person. (19)

emotional development. The recognition of feelings or emotions and the expression of those feelings. (4)

emotional disorder. A limitation in the way a person functions emotionally and socially. (21)

emotional neglect. The failure to provide children with love and affection. (19)

endometrium. The inner lining of the uterus. (5)

entrepreneurship. A business that is owned and operated by one person. (22)

entry-level job. A job that requires little or no education and training after high school. (22)

enuresis. Bed-wetting, which may be caused by physical or emotional problems. (13)

environment. Everything in a person's surroundings. (4)

epidural. A regional anesthetic that can be injected into the spinal cord during labor to take away feeling in the lower half of the body. (9)

episiotomy. Small cut made at the opening of the birth canal to allow more room for a baby to be delivered. (9)

Erikson's theory of personality development. In this eight-stage theory, each stage presents conflicts that require individuals to modify their personalities and adjust to their social environment. (16)

ethnic diversity. Representation by more than one cultural or ethnic group. (3)

ethnic group. A group of people with a common racial, national, tribal, religious, or cultural origin or background. (1)

ethnic identity. How a person sees himself or herself as a member of a particular ethnic group. (1)

extended family. Family unit that includes all relatives in a family, such as grandparents, aunts, uncles, and cousins; family that extends beyond the immediate family. (3)

F

fallopian tubes. Two tubes through which an egg travels to the uterus; fertilization often occurs here. Each fallopian tube connects to the uterus at one end and lies close to an ovary at the other end. (5)

family. Two or more people who are related by birth, marriage, adoption, or other circumstances. (3)

Family and Medical Leave Act. Law that allows certain employees to take up to 12 weeks of unpaid leave after the birth or adoption of a child, when a family member is seriously ill, or when the employee is seriously ill. (8)

family life cycle. Six-stage cycle that explains how families change over time as they expand and contract in size. (3)

family-centered childbirth. Childbirth method based on the belief childbirth affects the family as a unit. (9)

family planning. A couple's commitment to making decisions about their reproductive capabilities; includes decisions about the number, timing, and spacing of any children born. (5)

fetal alcohol syndrome (FAS). A pattern of physical and mental disabilities caused by excessive or steady alcohol consumption during pregnancy. (7)

fetus. The name for a developing baby from the ninth week of pregnancy until birth. (6)

flexibility. The ability to adapt to new and different circumstances; one of the qualities needed for effective parenting. (1)

fontanel. Soft spot on the top of a baby's head. (10)

Food Guide Pyramid. An outline of what to eat each day based on national guidelines for healthy eating. (7)

foster family. A family unit that serves as a substitute family for a child. (3)

Freud's theory of personality development. A theory based on three aspects of human functioning that Freud labeled the *id*, the *ego*, and the *superego*. (16)

G

gangs. Groups of bullies who seek to inflict power through physical means. (19)

gender role. A person's behaviors, attitudes, and beliefs about men and women. (13)

gene. The basic unit of heredity; genes carry all the characteristics that will transfer from parent to child. (5)

genetic counseling. Counseling that offers scientific information and advice about heredity. This advice is based on medical studies and family histories, especially the risks of congenital disorders. (5)

gifted. A child who has outstanding skills in either a general sense or a specific ability. (21)

goal. A direction or end toward which you work. (2)

growth. A process that begins at the moment of conception and continues until adulthood. (4)

guidance. Directing, supervising, and influencing a child's behavior. (17)

H

hereditary. Genetically passed from a parent to an unborn child. (2)

heredity. All the traits that are passed down from one generation to the next. (4)

heritage. All that has been passed down through generations in a family. (1)

HIV (human immunodeficiency virus). A virus that causes the disease AIDS. HIV is often transmitted sexually; has no cure. (6)

hyperactive. Being overly and uncontrollably active. (21)

I

identification. Unconsciously adopting the behavior patterns of another person. (17)

imaginative play. A type of play in which children pretend to be persons or objects other than themselves. (13)

"I" messages. Sentences that describe a thought, feeling, or other experience in the singular first person manner. (4)

imitation. Intentionally copying the behavior of others. (17)

immunization. Treatment that prevents people from developing certain diseases. (11)

incest. Sexual activity between persons who are closely related. (19)

inclusion. Practice of placing students of varying abilities in the same class. (21)

independent adoption. Adoption in which adoptive parents do not use an adoption agency. (5)

Individualized Educational Plan (IEP). A written agreement that sets educational goals for a student with disabilities; it is made between the student, his or her family, teachers, and the school. (21)

infant. Child from birth to one year of age; a baby. (11)

infant mortality rate. Rate that indicates the average number of infant deaths per 1,000 live births. (2)

infertility. Inability to conceive despite having intercourse regularly for at least one year. (5)

intellectual development. The development of a person's mental and thinking abilities. (4)

interests. Activities that appeal to a person over a period of time. (22)

Internet. A computer linkup of individuals, groups, and organizations in government, business, and education. (3)

in vitro fertilization. Assisted reproductive technology in which an egg is removed from a woman's ovary and fertilized with a man's sperm in a glass dish. The fertilized egg is later transferred to the woman's uterus, where it should implant. (5)

J

job. Work a person does to earn money; a single work experience. (22)

job sharing. An employment situation in which two employees share one full-time position. This can allow both employees more time to be with their families. (8)

K

Kohlberg's theory of moral development. A theory based on three levels of moral development that Kohlberg labeled the *preconventional, conventional,* and *postconventional levels.* (16)

L

Lamaze method. Type of prepared childbirth method in which parents attend weekly classes to learn what to expect in the final stages of pregnancy and during labor and delivery. (9)

large motor skills. Skills that require the use of the large muscles of the body, such as the trunk, neck, arms, and legs. (11)

leadership. The ability to direct and influence others. (22)

learning disability. Type of disability that involves a limitation in the way a person's brain sorts and uses information. (21)

Leboyer method. Childbirth method that focuses on the birth experience of the baby; it makes birth process less shocking and more comforting for the baby. (9)

life skills. The eating, dressing, and grooming skills children must learn in order to provide routine care for themselves. (12)

lifestyle. The typical way of life a person chooses for himself or herself. (3)

lisping. Speech pattern that may occur in preschoolers because they still have difficulty pronouncing some sounds, such as the *s* sound. (13)

logical consequences. Results set by parents to show what logically happens following certain acts of misbehavior. (17)

long-term goals. Goals you want to accomplish months or years from now. (2)

M

Maslow's hierarchy of human needs. A theory that arranges human needs in order of their priority. Lower-level needs must be met before higher needs can be recognized and fulfilled. (16)

maturation. The overall process of growth and development from infancy to adulthood. (4)

menstruation. The monthly shedding of the extra growth of the endometrium that sloughs off and passes out of the uterus and through the vagina. (5)

mental disability. Type of disability involving limitations in the way a person's mind functions. (21)

mental retardation. A condition that exists before age 18 and includes both intellectual functioning at a level that is significantly below average and deficits in adaptive behavior. (21)

miscarriage. The natural ending of a pregnancy before the fifth month; spontaneous abortion. (6)

mitten grasp. Grasp made with the palm and fingers opposing the thumb. (11)

moral development. The gradual process of learning to behave in ways that reflect an understanding of the difference between right and wrong. (1)

morals. Beliefs people have that help them distinguish between right and wrong behavior. (1)

multicultural. Including people from more than one cultural or ethnic group. (3)

multiple classification. Intellectual understanding that objects may fit into more than one category. (14)

N

nanny. A specially trained child care provider who provides 24-hour child care. (20)

natural consequences. Results that naturally occur when a certain behavior is performed. (17)

negative reinforcement. Response to a behavior that makes a person less likely to repeat the behavior. (17)

nonverbal communication. Any means of sending messages without using words. (22)

nuclear family. A family that includes a husband, wife, and the biological or adopted children they have together. (3)

nurturance. Loving care and attention; one of the qualities needed for effective parenting. (1)

O

object permanence. Concept that unseen objects have not necessarily disappeared. (11)

obstetrician. A doctor who specializes in providing medical care for pregnant women and delivering babies. (7)

open adoption. Adoption in which there is some degree of contact between the birthparents and the adoptive family. (5)

ovaries. Two almond-shaped organs in which a woman's eggs are made and stored. (5)

ovulation. The process by which the ovaries release a mature egg each month. (5)

P

parallel play. Play in which two children play separately, but beside one another, in the same activity. (12)

paraprofessional. A person with education and training beyond high school to prepare for his or her work. (22)

parental leave. Paid or unpaid leave from work to tend to parenting duties; is called *maternity leave* for mothers or *paternity leave* for fathers. (8)

parenting. The name given to the process of raising a child. (1)

parliamentary procedure. An orderly method of conducting business in a group setting. (22)

pediatrician. A doctor who specializes in providing medical care for infants and children. (8)

peer violence. Violence among people of the same peer group; often violence among children. (19)

permissive. Style of parenting in which parents allow their children to do whatever they want. Very little, if any, consistency, limits, guidance, and discipline are used. (17)

personal priorities. Principles, concepts, and beliefs a person holds as important. (1)

physical abuse. Intentional infliction of physical injury on a child. (19)

physical development. The changes in a person's size, height, or weight. (4)

physical disability. Type of disability involving limitations of a person's body or its function. (21)

physical neglect. The failure to provide sufficient food, clothing, shelter, medical care, education, guidance, and supervision for a child. (19)

Piaget's theory of intellectual development. A theory that states that people pass through four distinct stages as they develop intellectually. (16)

pincer grasp. A refined grasp in which objects are picked up with just the thumb and forefinger. (11)

placenta. A special organ formed during pregnancy that functions as the interchange between the developing baby and its mother. (6)

play group. Informal group in which parents arrange for their children to play together on a regular basis in each other's homes. (20)

positive behavior. Behavior that is acceptable, healthy, and satisfying for the person using it and others around him or her. (17)

positive reinforcement. A response that makes a person more likely to repeat a behavior. (17)

postpartum depression. Period of depression a woman may feel, for various reasons, after giving birth. (9)

postpartum period. Period of time following delivery of a baby when the woman recovers from pregnancy and childbirth; lasts from delivery until about six weeks later. (9)

pregnancy-induced hypertension (PIH). A complication of pregnancy that affects a woman's kidneys, heart, or blood circulation. (6)

prejudice. An unfair opinion or judgment formed about people of another group without getting to know them. (3)

prenatal care. All the special care a woman and her baby need during pregnancy; includes obtaining medical care, monitoring nutrition and weight gain, exercising, and avoiding factors that increase health risk. (7)

prenatal development. All the development that occurs between conception and birth. (6)

prepared childbirth. Birth in which both parents have been taught about the birth process, often in childbirth classes. (8)

preschooler. A child who is three, four, or five, years old. (13)

primary caregiver. The person who spends the most time with a baby. (8)

primary sex characteristics. Physical changes related to the development of the reproductive organs during puberty. (15)

problem ownership. Determining who owns and is most concerned with or upset by a problem. (4)

professional. A person who has advanced training and education in a specific area. (22)

puberty. The process through which the body becomes capable of reproduction. (15)

punishment. Penalty a person receives for doing something wrong. (17)

R

references. Persons other than relatives whom employers can call to discuss a job applicant's qualifications for employment. (22)

reflexes. Automatic reactions a baby has to certain stimuli. Examples are the rooting, grasping, stepping, Moro or startle, and Babinski reflexes. (10)

regression behavior. Reverting to past behavior a person has outgrown; commonly occurs when a child is in crisis. (18)

responsibility. Accepting and meeting obligations without reminder or direction; being accountable for one's actions. (17)

resume. A document that contains detailed information about your education, work experience, and qualifications for employment. (22)

reversibility. Concept that objects can return to their original condition after they have been changed. (14)

Rh factor disorder. A disorder that can complicate pregnancy. It occurs when an Rh- mother gives birth to a baby who is Rh+. (6)

role. A set of behaviors related to a certain function you assume in life. (2)

rubella. A virus that can complicate pregnancy, causing miscarriage, stillbirth, or congenital disorders; also called *German Measles*. (6)

S

school-age years. The years in childhood between ages six and twelve. (14)

secondary sex characteristics. Body changes during puberty that are not directly related to the development of the reproductive organs. (15)

self-care children. Children who stay home alone and must attend to their own needs until their parents return home; sometimes called *latchkey children*. (14)

self-concept. The mental image a person has of himself or herself. (4)

self-control. The ability to govern one's own actions, impulses, and desires. (17)

self-demand feeding. Method of feeding a baby in which feeding times are determined by the baby's hunger rather than by a set schedule. (10)

self-esteem. How a person feels about his or her self-concept. (4)

separation anxiety. Overwhelming fear shown by infants when their primary caregivers are not in sight. (11)

seriation. The ability to order groups of things by size, weight, age, or any common property. (14)

sexual abuse. Forcing a person to observe or engage in sexual activities. (19)

sexually transmitted diseases (STDs). A number of infections and conditions that are passed from one person to another through sexual contact. (6)

Shaken Baby Syndrome. A set of symptoms that occur when an infant or small child has been violently shaken. (19)

short-term goals. Goals you hope to accomplish soon, within a few days or months. (2)

siblings. Brothers and sisters. (17)

single-parent family. A family that includes one parent and his or her biological or adopted children. (3)

small motor skills. Skills that require the use of the small muscles of the body, such as those of the eyes, hands, feet, fingers, and toes. (11)

social development. The process of learning to relate to other people. (4)

sperm. Male sex cell that carries 23 chromosomes from the father and will unite with an egg to create a baby. (5)

stepfamily. A family that includes a married couple, each spouse's children from previous relationships, and any biological or adopted children they have together. (3)

stereotypes. Widely-held beliefs that all members of a group are alike. (3)

stillbirth. The natural ending of a pregnancy after the fifth month; spontaneous abortion. (6)

stranger anxiety. Intense fear of strangers that occurs in the last half of the first year. (11)

stress. The tension caused by a condition or situation that demands a mental or physical adjustment. (14)

stuttering. Speech pattern in which long pauses are injected into sentences, sentences are stopped midway and started again, or one sound or phrase is repeated. (13)

sudden infant death syndrome (SIDS). A syndrome in which a seemingly healthy infant dies without warning; more common among infants of parents who smoke. (7)

support group. A group of people who share a similar problem or concern and hold meetings to talk, listen, and support one another. (4)

support system. People, institutions, and organizations that people can turn to in times of need. (4)

T

teachable moments. Spontaneous learning experiences that can be used to expand children's natural curiosity. (12)

teamwork. Involves working with other people to achieve common goals. Teamwork is vital in almost every career. (22)

technology. The use of scientific knowledge for practical purposes. (3)

temper tantrums. Violent outbursts of negative behavior common in toddlers and some preschoolers. (12)

testes (testicles). Two oval-shaped organs in which sperm are produced. (5)

time/life line. A graph that represents goals a person or couple plans to reach throughout life. (2)

time-out. Punishment involving the removal of a child from the presence of others for a short period of time. (17)

toddler. A child from his or her first birthday to his or her third birthday; children ages one and two. (12)

traditional childbirth. Childbirth method in which attention is focused on the health of the mother and baby and on the woman's comfort; anesthetics are given as needed, and the baby's health is monitored. (9)

trial and error. Choosing behaviors through a process of testing. Children keep trying new ways of doing something until they find one that works. (17)

trimester. A three-month period. Pregnancy consists of three trimesters. (6)

U

ultrasound test. A prenatal test in which sound waves are used to create a "map" of the fetus. It shows the position and development of the fetus. (7)

umbilical cord. A flexible cord that contains blood vessels and connects the placenta to the developing baby. (6)

uterus. A hollow, muscular organ which holds and nourishes a fertilized egg as it develops. (5)

V

vas deferens. Two long, thin tubes in the male which connect the epididymis to the ejaculatory duct; mature sperm are stored here. (5)

visitation rights. A parent's court-ordered rights to visit his or her child during certain times and conditions; commonly granted to the parent who does not live with the child following a divorce. (18)

W

weaning. Phasing out of taking milk from a breast or bottle. (11)

"we" messages. Messages that imply two or more people are jointly involved and affected by a problem situation. (4)

Y

"you" messages. Messages that place all the blame for a problem on others, creating defensiveness and resistance. (4)

Z

zygote. Single-celled organism that is formed when the separate nuclei of sperm and egg combine into one nucleus. (6)

Photo Credits

1-3 David Hoppper
1-4 Gerber Products
1-5 Nancy Henke-Konopasek
1-6 Scott Gauthier
1-8 David Hopper
1-9 Texas Dept. of Commerce, Richard
    Reynolds
1-10 David Hopper
1-11 Landscape Structures, Inc.
Chapter 2 opening photo: David Hopper
2-2 David Hopper
2-3 David Hopper
2-7 Thornridge High School
2-10 Jose Nieto
2-13 Cholla Runnels
3-10 Landscape Structures, Inc.
Filler: David Hopper
4-1 Bristol-Meyers Squibb Co.
4-2 BigToys
4-3 BigToys
4-5 David Hopper
4-10 David Hopper
Chapter 5 opening photo: David Hopper
5-1 David Hopper
5-3 David Hopper
5-6 Women's Center Hospital
Chapter 6 opening photo: March of Dimes
    Birth Defects Foundation
6-4 National Foundation—March of
    Dimes
6-6 March of Dimes Birth Defects
    Foundation
6-8 March of Dimes Birth Defects
    Foundation
7-8 David Hopper
7-11 Women's Center Hospital
8-2 Billie Hainsey
8-3 Billie Hainsey
8-5 Olympia Fields Osteopathic Hospital
8-8 Cholla Runnels
8-9 Monica Willson
8-12 Todd Scheffers
8-15 Monica Willson
9-5 Cholla Runnels
9-7 Women's Center Hospital
9-8 Women's Center Hospital
9-14 Matthew Hodges
9-15 Women's Center Hospital
10-1 Monica Willson

10-3 Nancy Henke-Konopasek
10-4 Susan Hutter
10-5 Monica Willson
10-7 Jacob Cullen Darlinger
10-10 Johnson & Johnson Baby
    Products Co.
10-11 Johnson & Johnson Baby
    Products Co.
10-14 Nancy Henke-Konopasek
10-15 Billie Hainsey
11-1 Bonnie Ford
11-2 Cholla Runnels
11-4 Cholla Runnels
11-5 Cholla Runnels
11-7 Cholla Runnels
11-8 Cholla Runnels
11-10 David Hopper
11-12 Monica Willson
11-13 Monica Willson
11-14 Monica Willson
11-18 Billie Hainsey
11-19 David Hopper
12-2 Todd Scheffers
12-5 Cholla Runnels
12-7 Ross Laboratories
12-8 Susan Fincher
12-10 Susan Fincher
12-12 Ross Laboratories
12-15 Nancy Henke-Konopasek
12-18 Cholla Runnels
13-2 Pam Ryder
13-4 David Hopper
13-5 Cholla Runnels
13-6 Nancy Henke-Konopasek
13-7 Nancy Henke-Konopasek
13-8 David Hopper
13-12 Cholla Runnels
13-14 David Hopper
13-15 Cholla Runnels
13-16 Billie Hainsey
13-18 Cholla Runnels
13-20 David Hopper
Chapter 14 opening photo: GE Plastics
14-3 State of New Hampshire: David
    Brownell
14-4 Johnni Laschober
14-6 David Hopper
14-8 Cholla Runnels
14-12 Cholla Runnels

Index

A

Abilities, 523, 524
Abstinence, 365
Active listening, 88, 89
Adolescence, 359
Adoption, 52-54, 112, 113
Adoptive families, 52
Afterbirth stage, 189
Age, factors in parenting, 41, 42
Agency adoption, 112
Aging stage, family life cycle, 65, 66
AIDS (acquired immunodeficiency
    syndrome), 134
Alcoholism, 451
    teens and, 363, 364
Allowances, 414
Alternate play behavior, 316
Alternatives, 46
Amniocentesis, 143
Amniotic fluid, 121
Anemia, 146
Anorexia nervosa, 362
Apgar test, 193
Aptitudes, 523
Artificial insemination, 112
Attention deficit/hyperactivity disorder
    (ADHD), 501-503
Au pair, 474
Authoritarian, 404
Authoritative, 405
Autonomy, 384
Awareness improvement of infants, 243

B

Babinski reflex, 210
Baby supplies, 163-169
    bath, 168
    bedtime, 168, 169
    clothing, 166, 167
    diapers, 165, 166
    furniture, 164, 165
    mealtime, 168
    travel, 169
Bathing newborns, 214
Beginning stage, family life cycle, 63
Behavior, 401-408
    authoritarian guidance, 404
    authoritative guidance, 405
    direct teaching, 402, 403
        identification, 403
        imitation, 403
        permissive guidance, 404, 405
        reinforcement, 403, 404
        trial and error, 403
Binge eating disorder, 362
Birth center, 163
Birthing room, 162, 163
Blastocyst, 121
Bonding, 195-197
Brazleton scale, 193
Breast-feeding, 169-172
Breech delivery, 192
Bulimia nervosa, 362
Bullying, 460

C

Career plan, 526
Careers,
    accredited child care programs, 527, 528
    child care personnel, 516
    child care settings, 528
    children's librarians, 518
    communication skills, 531, 532
    definition, 515
    developing a career plan, 526
    education programs, 528
    employability skills, 534, 535
    entrepreneurship, 522, 523
    entry-level openings, 527
    factors in parenting, 37-39
    health services, 519
    interviewing for a job, 533, 534
    leadership, 530
    nannies, 517
    parent educators, 520
    part-time employment, 532-534
    personal characteristics needed to work
        with adult family members, 525
    personal characteristics needed to work
        with children, 524, 525
    preparation, 529-535
    products and services for children, 521
    qualifications, 524-526
    resume, 533
    risks in teen parenting, 44, 45
    self-assessment, 523, 524
    social workers, 518
    student organizations, 529

teachers, 517
teamwork, 530, 531
trends affecting, 526-529
working directly with children and
    families, 516-519
working on behalf of children and
    families, 519, 520
writers, artists, entertainers, 521
youth and recreation leaders, 518
Certified nurse-midwife, 139
Cesarean delivery, 192, 193
Characteristics of strong families, 82-85
communicating, 83, 84
managing resources and
    sharing responsibilities, 84
sharing family rituals and traditions, 85
sharing moral standards, 85
spending time together, 83
Chat room, 422
Child abuse, 453-458
abusers, 455-457
caregivers and, 456, 457
definition, 453
Shaken Baby Syndrome (SBS), 454, 455
stopping, 457, 458
Child care, 471-489
adult-child ratio, 481
characteristics of caregivers, 481, 482
church-linked, 476
concerns of parents, 483-485
consistency, 482
cooperative, 477
deciding to use, 472
definition, 471
drop-in centers, 479
employer-sponsored, 476
evaluating, 482, 483
government-sponsored, 475, 476
in the caregiver's home, 474, 475
in the child's home, 473, 474
managing the child care
    experience, 485, 486
nationally franchised centers, 478, 479
physical setting, 480
play groups, 478
privately owned centers, 478
program, 480
school-age, 479, 480
selecting, 480-482
types, 473-480
university-linked, 476, 477
Child Development Associate Credential
    (CDA), 516
Child development charts,
infants, 255-263
preschoolers, 319-322
school-age children, 352-355

teens, 373
toddlers, 290-295
Child development theories, 379-399
Child neglect, 453-458
Child services careers, 515-537
Child support payments, 440
Childbearing stage, family life cycle, 64
Childbirth, 183-203
bonding, 195-197
breech, 192
Cesarean, 192, 193
family-centered, 190, 191
hospital procedures, 185
Lamaze, 191, 192
Leboyer, 192
medications, 186, 187
methods, 189-193
neonatal care, 193-195
postpartum period, 197-200
signs of labor, 183, 184
stages of labor, 187-189
traditional, 190
Childbirth preparation decisions, 159-161
birth center, 163
birthing room, 162, 163
choosing a caregiver, 176, 177
choosing a pediatrician, 177, 178
employment decisions, 173-176
hospital delivery room, 161, 162
Children with special needs, 496-506
definition, 496
emotional disorders, 503
gifted, 503-506
inclusion, 506
learning disabilities, 500-503
mental disabilities, 497, 498
physical disabilities, 499, 500
Chlamydia, 134
Chorionic villi sampling (CVS), 142
Chromosome, 108
Church-linked child care, 476
Circumcision, 195
Closed adoption, 113
Clothing, newborns, 166, 167
Colic, 218, 219
Colostrum, 170
Communication, 86-94
active listening, 88, 89
definition, 86
"I" messages, 90
problem ownership, 90
skills, 531, 532
techniques, 88-91
"we" messages, 91
"you" messages, 90, 91
Community influences, 70
Community resources, 94-97

Competitive sports, 331-334
Computer software and the Internet, 421-423
Conception, 119, 120
Concrete operational stage, Piaget, 381, 382
Conformity, 346, 347
Congenital disorders, 109
Consequences, 46
Conservation, 338, 339
Contractions, 184
Conventional level, Kohlberg, 392, 393
Cooperative child care, 477
Cooperative play, 284
Couples without children, 60
Cradle cap, 215
Crises, 449-469
    alcoholism, 451-453
    child abuse and neglect, 453-458
    definition, 449
    domestic violence, 459, 460
    drug abuse, 451-453
    gangs, bullies, and peer
        violence, 460-462
    missing children, 462, 463
    suicide, 463-466
    unemployment and financial, 450, 451
Cultural bias, 68
Cultural influences, 66, 67
Cultural traditions, 22
Custody, 439

D

Death, 443, 444
Decision-making,
    baby supplies, 163-169
    breast-feeding, 169-172
    caring for the baby, 172-178
    child care, 472
    childbirth, 159-161
    formula-feeding, 169-172
    parenting, 159-181
    place of birth, 161-163
    skills, 366
    teens, 366
Decision-making process, 46, 47
Dedication, 14
Delivery stage, 188, 189
Despair (Erikson), 388, 389
Development, 77-80
    definition, 78
    emotional, 79
    intellectual, 78
    patterns, 79, 80
    physical, 78
    rate, 80
    sequence, 80

social, 79
    trunk outward, 79, 80
    uniqueness of children, 80
Diaper rash, 217
Diapers, 165, 166
    newborns, 217
Dilation stage, 187, 188
Direct teaching, 402, 403
Discipline, 402
Diversity, 67
Divorce, 435-440
    after the divorce, 440
    children's reactions, 437-439
    legal proceedings, 439, 440
Domestic violence, 459, 460
Drop-in child care, 479
Drug abuse, 364, 452
    teens, 364
Dual-career families, 39
Dual work roles, 433-435
Dysfunctional family, 449

E

Eating disorder, 362
Education and health, 491-513
    adjustment to school, 494
    children with special needs, 496-506
    encouragement, 493
    homework, 494, 495
    inclusion, 506, 507
    Individualized Education Plan, 498
    parents' roles in education, 492-496
    parents' roles in health care, 507-510
    teachable moments, 493
Education risks, teen parenting, 44, 45
Egg, 106
Ego, 389
Egocentric, 278
E-mail, 72
Embryo, 121
Emotional abuse, 453, 454
Emotional changes, teen parenting, 43, 44
Emotional development, 79
Emotional development of infants, 249-252
    emotional responses, 251
    fear, 250, 251
    separation anxiety, 250, 251
    special objects, 249, 250
    spoiling babies, 252
    stranger anxiety, 250
Emotional development of preschoolers, 312-317
    gender roles, 315
    nightmares, 317
    play, 316, 317
Emotional development of school-age
    children, 342-347

conformity, 346, 347
parents and friends, 345, 346
Emotional development of teens, 366-372
dating, 369, 370
friendships, 368, 369
self-concept and self-esteem, 371, 372
Emotional development of toddlers,
282-288
guiding behavior, 286, 287
separation anxiety, 285, 286
temper tantrum, 287, 288
toys and play, 284, 285
Emotional disorder, 503
Emotional neglect, 454
Employer-sponsored child care, 476
Endometrium, 107
Entrepreneurship, 522, 523
Entry-level job, 516
Enuresis, 306
Environment, 81
Epidural, 186
Episiotomy, 189
Erikson's theory of personality
development, 382-389
Esteem needs (Maslow), 391
Ethnic diversity, 67
Ethnic group, 22
Ethnic identity, 22
Exercise during pregnancy, 150
Expectations about children and
parenting, 31-33
Extended family, 59, 60

F

Fallopian tubes, 107
Families,
adoption, 52-54
balancing work roles and, 431-435
birth, 52
characteristics of strong families, 82-85
child care options, 56-59
community influences, 70
concerns, 431-447
crises, 449-469
cultural influences, 66, 67
definition, 51
diversity, 67-69
divorce, 435-440
extended, 59, 60
family structures, 55-60
formation, 51-55
foster, 54, 55
functions, 60, 61
influence of marital relationships on
children, 82
lifestyle influences, 69, 70
marriage, 52

media influences, 70, 71, 419-423
morals, 21
moves, 444, 445
nuclear, 56
primary nurturing unit, 81, 82
remarriage and stepfamilies, 441
roles, 62, 63
serious illness, 442, 443
single-parent, 56-58
technological influences, 71-73
uniqueness, 66-73
Family and Medical Leave Act, 175
Family life cycle, 63-66
Family planning, 103-117
advantages, 103, 104
definition, 103
factors that influence decisions, 104, 105
genetic counseling, 109
heredity, 107, 108
infertility, 110, 111
issues, 108-114
reproduction, 106-108
Family services careers, 515-537
Family structures, 55-60
couples without children, 60
extended families, 59, 60
nuclear families, 56
single-parent families, 56-58
stepfamilies, 58, 59
Family-centered childbirth, 190, 191
Fears, infants, 250, 251
Feeding newborns, 212-214
Fetal alcohol syndrome (FAS), 152
Fetus, 121
Finances, factors in parenting, 37
Financial crises, 450, 451
Financial risks, teen parenting, 45, 46
Flexibility, 14, 15
Fontanel, 206
Food Guide Pyramid, 144-147
Formal operational stage (Piaget), 382
Formula-feeding, 169-172
Foster family, 54, 55
Freud's theory of personality
development, 389, 390
Furniture, baby, 164, 165

G

Gangs, 460
Gender determination, 120
Gender roles, 315, 425, 426
Gene, 108
Generativity (Erikson), 388
Genetic background, factors in
parenting, 41, 42
Genetic counseling, 109
Genital herpes, 133, 134

Gifted children, 503
Goal,
    definition, 34
    factors in parenting, 34-36
Gonorrhea, 133
Government-sponsored child care,
    475, 476
Grandparents, 65, 66
Grasping reflex, 210
Growth, 77-80
Guidance, 401-429
    behavior, 401-408
    consistency, 406
    definition, 402
    discipline, 405, 406
    honesty, 416-418
    media influences, 419-423
    misbehaving, 406-408
    punishment, 407, 408
    reasonable limits, 405, 406
    responsibility, 410-416
    role models, 408
    sexuality, 423-427
    sibling relationships, 408-410
Guilt (Erikson), 384, 385

H

Handedness, 304
Health, factors in parenting, 41, 42
Health and education, 491-513
    caring for sick children, 509
    childhood diseases chart, 510
    children with special needs, 496-506
    parents' roles in health care, 507-510
Health risks during pregnancy, 151-153
Health risks, teen parenting, 42, 43
Hereditary, 42
Heredity, 80
    role in reproduction, 107, 108
Heritage, 22
Herpes, 133, 134
HIV (human immunodeficiency virus), 134
Honesty, 416-418
Hospital delivery room, 161, 162
Hyperactive, 502

I

Id, 389
Identification, 403
Identity (Erikson), 386, 387
Illness, serious, 442, 443
Imaginative play, 317
"I" messages, 90
Imitation, 403
Immunization, 253
Incest, 454
Inclusion, 506
Independent adoption, 112

Individualized Educational Plan (IEP), 498
Industry (Erikson), 385, 386
Infant mortality rate, 43
Infants, 227-265
    child development charts, 255-263
    definition, 227
    emotional development, 249-252
    intellectual development, 240-248
    medical checkups, 253
    physical development, 228-240
    social development, 249-252
Inferiority (Erikson), 385, 386
Infertility, 110-114
    adoption, 112, 113
    artificial insemination, 112
    choosing an option, 113, 114
    fertility drugs, 112
    in vitro fertilization, 112
    surgery, 112
Influences on parenting decisions, 30-34
    desire to be parents, 31
    desire to influence a partner, 34
    expectations about children, 32, 33
    expectations about parenthood, 31, 32
    expressing marital love, 30
    pressure from family and friends, 33
Initiative (Erikson), 384, 385
Integrity (Erikson), 388, 389
Intellectual development definition, 78
Intellectual development of infants,
    240-248
    associations, 243, 244
    awareness improvement, 243
    brain growth and development,
        241, 242
    language development, 246-248
    learning by imitation, 246
    learning though play, 246
    memory development, 242, 243
    noticing similarities and differences, 245
    object permanence, 245, 246
    problem solving, 244, 245
    related to physical development, 242
Intellectual development of preschoolers,
    306-312
    language, 306-312
    reading and math, 311, 312
Intellectual development of school-age
    children, 336-342
    advances in thinking patterns, 338, 339
    conservation, 338, 339
    multiple classification, 338
    reversibility, 339
    school adjustments, 339, 340
    schoolwork and homework, 340-342
    seriation, 338
Intellectual development of teens, 365, 366
    decision-making skills, 366

Intellectual development of toddlers, 277-282
  books, 280, 281
  language, 281, 282
  toys and play, 279, 280
Interests, 523
Internet, 72, 421-423
Intimacy (Erikson), 387, 388
In vitro fertilization, 112
Isolation (Erikson), 387, 388

J

Job, 515
Job sharing, 174

K

Kohlberg's theory of moral development, 392, 393
  conventional level, 392, 393
  postconventional level, 393
  preconventional level, 392

L

Labor, 183-189
  afterbirth stage, 189
  delivery stage, 188, 189
  dilation stage, 187, 188
  signs of, 183, 184
Lamaze method, 191, 192
Language development,
  infants, 246-248
  preschoolers, 306-312
  toddlers, 281, 282
Large motor skills,
  active play, 302
  definition, 228
  pace, 231-233
  preschoolers, 300-302
  rolling over, 229
  sitting, standing, and crawling, 229, 230
  taking steps, 230
  toddlers, 268, 269
  voluntary body control, 228, 229
  walking, 230, 231
Latchkey children, 347, 348
Launching stage, family life cycle, 64
Leadership, 530
Learning disability, 500-503
Leboyer method, 192
Legal responsibilities and rights, 18-33
Life skills,
  definition, 273
  dressing, 305
  eating, 304, 305
  grooming, 305, 306
  preschoolers, 304-306
  toddlers, 273-275
Lifestyle, 69, 70

Lisping, 310
Logical consequences, 408
Long-term goal, 35
Love and acceptance needs, Maslow, 391

M

Marital love, 30
Marital relationship, factors in parenting, 36, 37
Maslow's hierarchy of human needs, 390-392
  esteem needs, 391
  love and acceptance needs, 391
  physical needs, 391
  safety and security needs, 391
  self-actualization needs, 391, 392
Maternity clothes, 154, 155
Maturation, 78
Media influences, 70, 71, 419-423
  computer software and the Internet, 421-423
  music, 421
  television, 419, 420
Medical care during pregnancy, 139, 143
Medical checkups,
  infants, 253
  preschoolers, 318
  school-age children, 351
  teens, 372
  toddlers, 289
Memory development of infants, 242, 243
Menstruation, 107
Mental disability, 497, 498
Mental retardation, 497
Mid-years stage, family life cycle, 64, 65
Miscarriage, 130, 131
Missing children, 462, 463
Mistrust (Erikson), 383
Mitten grasp, 234, 235
Moral development, 20-22
Morals, 21
Moro or startle reflex, 210
Moves, 444, 445
Multicultural, 67
Multiple classification, 338
Multiple roles, 39, 431-435
Music, 421

N

Nanny, 474
Nationally franchised child care, 478, 479
Natural consequences, 407
Negative reinforcement, 403
Neonatal care, 193-195
  circumcision, 195
  emergency, 193
Newborns, 205-223
  bathing, 214

caring for, 211-219
crying, 218, 219
diapers, 217
dressing, 216, 217
feeding, 212-214
hearing, 208, 209
holding, 211
physical characteristics, 206, 207
reflexes, 209
sense of touch, 209
sight, 207, 208
sleeping habits, 211, 212
smell and taste, 209
Sudden infant death syndrome (SIDS), 212
Nightmares, preschoolers, 317
Nonverbal communication, 531
Nuclear family, 56
Nurturance, 15, 16
Nutrition during pregnancy, 143-149

O

Object permanence, 245, 246
Obstetrician, 139
Open adoption, 113
Ovaries, 107
Ovulation, 107

P

Parallel play, 284
Paraprofessional, 516
Parental leave, 175
Parenting,
    adjusting to, 219-221
    child's self-concept, 91, 92
    child's self-esteem, 93, 94
    definition, 13
    education and health, 491-513
    factors to consider, 34-42
    infants, 227-265
    influences on parenting decisions, 30-34
    managing stress, 221
    myths, 16-18
    nurturance, 15, 16
    parent-child relationships, 85-94
    preschoolers, 299-325
    qualities needed, 14-16
    resources, 94-97
    responsibilities, 18-23
    rewards, 23, 24
    school-age children, 327-357
    strategies, 394
    teens, 359-375
    theories and guidelines, 379-399
    toddlers, 267-297
Parenting stage, family life cycle, 64
Parenting styles,
    authoritarian, 404
        authoritative, 405
        permissive, 404, 405
Parliamentary procedure, 529
Part-time jobs, 414-416
Patterns of development, 79, 80
Pediatrician, 177
Peer violence, 460
Permissive, 404, 405
Personal priorities, 20
Physical abuse, 453
Physical development, 78
Physical development of infants, 228-240
    eyesight, 233
    large motor skills, 228-233
    mitten grasp, 234, 235
    pace, 231-233
    pincer grasp, 235, 236
    related to intellectual development, 242
    rolling over, 229
    safety, 236, 237
    sitting, standing, and crawling, 229, 230
    sleeping patterns and problems, 240
    small motor skills, 233-236
    solid foods, 236-238
    taking steps, 230
    teething, 239, 240
    voluntary body control, 228, 229, 233, 234
    walking, 230, 231
    weaning, 239
Physical development of preschoolers, 299-306
    active play, 301, 302
    enuresis, 306
    handedness, 304
    large motor skills, 300-302
    life skills, 304-306
    safety and dangers, 303
    small motor skills, 302-304
Physical development of school-age children, 329-336
    physical fitness and competitive sports, 331-334
    safety, 334-336
Physical development of teens, 360-365
    alcohol, 363, 364
    boys, 361
    drug abuse, 364
    eating disorders, 362, 363
    girls, 362
    sexual health, 364, 365
    tobacco, 363
Physical development of toddlers, 268-277
    dangers and safety, 271, 272
    large motor skills, 268, 269
    life skills, 273-275
    small motor skills, 270
    teething, 275, 276
    toilet learning, 276, 277

toys and play, 270-273
Physical disability, 499, 500
Physical fitness and competitive sports,
    school-age children, 331-334
Physical needs (Maslow), 391
Physical neglect, 454
Physical safety, school-age
    children, 334-336
Piaget's theory of intellectual develop-
    ment, 379-382
    concrete operational stage, 381, 382
    definition, 379
    formal operational stage, 382
    preoperational stage, 381
    sensorimotor stage, 380, 381
Pincer grasp, 235, 236
Placenta, 121
Play,
    imaginative, 317
    infants, 246
    preschoolers, 284, 285, 316, 317
    toddlers, 279, 280, 284, 285, 288
    types, 284, 285
Play groups, 478
Positive behavior, 401
Positive reinforcement, 403
Postconventional level (Kohlberg), 393
Postpartum depression, 199
Postpartum period, 197-200
    checkup, 200
    definition, 197
    emotional changes, 199
    exercise, 200
    going home from the hospital, 198, 199
    mother's hospital stay, 197, 198
    physical changes, 199
    rest, 199
Preconventional level (Kohlberg), 392
Pregnancy, 119-137
    complications, 130-134
    conception, 119, 120
    couple's relationship, 128, 129
    emotional changes, 127-130
    gender determination, 120
    husband's emotions, 128
    miscarriage and stillbirth, 130, 131
    physical changes, 126, 127
    pregnancy-induced hypertension
        (PIH), 131
    prenatal development, 121-124
    Rh factor disorder, 132
    rubella, 131, 132
    sexually transmitted diseases
        (STDs), 132-134
    signs of, 125, 126
    tests, 126
Pregnancy-induced hypertension
    (PIH), 131

Prejudice, 68
Prenatal care, 139-157
    alcohol, 152
    caffeine, 153
    checkups, 141, 142
    definition, 139
    dietary supplements, 149
    exercise, 150
    first medical visit, 140, 141
    health risks, 151-153
    illegal drugs, 151, 152
    maternity clothes, 154, 155
    medical care, 139-143
    medical checkups during
        pregnancy, 141, 142
    medications and over-the-
        counter drugs, 151
    nutrition, 143-149
    prenatal tests, 142, 143
    rest, 154
    salt, 149
    smoking, 152, 153
    water, 148
    weight gain, 149, 150
    X rays, 153
Prenatal development, 121-124
    month-by-month development, 121-124
Preoperational stage (Piaget), 381
Prepared childbirth, 159
Preschoolers, 299-325
    child development charts, 320-322
    definition, 299
    emotional development, 312-317
    intellectual development, 306-312
    medical checkups, 318
    physical development, 299-306
    social development, 312-317
Primary caregiver, 176
Primary sex characteristics, 360
Priorities, 20
Privately owned child care centers, 478
Problem ownership, 90
Problem solving, infants, 244, 245
Professional, 516
Puberty, 360
Punishment, 402

R

Rate of development, 80
Readiness for parenthood, 39, 41
Readiness for school, 328, 329
References, 533
Reflexes, 209-211
    Babinski, 210
    grasping, 210
    Moro or startle, 210
    rooting, 209, 210
    stepping, 210, 211

Regression behavior, 437
Relationships, effective parent-child, 85-94
Remarriage, 441
Reproduction, 106-108
    genetic counseling, 109
    heredity, 107, 108
Resources for parents, 94-97
Responsibilities of parenting, 18-23
    fulfilling children's emotional,
        intellectual, and social needs, 20
    fulfilling children's physical needs, 19, 20
    fulfilling legal responsibilities
        and rights, 18, 19
    loving children, 19
    promoting moral development, 20-22
    take care of themselves, 22, 23
    teaching about heritage and culture, 22
    wanting and preparing for children, 19
Responsibility, 410-416
    allowances, 413, 414
    definition, 410
    part-time jobs, 414-416
    volunteer work, 412, 413
Rest during pregnancy, 154
Resume, 533
Reversibility, 339
Rewards of parenting, 23, 24
Rh factor disorder, 132
Rights of parents, 18-23
Role confusion (Erikson), 386, 387
Roles, 39
    family, 62, 63
Rooting reflex, 209, 210
Rubella, 131, 132
Runaways, 462, 463

S

Safety,
    chat rooms, 422
    preschoolers, 303
    school-age children, 334-336
    toddlers, 271, 272
Safety and security needs (Maslow), 391
School adjustments of school-age
    children, 339, 340
School-age child care, 479, 480
School-age children, 327-357
    child development charts, 352-355
    emotional development, 342-347
    intellectual development, 336-342
    medical checkups, 351
    physical development, 329-336
    readiness for school, 328, 329
    self-care, 347, 348
    social development, 342-347
    stress, 348-350
School-age years, 327

School violence, 461, 462
Secondary sex characteristics, 360
Self-actualization needs (Maslow), 391, 392
Self-care children, 347, 348
Self-concept, 91, 92
    teens, 371, 372
Self-control, 402
Self-demand feeding, 213
Self-esteem, 93, 94
    teens, 371, 372
Sensorimotor stage (Piaget), 380, 381
Separation anxiety, 250, 251
    toddlers, 285, 286
Sequence of development, 80
Seriation, 338
Sexual abuse, 454
Sexuality,
    guiding healthy development, 423-427
    gender roles, 425, 426
    questions children ask, 424, 425
    teens, 426, 427
Sexually transmitted diseases (STDs),
        132-134
    chlamydia, 134
    genital herpes, 133, 134
    gonorrhea, 133
    HIV/AIDS, 134
    pregnancy and, 132-134
    syphilis, 133
Shaken Baby Syndrome (SBS), 454, 455
Shame (Erikson), 384
Shoplifting, 418
Short-term goal, 35
Sibling, 408
Sibling rivalry, 409, 410
Single-parent family, 56-58
Sleeping patterns and problems of
    infants, 240
Small motor skills,
    definition, 233
    eyesight, 233
    handedness, 304
    mitten grasp, 234, 235
    pincer grasp, 235, 236
    preschoolers, 302-304
    toddlers, 270
    voluntary body control, 233, 234
Smoking, teens, 363
Social changes, teen parenting, 43, 44
Social development, 79
Social development of infants, 249-252
    fear, 250, 251
    separation anxiety, 250, 251
    special objects, 249, 250
    spoiling babies, 252
    stranger anxiety, 250
Social development of preschoolers,
    312-317

gender roles, 315
play, 316, 317
Social development of school-age
children, 342-347
conformity, 346, 347
parents and friends, 345, 346
Social development of teens, 366-372
dating, 369, 370
friendships, 368, 369
self-concept and self-esteem, 371, 372
Social development of toddlers, 282-288
guiding behavior, 286, 287
separation anxiety, 285, 286
temper tantrum, 287, 288
toys and play, 284, 285
Social influences, factors in parenting, 33
Special needs, children with, 496, 506
Sperm, 106
Stagnation (Erikson), 388
Startle reflex, 210
Stealing, 417, 418
Stepfamily, 58, 59, 441
Stepping reflex, 210, 211
Stereotype, 68
Sterilization, 114
Stillbirth, 130, 131
Stranger anxiety, 250
Stress, 22
children, 348-350
Student organizations, 529
Stuttering, 310
Substance abuse, 452, 453
Sudden infant death syndrome (SIDS), 153
Suicide, 463-466
factors leading to, 464, 465
preventing, 466
warning signs, 465, 466
Superego, 390
Support group, 96
Support system, 95
Syphilis, 133

T

Teachable moments, 279
Teamwork, 530, 531
Technological influences, 71-73
Technology, 71
chat rooms, 422
computers, 421-423
e-mail, 72
Internet, 72
Teen parenting, 42-46
career risks, 44, 45
education risks, 44, 45
emotional changes, 43, 44
financial risks, 45, 46
health risks, 42, 43
social changes, 43, 44
Teens, 359-375

child development charts, 373
emotional development, 366-372
intellectual development, 365, 366
medical checkups, 372
physical development, 360-365
social development, 366-372
Teething,
infants, 239, 240
toddlers, 275, 276
Television, 419, 420
Temper tantrum, 287, 288
Testes, 106
Theories and guidelines, 379-399
Time/life line, 35
Time-out, 408
Tobacco, 363
Toddlers, 267-297
child development charts, 290-295
definition, 267
emotional development, 282-288
importance of play, 288
intellectual development, 277-282
medical checkups, 289
physical development, 268-277
social development, 282-288
Toilet learning, 276, 277
Toys and play, 284, 285, 288
Traditional childbirth, 190
Trial and error, 403
Trimester, 119
Trust (Erikson), 383

U

Ultrasound test, 142
Umbilical cord, 121
Unemployment, 450, 451
University-linked child care, 476, 477
Uterus, 107

V

Vas deferens, 106
Verbal communication, 531
Visitation rights, 440
Volunteer work, 412, 413

W

Weaning, 239
Weight gain during pregnancy, 149, 150
"We" messages, 91
Work roles,
balancing with family, 431-435
managing dual, 433-435
Written communication, 531, 532

Y

"You" messages, 90, 91

Z

Zygote, 120